Praise for Geoffrey Wawro's *Quicksand*

"Wawro's considerable talent for seamlessly blending military, social, and political history (as well as his extensive archival elbow grease) makes [*Quicksand*] a success."
—*Booklist*

"A keen-eyed, sweeping survey of the depressingly familiar erroneous U.S. policy in the Middle East since the Balfour Declaration in 1917. . . . An excellent argument for the necessity of careful sifting of historical precedent and error."
—*Kirkus Reviews*

"A coherent and highly readable analysis of American involvement in the Middle East over the past century. . . . Wawro successfully provides the big picture."
—*Library Journal*

"A bold and comprehensive account of America's involvement in the Middle East. *Quicksand* cannot answer the haunting question posed by General David Petraeus during the 2003 invasion of Iraq—'Tell me how this ends?'—but Geoffrey Wawro's history does reveal how an extraordinary tale of idealism, politics, force, and miscalculation began and unfolded over the past century."
—Rick Atkinson, author of *An Army at Dawn*

"Wawro does a terrific job of explaining why America's Middle East policy has been so wrongheaded for so long, and how it has gotten the United States into so much trouble in recent years. *Quicksand* should be required reading for everyone in Washington who has a hand in formulating policy toward the Arab and Islamic world."
—John J. Mearsheimer, R. Wendell Harrison Distinguished Service Professor of Political Science, University of Chicago

"Foreign policy is a chief responsibility of any American president, yet readers of Geoff Wawro's *Quicksand* will be shocked by the history he describes—presidents, members of congress, and lobbyists who consistently sacrificed statesmanship to expediency, leaving the U.S. stuck in the Middle Eastern quicksand Wawro so richly describes."
—Newt Gingrich, former speaker of the U.S. House of Representatives

PENGUIN BOOKS

QUICKSAND

Geoffrey Wawro is the General Olinto Mark Barsanti Professor of Military History and director of the Military History Center at the University of North Texas. Wawro has hosted many programs on the History Channel and taught for several years at the U.S. Naval War College. He received his BA from Brown and his PhD from Yale, and he lives in Dallas, Texas.

QUICKSAND

America's Pursuit of Power
in the Middle East

GEOFFREY WAWRO

PENGUIN BOOKS

PENGUIN BOOKS

Published by the Penguin Group

Penguin Group (USA) Inc., 375 Hudson Street, New York, New York 10014, U.S.A.
Penguin Group (Canada), 90 Eglinton Avenue East, Suite 700, Toronto,
Ontario, Canada M4P 2Y3 (a division of Pearson Penguin Canada Inc.)
Penguin Books Ltd, 80 Strand, London WC2R 0RL, England
Penguin Ireland, 25 St Stephen's Green, Dublin 2, Ireland (a division of Penguin Books Ltd)
Penguin Group (Australia), 250 Camberwell Road, Camberwell,
Victoria 3124, Australia (a division of Pearson Australia Group Pty Ltd)
Penguin Books India Pvt Ltd, 11 Community Centre, Panchsheel Park, New Delhi – 110 017, India
Penguin Group (NZ), 67 Apollo Drive, Rosedale, North Shore 0632,
New Zealand (a division of Pearson New Zealand Ltd)
Penguin Books (South Africa) (Pty) Ltd, 24 Sturdee Avenue,
Rosebank, Johannesburg 2196, South Africa

Penguin Books Ltd, Registered Offices:
80 Strand, London WC2R 0RL, England

First published in the United States of America by The Penguin Press,
a member of Penguin Group (USA) Inc. 2010
Published in Penguin Books 2011

1 3 5 7 9 10 8 6 4 2

THE LIBRARY OF CONGRESS HAS CATALOGED THE HARDCOVER EDITION AS FOLLOWS:
Wawro, Geoffrey.
Quicksand : America's pursuit of power in the Middle East / Geoffrey Wawro.
p.   cm.
Includes bibliographical references and index.
ISBN 978-1-59420-241-4 (hc.)
ISBN 978-0-14-311883-1 (pbk.)
1. United States—Foreign relations—Middle East.   2. Middle East—Foreign relations—United States.   3. United
States—Foreign relations—20th century.   4. United States—Foreign relations—21st century.   I. Title.
DS63.2.U5W39   2010
327.73056—dc22   2009031608

Printed in the United States of America
Designed by Marysarah Quinn
Maps by Jeffrey L. Ward

FOR MATIAS AND WINSLOW

CONTENTS

QUICKSAND

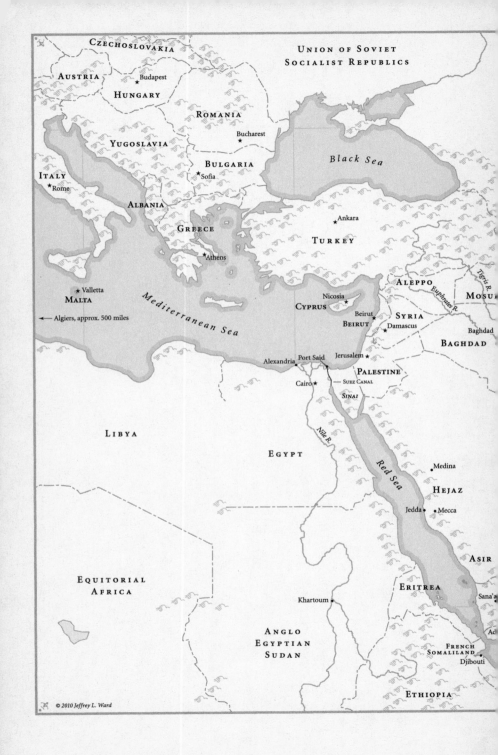

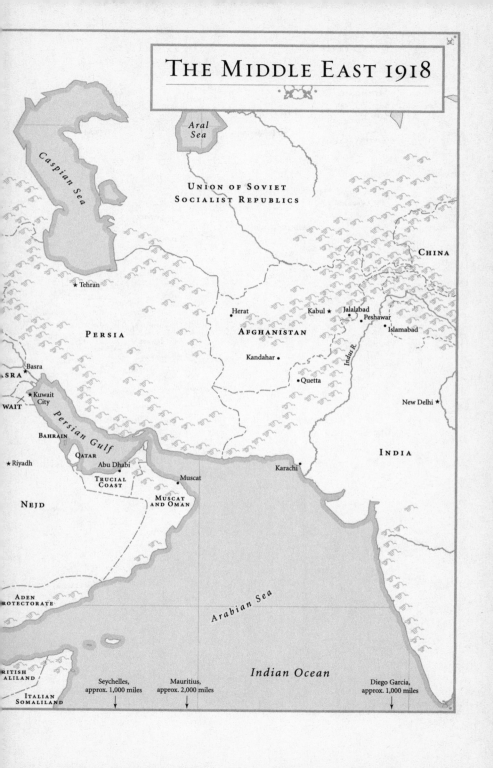

THE MIDDLE EAST 1918

Aral
Sea

Caspian Sea

UNION OF SOVIET
SOCIALIST REPUBLICS

CHINA

★ Tehran

PERSIA

• Herat
Kabul ★
Jalalabad
• Peshawar
• Islamabad

AFGHANISTAN

Indus R.

• Kandahar

• Quetta

New Delhi ★

Basra
★
SRA

★ Kuwait
City

WAIT

Persian Gulf

BAHRAIN

QATAR

Abu Dhabi

TRUCIAL
COAST

Karachi •

INDIA

★ Riyadh

MUSCAT
AND OMAN

• Muscat

NEJD

ADEN
ROTECTORATE

Arabian Sea

RITISH
ALILAND

Indian Ocean

ITALIAN
SOMALILAND

Seychelles,
approx. 1,000 miles
↓

Mauritius,
approx. 2,000 miles
↓

Diego Garcia,
approx. 1,000 miles
↓

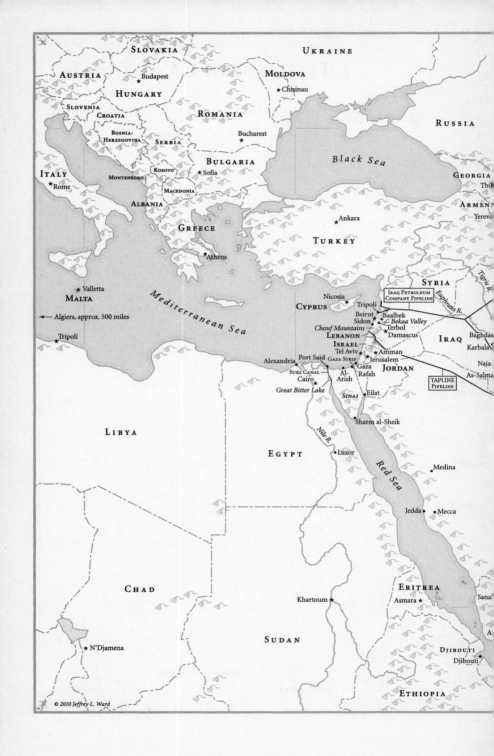

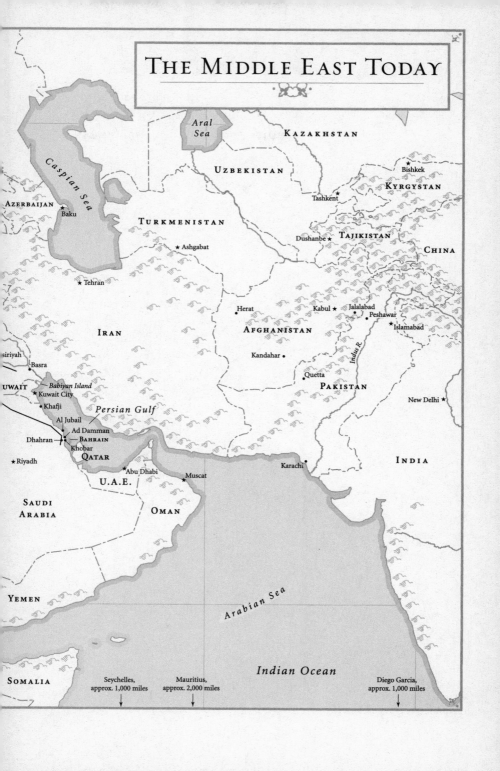

THE MIDDLE EAST TODAY

INTRODUCTION

"THE ARAB QUESTION is a regular quicksand," British foreign secretary Sir Edward Grey grumbled as the nineteenth century turned to the twentieth.[1] Now, at the start of the twenty-first century, American officials feel Grey's pain. They regarded the terror attacks of 9/11 with shock and consternation, and probably looked for a book that would explain how the United States had earned such blistering unpopularity in the Middle East, how it had gone from being—in the words of a British intelligence officer in Cairo in 1919—"the only great power acceptable to the Arabs" to one that is quite unacceptable.[2] When asked in 1933 how and why he had chosen *Americans*—and not the more proximate British, French or Germans—to develop the oil fields of Saudi Arabia, King Ibn Saud replied that he had made his decision after "a careful study of the statements of Woodrow Wilson and of American history." He could have *only* an American company develop his oil. Why? Because "Americans work hard! They get the oil and they don't get into politics."[3]

How did the United States migrate from that disinterested point to the situation we are in today, where virtually every regime in the Middle East deplores (or affects to deplore) our meddling in its politics and culture? I was surprised to discover that no such book exists. There are hundreds of books on the nations and politics of the Middle East and hundreds more on American involvement with specific regimes and episodes, or on themes like terrorism, oil, Islam and imperialism, but where is the book that traces the twisting path from the Balfour Declaration to the Bush Doctrine of 2002: from Washington's first tentative steps into the Middle East during the Woodrow Wilson administration to the brusque, sweeping changes proposed by George W. Bush in the lead-up to wars in Afghanistan and Iraq?

This book aims to fill that gap in the literature with a close analysis of three things. First, America's entry into the Middle East; second, America's cultural, political and military impact on the region; third, the global tremors that are cracking outward from that impact. *Quicksand* inevitably begins with the European period of control in the Middle East, for those decades between 1915 and 1956 created stubborn Muslim attitudes toward Western power and culture that have dogged every American effort to penetrate the region. This book will examine the degree to which the old European imperial powers, who shunned American plans for a "New Middle East" at the dawn of the twenty-first century, are themselves responsible for the worst, seemingly inexpugnable features of the Old Middle East. Indeed how have American policies been constrained (or ruined) by the legacy of British, French, German and Italian machinations in the Middle East in the modern period? How have our relationships in the Middle East been fouled by Russian mischief during the Cold War?

How exactly did America's "special relationship" with Israel take shape? On what grounds did Washington buck Arab opinion and recognize the state of Israel in 1948? Has the gamble—for that is undeniably what it was—paid off, or has it weakened us as a global power? How have the Middle Eastern nations and their militant fringe groups behaved? Do they have legitimate, soluble grievances with America, Israel and the West or, as British novelist Martin Amis has written, are they *agonistic*, which is to say marked by "darkness . . . , sequestration, the shockingly bitter and unappeasable self-exclusion from the planet, with its fear of comparison, its fear of ridicule, its fear of truth."[4] Amis made that chilling observation about militant Islam in 2002. In 1942, an American agent in Morocco reported the same difficulty: "Muslims," he wrote, "have an incurable tendency to dissect instead of implement their dissatisfaction." This American agent traced it to the "drastic manner" with which the French quelled civil disorder and political dissent, but that may be placing too much blame on the French and not enough on the Muslims themselves.[5] There is an old Arab saying that "a ruler is *naturally* opposed by half of his subjects."[6] What explanation is there for such ruinous political behavior, and what are its consequences? We shall see.

Quicksand asks how America's pursuit of basing rights and tactical advantage in the Middle East since 1945 has affected our larger grand strategic interests. In other words, what is the *real* price of the Israeli alliance or a Saudi or Iraqi air base? Iraq 2003 provides a swift rebuke; Cheney, Rumsfeld and the neocons premised that war on an easy, cheap (less than $50 billion) victory and a long lease on Iraqi bases. Instead, we have paid with more than four thousand dead, thirty thousand wounded and an estimated $3 trillion in direct and indirect war costs, and we have scant hope of secure bases in Iraq after the war. Have the military benefits been overwhelmed by the political and financial costs? As a historian I have tried to place America's current options over the trails cut by past performance. In this crucial enterprise, I am guided by the reasoning of that great conservative thinker Edmund Burke: "When things go wrong we are always tempted to ask not how we got into this difficulty, but how we are to get out of it . . . to consult our invention and to reject our experience." Yet, Burke concluded, such thinking is "diametrically opposed to every rule of reason, and every good principle of good sense." The study of *history* is the key to "correct our errors if they should be corrigible; or at least to avoid a dull uniformity in mischief, and the unpitied calamity of being repeatedly caught in the same snare."[7]

To illuminate those persistent snares of history, I have researched in military, intelligence and diplomatic archives in Washington and London. I have read through the vast published literature on Middle Eastern history, but I want to know—and I know that the reader will want to know—how American decision makers felt and reacted at every critical juncture of America's advance into the Middle East since 1917. Did we recognize the vague dangers that later formed into real threats? Did we attempt to repair the damage done by European imperialism, or merely settle into the wreckage in our own American way? The book is deliberately based on Western, English-language sources, because it sets out to understand how the United States as a great power ventured into the Middle East, and how it fortified itself for a long stay. Did we take advice from regional experts like the British and French, or ignore them? Our recent efforts to "transform" the Middle East have gone shockingly badly. While reading Anwar Sadat's memoirs, I was struck by a sentence that seemed to apply exactly to the "groupthinking" George W. Bush administration: "It is quite extraordinary how people can live with delusions big enough to transform illusions into reality, reality into illusion."[8] The sort of history contained in this book, not delusions, should always be the guide of American policy and strategy.

For all their expertise, regional experts have never agreed on a single way to transliterate Arabic, Farsi or Hebrew names and titles. The titles themselves are a regular mystery. A British expert ordered to shed light on Middle Eastern honorifics in 1944 explained them this way:

"*Sherif:* much confusion about this; *Seyyid:* much abused in many countries; *Emir:* a prince of a blood, but can also be used for a provincial governor; *Sheik:* widely applied to tribal personages, but also townsmen of consequence and senior bureaucrats; *Bey:* often used in preference to *sheik* by persons who would have merited a title in the old Turkish system and dislike the association of '*sheik*' with age or desert life; *Abu:* generally a nickname, 'father' or 'daddy,' thus, Colonel Glubb is *Abu Hunaik,* 'Daddy Little Jaw'; *Haji:* convenient title for anyone who would merit no other title; *Effendi:* still applied to persons not entitled to *sheik* or any other title; *Ibn* means like its variant *Bin* 'son of,' replaced sometimes by article *al,* which means 'of the house of,' as in the current king of Saudi Arabia 'Abdul-Aziz ibn (son of) Abdurrahman al (descendant of) Faysul al (of the house of) Saud.'"[9]

As that last reference to King Ibn Saud suggests, great powers and individual analysts rendered names randomly and unscientifically. Most were tolerant of shifting spellings; some were not. Percy Cox, the British administrator who ran Iraq in the early 1920s, would cross out every reference in his reports to Ibn Saud and replace it with Bin Saud.[10] That man, the first king of Saudi Arabia, was alternately called Abdul Aziz or Abd al-Aziz; his family Saud or Sa'ud; his Red Sea capital Jidda, Jedda or Jeddah; his fourth son Faisal, Feisal or Faysul; his chief rival Hussein or Husain or Hussayn. In this book I have tried to be as legible and consistent as possible, fully sharing—in my own ignorance of Middle Eastern languages—Lawrence of Arabia's frustration with Arab orthography: "There are some 'scientific systems' of transliteration, helpful to people who know enough Arabic not to need helping, but a washout for the world. I spell my names anyhow, to show what rot the systems are."[11]

Contemplating the spreading rot of Nazism in 1942, before the first American landings in North Africa, a general staff planner in Washington proposed basing the entire Allied war effort on the broader Middle East: a "line of strategic centers from French Morocco to India," a "six thousand mile-long chain of force around Hitler in Europe" from Casablanca to Karachi. Unable to penetrate the bunkers, minefields, beach obstacles and shore batteries of Hitler's Fortress Europe, the United States and Britain would strangle the Nazis and the Fascists from a distance. The

Allies would sever Axis connections to the Japanese Empire, seize the ports, air bases and oil fields of the Middle East, and then begin to shorten the six-thousand-mile chain, crushing Hitler and Mussolini from the outside in.[12] Russia, on the ropes at Stalingrad, would be relieved by the diversion and sustained by American and British supplies shipped up the Trans-Iranian railway from the Persian Gulf to the Caspian Sea.

Like the great English historian Arnold J. Toynbee, who wrote strategic assessments for Churchill after 1940, American strategists perceived the indispensability of the Middle East for both sides in World War II. It was the hub of three continents: Europe, Africa and Asia.[13] The completion of the Suez Canal in 1869 and the introduction of long-distance air routes in the early twentieth century had given the Middle East even more importance as "the shortest route between the two chief concentrations of population and power in the world of the twentieth century": between the world of India, East Asia and the Pacific and the world of Europe, America and the Atlantic. "Command of the Middle East," Toynbee noted, "carried with it the power of keeping open the direct routes between those two geographical poles, or closing them, or forcing them open again."[14] An American in Tehran during the war observed the importance of Iran to Russia's survival: "The bulk of the aid that the Russians use to fight, to survive, reaches them through the Persian Gulf to Abadan and then on by rail to Azerbaijan. And where the hell would they be without the essential supplies we move to them through Iran?"[15]

Also in 1942, in Buenos Aires, Argentina, the German air and naval attaché briefed a group of rich Nazi industrialists on Hitler's strategy for the year ahead. The führer would abandon the push toward Moscow and instead thrust south to the Middle East, driving through Turkey, Iraq, Iran and Afghanistan. The Wehrmacht would shear off Soviet Central Asia, seize the oil fields on the Caspian Sea and the Persian Gulf, and annex Russia's most vital assets: the wheat fields of Ukraine and the ores and heavy industry of the Donetz basin. In those last months of German success, before the twin blows of El Alamein and Stalingrad, the Allies confronted the real possibility that the Germans, Italians and Vichy French would converge victoriously on Syria, Iraq, Iran and India from two directions: east from Libya and Egypt and south from Turkey and the Caucasus.[16]

Those Allied and Axis planners and dreamers of 1942 were applying the new tools of the Middle East—oil wells, pipelines, telegraphs, ports, airfields, hardened roads and the Suez Canal—but also the lessons and dreams of *history*. The Middle East had been a pivot of world rivalry since antiquity, when the armies of Cyrus,

Darius, Xerxes, Alexander and Caesar fought to control the region. The Dark Ages were not "dark" at all in the Islamic Middle East, where the splendid capitals at Baghdad, Medina, Damascus, Kufa and Basra dazzled European travelers with their palaces, libraries, gardens and fountains. "Live long, O Caliph, to thy heart's content / In scented shade of palace minarets," an Arab poet wrote of the enriching trade and civilization that flowed across the Fertile Crescent from the Euphrates to the Nile and tempted first the Crusaders, then Genghis Khan and Tamerlane, to descend with their plundering hordes.[17] Crusaders sailed from Europe to snatch a piece of that civilization in the eleventh century, and trade caravans rumbled across the vital headland between the Mediterranean and the Indian Ocean—from Beirut to Basra—carrying silks, jade, tea and spices to the West; gold, silver, ivory and slaves to the East.

Driving home with ferocity a point that Nazi panzers would rediscover centuries later—that the Middle East is just one stage in the great steppe and desert belt that runs from North Africa all the way to the Pacific—Tamerlane swept down with his mounted Mongol armies toward the end of the fourteenth century and seized Damascus, Baghdad, Isfahan and Shiraz. To close the steppe belt against pursuers or imitators, Tamerlane despoiled it: slaughtering peasants and piling their skulls into pyramids, pulverizing roads and bridges, and wrecking the marvelously advanced irrigation systems of Mesopotamia and Persia to create a desert. His assaults on local culture were even fiercer. When the Persian poet Hafiz crooned to his Shirazi lover that he would "give Bukhara and Samarkand for the mole upon her cheek," Tamerlane summoned Hafiz and bellowed: "Miserable wretch, I subjugate continents to adorn Bukhara and Samarkand and you would sell them for the mole of a Shirazi wench?"[18] Western empires like the Venetian Republic rose and fell with these turbulent rhythms of the Middle East, Gibbon sadly reporting that "grass grew up in the fair and pleasant streets of Venice" after the Mongols and then the Turks had smashed their way down to the Mediterranean coast from Central Asia, thinning and then redirecting the enriching Silk Road caravan trade.

For centuries thereafter, the Middle East stagnated. European navigators opened up the Cape sea route around the southern tip of Africa, putting the old caravans out of business and flinging the Middle East into unaccustomed poverty and insignificance. Napoleon Bonaparte tried to rip Egypt, Palestine and Syria away from the Turks in 1798, but exhausted his armies marching up and down dry, pestilential tracks before abandoning the mission and fleeing home to France in defeat. Finishing his tour of the Middle East in the early 1840s, British historian Alexander King-lake arrived on Mount Lebanon and stared thirstily toward the Mediterranean and the West:

> I clung with my eyes to the dim, steadfast line of the sea . . . I had grown well used of late to the people and the scenes of forlorn Asia—well used to the tombs and ruins, to silent cities and deserted plains, to tranquil men, and women sadly veiled; and now that I saw the even plain of the sea, I leapt with an easy leap to its yonder shores, and saw all the kingdoms of the West in that fair path that could lead me from out of this silent land . . . Behind me I left an old and decrepit world; religions dead and dying;—calm tyrannies expiring in silence.[19]

The completion of the Suez Canal in 1869 revived the strategic importance of the Middle East. The hinge region had always been crucial to powers wanting to check the spread of their rivals, but it was now more crucial than ever. Writing from Calcutta in 1917, a British officer found that the Middle East—that "neck of land between the settled states of the West and the unsettled states of the East"—had recovered its importance "for any power with interests in the Indian Ocean and the Persian Gulf."[20] Just as the Turks had closed the Venetian roads across the Middle East in the fifteenth century, Britain worried that the Germans would do the same to the British routes in the twentieth. Thus, Kaiser Wilhelm II's visit to the Tomb of Saladin in Damascus in 1898 was viewed in London as a deliberate provocation, the young kaiser posing as the champion of the oppressed Muslims against British and French colonialism. It was barefaced but effective humbug: "every Bedouin of the desert is thus persuaded that Germany is a friend of the Arabs," a German diplomat cynically jotted at the time.[21] With the Berlin-Baghdad Railway advancing in 1903 and a big German port under construction at the head of the Persian Gulf—both concessions wrung from the Turks when Britain was distracted by the Boer War—the Germans were poised to cut off Britain's land and sea connections with India and China. The Germans buttressed their position by rebuilding the beaten Turkish army after its defeats in the Balkan Wars and lending critical diplomatic support to the sultan after the Armenian massacres. With the Germans pressing down from Asia Minor, Britain fought World War I as desperately in the Middle East as it did in Europe, detaching precious troops for a great "push" from

Cairo to Damascus and inciting the Arabs to rise up and expel the German-backed Turks from their chain of garrisons in Syria and Arabia.

Part of the British war strategy was Israel. To weaken the Ottoman Turks and drive a wedge between the German and Austro-Hungarian governments and their Jewish subjects (and bankers), British foreign secretary Arthur Balfour conceived the idea in 1917 of a "Jewish national home" in Turkish Palestine. Though Arabs outnumbered Jews ten to one in Palestine—and American president Woodrow Wilson was enjoining the Allies to consult populations and assure "national self-determination" after the war—the British calculated that a dependent state of grateful European Jews would secure their flank on the Suez Canal and give them a solid foothold on the Levant. "Who will begrudge the Jewish people that little notch which is Palestine?" Britain's foreign secretary mused as he put finishing touches on what would shortly be called the "Balfour Declaration" near the end of World War I.[22] Were more shortsighted words than those *ever* spoken?

The British position after World War I was fatally undermined by this mushy imprecision on the fate of Palestine, but also by wider equivocation toward the Arabs. The British had sought an Arab uprising against the Turks in 1916 in exchange for the promise of independence and "Arab union." Though the latter ambition was more an Arab than a British affair, independence and self-determination for the largely Arab *vilayets*, or provinces of the Ottoman Empire, were British promises that were never redeemed. Instead, the British endorsed the "Jewish national home" in Palestine and carved Iran, Iraq, Arabia and Syria into British and French postwar spheres of influence. Britain spent the interwar period alternately battling and coddling Arab nationalists. London's strategic need for Iraqi oil and a Jewish-administered rampart next to Suez undercut all their appeals to the Arabs. Yet their every concession to the Arabs enraged the Jewish settlers who began flooding unstoppably into Palestine after the Nazi rise to power in Germany in 1932. With Hitler passing anti-Jewish laws and threatening genocide, the Jews of Europe seized on Arthur Balfour's 1917 declaration as the legal basis for a legitimate, internationally recognized Jewish state.

World War II further frayed the fabric of the Middle East. The British, thrown back at Dunkirk and down to their last armored division in 1940, deployed it not on the beaches of Sussex, but in Egypt, where it was sent to repulse Rommel's expected push from Libya toward the Suez Canal and then on to the Persian Gulf. British victory in that campaign ensured that London would cling doggedly to its Middle Eastern colonies after the war. They had become symbols of British greatness and resolve. The French, who had dug in to their Syrian, Lebanese and North African colonies during the interwar period, dug in even deeper under the blows of the Germans. Battered in Europe, the Vichy French saw their eventual resurrection in both the Arab West ("al-Maghrib") and the Arab East ("al-Mashriq"). They would rebuild French glory in the Mediterranean and Middle East and enlist themselves (and their Arab protégés) in the Nazi New Order, which optimists were already calling the "New Europe." In the New Europe, Hitler would need Middle Eastern oil, ports and air bases, and the French would provide them, in exchange for a larger role in German plans. Those German plans for the Middle East were unremittingly bleak. When not secretly promising Arab territory to the French, Italian and Spanish fascist regimes, Hitler publicly incited the Arabs to kill Jews and Englishmen. He and his clients—like Haj Amin al-Husseini, the leading Muslim cleric in Jerusalem—adduced murky "imperialist-Jewish plots" to frighten the Arabs and win them to the side of the Third Reich.

The Israeli-Palestinian conflict, perhaps manageable before World War II, became utterly unmanageable after it. Hitler and his fascist allies had slaughtered six million Jews and driven two million into wandering exile. As wretched European "DPs," or displaced persons, the Jews needed a home. With most of the world—including the United States—closed by pointedly anti-Jewish immigration quotas, Palestine beckoned. But the British—beset by Palestine's furious Arab majority—balked, refusing to let the Jewish refugees land in large numbers. In the most notorious instance, the British sent the fully loaded ship *Exodus* from Haifa back to European waters before forcing the Jewish passengers, who had survived the Nazi death camps, to debark in Germany, of all places.[23] The predicament—insouciantly created by Arthur Balfour in 1917—had become heavy and careworn. Yet the Jewish survivors would not hear "reason"—like the Arab demand that Jewish refugees be distributed proportionately among the member states of the United Nations—and the Arabs of Palestine would not accept the Jews, whom they regarded as European interlopers. The British spent the next three years separating the two sides (Palestinian Arabs and Jewish settlers) and trying hard to enact a compromise before abruptly dumping the mess into the lap of the United Nations in 1948 and leaving. It was the inglorious end of the British Empire.

The United States of America strode confidently in to fill the gap. The State Department's Division of Near Eastern and African Affairs predicted that the Middle East would provide "an easy, almost automatic American harvest of influence."[24] Though some skeptics—like Colonel "Wild Bill" Donovan of the Office of Strategic

Services (OSS), the forerunner of the CIA—warned that the Middle East would shortly become "a political and economic jousting ground," a "new Balkans," a "birthplace of many international conflicts," presidents Franklin Roosevelt and Harry Truman were less cautious.[25] Roosevelt tried, as Cordell Hull put it, "to talk both ways" on the question, reassuring the Arabs one day, the Jews the next. Leaving a meeting with FDR in 1944, a State Department analyst muttered, "I've read of men who thought they might be King of the Jews and other men who thought they might be King of the Arabs, but this is the first time I've listened to a man who dreamt of being King of *both* the Jews and the Arabs."[26] Truman, true to his nature, had more pragmatic aspirations. There were more Jewish voters in America than Arab ones and the Jewish lobby was better organized. Thus, Truman gave almost unconditional political support to Israel and tended to make light of the severe damage which that position wrought on his cabinet and his relations with the Arab states. His secretary of state, George C. Marshall, regularly complained that Truman was too quick to compromise the United States on vital "international questions" in order "to pick up a few [Jewish] votes" at home.

In their haste to contain Moscow's drive to the Persian Gulf and the Mediterranean—which flared into the Azerbaijan, Greek and Turkish crises between 1945 and 1949—FDR and Truman did not pause to learn much from Europe's tortured history in the Middle East. Warnings like this one—from the French resident-general in Tunis in 1950—went largely unheeded: "Here you are dealing with a people of a completely different order of ideas, of ways of thinking, of customs and traditions from those of Western peoples. These differences are the heritage of centuries."[27] It was as if the Americans actually believed the improbable Arab saying that "what is past is dead." To Roosevelt and Truman, the British and French were on the way down, the Americans on the way up. The Middle East would be sorted out with tried-and-true American methods: cash money, big grins and a slap on the back. U.S. ambassadors, investors and military advisory groups dispatched into the region were hopeful. Unlike the British or French, the Americans had no rancid imperial history. Washington was an honest broker, its emissaries on solid ground. "Egypt trusts the United States," the Egyptian ambassador told the American secretary of state in January 1945. "You are a disinterested country."[28] Others—Arabs and Americans—were not so sure. A bright State Department analyst (and future Cold War historian), Herbert Feis, detected "murmurous anxieties traveling their way along the air-conditioned corridors of the Navy and Interior Departments, and filtering through the latticed doors of the State Department." Feis and his anxious colleagues worried in 1947 that the Middle East was not solid ground at all. It was quicksand. "There we enter strange territory, troublesome lands, and encounter suspicious rivals. What of our rather stumbling course thus far?"[29] Faced, more than sixty years later, with the same unresolved problems and perplexities, we must now ask that question again and determine whether we have shored ourselves up or driven ourselves deeper and more inextricably into the mud.

Even a stumbling course benefits from signposts, and the reader will want some for this long book. *Quicksand* sets out to discover and elucidate the countries, interests, raw materials and ideas that have lured us to the Middle East and snared us there. The book's structure is chronological, which is the only way to convey the accumulating pressures that have lodged America in the Middle East. The creation of Israel with crucial U.S. backing is one of the most important events in this book, and every subsequent discussion of Israel builds upon the findings in chapters one and three. Some readers may be perturbed or merely surprised by the portrait of Israel and U.S.-Israeli relations that emerges in this book, but the facts lead there; indeed my approach to Israel is no different from my approach to every other country in this book. It is solidly rooted in American and British archives, journalism—"the first draft of history"—and scholarly literature.

"Oil" is the title of chapter two, which indicates the other chief driver in this book. The West's need for Persian Gulf oil and gas after World War II, when U.S. supplies peaked and began to decline, suggested a corresponding need to *control* that oil, especially in the face of continual Soviet threats to control it. That early Cold War mind-set hardened into dogma that persists to this day—we cannot imagine a world without the Saudi oil pump, and the princes in charge. Throughout the book, Washington ponders intriguing alternatives to the retrograde Saudis, but always goes back to the Saudi princes: "Better the enemy that you know." *Quicksand* spools out the alternatives in real time, giving a sense of turning points that were not taken but also of the intractability of politics in the region. Alternatives—like Nasser's Arab nationalism—have beckoned, but each time U.S. presidents tiptoed up to them, fearful of Saudi and Israeli tantrums, they were insulted, rebuffed, or presented with long lists of demands that no responsible government could satisfy. U.S. decision makers have always been acutely aware of the stakes in the Middle East. From the 1940s on, every administration has acknowledged the depressing tendency of Middle Eastern governments to fall into corruption, economic stagnation, repression and sectarian squabbles. Where strongman rule faltered, mass movements—Arab nationalism, Sunni fundamentalism, Shiite revolution—suggested themselves, in the Arab and Persian street, as the only virtuous way forward. The book looks at the seductive appeal those mass movements have had for the peoples of the Middle East and the deadly threat they have seemed to portend for American interests, which have always preferred bilateral relations with reliable strongmen in states like Saudi Arabia, imperial Iran or the Egypt of the free officers. Our preference for states over transnational movements is understandable, but we have so often attached ourselves to the wrong states or the wrong leaders. In our analysis of the transnational movements, we have consistently overestimated the threat posed by Nasser, the Baathists and the Arab nationalists. In the case of the shah, we evinced an odd confidence in his staying power even as the revolutionary pressures accumulated around him. We notoriously underestimated the threat of al-Qaeda—Bush 43 harrumphing as he took office that he was "not gonna swat flies"—until the flies, each loaded with thirty tons of jet fuel, had leveled the Twin Towers and a wing of the Pentagon.

Quicksand marvels at the ability of bright American strategists to get things wrong, usually under the influence of the Cold War, the "long war" against terrorism or the domestic political pressures generated by the Israel and oil lobbies. The utility of Western armed force in the region is another overarching theme. Every president from Truman to Clinton felt certain that inserting Western forces into the Muslim Middle East was asking for trouble. The Suez Crisis, the Six-Day War, the Yom Kippur War and Operation Desert Storm were contested against a backdrop of doubts. Eisenhower rolled back the (successful) Anglo-French assault on Suez precisely because he didn't want Western forces destroying Western influence among the peoples of the Middle East. He kept his intervention in Lebanon small in size and scope so as not to ignite a regional backlash. Johnson and Nixon agonized over the extent and nature of support they would provide Israel in 1967 and 1973, fearing the odium of Arab governments. And George H. W. Bush narrowly secured congressional approval to liberate Kuwait in 1991, when many agreed with the estimation of Senator Pat Moynihan that "nothing large happened," only that "a nasty little country invaded a littler but just as nasty country." What good could U.S. forces achieve in such an environment? Was such a war even worth the bones of a single American GI?

With this background in hand, readers will appreciate the great conceptual leap taken by George W. Bush and his neocons, who startlingly decided that the Middle

East *was* ready for U.S. military activism—and fertile ground for a "freedom agenda" that would be transmitted from Washington and lowered over the grateful peoples of the Middle East. What was perhaps most striking about the George W. Bush administration was its willed ignorance of history. Presidents like Truman, Eisenhower, Kennedy, Johnson and Bush 41, who aligned themselves against popular Arab leaders or movements, did so with the knowledge that they were courting trouble. Bush 43—the self-styled "gut player"—had none of that prudence, and the Obama administration will be harvesting his failures for a long time to come.

My last hope for this book is that it will be as entertaining as it is illuminating. "History," Winston Churchill once wrote, "with its flickering lamp, stumbles along the trail of the past, trying to reconstruct its scenes, to revive its echoes and kindle with pale gleams the passion of former days." I know that *Quicksand* will occasionally stumble, but I hope that it will reconstruct, revive and kindle as well.

CHAPTER I

ZION

COULD THERE HAVE BEEN a less discerning man than Arthur Balfour to draw the battle lines of the modern Middle East? As British foreign secretary in 1917, the sixty-nine-year-old Balfour carelessly issued what came to be called the "Balfour Declaration" in an open letter to Baron Walter de Rothschild. "His Majesty's Government view with favour the establishment in Palestine of a national home for the Jewish people, and will use their best endeavors to facilitate the achievement of this object."

Languid and aristocratic to his fingertips, Balfour was not a clear thinker. Reflecting on his thought processes one day, he said, "I can remember every argument, repeat all the pros and cons, and even make quite a good speech on the subject. But the conclusion, the decision, is a perfect blank in my mind." His powers of observation were little better. Lord Vansittart said that Balfour "viewed events with the detachment of a choirboy at a funeral service."[1] He combined dreamy romanticism about the "Jewish tribes of Israel" or the "Bedouin of the desert" with ruthless arrogance in every other department. "The only thing which interests me in the Caucasus is the railway line which delivers oil from Baku to Batumi," he irritably scribbled in 1918. For the rest, "the natives can cut each other to pieces, for all I care."[2] George Curzon, who would succeed Balfour as foreign secretary, deplored Balfour's carelessness: "His charm of manner . . . blinded all but those who knew him from the inside to the lamentable ignorance, indifference and levity of his regime. He never studied his papers, he never knew the facts . . . and he never looked ahead." Asked what he thought Balfour's place in history would be, Prime Minister David Lloyd George replied, "He will be just like the scent on a pocket handkerchief."[3]

The one place where Balfour's influence did not evaporate was the Middle East. Even as Balfour's 1917 declaration of a "Jewish national home" in Palestine wended its way across Europe—provoking jubilation in the Jewish ghettos of Russia and the Balkans—it was clear that the foreign secretary was saddling the British Empire with a heavy liability. After all, Zionist efforts to settle in the Egyptian Sinai had earlier been rejected by British governments on the grounds that "the establishment there of a large society of Austrian, Russian and Rumanian Jews would entail a material increase in the existing complications of the machinery of government."[4] Logically, Zionism would impose no less serious complications in Palestine, whose Arabs, in the heat of World War I, were sniffing the fumes of their own "Palestinian" nationalism for the first time. To Balfour's pledge to support the settlement of European Jews in Palestine, Curzon raised the obvious objection: "What is to become of the *people* of the country?"[5] There were more Arabs than Jews in Palestine—ten times as many in 1917—and they had been clashing with "Zionist" settlers for twenty years before the declaration. Their battles would only intensify as a result of Balfour's intervention. Balfour, however, apparently believed that there were hardly any Arabs in Palestine, just a few scattered Bedouin tribes and a lot of "Turks," who, in 1917, were Germany's ally and Britain's enemy and therefore—in Balfour's eyes— fair game to be "driven out" and replaced with European Jews.[6]

HERZL AND THE ZIONIST IDEA

Zionism—the quest for a Jewish national home in Palestine—was the brainchild of Theodor Herzl. A thirty-four-year-old reporter for Vienna's *Neue Freie Presse* in 1894, Herzl went to Paris to cover the unfolding Dreyfus Affair, the sensational trial and public degradation of Captain Alfred Dreyfus. Dreyfus, a French Jew, had been the target of a vicious anti-Semitic campaign wielded by the French army to discredit republican government and distract attention from its own slipshod security arrangements. Though framed by his colleagues—Dreyfus would be pardoned five years later—this possibility did not at first even register in even the most enlightened circles. With Dreyfus destined for life imprisonment on the leper colony of Devil's Island, seven miles off the coast of French Guiana, France's otherwise moderate and gentle Socialist leader, Jean Jaurès, thought the vile place too good for Dreyfus. The captain deserved a bullet in the head, in his view. The French public considered the poor, misused army officer a "Judas," a "traitor," a "fetid Jew." Each accusation was founded on the alleged homelessness and perfidy of wandering, huckstering "Israelites." From his post in Paris, Herzl watched the proceedings in horror: "The enormous majority in France wanted to damn a Jew and, in this one Jew, all Jews," he wrote. That this happened in "republican, modern, civilized France, one hundred years after the Declaration of the Rights of Man," struck Herzl as particularly appalling. Pogroms happened regularly in backward Russia and Austria-Hungary, but standards were thought to be quite a bit higher in France. Herzl recalled Lord Byron's *Hebrew Melodies*, which had pricked the conscience of an earlier generation:

> The white dove hath her nest, the fox his cave.
> Mankind their country—Israel but the grave.[8]

Two years later, Herzl published the pamphlet that would become the foundation stone of the state of Israel: *Der Judenstaat*, or "The Jewish State." That was its polite translation; the correct translation, defiantly formulated by Herzl to mock the anti-Semites, was "The Jew State." Herzl was not the first to float the idea of a Jewish state. In the course of his invasion of Egypt and march toward Syria, Napoleon Bonaparte had invited the Jews "home" to Palestine in 1798. Great Britain's long-serving prime minister and foreign secretary Lord Palmerston had urged the creation of a Jewish state to enrich and buttress the Ottoman Empire in the 1830s, and Benjamin Disraeli—British prime minister in the late 1870s—had anonymously submitted a pamphlet called "The Jewish Question within the Eastern Question" to the Congress of Berlin, convened to settle the fate of the Ottoman Empire in 1878. Disraeli's central argument had been that since the Ottoman Empire, the "Sick Man of Europe," was bound to collapse in the years ahead, Britain ought to anticipate the collapse by amputating Palestine and settling European Jews there, who would develop "within half a century" into a compact, rich, pro-British nation.[9]

Herzl moved beyond such traditional power diplomacy to give Zionism a modern twist.[10] Eager to counter anti-Semitism with an idea no less "voluptuous," Herzl hit upon "Labor Zionism," which melded the old traditions of Judaism with the new appeals of socialism and the nation-state. Even secular Jews, with no religious interest in returning to Zion, might be lured there by the promise of secure borders, reliable police protection, a seven-hour workday and fair wages. "Ghetto Jews" would probably flock to the new state to worship and work in peace. Herzl planned to invite or extort funding for the enterprise from rich, assimilated Jewish families like the Rothschilds, Goldschmidts, Anspachs and Montefiores, who would either open their wallets or—he threatened—see their fortunes destroyed by furious Jewish mobs.[11]

Though many mocked Herzl's chutzpah—wags dubbed him "King of the Jews," the "new Moses" or the "Jewish Bismarck"—the Zionist founder plunged into an international campaign to create a Jewish state, writing to emperors, kings, presidents, the pope and the sultan. In 1895, he visited Baron Maurice de Hirsch, a rich Bavarian Jew, and scolded him for subsidizing the flight of persecuted Russian Jews to agricultural colonies in Argentina. The Jewish state *had* to be Palestine, Herzl insisted. A poor, neglected strip of two disconnected Turkish provinces—the *vilayet* of Beirut and the *sanjak* of Jerusalem—Palestine was a malaria-infested backwater, but could be so much more. Under intensive Jewish settlement and development, Herzl argued, it would become the biblical "land of milk and honey" again and be an avowedly modern place with a progressive slogan: "Faith holds us together, science makes us free." It would also be a wholesome place, where "Jew boys would become young Jews" and regain a dignity trampled by European bigots. "You breed beggars," Herzl scolded Hirsch. "As long as Jews are passive recipients of charitable funds, they will remain weaklings and cowards."[12]

Still, Zionism did not catch on. Wealthy European Jews feared its socialist planks and rejected as lunacy Herzl's apocalyptic prediction of a day when anti-Semitic regimes would revoke the citizenship of European Jews. Even active philanthropists like Edmond de Rothschild, who was funding nineteen Jewish settlements in Palestine by 1903, worried that Jewish settlers in the Holy Land would choose an easy life of handouts over real work. Many of Europe's great Jewish intellectuals—thinkers like Sigmund Freud, Stefan Zweig and Karl Kraus—were even less supportive. "Why should we go to Palestine?" Zweig puzzled. "Our language is German and not Hebrew, and beautiful Austria is our homeland . . . Why does [Herzl] . . . place arguments in the hands of our worst enemies and attempt to separate us, when every day brings us more closely and intimately into the German world?" (Austrian Nazis would drive Zweig to exile in 1934. He committed suicide in Brazil in 1942.) Frustrated, Herzl suffered a heart attack and died at the age of forty-four in 1904, repenting the apparent failure of his idea. The London Rothschilds, he grumbled, were "vulgar, contemptuous, egotistical people." Future Zionists would need to come forward, as Herzl himself had predicted years earlier: "Better mechanics than myself will be found to carry the work out . . . The world needs the Jewish State; therefore it will arise."[13]

Life in "Israel," meanwhile, continued much as it had for centuries. It was a largely Arab place in which a steady trickle of European Jews mixed with the several thousand Sephardim who had lived in Palestine since their removal from Spain and North Africa in the fifteenth century. Arriving Jewish settlers tended to overlook the Arabs, who concentrated in rural villages dotted around the hill country of the interior and shunned the coastal plain and the Jordan and Jezreel valleys marked out for settlement by the Zionists because of the dangers of malaria and Bedouin raiders.[14] Looking around in the 1860s, Mark Twain had found Palestine "a hopeless, dreary, heartbroken land . . . desolate and unlovely." Jericho had been "accursed," Jerusalem a "pauper village." Looking around in the 1890s, the Zionists noticed that there were Arabs there. "But there are *Arabs* in Palestine!" Herzl's early collaborator and ally Max Nordau had famously expostulated. "I did not know that! We are committing an injustice!" Other Zionists had no such qualms: "Outside Palestine," Ahad Ha'am wrote in 1891, "we are accustomed to believe that the Arabs are all wild beasts of the desert, a people akin to jackasses who do not understand what is going on around them." Zionist hard-liners criticized what they called "diaspora thinking": an overly solicitous concern for "what non-Jews say." To true Zionists, rapid unflinching settlement (and the displacement of Arabs) "to redeem the land of our forefathers" was the only way forward.[15] Although Herzl had cautioned Zionists to "expropriate gently . . . , discreetly and circumspectly," his followers took a harder line. "We cannot allow the Arabs to block so valuable a piece of historic reconstruction," the London-born Zionist Israel Zangwill wrote in 1921. "'We must gently persuade them to 'trek.' After all, they have all Arabia with its million square miles . . . There is no particular reason for the Arabs to cling to these few kilometers. 'To fold their tents' and 'silently steal away' is their proverbial habit: let them exemplify it now."[16]

JEWISH SETTLEMENT

To give the Arabs a push, hundreds of Jews debarked in Palestine every year, betting that they were safer in a foreign land under the protection of their European consuls than they would be in their European motherlands under the dubious protection of anti-Semitic troops and gendarmes and, in the case of Russia, under outright attack from the "Black Hundreds," vicious anti-Semitic gangs that struck Jewish villages and quarters with impunity. Zionists called the period from 1904 to 1914 the second aliyah, or "ascent," to Palestine. The first had been 1882 to 1903, after Russia's tsar Alexander III had passed laws barring Jews from the professions and banning them from all Russian towns and villages with fewer than ten thousand inhabitants expressly to "cause one-third of the Jews to emigrate, one-third to accept baptism, and one-third to starve." Under pressures like those, thirteen thousand Jews emigrated to Palestine from Odessa alone between 1905 and 1910.[17] Yet at least as many European Jews departed every year to return to Europe, frustrated by Palestine's filth and diseases and the Turkish bureaucracy, which, belatedly worried by the spread of Judaism, had begun to obstruct Jewish land purchase. Herzl himself had tried to buy Palestine from the Ottomans in 1896, but had been rebuffed by Sultan Abdul Hamid II: "When my empire is partitioned, perhaps [the Jews] can get Palestine for nothing, but only our corpse can be divided. I will never consent to vivisection."[18]

For the Zionists, vivisection seemed an increasingly attractive option. Turkish citizenship was out of the question, for civil rights, government jobs and favorable tax rates were largely reserved for Muslims in the Ottoman Empire. Legal residence in Palestine was increasingly difficult, and clandestine immigration defeated the whole purpose of Herzl's project for a "public, legal homeland." There were eighty-five thousand Jews living in Palestine on the eve of World War I—a higher per capita ratio of Jews than in any country in the world—yet they struggled to sink their roots in a land that contained six hundred thousand Arabs.[19] The prejudices of the Turkish sultan had acquired an even harder ideological edge after the Young Turk Revolution of 1908. Arab members of the new Ottoman parliament protested that European Jews were eroding the Muslim majority in Palestine, and colonizing it.[20]

There was truth to that accusation. A common Zionist tactic in the early 1900s was to purchase Turkish land in Palestine, drive off the Arab peasants, or fellaheen, settle Jewish immigrants and then place the property under the control of a Russian, German, French or British foreman to remove it from Ottoman jurisdiction (because citizens of European great powers could not be summoned to Turkish courts) and to fend off title claims by the angry, dispossessed fellaheen. When lawsuits did arise in Turkish courts, the Jews proved no less adept than Turks or Arabs at bribing Ottoman judges to secure ownership of disputed property.[21] The impact of Jewish purchases on the Arab natives of Palestine was often heartrending. Negotiating for the purchase of some Arab land in eastern Galilee in 1919, a Zionist agent was conflicted by what he saw around him: "I sat in the tent and wrapped up the negotiation . . . For long afterwards I did not cease hearing the sad melody of the Bedouin men and women who gathered by the sheik's tent that evening, before they left the village of Shamasin near Yama, which is [today] Yavneel." The songs were "lamenting their bad luck, which was forcing them to leave the cradle of their homeland."[22]

Some Arabs proved less fatalistic. In Constantinople and Jerusalem, militant anti-Jewish associations sprang up to oppose further Zionist settlement in Palestine. Barred from the port city of Jaffa, hundreds of Jews built a new town on the periphery, which they named Tel Aviv, or "Hill of Spring."[23] With a foothold on the coastal plain, the Zionists then took aim at Palestine's interior: Judea, Samaria and Galilee, as well as the fertile valleys of the Jordan and the Jezreel. Touring Palestine in 1919, an American fact-finding mission dispatched by President Woodrow Wilson reported that, in meetings with Zionists, "the fact came out repeatedly . . . that the Zionists looked forward to a practically complete dispossession of the present non-Jewish inhabitants of Palestine, by various forms of purchase."[24]

Turkey's decision to ally with Germany against Russia, France and Britain in World War I nearly extinguished Zionism. To preempt internal sedition in favor of the Triple Entente, the Turks in 1914 began expelling Russian Jews from Palestine. By January 1915, seven thousand European Jews had fled the Holy Land, and twelve thousand more had taken Turkish citizenship as a hedge against persecution. As non-Muslims, most were assigned to backbreaking labor crews for the duration of the war. They built roads, quarried stone and constructed mud and sandbagged fortifications. Determined to break the Jews as a potential "fifth column" of the Entente powers, Jamal Pasha, Palestine's Turkish military governor, closed Zionist newspapers, banned Jewish rallies, voided Jewish land titles and incited Arabs to raid Jewish farms and shops. Famine killed thousands across Syria, Lebanon and

Palestine as the Turkish army requisitioned livestock and food and imports dried up. In four years of war, the Jewish population of Palestine plunged from eighty-five thousand to sixty-five thousand, most of the victims starved, killed or expropriated by the Turks. Herzl would have rolled in his grave; what little progress Zionism had made over the years was undone by a few months of terror and famine.

BRITISH IMPERIAL STRATEGY

Although the British had never shown more than tepid interest in Zionism— Colonial Secretary Joseph Chamberlain had offered Herzl a wedge of British Uganda, not Palestine, for colonization in 1903—the Jews suddenly appeared to serve a strategic purpose in World War I and its confused aftermath. In control of Egypt, Jordan and Iraq after leading the Arab Revolt and successfully repelling Turkish attacks toward Suez, British prime minister David Lloyd George now wanted Palestine—"the strategic buffer of Egypt," according to George Curzon—as well. Yet he could not simply annex the territory without offending his European allies and American president Woodrow Wilson, whose Fourteen Points insisted on national self-determination and the peaceful, consensual formation of nation-states.

The United States of America was more than a minor obstacle as World War I wound down. Angered by the land-grabbing of the British in Palestine and Iraq and the French in Syria and Lebanon, Woodrow Wilson dispatched a commission to the region in 1919 to discover—in true American style—the feelings of the actual inhabitants of those places. The roving commission had been suggested to Wilson by his old friend Howard Bliss, who had journeyed to Paris to meet with Wilson and warn him against British and French designs on Arab territory. Bliss, son of the founder of the American University of Beirut, implored Wilson "to ask the Arabs of Palestine what *they* wanted." (Predictably, British foreign secretary Curzon judged this interest in the views of Palestine's inhabitants "the most absurd and inappropriate idea in the world.")[26] But Bliss's love for the region dovetailed neatly with President Wilson's love for democracy and plebiscites; thus, the president authorized the King-Crane Commission, named for Henry King, president of Oberlin College, and Charles Crane, a leading Chicago industrialist and Democrat. Traveling through Palestine in 1919, King and Crane made a surprising discovery. The Arabs—even the Bedouin in the desert—wanted nothing to do with the British or the Jews. Of 260 communities surveyed, 220 spoke emphatically against Zionism and the Balfour Declaration.[27] What the Arabs really wanted were the *Americans*. With the prospect of Palestine, Jordan, Iraq, Syria and Lebanon falling under British and French control—as "mandates," or temporary colonies, of the League of Nations—a majority of Arabs polled by King and Crane asked for American protection, for an American mandate that would not carve the region into Anglo-French spheres of influence and a Jewish national home. "Nearly the entire public wishes the Mandate to be given to the [United States], because they have seen that England promised to give the Jews Palestine as a national home," an Arab writer in Jerusalem asserted in 1919.[28]

Beset by American idealism and French acquisitiveness, British prime minister Lloyd George badly needed an ally in Palestine. Enter the Zionists. Chaim Weizmann, a Russian émigré and forty-year-old chemistry professor at the University of Manchester, proved to be one of the adepts of a new generation of Zionists. Using his connections to Herbert Samuel—Britain's Jewish postmaster general—Weizmann exerted extraordinary influence on Lloyd George's war cabinet, pushing the prime minister, Balfour, Jan Smuts and Alfred Milner in the direction of a Jewish state, with the assurance that they would be "granting the Magna Carta of Jewish liberation." Weizmann's rhetoric was celestial, but his trump card was earthly, something the British *needed* to justify taking Palestine, evicting the Turks, turning out their wartime allies and disappointing the Americans: "a British protectorate over a Jewish homeland."[29]

Thus, the state of Israel—still just a gleam in the Zionist eye—cropped up as the savior of British imperial strategy in the 1920s, a course that Herzl had unsuccessfully proposed to British colonial secretary Joseph Chamberlain in the 1890s.[30] Just as Whitehall had been careful to insert a British "advisory role" into Emir Faisal's Arab Revolt in 1916 to shape any postwar Arab government in Arabia and Iraq—virtually assuring Britain the whip hand in the postwar oil-rich Gulf—it now viewed the Jews of Palestine as the perfect pretext for British imperial control of the strategic coastal strip from Gaza north to Acre. Stumbling in Iraq—"The people of England have been led in Mesopotamia into a trap from which it will be hard to escape with dignity and honour . . . things have been far worse than we have been told," T. E. Lawrence reported from Baghdad in 1920—the British needed Palestine more than ever.[31] With Lawrence predicting "disaster" in Iraq—"our unfortunate troops . . . are policing an immense area, paying dearly every day in lives for the willfully wrong policy of the civil administration"—the British cabinet began to envision Palestine as the indispensable "land bridge" joining India and Egypt: "a non-stop ribbon of British Empire 'pink' between the Atlantic and Pacific oceans in the atlases of the world."[32]

Not content to become a mere ribbon of pink on British maps, Chaim Weizmann *was* happy to promise the British that a Jewish-dominated Palestine would become "an Asiatic Belgium."[33] Indeed, Weizmann's phrase was carefully chosen to lure the British. Just as neutral Belgium blocked the shortest invasion routes to England from Europe, Israel would fend off looming threats to the Suez Canal, the Iraqi oil fields and Egypt. The Turks had flown regular air raids over Port Said during World War I from bases in Palestine. They had tried repeatedly to cripple British shipping in the hundred-mile-long canal. After the war, London vowed to prevent "any great power from establishing air bases along the frontier of Egypt."[34] A British-directed Israel would hold the eastern frontier.

Lloyd George's pragmatic view of the situation seeped down to his trio of undersecretaries for Near Eastern Affairs: Mark Sykes, Leopold Amery and William Ormsby-Gore. Like the American neocons in 2001, these men saw the Middle East as a strategic crossroads that was theirs for the taking. Palestine not only offered flank protection for Egypt and Suez, it was also the Mediterranean outlet for Britain's oil pipeline from the Iraqi fields of Kirkuk and Mosul, a stop on the international air route to India and the start of the desert motor road to Asia.[35] "From the purely British point of view," Sykes told Amery in 1917, "a prosperous Jewish population in Palestine, owing its inception and its opportunity of development to British policy, might be an invaluable asset as a defense of the Suez Canal against attack from the north and as a station on the future air routes to the East."[36] In a secret letter to Britain's Cairo headquarters in May 1917, Foreign Secretary Balfour divulged that he was sending Weizmann out to Egypt "with full permission to work for a British Palestine." Balfour assumed that the Zionists would work hand in glove with British interests.[37] Though the British foreign secretary had discreetly heeded Russian opposition to the Zionists until 1917, Tsar Nicholas II's abdication in March untied his hands. Balfour increasingly viewed the Zionists as a useful "back channel" into Russia's heavily Jewish Bolshevik Party as well as a lever to divide German Jews from the kaiser and pull the large Jewish populations of Austria-Hungary away from the Central Powers.[38]

In Palestine itself, Balfour and Sykes were eagerly anticipating Field Marshal Edmund Allenby's thrust north toward Jerusalem in the fall of 1917, which rolled over Gaza, Beersheba, Jaffa and Jerusalem under a cloud of high explosive and

poison gas. To mollify Woodrow Wilson and the French (the Russians would conveniently remove themselves from the bidding by their Bolshevik Revolution in
October 1917), the British now needed a credible client in Palestine, a colonial people to "protect" and nurture toward independence. Weizmann and other leading
Zionists rushed into this embrace. Having persuaded Britain's Near Eastern desk
to begin using the term "Jewish nationalism" in connection with Palestine—at a
time when sixty-five thousand Jews comprised just 10 percent of the Palestinian
population—the Zionists would now piggyback on the British to go all the way and
secure a Jewish state.

"The Jews "have been exiled, scattered and oppressed," Balfour told Harold Nicolson in 1917. "If we can find them an asylum, a safe home in their native land, then
the full flowering of their genius will burst forth and propagate." Balfour had clearly
come a long way since authoring the Aliens Act in 1905, which had barred the UK
to Russian and Polish Jews fleeing pogroms on the Continent, to appease anti-
Semitic British conservatives (like Balfour himself). Balfour, of course, was the classic "Christian Zionist," a Protestant devoted to Zionism as a way to exile, not
integrate, Jews, whom he regarded as an indigestible "people apart." But Balfour's
sudden solicitousness for Jews struck many contemporaries as sentimental nonsense, for Palestine had not been "native land" to Jews for thousands of years. The
Old Testament *was* saturated with references to a Jewish "return" to Palestine—an
article of faith not only for Jews, but for many Protestant sects—but 90 percent of
Palestine's "natives" in 1917 were Arabs.[39]

But the British in 1917 needed to head off a late promise by Balfour's rival in
Berlin, German secretary of state for foreign affairs Richard von Kühlmann, to create a Jewish state in the Holy Land. Worried about direct appeals to German and
Eastern European Jews by the London Zionists, Kühlmann invited Jamal Pasha, the
Turkish governor in Palestine, to a meeting in Berlin with the leading German Zionists. Kühlmann dangled the promise of a Jewish homeland in Palestine in exchange
for continued Jewish investment in German war bonds. For Balfour, coping with
the Russian collapse on the eastern front, Italy's defeat at Caporetto, a French army
mutiny and heartrending British casualties at Passchendaele, the Palestine issue
exposed a rare German vulnerability. If Balfour, not Kühlmann, got credit for the
Jewish national home, then Britain might strike a political and financial blow
against the Central Powers.[40]

A prompt British declaration in favor of a Jewish state might also stiffen the new
Russian government, or so Weizmann hinted in a letter to Balfour in October 1917:

"Jews are now playing an important role in Russia, but they are against the Allies and for the Germans, yet almost every Jew in Russia is a Zionist. If they can be made to realize that the success of their Zionist aspirations depends on the Allied expulsion of the Turks from Palestine, then we can enlist them in our favor."[41] Weizmann's suggestion was picked up in revolutionary Petrograd, where a high-ranking British envoy, General Charles Barter, implored London to proclaim a Jewish national home during the seizure of power by Lenin's predominantly Jewish politburo: "Would it be possible for the Allies to make some sort of conditional promise that in the event of a successful termination of war Palestine would be given to the Jews? Such an announcement would immediately have a powerful effect in this country where Jewish influence is great and where craving for the promised land and distinct nationality is greater even than in England."[42]

AMERICAN JEWS AND ZIONISM

The British also needed to *justify* their occupation of Palestine in the new Wilsonian age of national self-determination. Employing U.S. Supreme Court justice Louis Brandeis—the president of the American Provisional Executive Committee for Zionist Affairs and the American-born son of Czech Jews—as an intermediary, Balfour and Weizmann persuaded President Wilson to back the Jewish state in October 1917. It was not easy. As in Britain, there was a deep gulf in American Jewish opinion: on one side stood Judge Brandeis and the two million largely poor Jewish immigrants who had arrived in America between 1882 and 1914; on the other side stood older, wealthier Jewish "assimilationists" like Jacob Schiff, Solomon Loeb, Louis Marshall and Otto Kahn. There was a clear class and ethnic division: uptown German-born "patricians" versus downtown Russian-born "tramps." Philosophically, wealthy American Jews like Schiff feared that Zionism would revive old prejudices against rootless "international Jews." Schiff considered Zionism a menacing development: "The establishment of a Jewish nationality in Palestine founded on the theory of Jewish homelessness must have the effect throughout the world of stamping the Jews as strangers in their own native land, and of undermining their hard-won position as citizens of those lands."[43]

Yet crucial political arithmetic in the United States favored the Zionists. Between 1900 and 1914 a yearly average of one hundred thousand Jewish immigrants—

largely from Russia, Rumania and Austria-Hungary—had entered the United States. Most settled on the East Coast—New York City alone absorbed 70 percent of the inflow—and the rest drifted westward to form cohesive pockets in politically vital cities like Chicago, Cleveland, Cincinnati and St. Louis.[44] By the time of the Balfour Declaration, Zionism had become a domestic political cause in America, and faced with this tough issue in 1917, President Wilson punted. He had his principal aide, Colonel Edward House, and his secretary of state, Robert Lansing, inform the British embassy that "everything like active participation in the [Zionist] movement would be avoided" by the U.S. government. Not because the president feared Arab opinion, but because he didn't want to alienate rich donors like Schiff and Loeb: "Too intimate relations with the Zionists would alienate the opposing Jewish faction." Late in the war, Wilson finally succumbed to heavy pressure from Brandeis, Balfour and a sequence of noisy Zionist rallies across America in 1917. He gave the Balfour Declaration his seal of approval. Like Balfour and Lloyd George, Wilson also calculated that he might use the Zionists—who had millions of adherents in Russia—to help steer the Bolshevik Revolution into more moderate channels.[45]

With Wilson's wary assent, the Balfour Declaration appeared in November 1917, pledging to "facilitate . . . the establishment in Palestine of a national home for the Jewish people." This was a dilution of first drafts of the declaration, which had Britain "securing," not merely "facilitating," the national home, but joy broke out in the Jewish quarters of Europe anyway, confirming for a moment the tactical wisdom of the declaration. "More than half the population here is Jewish," Britain's consul wrote from Odessa. "They are engaged in vast demonstrations and proces-sions before the British and American consulates." The consul counted 150,000 marchers, mainly Odessan Jews, and thousands of skinny refugees from Rumania.[46] Though the declaration guaranteed that "nothing shall be done which may preju-dice the civil and religious rights of existing non-Jewish communities in Palestine"— later the British rationale for blocking Jewish immigration into the Holy Land—the declaration drew no fixed boundaries for the "national home."[47] Indeed Robert Graves would later cite the Balfour Declaration as a classic example of expository confusion in his handbook for writers, noting that "it allowed ardent Zionists to understand the word 'in' as meaning 'consisting of' rather than merely 'situated within the borders of.'"[48]

The Zionists evinced no confusion on the matter; they wanted historic Palestine "from Dan to Beersheba"—which was to say from Mount Lebanon to the Negev, including the headwaters of the Jordan and the springs of Mount Lebanon—but the British, who had seemed eager to grant those borders in 1917, buckled three years later under pressure from the French, who had their own Lebanese and Syrian projects to defend. Having shared Egypt uneasily with the French until 1882, the British had no desire to repeat the experiment, and since a truncated Palestine would serve Britain's strategic purposes as well as a large one, Britain bowed to the French demands. France took Syria and carved off its coastal strip of Lebanon. These two new French mandates physically encroached on Palestine, but not so much as to endanger British interests. The Royal Navy could dock at Haifa, an oil pipeline could be run from Iraq to the coast, British Egypt would have its eastern buffer and Britain could begin building direct road, rail and air routes from the Mediterranean to the head of the Persian Gulf.[49]

"A Land without People for a People without Land?"

After pleading unsuccessfully for a U.S. intervention against British pragmatism, Weizmann got to work building the Jewish state.[50] The Jewish settlers did not consider themselves a minority in Arab Palestine; rather they viewed themselves as the vanguard of the world's fifteen million Jews against a mere rump of six hundred thousand Arabs, who would be brushed away or swallowed up in a surge of immigration. Zionist propagandists tested the improbable idea that Palestine was a "land without people for a people without land." Weizmann later confessed that he accepted Balfour's offer of a "national home" as opposed to a "state" only because he knew that the British would not concede a Jewish state. The Jews themselves would have to effect the conversion later, by tactical moves on the ground.[51]

Still, new "facts on the ground" had to be physically staked out. The Zionists eagerly sought land in Palestine to dilute the Arab majority, but found it hard to get. Though the British had pledged in 1919 "to encourage close settlement by Jews on the land . . . to promote intense cultivation," they now devoted most of their funds to encouraging the Arabs, who received nearly five times more acreage than the Jews from British-controlled domains. General Reginald Wingate urged Balfour to funnel the Jewish immigrants to Palestine into "reservations or colonies" within a larger, Arab-run Palestine. Further concessions to the Zionists, Wingate warned, "must be made with utmost caution."[52] The British were not exactly pro-Arab. "I dislike them all equally," General Walter Congreve thundered. "Arabs and Jews and Christians, in Syria and Palestine, they are all alike, a beastly people."[53] Yet there were strategic and cultural currents in British Middle Eastern policy that belatedly ran against fulfillment of the Balfour Declaration. During the Great War, Britain had favored a Jewish state to undermine the Germans, woo the Bolsheviks and buttress the Suez Canal, but now that the war was over, Britain had to worry about the morale of its millions of Muslim subjects in the Middle East and South Asia. Why would Britain favor a small number of Jews in Palestine when it had a large Muslim empire to manage? Weizmann sensed the equivocation in London and wrote a scathing letter to Balfour in 1919: "The present system tends to level down the Jew politically to the status of the native." If not corrected in favor of the Zionists, the system would "tend toward the creation of an Arab and not a Jewish Palestine." This presumption of Jewish superiority irritated the British, who began to have doubts about their protégés even as they were installing them in Palestine. Zionism is "an embarrassment," William Ormsby-Gore confessed in February 1919. Ronald Graham agreed; Weizmann, he said, "has sold Britain a pup."[54]

But the pup was growing fast; thirty-seven thousand more Jews poured into Palestine between 1919 and 1923. Most of them were emigrants from Poland, Ukraine and Russia, driven out by civil wars, famine and pogroms. The British governor of Jerusalem, Sir Ronald Storrs, judged the new arrivals "maddeningly tiresome." Allenby's headquarters acknowledged in June 1919 that Arab "fear and distrust of Zionist aims grow daily" and that British support for a Jewish state would require a big, costly British army in Palestine for many years. As if to confirm that prediction, Palestinian Arabs promptly killed five Jews and wounded two hundred in a rash of anti-Zionist attacks. A British inquiry in 1920 ascribed this murderous Arab radicalism to three causes: Arab dismay at the pace of Jewish immigration, the Arab belief that the Balfour Declaration voided their own right of national self-determination, and Arab susceptibility to increasingly virulent pan-Arab and pan-Muslim ideas. In the "Jaffa riots" of May 1921, 47 more Jews were killed and 146 wounded.[55]

"The League [of Nations] requisitioned Palestine from its [Arab] owners to provide the Jews with a permanent abode and appointed Britain to act as billeting officer," Arthur Koestler quipped, and Herbert Samuel arrived as this "billeting officer"—the new high commissioner of Palestine—with the task of easing Arab-Jewish tensions. Though Samuel was a devoted Zionist—he had implored British foreign secretary Edward Grey in 1914 to use World War I to "rebuild the Jewish

Temple" in Palestine—he now hesitated to crack down on growing Arab violence. Indeed he may have spurred it by appointing Haj Amin al-Husseini to the post of grand mufti of Jerusalem in 1921. As the highest authority on religious law and a fiery orator, Haj Amin became the top political and religious leader of the Palestinian Arabs and swiftly centralized power in the Supreme Muslim Council, which was the Arab community's equivalent of the Jewish Agency.[56] Like Yasser Arafat years later, Haj Amin appropriated Palestinian funds—the *waqf*, or religious trust, generated £67,000 per year; the orphan funds another £50,000—and used them to entrench himself and foment violence. Little was spent on education and social work; much on agitators, propagandists and vigilantes.[57] Samuel was no match for this. "All my life a convinced Liberal . . . I was the last man to take a hand in any policy of oppression," he wrote. Though bolstered by squads of "Black and Tans"—skull-cracking British paramilitaries sent out from Ireland to help quell the violence—Samuel watched the mandate slide into violence.

"TREMENDOUS AND INDEFINITE LIABILITIES"

When nearly one hundred Jews and Arabs were killed in rioting in Jaffa in 1921, Samuel responded by slowing Jewish immigration. He felt constrained by events in Iraq, where the British were engaged against another Arab revolt. They could not afford a wider one in Palestine. Demoralized by Lord Northcliffe's influential newspapers, which ran the gamut from the *Times* to the *Daily Mail*, many in Britain now simply wanted to wash their hands of the entire Palestinian question. "Tremendous and Indefinite Liabilities in Mesopotamia and Palestine," shouted a tabloid headline in June 1920.[58] To reduce their liability, the British government moved swiftly to contain the Palestinian troubles. Though Balfour had envisioned Jewish farms on the eastern bank of the Jordan, Colonial Secretary Winston Churchill dashed that vision in 1921, when he created the new state of "Transjordan"—today's Hashemite Kingdom of Jordan—which was really just a poor wedge of desert that did not fall naturally into the territory of Palestine, Saudi Arabia, Iraq or Syria. Of all the artificial Middle Eastern countries formed at the San Remo Conference of 1920, Transjordan was the most artificial, which helps explain its continuing problems today.[59] Churchill conferred this new British mandate on Faisal's brother Abdullah, who ran the country on the backs of his British-officered Arab Legion. In return for loyalty and prompt observance of London's edicts, Abdullah—"a cheery-faced, shrewd, genial little man"—received a monthly salary, British advisers, a security guarantee and the vague promise of independence in the future. Churchill also moved to contain the "Jewish national home" within nine thousand square miles west of the Jordan, where Zionists would wield limited political power. The Jewish national home, Churchill wrote in a government white paper, did not imply "the imposition of Jewish nationality upon the inhabitants of Palestine," but merely "the further development of the existing Jewish community."[60]

Churchill's white paper, published in 1922, became official British policy. Having uncharitably tried to dump the Palestinian problem into America's lap in 1918—when Arthur Balfour had offered to transfer Palestine to U.S. "protection"—the British now worked feverishly to satisfy conflicting Jewish and Arab aspirations.[61] They had their work cut out for them, for the Balfour Declaration was proving just another effusion of what Curzon had called Balfour's "lamentable ignorance, indifference and levity." Saddled with a deteriorating situation—described by the *Evening Standard* as "holding the scales between the Jews and Muslims"—Churchill displayed more seriousness.[62] He firmed up the mushy language of the original Balfour Declaration and aimed to reassure the Arab majority that, as he bluntly put it, Palestine would *not* become "as Jewish as England is English."[63] But the Arabs rejected even this. An Arab delegation sent to London in 1922 argued that Palestine must be readied for immediate independence by the terms of the Covenant of the League of Nations. The Arabs were in no doubt as to who would win a plebiscite in an independent Palestine. A 1923 census showed that they comprised 80 percent of the Palestinian population, which now totaled 650,000 Muslims, 87,000 Jews and 73,000 Christians.[64] But the British balked, explaining that the Balfour Declaration predated the League covenant and effectively tied their hands. Observing that Iraq and Saudi Arabia already had Arab governments, propagandists in Palestine concluded that "self-government *here* will be granted only when the Jews have sufficient numbers to *benefit* by self-government."[65]

Arab nationalists despised the Jewish national home. Their nationalism was of recent vintage—born of prewar exasperation with the anti-Arab pan-Turkism of the Ottoman Empire—but nonetheless fervent for that. When British high commissioner Herbert Samuel offered the Arabs eight of twelve seats on a Palestinian advisory council, they refused. When Samuel asked them to form an Arab Agency, to balance the claims of the existing Jewish Agency, they refused again. Since the Arabs did not recognize the existence of a Jewish Agency, Musa Kazem al-Husseini declared, why would they need an Arab Agency? Out of ideas, Samuel concluded that this Arab political boycott left him no choice but to govern by decree. Instead of generating its own self-governing institutions—the point of League of Nations mandates—Palestine let itself be governed like a crown colony, Herbert Samuel churning out as many laws for Palestine each year as the British Parliament did for the entire United Kingdom. "We have merely carried on the Turkish administration with British officials," one Englishman sighed.[66]

While the Palestinian Arabs practiced what would come to be called "rejectionism," the Jews dug in deeper. The British had been vague from the start about their plans for the Jewish national home, allowing only that a "Zionist Organization" could establish a "Jewish Agency" to collaborate with British officials in Palestine "to assist and take part in the development of the country." The British tiptoed around the issue of sovereignty, lest they inflame the Arabs or disappoint the Jews. Puzzled by the whole Palestinian question, American secretary of state Robert Lansing took Chaim Weizmann aside at the Paris Peace Conference and asked him, "What exactly is meant by the phrase 'Jewish national home'?" Lansing was worried that a Jewish state implanted in the Holy Land by British imperial interests and tens of thousands of Eastern European immigrants would contradict American president Woodrow Wilson's Fourteen Points, which emphasized transparent diplomacy and the right of populations to determine their political future. Weizmann replied carefully, "The Zionist Organization did not want an autonomous Jewish government, but merely to establish in Palestine . . . an administration, not necessarily Jewish, which would render it possible to send into Palestine 70,000 to 80,000 Jews annually." The Jews would arrive from many lands speaking many languages, and it would take a generation for Hebrew schools to make their children "as Jewish as the French nation is French and the British nation British." Only then, Weizmann reassured Lansing, sometime in the future, when Jews were a solid majority, would they "establish such a government as would answer to the state of the development of the country and to their ideals."[67]

That was for public consumption; privately, the Zionists knew that the future was *now*. Indeed at the Paris Peace Conference, British prime minister Lloyd George had quietly pressed the Zionists to move swiftly, before the other great powers or the Arabs looked too closely at just exactly what was going on in Palestine: "You have to take your chance now, before the political world freezes. As soon as it is frozen, nothing can be moved." Thus, the Jews dashed ahead at full speed. They opened Hebrew University in Jerusalem in 1925 and created a Jewish government and civil society from scratch: a national assembly, two dozen political parties, town and rabbinical councils, a Hebrew press and collective farms, or kibbutzim. Weizmann used the lever of Jewish relief funds to win over the impoverished Orthodox Jews of Jerusalem, who, until the 1920s, had piously resisted the secular Zionists.[68]

Immigration from Eastern Europe and Germany surged. A great wave of Polish and Ukrainian Jewish immigrants arrived to swell the Jewish population of Palestine to 154,000 in 1930. A typical immigrant was Golda Meyerson—the future Israeli prime minister Golda Meir—who arrived from Kiev (via Milwaukee) to find work in the political department of Chaim Weizmann's Jewish Agency. She worked alongside other immigrants like David Gruen and Levi Shkolnik, who came from Poland and Ukraine to make better lives and took the surnames Ben-Gurion and Eshkol. The threats of Hitler and other European fascists drove two hundred thousand more European Jews into Palestine between 1932 and 1938. This Nazi-induced emigration radically changed the demography of the British Mandate: Jews had been 4 percent of the Palestinian population in 1882, 13 percent in 1922, 28 percent in 1935 and were already at 30 percent when World War II broke out in Europe.[69]

Nazi, Soviet, Polish, Hungarian and Rumanian racial policy conferred a new and unexpected legitimacy on Jewish demands for a state of their own in Palestine. Tel Aviv, a sparse little suburb of Jaffa in 1920, was a Jewish city of 160,000 twenty years later. An American visitor in 1947 remarked that "the town resembles a Central European dream of a Riviera resort, and entering it one enters a world, wholly different from the essentially eastern culture of Nazareth, Hebron or Beersheba." Indeed, in Tel Aviv, a purely Jewish city, "it was easy to forget the Arabs" altogether.[70] Jerusalem and Haifa built modern Jewish quarters in the 1920s, and more than a hundred Jewish agricultural and industrial settlements spread across the mandate, producing citrus fruits, vegetables, textiles, clothing, lumber, stone and cement.[71]

Visitors were impressed. Eleanor Rathbone, a British member of Parliament who toured Palestine in 1934, returned "crazed with the tremendous work" in the Jewish areas.[72] Kermit Roosevelt, Jr., the grandson of Teddy and cousin of FDR, was less crazed by Zionist crop yields in Palestine, which he described as "propaganda farming" accomplished—even in deserts—more by charitable subsidies from rich Jewish benefactors in Vienna, Paris, London and New York than by the sweat of

Jewish brows in Palestine. Like the Jewish Agency in Palestine, the Zionist donors abroad were concerned to "make the desert bloom" at *any* price so that the Jewish settlers could be made to look industrious and the Arab inhabitants slothful. Yet despite massive subsidies, Jewish farmers were unable to produce more than a third of Jewish food requirements. Roosevelt described his visit to a kibbutz where "they had spent one million American dollars to keep a couple of hundred acres of land in pretty regular production. To eat a carrot or a melon produced off that land is like eating solid 22-carat gold. Arabs say that no human being can afford such a diet—even if his money does come from abroad."[73]

While the rest of the world limped through the Great Depression, Palestine experienced a boom in the 1930s. Haifa ran a desert pipeline down to Kirkuk for the Iraq Petroleum Company, and opened a deepwater port in 1933 and an oil terminal in 1934. The Palestine Electric Corporation constructed a hydroelectric system along the Jordan River Valley. Palestine Potash Company Ltd. built a big plant on the Dead Sea, and Jewish agriculture took off, shipping fifteen million cases of oranges, grapefruits and lemons by 1939, a fivefold increase over ten years. In all, Jewish firms in Palestine absorbed £80 million of investment in the 1930s—much of it from overseas philanthropists—which fueled the expansion.

Arabs naturally profited from the bigger tax base, bigger domestic market and improved services, but the rising tide lifted Jewish boats faster than Arab ones. Indeed Arab leaders felt themselves being flushed out of Palestine. With the fertile land in the valleys passing steadily into Jewish hands, Arabs were increasingly con-fined to congested hill villages. To slow the pace of land sales, Grand Mufti Haj Amin al-Husseini issued a fatwa, or religious order, in 1935 declaring Arabs who sold land to Jews "apostates" and denying them burial in Muslim cemeteries. But Arabs continued to sell their land, lured by the high prices being offered by Jewish purchasing agents.[74] Arab wages were also significantly lower. A Jewish road asphal-ter earned 250 piastres a day in 1935, an Arab 120; a Jewish orange picker earned 220 a day, an Arab 120; a Jewish laborer 120 a day, an Arab 70. America's consul general in Jerusalem noted an increase in Arab frustration in the 1930s. Wages remained low and land was disappearing. If there had been little Palestinian nationalism be-fore, there was a great deal now: "The non-Jewish native population of Palestine has developed a very strong nationalism. The Arabs have not done as much to develop the country, but this is no justification for one man taking away another man's house."[75]

"THE BIBLE IS OUR MANDATE"

Seesawing between support for the Arabs and support for the Jews, the British in 1927 formally recognized the "Knesset Israel": a single Jewish secular and religious community with wide powers of taxation and administration. The Arabs controlled most of the town councils in Palestine—wherever they were in the majority—but wielded no influence in the largely Jewish districts. This separation widened the cultural gulf between the two communities. Although the British apportioned education dollars proportionately by population, the Arabs relied entirely on public money for their schools, while the Jews received 85 percent of their education budget from private sources. The result was predictable. By 1937, young Jews in Palestine had universal access to primary education, near universal secondary education and broad access to Hebrew University. Arabs sank into darkness; in 1937, just 39 percent of Arab boys were at school, and only 17 percent of Arab girls. The schools themselves reinforced division. A British commission convened under Lord Peel in 1936 found that Jewish schools taught that "the national home was an exclusively and intensely Jewish achievement." Young Jews were not "expected to share their life in any way with the Arabs." And why should they? Jews in Palestine looked back two thousand years. "The Bible is our Mandate," David Ben-Gurion told the Peel Commission in 1936.

Fifty-year-old Ben-Gurion, who would go on to become Israel's first head of state, was in no mood to compromise. He had come to Palestine from Russia in 1906 to escape persecution and had worked first as a stone-breaker for Turkish road crews, then as a volunteer in the British army during World War I, and then as a kibbutznik. Ben-Gurion felt as entitled to Palestine as anyone, and he viewed rapid Jewish settlement by European immigrants like himself as a fine way to push out the Arabs. Settlements would be thrown up "to forestall as far as possible the geographical basis for possible partition or cantonization." Like settler groups today who deliberately build in the West Bank to deny it to the Palestinians, Ben-Gurion and the other Zionists in the 1930s built "on the outskirts of the country in order to secure, when the day comes, that the whole of Palestine will be Jewish, and not only a part of it."[76] Palestinian Arabs took a no less blinkered line, their schools teaching Arabic language and Islam "and no Hebrew and no Jewish history." Taking stock of this dangerous state of affairs, a British official concluded that Palestine in the 1930s was "divided into two watertight compartments, with no fusion at all between the Arab and European Jewish communities." In July 1937, Lord Peel formally recommended the partition of Palestine into separate Jewish and Arab states.[77] That was anathema to the Zionists, who would not even consider dividing Palestine. Weizmann, like the Israelis ever after, battled every impulse toward the "internationalization" of the Palestinian question, whether by the great powers, the League of Nations or the UN. "Any partition or dual or multiple control cannot benefit this country," Weizmann wrote. "Palestine must have *one* just and fair guardian, and only one."[78]

No one was in any doubt as to *whom* Weizmann wanted as that one guardian. To establish Jewish bona fides, Weizmann launched a full-blown public relations campaign. Rabbi Stephen Wise, a Hungarian immigrant who ran the Zionist Organization of America, hammered home the assertion that a Jewish state in Palestine was "one of the basic data of Western civilization." For the Arabs, Wise wrote in *Life* magazine, Palestine had "never been more than a neglected outpost."[79] Such statements were warped but effective. Wise also worked to split the British and Americans over the issue of Palestine. His stump speech—repeated on fund-raising tours around the United States—castigated the "bungling policies of the British in the Middle East" and repeated the joke that "my wife has given me a box of nails upon which to grind my teeth whenever I think of Great Britain." The strategy worked. The Democrats adopted the Jewish state in Palestine as a plank in their party platform. And leading Republicans like Wendell Willkie and Herbert Hoover declared that "power politics must not stand in the way of a Jewish national home in Palestine."[80] In the 1930s, Rabbi Wise's Zionist Organization proved adept at lining up big-name United States senators like William Borah, Harry Byrd and Millard Tydings to endorse Zionist declarations. "As Americans deeply concerned at the destruction of Jewish achievements," eleven senators wrote Cordell Hull in 1937, "we support the effort of the Jewish people to establish in Palestine a center of safety and security."[81]

AMERICA CLOSES THE DOOR TO "YIDDISH JEWS"

Ironically, this American benevolence sprang from an anti-Semitic root. New York Jews, who joined the locally recruited American 77th Infantry Division in World War I, were reviled by at least one New York newspaper as "sinister agents of Yid-

dish Bolshevism." That same division—which was 40 percent Jewish—had famously lost a battalion in the Argonne Forest in 1918 until a brave American
infantryman stole through German lines to alert American headquarters to the
battalion's whereabouts. The man who performed the rescue was Private Abraham
Krotoshinsky, a New Yorker whom one respectable newspaper identified for its
readers as "a little stoop-shouldered Polish Jew."[82] Polls in the United States on the
eve of World War II revealed that 60 percent of Americans took for granted that
"Yiddish Jews" were greedy, dishonest and pushy.[83] Congress severely limited Jewish immigration with the Emergency Quota Act of 1921 and the Immigration Act of
1924. The two bills were patently anti-Jewish (and anti-Catholic) in that they heavily favored Protestant immigrants from Britain, Germany and Scandinavia and
drastically reduced the inflow from Roman Catholic nations and the Jewish regions
of east Central Europe.

The impact on the United States was dramatic. Whereas nearly a million immigrants had entered America in 1920—including 119,000 Jews—*total* immigration
fell to just 150,000 in 1924, with paltry contingents from the three countries where
Europe's Jews were concentrated: just 603 immigrants from Rumania, 2,148 from
Russia and 5,982 from Poland.[84] World depression, unemployment and the passage
of American-style immigration acts in Argentina, Canada, Australia and South Africa shunted "Izzy Yidinski"—American slang for Jewish immigrants—toward his
last refuge: Palestine. When pressed by a delegation of Arab-Americans to clamp
down on this Jewish emigration to Palestine, Senator Borah of Idaho, a public supporter of Zionism, vented his private dislike of Jews: "I wish to Christ that they'd
all go to Palestine!"[85] In Britain, Tory MP Harold Nicolson—an outspoken "gentile
Zionist"—described a Jewish state in Palestine "as a way of confining Jews to a . . .
holiday camp, as a way of dealing with [Britain's] minority problem."[86]

In fact, as Nazi attacks on Jews intensified in the late 1930s, America and Britain
admitted only small numbers of Jewish refugees—or any other immigrants. In the
decade between 1933 and 1942, the United States accepted only 160,000 European
Jews, adding just 0.1 percent to the 3.6 percent of the American population that was
Jewish. Besieged by terrified German Jews, American consuls in Berlin, Hamburg
and Stuttgart rejected most visa applications on the grounds that the recipients
might become public charges in an economically depressed America. In the same
period, pressured by Washington, the British admitted 214,000 Jewish immigrants
to Palestine, which increased the Jewish fraction of the total population there from
17 to 30 percent.[87] Palestine, in short, beckoned as a convenient catch basin for Jew-

ish emigrants who were not welcome in America or Britain. Inexorably, it was becoming the distant "holiday camp" for Jews envisaged by Harold Nicolson.

"ESTABLISH TEL AVIV IN AMERICA . . ."

From this ignoble mix of motives, the U.S. government increasingly took the Zionist side in Palestine. From the domestic political standpoint, it could hardly afford *not* to. Until the 1930s, America, not Palestine, was the Jewish promised land, where 68 percent of European Jews emigrated, compared with just 3 percent to Palestine.[88] That explained Mussolini's assertion in 1941 that "if the Jews want a state, they should establish Tel Aviv in America."[89] To satisfy America's growing Jewish political constituency, Congress had passed a joint resolution supporting the Jewish national home in 1922, and groups of Congress members chimed in regularly thereafter to remind Great Britain of its responsibilities. "The British have fallen down completely in Palestine," New York congressman Hamilton Fish, Jr., expostulated in 1930. "They must maintain the Balfour Declaration, which was approved by the Principal Allied Powers and the U.S. Congress."[90] In 1936, publisher William Randolph Hearst chartered the Italian luxury liner *Conte di Savoia* to take an American senatorial commission to observe firsthand what Hearst's papers were calling "the Holy Land Crisis." The senators did not disappoint. "We found Palestine in a state of terror," New York senator Royal Copeland wrote from shipboard. The British had failed "to deal sternly with the [Arab] lawbreakers." Copeland and the others demanded a harsh British crackdown on the Palestinian Arabs: "The British must use stronger methods." Copeland also wanted the British to stop appeasing Arabs—to serve their wider imperial interests—and tilt more toward the Jews. "Great Britain is using Palestine as a political football for her imperial purposes," Copeland grumbled.[91] None of this political grandstanding pleased the U.S. State Department, which then, as now, perceived the insolubility of the entire Palestinian question. "I caution you not to push the British too hard," Undersecretary of State Wallace Murray told Senator Copeland on his return to Washington. "They may turn around and offer the Mandate to *us*."[92]

And who on earth would have *wanted* the Palestine Mandate? From its formal inception at the League of Nations in 1922, the British Mandate had been unworkable. Depressingly, the British and Americans had seen this coming. The King-Crane Commission to Palestine had concluded on a dire note: "The Peace Conference should not shut its eyes to the fact that the anti-Zionist feeling in Palestine and Syria is intense and not lightly to be flouted. No British officer, consulted by the Commissioners, believed that the Zionist program could be carried out *except by force of arms*."[93]

Of course the prospect of armed force contradicted the Balfour Declaration itself. The British object in 1917, as Mark Sykes had written at the time, was "not to form an autonomous or independent Jewish state, but to find a center for Jewry under British Dominion." In such a British-controlled Palestine, "the Jews would rule themselves as churches do in organized states and not on a territorial basis, which would imply dominion over other races."[94] Yet what Weizmann was pursuing after 1919 was just that: Jewish independence, autonomy and dominion in Palestine. Here was the unbridgeable contradiction of Britain's "double undertaking": the Balfour Declaration and the Palestine Mandate. Both sides, Jews and Arabs, viewed any compromise as a deep betrayal. A Lebanese witness spoke of the "monstrous absurdity" of the British-built mandate, where Arabs were "determined to assert their language, religion and culture" as a nation, while the offsetting "Zionist policy was to oppose and prevent national independence until the Jews became a majority."[95] Arthur Koestler, a Hungarian-born Jew who lived in Palestine from 1926 to 1929, fretted at the obstinacy of his Zionist colleagues, describing them as "this race of eternal victims with its flayed skin and exposed nerves."[96]

Yet who could blame the Jews for their nervousness? Having settled into their national home in the 1920s, they found themselves under withering attack from their Arab neighbors in the 1930s. With Britain's protective presence reduced to a single RAF squadron and two armored car companies in 1926, Arab nationalists renewed their attacks on Jewish towns and settlements three years later. In a single week of fighting in August 1929, 133 Jews were killed and 339 wounded. The spark for the violence was a Jewish attempt to halt new Arab construction near the Wailing Wall—the last fragment of Herod's Temple—in Jerusalem. The Arabs retaliated by desecrating the wall, snatching out the little rolled-up prayers in the crevices and burning them. Running battles erupted in Jerusalem and across the mandate; 116 Arabs were killed and 232 wounded, most by British gunfire. "The fundamental cause of the outbreak," Sir Walter Shaw's Commission of Enquiry found, "was the excessive [Jewish] immigration" of the 1920s, which would only increase in the

1930s. For the Arabs, Shaw concluded, "there is racial animosity and political, national and economic disappointment. The Arabs see the Jewish immigrants not only as a menace to their livelihood, but as a possible overlord of the future."[97]

THE NAZI RISE TO POWER AND ITS IMPACT ON PALESTINE

The Jews saw things differently because of events in Europe. Hitler's virulently anti-Semitic Nazi Party received a majority of German votes in 1932 and seized absolute power against little opposition the following year. Scenes of Jews on their knees scrubbing sidewalks in German towns became commonplace, and Jewish emigration to Palestine surged. From 1933 to 1939, 235,032 Jews—mainly Germans and Austrians—landed in Palestine. Those were the "official numbers"; unofficially, thousands of illegal immigrants—barred by British quotas—also landed. Fifteen thousand "visaless" Jews arrived in Palestine from German-occupied Europe in 1939–40.[98] This influx, caused by German persecution, destroyed whatever hope the Palestinians had of limiting Jewish immigration. Nazism, more than any other single factor, made the Holy Land Jewish. In 1936, 384,000 Jews comprised 30 percent of Palestine's total population of 1.3 million, up from 13 percent in the early 1920s. In 1938, the German menace had become so grim that U.S. president Roosevelt organized an international conference in Evian, France, to consider ways to rescue Europe's Jews. Roosevelt's delegate to the conference blasted the Germans—and their "semi-fascist" imitators in Rumania, Poland, Hungary, Latvia and Lithuania— for their "uncivilized" behavior and its chaotic impact on Palestine. The Jewish population of Germany—721,654 in 1932—had been reduced by murder and forced emigration to 286,000 in 1939, loosing hundreds of thousands of destitute emigrants on the world. This was an atrocity with global consequences. "This forced and chaotic dumping of unfortunate peoples in large numbers pushes anarchically upon the receiving states," the American delegate said. The Germans, Austrians and other anti-Semitic states, he concluded, continued to "toss large sections of their populations lightly upon a distressed and unprepared world." The result was predictable: "general unrest and . . . international strain."[99]

Once in Palestine, the Jewish refugees—even before the full horror of the Holocaust became known—were in no mood to compromise with the British or the

Arabs. "The British government cannot humiliate us by introducing racial legislation against us here in *our* country," the Jewish Agency declared in 1940. "This is not Germany."[100] Of course it was not yet Israel either, but that did not matter to the immigrants. The Holocaust, the German slaughter of 6 million Jews during the Nazi era, overrode all other considerations. Of the 3.5 million Jews who had lived in Poland before the war, only 100,000 remained alive in 1945. Only 20,000 of the 800,000 Jews in Germany and Austria survived the war. One-third of France's Jews were exterminated; the Jewish population of the Netherlands was entirely wiped out. Jews who survived and escaped to Palestine would never again tolerate threats to their existence, least of all the casual genocidal rhetoric spouted by the mufti and other Arab leaders. Germany, in short, first accelerated Jewish immigration to Palestine in the 1930s, then hardened Jewish attitudes in the 1940s, vastly complicating British, Arab and, eventually, American efforts to control Jewish settlement.[101]

"WE HAVE TAKEN THEIR COUNTRY . . ."

The combination of German genocide in Europe, well-organized Jewish emigration to the Holy Land and great power patronage should have given the Palestinian Arabs pause. Harry St. John Philby, who spent thirty years advising Saudi king Ibn Saud and sided with the Arabs in Palestine, nevertheless concluded that "the Arabs had mainly themselves to blame" for their steady loss of influence in Palestine in the 1930s. They rejected the very idea of partition and refused to accept even restrictive British quotas on Jewish immigration. Philby detected "a curious mixture of obstinacy and optimism" in the Arab attitude wholly unjustified in view of their worsening odds. The Arabs, he argued, would have been wiser to "aim at an obtainable *quid pro quo* at the expense of an undeniable right, which would never be recognized by those who had all the necessary might to defend the wrong."[102] The Arabs, in other words, ought to have cut a deal while they still held a strong hand. Instead, the Arab leadership flailed ineffectively in ways that cast them in an unflattering light.[103] Faced with Arab obstinacy and the acceleration of anti-Semitic attacks in Europe, the League of Nations and the Western democracies tilted toward the Zionists.

A full-blown Arab revolt broke out in Palestine from 1936 to 1939. Triggered by rioting against British rule in Egypt and attacks on the French administration in Syria, the Palestinian revolt was coordinated by Arab "national committees" formed to plunder Jewish property and drive out the British occupiers and Jewish interlopers. "What Arab cannot do his math," David Ben-Gurion worriedly scribbled, "and understand that immigration at the rate of 60,000 a year means a Jewish state in *all* of Palestine? Why," Ben-Gurion went on, "should the Arabs make peace? . . . We have taken their country. Sure, God promised it to us, but what does that matter to them? Our God is not theirs. We come from Israel, it's true, but 2,000 years ago, and what is that to them?"[104] The British, who had drawn their Palestine garrison down to a few armored cars and air patrols, rushed two army divisions in to contain the revolt. While awaiting those reinforcements, the British deployed a Jewish militia called the Hagana (Hebrew for "defense") against the Arab rebels, undermining London's later efforts to outlaw the militia, which eventually became the Israeli army.[105] The ensuing repression by the British and the Hagana dealt a heavy blow to the Arab cause in Palestine: their best fighters were cut down, and the Arab movement itself splintered into a feud between the ruling cliques—the grand mufti's Husseini party and the Nashashibis. Both families were old Jerusalem aristocrats. The Husseinis based themselves on the mufti's religious authority; the Nashashibis on the extensive patronage of the Jerusalem mayor's office.[106] The Nashashibis (who received secret Jewish subsidies) were more moderate and willing to coexist with the Zionists, whereas the Husseinis (who received secret British subsidies) insisted on a complete halt to Jewish immigration and nation-building and used the issue to arouse the "Arab street" and erode Raghib al-Nashashibi's base. The Husseinis prevailed, as did their party line: an exclusively Arab-run Palestine with only civil and religious rights for Jews already in Palestine.[107] Britain's Peel Commission, convened to discover the cause of the uprising, concluded that it flowed from "the desire of the Arabs for national independence" and "their hatred and fear of the establishment of the Jewish National Home." The Arabs also feared the "intensive character of Jewish nationalism in Palestine" and the "'modernism' of many of the younger immigrants," which insulted Islam. With frightened Jews pouring into Palestine from Germany and Eastern Europe by the tens of thousands, the Arabs, Lord Peel reported, "foresee not national independence in the Arab sense, but self-governing by a Jewish majority."[108]

That, the British concluded in 1937, was the essential "paradox of Palestine." Like the Arabs of Iraq or Syria, the Arabs of Palestine were ready to govern themselves, as were the Jews. But so long as the two peoples were joined under the British Mandate, self-government was, as Peel exasperatedly put it, "impracticable," because "the Mandate . . . created that antagonism and keeps it alive" by continually shifting the Jews and Arabs around like two mismatched children on a seesaw. Yet Britain could not simply walk away from the mandate "because we cannot . . . both concede the Arab claim to self-government and secure the establishment of the Jewish National Home." Peel ended by urging partition of Palestine into two states: the Jews in the north and west, the Arabs in the south and east, with a corridor to the sea at Jaffa. "The answer to the question 'Which of them in the end will be given Palestine?' must surely be 'Neither.' . . . but . . . we see no reason why, if it were practicable, each race should not rule part of it."[109]

Partition, however, posed at least as many problems as the mandate itself. The British Partition Commission formed in 1938 discovered that the patchwork pattern of settlement in Palestine meant that even a carefully drawn Jewish state would inevitably include an enormous Arab minority, as large as 49 percent. The Palestinian grand mufti declared that he would accept no partition because whatever the Jews got "would merely be a springboard from which to leap on more."[110] Thus, the British White Paper of 1939 on Palestine concluded that partition would never work. "Relations between the Arabs and the Jews in Palestine must be based sooner or later on mutual tolerance and goodwill."

To concoct "goodwill" from a poisoned environment, the British cracked down hard on Jewish immigration and land purchases. The British White Paper of May 1939 fixed Jewish immigration to Palestine at just ten thousand annually for five years, this at a time when the Nazis were hounding a hundred thousand Jews a year out of Germany and Austria. The white paper pledged to admit just seventy-five thousand Jews to Palestine by 1944, when immigration would stop altogether "unless the Arabs of Palestine are prepared to acquiesce in it."[111] Worried about opinion in Iraq, where the mufti's allegations of "Anglo-Jewish plots" roiled the Arab street, the British tilted increasingly toward the Palestinians. That explained the expansion of Jewish terror groups like the Irgun and the Stern Gang in this period. Jewish terrorists resented British efforts to buy peace with their Arab subjects at a time when the Germans were expropriating and killing Jews in Europe. In May 1941, Anthony Eden pledged Britain's support for the goal of Arab unity, which, if taken to its logical end, would have squeezed out the Jewish national home.[112] The timing of those British moves—coinciding with Hitler's genocidal campaign against the

Jews in Europe—was appalling. But the British felt that they had no other means to calm Arab opinion.[113] British destroyers diverted new Jewish immigrants away from Palestine to ports in Mauritius and Cyprus, and Jews were forbidden to purchase land in two-thirds of Palestine.

THE PALESTINIANS AND THE AXIS

For the Jews, British pressure was baffling. While the Jews of Palestine registered 136,000 men and women for British military service in the war, the Arabs allied themselves with the Germans and Italians. With the outbreak of war, Grand Mufti Husseini fled into exile and dedicated himself to a policy of collaboration with the Axis. Both Husseini and his personal secretary, Osman Kamal Haddad, were sustained in the war by German and Italian subsidies. They repeatedly proposed anti-British uprisings in Iraq, Jordan and Palestine to weaken the Allies, take pressure off the already faltering Italian war effort, and assure bountiful oil supplies and investments to German industry after the war.[114] Sentenced to death by the British, Husseini fled to Iran, where he took refuge in the German embassy. When the British and Russians invaded Iran in 1941, Husseini escaped again, this time to Rome, where he made regular pro-Fascist radio broadcasts and offered to raise an Arab Legion to fight under the swastika flag.[115]

Meeting with Nazi foreign minister Joachim von Ribbentrop in November 1941—when Haj Amin Husseini moved on to Berlin to run the Nazi-inspired and funded Büro des Grosmuftis, or Office of the Grand Mufti—Husseini promised an Arab army and Arab sabotage against Allied installations in return for a German promise to permit an Arab federation of Syria, Palestine, Jordan and Iraq after the war. "The Arabs are ready to join the struggle at Germany's side," Husseini assured Ribbentrop. "The Arabs believe that a German victory will not only be good for the Germans, but for the entire world." Apprised of Husseini's declaration of a jihad—"I, Mufti of Palestine, declare this war as a holy war against the British"—Hitler still refused to commit.[116] He did not want to alienate Mussolini, who had his own expansive designs on the Middle East, or undermine his Vichy French ally in Syria and North Africa, or disappoint German imperialists, who coveted the ores, phosphates and oil of the Middle East. Hitler merely noted Husseini's "Aryan blue eyes" and agreed that the Arab and the German had identical enemies: "the Jew, the English-man and the Communist."[117]

How, the Jews in Palestine wondered, could the British appease such people? Whereas large numbers of Zionists had volunteered for British military service, the Palestinians had dragged their feet. The Jews reasoned, as the Zionist monthly *New Judaea* put it in 1940, that ardent Jewish military service—juxtaposed with Arab languor—would force London to "drop the nebulous term 'Palestinian'" and simply talk about *Jews* in connection with the Holy Land.[118] They far preferred the utilitarian logic of the American Republican presidential candidate Wendell Willkie, who stopped in Jerusalem during the war to declare that "those who contributed the most to the war effort would receive the most at the final settlement."

Willkie's comments worried the Palestinian Arabs. Fewer than 1 percent of them had volunteered to fight with the Allies; nearly 4 percent of the Jews had, including the twenty-six thousand troops of the "Jewish Brigade" armed and mobilized by Churchill in 1944.[119] The French were even more encouraging. Until the 1960s, they were Israel's stoutest ally. "*Who* had ever established the right of the Arabs to the *whole* Middle East, to the exclusion of all foreign elements?" General Charles de Gaulle wondered after the war. "The Arab states had been created artificially after the First World War. Throughout their history the Arabs had *always* been subject to foreign domination. One after the other, the Romans, the Byzantines, the Mamelukes and the Turks had been their masters. In the name of what *principles* are the Arabs now claiming the domination of the whole Eastern Mediterranean?"[120]

The Zionists relished this French disapproval of Arab aims. In a meeting with the Soviet ambassador in London in 1941, Weizmann hinted that he would drive a million undeserving Palestinian Arabs into Iraq, Syria and Transjordan after the war and settle four million European Jews in their place. The Arabs' "laziness and primitivism turn a flourishing garden into a desert," Weizmann growled.[121] Jewish settlers would make the desert bloom.[122]

JEWISH TERRORISM

But first the Jews would make it burn. In 1940, the Avraham Stern Gang—*Lechi* in Hebrew, or "fighters for the freedom of Israel"—formed in Tel Aviv. Like the other

Jewish terrorist group, Irgun Zvai Leumi, which counted twenty-nine-year-old Menachem Begin (a new immigrant from Poland) among its members, the Stern Gang took on the really execrable paramilitary operations considered too outrageous for the Jewish Agency's illegal but semirespectable Hagana: assassinating British officials and slaughtering unarmed Arab villagers in revenge for attacks on Jewish settlements. Begin, who rose to command Irgun (and would govern Israel from 1977 to 1983), was a particularly virulent Zionist. In February 1944 his terrorist faction actually declared war on Great Britain—Stern sought funds for the conflict from the Nazi ambassador in Syria—and set as its war aim a vast Israel extending from the Euphrates to the Nile, from Iraq to Egypt.[123]

Directed by Hagana staff officers, the Stern Gang and Irgun Zvai Leumi undertook a sequence of devastating attacks on the British administration and nearly killed the British high commissioner in Jerusalem, Sir Harold MacMichael, in August 1944. Seven assassins were seen running from the scene into a nearby Jewish settlement. When the British protested this new "ruthlessness," the hard-nosed chairman of the Jewish Agency, David Ben-Gurion, chose to interpret the protest as a "slanderous and anti-Semitic attack . . . part of a systematic whispering campaign against the Jewish future in Palestine."[124] This, of course, would become a frustrating pattern in Israeli foreign policy over the years: legitimate protests dismissed as "anti-Semitism."

In November 1944 in Cairo, the Stern Gang gunned down Walter Guinness, Lord Moyne, who was heir to the great Irish beer fortune and Britain's minister resident in the Middle East. A Stern Gang handbill, distributed after the killing, called Moyne the tool of a "hostile British policy" and "the arch-enemy of the Jewish people's aspirations for freedom in their country."[125] A classified British report on terrorist activities in Palestine in 1944 found the Jews far more dangerous than the Arabs: "The totalitarian organization and regimentation of the *Yishuv* has negated free thought and speech; growing numbers of young Jewish men and women have been infected by the gangster virus." Jewish youth were enlisting in large numbers to "fight a war of liberation for the rescue and admission into Palestine of Europe's Jews."[126] To this end, Irgun terrorists shot up British offices and in May 1945 declared that VE-day was D-day to them: they would make Palestine Jewish by *any* means.[127]

To London's dismay, Irgun, Stern and Hagana attacks escalated after VE-day. In just three days in June 1945, the Jewish militias inflicted £300,000 of damage. They cut the Haifa-Kirkuk oil pipeline, tore up railway tracks, bombed train stations, blew

up a British Officers' Club and kidnapped British officials. In July 1946, Jewish terrorists blew up the south wing of the King David Hotel in Jerusalem, killing eighty-
six British officials and five visitors. Britain's police chief in Haifa deplored the
terrorism and described Begin as "a ruthless thug who made Al Capone look like a
novice."[128] Winston Churchill, a longtime Zionist supporter, gave a blistering speech
to the House of Commons after Lord Moyne's assassination in Cairo: "If our dreams
for Zionism are to end in the smoke of assassins' pistols and our labors for its future
to produce only a new set of gangsters worthy of Nazi Germany, many like myself
will have to consider the position we have maintained so consistently and so long
in the past . . . These wicked activities must cease and those responsible for them
must be destroyed root and branch."[129]

Like Yasser Arafat's PLO years later, the Jewish Agency of Chaim Weizmann and
David Ben-Gurion publicly disowned the terrorists—deporting 279 of them after
the Moyne assassination—but there was a good deal of collusion between Jewish
officials and the terrorists to advance the Zionist program. "Already," a British historian wrote, "official Zionism was descending its spiral of intrigue, deceit, flattery
and corruption." Arthur Koestler called those Zionist deceptions "the main cause
of that ambiguous twilight in which the birth of the new state was shrouded." International observers simply did not *believe* statements from the Jewish Agency. In
a March 1948 diary entry, a Jewish soldier explained why: "The average Englishman
in Palestine doesn't like us and doesn't believe us. One reason is that we have plugged
him with too much propaganda."[130]

"THE REALLY DANGEROUS PEOPLE . . ."

Arab propaganda was scarcely more credible. Incredibly, the grand mufti—who had
organized Muslim "black legions" for Himmler's SS and encouraged genocide and
rapine from Berlin—published a statement in the *New York Times* in October 1946
positioning himself as a great Arab nationalist with the right "to form a democratically constituted government in Palestine." Unable to return to Jerusalem, the
mufti lived in exile in Egypt, where the Yugoslavs sought his extradition for atrocities committed by Bosnian Muslim units raised and blessed by the mufti.[131] But
scores of less prominent pro-German Palestinians returned to positions of power
in the Arab community after the war. Indeed, most Arab Nazis and Axis agents had

been released by the British and Free French by 1944, and many of them had risen to leadership positions in Egypt, Palestine, Iraq, Syria and Lebanon.

In Palestine, Hussein al-Khalidi, Auni Abd al-Hadi and Musa Alami returned to general acceptance as official leaders of the Palestinian Arabs. A half dozen Palestinians arrested and deported during the 1936–39 disturbances were allowed by the British to return in 1945. Many of them were notorious gang leaders and assassins: Shakir Abd al-Aziz, Abd ul-Hamid Jaulani and Fawzi Jarrar. Even those Palestinians like Jamal al-Husseini, captured on their way to Berlin and detained in Rhodesia for the duration of the war—and described by Colonial Secretary Lord Cranborne as "the really dangerous people"—were released by the British and permitted to return as "spokesmen of Palestine's Arabs." Only the mufti himself had put himself beyond the pale with his demoniac speeches and SS affiliation. The rest of the Palestinian leadership returned to a hero's welcome.[132] Even the moderates among them rejected a Jewish state. Musa Alami, a liberal Palestinian leader, had famously told Ben-Gurion in 1934 that the most the Jews could expect from the Arabs was a small enclave around Tel Aviv within a wholly Muslim Palestine. When Ben-Gurion objected that Jewish investment and development would benefit *everyone* in Palestine—Muslims, Jews and Christians—Alami replied that he "would prefer that the country stay poor and desolate for another hundred years, until the Arabs could develop it themselves."[133]

CHAPTER 2

OIL

ARABIA WAS EVEN POORER and more desolate than Palestine in the 1930s. To Westerners, the Kingdom of Saudi Arabia was simply "Arabia Deserta," a largely vacant place of scorched deserts. The British explorer Sir Wilfred Thesiger called it "a bitter, desiccated land which knows nothing of gentleness or ease," just fire-blacked stones at scattered campsites and "a few faint tracks polished on the gravel plains." Thesiger observed that an Arabian province the size of an English county might subsist on a single well that would "run dry after watering a few score camels." There the temperature regularly "reached 120 degrees in the shade—and there is no shade," just salt flats, sterile white sands, half-buried palms, empty wadis and jagged bare mountains in the distance. In 1917, a rare flood raced through the Wadi Dawsir after heavy rains. The Bedouin loped on their camels to the governor to warn him that the flood was approaching his oasis and he laughed hysterically in their faces: "Bring me a coffee-cup, and I will *drink* the flood."[1]

Like Thesiger and the sun-stricken governor of Wadi Dawasir, Lawrence of Arabia found the conditions unbearably hard. "Death in life," Lawrence called his grueling months in Arabia during World War I. "Men live here," Thesiger observed, "only because it is the world into which they were born. They know no other way."[2] An American traveler in the 1940s considered that here in the desert "war *is* life's proper schedule," but not war between men, rather war "against the elements.

Death by starvation, thirst or epidemic disease is an ever-present companion to life."[3] It was a companion in the cities too, even in the capital. An American diplomat in Jedda in 1947 complained of the pestilential conditions there. Just about everyone outside the embassy walls was sick with something—"flu, bronchitis, malaria, measles, tuberculosis, asthma, rickets, gastritis, malnutrition, or tropical ulcers"—and they all ended up in the American embassy medical clinic because of "the total inadequacy of the [Saudi] medical service."[4] There was no escape either. U.S. Army engineers sent to survey and recommend improvements to Saudi Arabia's roads in 1944 were appalled. "We have completed our reconnaissance of 3,315 miles of road in Saudi Arabia. For the most part, roads as such do not exist except for camel tracks." What roads there were had vanished beneath sand seas. "Two years minimum of blasting, grading, ditching and marking" would be needed to make just a few hundred miles of road serviceable.[5]

Saudi Arabia had been a death-inducing wasteland for centuries. There, in the western region of Hejaz, traders established the towns of Mecca and Medina on the caravan routes connecting Muscat, Mesopotamia, Egypt and Africa. In AD 570, the prophet Muhammed was born in Mecca, and in his lifetime he saw most of the Arabian Peninsula pulled together under Muslim Arab rule. The Turks took nominal control of Arabia in the sixteenth century, but Arab clans and tribes wielded real power in the principal regions: the Najd, the vast central plateau around Riyadh; the Hasa, the eastern province along the Persian Gulf coast; and the Hejaz, the western holy land surrounding Mecca and Medina.

WAHHABISM

Returning to his native Najd in 1740 after a long residency in Basra and Damascus, a middle-aged Abdul Wahhab began preaching a fundamentalist Islam reduced to the simplicity that had characterized it "before the tide of Arab conquest had laid the wealth and luxury of Asia at the feet of the Arab conquerors." Like Osama bin Laden today, Wahhab was a "Salafist." *Salaf,* which means "predecessors," refers to Muhammed's seventh-century disciples who absorbed and transmitted his piety. That, of course, was easier to do in the seventh-century desert, where thirsty, hungry men could stare Allah and eternity unflinchingly in the eye without material or carnal distractions. But Wahhabism crept out of the deserts and became a distinct school of Sunni Islam after the prophet's death, when Wahhab gave Salafism a political twist by naming the House of Saud the defenders of Arabian virtue. He denounced "the loose-living at Mecca and the idolatry in Medina" and co-opted the al-Saud family—the dominant clan in the Najd—with his perfervid preaching.[6] Most of the other tribes followed the example of Wahhab and the Sauds and returned—at least superficially—to fundamentalist Islam. This "Wahhabism"— borne on Saudi camels and scimitars—spread from the Najd into the Hejaz and gradually became the dominant sect in Arabia. Morale and motivation among the Wahhabi Ikhwan, or brethren, was never a problem, for Abdul Wahhab had licensed them to rape, rob and kill anyone who resisted his teachings.[7]

In Istanbul, the capital of the Ottoman Empire, the Turkish sultans interpreted Wahhabism as sedition. Arabia—riven by tribes and factions—was difficult to govern even in the few enclaves where the Turks managed to install emirs, or governors, amid the roistering clans. Wahhabism's rejection of Sunni orthodoxy made the task even harder. Yet two determined Turkish military campaigns in the early nineteenth century failed to wipe out the Wahhabis. Coercion having failed, the Turks tried diplomacy. In the 1860s, Sultan Abdulaziz in Istanbul tried to refashion his tottering Ottoman Empire into a modern European state. The sultan and his viziers conceded local governments, responsible ministers, tighter finances, fairer taxes, military modernization, better schools and land and social reforms. In Saudi Arabia, they tried to wean Arabs from raiding and brigandage and settle them instead on rice and date farms to protect them "from the evil of Bedouin Arabs and tribes," whom the sedentary Turks called "vermin."[8] Of course some "vermin" were more useful than others, and at the turn of the century, the Turks helped the Rashid family push the Sauds out of power in the Najd and the Hasa.

IBN SAUD

The Turkish-backed Rashids seized and held power in Arabia only from 1890 to 1902, when a twenty-six-year-old desert prince named Abdul Aziz Ibn Saud burst from his Kuwaiti exile with two hundred camel troops to reestablish independent Wahhabi control of a region that was nominally an Ottoman *sanjak*, or province.[9]

Six feet three inches tall, rugged and handsome, Ibn Saud made a powerful first impression, which explained why the British and the al-Sabah rulers of Kuwait had sheltered him as an eventual hedge against Turkish expansion into their profitable domain at the head of the Persian Gulf. As an investment, Ibn Saud paid off. He was charming, shrewd and physically brave—essential qualities in the rough-and-tumble world of the Arabian desert—and sufficiently pious to rally even the most fervent Wahhabis: "[H]e believed that Islam is all in all," a British analyst wrote in 1944.[10] Ibn Saud named his shock troops the Ikhwan, or Salafist Sunni brethren, who left their tribes and sold their horses, camels and other property to join ascetic Wahhabi hamlets and resume the old Arabian sport of cutting the Ottoman telegraph between Damascus and Medina, a sport only briefly suspended by the more pliant Rashids.[11] Dressed in coarse white shirts and head scarves—symbols of Muhammed's austerity—the Ikhwan troops set the tone in the lands under Saudi control. Called Jund al-Tawhid—"soldiers who enforce the oneness of God"—they struck fear into every oasis and town they approached. The Ikhwan had the power to plunder or kill anyone suspected of impiety. They had a reputation for "ignorance and ferocity," and orthodox clerics rued their "perverted fundamentals," but the Ikhwan brothers nevertheless enjoyed the unstinting support of Ibn Saud, who used their regular jihads to expand his growing realm.[12] With Wahhabi raiders gathered on his frontiers, Sheik al-Sabah of Kuwait, another slackly governed Ottoman province, appealed for British protection in 1899 and got it, an accident of history that would eventually blossom into full-fledged independence, oil riches, nationhood and eternal Iraqi regret over the "lost province of Kuwait."

With the Ottomans distracted after 1908 by the Young Turk Revolution as well as the overthrow of Sultan Abdul Hamid II, the struggle with Italy for Libya, and the two Balkan wars, which ripped away the last Turkish provinces in Europe, Ibn Saud found himself free to unleash the cruel Ikhwan brethren in a broader struggle for control of the Najd and the Hasa. There too the Turks crumpled, weakly confirming the usurper Ibn Saud as *wali*, or "protector," of the Arabian Peninsula.[13] In 1913—with the Turks pinned down in the Second Balkan War—Ibn Saud's mounted columns reduced the Turkish forts in Arabia one by one, lashing together scaling ladders from date palms and well ropes and surging over the walls in the dead of night.[14] For the Turks, those sneak attacks in the Hasa were the beginning of the end. Until 1913 they had effectively pressed "Wahhab's rebel horde" into the arid, inland Najd. Now, with control of Arabia's eastern coast as well as the interior, the Saudis would either continue to expand or sell their new conquests to the ubiquitous British, who already controlled Yemen, Oman, Bahrain and Kuwait and had designs on Saudi Arabia as well.

Neither scenario was acceptable to the Turks. To them, Saudi Arabia was strategically vital for two reasons: its holy places in the west buttressed Istanbul's religious authority, and its central and eastern provinces—the Najd and the Hasa—impeded British access to Kuwait, Bahrain and Iraq. With forty-year-old Ibn Saud in the saddle in Riyadh, the door was open to further Wahhabi inroads and deeper British imperial probes along the Persian Gulf. Further west, the Hejaz and its holy places—key struts of the Ottoman caliphate, or religious leadership—remained in the hands of the Turkish-appointed "Sherifians" until World War I. The "Sherifians" were the Hashims, or "Hashemites," who were bitter rivals of the Sauds. To slow down Ibn Saud—despised by the gentler Hashemites as a barbaric warlord—the Turks had appointed Emir Hussein, the leading Hashemite, as their chief magistrate, or sherif, of Mecca in 1908.

Worried by Ibn Saud's charisma and ambition, the Turks tried to buy him off but were rebuffed with words that must ring false to the notoriously loose-living Saudi royal family today. "You have been content to be rulers without realizing the responsibility of rulers to take thought for the welfare of their subjects," Ibn Saud scolded the sultan. The House of Saud would do better for the Arabs, he vowed. They would behave differently from the other desert princes and the Ottomans, and *not* let their energy and principles "wilt in contact with the wealth and luxuries of the conquered provinces."[15]

"PROTECTING THE PURITY OF ISLAM"

World War I, which exploded in the midst of these wrenching political changes, was pivotal for Arabia. Great Britain viewed the region as vital to the security of the British Empire. One of the short routes from London to India passed through Suez; the other along the Tigris and Euphrates rivers and through the Persian Gulf. Britain had traditionally controlled this area, despite its nominal allegiance to the Ottoman Empire, through treaties of protection with the various Arab sheikhs in Saudi Arabia, Bahrain, Qatar and Kuwait. Indeed, Saddam Hussein's invasion of

Kuwait in 1990 would be based on the historically interesting argument that the sheikhdom was really Iraqi because it had been illegally detached from Ottoman Basra during World War I.

Determined to hold their fractious empire together, the Turks dangled some attractive options before the Arab princes of the Najd and the Hejaz in 1914, but the British and the French, who wielded considerable influence with the Sauds and Hashemites, determinedly closed off those options. Faced with the inconvenient fact that there was actually much to commend the modernizing German-allied Turkish government—it had been secular and constitutional, with expanding trade, industry and railways, a functioning judiciary and the rule of civil law since the Young Turk Revolution of 1908—France and Britain weirdly declared that Western progress and modernity were actually quite evil. Groping for a lever to move the Arabs against the Central Powers, French propaganda dubbed the modernizing Turks "a foreign and half-believing folk." They were foreign because they were Turks, not Arabs, and half believing because their rising men were secular officers like thirty-four-year-old Mustafa Kemal—the future Atatürk—who enjoyed whiskey, women and automobiles, spoke fluent French and waltzed gracefully. By supporting the Hashemite Sherif Hussein of Mecca against Westernizing Young Turks like Mustafa Kemal, France and Britain claimed to be "protecting the purity of Islam." One French newspaper fretted (surely disingenuously) that "the Germans and Turks will deprive Islam of its dogmatic and supernatural meaning by introducing the creed of modern Germanism, falsifying religious ideals and leavening the ancient religion of Muhammed with the spirit of modernity."[16] Those early-twentieth-century British and French machinations were astonishing. Trying to modernize the Ottoman Empire against Muslim superstition and British and French sabotage, the Young Turks felt, as one historian put it, "like a troupe of actors trying to improvise a five-act play before a crowd of violent, heckling devotees of Shakespeare."[17] They never stood a chance.

Britain's Balfour Declaration would have undermined even the wiliest Anglo-French sabotage. "It made a profound impression on . . . Muslims," General Reginald Wingate wrote Balfour from Cairo in 1917. "They view with little short of dismay the prospect of seeing Palestine and even eventually Syria in the hands of Jews, whose superior intellect and communicative abilities are feared by all alike." Arab fears, Wingate concluded, tended to reinforce "German-inspired Turkish propaganda."[18] In league with the Germans, who had plans to exploit the Berlin-

Baghdad railway, the Turks were offering *ihtilaf*, or "decentralization": a self-governing Arab state under nominal Turkish suzerainty.[19] Such a reformation, while good for the Arabs, would not have served British or French imperial interests. London and Paris needed physical control of the Middle East after the war, and thus searched for tractable puppets like Emir Hussein of Mecca. "Should the war lead to the breaking up of the Turkish Empire," British prime minister Herbert Asquith announced, then "the province of Hejaz [must] come under the special consideration of the British government."[20] Mecca and Medina had deep religious significance for the Muslims of the British Empire, and the Hejaz could be a foothold for British oil interests. There was indeed, as German commentators wrote during World War I, something "contemptible and backward" in those British and French tactics, but they worked in the short term.[21]

As fighting raged in Europe and the British army absorbed horrific casualties at Mons, Loos and the Somme, British headquarters in Cairo sent Captain T. E. Lawrence to meet with Emir Hussein, the Hashemite sherif of Mecca, and persuade him to raise an Arab revolt against the Turks. The British and French, increasingly interested in an "eastern strategy" to reduce the gruesome casualties on the western front, induced Emir Hussein to declare the independence of the Muslim holy places and crown himself "king of the Hejaz" in 1916. London and Paris hoped that the ensuing Arab Revolt would divert Turkish and German troops from the eastern and western fronts to a costly new front in the Middle East. Not surprisingly, Ibn Saud interpreted the British move less as an attack on the Turks than as one on himself, and he met the British and Hashemite challenge by attacking the last Turkish outposts in his own enlarged kingdom along the eastern coast, while Hussein annexed most of southern and western Arabia to the Hejaz. From Cairo, Ibn Saud received his own version of Emir Hussein's Lawrence: Captain W. H. I. Shakespear. Poor Shakespear was promptly killed in action while directing Ibn Saud's artillery near Zilfi in 1915. Shakespear of Arabia was as seasoned and respected by the Arabs as Lawrence, and his premature death reportedly "left Ibn Saud to sulk in his tents," reducing him "to relative insignificance as a factor in Arabian politics."[22]

Without a British mentor, Ibn Saud watched leadership of the Arab Revolt gravitate to Sherif Hussein, who threw his forces into what one historian called "the world's first oil war." While Hussein's troops battled on the Arabian Peninsula, a British army in Persia attacked into Iraq to seize Basra, buffer the big British wells and refineries at Abadan, and make the Persian Gulf a "British lake."[23] Lawrence tried and failed to get the Saudis to open a third front against the Turks. In his dispatches to Cairo and London, Lawrence blasted Ibn Saud for his immobility and for the parochialism of his "Wahhabite missionaries," who had unhelpfully denounced all Shiites and even orthodox Sunnis like Emir Hussein and his son Faisal as "*kafirs*," or infidels, deeply eroding Lawrence's efforts to build a broad anti-Turkish Arab coalition. The Saudis "preach an exaggerated fatalism," Lawrence reported in 1917. "'God does everything'; they forbade medicine to the sick, discouraged trade, building and forethought. A favourite saying was, 'If a man falls into a well, leave it to God to pull him out.'"[24]

Ibn Saud's embrace of this Wahhabi fatalism was motivated by a desert realpolitik that would permanently mark Saudi Arabia. In 1917, Lawrence observed that the "Wahhabi sect" had withered away over the centuries only to be abruptly and purposely revived by Ibn Saud to drive a wedge between the emir of Mecca's "rich and comfortable towns"— "fond of silk and tobacco and not too fond of prayer"— and the poor, uncomfortable desert nomads.[25] With a small, weak army and a host of competing tribal sheikhs, Ibn Saud expanded his reach on the Arabian Peninsula by gathering in the Bedouin and allying everywhere he went with the *mutawwa*— Koran-reading "men of religion"—who clustered in the towns and oases that Ibn Saud absorbed in the first thirty years of the twentieth century. Most of the Saudi emir's new subjects were poor illiterates, and Ibn Saud—a stranger and an interloper everywhere he went—relied on the *mutawwa* to explain and legitimize his new state and persuade his growing body of subjects to perform military service and pay taxes. Naturally, the intercession of the holy men on Ibn Saud's behalf—they proclaimed him imam, or religious leader, wherever he went—came with a price. A pious man to begin with, Ibn Saud was forced to redouble his piety and embrace Salafist doctrines and rituals as well as the clotted clerical bureaucracy in Riyadh that so annoyed the efficient Lawrence.[26] Invited by the British to Basra during the war, Ibn Saud was treated to a display of the latest technologies. The British were hoping to nudge him into the modern age under British, not German, tutelage. He was whisked to Basra in a British train, then taken to inspect British heavy artillery, airplanes and the bustling, mechanized wharves on the Shatt al-Arab waterway dividing Iran and Iraq. At a British field hospital, the disbelieving king was x-rayed and shown the bones of his own hand under the roentgen rays. His British escorts waited eagerly for a reaction, but the famously laconic king's only comment was: "It is good for us to see your might."[27] That was the Saudi royal family in a nutshell: they made a virtue of primitivism, and gave nothing away.

THE END OF THE CALIPHATE

The rival Hashemite and Saudi emirs grated against each other until 1924, when, in faraway, newly secular Istanbul, Kemal Atatürk abolished the office of the caliph. This was a step with far-reaching consequences. The caliph was Islam's pope—the spiritual leader of Sunni Islam and the symbolic successor to the prophet—whose holy writ extended from Cameroon across to Indonesia and up through the Indian subcontinent to the Middle East and Soviet Central Asia. In Transjordan, Emir Hussein, who had denounced the caliphate during the Great War as a seventh-century office that was "grammatically absurd and blasphemous" in the twentieth, swallowed his objections and proclaimed himself the new caliph of Islam.[28] Hussein saw the caliphate as a convenient club with which to beat Ibn Saud, but the British Empire, with its millions of Muslim subjects around the world, also lurked behind the move. Ever since their defeat of the Ottoman Empire in 1918, the British had been looking to transfer the caliphate to a pliable Arabian regime in the Hejaz whose "geographical position would interpose it as a wedge between the Islam of Africa and that of India." Such a regime, a British analyst concluded in 1917, needed to "be strong enough to *pose* as an independent sovereign" but weak enough to be manipulated from London.[29]

Fully apprised of this British and Hashemite bid for leadership of the Muslim world—and with little to lose, the British having just terminated their monthly subsidy to Ibn Saud—the Saudis struck back furiously.[30] Ibn Saud's Ikhwan army invaded the Hejaz in 1925 and seized Mecca and Medina, where the Wahhabi troops briefly earned international opprobrium by firing into the tomb of the prophet to expel the Hashemite defenders. Thwarted in their bid to place the Hashemites in control of Arabia and the holy places, the British discreetly withdrew Sherif Hussein to Cyprus. This was a turning point in Saudi history. Hussein was moderate and relatively secular. In a conversation with Lawrence of Arabia in 1917 he had vowed to "reduce friction between the [Muslim] sects, restrain extremists, persuade moderate Sunnis and moderate Shiites to meet together under his presidency and to purge Islam of the lunatic idea that it is a polity bound temporally to a single infallible head."[31] The caliphate, which the British had planned to confer on Hussein to give force to his moderation, languished. Its next claimant would be Osama bin Laden.

In December 1925, Ibn Saud's troops cut through the barbed wire and mine-fields girding Jedda and added that last British outpost on the Red Sea to the expanding Wahhabi state. There the Saudis gave a glimpse of the draconian way in which they would treat believers and infidels alike. Jedda, which means "grand-mother," was reputed to be the last resting place of Eve, the grandmother of the human race. Her vast mausoleum was a holy place for many, but the Wahhabis—who forbade the veneration of tombs—smashed it down and ground the rubble into dust.[32] Confronted with the usual diplomatic "capitulations" that the Christian great powers had imposed on weaker empires like Turkey and China in the nine-teenth century to protect the rights of Europeans, Ibn Saud coldly announced that he would "tolerate no criticism or interference with God's law on earth."[33] None of the great powers—let alone moderate Muslim states like Persia or Egypt—was in a mood to recognize this grim new kingdom, which merely reinforced the irony that the atheistic Soviet Union was the first country to confer formal diplomatic recog-nition on Ibn Saud's Wahhabi state in 1926. Not to be left out, the rest of the great powers reluctantly followed suit.

THE BIRTH OF SAUDI ARABIA

Now "King of Hejaz and Najd and its Dependencies," forty-five-year-old Ibn Saud worried that the new title lacked zest and did not sufficiently exalt the conquering family. Thus, in 1932, the Kingdom of Najd and Hejaz and its Dependencies became simply "the Kingdom of Saudi Arabia," which meant "the Arabia of the Sauds." When tribesmen in one desert village put about a rumor that the king was impotent because of a war wound sustained against the Turks, Ibn Saud descended on the village with his retinue, selected an attractive virgin, married her on the spot and bore her immediately to the royal tent to assert his sovereignty.[34]

The "state and its countries and lands are to God, and then they are *mine*," Ibn Saud affirmed, and one of his first acts—after purging the most fanatical Ikhwan brothers—was to decree that every member of his extended family was of royal blood. The king hoped to replace fanaticism with nepotism as the kingdom's ruling principle. Blood was the glue of the Bedouin tribes and no Bedouin—including the Sauds—owed anything to anyone (except a guest) outside his family. "God have mercy on me and Muhammed and no one else beside" went an Arabian desert prayer.[35] Since the Saudi king had at least 45 sons and 125 daughters by more than 200 wives, the royal family in its palaces in Riyadh and Jedda mushroomed alarmingly and began to gobble up public revenues.[36] To hedge against the inevitable scandals that would attach to the king's extravagant sons and nephews, Ibn Saud conferred authority for all Saudi law and morality on the Wahhabi ulema, or priesthood, which claimed for itself direct knowledge of God's will and dealt as severely with Saudi morals as the princes did with the public purse. The mosque—in all its obscurantism—would be made to serve as a stand-in for democracy. When U.S. secretary of state John Foster Dulles referred years later to "Saudi public opinion," a Dutch colleague snapped back, "In Saudi Arabia there is no such thing as public opinion."[37]

Over the years, the joyless Saudi clerics would wage war on the modern age. Ibn Saud had tended toward pragmatism: "Allah gave Arabia the true faith," he liked to say, "and he gave the Western world the iron." As guardian of Mecca and Medina, it was Saudi Arabia's peculiar task to make use of the West's "iron"—its advanced technology—while laboring to keep Islam pure.[38] That was an uphill battle in the bawdy, materialistic twentieth century. "Saudi Arabia lags far behind the northern Arabs by not having gone through the Western colonial mill," a British diplomat observed. "The British and French Mandates meant having to rub along with the technologically advanced foreigner."[39] Isolated by their deserts and pre-oil poverty, the Saudis never had to rub along with *anyone*. Thus—incredible as it seemed to the rest of the world—the Wahhabi clerics in the 1930s tried to ban tobacco, and then attempted bans on cars, airplanes, telephones, modern hospital equipment, photography, record players, cinemas, radios and television. All of them were seen, like alcohol, to be contrivances of the devil engineered to destroy the faith and peace of believers. Ibn Saud made occasional stands against the clerics, but was generally forced to accede to them because they were the glue that held the country together.[40]

A politically correct language evolved in Saudi Arabia to describe the regular collisions between religion and what was obliquely called "civilization," or *tamaddun.* Civilization—the secular education and culture of the West—was desperately needed to develop and irrigate the hardscrabble desert kingdom, so hundreds of young Saudi males were dispatched to colleges in Syria, Egypt, Britain, France, Germany and the United States. Most of them relished their new surroundings.[41] Naturally, a gulf began to open between such privileged, rather liberal Saudis and the fundamentalist poor, who had never had their eyes opened by foreign travel or education. The first truck to jounce into the Saudi town of Hauta in the 1940s was taken for a demon and publicly torched in the marketplace. When a Wahhabi cleric flew to Cairo for meetings, he refused to have a passport photo taken on the grounds that cameras were infernal machines, an unscientific claim that both the Saudi and Egyptian governments accepted.[42] This conservatism collided violently with urbanization and rationality. The populations of Riyadh, Medina and Jedda quadrupled in the first twenty years of the kingdom; Damman, Dhahran and Mecca grew nearly as fast.[43]

In the years after World War I, no one suspected that Saudi Arabia would shortly become the world's gas station. In the 1920s, the British, who controlled most Persian, Iraqi and Arabian oil production to fuel the Royal Navy, had freely conceded the deserts and offshore waters of Saudi Arabia to America's Standard Oil and Texas Fuel companies after failing to locate impressive quantities of oil in their own concessions around Bahrain Island. Oddly, the British considered Saudi Arabia entirely dispensable in the 1920s and 1930s. Their prime concerns on the desert peninsula were to monitor "Bolshevik agents," who mingled with the pilgrim throngs to Mecca, and to eradicate cross-border raids by Wahhabi "Ikhwan elements" into Kuwait and Iraq. The first task was rendered easier in the 1920s because Moscow deemed the Saudis "too ignorant and ill-fitted to assimilate the advanced Soviet ideas," and because the Soviet *rezident* in the kingdom was "a confirmed drunkard, who [drank] six or seven liters of wine per day, besides liquors."[44] The second task, a British analyst noted, was far more easily accomplished in the twentieth century than it had been in the nineteenth: "Desert warfare is no longer a threat because air warfare has taken the gilt off the gingerbread. Raiders can now be killed with aircraft before they get away with the loot."[45]

As for the real loot—the "black gold" lodged beneath Arabia's desert sands—it needed to be "proven up" before the British would get really interested. With crude oil selling for just a dime a barrel during the Depression, no oil company wanted to waste money drilling into Saudi Arabia's unproven geology or ferrying the small quantities they did extract over to the British refinery at Bahrain on barges.[46] The United States was not much more hopeful; though eager to break into the British-run Gulf, Washington did not bother establishing diplomatic relations with Saudi Arabia until 1933, and would not get around to opening an embassy until 1944. Before the oil boom, the kingdom was a poor country that produced nothing but dates, wheat, barley, hides, camels, horses, donkeys and sheep.[47] It lived from a peculiar kind of tourism: the thousands of pilgrims, or hajji, who journeyed to Mecca and Medina every year to visit the holy places. In the 1920s, a hundred thousand Muslim pilgrims entered the Hejaz every year, each spending an average of fifty dollars on tolls, transport, customs, room and board. Those rather paltry expenditures in western Saudi Arabia formed the mainstay of Saudi public revenues before the discovery of oil in commercial quantities on the east coast. As late as 1944, the Saudis were earning nearly seven times as much from pilgrims (13 million riyals) as they were from oil (2 million riyals).[48] Thus, Ibn Saud's seizure of the holy shrines from the Hashemites in 1925—when 130,000 pilgrims descended on Mecca—had been an economic as much as a strategic or religious move, but even hajj revenues in a good year were not enough to fund a growing state.

THE SAUDIS STRIKE IT RICH

In 1931, Ibn Saud hired American mining engineer Karl Twitchell to prospect for oil along the Saudi coast across from Bahrain Island, where the British had drilled several productive wells (and would hit pay dirt in 1932). Ibn Saud had covetously watched the rich growth of other nations' revenues after British explorers found oil in Iran in 1908, Kuwait in 1924 and then the great, gushing Iraqi Kirkuk field in 1927.[49] The Saudi king wanted a piece of the action. Poking around Saudi Arabia, Twitchell found promising core samples beneath the peaks of Jebel Dhahran and hired Standard Oil of California to widen the search. The work was arduous; in the first sweeps across four hundred thousand square miles of Saudi desert—an area more than one-fifth the size of the continental United States—American geologists spent more time heaving their jeeps out of sand dunes and gullies than tapping rocks. Some oil was found in June 1932, but each well—dry or wet—cost a quarter of a million dollars just to drill, an intimidating proposition in those lean Depression years. Having spent most of the 1930s drilling too close to the surface of the Saudi desert, American explorers bashed down to 4,727 feet in 1938 and finally struck oil in what were judged "commercial quantities."[50] By 1939, Standard Oil was drilling the entire length of the Dhahran peninsula and was pumping thousands of barrels a day up a thirty-nine-mile pipeline to the new harbor and oil terminal at Ras Tanura.

Twitchell and the Saudis had gone fishing for a cod and caught a whale. A desert kingdom that had derived no profit at all from its eastern provinces and had no prospect of repaying its $600,000 foreign debt in 1930 was effortlessly raking in $1 million per year in oil field fees and royalties by 1939. For every barrel of hot oil the Americans pumped to the surface, they paid King Ibn Saud a royalty of seventy-five cents.[51] For the Saudis, a royal adviser remarked, "the oil story was a veritable romance, surpassing the most improbable tales of the Arabian Nights in its astonishing evolution from the first laborious steps of the American geologists in the desert to the discovery and exploitation of a liquid El Dorado, far down in the bowels of the earth."[52] Indeed, by the time the Germans invaded France in 1940, geologists were confidently estimating that the Persian Gulf region contained 42 percent of the world's oil reserves. Most of the known reserves were in Iran, Iraq and Kuwait, but, even in its baby shoes, Saudi Arabia accounted for 19 and 8 percent of Mideast and world totals, respectively. That potential, as well as keen American interest, explained Saudi Arabia's independence. Instead of being colonized like Iraq or Kuwait, Saudi Arabia's American mentor ensured that the House of Saud remained sovereign, the better to be exploited by Washington.[53] "In all surveys of the situation," an American analyst wrote, "the pencil came to an awed pause at one point and place: the Middle East . . . Stolid geologists flew over the structures outlined in the desert sands, and thereafter spoke as men who had been granted a peep into the bounties of creation."[54] And in the Middle East, Saudi Arabia stood out above all others: "When you talk about oil out here," a driller at Dhahran remarked in 1947, "remember that we've barely begun to look for oil properly. Even so, proven reserves—oil that we know is in the fields already explored—are at least equal to those of the entire Western hemisphere." It had taken Americans ninety years since first drilling for "rock oil" in 1859 to find thirty billion barrels of the stuff in U.S. fields. The Saudis had found thirty-two billion barrels in a decade, and they were only scratching the surface.[55]

HOSTAGES TO FORTUNE

Washington was never comfortable with the Soviet Union's menacing proximity to such a vital resource area. When would the Red Army push south to the Persian Gulf?[56] Heavy American investment in the oil enterprises of northeastern Arabia had, as Arnold Toynbee wrote, "given hostages to fortune." A CIA memorandum in

1949 warned that "Saudi Arabia is to all practical purposes completely defenseless against modern methods of attack."[57] And Western oil production had the unfortunate effect of crowding together "an uncomfortable number of valuable strategic and economic assets in the Middle East within a compass that was relatively small") when approached by Soviet combat aircraft or tracked vehicles. Those postwar "wells of power" ran in a continuous belt from Baku south to Kirkuk, Abadan, Kuwait and Dhahran. They were densely packed in the great basin of the Tigris and Euphrates rivers and the Persian Gulf. "Russian tanks," Toynbee lyrically concluded, might soon "be in a position to bear down in the tracks of Hyksos chariot wheels and Scythian and Mongol horsemen from the Qarabagh to the River of Egypt."[58] The military onslaught would be in the Middle East—from Herat in Afghanistan (Toynbee's "Qarabagh") west to the Nile—but the economic shock would be felt in America and Western Europe.

For their part, the Soviets felt at least as vulnerable as the Americans in the Middle East. With Turkey and Iran governed by hostile, pro-Western regimes, Russia feared an Anglo-American naval or air attack from the south. Such fears had partly motivated the Nazi-Soviet nonaggression pact in 1939, when Stalin viewed a cooperative relationship with Germany as an effective way to bar the Black Sea straits—"Britain's historic gateway for an attack on Russia"—and extend Soviet influence down to the Persian Gulf.[59] Both camps—the oil-thirsty Western democracies and the fragile Soviet bloc—felt vulnerable and exposed to sudden and overwhelming attacks from the other.

And so, both sides—the Americans and the Soviets—struggled fiercely for control of the region. In 1945 it was home to 350 million Muslims—then one-seventh of mankind—and the region pumped out a billion barrels of crude every year. In a letter to presidential adviser Chip Bohlen after the war, William Eddy, a former American ambassador to Saudi Arabia and OSS agent in the Middle East, called the arc from Pakistan to Morocco the "only remaining important area not yet committed in the world struggle for power." It contained "vast resources of manpower, food and oil, and the strategic bases and warm water ports which would be indispensable in a *third world war*."[60] Kermit Roosevelt, Jr., who had run American intelligence operations out of Cairo during World War II, argued in 1947 that the Muslim peoples of the Middle East were the key cultural bridge between "Occident and Orient." Winning them over was essential to building "one world" of freedom and free markets, as opposed to three, of capitalism, communism and poverty.[61]

"IBN SAUD'S FAIRY GODMOTHER"

To build barriers against a Soviet push into the Middle East, the Americans piled into Saudi Arabia. The British, who had traditionally paid and protected Ibn Saud, marveled (and grumbled) at America's largesse. With World War II over, the British slashed their annual subsidy to Ibn Saud to the bone. Washington went in the opposite direction, "erring on the side of over-generosity." Whatever the Saudi royals wanted, they were given. Generosity took many forms but was mainly a can-do American willingness to satisfy all the king's needs instantly. In January 1945, Ibn Saud complained to the American ambassador of the embarrassment he had felt in having to drive Egypt's King Farouk to the Hejaz to see the Muslim holy places in "supply trucks," because he had no cars. Within days, the American ambassador had procured a $400,000 shipment of Ford and Packard cars and spare parts as well as a supply of tires, which he shipped over from Cairo and humbly presented to the Saudi monarch as a gift from the United States.[62]

That was the sort of opulence that poor, declining Great Britain—whose every budget item came under cold scrutiny in the House of Commons—could not even begin to contest. When Ibn Saud met with Churchill and Roosevelt on their way home from Yalta in February 1945, the Americans sent a cruiser and a destroyer into the Suez Canal to ferry the king between his meetings with the U.S. president and the British prime minister.[63] When the principal Saudi princes—Faisal, Fahd, Abdullah, Saud and Nawwaf—convened in Jedda in April 1945 to see Foreign Minister Faisal off to San Francisco for the founding UN conference, the U.S. government covered all their costs. An American plane was detached to carry the princes to the fleshpots of Cairo, and a second (secret) flight followed after dark with Prince Faisal's mountains of luggage and his three personal slaves, who would serve the Saudi foreign minister in the "land of the free." "These American efforts to impress usually miss the mark," the British Foreign Office sniffed. But really, they didn't.[64]

By the end of World War II, Saudi Arabia's oil fields alone were producing as much oil as all the other oil fields of the Middle East combined.[65] This was a bounty that the Americans were determined to reap, and the Saudis relished the American attention. Prince Faisal, the forty-one-year-old Saudi foreign minister, was described by a British analyst as "a feebler version of his father." Reared in the soft surroundings of Mecca and notorious for the "excessive delight he had taken in the harem from his youth upwards," Faisal was a scandal because of his regular hops across the border to party in Kuwait. He had visited the United States with his half brother Khalid in 1943 and had sipped so deeply from the American cup that State Department auditors had grown concerned at the nature of American subsidies to the Saudis. How could they be justified or even adequately reported in a transparent republic that deplored corruption and waste? "The Department of State has spent $15,000 on visits of the Saudi princes. Are we justified in spending these amounts?" one anxious State Department official queried another. When Faisal and Khalid visited in 1943, they had partied their way from New York to Washington, down to Miami and across to Las Vegas, spending all the way. "Bills are still coming in from that trip," a State Department accountant grumbled in June 1945. Needing Saudi friendship, America doubled down. When Faisal came to sign the UN pact in April 1945, the State Department gave him $3,350 to play with. That was the equivalent of $34,000 today—not bad for "walking-around money."[66] Even greased with U.S. dollars, the Saudi-American alliance was never a natural fit, but Riyadh was able to explain it with reference to the Soviet threat. In 1948, Ibn Saud's foreign ministry described the growing American presence at Dhahran and elsewhere as "necessary to protect the kingdom's completely defenseless oil installations."[67] Americans were infidels, but they were still "people of the book"—Christian and Jewish monotheists like the Muslims—who could unite in Dar al-Islam (the "territory under God's law") for regrettable but inevitable forays into Dar al-Harb (the "territory of war") inhabited by the Soviet atheists.[68]

Gradually, a British analyst observed in 1945, the State Department became "Ibn Saud's fairy godmother," showering him and his princes with "unlimited generosity."[69] The CIA pointed out that Saudi Arabia's backwardness gave Washington considerable leverage. The kingdom had "no industrial potential, a low standard of education, and poor port and transportation facilities." Its only asset was oil money, which it traded for American deliveries of just about *everything.*[70] The American objectives were oil, a lucrative export market outside the British sterling area, the big airfield and telecommunications hub at Dhahran, and foreign sales of American weapons. In 1949, Ibn Saud was spending 33 percent of the Saudi budget on the military, and "there [were] no limitations" on what he might spend on ground, air and naval forces despite having just 1.3 million men of military age in his kingdom of 6 million men.[71]

The British cautioned that this American-style access to the kingdom came with a hidden cost.[72] "The Americans," a British official wrote in March 1945, "have a too permissive conception of permissible activity in territory which is the spiritual metropolis of hundreds of millions of Muslims." This "new phenomenon of American economic imperialism in Saudi Arabia" would severely damage "Arab goodwill." The region was almost impenetrably complex and the Americans would almost certainly mess it up. After all, the Englishman concluded, "this is not Panama or San Salvador," places the Americans had some experience messing up.[73] Herbert Feis, at the U.S. State Department, agreed. "Where did defense end and ambition begin?" he asked in 1946. "Where was the line between inert neglect, legitimate and friendly expansion of the national interest, and provocative intrusion?"[74] Ibn Saud pondered the same question in the 1940s. "People are saying that my country is an American colony . . . Ibn Saud has given his country to the United States, even the Holy Places," he grumbled to the American ambassador.[75]

Little Arab oil actually trickled into Allied gas tanks during World War II because the fighting in the Mediterranean closed off that transport route and because the Allies did not have enough tankers to carry tons of Persian Gulf oil around the South African Cape to the west. Some Iraqi oil made it from Kirkuk and Mosul down an 850-mile pipeline to the British refinery in Haifa, but it was generally easier to produce the oil in Texas, Mexico or Venezuela and then ship it through the Caribbean to Europe and North Africa. Kuwait—with one-third of known Middle East reserves and one-seventh of the world's—actually closed its oil fields from 1942 to 1945. Indeed, Western markets were so inaccessible owing to the fighting in North Africa and the U-boats in the Mediterranean and Indian Ocean that Middle Eastern oil field workers were laid off and their wells plugged until the last months of the war.[76] Having tasted real riches in the 1930s, Ibn Saud was abruptly and humiliatingly reduced—for the duration of the war—to a ward of the British, who sent him food and paid him a $12 million annual subsidy. During the conflict, the United States began jockeying for postwar domination. Forbidden by Congress to extend Lend-Lease aid to neutral Saudi Arabia until the last months of the war, FDR advanced loans and aid through the British. The cash, food, machinery and vehicles supplied to the Saudis every year by the British were really diverted American Lend-Lease materials, and—stressing that fact—one American oilman wrote in 1941 that he "didn't want the British to run away with all of the credit on this thing."[77]

"THE CENTER OF GRAVITY OF WORLD OIL PRODUCTION"

He needn't have worried. British relations with Saudi Arabia had been prickly since the Saudi takeover of Mecca and Medina in 1924, when the British had grudgingly abandoned the Hejaz while endeavoring to box Ibn Saud in from their client kingdoms in Iraq, Kuwait and Jordan.[78] When Roosevelt described British imperialism to Ibn Saud in 1945 as "working to bring freedom and prosperity to the world on condition that it be brought by *them* and marked 'Made in Britain,' " the Saudi king hooted with complicit laughter: "Never have I heard the English so accurately described!"[79] As the breathtaking extent of untapped Saudi oil reserves (and tapped-out American ones) dawned on Harold Ickes—FDR's wartime petroleum administrator—the American official pushed hard to shoulder aside the British and secure direct American Lend-Lease aid for Saudi Arabia in 1943. "The center of gravity of world oil production is shifting from the Gulf [of Mexico]-Caribbean areas to the Middle East–Persian Gulf areas," Ickes wrote the president.[80] Secretary of the Navy James Forrestal warned Dean Acheson in December 1944 that the reliance of the U.S. Navy and Army Air Corps on a steady supply of "refined petroleum products" on every continent was so acute that "the orderly development of the oil resources of the Mesopotamian Basin and the Persian Gulf [had become] a strategic interest of the U.S."[81]

Herbert Feis of the State Department's International Economic Affairs bureau underlined that strategic importance of Middle Eastern oil two years after the war. "Nature," he wrote, "now compelled a self-protective [American] effort to control the golden pools of Bahrain and Saudi Arabia . . . There is only one good storage place for immense amounts of oil—underground in the pools in which they are discovered." Feis and the State Department took it "for granted that American interests needed actual physical control of or . . . assured access to adequate sources of supply."[82] Meanwhile, Stalin's budding interest in Middle Eastern oil—and the age-old Russian desire to control a port on the Persian Gulf—served only to accentuate the immense strategic value of Saudi Arabia. After Stalingrad, the Soviets requested an annual allotment of twenty million tons of Gulf oil, and Stalin looked for ways to wangle a one-third Russian share in "Arabian oil companies" like the British venture in Kuwait or Standard Oil's Saudi concession. After the war, the

Soviets sought reparations—in the form of Arab or Iranian oil deals—for the massive damage the Germans had done to their oil infrastructure.[83]

Harold Ickes sought to deflect the Russian challenge and warned the president that America was foolishly draining its own oil patch to power the rest of the globe. The process had been well under way even before the war, when oil sailed in 1938 from west to east at a rate of 700,000 barrels a day, and the United States exported nearly three times more oil (447,000 barrels) than it imported (170,000 barrels).[84] Japan resolved on war with the United States (and the sneak attack on Pearl Harbor) only after America—Japan's biggest oil supplier—cut off all exports in July 1941 to protest Japan's seizure of French Indochina. The world's oil dependence on America only intensified during World War II. With just 32 percent of the world's reserves in 1944, the United States was producing 64 percent of the world's oil and burning it up in the global operations of the Allied coalition's gas-guzzling armored divisions, fleets and air forces. With 42 percent of known world oil reserves, the Middle East, cordoned off by war and its own rickety production facilities, was supplying less than 4 percent of world production.[85] Ickes called for a radical shift, and Roosevelt implemented it on a muggy July afternoon in 1944, when he attempted to purchase the Arabian-American Oil Company (Aramco) and make it a U.S. government agency.

Plans for American government investment in Aramco, which had been founded as a joint Saudi-American private venture in 1933, reflected Washington's determination to seize leadership in world oil markets from the British. By late 1943, the United States had shipped $586 million of oil to Great Britain under Lend-Lease and was projecting shipments of $60 million a month for 1944. Churchill offered to repay *in kind* the American oil once the Axis fell and the pipelines from Iran and Kuwait were running full tilt again, but James Byrnes—FDR's director of war mobilization and Truman's first secretary of state—rejected such an arrangement on the grounds that postwar oil reparations from British wells would "seriously injure American concessions and interests in Saudi Arabia" by creating too much supply. It would be better, Byrnes shrewdly argued, for American companies simply to redivide the oil fields and pipeline routes of the Middle East with the British; that would be payment enough.[86]

What Roosevelt, Truman, Byrnes and Ickes had in mind was nothing less than a basic restructuring of global oil supply and consumption. On the eve of World War II, the United States, Mexico and Venezuela had supplied 77 percent of Western Europe's oil. During the war, the United States had fueled the Allied war effort.

Now Ickes and other prominent Americans noticed that the American well was running dry. New oil discoveries in the United States had exceeded consumption in every year between 1928 and 1940, but the trend reversed in 1941. With U.S. production increasing from 3.2 million barrels a day to 5 million barrels a day that year—and consumption projected to increase as the war continued and when the car-crazy, house-buying troops came home—America began cutting deep into its reserves.[87] In March 1943, the Presidential Committee on International Petroleum Policy reported that future American demand for oil—for wartime, but also postwar consumption once rationing was lifted—would exceed domestic production.[88] Five U.S. senators who circled the globe in the fall of 1943 to assess the war effort complained in the *New York Herald Tribune* that American oil—the essential lubricant in the mechanized American way of war and the suburban American way of life—was being burned up in irreplaceable quantities while the best Rumanian and Russian fields were in German hands and the British hoarded their Middle Eastern reserves. "Each ship, truck, tank, and plane that came out of the hands of its builders was an added claim against American underground reserves."[89]

To conserve dwindling American reserves for the future, Roosevelt's administration, which feared that it would be unable to "oil *another* war" after this one, planned to shift Europe's postwar supply from the United States to the Middle East.[90] That would relieve pressure on American stocks, but also burn up vulnerable Middle Eastern oil first and leave secure American and Caribbean sources intact for the contingency of World War III.[91] "All our national interests demand the development of Middle Eastern reserves," Kermit Roosevelt, Jr., concluded in 1947.[92] Thwarted in their bid to own and operate Aramco as an arm of the federal government, FDR's "old curmudgeons"—Harold Ickes and Jimmy Byrnes—did finally compel the British to cede larger tracts of Iraq, Kuwait and Bahrain to American oil companies and to recognize Saudi Arabia as an exclusively *American* sphere of influence. By 1944, the Persian Gulf reserves under U.S. control had risen from 13 to 42 percent. The actual increase in oil in the ground—in view of the prewar Saudi oil strikes—was 1,900 percent, enough eventually to replace the sixty billion barrels of American oil burned up in the struggle to defeat Germany and Japan.[93] Using America's enormous wartime leverage as the "arsenal of democracy," Ickes and Byrnes also persuaded London to agree to American refinery and pipeline projects in Saudi Arabia that would gradually wean Europe from American oil and put it on a steady diet of British- and American-produced Middle Eastern oil. Before pipelines, the only way to get Arabian oil to European markets in the 1940s was by dispatching empty tankers through the Suez Canal, down the Red Sea, around the Arabian Peninsula and up the Persian Gulf, and then back along the same route with full tanks. Each round trip burned up twenty days of travel, seven thousand miles of fuel and about forty thousand dollars' worth of Suez tolls, all of which were saved by trans-Arabian pipelines terminating in Lebanon or Palestine.[94]

All of these American oil and infrastructure deals were pursued against a background of wartime power politics that did not commend the Saudis as an ideal ally in this war, or any other. King Ibn Saud was neutral in World War II. Leaning toward the Allies, he hedged his bets with the Axis. The Saudi dynasty had watched Italian designs on the Middle East warily since 1919, when the Italian government had tried to annex the Antalya district of southern Turkey as well as Yemen at the Paris Peace Conference. Thwarted then, the Italians tried again under Mussolini. They signed a "treaty of friendship" with Yemen in 1926, and aided the Yemeni leader—the imam of San'a—in his border war with Saudi Arabia in 1934. Determined to break the British grip on Suez—"the bars of the Italian jail"—Mussolini took aim at the southern entrance of the Red Sea as well. In a European war, he would seize the seventy-five-square-mile British enclave at Aden and link it to the growing port of Assab in Italian Eritrea, just forty miles across the Strait of Bab-el-Mandeb. Joined to the burgeoning Italian presence in Ethiopia, Libya and the Dodecanese Islands, those Arabian annexations would give Fascist Italy control of key maritime choke points.[95] When Fascist Italy invaded and annexed Ethiopia in 1935–36 against feeble League of Nations opposition, Ibn Saud felt confirmed in his belief that the League, which sporadically showered nonmember Saudi Arabia with brochures on the evils of slavery and misogyny, was an empty husk properly ignored.[96]

Skeptical of British and League security promises after the Italian conquest of Ethiopia, Ibn Saud cozied up to the Axis "Pact of Steel." In 1939, he accepted a symbolic gift of Italian arms—ten howitzers, one tank, six planes and six slots for Saudi pilots in Italian flight schools—and assured a German envoy that he was looking for Hitler's help "to free Arabia from British influence." Saudi Arabia, the king protested, was in the same predicament as Nazi Germany: "encircled" by hostile powers. The British had shrewdly installed Hashemite kings in Iraq (Faisal) and in Jordan (Abdullah) and had backed Sherif Hussein in the Hejaz until 1925. Ibn Saud also needed Hitler's protection against Mussolini. The Italians coveted Yemen, which, before the commercial production of oil, easily trumped Arabia as a strategic asset; hence the ancient Arab saying "If the Yemen goes, Islam is gone." A great power established in the high fertile tablelands of Yemen would be master of the Hejaz and the Muslim holy places at Mecca and Medina, which lay across the border.[97]

Ibn Saud proceeded cautiously in World War II. Britain and Italy seemed poised to carve up his kingdom, whereas the Germans—whom the Saudi king regarded "with great respect and wonderment"—had no plans (as far as Ibn Saud knew) to annex or control Arab territory.[98] Part of this was diplomatic playacting, but there were hard interests at stake too, and the Saudis clearly pursued them in league with the Nazis. In 1941, Ibn Saud sent a royal envoy to Vichy to negotiate for the eventual cession—by the victorious Germans, Italians and Vichy French—of Syria, Lebanon, Jordan and Palestine to the Saudis, who would establish a new German-aligned Arab kingdom under Ibn Saud.[99] Pressed by the British to declare war on the Axis powers in 1942, Ibn Saud refused. The Saudi king disingenuously informed the British ambassador that he was not authorized to take his kingdom into the war because Mecca and Medina were the spiritual property of *all* Muslims: "I would be like the man riding into battle on a borrowed camel, beating it with a friend's stick."[100]

Ibn Saud was also careful to improve relations with the British and Americans. He recklessly—in the view of his advisers—proclaimed his confidence that Great Britain would not be defeated in the dark days of 1940, and he relocated Fascist Italy's legation in Jedda to a remote quarantine island in 1942 as a sop to Washington and London. Only in March 1945, when it became apparent that membership in the Grand Alliance against Germany and Japan had become a precondition for membership in the new United Nations Organization, did Ibn Saud finally ditch neutrality and join the Allies. In adhering to the alliance, Ibn Saud was careful to exclude Mecca and Medina. Fifty years later, Osama bin Laden would foment holy war to protest "infidel" American bases near the sacred Hejaz. Ibn Saud saw that threat coming in 1945: "We exclude from this declaration the zone of [Mecca and Medina] . . . They are the zone of safety and peace for all those who live there and all those Muslims who come to them."[101] Meeting with American ambassador William Eddy in July 1945, Ibn Saud insisted that all American personnel in the kingdom confine themselves to the Dhahran peninsula or the embassy and consulates. "The King," Eddy wrote, "anticipates violent criticism from the reactionary sheikhs and fanatics if any foreigners leave the Dhahran–Ras Tanura area for the interior of the country."[102]

Ibn Saud's exclusion of the Hejaz and indeed the entire "interior" of Saudi Arabia from his last-minute American alliance posed no problems for Washington, which had its gaze firmly fixed on Saudi Arabia's Dhahran peninsula. Dhahran, on the kingdom's east coast, was far from the western holy places. Its air base, the American ambassador remarked, was like "an immense aircraft carrier lying athwart the principal air traffic lanes of the world, a natural fueling stop for aircraft flying from Europe or North Africa to India and the Far East." With fresh memories of World War II, American strategists were taking precautions for World War III: "If the Mediterranean is closed again by war, Saudi Arabia, Yemen and Iraq will be the *only* Arab states the U.S. will have access to via the Central African airfields." And Saudi Arabia was the best of the three—"more sheltered geographically than Iraq and better facilities than primitive Yemen." Militarily, Saudi Arabia had become a "key asset" in the Cold War, more valuable than Greece, Turkey or Pakistan because of its central location, expansive desert land mass (perfect for absorbing and exhausting Soviet thrusts), natural airfields and ideal flying conditions. "Considering land masses from the point of view of global warfare," Ambassador J. Rives Childs wrote from Jedda in December 1948, "Saudi Arabia is a key piece of the U.S. front line defense."[103]

THE GREAT OIL PUDDLE EXPANDS

Saudi oil, of course, provided more incentives. Secretary of the Navy Forrestal reminded Secretary of State Byrnes in July 1945 that Saudi Arabia was "one of the three great [oil] puddles left in the world." The rich sedimentary deposits trapped in the sloping shelves of the Persian Gulf promised colossal, accessible quantities of crude.[104] In 1944–45, Aramco built a big refinery at Ras Tanura that produced fifty thousand barrels a day and ran a submarine pipeline from the Dammam field to the Bahrain refinery to churn out more finished product. Dhahran, site of Aramco headquarters—a sprawling gray-walled complex nicknamed "the Kremlin"— became an American colony in the years after 1944, with two thousand American staff, an American air base, a brand-new American consulate and daily company flights from New York to Dhahran and back again on DC-6Bs affectionately called "Flying Camels." When Kermit Roosevelt, Jr., visited Dhahran in 1947 he noted that it had become "the biggest American settlement between Paris and Manila."[105]

In 1947, American engineers began work on the Trans-Arabian Pipeline—better known as "Tapline"—a 754-mile, thirty-inch pipe from Saudi oil wells to the Lebanese coast, which would deliver a dramatic increase in supply to the European market. Tapline was a marvel. It was finished in 1950 when American crews from Bechtel, working west, and Williams Brothers Overseas Company, working east, joined the last welds on a sweltering desert plateau in Syria. Tapline had been clapped together from 200,000 sections of steel pipe, each section containing enough steel to make two Chevy station wagons. Once fastened together, each gleaming mile of pipe could be filled with 4,400 barrels of oil, and there were 754 miles of pipe snaking through four countries: Saudi Arabia, Jordan, Syria and Lebanon. During normal operations, 5 million barrels of oil sloshed along Tapline, each drop of oil spending exactly sixteen days in transit from Arabia to the Mediterranean, where 330,000 barrels spilled into the old Phoenician port of Sidon every day.[106]

At a price of $250 million, Tapline cut in *half* the cost of transporting Gulf oil by tankers through the Red Sea and Suez to Europe. It became a key cost-cutter in President Harry Truman's European Recovery Plan, which envisioned shifting all Marshall Plan countries to 80 percent reliance on Middle East oil by 1951, once Middle Eastern export facilities caught up with the region's surging production. In 1949, the Middle East produced 830,000 barrels per day, but could cram only a third of that into the available tankers and pipelines. Tapline was the game-changer.[107] And Harold Ickes planned to augment Tapline with a "strategic reserve" of 1 billion barrels of Saudi oil that would be left in the ground "for war, if needs must, and for peace, in any event." There, Ickes met stout resistance from senior Texas senator Tom Connally, whose constituents feared that cheap Saudi oil would depress the price of their "Texas tea," and Republican isolationists like Ohio senator Robert Taft, who rather startlingly dropped a line from Horace into the Senate's discussion of Ickes's petroleum reserve plans: "Iccius, are you now looking enviously at Arabia's rich territory?"[108]

Ickes was. By 1945, the U.S. Navy was already fueling its Pacific operations from American wells in Bahrain.[109] U.S. Army Air Corps and supply units had been staging through the Middle East on their way to the Pacific theater and running the important supply route from Iran to Russia. After the war, the United States remained. Wallace Murray, head of the State Department's Near Eastern bureau, wrote Dean Acheson a top secret memo in January 1945 describing the undiminished strategic importance of Saudi air bases and overflight rights. Dhahran had been a key staging area in the world war, and the ability to overfly the Arabian Peninsula had shaved 220 miles off the flight from Europe to the Far East and provided emergency landing areas in the desert. In 1948, the Pentagon planned to base eighty to a hundred B-29s at Dhahran to pound the Soviets if they struck south to the Gulf.[110] Those "aviation positions"—to say nothing of Saudi oil—would be as critical in a cold war as a hot one. And the Middle Eastern regimes voiced few objections: nationalist leaders like the shah of Iran and the sultan of Morocco requested arm's-length U.S. investment and technology to replace manipulative British and French imperialism. The Saudi foreign minister, Prince Faisal, told U.S. ambassador William Eddy in 1945 that America needed to reject isolationism and replace Great Britain as "the hand that measures [Saudi Arabia's] food and drink."[111]

America didn't need to be asked twice. In a decade of feverish activity, U.S. oil companies—spurred by planners in Washington—sucked up nearly half the proven oil reserves of the Middle East. Pressured by the American government, the British were forced to yield a quarter share of the Iraq Petroleum Company (IPC), a half share of the Kuwait Oil Company (KOC) and all the exploitable reserves in Saudi Arabia and Bahrain.[112] The Americans were particularly drawn to Saudi Arabia, where, as one engineer put it, the oil—pressed to the surface by bubbles of natural gas—"literally blew itself out of the ground." In Texas in the 1950s, the average well was eking out just thirteen barrels of oil a day, and that meager sum with pumps laboring around the clock. In Saudi Arabia's Ain Dar field near Dammam, the wells produced sixteen thousand barrels a day *without pumps*. And, in contrast to Texas, there seemed to be no end to the Saudi reserves. The three thousand Americans working in Dhahran had increased Saudi daily production to three hundred thousand barrels in 1948, which converted the kingdom into the world's fifth largest producer after the United States, Venezuela, Russia and Iran.[113]

FDR's plan to shift Europe from American to Middle Eastern sources of oil was happening; in 1950, the *Economist* reported on the inexorable sprawl of "the fantastic, artificial American oil town of Dhahran." It had an international airport, a $50 million refinery, three marine terminals and hundreds of miles of new paved roads.[114] With Aramco stock wholly owned by American companies—the future Exxon, Mobil, Chevron and Texaco—who split oil profits fifty-fifty with the House of Saud, the United States looked forward with hope. They gave the Saudi oil towns American-style nicknames—"the friendly city" (Abqaiq) or "the home of safety" (Ras Tanura)—and strung oil rigs along the azure coast that shimmered by day and then flared and glowed all night.[115] Saudi Arabia had become an irreplaceable strategic asset for the United States, ramping up production from 164,000 barrels per day in 1946 to 300,000 barrels per day in 1948 and to 476,000 barrels per day in 1949 (and to 10 *million* barrels a day in 1979).[116] By 1950, Saudi Arabia's Aramco was producing 546,000 barrels a day and employing 16,000 people in field operations: 2,300 Americans, 10,700 Saudis and 3,700 others. On a visit to Aramco's Dhahran offices in 1950, the American assistant secretary of state for Near Eastern Affairs had only oil on his mind: "What was the best idea they had of reserves? Were pressures holding up? Was there a good water drive to the oil reservoirs? What were gas-oil ratios? Had they mapped new structures to drill? How could production be stepped up?"[117] Increased Saudi production was a key facet of U.S. Cold War strategy: it would supply Western Europe and Japan with the low-cost energy that they needed to recover, modernize and defend themselves after World War II.[118]

"IF ONLY ALLAH HAD NOT DRENCHED OUR LANDS IN OIL"

The Middle Eastern peoples, Arnold Toynbee warned during World War II, "would be the first victims of this international explosion into their domain." Yet the foreigners did troop in, "from the uttermost ends of the earth," bearing strange doctrines.[119] Aramco had originally promised to import no more than "one hundred men," damned but essential nonbelievers, to run oil operations.[120] But that original hundred had grown to thousands with the demands of modernization. Some were welcome—campaigning vigorously against malaria, smallpox and illiteracy—but others were recognized as interested only in marketing the region's oil. In Iraq, a young Arab bitterly complained to an American visitor during World War II that "if only Allah had not drenched our lands in oil, maybe the British, the Russians, the French and even the Zionists would leave us alone and even let us live in peace and freedom."[121]

Harry St. John "Jack" Philby, who advised the Saudi royal family from 1917 until 1955, described the shock effect of Western technology and American ideas in the 1930s and 1940s on the people of Allah: in less than a decade, an Arab civilization that had lived simply for four millennia was hit by "an all-embracing social revolution, consciously based on Western but mainly American models and ideals." One of the oldest models in the world was supplanted in just a few years by one of the newest, pasting "a veneer of the new civilization in place of the precious traditions of an ancient culture."[122] An American worker in Saudi Arabia in the 1950s put it more crudely: an entire people had passed "from ragheads to riches" in the blink of an eye. Oil royalties were enriching the kingdom, and Aramco was spending $140 million a year on supplies and infrastructure, creating a new middle class of Saudi dealers and contractors. In 1957, Aramco's thirteen thousand Saudi employees earned an average annual salary of $1,300, which was twenty-six times the Arab average of $50.[123]

Though pleased with the wealth, Ibn Saud lamented the social and cultural changes: "Who could have thought even a few years ago," he exclaimed in 1948, "that I should live to see liquor and drugs coming into Riyadh? . . . If it were in my power to choose, I would have doomsday now!"[124] Reflecting on his many visits to the Arabian Peninsula both before and after the discovery of oil, the British explorer and travel writer Wilfred Thesiger wrote that doomsday, of a sort, had already arrived:

> If anyone goes there now looking for the life I led they will not find it, for technicians have been there since, prospecting for oil. Today the desert where I traveled is scarred with the tracks of lorries and littered with discarded junk imported from Europe and America. But this material desecration is unimportant compared with the demoralization which has resulted among the *Bedu* themselves. While I was with them they had no thought of a world that was other than their own. They were not ignorant savages; on the contrary, they were the lineal heirs of a very ancient civilization.

Droughts and other privations had given them the "self-discipline they craved," but the Western oil boom had "driven them out of the desert into towns where the qualities which once gave them mastery [were] no longer sufficient." Drought and tribal conflict had killed them before, but now, Thesiger grimly concluded, "it is not death, but degradation which faces them."[125]

Degradation, at the hands of the rich, opportunistic West, kicked into high gear. Westerners like Thesiger certainly romanticized a Bedouin life that was at least as brutal and dangerous as it was noble and austere. Travelers in the pre-oil days described murderous daylight raids on oases, brigandage and a general unwillingness to venture outdoors anywhere after dark. But there *had* been something of the noble savage in the old Arabian. That nobility of spirit and self-confidence was washed away by the flood of petrodollar royalties, which rose from $13 million a year in 1946 to $172 million a year just five years later.[126] The flood of greenbacks overwhelmed a primitive administration that had been designed to run a poor desert kingdom. Jack Philby noted that the Saudi state in the 1940s had no proper accounting office, auditors or even dollar reserves. The kingdom was "devoid of any of the technical devices" of the West, and the all-important ministry of finance was "reduced to the status of an agency for producing funds for this scheme or that, without regard to the merits of the schemes themselves, or to the genuine availability of the money." Indeed the only iron law in Saudi administration became "the king's overriding pleasure," which made for rampant inefficiency and corruption. When Parker Hart arrived as President John F. Kennedy's new ambassador to the kingdom in 1961, he evaluated Ibn Saud's eldest son—King Saud—and the entire royal family and warned the White House that their "extravagance" and "enormous wastage of funds" would pose problems.[127] Philby noted the severe social and cultural strains that resulted from such wastage and extravagance. The Wahhabi clerics, who had vastly expanded their powers in the 1920s, felt themselves under unremitting attack. The "tide of royalties from oil [was] seeping irresistibly into every stratum of society . . . The saturated soil could only breed the brine of corruption . . . The old weeds of vice, ruthlessly trampled down and uprooted by the old desert fanatics, were flowering again."[128]

Mike Cheney, a young American who went to work on Saudi construction projects for Bechtel and Aramco in 1948, observed that Saudi Arabia was "a tenth century society in the midst of a convulsive leap into the twentieth," a nation transitioning "from the camel to the Cadillac . . . here grizzled *imams* preached reaction to a nightshirted new proletariat already dreaming of forbidden things like the ballot box and the union shop, ham sandwiches and Marilyn Monroe."[129] For many Saudis, the contrasts were hard to stomach. Ambassador Eddy had cautioned Washington in 1945 "to remember how undeveloped the country is, and to prevent the impact of the sophisticated races of the West from spoiling an Arab race by rushing in too rapidly." The changes America was bringing to Saudi Arabia, Eddy warned, had been gradually implemented "through a period of 1,000 years in other countries."[130] Saudi Arabia did not absorb the shock. Saudi oil royalties in 1948 alone came to $28 million, which landed as a lump sum in the royal purse before streaming into various development projects.[131] Bechtel alone was doing $500,000 a month of public works in the kingdom in 1948, building roads, harbors and reservoirs.[132] Yet Mike Cheney worried about "the cloudy realms of the Saudi mind—a mind imbued with the mores of tribal society, impregnated with the desperate Arab pride, bound by the structures of Wahhabi Puritanism, and then thrown into close and constant contact with a completely alien culture." Under American tutelage, the simple desert life was traded for the city and the automobile and, as Eddy put it in 1945, "a total dependence on Western imports and technologies."[133] The well-meaning American purveyors, Cheney discovered, had a "shattering effect on the narrow, veiled mind of the peninsular Arab." With their "glittering possessions, technical skills, easy self-confidence and freedom of thought and action," the Americans made the Saudis doubtful, bitter and inauthentic in their own eyes.[134]

Many American actions struck the Saudis as narrow and veiled in their own way. In 1944, the U.S. government sent a routine shipment of riyals—the silver coin of Saudi Arabia, each worth about 30 cents—to the royal palace at Jedda as part of wartime assistance. U.S. Army headquarters in Cairo decided that it needed to make a photo op of this American generosity and thus flew a colonel, two majors, a captain, two lieutenants and a squad of infantry to collect the cash in the port of Jedda, hand it to the king and mug for the cameras with a suitably "grateful" Saudi monarch. When the American officers landed at Jedda airport, they were met by Ambassador Jimmy Moose, who wondered why they had come. They explained, and he replied that the cash had already been unloaded and delivered to the national bank. He told them a funny story about the officious, glowering American military police who had escorted the shipment to the bank with their rifles leveled at the crowds that they passed, not apparently knowing that "punishment for theft is drastic in Saudi Arabia—for the first offense you lose your hand, for the second your head. So there is little stealing, and no one would think of taking from the king."

Moose said good-bye to the officers, but they refused to return to Cairo. There had been no speeches of thanksgiving or photos of a beaming, grateful Saudi king and finance minister. Wait, Moose replied, Saudi Arabia has been receiving British and American subsidies for years, and this is a minor and merely symbolic one. Why would the Saudis celebrate it? Plus, he delicately added, how dare a collection of junior officers and enlisted men—even American ones—demand an audience with a *king*? The Americans persisted; they wanted pictures of the smiling king and his finance minister with a cascade of silver riyals streaming through their fingers. Moose was embarrassed, and the Saudi finance minister, Sheikh Abdullah Suleiman, was furious. Kermit Roosevelt, who was present, recalled that Sheikh Abdullah assumed that the Americans must be drunk. A compromise was reached: sacks of riyals with American markings were extracted from the bank vault, the grim-faced American soldiers with rifles were photographed handing them to Saudi royal guards with scimitars, and Sheikh Abdullah was photographed accepting a slip of paper from the American colonel.

[The king, who had been shielded from the worst of the embarrassing affair by his minions, then threw a banquet to honor the American delegation. The Americans grumbled about the lack of cocktails—Moose explained that alcohol was forbidden in the kingdom—and fresh-pressed tomato juice was served instead. Moose and Roosevelt watched in horror as the American officers raised their glasses and, ignoring the Saudi king, gestured toward the medical officer in their entourage and bawled: "Hey, doc! Is it okay to drink this stuff?" No, it wasn't. "Don't touch it!" the officer yelled back. As each plate arrived, the men and officers shouted, "Give us the word, doc! Safe to eat this stuff?" The answer was invariably "no." The Arabs at the table "sat with faces politely blank," enduring the rudeness—"they are also proud people." A U.S. Army photographer wedged in between the Saudis and their plates to snap candids, which was "not at all in conformity with the grave courtesy of traditional Arab hospitality." The Saudis continued to sit silently while the American captain described his crossing from Egypt on a navy ship that served "pork chops every day"; pork to a Muslim is as filthy and forbidden as alcohol. Kermit Roosevelt cringed at the memory: "It was as if an American host entertaining foreigners had seen them refuse his steak, potatoes and salad as unclean and had then heard one say to another, 'Oh, we had a fine meal on the way over; we dined on horse manure.' "[135])

Educated Saudis resented such yawping insensitivity. At a meeting in Riyadh in 1948 between the American ambassador and several Saudi ministers, the Saudi deputy foreign minister requested American aid and material to build a mechanized army of eighty thousand troops. The ambassador replied: "Do you really think that even with unlimited funds and every military factor favorable that we can rely on *Saudi* troops to defend this area? It took the United States years to organize its own defense; what can be expected from Saudi Arabia?" That was crushing enough; his next words—meant to console—were even more so: "We all have our respective talents and for some reason God seems to have given Americans mechanical aptitude . . . Saudis have talents along other lines—art and poetry for example."[136] Perhaps he gleaned these attitudes from his British colleagues, who were at least as deprecating: "Saudi Arabia has little to offer except grief . . . None of the Saudi officials have shown any practical interest in the proper maintenance of the military equipment which they have, which is all going to rust and ruin. They are like young children playing with toys."[137]

"'OILISM'. . . IS THE EVIL IN THE WORLD TODAY"

Focused on Saudi oil, the Americans did not worry much about Saudi self-esteem. The Saudi kings had governed untrammeled by any check and balance other than the sharia, or Islamic law, since the kingdom's foundation in 1926. As William Eddy bluntly put it in 1945, "the importance of the country is due solely to the presence of oil deposits," and access to those deposits, British prime minister Anthony Eden sourly noted in the 1950s, was easily purchased with "a few jeweled Cadillacs."[138] Eddy, who also worked for Aramco until his death in 1962, oversaw boom years for Saudi oil. Even the bountiful finds of the 1940s were eclipsed by discoveries after 1950, when American petroleum engineers bored into the famed Ghawar field southwest of Dhahran. Ghawar's reservoirs proved on closer examination to be a single sea of oil: 170 miles long and 20 miles wide. That one underground pool contained 130 billion barrels of oil—far more oil, in other words, in a single Saudi field than was contained in the entire United States.[139] With resources like that—and a $700 million American investment in Saudi infrastructure by 1956—it was perhaps inevitable that the United States would sweep Saudi resentments under the carpet.

"Aramco will give anything for a quiet life, so long as they can continue to draw their profit," a British analyst acidly observed in June 1956.[140] With Eisenhower and the Republicans in charge in the 1950s, the Democrats did not resist the temptation to score points off the opulent Saudis. Representative George McGovern jeered in 1957 at King Saud's "vast array of air-conditioned Cadillacs, luxurious palaces, slaves, concubines and revelry beyond imagination." Some of it was purchased with petrodollars, some with American baksheesh, and the king enjoyed all this while "the populace languished in poverty." Senator Hubert Humphrey, who was positioning himself for a run at the White House in 1960, joined in the Democratic criticism of Eisenhower's efforts to marginalize Egypt's Nasser and base the U.S. position in the Middle East on the House of Saud: "Our Middle Eastern policy is in pretty sad shape if it relies on the assurances and alleged friendship from the King of Saudi Arabia."[141] To deflect criticism like that—which would evaporate the moment the Democrats regained the White House in 1960—Aramco glibly defined Wahhabis to puzzled Americans as "Muslim Unitarians." This would have been news to the oppressed Shiites of Saudi Arabia, who had been classified as *rafida*—

contemptible "rejecters of the faith"—by the Wahhabi clerics ever since the brutal annexation of their settlements by Ibn Saud's Ikhwan army in 1913. (Saudi Shiites were a low caste that provided sweepers and lavatory cleaners for the kingdom; their word was not generally accepted, and a Shiite in a lawsuit against a Sunni had no hope.)[142] Another Aramco analyst asserted that Wahhabism was merely Islam's "Reformation," a virtuous purging of corrupt old institutions by Muslim Martin Luthers.[143] Those American efforts to paper over the invidious teachings and distortions of the Saudi schools and mosques were understandable. Because of their close identification with Israel and their political need to play down the oil issue, successive American administrations effectively "subcontracted" policy in Saudi Arabia to Aramco, which had no incentive to criticize Saudi culture or domestic arrangements. It was in this context that British prime minister Winston Churchill declared in 1954 that "'oilism' and not colonialism is the evil in the world today."[144]

"We are all oilists now" might as well have been the mantra in the United States. Speaking to an annual meeting of petroleum engineers in New Orleans in February 1957, Mobil Oil chairman Brewster Jennings warned that the "Free World countries outside the Iron Curtain" were consuming 16 million barrels of oil a day in 1956. Of that total, 60 percent—9.6 million barrels—was consumed in the United States; plus, demand was growing 5 percent year over year in the United States, and 12 percent in Western Europe. (By 2009, Americans would be burning 21 million barrels of oil per day.) With just 20 percent of world reserves, the United States was still producing 50 percent of the world's oil to slake the global thirst, and U.S. wells were running dry as a result. Of American reserves of 94 billion barrels in 1956, 58 billion had already been produced and consumed (and American reserves would dwindle to just 21 billion barrels by 2008). Venezuela, meanwhile, had burned through more than a third of its 21 billion barrels of reserves.

The Middle East, by contrast, seemed inexhaustible and able to fuel almost unlimited Western growth. Superficial exploration in Iran, Iraq and Saudi Arabia had by 1956 "proved up" more oil than had *ever* been found in the entire United States. Indeed, the vast reserves of the Middle East explained the great paradox of the 1950s: although the Western world needed more and more oil, it had discovered so much so quickly in the Persian Gulf area that it became in some sense expendable. When Iranian prime minister Muhammed Mossadeq nationalized the Anglo-Iranian Oil Company in 1951 and the British retaliated by demanding an international boycott of Iranian-produced oil, the world complied. There was so *much* oil in the Middle East that the world could do without Iran's.[145] It was easy to see why: just

1,500 wells in the Persian Gulf in 1956 had uncovered 105 billion barrels of reserves, which was 11 billion more barrels than the United States had found at the bottom of its 1.5 *million* wells. And how the oil flowed in those Middle Eastern wells! The average American well in 1956 was yielding just 12 barrels per day, while the average well in the Persian Gulf was gushing 500 barrels per day. In Texas, where the cream had already been skimmed from the top of the bottle, it took a mile of hole to get as much oil as five feet of hole in Saudi Arabia—and the Saudis were only getting started.[146]

This abundance of Arab oil created dependency. By the mid-1950s, Western Europe, busily rebuilding from the destruction of World War II, relied on Middle Eastern sources for over 90 percent of its oil. By then, the United States was consuming most of its own production, wringing 50 percent of world production in the 1950s from just 12 percent of world reserves. Aramco estimated that by 1965 the United States would be importing 3 million barrels of oil a day to meet domestic needs. By 1975, the United States would be importing 25 percent of its domestic consumption. It seemed obvious where the oil would come from. With over 75 percent of the total oil resources of the non-Communist world, the Middle East— with its 230 billion barrels of reserves—had become an inalienable strategic asset. In 1956, American companies controlled 58 percent of Arabian production. Oil had become the single largest American investment in the eastern hemisphere—worth $750 million—and Saudi Arabia had become the world's indispensable "swing producer." With the ability to increase daily production by 1 or 2 million barrels, the Saudis ironed out price swings and kept oil cheap. The price actually *fell* from $1.80 a barrel in 1963 to $1.20 a barrel in 1969.[147]

But the degree of actual American *control* over that vital asset was always in doubt.[148] The American-Saudi love-hate relationship was succinctly described by Crown Prince Saud in 1947. First he chided the State Department for a "continued American occupancy of Dhahran [that] was considered proof to the Arab world that the Saudi king was subservient to American interests"; then he turned around and sought guarantees from the State Department that America would "maintain the territorial integrity of Saudi Arabia."[149] In the mid-1950s, Saudi Arabia very nearly went to war with Great Britain to annex the oil-rich Buraimi oasis from the British protectorates of Abu Dhabi and Oman. Although Britain protested in Washington—"we cannot allow this primitive, irresponsible and expansionist power to seize control of [even more oil] sources"—President Eisenhower bluffly insisted "that the whole Arab Peninsula belonged, or ought to belong, to King Saud."

When the British countered that legally and historically it didn't, Eisenhower (lamely) replied, "People in general are very ignorant and tend to think it does."[150] Despite this willed ignorance and the blank check for Saudi security, Washington received few tangible benefits in return, other than Aramco's revenues. When the Americans pulled together a regional alliance of Middle Eastern states in the 1950s to contain the Soviet Union—the Baghdad Pact—the Saudis refused to join, despite Washington's desperation to attract Arab member states. When President Eisenhower tried to draft King Saud into a coalition to oppose the "Sovietization" of Syria and Iraq in 1957–58—"exert your great influence to the end that the atheistic creed of Communism will not become entrenched at a key position in the Muslim world"—Saud dodged, blaming the whole crisis on American support for Israel, without which "the situation would not have reached the present point."[151]

"MAKE SAUD THE GREAT GOOKETY GOOK OF THE MUSLIM WORLD"

Meeting with the British, Ike suggested that Washington and London work together to "make Saud the great gookety gook of the Muslim world."[152] Unfortunately, Washington's "gookety gook" stolidly ignored American requests to help mediate the Arab-Israeli dispute and subsidized Middle Eastern governments like Egypt and Syria and emerging Palestinian terrorist groups that were hostile to the United States. In 1961, King Saud stunned the Americans by terminating their lease on Dhahran airfield, which had been a vital hub linking American operations in Europe and Asia since World War II.[153] The Saudis were "anti-Western," quietly "subversive" and "neutralist," a British foreign ministry official noted. Evelyn Shuckburgh, principal aide to Foreign Secretary Anthony Eden in the 1950s, thought the degree of American support for Saudi Arabia was unfathomable: the "Saudis enjoy a remarkable degree of sympathy in Washington and there is, in effect, a kind of blind spot toward their misdeeds."[154]

As America and Saudi Arabia squirmed in this uneasy embrace, yet another complicating factor obtruded: Israel. The House of Saud had been denouncing the Zionists as "marauders" and "land grabbers" since the 1930s, and the Americans had never won the Saudis over to Washington's supportive position. Ibn Saud gave an interview to *Life* magazine in 1943 in which he bluntly stated the Arab case against

Israel: "I cannot find that the Jews have any justification for their claims to Palestine." They had been "captured, slaughtered and scattered by the Romans," who, in turn, had been conquered by the Arabs. "That was 1,300 years ago. If the Jewish argument is to be logically applied we shall have to turn out of their homes many races up and down the world who think themselves the rightful owners of the land they live in."[155] That same year—as U.S. troops invaded Italy and American carriers drove closer to Japan—Ibn Saud wrote a personal letter to President Roosevelt imploring him not to forget the Palestinians amid "this immense world conflict of nations." Zionist propagandists, Ibn Saud warned, were "exploiting the American people's ignorance" to "annihilate the Arabs of Palestine."[156] A worried American ambassador in Jedda feared that Saudi Arabia—"more stable than any Arab state because public opinion is a reflection of the will of Ibn Saud"—could be alienated and driven into opposition by the Israel issue. "How long will Ibn Saud's patience endure in the face of the persistent rebuffs we've given him in the form of our Palestine policy—our admitted pro-Israel policy?"[157]

ON GREAT BITTER LAKE

In 1945, King Ibn Saud met with President Franklin D. Roosevelt during the American president's passage through the Suez Canal on his way home from his Yalta meetings with Churchill and Stalin. It was the last of many foreign trips for FDR, who would die two months later. For sixty-nine-year-old Ibn Saud, it was his first foreign trip since his only other one, to Basra, thirty years earlier. Before leaving Saudi soil, he took the American ambassador aside and made clear his position on the Jewish national home in Palestine: "Our holy book says this of the Jews. They are against you in the present day and they will be so until the end of the world. It is a struggle for life and death for the Arab against the accursed Jew."[158] Ten days later, Ibn Saud was borne from Jedda to the Great Bitter Lake in the Suez Canal aboard the USS *Murphy*. Once on the lake, the brackish midpoint of the canal between the Red Sea and the Mediterranean, the king was hoisted aboard the cruiser USS *Quincy*, where President Roosevelt was resting after his thousand-mile flight from Sevastopol.[159]

The surroundings at Roosevelt's summit were altogether different from a Washington conference room. Ibn Saud—tall, broad shouldered, bearded, one eye nearly closed by a cataract, limping from old war wounds—had converted the *Murphy* into a royal pavilion, with awnings, rugs and upholstered chairs. Seven-foot slaves brewed coffee in the gun turrets and padded in and out of the royal presence on thick rugs laid from the fantail to the forecastle.[160] Roosevelt was struck and demoralized by the dogged way Ibn Saud worked the issue of Palestine. He later told a friend that "of all the men he had talked to in his life, he had got the least satisfaction from this iron-willed Arab monarch."[161] As guardian of the Muslim holy places, Ibn Saud felt bound to defend "Muslim religious considerations and Arab nationalist sentiment" at every turn. Not to do so, an American intelligence report suggested, "would lose him the respect of his co-religionists, threaten his influence with the Wahhabis, and even cause his overthrow."[162] Each time FDR tried to shift the subject away from Palestine, the Saudi king swerved back "to expound the case of the Arabs and their legitimate rights in their lands." Ultimately, Roosevelt abandoned politics and shifted to small talk. "I am a farmer," he improbably told the Saudi king. Gazing across to the Egyptian desert, he lightly suggested that Ibn Saud develop his water resources, irrigate his parched desert lands and "make room" for a bigger Arab population. Undeterred, Ibn Saud swerved back again: "We will not engage with any enthusiasm in the development of our country's agriculture and public works if that prosperity will be inherited by the Jews!"[163]

In his own meetings with Ibn Saud in Egypt, Churchill—groping for an "exit strategy" from Britain's exasperating Palestine Mandate—encountered the same obstinacy on the Arab-Jewish question. "We have supported and subsidized you for twenty years," Churchill reminded the Saudi king. "Now you can help us by restraining Arab fanaticism in Palestine and effecting a compromise with the Zionists." Seated comfortably beside Churchill on the patio of King Farouk's Auberge du Lac at Fayoum, overlooking the lake and surrounded by fields of cotton, clover and tomatoes, Ibn Saud glared at the British prime minister. "I will help the Allied cause," he said, "but I cannot destroy my soul and honor as a Muslim by compromising with Zionism."[164] Returning to Jedda, Ibn Saud, who had restrained himself in the presence of Roosevelt and Churchill, let fly at the American ambassador: "If America chooses in favor of the Jews, she will have repudiated her friendship with us, and it will be proof that America is content to see the annihilation of the Arab race."[165]

CHAPTER 3

EXODUS

HAVING NARROWLY ESCAPED real annihilation in Hitler's gas chambers, Jewish immigrants to Palestine after 1945 ignored the protests of spectators like Ibn Saud. Freed from the Nazi death camps, thousands of Jewish survivors flooded into Palestine. They regarded British immigration caps and quotas as attempts, as Ben-Gurion acidly put it, "to seclude Jews in a special Jewish *Lebensraum*."[1] (Ben-Gurion at the time was trying to win approval of a scheme to pay Iraq £10 million to accept five hundred thousand Palestinian refugees in what would have become a special Muslim lebensraum east of the Jordan.) The Zionists worried about the implications of a secret demographic report prepared by the Jewish Agency in 1944, which predicted, with astonishing foresight, that Arab birthrates—the highest in the world—would overwhelm the effects of even massive Jewish immigration by the year 2001.[2] The report concluded that even a million European Jewish immigrants—unthinkable under the prevailing 1939 white paper—would assure only a fleeting Jewish majority. (In this respect, Yasser Arafat was correct in asserting that "the womb" would be the secret weapon of the Palestinians in their struggle with the Zionists.)

The future of "mutual tolerance and goodwill" desired by Lord Peel in the 1930s seemed farther off than ever. Political and ethnic strains were at a breaking point, and the mollifying economic good times of the 1930s had been replaced with infla-

tion and stagnation in the 1940s.[3] The Anglo-American Committee of Inquiry assembled in 1946 felt bound to assure both sides that in postwar Palestine "Jew shall
not dominate Arab and Arab shall not dominate Jew" and that an independent
Palestine "shall be neither an Arab nor a Jewish state." Yet neither the Jews nor the
Arabs were reassured by those Allied pledges, which rang hollow anyway in view of
rising American pressure in favor of the Jews.

AMERICA'S ISRAEL LOBBY TAKES SHAPE

President Franklin Roosevelt—worn down by the war and cancer—seemed confused
by the basic facts of Palestine. In one letter he sent to Secretary of State Cordell Hull,
FDR imagined that Britain had created the Palestine Mandate not to settle Jews
alongside Muslims and Christians in the Holy Land, but simply "to convert Palestine
into a Jewish Home." In another, he uncritically accepted false Zionist claims that
Arab immigration into Palestine since the 1920s had been increasing by the same
multiples as Jewish immigration.[4] In fact, Jewish immigration had fed a tenfold increase in the Jewish population of Palestine between 1919 and 1946, while the Arab
population had merely doubled in the same period.[5] Roosevelt had been harshly
reminded of Arab indignation at these facts on the ground in his summit with King
Ibn Saud in 1945, when the Saudi king had railed against the Jewish home and its
American supporters and growled to his American ambassador that "no matter how
great the force of money and arms mobilized for the Jews, we shall elect to perish to
the last Arab rather than live under Jewish rule."[6] The question of Palestine, in short,
was as fraught in 1945 as it would be sixty-five years later, and sixty-three-year-old
Franklin Roosevelt was not the man to solve it. "For all his charm and skill as a political leader, [he] was, when it came to foreign policy, a very superficial man, ignorant [and] dilettantish," George Kennan witheringly wrote.[7] Ignorance and
dilettantism certainly marked Roosevelt's halfhearted mediation between the Zionists and Arabs. Above all, FDR watched the twentyfold increase in *America's* Jewish
population since 1882: from 250,000 to 4.8 million. That was a lot of voters. Prodded
by active Jewish lobbies like Louis Brandeis's Federation of American Zionists and
Joseph Proskauer's American Jewish Committee, Roosevelt had battled British attempts to limit Jewish emigration to Palestine since 1936 and had blasted the British
White Paper of 1939 for discriminating against Jews and "closing off their only ave-

nue of escape."[8] With presidential elections in 1940 and 1944, FDR, like Truman after him, succumbed completely to the domestic political arithmetic sketched by Judge Bernard Rosenblatt in the *Zionist Review* at the start of Roosevelt's fourth term:

> New York is entitled to 47 electoral votes, while only 266 electoral votes are necessary to elect a President. Whether the vote of the State of New York goes to one party or another (by relatively few votes in a population of over 13 million) will make a difference of 94 votes in the electoral college, so it may be readily understood why a presidential contest may hinge on the political struggle in New York, and to a lesser extent in the large States of Pennsylvania (36 electoral votes), Illinois (27) or Ohio (23) . . . Now, New York, Illinois, Ohio, as well as the populous States of Massachusetts and New Jersey are normally "doubtful," that is, they may swing to one party or another by a mere few thousand votes . . . Perhaps 90 percent of the Jewish population of the United States is concentrated in these doubtful States.[9]

The American public—saddened by Jewish suffering and largely unaware of Arab claims in Palestine—eagerly embraced the Zionist propaganda that appeared in every major American newspaper and many minor ones too. The Jewish propaganda was ingenious, appealing at the same time to American sentimentality and anti-Semitism, as in this ad, which ran in the *New York Times* in April 1943:

> Germany exterminates the Jews in Europe and Britain bars the way to their rescue. America is not asked to open *her* doors to the uprooted people. Open wide the doors of Palestine![10]

Jewish access to the White House and State Department was also remarkable. White House counsel Clark Clifford was a devout Zionist, and Edward Stettinius, FDR's last secretary of state and Truman's first, engaged in long, apparently infuriating meetings with Jewish lobbyists like rabbis Stephen Wise and Hillel Silver. In January 1945, Stettinius recorded the following conversation with New York congressman Sol Bloom:

BLOOM: Hello, Ed.
STETTINIUS: How are you, boy? I'm sorry not to have called you back sooner.

BLOOM: I want to tell you something. I am getting sick and tired of these
    rabbis, and how they want to come down to see you. I told them to cut it
    out; don't you know he is busy?

STETTINIUS: You have called me and have found that I have left town.

BLOOM: I am tired of it.

STETTINIUS: I am out of town for good now.[11]

In or out of town, Stettinius, FDR and Truman by 1945 had rallied entirely to
the Jewish position on Palestine. Twenty-five percent of New York's eight million
inhabitants were Jewish, and Palestine was their wedge issue.[12] There was also a
humanitarian angle: stunned by the scenes of squalor and cruelty in the liberated
Nazi death camps, the United States took the Jewish side even more forcefully in
Palestine after the war. "Of all the inhuman and tyrannical acts of Hitler and his
Nazi lieutenants," Secretary of State Cordell Hull declared on the twenty-fifth
anniversary of the Balfour Declaration in November 1942, "their systematic persecution of the Jewish people—men, women and children—is the most debased."[13]
The British Labour Party—Zionist since World War I *except* when actually in power
in 1929–31—believed that Hitler's Holocaust had so fundamentally broken the
course of human history that some dramatic fix (in Palestine, not England) had to
be found: "There is an irresistible case [for the Jewish state] now, after the unspeak-
able atrocities of the cold and calculated German Nazi plan to kill all Jews in Europe." Surely the Arabs of Palestine could be relied upon to do the right thing and
relocate: "They have many wide territories of their own; they must not claim to
exclude the Jews from this small area of Palestine, less than the size of Wales . . . Let
the Arabs be encouraged to move out, as the Jews move in."[14]

In June 1943, President Roosevelt and Under Secretary of State Sumner Welles
met with Jewish Agency chief Chaim Weizmann in the White House. Straining to
maintain good ties with the Arabs and the Jews, FDR told Weizmann that he had
got Churchill to agree to "call together the Arabs and Jews of Palestine" for negotiations. Weizmann wanted nothing to do with negotiations. "The Arabs," he told
Roosevelt, "must be told beforehand that the democracies meant to affirm the Jewish rights to Palestine." Welles reminded Weizmann that King Ibn Saud had "been
writing unpleasant letters recently" to FDR to demand a halt to Jewish emigration
to Palestine, which risked making the Arabs a minority in their own country. "Ibn
Saud is a desert prince," Weizmann scoffed. "He is very much removed from world
affairs." Welles hastened to agree: the Saudi king's suggestions were "of course

childish." There were now six hundred thousand Jews in Palestine and twice that number of Arabs. While most of the Jews lived in towns, most of the Arabs lived in rural areas as farmers, shepherds and nomads. Surely there was room for more Jews in town *and* country. (Four years later, during the partition of Palestine, Weizmann would coax the entire Negev Desert out of Truman using the same argument.)[15] Roosevelt keeled over. "The Arabs have done badly in this war," he agreed. "They have vast, undeveloped countries." He pondered for a moment, then trailed off: "Perhaps the Jews can help with this development . . ." Like a teacher coaching a pupil, Weizmann eagerly nodded: "The Arabs will not revolt if they know the democracies really mean business."[16]

Weizmann certainly meant business. In early 1944, the Jewish Agency began purchasing small boats and lighters in the Balkans to carry illegal Jewish immigrants across to Palestine. The unexpectedly rapid Soviet advance through Eastern Europe had freed the 250,000 Jews of Rumania from Hitler's clutches. Thousands of them tried to migrate to Palestine. Palmach infantry—the shock troops of the Hagana— were given naval training to assist the landing of incoming Rumanian Jews, using force if necessary. Any British obstruction of immigration was conflated with Nazism. "The Thames flows into the Rhine" was a favorite slogan of *Mivrak,* the biweekly Stern Gang paper, which meant that Britain's treatment of the European Jews was as bestial as Germany's.[17] A British intelligence officer assigned to study the new Jewish naval units found that they were intended to goad the British or Arabs into counterattacks "thereby releasing a storm of atrocity propaganda" that would "unite Jewish Zionists and anti-Zionists across the world and divide Britain and the U.S." Once the British or Arabs stepped in to obstruct the Jewish immigrants— Rumanians now, Poles later—"it would be easy to invoke humanitarian sentiment on behalf of the refugees from Europe."[18]

The United States was more prone to humanitarian sentiment than any other great power, and in 1944 both the U.S. Senate and House of Representatives debated—in Secretary of State Cordell Hull's words—"alarming resolutions" that trampled on thirty years of Jewish-Arab negotiation in Palestine and threatened to drive a wedge between Britain and the United States, just as the Zionists intended. According to the U.S. Congress, Britain now had an *obligation* to throw open the doors of the Holy Land to *unlimited* immigration "so that the Jewish people may reconstitute Palestine as a free and democratic Jewish Commonwealth."[19]

When Army chief of staff General George Marshall and Navy secretary James Forrestal persuaded Congress to postpone debate on the resolutions until after the war—Marshall and Forrestal saw clearly the political damage that the congressional resolutions would do to U.S. interests and basing rights in the Arab Middle East— the House went ahead and debated and resolved anyway, in favor of a Jewish state. With New York governor Thomas Dewey, the Republican presidential nominee in 1944, calling loudly for "the reconstitution of Palestine as a free and democratic Jewish commonwealth," FDR made a point of meeting publicly with Zionist leaders to affirm that a Jewish state in Palestine—swelled by unlimited European immigrants—was a Democratic Party objective too.[20] Lost in the American corridors of power were voices like that of Ibn Saud, who wrote witheringly to the White House: "In the name of humanity it is proposed to force on the Arab majority of Palestine a people alien to them, to make these new people the majority, thereby rendering the existing majority a minority."[21]

Roosevelt died in office in April 1945. His last brush with the question of Palestine was during his meeting with Ibn Saud on board the USS *Quincy* in the Suez Canal on the way home from Yalta in February 1945. There FDR had tried to persuade Ibn Saud of the "equity" of settling displaced European Jews in Palestine but received no encouragement from the Saudi monarch, who had called the Jewish national home "a tissue of deceit and trickery."[22] If the Jewish settlers were allowed to remain in Palestine, Ibn Saud prophetically warned Roosevelt, "the outwardly prosperous country [would be] torn from within with strife and drenched with blood."[23] Understanding at last that he could not "talk both ways" indefinitely on the Arab-Jewish question, FDR lost his earlier enthusiasm for a Jewish state. After Yalta, the American president resolved to reconvene congressional leaders to "re-examine our entire policy on Palestine." There would be no easy or dramatic solutions. Sounding just like despondent leaders today, FDR awaited a miracle: "Some formula, not yet discovered, would have to be evolved."[24]

THE TRUMAN TOUCH

But those were the tired musings of a dying man. President Harry Truman, younger and healthier than his predecessor, was also blunter. Truman, who relished domestic politics more than foreign ones, was much less concerned than FDR to appear impartial in the Middle East, and he lost no time taking up the cudgels for a Jewish state in Palestine. Truman, a staunch supporter of Zionism as a senator, now, as president, saw the matter simply: there were five million Jews in the United States and most of them voted. Moreover, settling the uprooted Jews of Europe in Palestine was politically popular in the United States among all classes and religions. Americans had overlooked the early phases of the Holocaust because of Nazi secrecy but had watched in horror the last German effort to exterminate the nine hundred thousand Jews of Hungary in 1944–45 as breaking news. With Adolf Eichmann openly deporting twelve thousand Hungarian Jews a day by train to Auschwitz, Americans predictably sided with the Zionists on humanitarian grounds.[25] Americans felt natural sympathy for Jewish victims of the Holocaust and were influenced by well-wrought Zionist propaganda—"hundreds of thousands of Jews at present rotting in Nazi concentration camps might have become valiant soldiers in the cause of the UN if not for the policy of the British government"—as well as by the sermons of Protestant ministers, who found all the justification needed for the Jewish national home in the books of Judges, Samuel, Kings and Chronicles.[26]

Against this peculiarly American backdrop, President Truman in August 1945 asked British prime minister Clement Attlee to tear up the White Paper of 1939 and immediately open Palestine to mass Jewish immigration. In the American-occupied zone of Germany, General Dwight Eisenhower settled Jewish "DPs," or "displaced persons," on requisitioned German farmland to learn basic agricultural skills before their departure to Palestine. Ike dispatched weekly military flights to Palestine to bring back Zionist teachers and Hebrew instructors for the European DPs.[27] The ramifications of this American policy cut deep: Neville Chamberlain's prewar controls on immigration had been designed to perpetuate a population in Palestine of ten Arabs for every six Jews. Unrestricted immigration and large Jewish families would tip the ratio the other way.[28] On VE-day, there were at least a hundred thousand Jewish survivors languishing in the abandoned German death camps. There were four hundred thousand more Jewish DPs streaming westward out of Poland, Hungary and Rumania toward the British and American zones of occupation.[29] Indeed, there were so many DPs that the Red Cross's International Tracing Service, created to count refugees and reunite families, crammed sixteen *miles* of shelves with their records.[30]

To cope with the crisis, Truman demanded an immediate hundred thousand immigration certificates to Palestine from the British. A White House report on DPs in September 1945 urged immediate mass emigration to Palestine: "We appear to be treating the Jews as the Nazis treated them, except that we do not exterminate them. . . . They are in concentration camps in large numbers under our military guard instead of S.S. troops."[31] Further east, the Jews were far worse off; in Poland in 1946 there were bloody pogroms designed to drive off returning Holocaust survivors. In April 1946, Truman moved to force Britain's hand. He had agreed to admit 39,000 Jewish DPs to America annually, but the number of Jewish DPs in the U.S. occupation zone in Germany stood at 250,000. Truman issued a statement from the White House applauding the British for their decision to revoke the land transfer restrictions of 1940 and immediately grant the hundred thousand immigration certificates to Jewish refugees in Europe. This, Truman declared, would "permit the further development of the Jewish national home" (and take pressure off American and British immigration officials). Unfortunately, Attlee had never agreed to the measures. The next day, Attlee stated that new immigration and land transfers were quite impossible in view of dwindling British military resources and the rapid growth of illegal Jewish and Arab military formations. New immigrants and settlements would mean full-scale civil war.[32] Privately, Attlee and Foreign Secretary Ernest Bevin were furious at Truman's freelancing. In his haste to win votes at home, Truman had trampled on Britain's imperial interests. In the midst of independence and defense treaty negotiations with the Jordanians and Egyptians, Bevin now found himself exposed to harsh attacks for his acceptance of the American line on Jewish immigration.[33]

In September 1946, the Arab League, meeting in London, rejected British and American proposals to concede local autonomy to Jewish and Arab communities in Palestine as a first step toward eventual federation or partition. No, the Arabs replied, "Palestine will be a unitary state with a permanent Arab majority." Jews with ten years of residence would be given Palestinian citizenship and Jews might hold up to one-third of the seats in a Palestinian parliament, but Palestine would always be an *Arab*, not a Jewish, state.

Palestine's Jewish Agency—run by Chaim Weizmann, Moshe Shertok and David Ben-Gurion—also rejected the Anglo-American proposals. In 1944, Weizmann had pronounced *water* the chief factor compelling Palestinian unity under a Jewish state. Palestine could not be partitioned into Jewish and Arab states, Weizmann told a gathering in London, because the water was in the north and the vast "new" territories in need of population and irrigation were in the south. "If you want to irrigate the Negev with the waters of the Jordan, you cannot cut Palestine into two, because then development becomes impossible."[34] This water question would bedevil Israel and Palestine into the twenty-first century, and with such geological and economic arguments in mind, the Zionist Congress, meeting in Basel in December

1946, judged federation or partition "a travesty of Britain's obligations under the Mandate." Instead, the Zionists demanded that the path be left open for "Palestine to [be] established as a Jewish Commonwealth integrated into the structure of the new democratic world." The words "commonwealth" and "democratic" were the euphemisms—the British called them "screens"—most frequently deployed by the Zionists to preempt Arab objections to the religious basis (and prejudices) of the proposed Jewish state.[35] The Zionists demanded unchecked immigration and full powers to the Jewish Agency—still technically an auxiliary of the British—to "build the country."

The British were stymied. On one side stood Arabs demanding an Arab state with a permanent Arab majority. On the other stood Zionists demanding uncontrolled immigration from Europe and a "Jewish commonwealth." A British report in 1946 compared the Jewish tendency to behave as if there were no Arabs in Palestine with the Afrikaner exclusion of blacks in South Africa. In Palestine, a British analyst wrote, the Jews "behave as a *Herrenvolk*"—a "master race."[36] Attlee wearily formed yet another commission. "If all the books of statistics prepared for the nineteen commissions that have had a shot at the problem were placed on top of one another they would reach as high as the King David Hotel," the mandate's chief secretary groaned. This one had another stab at compromise, granting ninety-six thousand immigration certificates for 1947 and 1948—less than half the number desired by the Americans—and converting the mandate into a trusteeship, to prepare Palestine for independence in five years. The plan was hopelessly optimistic, and one senior British official confessed that since World War I the British had never really had a viable policy for Palestine: "Nothing but fluctuations of policy, hesitations . . . , no policy at all."[37]

Both the Arab delegations and the Jewish Agency rejected Attlee's latest fluctuation. Since a trusteeship needed cooperative beneficiaries, Britain found itself again at an impasse. Attlee gave up, and instructed Bevin simply to hand the mandate and all its problems over to the newly formed United Nations. In February 1947, Bevin did just that:

There are in Palestine about 1,200,000 Arabs and 600,000 Jews. For the Jews, the essential point of principle is the creation of a sovereign Jewish state. For the Arabs, the essential point of principle is to resist to the last the establishment of Jewish sovereignty in any part of Palestine. . . . There is no prospect of resolving this conflict by any settlement between the parties. . . .

We have, therefore, reached the conclusion that the only course now open to us is to submit the problem for the judgment of the United Nations.[38]

MARTIAL LAW

Bevin and Attlee, grizzled Labourites who had come of age in the working quarters of London and Bristol, would probably have liked to exhume Earl Balfour's bones and grind them underfoot. Bevin's surrender in 1947 was as good a postmortem on Balfour's credulous hopes as any. With the Jews and Arabs battling to gain the upper hand before the UN sat in judgment, the fighting resumed. In 1947 Britain proclaimed martial law and split the mandate into military-run "security zones." During World War II, the population of Palestine had grown to 1.9 million. Thanks to immigration, there were now 625,000 Jews, a full third of the population. To encroach on Arab lands, the Jews embarked on a more aggressive settlement policy. "What land we had was scattered a bit here, a bit there, with the Arabs owning what was in between," Yohanan Ramati wrote in 1951. To link up the Jewish enclaves and chase off Arab squatters, "we bribed the British, the *mukhtars* of the Arab villages, and the *fellaheen*. We also went to court over some of [the disputed land], and in other places beat up a few Arabs." Zones of Palestine that the British had never even considered for inclusion in a future Jewish state ultimately devolved to Israel because of forty-two Jewish settlements rapidly erected around Beisan and north of Gaza in the late 1940s. The Jewish settlements drove the Arabs out by not giving them jobs: "The Arab population tended to disappear from Jewish-owned land . . . where the employment of non-Jewish labor was explicitly debarred." Landless Arabs now drifted into the cities, ports and orange groves looking for homes and work.[39]

For the Truman administration, the Palestine question, initially regarded as a manageable international problem with a big domestic payoff, was finally recognized for what it was: a chronic, destabilizing crisis. On one side stood the Jews and the UN. The Jews, publicly at least, desired the formal partition of Palestine into Jewish and Arab states; the UN General Assembly had actually endorsed such a policy by a vote of thirty-three to thirteen. On the other side stood the angry Arab states and the furious Palestinian Arabs, who wanted a one-state solution with a permanent Arab majority. For the United States, now assuming the role of world leader, Palestine was a losing proposition for the simple reason that contingents of

Jewish emigrants to Palestine small enough not to alarm the Arabs would inflame the Jews, and contingents large enough to appease the Jews would inflame the Arabs. Appeasing the Arabs would harm Truman at home; appeasing the Jews would harm him abroad. That was the American security dilemma felt as keenly by Truman in 1948 as by Barack Obama sixty-two years later.

PALESTINE AND THE U.S. ELECTIONS OF 1948

Lord Inverchapel, Britain's ambassador in Washington, observed in January 1948 that President Truman was boxed in; he could not now take a pro-Arab line and oppose partition. "The Administration *cannot* reverse policy . . . without encountering intense pressure from Zionists and also non-Jewish elements who want the United Nations to succeed." Truman worried that support for the Arabs would cost him Jewish votes as well as non-Jewish Democrats who would defect to Henry Wallace's Progressive Party if the president did not take up the cudgels for the UN in Palestine. Wallace, who served as Roosevelt's vice president from 1941 to 1945, judged all American efforts to appease the Palestinians in 1947–48 "a sellout for Arab oil."[40] And of course there were the Republicans, who watched and waited: "The Republican presidential aspirants, Dewey and Taft, are on the watch for *any* chance to impale the Administration on the horns of the Palestine dilemma."[41] Governor Dewey, the State Department's Near Eastern expert Loy Henderson recalled, "was almost constantly criticizing Truman for failure to give full support to the Zionists. If Truman had taken positions [against the Jewish state], he would almost certainly have been defeated in the November [1948] elections."[42]

Finally, there was the unresolved problem of immigration. To draw down the pool of DPs in Europe, Illinois representative William Stratton had introduced a bill in the House in April 1947 calling for the admission of a hundred thousand refugees a year to the United States for four years, but the "Stratton Bill" never even made it out of committee, nor did a similar bill in the Senate even make it to committee. The "Displaced Persons Act of 1948," eventually signed by Truman, was amended in the House and Senate to exclude as many Jews and Catholics as possible by manipulating national quotas and preferences. Truman signed the bill reluctantly, noting publicly that it did little to solve the problem of *Jewish* refugees and that it "discriminates in callous fashion."[43] Plainly the American people and their elected representatives wanted the ongoing crisis of Jewish DPs solved in Palestine, not America.[44]

The British embassy, delighted to be rid of the Palestine problem, found the Americans to be curiously incapable of mediating in the Holy Land. Truman—with his flanks exposed to Wallace on the left and Dewey on the right—proved "extremely unwilling to court risks in an election year," Inverchapel reported from Washington. "It is almost inevitable that the [Truman] Administration will continue to be swayed in its Palestine policy by domestic rather than international considerations." For his part, Truman was unapologetic. Meeting in late 1945 with a conference of State Department officials who were up in arms over his unpopular—among Arabs—support for the Zionists, Truman refused to bend: "I am sorry, gentlemen, but I have to answer to hundreds of thousands who are anxious for the success of Zionism: I do not have hundreds of thousands of Arabs among my constituents."[45]

"PEOPLE IN STATE ARE BITCHING THINGS UP"

Although Secretary of State James Byrnes was a loyal Truman appointee, the career ranks of the U.S. State Department rebelled. Loy Henderson and the Near Eastern Affairs bureau viewed Israel as poison to American interests. Like presidents Nixon and George W. Bush, Truman responded by shifting the Palestine question from "the career men of the State Department" to the White House.[46] Truman handed the Palestine portfolio to Clark Clifford and the White House counsel's chief advisers on Palestinian affairs, David Niles and Max Lowenthal. Niles, a naturalized Polish Jew, served as White House liaison to the Zionist Organization's Washington office. Lowenthal, an acolyte of the late Justice Brandeis, had close connections with Weizmann's Jewish Agency. Like the neoconservatives clustered around Paul Wolfowitz and Doug Feith after 9/11, Niles, Lowenthal and their influential allies, Abraham Feinberg and Eddie Jacobson, were determined to break the back of the pro-Arab State Department. "People in State are bitching things up," Niles wrote Lowenthal in May 1948. Lowenthal, whom Truman called the White House's "backroom boy," agreed. "There has to be a house-cleaning in State, or someone in State on Palestine matters who is trustworthy." Lowenthal bluntly pitched American support and early recognition of a Jewish state in Palestine as the most expedient way to secure votes in U.S. elections.[47]

The more equitable Clark Clifford often balked at their advice. Lowenthal's memos, Clifford observed, amounted to "carefully-screened facts assembled to 'prove' whatever point Lowenthal is trying to make." The "one premise implicit in all of his memoranda was that the U.S. should support the Zionist cause, come what may." Still, Clifford also believed that Truman needed Jewish votes (and gifts) to secure his political future. Under relentless White House pressure like this, Loy Henderson was forced out of the Near Eastern bureau and shipped off to become U.S. ambassador to India in 1948.[48] James Forrestal, now secretary of defense and no friend of the Zionists, deplored the "squalid political purposes" of Niles, Lowenthal and Clifford and, like George Marshall—Truman's secretary of state after Byrnes's resignation in 1947—insisted that "United States policy should be based on United States *national* interests and not on *domestic political considerations.*"[49] George Kennan, on Marshall's policy planning staff, echoed that view, asserting that Truman was permitting himself to be "guided not by the national interest, but by other considerations."[50]

Kennan's view was also the British view. George Kirk considered that Truman's excessively political line on Palestine had converted an already fraught situation "into the grim realization of a Marx Brothers phantasmagoria."[51] In his New Year's 1948 instructions to his Washington embassy, Foreign Secretary Ernest Bevin told Lord Inverchapel to inform the White House that most Arab leaders wanted to solve the Palestinian problem so that they could turn to internal matters, but needed concessions from the Jews to mollify "popular opinion." Were the Jews to emerge from partition holding "the major part of their claims," Bevin feared that revolutionary upheaval would follow. "The positions and lives of the Arab leaders would be most insecure, a change of regime would follow, Communist or fanatical pan-Islamic." This, according to the British, was the reason the Arab states armed and financed Arab guerrillas in Palestine. Having roused their own masses with "intemperate propaganda from above" in the 1930s and 1940s, they found themselves with no room for maneuver in 1948. If they tolerated Jewish claims in Palestine, they would "give too great a handle to their extreme opposition." From London's perspective, there was only one way forward: "To avoid war, a strong American intervention with the Jews is necessary."[52] Paul-Henri Spaak, the influential prime minister of Belgium, seconded this view, telling the U.S. State Department in April 1948 that Palestine needed to be a single, federated state in which the majority would rule and Jews would enjoy a "large measure of autonomy."[53]

Truman still hoped to muddle through. He had his hands full defending Greece and Turkey against communist encroachment and rescuing Berlin from a Soviet blockade. He had little time to spare for Palestine. While America's UN ambassador assured the secretary general that "we're prepared to take a strong line with the Jews, to put politics on ice," Clark Clifford was quietly cultivating Truman's domestic garden by applauding the Balfour Declaration, advocating a Jewish state and quoting lines to Truman from Deuteronomy: "Behold, I have set the land before you: go in and possess the land which the Lord swore unto your fathers, Abraham, Isaac and Jacob, to give unto them and to their seed after them."[54] Florida senator Claude Pepper, writing in the *New York Times* in August 1947, demanded that the Jews be granted "the sustaining heritage of Palestine."[55] Claude Pepper was just one of many influential liberal senators who saw opportunity in Palestine: a new state of "Israel" would pay off internally with Jewish votes, but would also pay external dividends. Israel would widen the scope of the UN—by giving it a peace to administer in Palestine—and would weaken British imperialism by plucking away another of London's mandates. This convergence in the late 1940s of American Anglophobia and zeal for the UN was bad news for the Arabs of Palestine. The fact that the British favored the Arabs was just one more reason for the Americans to favor the Zionists. The Arabs could feel this American temporizing in their bones. Meeting in April 1948 with Warren Austin, Truman's ambassador to the UN, General Jamal el-Husseini, chairman of the Palestine Arab Higher Committee, warned that "unless the U.S. changed its attitude toward Palestine, the Arab states might in despair turn to the USSR." Impossible, Austin replied. The Soviet Union was a godless state with no respect for Islam or ancient traditions. "Despair often drives people to do things contrary to their own best interests," Husseini replied.[56]

Political lobbying clouded the apprehension of best interests in America as well. "We could have settled this Palestine thing if U.S. politics had been kept out of it," President Truman groused. He particularly resented the influence of Moshe Shertok and Chaim Weizmann in American politics. In a letter he drafted to Weizmann in December 1947, Truman wrote, "I don't think I ever had as much pressure and propaganda unnecessarily aimed at the White House as I have had in this instance."[57] William Eddy, America's ambassador to Saudi Arabia from 1944 to 1946, complained to the Joint Chiefs of Staff in 1948 that Truman's "pro-Zionist policy" had caused "the prestige of the U.S. government among the Arabs to vanish."[58] Secretary of State Marshall could barely keep his anger at the Jewish lobby in check. He never supported partition, and bluntly told Truman at a meeting on Palestine in May 1948 that Truman was putting "the great office of the President" at risk by permitting domes-

tic political concerns to shape strategy and policy. That meeting, three days before
the British pullout, was—according to Clifford—the scene of "the sharpest rebuke"
ever delivered to Truman, and perhaps to any president in the Oval Office. Marshall
told Truman that if the president supported a Jewish state in Palestine, then his
secretary of state would have no choice but to vote against him in November.[59]

THE UN'S FIRST GREAT TEST

The UN too pondered its choices. "The problem of Palestine is insoluble," the organization's special committee for the mandate grumbled in 1947.[60] Whereas the
British and the Arabs viewed the solution as an Arab state with guarantees for a
Jewish minority, the Truman administration—despite fierce misgivings in the
cabinet and at the State Department—saw partition as the only solution that would
bring closure to an ongoing international problem and satisfy the millions of Jewish voters in America. Partition was also the only solution that would jibe with
America's severely downsized military. Focused on domestic programs and European reconstruction after World War II, Truman had ordered sharp defense cuts,
slashing the $30 billion budget submitted to him by the service chiefs in 1948 to just
$14.4 billion.[61] That was roughly the same sum that Truman would invest in the
Marshall Plan. With few troops or tanks and a defense posture geared toward nuclear airpower, Truman, preoccupied with the Cold War, had no practical means
to intervene in Palestine and keep the peace between Jews and Arabs anyway.

Washington's campaign for partition at the UN was concentrated and firm.
Looking back from the perspective of the 2000s, when Americans evince skepticism
about the United Nations, it is remarkable to recall the high hopes Americans
vested in the UN in the late 1940s. During World War II, FDR had floated the idea
of "four policemen" running the world after the war: the United States, the USSR,
Britain and China. That notion of four global gendarmes had polled badly among
American voters and members of Congress, who thought that such a "cabal of big
powers" would be no different from the vicious cabals that had caused two world
wars. American isolationists wanted, as usual, to be left alone, and American internationalists wanted a return to the "collective security" advanced by Woodrow
Wilson in 1919. To rally America's internationalists and to coax the isolationists off
the sidelines, FDR had advocated the UN, which was a clever fusion of Wilson's

discredited League of Nations (the General Assembly) and the stillborn "four policemen" idea (the Security Council). Ideologically, Congress and the American
public were unwilling to assume responsibility for the "free world" unless the task
was transmitted through a virtuous world organization, not grubby tyrants like
Stalin or the selfish old European empires. (Stirring and prescient in retrospect,
Winston Churchill's "Iron Curtain Speech" in Missouri in 1946 had been damned
at the time by Walter Lippmann as a "catastrophic blunder" designed to ignite great
power rivalry and bring the world to the brink of war.)[62] FDR may have "perpetu-
ated an adolescent idealism among the American people" by making exaggerated
claims for the UN, but he succeeded, and prevented the United States from slipping
back into isolationism as it had done after World War I.[63] Moreover, the UN was a
convenient strategic vehicle to "Americanize" the world: to stymie Soviet competition with the offer of American social, economic and political liberalism.[64] Thus, by
the time the Palestinian partition crisis arrived in 1948, the UN was ready to administer disputed lands and Washington was spoiling for an opportunity to showcase
the constructive potential of the UN and detach itself from any affiliation with
"British imperialism."

TRUMAN PRESSURES THE UN

For the Arabs, this all amounted to the perfect storm. For Truman, already absorbed
with the Prague coup, which saw Czech president Eduard Benes toppled by the
communist Klement Gottwald in February 1948, and the steady defeat of Chiang
Kai-shek's Chinese nationalists by Mao Zedong's communists, things were even
stormier. The last thing Truman wanted was to make big decisions in the Middle
East, but Jewish leaders like New York congressman Emmanuel Celler and Joseph
Proskauer—also president of the American Jewish Committee—forced him in that
direction. Celler demanded that Truman squeeze the undecided delegations of
Greece, Haiti, China, Ecuador, Liberia, Honduras and Paraguay. Proskauer urged
the same treatment for the Philippines. In an age when there were only fifty-seven
countries in the United Nations General Assembly, Truman's "pressure boys" were
exerting a full-court press, and their tactics worked. On November 29, 1947, the UN
voted for the partition of Palestine, thirty-three to thirteen, with ten abstentions.
Having feared a Soviet veto up to the last minute, the Zionists were overjoyed by

Russia's support, which stemmed from Stalin's desire to split the British and Americans over the issue of a Jewish state and win the gratitude of the Zionists. "What's happened to us in connection with the Soviet Union is a real miracle," Moshe Shertok exulted.[65] Not really: although the Soviets would shortly emerge as the arsenal of Arab states committed to the annihilation of Israel, in the late 1940s they saw a partitioned Palestine as a win-win. The Jewish state could be counted upon to move ruthlessly against "reactionary" and "semi-fascist" elements like the grand mufti's circle and the Muslim Brotherhood, and Arab Palestine, shorn of its Nazi sympathizers, would become a pro-Soviet "anti-colonial state." The Soviets would have their cake and eat it too. Thus, Andrei Gromyko, the young Soviet ambassador to the UN, welcomed the American-sponsored partition plan.[66]

THE PARTITION OF PALESTINE

Though there were half as many Jews as Arabs in Palestine—625,000 Jews versus 1.3 million Arabs—the Jews nevertheless received the bulk of Palestine from the UN. The Jews got 5,700 square miles; the Arabs 4,300 square miles.[67] The Americans were not alone in pressing the broad Jewish claims, which stunned and infuriated the Arabs. France's Charles de Gaulle supported the enlarged Israel as "just reparations" for Jewish suffering in World War II and as a way to slow the spread of revolutionary pan-Arabism, which threatened the French position in Algeria, and further weaken the British position in the Middle East.[68] Herschel Johnson, who had spearheaded the American campaign at the UN and had nearly broken under the pressure, was rhapsodic, uttering words that rivaled Balfour's—"who will begrudge the Jewish people that little notch which is Palestine?"—in their credulity. Reflecting on the prospects for partition, Johnson declared that the boundary between the Jewish and Arab states of Palestine will "be as friendly as the boundary which runs for 3,000 miles between Canada and the United States."[69] Johnson's boss, UN ambassador Warren Austin, was less optimistic. To him, the future looked bleak. A separate Jewish state in Palestine "will have to defend itself with bayonets forever, until extinguished in blood."[70]

The blood gushed in April 1948, when British troops evacuated Palestine and Jewish and Arab militias began fighting for the inheritance. In Haifa, where seventy thousand Jews lived alongside seventy thousand Arabs, Arab demonstrators rallied to "throw the Jews into the sea" before they could "take our land."[71] The Arabs were too late. Even before the last British units sailed in May, the Jewish Hagana had rousted the Arab populations of Haifa, Acre, Tiberias and Safad. Operating in eight hundred homemade armored cars clapped together in the Jewish settlements, the Hagana fought running battles along the Tel Aviv–Jerusalem road.[72] That spring campaign was horribly capped by the "massacre of Deir Yassin," where Irgun and Stern Gang units plundered and then murdered 107 Arab men, women and children. Yitzhak Levy, a Jewish commander, noted the "great cruelty" of his troops in his after-action report: "Whole families—women, old people, children—were killed . . . prisoners were murdered viciously by their captors."[73] The British, concerned only to defend their evacuation routes and remove 210,000 tons of supplies, looked the other way. In April 1948, Haifa was half Jewish and half Arab. By May, it was almost entirely Jewish. Only four thousand of seventy thousand Arabs remained, confined to a ghetto around Wadi Nisnas.[74] The Hagana laid siege to the beloved Arab city of Jaffa; by May, they had evicted the entire Muslim population of ninety thousand by turning their howitzers on the Arab neighborhoods and lobbing in shells. "The spectacle was shocking," a Hagana report noted. "A terrible panic arose and . . . those running trampled each other underfoot."[75] Jewish units did the same to the all-Arab town of Acre, which, like Jaffa, had been reserved for the Arabs by the UN. In Tiberias, Jewish mobs plundered the Arab bazaar, carrying off beds and refrigerators and settling into Arab shops and homes. "Shame covers my face," a Jewish officer wrote in his account of the battle.[76]

The UN partition plan had granted the Jewish state 55 percent of British Palestine, including the rich coastal plain from Haifa south to Jaffa, eastern Galilee and the Negev Desert. The Arab state received Samaria and Judea (the heart of today's West Bank), western Galilee and its lovely port of Acre, and the southern coast from Isdud (now Ashdod) through the Gaza Strip to a stretch of desert along the Egyptian border. The UN declared Jerusalem and Bethlehem off-limits to either state. Because of their religious significance to Muslims, Jews and Christians, they were grouped in an international zone. George Wadsworth, the American ambassador to Iraq, proposed making Jerusalem "a spiritual Yellowstone Park" for men and women of all faiths to revere and enjoy.[77] Neither side was pleased with the partition. The Arabs criticized the quantity and quality of land given to the Jews, as well as the enormous Arab minority left inside the borders of the Jewish state (325,000 Arabs in a total population of 823,000). The Jews publicly praised the partition, but secretly plotted to seize all of Palestine. "We must copy the Poles, who exploited the confusion and war weariness in 1918 to occupy [Lithuanian] Vilnius and present the world with a fait accompli," Ben-Gurion jotted.[78] Now, with the British army in full retreat and the world distracted by other things, Ben-Gurion rushed to implement the fait accompli.

"KILL THE JEWS!"

Attacking along the donkey tracks that threaded into Jerusalem, Jewish troops tried to relieve the beleaguered synagogues of the Old City but were driven back by Jordanian Bren gun carriers, scout cars and pack howitzers, all rather confusingly led into action by a few dozen British officers seconded to King Abdullah's Arab Legion.[79] South of Bethlehem, four Jewish settlements at Kfar Etzion were surrounded and wiped out by the Jordanians, who accepted the surrender of the settlers and then slaughtered them in cold blood, screaming, "*Idbah al yahud!*"—"Kill the Jews!"[80] To isolate the Jewish settlements, the Arabs blocked the roads between them. Outgunned by the Jews, the Arabs' only hope was to control the Palestinian roads to prevent the Jews from combining their scattered formations. When the Jews ran the roads in armored trucks and buses, the Arabs ambushed them. The Jews retaliated, flinging Molotov cocktails at Arab cars and trucks and advancing into Arab villages to "uproot them." Young Ariel Sharon—nicknamed "Arik"—cut his teeth in this bloody civil war, which, on the Jewish side, suppressed all "political-moral considerations" to facilitate an "active defense" by preemptive terror attacks. Until April 1948, the Arabs enjoyed a string of successes. They isolated the Jews in the Negev from their fellows in the coastal plain and walled off western Galilee and Jerusalem as well, which persuaded men like Sharon to take the gloves off and start slaughtering Arab civilians. There was some soul-searching on the Jewish side— "This recalls Lidice," one Jewish mayor protested, referring to the Nazi slaughter of an entire Czech town in 1942—but hard-liners carried the day. "It is not enough to hit huts," a Hagana general coldly uttered. "People too [must be hit]."[81]

With little external support, the Palestinian Arabs wilted under Jewish fire. The Israelis established conventional superiority early on. Many Jews had served in British units raised in Palestine, and additional weapons were procured through bribes to British soldiers and supply officers. A British raid on a Hagana arsenal in 1946 turned up hundreds of army rifles, mortars, machine guns, antitank rifles, a half million rounds of rifle ammunition, five thousand grenades, five thousand mortar bombs, eight hundred pounds of explosive and even Bren gun carriers quietly "liberated" from British garages.[82] That weapons cache was a rare success for the British, who were usually driven away from Jewish settlements with the very guns and bombs they were searching for.[83] With firepower like this, the Hagana in 1948 comprised thirty thousand redoubtable frontline troops with an equal number of reserves and augmented by the ruthless four thousand irregulars of the Irgun and Stern Gang.

Against this disciplined, well-equipped Western-style army—it would shortly be renamed the Israeli Defense Force (IDF)—the Palestinian Arabs deployed in loose *jihadiyya*, or "fighting societies." The fighting societies were regional, not national, and had no reserves, logistics or supreme command. Although as many as thirty thousand Palestinian Arabs took up arms in 1948, the British estimated that there were no more than twenty-five hundred reliable Arab fighters in Palestine, and they were sundered into lightly armed bands of fifteen to fifty men. Moreover, the Arabs, who rarely contested British arms searches in the Jewish style, had nothing like the firepower of the Hagana. As a British intelligence report noted in 1945, "The Arab does not favor a weapon which expends ammunition rapidly or requires careful maintenance." In fact, the Arabs had hardly any light automatics, and few grenades, mortars or mines.[84] They relied on "disorganized guerrilla warfare and had a total lack of logistics and supplies."[85]

Politically, the Palestinians were split into competing political factions like the Arab Higher Committee (AHC), the Arab League Military Committee and its Arab Liberation Army (ALA), and the Muslim Brotherhood in Egypt. They battled each other when not battling the Hagana. "Amongst the Arabs there is a total failure to organize because of local jealousies," a British officer wrote in January 1944.[86] The Palestinian Arab movement had never recovered from the debilitating feud between the leading Husseini and Nashashibi families, and all cohesion had evaporated during the war, when the mufti lived in exile and his principal Husseini partisans were in British jails in Rhodesia. A British intelligence report predicted that, under these demoralizing circumstances, Palestinian nationalism would die out and be swept up in a broader pan-Arab nationalism.[87] A British official who inspected Arab units in northern Galilee in March 1948 did not bother to conceal his contempt. The troops had no artillery, mortars, machine guns or medics, but had no worries either: "The men of this village behave like a bunch of schoolchildren, wanting a parade to show off their weapons, to let me see how tough they are and ready to fight the Jews, and how sorry they are that there are no Jews [nearby] to kill."[88]

"MAKE THE ARABS TREK"

When the Jews did march into range, it was they who did most of the killing, not the Arabs. Whereas Jewish kibbutzim were built for war—fortified with trenches and bunkers—Arab villages collapsed under a few mortar rounds. In the sharpest phase of the civil war—December 1947 to May 1948—the Palestinian Arabs failed to capture a single Jewish settlement, while the Jews seized two hundred Arab towns and villages.[89] The Hagana had a proper general staff, which devised the "Dalet Plan" in 1948. That plan set out very plainly that the war of 1948 would be used not only to defend Jewish areas, but to gain control of lands allotted to the Arabs by the UN partition. Jewish settlements and concentrations would be augmented by Arab population centers "located inside or near our defensive system in order to prevent them from being used as bases." "In each attack," Prime Minister Ben-Gurion told his commanders bluntly, "it is necessary to give a decisive blow, ruin the place, kick away the inhabitants."[90]

By the spring of 1948, more than a hundred thousand Arabs had fled their homes in Haifa, Jaffa and Jerusalem, the coastal plain and the Jordan Valley. Some fled into solid Arab towns like Nazareth, Nablus and Bethlehem; others over the border into Jordan, Syria and Lebanon, or by ship to Cyprus. This was part of a deliberate Jewish strategy to "make the Arabs trek," but also the result of Arab fumbling. The Arab militias fought halfheartedly and tended to evacuate Arab villages near the line of fire, not grasping that waiting Jewish settlers would rush in to take their places. The mufti's efforts to halt the exodus and keep a physical Arab presence in the expanding Jewish national home collided with Arab panic. Although the mufti and the Arab Higher Committee ordered Palestinian Arabs to remain in place and fight the Jews, Palestinian Arab officials did a brisk business selling emigration certificates to frightened Arab evacuees.[91]

THE STATE OF ISRAEL IS BORN

The British army was supposed to remain in Palestine and keep the peace until August 1948. But its attention was slipping. Broken by World War II and sustained through the cold winter of 1947–48 by U.S. aid, the British government saw little point in expending scarce funds on a situation that had been radically changed by the surge of Jewish immigrants into Palestine and the UN resolution of November 1947.[92] Relinquishing the mandate and withdrawing British troops three months early on May 14, 1948, seemed a sensible economy and a facing of facts on the ground. Upon hearing of the British scuttle, Chaim Weizmann rushed his representative in Washington, Aubrey Eban, the future Israeli foreign minister Abba Eban, to meet with Clark Clifford and tell him that a "State of the Jews"—"Israel" would be a last-minute name change—would shortly be proclaimed. Israel proclaimed statehood later that day across its old settlements and newly conquered Arab territory. One of Israel's first acts was to void the British White Paper of 1939 and invite "home" thousands of immigrants from the DP camps in Germany, France and Cyprus. To snuff out the "Zionist entity" before it could sink its roots, the armies of Egypt, Iraq, Jordan, Syria and Lebanon immediately declared war and invaded the new state of Israel.

Until 1948, Egypt had lived in isolation from the broader Arab world. It had passively watched the Arab Revolt against the Turks and rebuffed Palestinian appeals for help against the Jews when the Balfour Declaration was announced. "Go back and make your peace with the Jewish settlers," Prime Minister Saad Zaghloul had told a Palestinian deputation. "They too are Semites, and the British will keep them under control." Egypt until 1948 had taken a more European outlook—as befitted a country that had been created by Farouk's Europeanizing dynasty—and resisted the Arab nationalism that began to take hold in Damascus and Baghdad in the late nineteenth century. All that changed in 1948. Suddenly, with Jewish soldiers and terrorists slaughtering and evicting the Arab inhabitants of Palestine and driving three hundred thousand refugees into the neighboring states, the Egyptians were forced into the Arab world. They became the political leaders of the Arab League—to forestall Baghdad's ambition to rule the Fertile Crescent from Beirut down to Basra—as well as the core of the Arab military coalition against Israel or any other threat, a role they would retain until 1973. This steady, altogether improbable unification of the Arab world ground forward because of Israeli behavior in Palestine, which the Israelis did not even bother to keep secret at first. We are "cleansing" Palestine of Arabs, Yigal Allon boasted in *Ha Sefer Ha Palmach.*[93]

TRUMAN DEFIES THE "STRIPED-PANTS BOYS IN THE STATE DEPARTMENT"

President Truman was curiously unfazed by these developments. Eager to beat Moscow to the punch and to assert his independence from the cautious "striped-pants boys in the State Department [who] are against my policy of supporting Israel," Truman recognized the new state of Israel on the day it was proclaimed, May 14, 1948.[94] Secretary of State George Marshall was furious. He had just warned Abba Eban that America would not "bail out" the Zionists if they declared independence. In an emergency meeting called to discuss the recognition question, Marshall declared that "the great dignity of the office of President would be seriously diminished" if Truman subordinated an "international problem" to a "transparent dodge to win a few votes." Undersecretary of State Robert Lovett chimed in that Truman was "buying a pig in a poke," a state with high strategic costs and dubious benefits. No wonder the Jewish Agency in Palestine privately referred to Marshall's State Department as "bastards," or "*momzerim*."[95]

Dean Rusk, who had just joined America's UN delegation, struggled with the "anomalous situation" created by the Arab invasion and U.S. recognition of Israel. Without American recognition, the Zionists had no international rights or standing. Truman's precipitate decision to recognize the new state—against Marshall's advice—gave the "Israelis" new rights and privileges, which worried Rusk: "The Jews will run to the Security Council with the claim that their state is the object of an armed aggression and will use every means to obscure the fact that it is their *own* armed aggression against the Arabs inside Palestine which is the cause of the Arab counter-attack." Israel did just that, and although the United States maintained its arms embargo, it privately conveyed its support to the Israelis as well as a $100 million loan. Rusk considered U.S. support of Israel in 1948 "morally indefensible." In the first phase of the war, the Israelis had driven 300,000 Arab refugees out of the wedge of Palestine allotted to the Jews by the 1947 partition plan. In the second phase of the war, after the American recognition of Israel and the Arab invasion of Palestine—on behalf of the refugees—the Israeli army and paramilitaries advanced into the wedge of Palestine allotted to the Arabs and evicted 450,000 *more* refugees in a successful effort to destroy the Palestinian claim to Palestine through ethnic cleansing.[96] For the United States, which took Israel's side in this episode, the experience of 1948–49 was just what George Marshall had said it would be: political poison contrary to "American national . . . [and] strategic interests."[97]

Dean Rusk fretted that "from the aspect of our relations with the Middle East and of our broad security interests in that region, it would be almost fatal to pit the forces of the U.S. . . . against the governments of the Arab world." With the Hagana and Irgun rampaging through Arab quarters and villages, Rusk at the UN recommended emergency surgery: "Combine now with France and Great Britain to force a *modus vivendi* . . . Abdullah of Jordan will get a corridor across Palestine to the sea at Jaffa; Ibn Saud will get a port at Aqaba, and the Syrians will get some northern territory, leaving the Jews a coastal state running from Tel Aviv to Haifa. The UN could bless the deal."[98] Rusk and Marshall were looking for ways to deliver a Jewish state for Truman without inflaming the entire Arab world. In New York, E. B. White, stunned by the horrors in Palestine and the recent invention of weapons of mass destruction, penned a weirdly prophetic warning:

> [Manhattan] for the first time in its long history is destructible. A single flight of planes no bigger than a wedge of geese can quickly end this island fantasy, burn the towers, crumble the bridges, turn the underground passages into lethal chambers, cremate the millions. . . . In the mind of whatever perverted dreamer might loose the lightning, New York must hold a steady irresistible charm.[99]

The U.S. oil lobby—headquartered on that destructible island of Manhattan—also criticized Truman's support for Israel. An Aramco executive warned, "The United States is jeopardizing the good will of 30,000,000 Arabs and 220,000,000 Muslims, risking the loss of its cultural and educational leadership in that part of the world, the sacrifice of many hundreds of millions of dollars of investments . . . and the strategic loss of access to air and naval bases throughout the entire Muslim world."[100] A Bechtel employee in Khobar on the day of the American recognition recalled the resentment that welled up among his hosts—an ordinary Saudi family—when they heard the news on the radio of Truman's decision to recognize the Jewish state: "Amrika say—is okay—Israel. President Truman, he give order—Amrika will keep Israel." In the streets outside, black-robed women wailed despondently and crackly radio voices bellowed through static cries of "*Falastin, Falastin!*"[101] The Saudis and Syrians promptly threatened an oil embargo: the Saudis might withhold their oil and the Syrians might block Tapline—Standard Oil's pipeline from Saudi

Arabia across the Golan Heights to Sidon on the Lebanese coast, which was under construction. But the White House downplayed the threat. "The Arabs need us more than we need them," Clifford told Truman. "They must have oil royalties or go bankrupt." The greater threat, in Clifford's eyes, was any "shilly-shallying appeasement of the Arabs," which would cast America "in the ridiculous role of trembling before threats of a few nomadic desert tribes" and earn the "contempt" of serious players in the Cold War, like "Russia or Yugoslavia."[102]

WAR

The Arabs planned to destroy Israel with or without American shilly-shallying. Their casus belli—that Palestine was a single country whose political future had to be determined by the Arab majority—was immediately rejected by the Americans as "the highest type of evidence of the international violation of the law."[103] No less an authority than the United Nations had authorized partition and a Jewish state. Enjoying the advantages of tactical surprise on the frontiers and heavy weapons—tanks, artillery and aircraft—the Arab armies initially made great gains in May 1948, cutting into areas allotted to the Jews by the 1947 UN resolution. Egypt controlled the Negev, the Jordanians and Iraqis pushed toward Tel Aviv, and the Syrians invaded eastern Galilee. Accustomed to fighting in platoons and companies with light weapons, the Jewish forces were no match for the regular Arab armies and they suffered 4,000 casualties in the weeks after the Arab onslaught. By July, however, the Israelis had turned the tide.[104] Whereas the Arab states—who never put more than 55,000 troops in the field in this little war—watched their ammunition and equipment dwindle under a UN arms embargo, the Israelis mobilized 115,000 men and women and successfully reequipped with critical shipments from the Czechs, who ignored the embargo.

The vast size of the Arab countries bounding Israel accounted for the "David and Goliath" legends that circulated after the war, with plucky little Israel fighting off an Arab giant. In fact, Israel was Goliath and the Arab coalition—with its small, brigade-strength Egyptian, Jordanian, Syrian and Iraqi contingents—was David.[105] In December 1948, the newly christened IDF—created to facilitate the fusion of the Hagana with the Stern Gang and Irgun—outfitted itself with tanks, artillery and combat aircraft, shifted to the offensive, knocked out the Iraqis, Jordanians and

Syrians, and then turned its fire on the Egyptians. Between February and July 1949 the Israelis imposed cease-fires on all of their Arab neighbors. The Arab states did not cooperate with each other, and they all underestimated the Israelis, who seized 80 percent of Arab Palestine in their counterattacks.[106] "We were complacently expecting the Jews to run away the moment they saw us," an Egyptian general recalled.[107] Entering Jerusalem, Ben-Gurion noted approvingly that "there are no strangers here," by which he meant no Arabs. "One hundred percent Jews. Since Jerusalem's destruction in the days of the Romans, it has not been so Jewish as it is now." He concluded on a menacing note: "I do not assume that this will change."[108] The Palestinian Arabs were the principal losers, driven into exile and squalid camps. "The Palestinian refugee problem," Benny Morris observed in his account of the war, "was the main expression of that defeat." Between 1947 and 1949, 750,000 Palestinians were driven from their homes and about 160,000 remained behind. Only about 5,000 Jewish civilians fled the Arab areas, and they were quickly absorbed into the greatly enlarged Jewish state. "We put new immigrants in Arab houses," Ben-Gurion smiled. The Palestinians no longer had houses; theirs were occupied by the IDF and inflowing waves of Jewish settlers.[109]

REFUGEES IN A U.S. ELECTION YEAR

For the Americans, the Jewish mopping-up operations posed a critical test. Would Washington intervene—British style—to maintain a balance between the Jews and Palestinians, or pursue a different solution? Would Washington force Israel to release Arabs from newly created "ghettos" in the Jewish zone, and to take back and resettle the hundreds of thousands of Arab refugees the Hagana had driven out of Palestine in 1948? The Israelis were unrepentant; the Arab League, after all, had trumpeted the Arab invasion in May 1948 as an opportunity not merely to defend the Palestinians, but to fight "a war of extermination and a momentous massacre, which will be spoken of like the Mongolian massacres and the Crusades."[110] As tone-deaf then as they are now, the Arab states permitted the Jews to cloak their aggression in a claim of national defense. Still, Israel's own savagery was hard to stomach. A British report from Haifa in October 1949 described the Arabs there being ejected from their homes and packed into stifling quarters. Villages in Galilee had been "forcibly emptied" and force-marched to Nazareth, where they were handed over to the Red Cross for feeding or removal. Arab villagers were forbidden to farm, and Jewish squatters and immigrants were presented with the titles to Arab property. The British consul general in Haifa drove out from the city and counted along the main road "at least twenty [Arab] villages blown up by the Jews . . . thus cleared completely for the accommodation of Jewish settlers."[111]

The UN naturally looked to the Americans for a remedy, but domestic politics in an election year made redress of the Israeli atrocities difficult. Fighting an apparently losing campaign against Republican challenger Tom Dewey—who had wide projected leads in the electoral college and the popular vote as late as November 1948—Truman was in no position to alienate Jewish voters at home. As in 1944, Dewey and the Republicans again had a strong Israeli plank in their platform, pledging "full recognition" and "development aid" to the Jewish state.[112] With Israeli forces hammering the Egyptians in the Negev and Britain and China—and Secretary of State George Marshall—calling for sanctions against Israel in October, Truman led a spectacular rally in New York's Madison Square Garden in which he boasted of his unflinching support for Israel and his determination to block any sanctions. "Israel," Truman declared, "must be large enough, free enough, and strong enough to make its people self-supporting and secure." The Jews were taking over Palestine "in a way perhaps comparable to the winning of the American West."[113] Neither Truman nor Dewey would force the Israelis to give back Arab territory annexed in 1948.[114] Truman secretly directed Marshall to "avoid taking positions on Palestine before November 3, the day after the presidential election." The president wanted to keep some leverage over Israel without alienating America's Jewish voters on election day. The close Truman-Dewey race and the importance of the Jewish vote gave the Israeli military all of October and November 1948 to work unmolested. It stepped up its offensives and annexed the entire Negev, absorbing the vast Arab pockets around Beersheba and El Auja. While this was going on, Golda Meir and Teddy Kollek—the future mayor of Jerusalem—were in the United States raising $50 million for the purchase of weapons for the IDF.[115]

James MacDonald, Truman's special representative in Tel Aviv, concluded in November 1948 that it was hereafter "unrealistic politically and militarily" to force Israel back to the November 1947 UN boundary lines or to demand the return of Arab refugees. Even if the United States did try to implement sanctions to compel Israel to heed the UN resolution passed on December 11, 1948, which called for the repatriation or compensation of all Palestinian refugees, the Soviets—who still courted Israel as a possible socialist ally and had officially condemned the Arab invasion in May 1948 as "unprovoked aggression on the lawful rights of the Jewish people"—would opportunistically step in to "bust" the sanctions and pick up Israel as a convenient base in the eastern Mediterranean.[116] Like so many American policy makers in the early days, MacDonald was an optimist. America must not "keep in step with Britain" and repeat London's "decade of mistakes and humiliations," but set off on its own new course. MacDonald had no winning policy recommendations, just a general sense that the British had been inept. But his views fit with Truman's view that Israel must not be pressured. When Secretary of State Marshall threatened to resign over the president's unwillingness to roll back Israel's "chauvinistic and imperialistic" gains with sanctions, the president ignored the threat and had a spokesman publicly declare that the United States would oppose any reduction in Israeli territory without Israel's consent.[117]

The only tense moment in the new American-Israeli relationship cropped up in December 1948, when the Israelis struck briefly into Gaza and al-Arish to trap an Egyptian army retreating from the Negev. Al-Arish was Egyptian and Gaza was held by the Egyptian army for the Palestinians, who had been granted a broad crescent of land north and south of Gaza by the original UN partition plan in 1947. Israeli attacks there could have triggered a British security guarantee to Cairo. Faced with the absurd prospect of a military clash with his closest Cold War ally because of Israeli freelancing, Truman instructed MacDonald to go to Prime Minister Ben-Gurion and Foreign Minister Shertok, who had changed his last name in the Israeli style to Sharett, and tell them that any invasion of Egypt or Jordan would "deeply disturb" Israel's relations with Washington and force the United States to "reconsider" its sponsorship of Israel's admission to the UN. In the mild language of diplomacy, those were hard words, and Sharett's reaction to them demonstrated that American pressure on Israel—if ever exerted—would probably work. Sharett's "fingers tightened around his pen and his face [became] white with tension."[118]

Driven humiliatingly out of Palestine, the Egyptian army consoled itself that it had clung to its positions there for a time "like the Russians at Stalingrad."[119] For the Israelis, the war of 1948 had been—in the words of the British Foreign Office—a convenient "test of American indulgence," and the Americans had measured up. The year 1948 had forged "an unbreakable Israeli-American combination."[120] British efforts to push the Israelis out of the Negev and keep control of the Gaza-Beersheba-Jericho road, which loosely connected Egypt and Jordan, went nowhere, to Israel's immense relief. Truman perceived those concerns as a last futile gasp of British imperial policy and, anyway, considered the matter trivial in comparison with the bigger problems faced by America. From summer 1948 through spring 1949, the United States was engaged in the Berlin airlift, feeding two million Berliners and staring down the Soviet Union in Central Europe. The Negev, Truman testily reminded the British ambassador, "is a small area not worth differing over."[121]

THE PALESTINIAN REFUGEE PROBLEM EMERGES

American distraction suited Israel's book, as did the headlong Palestinian flight into exile during the 1948 war, which solved a demographic problem that had appeared insoluble before the war. In the Jewish zone of Palestine staked out by the UN in 1947, there had been 498,000 Jews and 325,000 Arabs. It would have been difficult to erect a Jewish state on such a mixed demographic foundation. Now, after the three rounds of fighting between December 1947 and March 1949, the problem had been fixed. The war had cost Israel $500 million and 5,700 dead, but with what magnificent results: "The most spectacular event in the contemporary history of Palestine—more spectacular in a sense than the creation of the Jewish state—is the wholesale evacuation of its Arab population," Moshe Sharett rejoiced. Allotted 55 percent of Palestine in 1947, the Israelis now had 80 percent, and most of the conquered territory—2,500 square miles of previously Arab land—had been emptied of Arabs. "The reversion to the *status quo ante* is unthinkable," Sharett explained. He saw the flight of the Palestinians as a miraculous removal of Israel's otherwise indigestible Arab minority. "Even if a certain backwash is unavoidable, we must make the most of the momentous chance with which history has presented us."[122]

Some Arab sympathizers agreed with Sharett's conclusion, if not his methods. William Burdett, Jr., the American consul general in Jerusalem, surmised in February 1949 that "security in the long run will be served best if the refugees remain in the Arab states and Arab Palestine instead of returning to Israel." Burdett was not fond of the Zionists but concluded that "the U.S. has supported the establishment of a Jewish state, so it should insist on a homogeneous one." Were the Palestinian refugees to return, they would constitute a perennial gnawing "minority problem" and "a constant temptation for uprisings and intervention by neighboring Arab states."[123] Other Americans were not so sure. In 1949, the State Department asked how Israel's neighbors could be expected to settle as many as six hundred thousand

Palestinian refugees. The terrified Palestinian refugees who swarmed into the little Kingdom of Jordan entirely eclipsed the king's three hundred thousand subjects.[124] American critics also deplored Israel's repulse of any refugees plucky enough to return to Palestine and Tel Aviv's systematic confiscation of their homes and land. This violated UN Resolution 194 of December 1948, which called on Israel to permit all refugees who wished to return home and "live at peace with their neighbors" to do so. In April 1949, Truman pronounced himself "disgusted with the manner in which the Jews are approaching the refugee problem," and vowed to correct it. Taking the president at his word, George McGhee, assistant U.S. secretary of state and coordinator of Palestine Refugee Matters, invited the Israeli ambassador to lunch at the Metropolitan Club and offered to trade a $49 million American loan to Israel for better treatment of the Palestinian refugees. The Israeli ambassador looked McGhee in the eye and told him that Israel had no need to negotiate; it would get the money anyway. The Israeli ambassador was right: that afternoon, Truman picked up the phone and bluntly ordered McGhee to release the funds with or without Israeli concessions to the Palestinians.[125] In May 1949, Truman sent Ben-Gurion a querulous letter threatening to "revise [America's] attitude toward Israel" if Israel continued to reject the UN resolutions of 1948 on the Palestinian refugees, but Ben-Gurion continued to reject, and Truman continued to submit.[126]

U.S. compliance with even the most outrageous Israeli behavior stemmed from the usual lobbying buttressed by a strategic shift in Washington. The White House, Pentagon and State Department reoriented themselves after the 1948 war and the November 1948 U.S. elections. Instead of "alienating" Israel with threats of sanctions or territorial exchanges, Washington resolved—in the words of Undersecretary of State Robert Lovett—to "secure Anglo-American strategic requirements in the Middle East by winning the Israelis over into the Anglo-American camp."[127] Israel, in short, would become a strategic American outpost in the eastern Mediterranean, what Truman hopefully called "the industrial backbone of the Middle East."[128] Moreover, having just "lost" China and Indonesia to the communists and having just promulgated a "Truman Doctrine" for the defense of vulnerable states against subversion, Truman viewed the creation of a pro-American regime in Israel as a rare, invigorating success.[129]

John Foster Dulles, who was Governor Dewey's foreign policy adviser in 1948 and would be President Dwight Eisenhower's secretary of state from 1953 to 1959, told James MacDonald in December 1948 that the Arab-Israeli War had revealed three critical facts that America would need to reckon with in the years ahead: first, the impotence of the Arabs and the might of the Jews; second, the unreliability of the British, who had been proven wrong in all their predictions about the region; and third, that Washington would have to topple and replace British leadership in the Middle East.[130] Dulles and Marshall had both rued the ease with which Soviet propagandists had used British aims—to expand Egypt and Jordan and shrink Israel—to drive a wedge between the Israelis and the Western allies. The U.S. government would not let that happen again.[131] Britain would simply have to embrace the American plan for the region—a strong Israel—and drop its own: "an Arab fence to prevent Russian entry into the area."[132] Of course the American strategy engendered as many problems as it solved, and was founded on slapdash thinking: Israel, Truman averred, needed to exist and prosper because "of the promises made to the Jewish people in the First World War, [which] must be kept."[133] Thus, the United States bound itself permanently to Israel in 1948 because of casual British promises made in the heat of World War I to weaken the Central Powers and strengthen the entente. Needless to say, such conduct—based on domestic political considerations and a narrow-minded humanitarianism that succored the Jews but overlooked the plight of the Palestinians—disgraced the very idea of strategy. America's preferment of the Zionists, Kermit Roosevelt noted in 1947, turned the entire Arab world against the United States, crushed out moderate political forces in every Arab state and nourished reactionary, vengeful ones instead:

> Times of strife are hard on moderates. When you condemn outsiders it is easier to condemn them *in toto*. When you are fighting invasion from the West, it is less complicated to hate everything Western than it is to distinguish between some things that are bad and others that are good . . . and because the U.S. has pursued a wavering but generally pro-Zionist policy we have been the most bitterly attacked of all Western powers.[134]

Backed by Washington, the Israelis made no concessions to the Palestinians or the beaten Arab states. The Soviets also backed the Jews. Moscow scorned the Arab armies that had invaded Israel. They included German Nazi officers in Egyptian uniform, pro-Nazi Turkish officers and decidedly lumpen elements like the dregs sent by Iraq: "90 percent Shiite Arabs, the rest being Kurds." The Russians were not willing to write off the Israelis just yet. The Jews appeared far more modern, progressive and *usable* than any of the Arab contingents, which were "riddled with reactionary forces."[135] The Arabs, not the Jews, had started the war by seeking to prevent implementation of the 1947 UN partition plan. Let them now suffer the consequences. "I believe we should prevent the return of the Arabs," David Ben-Gurion declaimed in June 1948. "To allow their return would be foolish."[136]

Refusal to permit the return of the Palestinian refugees became Israeli policy.[137] Arab property was confiscated or destroyed. Deserted Arab villages were picked over and then burned to discourage their inhabitants from returning. The Hagana razed much of the Old City of Jaffa and most of the archaeologically rich Arab quarter of Tiberias, blasting and wrecking until they ran out of dynamite. Jewish settlers moved into the Arab quarters of big cities like Haifa; Jewish kibbutzniks harvested abandoned Arab fields—confiscated as "fields of saboteurs"—and sold the produce. Arab "land and houses are spoils of war," Moshe Sharett announced, "just compensation for the [Jewish] blood spilled."[138] Yosef Weitz of the Jewish Land Department was even blunter: Arab property was "good for [the] settlement of [our Jewish] brothers . . . This was [the reason for] our war." Although Aharon Zisling, Israel's new minister of agriculture, recognized the dangers of a seething, expropriated Arab diaspora on Israel's borders, he agreed with Sharett. "We must not give back to the Arabs even a shoelace," he said. Ezra Danin, of the Hagana intelligence service, concurred: "War is complicated and lacking in sentimentality. If the commanders believe that by destruction, murder and human suffering they will reach their goal more quickly—I would not stand in their way." The Palestinians, he concluded, "will do these things to us" if the Jews did not "do them first."[139]

Of course it was not as simple as all that. There was, as de Gaulle's adviser Raymond Aron later wrote, "another side to it." The gouging Israeli attacks in 1948–49 plowed 844,000 Palestinians out of their homes and into the neighboring countries, none of which were happy to be saddled with the social, political and financial demands of those refugees' upkeep. Jordan received the biggest influx, and the little Bedouin kingdom became essentially a Palestinian state: 391,000 Palestinians fled to Jordan, most to the West Bank, the rest to Amman and its environs. Since Palestinian elites were better educated and more politically experienced than the Jordanians, they were hard to assimilate, and the masses of less elite Palestinians threatened to make Jordan a "poorhouse," facts that King Abdullah made clear to the U.S. embassy in 1949.[140] An additional 5,000 refugees crossed to Iraq. Egypt absorbed 258,000 refugees; 250,000 of them settled in the Egyptian-administered Gaza Strip. Damascus reported 100,000 Palestinian refugees in Syria, and 90,000 more fled into Lebanon. The total calculated by the U.S. embassy in Cairo in 1949 was 844,000. In all, 75 percent of the Palestinian population had been uprooted and expelled from their homeland, leaving between 100,000 and 300,000 Arabs inside the new 1949 borders of the State of Israel.[141] Raymond Aron predicted for Israel an "infernal cycle of occupation and repression" that would gnaw away at the Jewish state's legitimacy "by violating the moral principles on which the state was based." Aron cautioned Israelis that the "moral danger [was] greater than the military danger" if Tel Aviv embarked on a long-term policy of Palestinian occupation.[142] Far-sighted Israelis saw this coming, even in 1948. The minister of agriculture, Aharon Zisling, who had earlier enjoined his colleagues to rob the Arabs down to their shoelaces, nevertheless worried that "we still do not properly appreciate what kind of enemy we are now nurturing outside the borders of our state. Our enemies, the Arab states, are a mere nothing compared with those hundreds of thousands of Arabs who will be moved by hatred and hopelessness and infinite hostility to wage war on us, regardless of any agreement that might be reached."[143]

The Bernadotte Plan

Count Folke Bernadotte, who had served as vice president of the Swedish Red Cross during World War II and then as UN mediator in Palestine after the British departure in May 1948, regretted the swift Israeli victory and ethnic cleansing and made a last stab at preserving an Arab presence in Palestine. He proposed internationalizing Jerusalem, converting Haifa into a free port and granting the Negev—destined in the 1947 UN plan for Jewish settlement—to Jordan in exchange for Arab recognition of Israel and Jewish annexation of the Arab enclave at Jaffa and Arab western Galilee. He also proposed an Arab corridor to connect up the Gaza Strip and the Arab lands on the West Bank, and a solid Arab presence in Jerusalem.[144] Flush with victory, the Israeli leadership was in no mind to give back, convert or grant anything. They wanted it *all*: the Negev, Jaffa, Upper Galilee, Jerusalem and no disruptive strips or corridors.

Bernadotte's proposals—aimed at a long-term solution that would pacify the region and coax acceptance of a Jewish state from the Arabs—seemed good for the Arabs and bad for the Jews. They reduced Israel to 2,124 square miles, less than half the land mass envisioned by the UN partition resolution of November 1947. The Negev was a particular Israeli concern: it would settle and employ tens of thousands of new immigrants, give sea access to the Indian Ocean and quite possibly—this was the Middle East, after all—provide the oil, gas and mineral deposits that would power the new state. Thus, the Israelis moved fast to crush Arab resistance, root out the last refugees and intimidate the UN. Some Israeli journalists tried to smear Bernadotte by whispering in their columns that his celebrated wartime liberation of fifteen thousand death camp inmates had involved collaboration with Himmler's SS. Others accused the Swede of being "an agent of Anglo-American imperialism" and "oil interests."[145] While the Israelis stewed, the "Anglo-American imperialists" scrutinized the Bernadotte plan. It seemed to offer long-term solutions to the Arab-Israeli conflict. In a meeting with President Truman on September 1, Secretary of State Marshall agreed that Israel would be strengthened for the long haul if it swapped land for peace. Marshall then wired British foreign secretary Ernest Bevin urging him too to endorse Bernadotte's plan. If the Jews and Arabs would not agree to the plan, Marshall wanted the UN to impose it "as the best possible basis for bringing peace to a distracted land." Bevin wired back his "wholehearted and un-qualified support" for Marshall's line of thinking.[146]

Marshall did not reckon with the power of the Jewish lobby. Israeli foreign minister Moshe Sharett successfully argued that the Arab states were trying to "ruin" Israel by "uniting to force Israel to take back refugees" and construct homes for them.[147] But the "refugees" were *Palestinians*, and the Israelis had deliberately and systematically destroyed their homes. Surely the Palestinians retained *some* rights in their native land. When Marshall in Paris publicly announced America's intention to implement the Bernadotte plan in the UN General Assembly, Rabbi Abba Hillel Silver, cochairman of the American Zionist Emergency Council, coun-terattacked at home in Washington. American Jews, he reminded Truman in a tele-gram, "relied on the loyalty of the American Government . . . and the personal pledge of the Democratic Party" to uphold a big Israel, not a little one. Rabbi Silver pronounced himself "profoundly shocked" by Secretary of State Marshall's support of the Bernadotte plan. His lobby group ran full-page ads in American newspapers blasting the Marshall policy. Silver's attack on the Democratic Party overtook Tru-man and Clark Clifford, who were on a campaign swing through Oklahoma. They both buckled under the Jewish pressure. Clifford phoned Undersecretary of State Robert Lovett in Washington—Marshall was in Paris—and warned him off: "The pressure from Jewish groups on the President is mounting." Lovett protested: to force Marshall to renounce Bernadotte's proposals "would label this country as violating its agreements with other countries and completely untrustworthy in international matters." The consequences, Lovett warned, "could be absolutely disastrous to us in the UN and elsewhere." Clifford didn't care. He ordered Lovett to stop pushing the Bernadotte plan, and Truman phoned Marshall in Paris and ordered him to make no further comments or commitments on Palestine.[148] With the Republicans poised to exploit any hint of Democratic support for the Arabs in the November elections, Truman gave Israel everything it wanted.

THE STERN GANG KILLS BERNADOTTE

When slanders about Bernadotte failed to scuttle the Swede's plan, Israeli terrorists turned their guns on the UN mediator. On September 17, Stern Gang assassins disguised in Israeli army uniforms flagged down Count Bernadotte's jeep in Jerusalem and shot him and his deputy at point-blank range. The terrorist attack was planned by the thirty-three-year-old future Israeli prime minister Yitzhak Shamir. Shamir and Begin, prominent Israeli terrorists in 1948, formed the Herut Party after Israel declared its independence. The party evolved into today's Likud.[149] With Bernadotte out of the picture, the Hagana launched Operation Ten Plagues in October with three brigades, which wheeled through the Negev, taking Beersheba and the southern coast and driving sixty thousand more Arabs into the Gaza Strip. Like Operation Yiftah in eastern Galilee in the spring and Operation Dani in July, the Negev offensive was intended not only to defeat Arab troops there—in this case the Egyptian army—but to link up scattered Jewish settlements by emptying the spaces between them of Arabs.

Terror was used to discourage the Arabs from ever returning to Israel, a fact noted by Britain's ambassador in Tel Aviv: "The lot of the Arabs in Israel today would make me chary of recommending their return to Israel."[150] Another British official deplored the "sickening jargon" developed by Israelis to describe the country's consolidation: " 'liquidation of the diaspora,' 'ingathering of the exiles,' 'tracks led to the border,' and the overworked Biblical tags like 'the desert shall blossom as the rose' and 'if I forget thee, O Jerusalem.' "[151] It was noisome to the British embassy but music to Ben-Gurion's ears; he visited Beersheba on October 30 and found, to his delight, that all the Arabs had fled. Most went to the Gaza Strip—a corridor twenty-five miles long and four miles wide under Egyptian military occupation—which became a haven for uprooted Palestinians. Sent to observe Gaza in late

1948, an American traveler wrote that it was an ugly town of twenty-five thousand swelled to eighty-five thousand by Palestinian refugees who "pack sidewalks, take up the vacant lots and the public market, occupy barnyards, and generally seem to fill in every empty space which the town might have had." Within a month or two there would be two hundred thousand more refugees crammed into Gaza.[152] Joe Alsop, who visited the Palestinian camps in his travels for the *New York Herald Tribune*, found them "horrifying: if you see them once, you can never forget your indignation against the Israelis for their callousness about the ... problem, against the Arab leaders, who have made political capital of the refugees' misery, against the Western nations and the UN, because the provision for the refugees is so pitifully inadequate, and against the very world we live in, for producing such horrors."[153]

The Spoils of War

The rough frontiers created in the fighting and cease-fires of 1948–49 have endured for sixty years. Israel became a contiguous nation extending from the beaches of the Red Sea north to Mount Lebanon. Instead of the half dozen strips, enclaves and pockets of Palestinian territory contemplated in the 1947 partition plan, Israel now confronted just two: the Egyptian-held Gaza Strip and the Jordanian-occupied West Bank (of the Jordan River). The occupation of those pockets would change over the decades, but they would remain stuck like indigestible morsels in Israel's windpipe. Demographically, the Jewish success was staggering. From a population of just 25,000 in 1882 and 65,000 in 1918, the Jews of Palestine had increased to 650,000 in 1948. The victorious war against the Arab states had removed the last obstacle to the foundation of the Jewish state of Israel and had converted the ethnically mixed state envisioned by the UN partition plan—498,000 Jews and 325,000 Arabs in the Jewish state—into one where Jews easily dominated with 650,000 of their own against a manageable Arab minority of 100,000.[154] The Jewish destruction of Palestinian hopes in 1948 also wrought a major change in the "Palestinian question" that the British and Americans immediately grasped. The question of Palestine—the ultimate disposition of its land and refugees—became internationalized: "an important part of the Arab nationalist program," an inextricable piece of the pan-Arab identity.[155] And why would it be otherwise? Many of the Arab states now contained debris of the Palestinian expulsion in their refugee camps. Touring them in 1949, U.S. assistant secretary of state George McGhee observed that "in all the camps I saw the utter despair of people living in tents or on the ground with only elementary nourishment and meager health facilities. They were underfed, bewildered and embittered. They asked why they couldn't go home. In many cases they could see their farms across the barbed wire. One would be hard put to find a more poignant example of human misery."[156]

The Egyptian coup of 1952 which brought Colonel Gamal Abdel Nasser to power boiled up from two immediate sources: fury at the military incompetence demonstrated in 1948 and nationalist pride inflamed by the Israeli triumph. Nasser smoothly converted "the Disaster"—or al-Nakba—into a challenge for the future. "We ourselves are responsible for the loss of Palestine . . . We did nothing but make speeches and hold meetings. We used to say that we would throw the Jews into the sea, but we didn't do it."[157] The well-organized and fundamentalist Muslim Brotherhood—al-Ikhwan al-Muslimun, which affirmed its determination to evict the Zionists—was one of the chief political benefactors of the Egyptian defeat in 1948.[158] If Western methods would not uproot the Israelis, perhaps Eastern ones would.[159] Pointing to two trends that would emerge in the years ahead, an Egyptian analyst warned the American ambassador that an Arab defeat could lead to extreme nationalism in one of two forms: either a "swing to Communism, or its reverse, a complete repudiation of Western influence and an Islamic religious revival."[160] British foreign secretary Ernest Bevin agreed, warning the Americans that their pro-Israel policy guaranteed the growth of "Communist or fanatical pan-Islamic regimes in the Arab countries."[161] Still, Bevin's lieutenant Hector McNeil wearily concluded, Israel was probably permanent and invincible: "As long as America is a major power, and as long as she is free of major war, anyone taking on the Jews will be indirectly taking on America."[162]

Truman's America waltzed carelessly into the future. President Truman assumed that Arab muttering and intransigence might be cured by a determined show of support for Israel. In the last years of his presidency, Truman granted Israel $277 million in aid, more aid to a tiny country with under a million inhabitants than he granted to all the Arab states combined. Like his successors, Truman supplied millions more by what Arab foreign ministers called "indirect American financing of Jewish immigration to Palestine": the charitable deduction of Zionist donations on U.S. income tax returns.[163] Truman's secretary of defense Louis Johnson worried about the strategic costs. The large Israel backed by Truman made "Russian aggression" all the more likely: it had spawned insoluble hatreds and a massive refugee problem in Jordan, Gaza, Lebanon, Syria and Iraq. In Johnson's view, the Arab-Israeli dispute "serves to perpetuate and aggravate conditions of insecurity, unrest and political instability, with attendant opportunities for Soviet penetration."[164]

TRUMAN'S LAST STAND

Brought belatedly to his senses, Truman did what he should have done before and after the Bernadotte assassination: he demanded that the Israelis accept the return of at least two hundred thousand Palestinian refugees to their homes and that they make real concessions, including the internationalization of Jerusalem and land corridors through the Negev to link Egypt and Jordan and give the Jordanians access to the Mediterranean. Marshall had already indignantly resigned. The new secretary of state, Dean Acheson, presented the demands to Israeli foreign minister Moshe Sharett in April 1949. Sharett and Prime Minister David Ben-Gurion rejected most of the American demands. Truman sent a "grave note" to Ben-Gurion insisting that the Israelis make the requested concessions. Unfortunately, the president was closing the stable door after the horse had bolted. Israel had what it wanted and had no need to make concessions. Truman's threat of "a revision of [America's] attitude toward Israel" was regarded in Tel Aviv as an empty threat. Sounding like Ariel Sharon fifty years later, Ben-Gurion defiantly told the Knesset, "We can be crushed, but we will not commit suicide." It was all theater. The only nation that could really crush Israel was America, and Ben-Gurion knew that the Americans would not pull the trigger. In May 1951, Truman invited Ben-Gurion to Washington, lunched with him in Blair House, threw his support behind a $500 million Israel bonds drive and pledged to support an Israeli request for $150 million in foreign aid. The following year, Truman assured Sharett—in words eerily like Balfour's in 1917—that his helpful attitude toward Israel was "the result of his knowledge and study of Israel's history from the days of Abraham." Where the Middle East was concerned, the "striped-pants boys of the State Department" and the Pentagon had been beaten again. The White House, Congress and U.S. Jewish leaders had won: their policy, defined in the war of 1948 and its messy aftermath, would henceforth channel and distort American strategy in the Middle East.

CHAPTER 4

AJAX

EVEN AS THEY TRIED to square the circle in Israel, Truman's "striped-pants boys" were fending off challenges to American leadership elsewhere in the Middle East. The Turkish and Azerbaijan crises of 1945–46 were the first Soviet attempts to "satellitize" key countries in the region. With a hundred thousand troops in northern Iran during World War II, Stalin had tried to fashion a Soviet puppet state out of Tabriz and northern Iran. The Kremlin had demanded "border revisions" in eastern Turkey as well as joint Soviet-Turkish control of the Dardanelles—the crucial straits connecting the Black Sea and the Mediterranean. Soviet annexations in Iran and Turkey would have dramatically shifted the momentum in the Cold War. Stalin had been pushing for a Soviet republic in northern Iran since the 1920s—he had quarreled with Lenin on the issue—and had even tried to wring the promise of one from the Nazis before Hitler's invasion of the USSR in 1941. After Russia's victory at Stalingrad—which mortally wounded Iran's prewar German protectors—Stalin began demanding Iranian territory and oil fields outright, and he placed additional pressure on the Turks in 1946 by arming the Kurds and urging them to secede.[1] Truman had resisted those Soviet probes: he dispatched the USS *Missouri* to Istanbul, placed American military units in Europe on a war footing and proclaimed the "Truman Doctrine" in March 1947 to deter "Soviet plans for engulfing the Middle East."[2]

THE COLD WAR IN IRAN

But the Soviets were just getting started. "Our ideology stands for offensive operations when possible," Molotov liked to say, "and if not, we wait."³ Blocked in Turkey
and Azerbaijan, the Soviets shifted pressure back to Iran. This time they acted more
delicately, operating through a Soviet-trained communist party—Hezb-e Tudeh-ye
Iran, or the "Party of the Masses of Iran"—that would try conspiracy, propaganda
and the ballot box to seat itself in power before heading for the desired "dictatorship
of the proletariat." But the Soviet hand was always visible: Tudeh demonstrations
of twenty-five thousand or more in Tabriz and Tehran were organized, paid and
delivered to their meeting points by Red Army trucks, which explained Tudeh's
powerful influence despite its paltry support nationwide. When Iranian police attempted to control the Tudeh demonstrations, they were disarmed by Soviet troops,
who remained in northern Iran long after the last shot had been fired in World
War II.⁴

Philosophically committed to the United Nations and the free development of
emerging democracies, the Truman administration nevertheless felt compelled to
operate aggressively against Soviet-backed parties like Tudeh. The Soviet coup in
Czechoslovakia in 1948 had prompted Truman's NSC to beef up the Office of Policy
Coordination (OPC), whose brief was to stop the spread of communism all over
the world—not just in Europe, but in places like Iran and Iraq as well. By 1952, the
OPC had merged with the CIA and had a staff of six thousand and an annual budget of $82 million, and helped devise American responses to Soviet moves like the
Prague coup, the Berlin blockade, the Korean War and Tudeh maneuvering in Iran.
Inevitably realpolitik trumped the "one world" idealism that had infused the United
Nations coalition in the months after World War II. Truman backed away from a
proposed UN trusteeship for French Indochina—throwing Vietnam back into the
arms of its colonial masters—in order to fortify Southeast Asia against communism
and justify American annexation of the formerly Japanese Northern Mariana Islands. Truman rearmed Germany and Japan in 1947 as barriers to the spread of
Soviet power—despite their recent instigation of the bloodiest war and genocide in
history. In Iran too, Truman vowed to get tough.

The Tudeh Party had been founded in 1920 and indoctrinated by a steady flow
of Bolshevik agents across Iran's borders with Russia and Azerbaijan. Tudeh mili-

tias had struggled to rip Tabriz and Iran's north—the areas occupied by the Red Army from 1941 to 1945—away from Tehran in the Azerbaijan Crisis. That was a new twist on the old Persian proverb: "When the British lion and the Russian bear move together, the fate of Iran will be sealed."⁵ The British lion had expressed itself as willing to loosen its grip on Iran, but the Russian bear tried to stay. That engaged President Truman, who had warned Stalin in January 1946 that the Soviets were threatening "the raw material balance of the world" by encroaching on Iran's oil.⁶ The Iranian shah—the dark, slim, rather mysterious twenty-seven-year-old Muhammed Reza Pahlavi—retook Tabriz and the other cities of the north in 1946, suppressed the Soviet-sponsored Kurdish and Azeri puppet regimes inside Iran and then outlawed Tudeh in 1949 (after party operatives had tried to assassinate him). Officially banned, Tudeh dived underground—forming a Soviet-style central committee and politburo—and by 1952 was estimated to have thirteen thousand dedicated members and forty thousand "fellow travelers" in Tehran, Kermanshah and Hamadan.⁷

LONDON'S CASH COW

Iran was still chiefly a British concern in the decade after World War II. Along with the Suez Canal and the Iraq Petroleum Company, Iran in 1950 was Great Britain's most prized overseas asset. The British-owned Anglo-Iranian Oil Company (AIOC) had enjoyed an enriching monopoly on the exploration, extraction and production of Iranian oil since 1901. With exclusive drilling rights to five hundred thousand square miles of Iran, the British government had fobbed Iranian monarchs off with below-market royalties and paid bribes to the tribes in Iranian Khuzestan—still the world's chief oil patch—to get the oil out. In 1952, when American oil companies were paying the Saudis and Venezuelans 50 percent of their profits, AIOC was paying a miserly 16 percent.⁸ "The British cut throats with a cotton knife," Iranians liked to say, and indeed, London's stingy royalties did seem as deadly to long-term Iranian development as a violent blow. And with the whole energy-consuming world recovering from World War II, AIOC's income kept growing: in 1950, AIOC banked more in a single year than it had paid in royalties to Tehran over the previous fifty years. AIOC routinely earned ten times more than it paid the Iranian government, and paid far more taxes to the British government than to Iran's. And the royalty agreement that generated such vast (British) bounties was not scheduled to expire until 1993.⁹

Sixty-nine-year-old Muhammed Mosaddeq stormed into office in 1951 thanks to deep frustration with Britain's apparently permanent profiteering in Iran. Development gurus like to say—as one did in 1947—that cheap Middle Eastern oil would permit new nations to skip railroads and leapfrog straight into trucks, cars, and planes. "Faraway lands can grow richer and healthier because of the treasure buried at the crossroads." But the people of the crossroads—the Iranians, the Kurds and the Arabs—wanted to be *paid* for the treasure that would magically make everyone wealthier.¹⁰ As early as 1944, Mosaddeq had unsuccessfully introduced a bill into the Iranian parliament that would have banned the foreign ownership and sale of Iranian oil.

British geologists had discovered Iranian oil in 1908. By 1913, the British government held a controlling stake in AIOC and moved to lock in that control by assisting in the 1921 coup that hoisted Reza Khan, a cunning, jackbooted Iranian Cossack, onto the Peacock Throne, making him just the latest shah, or king, of Iran. There had been other factors in Reza Shah's rise, chiefly the incapacity of the deposed Qajar dynasty, Reza's own thirsting ambition and Iran's fear of Bolshevik revolution and civil war, which loomed just over the northern border. Once in power, Reza Shah and his Pahlavi dynasty worked closely with London. To Iranian nationalists like Mosaddeq, the Pahlavis worked far *too* closely with the British. In 1933, Reza Shah extended AIOC's lease and monopoly on Iranian oil for sixty years, without any increase of the niggardly 16 percent royalty.¹¹ By 1951, Reza Shah was dead and his son Muhammed Reza, the brooding, thin-skinned product of a Swiss boarding school, had become shah of Iran. Muhammed Reza was intimidated and frustrated by Mosaddeq. They wanted many of the same things—the shah spoke in the late 1940s of Iran's need for "free public education, free hospitals and clinics, and economic improvements"—but Muhammed Reza wanted to introduce those reforms through a top-down "White Revolution." Mosaddeq was a colorful, reckless demagogue who wanted to ram changes up from the bottom. In the process, he would make powerful enemies among Iran's leading interest groups: the army and police, the landowners, the merchants, the religious leaders, the tribes, the vigilant foreign embassies and, of course, the monarchy.¹²

MOSADDEQ

Mosaddeq had been born into a rich, aristocratic family in 1882 and, as a teenage boy, had inherited his father's job as comptroller of Iran's Khurasan Province. Young Mosaddeq tackled the job intelligently, and developed an abiding contempt for monarchy after dealing with the various scandals tolerated by the Qajar kings in Khurasan, a contempt that he did not bother to conceal when elected in his twenties to the Iranian parliament, or *majlis*, as deputy from Isfahan. The last Qajar king responded by sending Mosaddeq into exile, which he spent at the École des Sciences Politiques in Paris before returning to Iran. When the Pahlavis ousted the Qajars in the coup of 1921, Mosaddeq was made finance minister, and then governor of Azerbaijan. Mosaddeq did not last in the latter post: his principles were unbending—a rare occurrence in biddable Iran—and when the shah refused to give Mosaddeq command of army units stationed in his province, Mosaddeq indignantly resigned. He was in his midforties and appeared to have burned his bridges for the last time.

Over the next thirty years, before the great showdown of 1952–53 with the British, Mosaddeq ducked in and out of exile, served as a *majlis* deputy from Tehran and held various jobs in the foreign ministry. Throughout, he became convinced that the Pahlavis had fallen too deeply into the pockets of the British and needed to be pulled out. He propounded a theory of "negative equilibrium," by which Iran would defend its sovereignty not by befriending any particular great power, but by keeping them all—Russia, America and Great Britain—at arm's length. The Iranians tried out "negative equilibrium" with disastrous consequences in the 1930s, when they invited in Nazi technicians and businesses to weaken the influence of the dominant British and Russians but then suffered an Anglo-Russian invasion and partition of the country in 1941 as a consequence.[13] Mosaddeq also believed that Iran needed to move down the Western track of development that he had studied and observed at "Sciences Po," namely, to modernize, secularize and codify the Iranian legal system. This would lead to trouble with Iran's powerful Shiite ulema, or clergy, which would eagerly assist in Mosaddeq's eventual removal.[14]

This tremendously able, experienced, proud and principled statesman would never have been thirty-two-year-old Shah Muhammed Reza Pahlavi's first choice for prime minister in 1951, but the shah's hand was forced by British intransigence. The shah and Mosaddeq agreed on the pressing need to obtain a larger share of oil profits from AIOC, and Mosaddeq was the man to obtain it. He dominated the "National Front" coalition of parties in the Iranian *majlis*—they had voted seventy-nine to twelve to confirm him as prime minister—and was respected by the Iranian people. "All of Iran's misery, wretchedness, lawlessness and corruption over the last fifty years have been caused by oil and the extortions of the oil companies," one radio commentator blared.[15] That summed up the mood of ordinary Iranians, and Mosaddeq pinned the blame squarely on the British. "You do not know how crafty they are," he told Averell Harriman. "You do not know how evil they are. You do not know how they sully *everything* they touch."[16] The shah, who resented British niggardliness at least as much as the National Front, appointed Mosaddeq as a battering ram to force the British to renegotiate the terms of their 1933 oil concession. If they would not shorten their lease and pay American-size royalties, Mosaddeq would nationalize their fields and facilities.[17]

Still, the king and his prime minister were anything but natural allies; the shah feared Mosaddeq and Mosaddeq loathed the shah. Although the prime minister had many planks in his platform, including land and tax reform and increased spending on social programs, the issues he and Iranian reformers cared most about were oil and democracy. Mosaddeq not only wanted to expel the British, nationalize AIOC and use the proceeds to transform Iran from its position as Britain's gas station into a modern nation with a flourishing, diversified economy, he also wanted to slash the prerogatives of the shah and increase the powers of the elected prime minister. To undermine the shah, Mosaddeq sent Iranian intelligence operatives into AIOC headquarters to seize lists of Iranian parliamentary deputies, bureaucrats, courtiers, officers and government ministers who had accepted cash bribes from the British to maintain London's monopoly rights and low royalties.[18] The ensuing corruption scandal blew the lid off the shah's cozy arrangements with AIOC, and Mossadeq had little trouble passing a bill through the *majlis* in May 1951 that brought the British oil company under Iranian government control and expropriated its assets.

MOSADDEQ NATIONALIZES ANGLO-IRANIAN AND BRITAIN APPEALS TO THE UN

Britain denounced Tehran's nationalization and appealed to the United Nations for relief. Mosaddeq traveled to New York in October 1951 to express the Iranian point of view: "If foreign exploiters continue to appropriate practically all of the income, then our people will remain forever in a state of poverty and misery."[19] Mosaddeq then stopped in Washington to meet with Truman and Acheson and repeated the arguments he had advanced at the UN. At Blair House, Mosaddeq gave a bravura performance, pleading for Truman's good offices: "I am speaking for a very poor country—a country all desert, just sand, a few camels, a few sheep." Acheson interjected that "with its sand *and* oil Iran [was] more like Texas" than a "very poor country." Mosaddeq burst out laughing, dropped the charade and, all agreed, instantly appeared twenty years younger.[20] Truman and Acheson were hugely impressed by the prime minister's wit and charisma—"his pixie quality and instant transformations"—and indeed transformations like the one being wrought in Iran by Mosaddeq were happening all across the world. Venezuela had hit Western oil companies with punitive new taxes in 1948, and the Saudis had followed suit in 1950, but expropriation and nationalization were extreme forms of "profit sharing" that few in Britain or America were prepared to accept. Mexico had nationalized its oil industry in 1938, setting off an Iran-style struggle with the United States that was not resolved until 1943, when the Mexicans paid $24 million in compensation and FDR responded gratefully by deepening the Good Neighbor policy.[21]

The British were less neighborly. They classified Iranian oil not produced by themselves as "stolen goods," and even the usually pacific Labour Party demanded punitive action.[22] "If Persia were allowed to get away with it," Labour's defense minister Emmanuel Shinwell declared in July 1951, "Egypt and other Middle Eastern countries would be encouraged to think that they could try things on; the next thing might be an attempt to nationalize the Suez Canal." Churchill, Anthony Eden and the Tories demanded an immediate "splutter of musketry" to scare the Iranians back into line. To nip the whole dreadful scenario in the bud—and keep an increasingly truculent Winston Churchill in line—Prime Minister Clement Attlee ordered the British military to prepare contingency plans for the "recapture" of AIOC's crucial Abadan refinery, which, with its storage tanks, pumps, pipelines, wharves, railways, tankers and thirty-seven thousand employees, was among Britain's biggest industrial plants in the 1950s and by far its biggest overseas operation.[23] For his part, Mosaddeq, an emotional man who regularly wept in public to drive home his points, proved quite reasonable. The British, he argued, had *already* reimbursed themselves for all their costs in wells, pipelines and refineries by a half century of miserly royalty payments. Still, he promised to pay some compensation—though certainly not the projected revenues for all oil that would have been produced and sold until the end of the British lease in 1993, as the AIOC had demanded—and remarked the irony that whereas the British were busy nationalizing their own coal and steel industries, they objected to an Iranian government's doing the same thing for its citizens. "Socialism is all right back home," one British diplomat grumbled, "but out here you have to be master."[24]

Certainly the British in 1951 believed that they *had* to make themselves masters of the Iranian house. Iran and Suez were the keystones of Britain's crumbling but still viable empire. "In peace and war," British foreign secretary Ernest Bevin reminded his colleagues in 1949, "the Middle East is an area of cardinal importance to the U.K., second only to the U.K. itself."[25] Declining relative to the superpowers in Washington and Moscow, London was determined to retain control of lucrative assets like the Suez Canal and the Iraqi and Anglo-Iranian oil companies, which physically projected British power and laid a hard foundation for Britain's soft postwar economy. The end of World War II had hit the UK economy hard. The simultaneous American termination of Lend-Lease aid and insistence on a "convertible" British pound at the Bretton Woods conference in 1944 had caused a slump. American Marshall Plan aid mitigated its worst effects, but the burdens of inflation, falling dollar reserves (required to convert sterling on demand) and chronic trade deficits caused by resurgent, U.S.-financed German and Japanese competition dragged Britain down in the 1950s. The *only* points of light in that dark sky were profits from British Middle Eastern oil investments and Suez tolls. Both revenue streams doubled in the late 1940s and early 1950s and would keep rising through the decade. "Oil," an American State Department analyst observed, "is a paramount consideration in British policy and thinking."[26]

The loss of India in 1947 and the Mau Mau Revolt in Kenya in 1952 only increased London's determination to cling to assets like AIOC.[27] It was a profit center that also conferred the intangible boon of prestige. A British diplomat in Kuwait observed that the British refinery at Abadan represented "something huge, a *symbol* which not even the most skeptical Arab could deny of British energy, British wealth, British efficiency and British industrial might." In the realm of the tangible, Persian Gulf oil had become the lifeblood of the British and Western European economies after World War II, and the wells in Iraq and Iran and Egypt's Suez Canal—still owned by European shareholders—were the heart and the main artery of the whole interlinked organism.[28] U.S. wartime plans to wean the British and Europeans from

Western hemisphere oil had succeeded beyond expectations. Whereas only 19 percent of British and Western European oil had come from the Middle East in 1938, fully 90 percent was coming from the Persian Gulf by the early 1950s. Of that total, 455 million barrels passed through the Suez Canal in tankers, and another 270 million barrels arrived on the Mediterranean coast in Syrian and Lebanese pipelines from Iran, Iraq and Saudi Arabia.[29]

Britain, which imported 146 million barrels of crude in 1955, not only needed oil, it needed sterling-priced oil—such as that produced in Iran and shipped through Suez—so as not to deplete its dollar reserves. Like America today, Britain in the 1950s "exported inflation" by printing pounds and requiring the nations in its "sterling area" to hold them for the purchase of goods and services. Countries like India or Botswana that held pounds for transactions such as the purchase of Iranian oil were, in effect, taxing themselves to maintain the British standard of living. The upheavals in Iran, Egypt and then Iraq in the 1950s would threaten an end to that blessed era. If Iranian, Egyptian and Iraqi nationalists broke free of British tutelage, seized control of their own natural resources and grasped the almighty dollar, British revenues would plummet, the pound would decline and Britain's "exported inflation" would boomerang when the nations of the "sterling area" dumped pounds to buy greenbacks. Britain would also lose the awesome "pricing power" it had through its control of the Suez Canal and Iranian oil; the same fuel oil that cost $3.95 a ton in Britain cost $8.30 a ton in Greece because of the opaque and profitable "freight rates" charged by the British (and Americans).[30] Britain, in short, felt compelled to cling to its oil fields, pipelines, tankers and Suez Canal base in the 1950s. If we let go, British diplomat Evelyn Shuckburgh gloomily confided to his diary, "we will be driven back to our island, where we shall starve."[31]

AMERICAN DOUBTS

America's role in what might have been an exclusively and tragic British episode was peculiar. The Roosevelt administration had insisted until FDR's death in 1945 that the United States would use its burgeoning power and influence to replace British and European imperialism all over the world with an equitable "one world" sensibility, to be implanted and extended through "Americanism"—the promise of

American-style social, economic and political freedoms—and the United Nations.[32]
Washington had picked out Mosaddeq's National Front party as the most likely
vehicle for Americanism and the best bulwark against Soviet communism and continued British imperialism. Allen Dulles, who would shortly become Eisenhower's
CIA director, had led Overseas Consultants, a consortium of U.S. oilmen, in their
efforts to devise American-led alternatives to AIOC's monopoly and to "make
things right in Iran." When Mosaddeq briefly resigned as prime minister in 1952, the
Soviets actually rejoiced: "The American agent Mosaddeq has been replaced."[33]

The Cold War complicated the American process of "making things right."
Truman had begun to understand that colonial vestiges like AIOC were the best
advertisements for communism. British treatment of the Iranians was pointedly
contemptuous, as Mosaddeq pointed out when describing the segregated British
communities in Tehran and Abadan. AIOC's employee handbook actually outlawed "the expatriate type of Britisher, who has married locally and acquired local
loyalties and contacts, cutting himself off from the British community."[34] It was with
far more sympathy than trepidation that *Time* magazine made Mosaddeq its "Man
of the Year" in January 1952. Mosaddeq was, *Time* trumpeted, the "Iranian George
Washington" and "the most world-renowned man his ancient race had produced
for centuries."[35] The British looked like unreconstructed redcoats by comparison.
They called Mosaddeq a "lunatic," a "buffoon in pajamas," an "Oriental character."
And Iran itself was no better; in British reports, it became a country of "Oriental
decadence."[36] In 1952, a State Department analyst warned that the British "were
clearly slipping from ally to albatross status in the Middle East." Their *image* abroad
might be as dangerous to long-term American interests as communism.[37]

Truman and Acheson—who deplored London's "rule or ruin policy in Iran"—
did restrain Britain's most aggressive impulses, dissuading them in 1951–52 from
invading Iran or assassinating Mosaddeq.[38] The British settled on a less violent,
two-track remedy. First, they would freeze Iran's sterling balances in London, stop
all exports to Iran, stop refining Iranian oil—which the Iranians, like the Arabs,
could not do themselves, relying instead on foreign companies—and insist on a
worldwide boycott of any Iranian oil that the Iranians did manage to ship. The
British assumed that once threatened with bankruptcy, Mosaddeq would swallow
his pride and sit down to negotiate a settlement to the nationalization dispute.[39] If
that economic approach failed—it did—the British would proceed down a second,
political track, which would be a coup d'état orchestrated by their Iranian protégés:

the shah, imperial officers, politicians, bureaucrats, journalists, clerics and tribal khans. The tribal leaders were particularly powerful in Iran because they had swept up so many of the weapons surrendered by the Iranian army in 1941, when Reza Shah had abdicated and Tehran had submitted to Russian and British occupation.⁴⁰ Warned by his own sources that a coup was in the works, Mosaddeq moved boldly to wrest control of Iran's 250,000-man military from the shah. In July 1952, Mosaddeq made himself defense minister, and then, with deliberate effrontery, named *himself* commander in chief of the Iranian armed forces.

Worried at the spread of Mosaddeq's power, the shah refused to yield the defense portfolio, and Mosaddeq—"a tall, thin, bent old man with a haggard yellow face and a dripping nose"—indignantly resigned.⁴¹ The shah heaved a sigh of relief and replaced Mosaddeq with Ahmad Qavam, a reliable old-guard conservative. Qavam, who had been selected for the job at secret meetings with British officials, was immediately recognized as a pawn, and Mosaddeq's National Front and Tudeh partisans streamed back into the streets to protest. Twenty-nine people died and hundreds were injured in the ensuing riots. Noting America's silence in the affair—which was naturally taken for complicity ("the Persians see a cloven hoof beneath the skirts of every robe")—Iran's leading Shiite cleric and president of the *majlis*, Ayatollah Abolqasem Kashani, summoned Ambassador Loy Henderson to complain. They met in Kashani's garden, where the cleric accused Washington of being "the dupe of British imperialism." The ambassador countered that even if that were so, British imperialism was dying and the new threat was Soviet communism. "Ah," Kashani mused, laying a soothing hand on the ambassador's knee, "it is not easy for the untutored peoples of the Middle East to appreciate American foreign policy. They are more concerned with the *actual* abuses of imperialism than with the *potential* dangers of communism."⁴²

Writing home to Washington, Henderson reported that he had assured Kashani that "the U.S. had *nothing* to do with Qavam's return to power," but Kashani had bought none of it. The ayatollah assumed, like most Iranians, that "America was with the British, and was behind Qavam too."⁴³ As the top religious leader in Iran, however, Kashani had his own ambitions. Enrolled in Mosaddeq's National Front for tactical reasons—there was no better alternative—he yearned for a less secular government that would preach the "unity of Islam" and increase the power of the mullahs.⁴⁴ Although Qavam would be hounded from office in less than a week by the pro-Mosaddeq protests, Washington noted Kashani's ambitions, and would soon make use of them.

The Return of Mosaddeq

Recalled to office by the chastened shah, Mosaddeq felt empowered. Furious with the British for conspiring with Qavam, Mosaddeq ordered troops to seize the Abadan oil refinery and expelled the entire staff of the British embassy and closed the facility—a walled, forested compound that sprawled across sixteen city blocks in central Tehran. Mosaddeq then broke diplomatic relations with Britain and expelled every British citizen living in Iran. Anticipating British reprisals, Mosaddeq refused even to consider "adequate compensation" for the British, ignoring the shah's argument that the British had "seen the writing on the wall" and were now ready for "rational negotiations."[45] The shah, naturally, was appalled. He had been taking a larger role in Iran's development since World War II and felt that he was making strides. He had been pushing the British—in alliance with Mosaddeq—for better oil royalties, had kicked off a seven-year plan of land reform and industrialization, had shrewdly extracted a $20 million trade agreement from the Soviets (to gain leverage with the Americans) and was close to securing a $100 million aid package from the United States and the World Bank. "The Shah had grown in realism, leadership and planning ability," an American negotiator in Tehran noted, whereas Mosaddeq increasingly appeared "like an ill-tempered, erratic old peasant continuing on the fringe of responsibility and reality."[46]

Two weeks after Mosaddeq shuttered the British embassy, Americans elected Dwight Eisenhower president and the British exhaled a sigh of relief. So did many Iranians. "People here think that Truman tags at the heels of the British and that Eisenhower will follow a more independent course and give Iran what it needs," the American consul in Tabriz wrote in November 1952.[47] Ike would give Iran "what it needed" all right. The general looked at the Iranian crisis through the lens of the Cold War and took a hard line that startled even British hawks.[48] After meeting with Eisenhower in March 1953, British foreign secretary Anthony Eden complained to Prime Minister Churchill that "the Americans are perpetually eager to *do* something. The President repeated this several times." Whereas the British wanted to do *nothing*, thus increasing financial pressure on Mosaddeq, who could not extract, refine or export oil so long as the British boycott on "stolen" Iranian oil was being observed around the world, the Americans worried that merely to let Iran's economy wither would play into the hands of Iran's Tudeh Party and invite Soviet intervention to "rescue" the impoverished Iranians. "If Iran goes down the communist drain it will be little satisfaction to any of us that legal positions were defended to the last," Truman reminded Churchill in 1952.[49] Iran falling into the communist camp, a State Department analyst wrote in 1953, would be far more damaging than any blows Mosaddeq might land on the sanctity of empire or contracts: "A loss of Iran might well mean a major Soviet threat to the remainder of the Middle East, including India and Pakistan, and hence the security of the United States." President Eisenhower concurred; in a letter to Churchill in May 1953, Ike warned that a British insistence upon "respect for contracts" would not justify "setting loose an endless chain of unfortunate repercussions" that might create "disaster for the Western world."[50]

To head off disaster, Eisenhower dispatched thirty-seven-year-old Kermit Roosevelt—the chief of CIA operations in the Middle East—to urgent meetings in London, where the British Foreign Office and MI6 pressed "a plan of battle" on Roosevelt. Mosaddeq had "regained control of the police, the army elements in Tehran, and the radio" and was leaning toward "autocratic government." The shah and Qavam were humbled.[51] The Tudeh communists and Kashani's religious schools were putting made-to-order "mobs" in Mosaddeq's hands whenever needed to crack heads and sway votes. Kermit, the grandson of Teddy and cousin of FDR, was a shrewd operator who privately deplored Britain's "shoddy, cynical intrigues" and striving for "political domination and economic exploitation" through a "sorry shaky lot of local politicians who were hardly worth owning." However, he publicly swallowed his doubts and counseled the British that Harry Truman would *never* have supported a Western-engineered plot against Mosaddeq, but "the new Republicans just might."[52] Roosevelt had a grudging respect for Tudeh—"it fills a need which badly needed filling for an adequate, progressive labor movement in Iran"— but felt that the party needed to be destroyed because of its Russian connections.[53] The Soviets were ruthless operators who needed, as CIA agent Miles Copeland put it, to be "matched perfidy for perfidy" in a program of "crypto-diplomacy" that would add steel to America's "romanticized" public diplomacy of freedom, democracy and human rights.[54]

EISENHOWER PONDERS A COUP

Not willing to wait for the January 1953 inauguration of the more forward-leaning Republicans, the British moved in late 1952, dispatching MI6's new head of station in Tehran, Monty Woodhouse, to Washington. Woodhouse bypassed the lame-duck Democrats and went straight for Eisenhower and the man who would be Ike's secretary of state—John Foster Dulles. Knowing that the new American president would have little sympathy for the British oil monopoly in Iran—which the Americans had been trying to whittle down since 1943—Woodhouse emphasized Mosaddeq's communist ties. Thwarted in Europe, where American troops, funds and will had stabilized the Cold War front along the line of the Iron Curtain, the Soviets, Woodhouse argued, were now turning their attention to the Persian Gulf. "In the Middle East, they have scarcely yet scratched the periphery. The weakest spot seems to be Iran."[55]

It was almost inevitable that the new Eisenhower administration would regard Mosaddeq as a communist. Secretary of State John Foster Dulles had run unsuccessfully for the United States Senate in 1949 on the slogan "Enemy of the Reds!" During the presidential campaign of 1952, the sixty-four-year-old Dulles had given speeches for Ike denouncing Truman and the Democrats for "appeasing" the communists and accusing Truman and Acheson of creating a "second China" in Iran through their too gentle handling of Mosaddeq. Dulles and Ike had pledged a global "roll back of the Iron Curtain" if elected.[56] In 1952–53, Eisenhower viewed Iran—"an area of 600,000 square miles between the Caspian Sea and the Persian Gulf"—as a vital hinge of Western interests. The Russians had sought to control this hinge "since the days of Peter the Great," and the Turks and the British had been blocking them for three hundred years. Now it was America's turn.[57]

Still, the modest gains for Tudeh under the umbrella of Mosaddeq's anti-British coalition did not justify a British assertion in late 1952 that "the only thing to stop Persia falling into communist hands is a coup d'état." Tudeh, as an American consultant at the time put it, was "much greater in the minds of certain officials than in reality."[58] Even as he courted Tudeh to widen his base, Mosaddeq was imploring the United States to intervene as an honest broker with the British.

Whereas Truman and Acheson had tended to view Mosaddeq as someone who might harness Iranian nationalism to stop the spread of communism, Monty Woodhouse and the British persuaded Eisenhower and Dulles that the opposite was true: that Mosaddeq was a Kerensky whom the Iranian communists would manipulate and then crush in a Bolshevik-style coup.[59] That British fear—not without basis, given Tudeh's plans for sabotage and assassination and the way they seeded the Iranian military and bureaucracy with revolutionaries—spread to Washington. There, cold warrior Charles "Chip" Bohlen, about to embark for the U.S. embassy in Moscow, fretted that "if Persia goes Communist, then Iraq and the rest of the Middle East will also ... We ought therefore to concentrate on saving Persia from Communism at all costs."[60] Because of the Soviet menace, no one in Washington was willing to let the Iranians work out this latest constitutional crisis on their own terms. "If Iran succumbs to the Communists, there is little doubt that in short order the other areas of the Middle East, with some 60 percent of the world's oil reserves, will fall under Communist control," Secretary of State Dulles told the National Security Council in early 1953.[61] Iran's 1906 constitution was the oldest in Asia, and it had always been torn by fights between the shah, the army, the landowners, the tribes, the *majlis*, the Shiite clergy and the merchant class. Mosaddeq's bitter struggle with the shah was splitting those constituencies into factions: some supporting the shah's despotism as good for public order and modernization, others deploring his tyranny, corruption, Western manners and extravagance. Left to their own devices, Iran's jostling interest groups would probably have descended from the heights of Mosaddeq's rhetoric to some temperate compromise. But would the Soviets and Americans leave them alone?[62]

For Washington, there were angles of attack in Iran less wrenching than the British-proffered coup, which Eden delicately called a "push from power."[63] Some CIA officials wanted to funnel support to Ayatollah Kashani or to pro-shah elements in the armed forces.[64] No one in the Iranian military was pleased with Mosaddeq's determination to cut the military budget to help pay for economic development, and many suspected that his plan to reduce the army and beef up the police was no more than a cynical ploy to purge pro-shah elements in the army. Indeed the Iranian military—described by an American visitor in 1947 as "corrupt and poorly disciplined" with "inadequate equipment" and "nonexistent morale" (how could it be otherwise with monthly pay for conscripts hovering around fifteen cents?)— nevertheless clung to the shah as its last, best hope for funds, prestige and power.[65] In the bazaar—the bustling world of Iranian shopkeepers and small business—there were other useful fractures caused by Mosaddeq's taxes, subsidies and policies. Restaurant and teahouse owners loved him; butchers, bakers and confectioners—who needed the British imports of meat, flour and sugar lost to the boycott—loathed him. Iran's labor unions were similarly split: some supported Mosaddeq; others opposed him. The Shiite clergy fell into a large camp of anti-Mosaddeq conservatives—called "quietists" because of their reluctance to take a visible role in the crisis—and a smaller group of pro-Mosaddeq radicals around Kashani. Rural tribes like the five hundred thousand–strong Qashgai, who were powerful in their tribal areas but also in the *majlis*, backed the prime minister, but large tribes like the Bakhtiari preferred the shah.[66] All of these fractures widened under the strain of the British boycott, which reduced Iranian oil revenues from $400 million in 1950 to $2 million in 1953. A sinking tide sinks all boats.[67]

Instead of watching, waiting and discreetly molding this crumbling Iranian scene, Washington lunged for a "quick fix": the British coup idea. Eisenhower and the Dulles brothers were also susceptible to economic arguments. CIA director Allen Dulles served on the board of J. Henry Schroeder, which had helped organize the Industrial Bank of Persia (the financing agent for AIOC), and Secretary of State John Foster Dulles sought new business for American oil companies and his friend John McCloy's Chase Manhattan Bank in Iran. Eisenhower cagily withheld his support for the British coup until March 1953, when AIOC formally agreed to concede U.S. companies a 40 percent share in the Iranian oil industry.[68] Dulles and other key players like Herbert Hoover, Jr., Dulles's adviser on oil policy, were also aware that even as the British plotted against Mosaddeq, they were weighing compromises like an increase in AIOC's oil royalty that would exceed the 50 percent that Aramco was paying the Saudis. From the American perspective, that was an idea at least as menacing as British threats to invade Iran or kill Mosaddeq.[69] The mere fact of the Iranian nationalization of AIOC was enough to engage the big American oil companies in the crisis; if the Iranian nationalization were allowed to stand, it might inspire similar measures in Saudi Arabia and the Gulf emirates. That would be "cutting the industry's own throat."[70]

Oilman and ambassador George McGhee observed in 1953 that "if it weren't for the Cold War, there's no reason why we shouldn't let the British and the Iranians fight it out." Unlike the situation today—when turmoil in the Middle East, Russia or Venezuela threatens to send world oil markets into shock—there was no shortage of oil in the world in the 1950s, and Iran before the boycott was producing just 660,000 barrels a day, which was 6 percent of ample world production of 11 million barrels a day.[71] Cheapskate AIOC was unlikely to boost its royalty beyond 50 percent—thus threatening the American deal with the Saudis—and even if Mosaddeq did push the British out, the Americans would probably benefit with new fields for exploration and growth. The Cold War, however, *was* a constant complication. What if Tudeh *were* only a fig leaf for Soviet encroachment? What if Mosaddeq—whom McGhee judged a "conservative" and a "patriotic Iranian nationalist with no reason to be attracted to socialism"—really *was* a weakling who would be swept aside by Soviet agents? The seventy-something Iranian premier (no one knew his exact birth date) was famous for his tearful outbursts and meltdowns. What if he fell apart at the wrong moment? Dulles allowed that Mosaddeq was no communist, but warned Eisenhower that "if Mosaddeq were to be assassinated or removed from power, a political vacuum might occur in Iran and the communists might easily take over." The Soviets might seize the onetime opportunity to encroach on Iran and "be free of any anxiety about their petroleum resources."[72] The probability of those outcomes was as likely as the desired American scenario: that Mosaddeq would turn his back on Tudeh and agitators like Ayatollah Kashani to become an "Iranian George Washington" committed to democracy, stability, free markets and the West.

America decided to assist British plans for a coup. Like the neocons, who later thought it would be simple to amputate Saddam Hussein, Dulles thought that it would be relatively easy to unpack Iran's National Front and put the most pro-American elements in power. In words that would resonate in Iraq in 2003 at least as much as they did in Iran in the 1950s, a senior State Department official protested that "if we are going to be Don Quixote going after the windmill, we should not force the poor windmill to be party to the deed." It was fanciful, in other words, to assume that Iran would tag along tamely with Western expectations.[73]

Still, not everyone believed that Ike and Dulles were being quixotic. CIA reports in March 1953 described growing, not shrinking, support for the shah. In street demonstrations, "pro-Shah and pro-Kashani groups [were] stronger than Mosaddeq's." The whole affair, the CIA concluded, would be no more than "an *opera bouffe* if Russia were not around the corner."[74] Since Russia *was* around the corner, Washington felt driven to act. Briefed on British plans for a coup by Dulles at a meeting of the NSC in March 1953, Eisenhower wrung his hands in frustration. He lamented that neither Dulles nor anyone else had yet figured out how "to get some of the people in these downtrodden countries to *like* us instead of hating us."[75] Dulles was fully prepared to be hated, if the price of being "nice" was too high. If Mosaddeq fell before Iran righted itself, the result would be "chaos and Tudeh."[76] And if the Tudeh stumbled into power through some negligence on America's part, Dulles and Ike would come under pitiless fire from red-baiters like Wisconsin senator Joe McCarthy and the House Committee on Un-American Activities.

The Soviets *were* ready to pounce in 1953. American intelligence gleaned "indications of a pro-USSR policy by Mosaddeq." The prime minister might expel U.S.

advisers, sever relations with Washington and "extend the Iron Curtain all the way to the Persian Gulf." He might endorse Tudeh's radical agenda in exchange for Soviet financial, economic and military aid.[77] Soviet radio broadcasts into Iran vilified "the vile, filthy Shah" and the "bogus governments" of *his* preferred prime ministers— Ahmad Qavam and Fazlollah Zahedi—and began to chip away at Mosaddeq too, to prepare the ground for a Tudeh coup: "The Shah would have been annihilated and the vile monarchy eliminated had the Mosaddeq entourage not brought shame on itself by fawning upon and flattering the Shah."[78] Mosaddeq, in Tudeh eyes, had become "a fascist dictator."[79] With the Soviets piping propaganda into Iran and providing Tudeh with material support and sanctuaries in Soviet Armenia and Azerbaijan, Dulles's increasingly hard line in Iran had a certain logic. Tudeh was still quite narrowly based—with about 8 percent support nationwide—but Mosaddeq was behaving erratically, and the Tudeh communists might use him to seize power in Iran. Then, Dulles grimly concluded, "in short order, the other areas of the Middle East . . . would fall into Communist hands."[80] The CIA briefed Dulles in March 1953 on the "consequences of a Soviet take over" in Iran and found them grim indeed: "Major loss of U.S. prestige in Cold War and . . . loss of entire Middle East except for Turkey."[81]

Washington Takes Charge

For Eisenhower, the logic of the domino theory was at least as compelling in the Middle East as in Southeast Asia. "When we knew what the [American] prejudices were, we played all the more on those prejudices," Monty Woodhouse reminisced.[82] In Ike's NSC, senior officials pondered a world in which 65 billion barrels of oil suddenly went missing, in which Europe lost 90 percent of its oil supply, in which the United States was forced to ration gasoline (to supply Europe), in which Europe expended the last of its dwindling dollar reserves to buy American oil and in which 18 percent of the world population went communist at a stroke.[83] Driven by these fears—as well as fear of what Senator Joe McCarthy might say about him— Eisenhower instructed Ambassador Loy Henderson to begin organizing an "anti-Communist" coalition of Iranians around rich, retired, fifty-six-year-old general Fazlollah Zahedi.[84] American coup planning went ahead, even as more sober analysts in the State Department reiterated that there was little danger of Iran actually going communist.[85] But needing to secure his flanks against the "red scare" in America—*Time* now called Mosaddeq's National Front "one of the worst calamities to the anti-Communist world since the Red conquest of China"—Ike authorized the CIA, which had set up an Iranian "war room" on Cyprus in 1953, to begin planning the removal of the Iranian prime minister and to spend $1 million in Iran "in any way that would bring about the fall of Mosaddeq." Having "lost" China and nearly Korea, America could not now "lose" Iran.[86] Zahedi, a tough old officer who had served in the Iranian Cossack Brigade under the shah's father, Reza, and had been jailed during the war for pro-Axis activities, was bought for the coup with appeals to his conservatism as well as the pledge of a £10 million payment in London, which Zahedi took pains to nail down before agreeing to lead a coup.[87]

The CIA promptly got to work. General Zahedi got $135,000; another $150,000 went to editors, journalists, politicians, prayer leaders and other opinion-makers; and $11,000 was handed over every week to deputies in the *majlis* to loosen them up for the expected coup and to arrange for "spontaneous" crowds to appear against Mosaddeq on coup day. Ayatollah Muhammed Behbahani, who spoke for the conservative Shiite establishment at Qom, accepted American bribe money to throw his support behind the shah and Zahedi.[88] Mobilizing the Iranian mullahs and the mobs was crucial because objective estimates of the Iranian political scene put Mosaddeq's approval rating at 90 percent despite the boycott-induced austerity. Mosaddeq was revered for his defense of Iranian sovereignty against British exploitation.[89] President Eisenhower's decision to remove Mosaddeq was hugely controversial; at least as many analysts in the State Department and the CIA opposed it as supported it. Dulles nipped that opposition in the bud in the disastrous "groupthinking" manner that would later be employed by the George W. Bush administration. In critical planning meetings, he included only those inclined to favor a coup against Mosaddeq, which was now being called Operation Ajax. Included were Dulles, his brother Allen, Secretary of Defense Charles "Engine Charlie" Wilson (best remembered for his phrase "What's good for General Motors is good for America"), Robert Murphy, Loy Henderson and Henry Byroade; excluded were all who openly opposed it. Opponents like the CIA's Tehran station chief, Roger Goiran, who called Ajax an illogical sellout to "Anglo-French colonialism," were reassigned and replaced with "team players."[90]

At the critical meeting in John Foster Dulles's office on June 25, 1953, where Ajax was officially launched, Kermit Roosevelt recalled that "the substantial group . . . had already concluded that anything but assent would be ill-received by [Dulles]."

"So *this* is how we get rid of that madman Mosaddeq," Dulles growled to the consternation of (silent) skeptics like Assistant Secretary of State for Near Eastern, South Asian, and African Affairs Henry Byroade, who sat and squirmed. "Accepting the fact that discussion would be useless, [Byroade] sat in silence, drumming his fingers on a knee, his black brows forming an uncompromising line that matched his equally straight, uncompromising mouth." Everyone understood that the American and British coconspirators had quite different agendas. The British wanted "to recover the AIOC oil concession." The Americans "were not concerned with that" but *were* concerned "with the obvious threat of Russian takeover." The mood at the meeting was restrained, with everyone taking his cue from Ambassador Loy Henderson, who had flown in from Tehran for the meeting. Henderson was not "really optimistic about our prospects of success" but nevertheless believed that Ajax was essential to stop Iran from "slipping under Russian control." Asked by Secretary of State Dulles to sum up, Henderson said, "I don't like this kind of business at all. You know that. But we are confronted by a desperate, a dangerous situation and a madman who would ally himself with the Russians. We may have no choice but to proceed with this undertaking." No one was comfortable with it—all were "on the positive side of noncommittal but not much," as Kermit Roosevelt recalled—but they plunged ahead anyway, reassured by CIA arguments that by restoring the shah to full powers they would be killing two birds with one stone: stabilizing Iran and buttressing Israel. Participants in the meeting were "strongly pro-Israel," and so Allen Dulles and Kermit Roosevelt "emphasized— separately, together, and as often as possible—that Iran was *not* an Arab country" and had excellent relations with Tel Aviv. "Saving Iran" from the communists would also save a key Israeli ally and oil supplier in the Middle East.[91] As the group filed out of Dulles's office, Roosevelt watched the secretary of state pick up the phone, presumably to call President Eisenhower and inform him of the decision to overthrow Mosaddeq.

Kermit Roosevelt sneaked into Iran from Iraq in July 1953 and made final arrangements for the coup. Mosaddeq attempted to thwart the impending coup by calling a national referendum in August that authorized him to dissolve a *majlis* that, shaped by CIA subsidies, had filled up with conservative opponents and bribed friends of General Zahedi. Mosaddeq's demand for new elections succeeded because he was popular, but also because the Tudeh Party launched a massive get-out-the-vote drive that veered into fraud—fifty thousand ballots were marked up at Tudeh headquarters and stuffed into the urns—and because Mosaddeq's many enemies boycotted the referendum, which led to lopsided returns for the prime minister. In Tehran, 161,062 voted with Mosaddeq, just 105 against.[92] Hoping to remove Mosaddeq quickly, Kermit Roosevelt approached Shah Muhammed Reza—who had been severely diminished by Mosaddeq's rising popularity—and begged him to sign an imperial *firman*, or decree, dismissing Mosaddeq from office and appointing General Zahedi. The shah, who held the meeting with Roosevelt in a parked car outside his palace on the paranoid assumption that Mosaddeq must have bugged the imperial residence, initially refused. He had no constitutional right to dismiss a prime minister and worried that moving against the most popular politician in Iranian history in league with the Western powers would endanger the Pahlavi family's hold on the Peacock Throne itself. With Mosaddeq's opposition routed—"they fear reprisal by government and Tudeh forces and [exhibit] an attitude of hopelessness and apathy"—what would stop the prime minister from simply abolishing the Iranian monarchy?[93]

"THE LAST ACT OF *FIGARO*"

As the shah tried to wriggle out of his part in Roosevelt's conspiracy, Roosevelt played his last card. He summoned General H. Norman Schwarzkopf—the father of the future Desert Storm commander—who had commanded the Imperial Iranian Gendarmerie from 1942 until 1948. Schwarzkopf senior had achieved celebrity and come to the attention of the Iranian royal family by heading the New Jersey State Police investigation into the Lindbergh baby kidnapping in the 1930s. He now went to the shah's White Palace in northern Tehran and was received by the king not in his study but outside in the gardens. The shah—still worried about bugs and terrified by the ubiquity of Mosaddeq's agents—expressed his fears of dethronement and civil war in frantic whispers. A British negotiator found the scene like "the last act of *Figaro*," with "unknown, dim figures lurking behind the rose bushes [and] everybody spying on everybody else."[94] Like Figaro, the master of palace intrigue, Schwarzkopf whispered back assurances that America and Britain would back the shah to the hilt and fly him safely off to exile if anything went wrong.[95]

Reassured, the shah signed the *firman* dissolving Mosaddeq's government on August 14, 1953, and dispatched a unit of imperial guards to arrest the prime minister. Tipped off, Mosaddeq had his own loyal troops waiting at his residence, who arrested the shah's troops and accused the Pahlavis of "plotting with foreign elements" against Iran. The shah reacted on that occasion just as he would in the face of the Ayatollah Khomeini's challenge in 1979. He ran away, first to his palace on the Caspian Sea and then to Baghdad, where he and Empress Soraya changed planes and kept on going, all the way to Rome. There, Shah Muhammed Reza finally sank down to rest in his favorite suite at the Excelsior Hotel. The CIA looked on in disbelief: by fleeing, the shah had demoralized all of his allies—Ayatollah Behbahani, disgruntled army officers, the dismissed *majlis* deputies, the Kurds and the rural tribes, which comprised 25 percent of the Iranian electorate—and emboldened not only Mosaddeq, but the Tudeh Party, which now called openly for the abolition of the "craven monarchy" and a turn away from the United States, which the Tudeh correctly identified as "a joint conspirator" in the British plot against Iran.[96] Gholam Mosaddeq, the prime minister's rising son, joined in the anti-American clamor, damning Eisenhower's "stupid diplomacy" and "brazen support" of British imperialism.[97]

The coup had collapsed because of the shah's timidity and Mosaddeq's popularity. With mobs hunting General Zahedi house to house in Tehran, Roosevelt hid the general in the basement of an American safe house. Meanwhile, Secretary of State Dulles flew to Rome to size up the shah, who had rather embarrassingly been photographed shopping with his wife while violence rocked Iran. Dulles disconsolately ordered Roosevelt to fold up Operation Ajax and return to Washington. But Roosevelt knew that despite Mosaddeq's tremendous popularity and charisma— "he could turn an audience into a prayer session or a raging monster"—the prime minister had made powerful enemies in the armed forces, the mosque and the bazaar.[98] Roosevelt almost single-handedly decided to give those enemies a last prod. He summoned into the streets the rioters and politicians that he had been sedulously buying since 1952.

In the streets, Roosevelt's protesters would denounce Mosaddeq's "tyranny" and demand the return of their "good king" from the boutiques of the Via Veneto. To create the right atmosphere for a counterrevolution, Roosevelt spent $50,000 buying vigilantes, who stormed around Tehran like Red Guards, pummeling innocent bystanders, throwing rocks into mosques, smashing shop windows and yelling, "Long live Mosaddeq and Communism!" Other American-funded vigilantes posed as supporters of the shah, and soon the competing mobs of hired thugs were fighting for control of the streets, the Radio Tehran station and the leading newspaper offices. Meanwhile, bewildered mobs of slum dwellers, bused up from southern Tehran with CIA subsidies, milled around to add to the confusion.[99] Prime

Minister Mosaddeq ordered the crowds to disperse, but they refused. The Iranian police and military, also in the pay of the plotters, refused to intervene and impose martial law.

AJAX

This American-engineered chaos required a solution, which was, of course, General Fazlollah Zahedi. He emerged from his CIA safe house on August 19, proclaimed himself "the lawful prime minister by the Shah's orders" and proceeded to crack down with the blessing of Iran's ayatollahs, who feared Mosaddeq's modernizing outlook and the influence of Tudeh's "Kremlin-controlled atheists." By now, Ayatollah Muhammed Behbahani had come to terms with General Zahedi. The Shiite clerics would dump Mosaddeq and support the shah in any deals he might cut with the Western powers and oil companies in return for the shah's creation of an "atmosphere of security" as well as his promise to uphold the supremacy of Shiite Islam. The shah agreed readily to those demands, which boiled down to nothing more than big budgets for the Qom establishment and its shrines and mosques, as well as a straitlaced insistence on respect for "public morality" and the ayatollahs.[100] With Behbahani's alliance of throne and altar in the works, the always supple Ayatollah Kashani ceased his dalliance with the Tudeh Party, dropped Mosaddeq like a hot potato and threw in with Ayatollah Behbahani's pro-shah conservatives, who had won over any mullahs still on the fence by writing them "black letters" on Tudeh letterhead threatening to kill them once the communists took power. (The fiercely ambitious Kashani considered himself the rightful heir to Mosaddeq and looked to the day—not far off—when his radical Shiite clerics would brush the shah aside to lead an "Islamic internationalist" movement into the global arena against the West.)[101] Iran's *bazaari*, or merchants—who had been alienated by Mosaddeq's taxes and a 50 percent plunge in the value of the riyal between 1951 and 1953—also rallied to the throne.[102]

Crowds swept out of the mosques and the bazaar bearing pictures of the shah, Behbahani and Zahedi. Some of the crowds, augmented by soldiers in uniform, moved with well-planned precision, busting political prisoners out of jail, seizing the headquarters of Mosaddeq's Iran Party and its newspapers as well as the Tudeh offices and papers, and, of course, the broadcast stations of Radio Tehran.[103] Kermit

Roosevelt and his CIA colleagues were nervous wrecks—"cigarettes and vodka-limes tasted awful"—but Zahedi was putting together a winning team and rallying the Iranian officer corps.[104] Whatever his other faults, Shah Muhammed Reza was extremely good to the military: he paid his officers well, procured expensive hardware from abroad and promoted regularly. Mosaddeq was not like that at all: he was far more interested in diverting resources from the military budget to internal development—and was believed to be planning to evict the large, well-heeled American military advisory group. Many Iranian officers had formed into the secret "Committee to Save the Fatherland" in 1952 and were now only too willing to rise against Mosaddeq. All the key generals had soured on Mosaddeq by August 1953: the commander of the Imperial Guard, the chief of the air force, the commandant of the Imperial Gendarmerie and all the tank commanders in Tehran.[105]

Six pro-shah tanks and their crews were sent to surround and shell Mosaddeq's residence, where just two tanks had been mustered in its defense. The pro-Mosaddeq tanks were quickly dispatched, and the elderly prime minister was observed fleeing over the garden wall. He was captured and flung into captivity, where he remained until his death in 1967. ("I dispense of everything. I have no wife, no son, no daughter, nothing. I see only my homeland before my eyes," he said at his trial.) The tribal leaders responded well in the provinces, where drivers were warned to clip a picture of the shah to their windshield, or suffer the consequences. One after the other, Iran's provincial capitals declared allegiance to the shah. Still in Rome, the shah answered a reporter's request for comment on the coup with amazement: "Can it be true?"[106] The shah returned to Tehran on August 22 and gratefully summoned Kermit Roosevelt to Saadabad Palace. They snacked on vodka and caviar and the shah raised his glass: "I owe my throne to God, my people, my army, to you, and to that undercover assistant of yours whom I shall not name." He was referring to CIA agent Miles Copeland (father of Police drummer Stewart), who had helped glue together the British and American halves of Operation Ajax.[107] Loy Henderson was present at the meeting and remarked that the shah was "a changed man—more confident and optimistic."

When Kermit Roosevelt returned to Washington, President Eisenhower pinned the National Security Medal on his chest and listened raptly to his account of Ajax. "It seemed more like a dime novel than a historical fact," Ike gushed.[108] Others were not so awed. It was, one critic put it, "a disaster, a slur nothing could whitewash," damning evidence of British imperialism and American connivance.[109] U.S. support for the British boycott—which closed all markets (and refineries) to Iranian oil—

amounted to economic sanctions against Iran and signaled that the U.S. priorities were to back the British, seat an anticommunist in power and secure an oil settlement that favored Western interests.[110] Explicable as those aims were in the context of the Cold War, they were naturally taken for unpardonable meddling in Iranian internal affairs. American advisers poured in on the heels of Mosaddeq, which changed perceptions of the United States in Iran and mocked Mosaddeq's program of "negative equilibrium." Mosaddeq, like Nasser after him, had sought to balance between the blocs so that no one power—neither Britain, America nor the USSR— would control or manipulate the Iranian scene.[111] "Negative equilibrium" was now dead and buried, as the shah slid gratefully into Eisenhower's pocket.

At his trial, Mosaddeq became an Iranian martyr, sounding the wounded themes of Shiite mythology and national pride that resound to this day in Iran's barbed relations with the United States: "My creed is the creed of the Lord of the Martyrs, Imam Husayn. That is, whenever right is at stake I will oppose any power." Only Iran mattered.[112] The American-sponsored removal of Mosaddeq, two Iran experts concluded, "branded itself on the Iranian public consciousness and became . . . a rallying cry of the revolution of 1978–79." Before the coup, Iranians had regarded "the British as malevolent and the Americans as benevolent."[113] After the coup, America put on the horns of Great Satan.

Truman and his State Department had viewed Mosaddeq as a tempestuous but useful democrat who might eventually promote American values and empower the Iranian middle class and other vital interests over the shah and his feudal clique. Visiting Iran in 1947, Kermit Roosevelt, who would shortly rescue the shah, had recorded that the "royal government is corrupt and inefficient," characterized by "unashamed graft, exploitation and almost open plundering by officials."[114] The irony, as another historian recently noted, "was that Mosaddeq was showing every sign of turning the country into just the kind of liberal democracy that the Western plotters were pledged to uphold."[115] Yes and no: Mosaddeq was a charismatic bourgeois with democratic aspirations, but he was ultimately destroyed by the same mob and demagoguery that he himself had created.

"Political forces which Mosaddeq himself encouraged in the past now require him to insist upon greater concessions [from] the British," the CIA had warned as the crisis ripened.[116] By harping on the "evils" of the British, Mosaddeq made a rational resolution of the crisis impossible. He would not deal practically with London, and his hard line made it impossible to accept anything less than total expropriation of British oil assets in Iran. If Mosaddeq settled for anything less,

Ayatollah Kashani jeered, the prime minister would be murdered like a dog. Mosaddeq backed himself out on a limb, and then began sawing it off. By alienating the mullahs, the shah, the army, the *bazaari* and other conservatives—by his rule by decree, his secularizing tendencies, his embrace of the Tudeh communists, his plans to decrease the (pro-shah) army and increase the (pro-Mosaddeq) police, his failure to *solve* the oil question through good-faith negotiations, his budget cuts and his resort to printing stacks of riyals to pay for his (reduced) government activities in the absence of oil revenues—Mosaddeq, much more than the CIA or MI6, created the conditions for his own removal.[117] He had provoked an economic and political crisis trusting in the lever of oil at a time when there was an oil *glut* in the world thanks to the development of "elephant fields" like Saudi Arabia's Ghawar. No one *needed* the 660,000 barrels per day that Mosaddeq was withholding. Despite the fact that Iranian gasoline amounted to one-third of Middle Eastern production and one-quarter of non-Western hemisphere world production and had powered most of the allied planes and vehicles in the Korean War, new sources were able to take up the slack and permit a thirsty world to chug serenely through Mosaddeq's nationalization crisis.

That economic fact of life—so different today, when illiberal regimes in Iran, Russia and Venezuela enjoy considerable leverage over their customers—was lost on no one as the British boycott of Iran's fields and refinery ground on, painlessly observed by all the big oil companies and yet costing the Iranian people and treasury an estimated $200 million between the start of the crisis in May 1951 and the end in August 1953.[118] As Allen Dulles later told NBC television, "The government of Mosaddeq was overthrown by the action of the shah. Now, that we encouraged the shah to take that action I will not deny." But it was the *action* of the shah and his Iranian allies. Washington consoled itself that it was merely playing what Allen Dulles and Miles Copeland called a "game of nations" with the USSR, which, in Iran, had players (the Tudeh Party and Kashani's entourage) who ultimately proved weaker and less appealing than the American players (the shah, General Zahedi and Ayatollah Behbahani).[119] Kermit Roosevelt met with Secretary of State John Foster Dulles after Ajax and explained that the operation had succeeded not because of British or American skullduggery, but because "the CIA's study of the Iranian situation convincingly showed that the Iranian people and most of the military wanted exactly the results the Eisenhower administration was seeking." If the Iranian people and military had not supported the result of Ajax, then Washington would have had to "give the job to the Marines."[120]

After the Iranian coup, Prime Minister Zahedi attended a victory party at the CIA offices in Tehran, approached the American station chief and said, "We are in, so what do we do now?" For the Americans, revised oil contracts and foreign aid to buttress the shah were the first orders of business. Washington would immediately send $68 million in emergency aid—and an additional $1.2 billion over the next ten years—but Zahedi would naturally have to deliver the American access to Iranian oil that John Foster Dulles and Herbert Hoover, Jr., had extorted from the British as the price of American support for Operation Ajax. Reminded by the Americans that he owed his throne to the United States, the shah grumbled that "any favor that the CIA had done him would be adequately paid for in oil." Indeed it would be. After the coup, AIOC tactfully changed its name to British Petroleum and, as promised in March 1953, sold a 40 percent share of its holdings in Iran to a largely American consortium: Standard Oil of New Jersey (Exxon), Socony-Vacuum (Mobil), Gulf Oil, SoCal (Chevron) and Texaco.[121] Sullivan & Cromwell, where the Dulles brothers remained partners, handled the sale, which effectively returned the production and distribution of Iranian oil to foreign hands. Profitable for American oilmen and lawyers—"one of the most attractive contracts to the oil industry in the Middle East"—the sale of AIOC's Iranian reserves to the Americans also profited the shah, who now claimed that he had "rejected any restoration of British control over oil operations in Iran," reduced the British stake and in so doing "defended Iranian nationalism."[122] He neglected to mention that Britain's losses were America's gains, which left Iran in the same state of subservience to foreign interests that it had found itself in at the onset of the crisis.[123]

Allen Dulles telegraphed British foreign secretary Anthony Eden in October 1953 to congratulate him on the successful outcome of Operation Ajax, which suggested new opportunities "to change to our advantage the course of events in the Middle East." Together, the UK and the United States had "closed the most dangerous gap in the line from Europe to South Asia." But Dulles's own analysts doubted the director's rhetoric. Even with massive "U.S. provision of arms and equipment," Iran would be held back for years, perhaps decades, by its sketchy infrastructure, limited transport, low level of education and endemic corruption. Iran's army of 120,000 was regarded as mediocre, and increasing it by a maximum effort to 400,000 troops would do little to slow the Red Army but would certainly bankrupt Iran.[124] "Persian forces are quite incapable of resisting Russian attacks," the British concurred. Worse, "Persian . . . civil administration would almost certainly collapse at the first sign of such an attack and the Shah would flee the country"—as he had during the coup attempt. Far from "closing the gap between Iraq and Pakistan," Operation Ajax and the enlistment of Iran in an anti-Soviet coalition would merely pull the Russians in deeper and "provoke a barrage of Russian threats and propaganda."[125] The United States would steadily be drawn in to buttress the shah, improve his military and suggest unpopular methods for internal security against the inevitable dissidents.

But that would be a problem for future American presidents. Eisenhower settled down to enjoy his easy victory. Ten thousand American military advisers flew into Iran between 1953 and 1963, bearing $535 million of American military equipment.[126] Beginning in 1954, disloyal mullahs, tribal chiefs, officers, politicians and students—the always problematic "urban left"—began to be purged, jailed or merely released from their government jobs or scholarships into unemployment. The shah's flight to Rome had caused him to lose face, which had to be viciously recouped. "Imagine under our system of values," an Iranian observed, "a monarch—the father of his country—who flees at the most critical moment and is shown buying jewelry with his wife!"[127] The shah moved aggressively to erase the stain. Three thousand alleged Tudeh members were fired from the civil service after the coup; the armed forces were purged of all suspected communists and "Mosaddeqists," and eighteen hundred pro-Zahedi officers were rapidly promoted to all the key military and police functions. The shah and Zahedi carefully rigged elections for the new *majlis* in 1954 to prevent the return of any National Front diehards.[128] A CIA team arrived in 1955 to begin training SAVAK, the shah's ruthless new national intelligence and security organization, and to cement the authoritarian regime that would hold power till the 1978–79 revolution. One CIA operative—Ted Hotchkiss—felt sullied by the experience. "I fought the fascists and the Nazis, [yet] we were becoming just like them."[129]

From the shah's perspective, fascist methods were required. SAVAK and the CIA unearthed a large Tudeh cell inside the Iranian military in 1954, after Tudeh airmen had protested the shah's coup against Mosaddeq by burning several Iranian air force jets on their runways. The shah, who loved nothing quite so much as high-tech foreign fighter jets, furiously responded by arresting 450 Iranian officers. All the captives were junior officers, but they were well educated and highly placed in sensitive jobs. According to CIA analysis, the Tudeh officers had been reporting to Moscow on the state of Iran's military since 1941 and had made ambitious plans to decapitate the Iranian state by simultaneously assassinating the shah, his prime minister, most of the cabinet, members of the *majlis*, the provincial governors and the key military commanders. Once the slate had been wiped clean of the "filthy Shah and his gangsters," the communists planned to thrust into power a ready-made Tudeh central committee and politburo.[130]

Iranians (and many Americans) still shed bitter tears over the Western-facilitated removal of Mosaddeq. The Eisenhower administration had held its nose and smashed a democracy in Iran. But Ike and Dulles consoled themselves—not without reason—that they had not acted alone, or merely in league with the British. Rather, they had facilitated the rise of strong but uncoordinated Iranian elements. This was in pointed contrast to the entirely hopeless Iranian regime change propagated by the George W. Bush administration in 2007–8, when President Bush and Vice President Cheney covertly sought $400 million for a ragtag band of Iranian fringe groups—believed to include Iranian Arabs, Baluchi tribesmen, drug-runners, Kurdish separatists and al-Qaeda-affiliated Salafists—that, even had they miraculously united to seize power, would have harmed, not helped, the American position in the Persian Gulf.[131] At least Eisenhower had the sense to base his coup on leading, credible Shiite and *Persian* elements. In his corrupt, cowardly way, the shah understood the requirements of the country better than Mosaddeq, who had veered into an increasingly erratic and left-leaning dictatorship. The shah, guided by the British and Americans, steered back to the middle and, as the CIA put it, cleverly used policy and patronage to piece back together the essential coalition needed to govern Iran: "the military leadership, violent and unreliable ultranationalists like Kashani, the old-guard conservative landowners, and the tribes."[132] Shah Muhammed Reza replaced Mosaddeq's "negative equilibrium" with a new policy of "positive nationalism," which he defined as "sovereignty and independence, *but in alliance with the United States.*" For imperial Iran, money would not be a problem; American aid was already flooding in—$45 million a year in the 1950s, $100 million a year in the 1960s—and a steady stream of oil revenues would keep the country flush and revolution-free for the next twenty-five years.[133]

CHAPTER 5

NASSER

EVEN AS IRAN SIMMERED DOWN, a bigger crisis was boiling up in Egypt, which was strategically at least as important as Iran. And in Egypt, money definitely *was* a problem.

To the Eisenhower administration—which had tussled with London over the proper course for Iran—the Egyptian dynasty of King Farouk was yet another embarrassing vestige of British empire, where "the palace clique, a polyglot collection of scoundrels who even down to the royal chauffeur swaggered under the titles of Pasha and Bey," seemed utterly incapable of modernizing effectively, adapting to the new forces of nationalism or even mounting a credible defense against communism or Islamic fundamentalism. Cairo often *seemed* rich, with its two million salaried government officials, twelve hundred big landowners, its rich merchant class and its horde of courtiers—pashas, beys and effendis—but that appearance deceived. The courtiers lived a charmed life, and many of them were not even Egyptian; they were Turks, Greeks, Italians, Albanians (like Farouk's father Fuad I) or Syrians who had arrived to work during the period of Ottoman rule. The *real* Egyptian was the peasant fellah in his mud hut in the Nile River Valley, who subsisted (in good times) on a few cents a day, barely scraped a living for his big family from a tiny quarter-acre plot and compounded crippling debts meeting his minimum living costs of $120 a year with an average annual income of just $40.[1] And

Egypt's problems had only *increased* since the British takeover seventy years earlier. The population had grown from two million to twenty million—and was growing 2 percent a year in the 1950s—but had not been absorbed and employed by new arable land or factory jobs. Most of Egypt in the 1950s was what it had always been—desert—so nearly 100 percent of the surging, wretched population of twenty million crammed themselves into 3 percent of Egypt's land mass. This made for a permanent crisis of health, living standards, social peace and crime, with hordes of destitute fellahs, tenant farmers, porters, donkey drivers and other day workers struggling to make ends meet. King Farouk himself was mugged while strolling through downtown Cairo in the 1940s.

Egypt's political tensions were as fraught as its social ones, with poor Egyptians increasingly loathing their rich king and pashas, and the fundamentalist, anti-Western Muslim Brotherhood, al-Ikhwan al-Muslimin, drawing its greatest strength not in the rural hills or grazing lands, but in the slums and student dormitories of Cairo, where secret membership by 1950 stood at about two million. Cairo, a visitor wrote in 1949, had become "not only the most cosmopolitan of Arab cities, but a capital seat of Arab xenophobia and a scene of some of the most violent mob action against foreigners."[2] "What is happening in the Arab world is not a revolution, but a revulsion," the U.S. ambassador to Cairo warned Washington.[3]

King Farouk seemed oblivious to it all; his annual income in 1950 was $4 million, and he drifted lazily between two palaces in Cairo, two in Alexandria, one in Inchass and one in Helwan. He owned two hundred red sports cars and limousines—the only red cars permitted in Egypt—and a fleet of yachts.[4] When America's assistant secretary of state for Near Eastern affairs visited Cairo in 1951 to press reforms on the royal house, he reported that Farouk "had degenerated by this time into his self-indulgent bad-boy period and seemingly took no interest in affairs beyond the intrigues of the palace." U.S. ambassador Jefferson Caffery was criticized by the Cairo press for "not taking a fatherly interest in reforming Farouk."[5] By the 1950s, the population density in the Nile Valley—three bedraggled fellahs per acre of arable land—was higher than even the most thickly settled parts of Europe or India and indeed made Egypt the most densely populated country in the world. In 1950, 95 percent of the Egyptian population lived in extreme poverty; 80 percent was illiterate. Just 5 percent of the Egyptian population possessed 95 percent of the country's wealth, and those families notoriously threw out more dinner leftovers every evening than a peasant and his half dozen dependents might consume in a fortnight. Disease raged virtually unchecked: 90 percent of Egypt's population suffered from trachoma; 60 percent had bilharzia; the rates of malaria, amoebic dysentery, elephantiasis, pellagra and hookworm were startlingly high.[6]

The British Empire was business, not charity, so British rule had done little to improve those appalling problems. Egypt spent a mere $2 million per year on public education in the 1920s, which was just half King Farouk's annual salary.[7] Britain's chief interests had always been the Suez Canal, Egyptian cotton and Egypt's absorbent market for British manufactured goods. London had taken control of Egypt in 1882, extorted a sixty-year lease on the Suez Canal in 1908 from an obliging Egyptian prime minister named Boutros Ghali (grandfather of the future UN secretary general Boutros Boutros-Ghali), declared Egypt a protectorate in 1914 and then made it an "independent kingdom" in 1922.[8] No one was fooled—the British did not even bother recalling their colonial high commissioner; they simply converted him into an ambassador, who continued, as before, to direct the Egyptian king "like a young schoolboy in the hands of a bluff, severe tutor."[9]

The British did as they pleased in nominally "independent" Egypt. In 1936, they forced a mutual defense treaty on Cairo that gave them unfettered access to Egypt's military bases as well as control of the Egyptian armed forces. Farouk, who succeeded his father, Fuad, just before the 1936 treaty was signed, looked on impassively. He would be coddled by the British just as his father had been. On the rare occasions when Farouk actually defied London—as in 1942 when the British chose his prime minister and Farouk rejected the British choice—the British would send tanks and infantry to get their way, rolling into the Abdin Palace grounds, training their guns on Farouk's windows and then dismounting from armored vehicles to demand (and get) Farouk's adhesion to their "suggestions." Farouk eventually gave up trying to be a head of state, and withdrew into debauchery: driving fast cars, partying in nightclubs and enjoying long, champagne-soaked holidays abroad. Gradually, this behavior made the British (and their choice of king) hated in Egypt. A Young Egypt movement sprang up in the 1930s, and its green-shirted mujahideen committed themselves to a nationalist jihad against Britain and Farouk.[10] Anwar Sadat, a young Egyptian army captain in 1942, recalled the pro-Nazi fervor that swept through Egypt during World War II. When the Germans invaded from Libya and pushed toward Alexandria, people lined up along the roads and cheered, "Forward, Rommel, forward!" In Cairo, Egyptian students and Muslim Brothers rallied to chant, "We are Rommel's soldiers!" General Aziz al-Masry agreed to fly to Rommel's headquarters in Libya to broadcast calls for mutiny in the Egyptian army, and General Muhammed Naguib, who would lead a revolt against Farouk after the war, bluntly informed the king that "I am ashamed to wear my uniform and request permission to resign."[11]

Egyptians applauded the Nazis out of exasperation with the British and Farouk's puppet dynasty. Although Farouk's brilliant nineteenth-century forefathers—Muhammed Ali and Ibrahim Pasha—had wrested Egypt from Turkish control in battle, Farouk himself performed so ineptly as Egypt's twenty-eight-year-old commander in chief in the 1948 war against Israel that he had exposed his kingdom afterward to nonstop subversion by nationalists, communists and religious fundamentalists. The CIA despairingly nicknamed Farouk "the Fat Fucker."[12] The British were only a little less harsh. "Where Farouk's own amusements and distractions are concerned, the king in him is fighting a losing battle against the man," the British ambassador in Cairo darkly observed in 1951.[13] Egyptians merely scoffed when the fat, balding, debauched Farouk proclaimed himself a sayyid, or descendant of the prophet, and announced his intention to become the Muslim caliph. Even Farouk had a keen sense of his limitations: "In a few years," he liked to joke, "there will be only five kings in the world—the King of England and the four kings in a deck of cards." CIA agent Kermit Roosevelt visited Farouk in 1947 and was struck by the decadence and hopelessness of his court: "I remember late one night watching one of the king's close relations by marriage swaying back and forth while the Scotch splashed in his glass to emphasize his words. 'They hate us,' he said thickly but earnestly. 'They look on us as a bunch of rich, no good Albanians. It won't be long now.' "

No, it wouldn't. Egypt, Kermit Roosevelt observed, was "a land of unhealthily violent contrasts where the rich grow richer, the poor grow poorer, and everyone grows more nervous." There was no governing class with any legitimacy, and trying to find one was "like courting a ghost or drinking with an invisible rabbit."[14] American strategists worried that if communists or Islamists—who opposed "all secular tendencies in Islamic nations"—were ever to take the offensive in this unhappy land, Farouk's British mentors would prove too weak, overstretched and politically compromised to stop them. Americans also resented Farouk's efforts to fence Egypt off from American influence after World War II. Indeed, one reason the United States became so cozy with Saudi Arabia was because Farouk and his British minders were being so difficult in the Mediterranean and the Red Sea. "Ibn Saud is much more friendly to the U.S. than is Egypt," an American diplomat wrote from Cairo in June 1949. "The Egyptians have not renewed our air transit rights, they do not encourage visits by U.S. Navy vessels, and their government is less than cooperative with the U.S."[15]

THE FREE OFFICERS REVOLT

Farouk's pro-British tilt explained the American decision to support Colonel Gamal Abdel Nasser's "Free Officers Revolt" against King Farouk in July 1952. With its central location and population of twenty-three million, Egypt—in American eyes—was the natural core and leader of the Arab world. Cairo was the greatest Arab city—far more impressive than Baghdad or Damascus—and Egypt, whether as a province, viceroyalty or kingdom, had never lost its national unity and identity. Egypt was still the richest Arab state, and Egyptians had led the push for the Arab League, which had been signed into life in Cairo in 1945 with an Egyptian bureaucracy and treasury. Cairo's al-Azhar University, which enrolled fifteen thousand religious students in the 1950s, was the nearest thing Sunni Islam had to a central religious authority. Egypt's press and media were read, heard and watched from Morocco to India. "Cairo," a CIA analyst concluded, "has become the Washington of the Islamic world" thanks to the energy of Nasser and the free officers, whom the Americans viewed as a far more redoubtable ally in the Cold War than King Farouk.[16] The free officers were relatively virtuous "new men": majors and lieutenant colonels from the lower middle class who knew and empathized with Egypt's desperately poor underclass. In the mid-1930s, Nasser had been rejected by both the Egyptian army and police as "unfit" because of his plebeian origins. Only in 1937, when the British abruptly expanded the Egyptian army because of the German and Italian threats, were peasants and petty bourgeois like Nasser finally let in. They never got on with Egypt's powerful effendi class—the rich, Turkish-descended playboys, officers and landowners of Farouk's court—and their free officer movement was fundamentally a social revolution.[17]

The free officers—who had formed into a pro-German secret society during World War II and joined the cheering crowds along Rommel's march routes—returned from the 1948 Arab-Israeli War convinced that the Arab world's "biggest battlefield is in *Egypt*," not Palestine, or anywhere else. They were anti-Zionist and anti-British and antimonarchical, and they viewed social revolution and diplomatic nonalignment as the best way to assert Egyptian independence and greatness. They blamed Farouk's Albanian-descended dynasty ("a family of non-Egyptians"), their corrupt courtiers and the no less corrupt politicians of Egypt's Wafd Party for the humiliating defeat at the hands of the Israelis and Cairo's ongoing subservience to London.[18] Wafd, or "delegation," was the Egyptian party of liberal nationalists that had sent a delegation to London in 1918 to request postwar independence from Western allies Woodrow Wilson, Georges Clemenceau and David Lloyd George. Their efforts in 1918 had been thwarted by the British, but also by Farouk's non-Arabic-speaking father, King Fuad I, who was cosseted by the British precisely so that he would obstruct demands for Egyptian independence.[19] By 1952, Farouk had become as loathsome to Egyptian nationalists as his father had been, and the Wafd had lost its Edwardian luster and subsided into legislative logrolling and corruption. What facts were permitted to emerge after investigation of the 1948 military defeat revealed that Farouk, his relatives, his advisers and the Wafd had all embezzled funds that had been appropriated for the army's invasion of Israel, which certainly helped explain the dismal failure of Egyptian arms. The Egyptian army fought that campaign with 1912 model Mauser rifles and without maps or tents, and one of Farouk's senior commanders, General Sirri Amer, was later convicted of embezzlement and drug trafficking during the war.[20]

From the American perspective, modern, practical *Egyptian* men like the free officers were the perfect nucleus for a new Egypt that would resist both arrogant British and evil Soviet empire. In 1952, the American embassy in Cairo urged the White House to resist pressure from the British and Israelis to leave Egypt as a British sphere and forge ahead to make it an American one. Egypt in the 1950s presented a "historic opportunity." In no other country in the Middle East "could immediate dividends in terms of security for the United States be received for such a relatively low expenditure of the U.S. taxpayers' defense dollars."[21] American hopes resembled those in Iraq fifty years later. Boosted by American aid and patronage, the free officers would evolve into a reliable ally who would have the legitimacy to resist Soviet blandishments and take otherwise unpopular decisions like enlistment in an American-led military alliance and the diplomatic recognition of Israel.[22] That, of course, was taking an awful lot on faith; indeed, Ambassador Jefferson Caffery's hopes were not unlike Vice President Cheney's in 2003. Both men felt that key countries—first Egypt, and then Iraq—could be molded into American beachheads in the Middle East. In the 1950s, Caffery, who called the free officers "my boys," felt certain that the mere offer of American friendship would induce Nasser and the free officers to "pay dividends." More likely was the prediction of Kermit Roosevelt in 1949 that Egypt and the rest of the Arab countries—demoralized by the extent of their social, economic and political problems—would continue to wield the issues of imperialism and Israel, "as the matador uses his red cape," to distract and entrance their unhappy citizens.[23]

COLONEL NASSER

Thirty-four years old in 1952, Gamal Abdel Nasser was the consummate matador and the quintessential Arab "big man." If, as a Lebanese commentator asserted, "Arab politics has always ridden on horseback," then Nasser was the man on the white horse.[24] Nasser's 1955 manifesto, *The Philosophy of the Revolution*—ghostwritten by his journalist friend Muhammed Heikal—observed that the Arabs were "wandering aimlessly in search of a hero." There were no other likely candidates for the role—"no one else is qualified to play it"—so Nasser "put on its costume." The playacting metaphor was apt, for Nasser's Arab nationalism, like Saddam Hussein's afterward, was always rife with hypocrisy, and the colonel had developed a youthful taste for drama, playing Julius Caesar in a school play when he was sixteen and pestering his school librarian with a stream of requests for heroic biographies, including books on Alexander the Great, Napoleon, Garibaldi, Bismarck, Atatürk, Hindenburg, Foch and Churchill.[25] Nasser had grown up in Alexandria, the eldest of eleven children. He had been in and out of jail as a boy for quarreling with his father, a postal clerk, and joining anti-British rallies. Anwar Sadat met Nasser for the first time in 1938, when they were both army captains at the Signals School near Cairo. Nasser, Sadat recalled, was a weirdly charismatic introvert. To acquaintances, the combination was powerful: Nasser came across as a striking, aloof, desirable man. Descended from the tall, dark Saidi clan of Upper Egypt, the colonel made a dramatic first impression and spoke stirringly. Still, intimates like Sadat warned of Nasser's narcissism, which blinded him to hard facts and deafened him to moderate advice, "erecting an almost insuperable barrier between himself and other people."[26]

That barrier would ultimately destroy Nasser, but initially it saved him, and launched his career. When the Egyptian Free Officers Organization was formed in 1939 to wrest independence from Britain, Nasser quietly joined but was overlooked by British intelligence. When the British arrested the leading Egyptian free officers—Captain Sadat and several others—in 1942, Nasser returned undetected from his garrison in Sudan and moved into the top job. He expanded free officer membership after the war, recruiting men "of outstanding performance," and created a cellular organization to defeat British efforts to infiltrate and unravel the network.[27] A major in the Arab-Israeli War of 1948, Nasser served in the ten-thousand-man Egyptian contingent and was trapped for several months in the trenches of the "Falluja pocket" between Jerusalem and Beersheba, where an Egyptian brigade withered under Israeli siege while the bulk of the Israeli army turned its attention to evicting as many Arabs as possible from Palestine.[28] After his return to Egypt, Nasser continued to expand the free officers, and the British continued to underestimate him, concluding that Nasser was harmless: "shy and retiring, in no way extreme or fanatical, not the inspiring type with powers of leadership, but more of a solid staff officer."[29]

In October 1951, Farouk's prime minister and head of the Wafd Party, Mustafa Nahas, revoked the Anglo-Egyptian Treaty of 1936, which he himself had signed into force fifteen years earlier. Nahas was attempting to appease rising militancy in Egypt, which had intensified because of Mosaddeq's struggle against the Anglo-Iranian Oil Company. Mobs of irregular "self-sacrificers," or fedayeen, formed in Egypt—some armed and trained by the Muslim Brothers, others by the free officers—and began attacking the British base in the Suez Canal Zone, which was a two-hundred-square-mile British-run enclave along the west bank of the canal. Sadat later described the fedayeen rioters in the class-conscious terms of the free officers that initially endeared the officers to the classless Americans: "It was . . . a violent expression of the suffering of more than 95 percent of the population, the broad masses who lived in great deprivation under a flagrantly capitalist and class-based system." Nahas and his Wafd Party, Sadat wrote, needed to be removed because they were "tool[s] in the hands of the king and the British . . . , at the expense of the people."[30]

PROJECT FAT FUCKER

The Egyptian riots around the Suez Canal Zone spread to Cairo in January 1952 and undermined an already feeble King Farouk. As profitable Korean War demand for

Egyptian cotton slackened, Farouk and Nahas resorted to various expedients to maintain a shred of popularity. They released the new Muslim Brotherhood leader Hasan el-Hodeiby from jail and encouraged him to stage rallies and attacks against British bases in Egypt. Washington was pleased to see the British under attack but, as in Iran, worried about a vacuum if the British hit back and Farouk collapsed. Who would replace Farouk? The Muslim Brotherhood? Communists? Those dire possibilities loomed large in 1952, when British troops counterattacked rioting Egyptian police and fedayeen and killed and wounded dozens in pitched battles. The Egyptians retaliated, attacking Europeans and setting fire to the Turf Club, Shepheards Hotel, the BOAC and Thomas Cook offices, Barclays Bank and almost every British-frequented bar, cinema and restaurant in Cairo. Seven hundred and fifty buildings were burned to the ground.³¹ Washington expressed alarm at the "natural propensity for frenzy" of the Arab mobs (which would be reprised years later in U.S.-occupied Iraq) and concluded that Farouk's regime now "gave off the smell of death." In Cairo, the CIA instructed Miles Copeland of Operation Ajax fame to start work on "Project FF"—as in Fat Fucker—to assist in the overthrow of Farouk by Nasser's free officers.³² Washington actually embedded Copeland in the Egyptian ministry of the interior as a "consultant," where he was free to head off British-organized purges of the free officers and draft plans for a November 1952 coup. When informed that Farouk and the British were preparing a crackdown, Copeland and Nasser moved the date forward to July.

On a steamy midsummer night, the free officers gathered at Camp Huckstep, an abandoned World War II U.S. Army post on the outskirts of Cairo, and then drove into the capital, where they filed into a slumbering Egyptian army headquarters and locked the duty officer and his guards inside a lounge. Warned of the coup by an indiscreet free officer, Farouk's war minister phoned army headquarters to order troops out against the rebels, but Sadat, already inside the building and working the switchboard himself, put the call through to Nasser, who pretended to be a night-duty officer, and coolly assured the war minister that nothing was amiss. Colonel Sadat, who nearly missed the coup because he had forgotten the revised date and gone to the movies, then coaxed the real guards out of the lounge where they were imprisoned, enlisted them in the revolution and ordered them to call army units in Cairo, Alexandria, Rafa, al-Arish, Luxor and the Western Desert, where undercover free officers were summoned to the telephone and given their orders.³³ Nasser calmed the jittery officers around him: "Tonight there is no room for sentiment; we must be ready for the unexpected." "Why do you speak to us in

English," one officer protested. "Because Arabic is not a suitable language to express the need for *calm*," Nasser said, laughing.³⁴

Since Nasser's organization had infiltrated every army post, the coup could be speedily arranged in any language. Tanks, towed artillery and infantry in trucks roared into the capital from the provincial garrisons and Cairo awoke on July 23, 1952, to a new government. Driving to Broadcasting House to announce the new regime that morning—a government purged of "traitors and weaklings"—Sadat saw "the streets . . . crowded with people as I had never seen them before. Men, old and young, women and children, were kissing each other, shaking hands, coming together in small clusters or large circles—but all the time in total silence. No shouts were heard."³⁵

NASSERISM

That may have been the last time an Arab government was inaugurated quietly and nearly bloodlessly—two dead and eight wounded—without burning tires and bursts of celebratory gunfire. Immensely pleased with the result, the United States threw its support behind Colonel Nasser's "transitional authoritarian regime" on the assumption that it would break with London, purge Farouk's corrupt effendis, foster regional stability, recognize Israel and prepare Egypt for a return of *real* democracy. Of course—as in Iraq in 2003—Washington should not have assumed so much, for Colonel Nasser was charting a radically new course toward Arab unity. Having watched the stagnant dynastic movements of the Sauds and Hashemites and the defeat of the Palestinians, Nasser hit upon a new idea deeply influenced by Lenin's Bolsheviks and the incremental Stalinist idea of "socialism in one country" to be followed by communism in many. Against the corruption of the Arab monarchies, Nasser contrasted pure, virtuous "Arab socialism": progressive policies that would unite the downtrodden Arab masses in a way that royal unions never could. Egypt would be the core of a great Arab power that would unite all the Arab lands under the progressive rule of Cairo. Even before he got started, Nasser was on a collision course with the Americans, who spurned Arab nationalism, reviled Arab socialism and pledged to defend the Arab monarchies—Saudi Arabia's in particular—against all challengers.

Almost immediately, Washington discerned the threat. Nasser's confidant Mu-

[handwritten in left margin: U.S. So-Communism / Think Communism]

hammed Heikal published the recipe for Arab nationalism in his newspaper, *Al-Ahram*: "First socialism in Egypt, then, with the gradual adoption of the Egyptian model in every neighboring land, Arab unification."[36] Nasser borrowed heavily from the Syrian ideas of Michel Aflaq's Baathists, or "revivalists," who dreamily called for a single, socialist Arab nation where all would work "without exploiting the efforts of others," where foreign businesses would be expropriated and where all public utilities, natural resources and industrial and transport services would be nationalized to ensure a "fair distribution of wealth." Such musings were unrealistic, but the Nasserites and Baathists thought that they would succeed where the Soviets had stumbled because they would "fuse nationalism and socialism into one entity" and focus less on "feeding the hungry and clothing the naked" than on liberating the repressed genius—the "hidden will"—of the Arab man.[37] *[handwritten: Threat to west · power]*

Those primal notions—will, manhood, genius—had a fascist feel, and indeed Nasser and later the Baathists found that they needed whipping boys no less than the Nazis, Fascists or Soviets to divert public attention from the contradictions of their failed policies. Internally, Nasser alternately flogged and coddled the middle class to gratify the Egyptian peasant. Twenty-four million of Egypt's thirty million citizens were fellaheen, and they adored Nasser for ramming through land reform and social services for the poor.[38] Externally, Israel and the pro-American Arab monarchies in Saudi Arabia, Iraq, Libya and Jordan became Cairo's chief whipping boys. Israel humiliatingly generated the same GDP as Egypt despite having just one-fifteenth of Egypt's population. The Israelis were so loathsome to the Arab masses that Nasser felt driven always to declare his eagerness "for the final conflict, the one that would wipe Israel off the map."[39] Nasser called himself the embodiment of all "progressive forces" and vowed to roll back monarchy, theocracy and Zionism wherever they cropped up in the Arab world. Then as now, Israel was the sole issue around which *all* Arabs would unite, but Nasser forged ahead with his contentious "Arab nationalism" anyway, in the sincere belief that he was tearing down the old to build the new: a powerful, secular union of Arabs, purged of Koran-thumping bigots, foreign settlers and bloodsucking imperialists.

Elected president of the United States shortly after Nasser's coup, Dwight Eisenhower rebuffed British attempts to talk about their widening Egyptian problem and enlist America's help in fixing it. Instead, Ike embraced the Egyptians. Perhaps guilt-ridden by the prospect of Operation Ajax, he grasped Nasser's Free Officers Revolt and the Suez Canal affair as the perfect opportunity to treat Egypt (and the new nations of the developing world) as an *equal*. "We must avoid the appearance of attempting to dominate the councils of the free world," Ike scolded British foreign secretary Anthony Eden. The new regime in Cairo must not be treated as if it were "not really important."[40] The free officers gratefully rushed to make contact with Washington. Anwar Sadat recalled polling his free officer colleagues in 1952 to discover if any of them actually knew someone in the American embassy. One of them knew the American military attaché, who was duly given a letter for the eyes of the U.S. ambassador.

Sixty-six-year-old U.S. ambassador Jefferson Caffery had a long history with the British and the Egyptians. The courtly southern gentleman had served on the American delegation at the Paris Peace Conference in 1919 and had deplored the way Egypt had been rudely bundled back into the British Empire over the objections of Cairo's Wafd delegates. Thirty-three years later, Caffery was determined to make things right. He liked the Egyptian nationalists and disliked the British, whom he considered "tragically incapable" of adapting to the postwar winds of change and the new world order.[41] With calculated effrontery, Caffery invited the entire Free Officers Constituent Council to dinner at his residence after the coup to congratulate them. Caffery and the Near Eastern desk at the State Department—filled with "Arabists" like him—expected nothing less than an "Egyptian renaissance" under Nasser.

But neither Caffery nor his supervisors reflected reigning opinion in Washington, where decision makers were far more focused on the demands of Soviet containment than on an Arab renaissance in Cairo.[42] By the time President Eisenhower stepped into the Oval Office in January 1953, the United States was lumbered with the leadership and defense of the "free world." Truman had wrought that transition by dropping two atom bombs on Japan, funding a thermonuclear arsenal, agreeing to German rearmament, joining NATO, drawing a line of containment around the Soviet Union with his Truman Doctrine and then going to war in Korea to arrest the spread of communism south from China and the USSR and to shore up Japan (and eventually Taiwan and South Vietnam) as American bastions in East Asia. Truman's National Security Council Document 68 (NSC-68)—inherited by Eisenhower and the Republicans—outlined American strategy for the Cold War: the Soviet Union, "because it possesses and is possessed by a world-wide revolutionary movement, . . . is the inheritor of Russian imperialism, and . . . is a totalitarian dictatorship," would be contained by thermonuclear bombs, bigger conventional forces and a ring of pro-American states.[43] Inevitably, the new American forcefulness and pragmatism were carried into the Middle East, where Turkey, Israel, Iran and then Egypt successively became fronts in the American struggle to contain Stalin. "As far as the sheer value of territory is concerned, there is no more strategically important area in the world than the Middle East," Eisenhower had told the Senate Armed Services Committee in August 1951 in his capacity as NATO commander. It is "the bridge to Africa and Asia, and we should bring the Arab world on our side."[44] Two years later, Ike was seated in the Oval Office, and he turned a sympathetic ear to British prime minister Winston Churchill's call for a "pro-Western front" stretched along the underbelly of the Soviet Union from Morocco to Pakistan.[45]

There were two ways to "bring the Arab world on America's side." There was the Iranian or Vietnamese way—set up a pliable, pro-American regime—or there was Caffery's way—support indigenous nationalists to earn their goodwill. The latter course seemed more "American" and ethical, but Eisenhower's secretary of state, John Foster Dulles, cautioned the president that "a policy of threatening or bulldozing the British" to support the inexperienced free officers would be counterproductive and potentially disastrous. All the free officers were violently anti- *anti-west* Israel, many of them were anti-Western and pro-Soviet, and the rest were resolutely "nonaligned" in the Cold War. Farouk, in contrast, was an Egyptian shah or Bao Dai, someone who could be aligned and steered down a pro-Western track. Moreover, America needed British support in the UN and at the Geneva Conference, where French Indochina was being partitioned; over the fraught question of German rearmament; and in Washington's unfolding coup against the Arbenz government in Guatemala, which British UN ambassador Pierson Dixon had bitterly called "the most flagrant act of aggression against a small state."[46] It would not be prudent to alienate the British in Egypt. They were needed urgently on the other fronts in the Cold War, and they seemed to be giving ground in Egypt gracefully anyway. Anthony Eden—more malleable than his mentor Churchill—had even hinted that he might one day agree to a British evacuation of the Suez Canal.

The first phase of Nasser's revolution in 1952 was soft. Nasser chose a wily old-guard politician, Ali Maher, as prime minister, and sent Sadat to Alexandria—where Farouk spent the summers—merely to request the king's abdication. With his palace ringed by rebel tanks and guns, Farouk acceded to the request, boarded the royal yacht *Mahroussa* with his wife, his four children, dozens of trunks and a stack of gold bars looted from the Bank of Egypt, accepted a twenty-one-gun salute and sailed off to exile in Naples. After wresting a promise from Farouk that he would send the historic yacht back to Egypt after his arrival in Italy—*Mahroussa* had been the first ship to pass through the Suez Canal in 1869—Nasser's Revolutionary Command Council (RCC) began to argue over just what sort of government Egypt would have now that Farouk and his kin had been dethroned and exiled. The most ardent free officers wanted revolutionary dictatorship and a Jacobin purge of the Wafd and other establishment parties; others, including Nasser, sought pragmatic cohabitation with old elites and a prompt return to parliamentary democracy. "If you begin with bloodshed you inevitably end in bloodshed," Nasser said. He even defended Farouk against hotheads like Wing Commander Gamal Salem, who wanted to kill, not exile, the king. "History," Nasser wisely countered, "will sentence him to death."[47]

When the RCC nevertheless voted seven to one for dictatorship, mass arrests and show trials, Nasser resigned his post and went home. The worried officers—deprived of their charismatic face—trailed him to his house and agreed that the existing parties would merely be instructed to "purge their ranks" and then be invited to "join the revolution."[48] Nasser seized upon this brief consensus to abolish the titles of pasha and bey—which were the coin of society in British Egypt—and to dictate a radical agrarian reform law, which broke up the big landed estates of the effendis and redistributed them to landless fellahs. In classic Egyptian fashion, the old parties did purge their ranks—of their youngest, most ethical members—and then rejected Nasser's land reform. The Wafd and the rest of the old guard were dominated by landowners and members of the phenomenally profitable Alexandria Cotton Exchange. For such men—6 percent of Egypt's population in 1952 still owned 65 percent of the land—real land reform would mean a loss of revenue and a loss of control over peasant sharecroppers, who were routinely ordered to vote their landlords or their designated creatures into parliament, or face eviction.[49]

TOWARD THE "UNITED ARAB REPUBLIC"

With Farouk and his ministers in exile, the British on the sidelines and Nasser's revolution already beginning to sputter, Egypt needed to be governed. The RCC's Arab nationalism required nonalignment with the superpower blocs in foreign policy and rapid internal development to make Egypt and any Arab states it might lure into a "United Arab Republic" a viable "third force" in world affairs.[50] That was the soaring theory—Egypt creating impregnable Arab "internal fronts" against the encircling superpowers—but the mundane reality, Sadat reminisced, was that "we had simply not prepared ourselves for taking over government posts." The Egyptian army officers had no idea how to govern but took on ministries anyway, to keep them out of the hands of the unreformed politicians, who had never been properly purged.

Sadat dolefully described the ramshackle way the RCC governed. Since the free officers were all of the same age and rank and fiercely competitive, they felt constrained to appoint General Muhammed Naguib prime minister and chairman of the RCC for no other reason than that "he was many years our senior" and hence more "respectable." General Naguib, who hailed from Khartoum, was an interesting man who had studied at Sandhurst and toured the Maginot Line after World War II. British advisers rated him "an absolute tiger for work" and approvingly noted that he had been wounded not once but three times in 1948. As Egypt's nominal head of state, Naguib was still a tiger for work, but of the wrong sort.[51] Before abdicating, Farouk had offered Naguib command of the army and a field marshal's baton if he would desert the RCC, but Naguib had turned him down, judging the fields for enrichment better under his *own* regime. Under Naguib's direction, corrupt officers descended into shabby alliances with corrupt politicians to gain control of the key ministries and patronage positions. "The word 'I' was on every tongue," Nasser recalled bitterly. Winston Churchill got to the essence of modern dictatorship when he told the House of Commons that the Egyptian experience under Naguib and Nasser was proving that "one of the disadvantages of dictatorship is that the dictator is often dictated to by others."[52] Colonel Sadat recalled feeling shamed by the way the free officers greedily adopted the habits of Farouk and the effendis, seizing control of perks and slush funds and doling them out to widen their circles of power.[53]

Alarmed at the seedy turn Egypt's revolution was taking, Nasser disbanded all political parties in January 1953, assumed dictatorial powers and proclaimed Egypt a republic. Nasser then confiscated all of Farouk's property—worth 70 million Egyptian pounds—and used much of what was not skimmed off by officers and other public employees to pay for rural clinics, hospitals and schools. In Cairo, Nasser used the military courts to arrest and jail opponents—old-guard officers and politicians, Muslim Brothers, union leaders and democrats—or simply those who annoyed him. In 1954, he had the six senior leaders of the Muslim Brotherhood arrested and executed.[54] He reportedly had a kind old effendi who had driven him to school as a child arrested. The man asked why. Nasser answered, "I have never forgotten that you made me sit in the front seat next to the chauffeur and not with you in the back seat."[55] Nasser erected a towering bureaucracy: the RCC, a council of ministers, a joint congress, a council for production and a council for services. Nasser's sclerotic "democratic socialism," which Western commentators like Walter Lippmann rather too hastily lauded as a "system of social justice," was actually coming to resemble Moscow's embarrassingly inefficient system. For the first time, the Soviets began to take an interest in Nasser as a possible client.[56]

THE MUSLIM BROTHERHOOD

As Egypt's velvet revolution hardened along these unmistakably secular and dictatorial lines, the Muslim Brotherhood finally rebelled. They denounced Nasser's RCC, which replied by disbanding the Muslim Brothers as curtly as they had disbanded secular parties like the Wafd or Prince Abbas Halim's Labour Party. Sadat noted the frightening response of the Ikhwan al-Muslimin: "waving napkins stained with blood and chanting slogans against the revolution."[57] Founded in 1928 by Hassan el-Banna, who feared the secularization of Egypt under British rule, the Muslim Brotherhood had adopted an overtly political program in the 1930s: first to expel the British "occupiers," then to wage jihad to rid Egypt of Westernizing tendencies. With Egypt in hand, the Muslim Brotherhood planned a far more ambitious campaign: to forge Arab unity, Islamic unity and eventually world unity, which, Banna declared, "is the aim and purpose of Islam." His program was chilling. Borders would be determined by creed, not nationality, and Muslims did not even need to be a majority to stake their claim: "Every region in which there is a Muslim who says, 'There is no God but God and Muhammed is his Prophet,' is a homeland for us, having its own inviolability and security."[58] When Prime Minister Ahmed Maher quite reasonably (and safely) declared war on Germany in 1945 to win a voice for Egypt in the UN and the peace talks that would follow the Axis surrender, he was gunned down for his "unpardonable act of subservience to British interests."[59] Nasser had no idea how *many* Muslim Brothers there were by the 1950s—anywhere from half a million to two million—but in rounding up the four hundred most visible leaders in January 1954, he fired the opening shot in Cairo's war against Islamist fundamentalism, which Hosni Mubarak is still waging in Egypt, as will his son Gamal.[60]

In theory, Nasser's revolution had two stages: in the first, the entire Muslim nation, or *umma*, would unite against the foreign occupier; in the second, the *umma* would turn its knives inward, to cut out exploiters, doubters and foreign agents. But Arab *ummas* were fractious even without the meddling of "traitors" and "foreign agents." In Egypt—a typical Arab country—over 80 percent of the population were illiterate peasants living in primitive conditions; another 10 to 15 percent were poor laborers, which left a narrow band of 5 percent or less of the population with enough land and disposable income to push their government one way or the other. The Muslim Brotherhood, Egypt's second biggest political grouping after the establishment Wafd, had no difficulty mobilizing the poor against the rich. "Under the impulse of sweeping emotion," one Arab critic of Nasser wrote, "it was easy to say 'the nation wanted this and that,' but rational analysis revealed the existence of *classes* in the nation whose wills and interests were often in conflict."[61] Taking stock of Nasser and his bombastic methods, Anthony Eden chided Eisenhower in 1953 for his blind faith in the colonel: "I am sure that neither of us have any illusions about the people we are dealing with."[62]

Eisenhower still hoped to take Nasser under his wing. Whereas the Truman administration had curtailed covert operations after World War II, Ike expanded them. He sent CIA agent Kermit Roosevelt to Cairo with $3 million to "harness Arab nationalism" for the United States.[63] While Ambassador Caffery dealt with General Naguib, Roosevelt was free to work on Colonel Nasser. They became fast friends, and Roosevelt began to implement CIA director Allen Dulles's plan to endow Egypt with an American-style intelligence agency: the al-Mukhabarat al-Ammah, or General Intelligence Service, which would gradually branch into a half dozen spy agencies employing fifty thousand operatives.[64] Despite its girth and the infusion of American know-how, Egyptians scoffed at their Mukhabarat. A popular joke in the 1950s had an Egyptian fox crossing the border into Libya. "Why did you leave Egypt?" the Libyan border guards asked. "Because camels are being arrested in Egypt," the fox answered. "But you're a *fox*!" the guards exclaimed. "Yes," the fox replied, "but God knows how long it will take the Mukhabarat to figure that out."[65] When the Mukhabarat faltered, the GIS's "public eye" took up the slack. The public eye comprised hundreds of thousands of Stasi-type informers and tipsters in hotels, shops, bazaars, cafés, street corners and offices. They reported on the activities of Egyptians and foreigners for small bribes, or baksheesh, and kept the regime informed about emerging threats and public opinion.[66]

Though there seemed little appreciable difference between the new Egypt and the old, many Americans retained their enthusiasm for the RCC. Ambassador Caffery asserted in 1954 that the free officers "had done more for Egypt in two years than all their predecessors put together before them."[67] Caffery's praise might even have been true given the awful inefficiency of kings Fuad and Farouk. Sadat estimated that the free officers had built more schools in 1953 than the Farouk regime had built in the previous twenty years.[68] The RCC's agrarian reform law, blocked in 1952 but muscled into force the following year, changed the character of the Egyptian countryside. Until 1953, Egypt had been maintained by Farouk as what one witness called a "cotton plantation to supply the Lancashire mills"; peasants worked like dogs (and sold their votes) for a pittance. Under Nasser, some fellaheen finally received parcels of land and a shred of dignity.[69] Nasser—who was impressed by Tito's wartime exploits and his postwar nonalignment—consulted with the Yugoslavs on ways to create an enlightened one-party state. On Tito's advice, Nasser fashioned Egypt into a Titoist dictatorship under the colonel's "Arab Socialist Union." Khrushchev and the Soviets tried to snip Nasser's Yugoslav connection, warning Nasser that "Tito is not a communist, he is a king," but Nasser viewed such warnings as advantages, not weaknesses, of the Tito system.[70]

"LIQUIDATING CAPITALISM"

Whereas Tito had used *his* Union of Socialists to meld the five peoples of Yugoslavia, Nasser crudely applied Egypt's version to meld "the five working forces of the Egyptian population: the peasants, workers, soldiers, intellectuals and national capitalists." The descent of Egypt into political and bureaucratic stagnation, which persists to this day, might be dated from that corporatist theory, which Nasser wrote into Egypt's national charter. Sadat recalled that RCC officials too often interpreted their "custodial role" over the "five working forces" as an excuse to confiscate private property, enrich themselves and fling rivals into prison. Although Nasser worked harder—eighteen-hour days—and was more ethical than most of his colleagues—he lived in a modest house, ate simple Egyptian fare and sent his children to public schools—there were rumors that "Mr. Clean" had squirreled away millions in numbered Swiss accounts.[71] Perhaps for that reason, Nasser was emboldened to "liquidate capitalism" despite having stipulated that "national capitalists" were one of Egypt's "five working forces."[72] His economic ideas were recipes for failure; he nationalized two hundred privately owned Egyptian companies, as well as the country's banks, insurance companies and cotton exporters. He tried to start new industries from scratch: "We want to gain workers [as opposed to peasants]—even if we have to build factories we don't really need to get them."[73] Mass meetings of the free officers—supper parties of fifteen hundred or more—revealed deep rifts in the revolution. Naguib pleaded for "unity"; Nasser querulously insisted that the RCC was "not liquidating itself" despite its many compromises with the old regime, and the Salem brothers—Wing Commander Gamal and Major Salah, despised by Sadat as "nervous, hot-tempered, unbalanced, exhibitionistic and insolent"—flailed Nasser and Naguib for their "weakness" and unwillingness simply to murder all "reactionary forces."[74] With no better way available to contain his enemies, Nasser resorted to the Faroukian expedient of *buying* them, but on a far bigger scale than the fallen king had attempted. Advised by an American consulting firm to employ no more than 180,000 civil servants and 50,000 soldiers in order to spare Egypt's finances, Nasser hired 1 million bureaucrats and 600,000 troops.[75]

Nasser began negotiating with the British in October 1954 for the evacuation of their Suez Canal base. Though slowed by his ballooning bureaucracy, Nasser remained a formidable adversary. His speeches in colloquial Arabic electrified the Arab street and effectively advanced Egyptian interests under the idealistic guise of Arab nationalism.[76] "Never since the Prophet Muhammed has one man enjoyed such prestige among the Arabs as Nasser," a Syrian diplomat marveled.[77] British foreign secretary and soon-to-be prime minister Anthony Eden viewed Nasser's rise with trepidation. "We cannot hope to maintain our position in the Middle East by the methods of the *last* century," he told the cabinet in February 1953, and rather surprisingly offered to evacuate all British troops, civil servants and contractors from Suez within seven years.[78] Eden also agreed to grant Sudan—Egypt's vast hinterland—its independence, thus satisfying another of Nasser's demands. Nasser and his cohorts regarded the Nile, whose headwaters streamed up from Sudan, as indivisible and wanted to unite Egypt and Sudan into a single country, for which Sudanese independence was the essential first step. Nasser accepted Eden's deal—muttering that non-Muslim separatism in southern Sudan, the origin of the Darfur genocide in the early 2000s, could only be an "imperialist plot"—and signed the Anglo-Egyptian Evacuation Agreement.[79]

For Washington, everything was going according to plan in the 1950s. Great Britain was voluntarily surrendering the Suez Canal, and Egypt seemed to be solidifying under a dynamic, genuinely popular new regime, which could be expected, as a CIA operative in Cairo put it, "to play Nebraska to our New York."[80] The Joint Chiefs of Staff and the State Department both advocated close ties and generous military aid to Nasser's Egypt, but President Truman, pressured by the Israel lobby, vetoed military aid and extended no more than a $10 million credit for Egyptian wheat purchases from American farms. The incoming Eisenhower administration was not much more generous. Here was the first jolt in the initially promising relationship. Although the Middle Eastern desks of the State Department wanted ever closer ties with Egypt—even at the cost of trouble with Britain, France and Israel—the European desks riposted that such ties would weaken the far more important Cold War Atlantic alliance with Great Britain and France: "If . . . guerrilla warfare starts with Egyptians shooting British soldiers with American ammunition, the results could be catastrophic."[81]

THE ISRAEL LOBBY INTERVENES

Truman's political reluctance to arm and strengthen the Egyptians was shared by Eisenhower. Though supportive of Egypt, he was quickly brought around to the Israeli point of view in Washington. Scornful of the Eisenhower administration's "moral and intellectual level," Israeli foreign minister Moshe Sharett vowed to train Eisenhower, Dulles and Secretary of Defense Charles Wilson—"a person of limited horizons and slow comprehension"—up to the more agreeable level of the Truman administration.[82] "Why is America seeking a security relationship with Cairo?" the Israeli embassy in Washington queried. "It is incomprehensible to the Israeli public that the United States should furnish arms to dictators such as [Egypt's] Naguib and [Syria's] Shishakli. Such action is *not* in the U.S. tradition." Israel, Secretary of State Dulles was informed, fit better with U.S. traditions. Tel Aviv would be a far better ally, with its own domestic arms industry, key airfields and eight divisions in the field. "[The Arabs] might be hesitant," an Israeli official declared, "but *we* are prepared to fight along with the West," against the Soviets or any other enemy.[83]

When the British tried to enlist the United States in the Baghdad Pact—which joined Britain, Turkey, Iraq, Iran and Pakistan in a security system in 1955—the Israelis expressed shock and intervened in Washington whenever Dulles seriously considered joining the alliance. The Israel lobby insisted that Washington *exclude* itself from such broad regional pacts and instead negotiate bilateral treaties with

Israel and any other states "willing to cooperate." Bilateral treaties were less likely to demand concessions on Palestinian land and refugees than regional pacts, which would make such concessions part of any regional security agenda. Tel Aviv in the 1950s strove to fence off Washington from any largely Arab organization that might weaken the U.S. government's special relationship with Israel. The Israelis also scuttled American efforts to broker a peace with the surrounding Arab states. "What price would Israel pay for peace?" Henry Byroade, the head of the State Department's Near Eastern office, asked the Israeli foreign minister in 1953. "None" was the answer. Israeli prime minister David Ben-Gurion coldly explained why: "Arabs have land thirty-six times [the size of] Israel, have water and oil, and hence do not *need* additional territory."[84] The Arab states would be given no option but to recognize as permanent the temporary borders agreed to (by Israel, Syria, Jordan, Lebanon and Egypt) in the General Armistice Agreements of 1949 and settle the Palestinian refugees on their *own* soil, while Israel distributed the land it had confiscated from the Palestinians during the war of 1948 to new waves of Jewish immigrants from Europe, North Africa and Iraq.

Ben-Gurion calculated that the future of Israel depended on making Jewish babies as fast as the Arabs made theirs, and on massive Jewish immigration. "The Western powers will only take Israel seriously when she has a population of at least 6 million," he told an Israeli officer in 1953. To get there, he sought no fewer than two million Eastern European immigrants in the 1950s. Though he disliked the temperament of these new postwar Zionists—"self-centered, city-bred softies"—they would just have to do.[85] This Israeli determination to reel in the diaspora caused embarrassment in Washington, which somehow had to explain to its Arab allies why a country that could not take back a half million Arab refugees could find room for four times as many Jewish immigrants.[86] With its Middle Eastern bastions in Egypt, Jordan and Iraq, London was at least as discomfited. "The centre of infection in the region is Israel," UK ambassador John Nicholls wrote from Tel Aviv in 1955, "and I believe that we must treat the Israelis as a sick people." Scarred by "2,500 years of Jewish history," they were "psychologically unstable and [not] capable of a mature foreign policy." Nicholls worried that the Israelis did not always "coolly reckon the odds" and were capable of a "suicidal policy."[87]

The Arab states were made to understand that they would have to live with whatever shocks Israel dealt to the region's delicate system. On Israel's independence day in April 1953, Ben-Gurion boasted that Israel had used immigration to increase its Jewish population from 650,000 to 1.45 million in just four years. Jewish settlements had doubled in that period and had expanded Israeli land under culti-vation from 175,000 acres (3.5 percent of the country) in 1948 to 875,000 acres (15 percent of the country) in 1953. Rapid development like that required water, which explained Israel's controversial effort to divert the Jordan River waters from the Syrian border into new Jewish settlements on the coastal plains and in the Negev Desert.[88] Hank Byroade, who counted himself among the State Department's "Arabists"—a few dozen Foreign Service officers who were anti-Israel and pro-Arab on the grounds that Israel had taken too much land and expelled too many refugees in 1948—pushed hard to stop the Jordan waters diversion. He also tried to persuade Dulles to assert that the Israeli Law of Return, which welcomed any Jew anywhere in the world to take Israeli citizenship, created legitimate security concerns for Tel Aviv's neighbors. Byroade was later forced by Dulles to apologize for his comments and reassure the Israelis that the rather mild pressure he had attempted to exert had reflected his "personal views," not the warmer, more political attitude of the Eisen-hower administration.[89] Thwarted in the 1950s, the Israelis won through in 1963, when they successfully diverted 75 percent of the Jordan River water into Israel.[90]

While Byroade mumbled his apologies, Ben-Gurion planned to use massive immigration to shift Israel's center of gravity from the cities and coast to the Negev. "This country isn't just a Jewish hotel," he snorted. Jews would have to leave the comfortable cities like Jerusalem, Tel Aviv and Haifa and settle in hardscrabble agricultural communities in the south, which would bring out the best in them. Israel's conception of the Negev—seized after a breach of the armistice of 1948—as a great frontier in need of settlement ran head-on into Nasser's insistence that the entire Negev be restored to the Arabs as a bridge between Egypt to Jordan.[91] Settling the frontiers and demilitarized zones around Israel was also a good way to seize additional Arab territory without resort to war. Moshe Dayan confessed as much years later:

> It worked like this: we would send a tractor to plow some place in the de-militarized zone where nothing could be grown and we knew ahead of time that the Syrians would shoot. If they didn't shoot, we would tell the trac-tor to move deeper, until the Syrians got mad and eventually fired on it. And then we would activate artillery and the air force . . . We thought . . . that we can change the armistice lines by a series of military operations that are less than war.[92]

(Nasser and the other Arab leaders were furious that Israel got away with calling itself a "status quo state" that only wanted peace and recognition, when Israel was actually engaged in a continual, creeping revision of the region's borders.)

In 1955, Hank Byroade left Washington to become U.S. ambassador to Egypt. He was chosen because of his Arabist outlook and also because, at forty-two, he was close to Nasser in age. When the two met, Byroade took an immediate liking to Nasser. The colonel, still in possession of the feeble arsenal inherited from Farouk, requested American military aid, and Byroade recommended a $28 million package of artillery, medium tanks and B-26 bombers.[93] Washington agreed, but on condition that the weapons never be employed in *offensive* operations. Those were the pacific terms of the American Mutual Security Act, which the Israelis would blithely violate the following year. Since the Egyptians were contemplating offensives against Israel and the British-run canal zone, they rejected the American terms as an infringement of their sovereignty and appealed to the more permissive Soviets. This had always been the nightmare of Ike and Dulles, and it quickly materialized. Initially patronizing where the free officers were concerned—the 1952 edition of the *Great Soviet Encyclopedia* had deemed the RCC a "reactionary . . . petit-bourgeois grouping serving . . . the interests of the Americans"—Nikita Khrushchev waved off those doctrinaire cavils and, after securing payment in cotton, shipped off a $100 million arms package to Egypt in 1955.[94]

Those first Soviet transfers of Czech arms to the Egyptians—quickly followed by Russian MiGs, Ilyushin jet bombers and tanks—represented a sea change in Moscow's approach to the Middle East. Until the 1950s, the Soviets had backed Israel—a country founded by Russian and Eastern European Jews—as their most likely lever in the Middle East, which was either dominated by the Western powers or split between a bewildering array of "reactionary" Muslim clerics, tribes and thrones, all quite religious and instinctively hostile to godless communism. ("We deny all morality taken from superhuman or non-class conceptions," Lenin had declared, which would not endear him to any but the most secular Muslims.)[95] Stalin's "Doctors' Plot" in 1953, cooked up to justify a purge of liberal Soviet Jews, began the shift away from Israel to the Arabs. Zionism in Soviet eyes suddenly became as odious a concept as Trotskyism or Titoism. *Pravda* summed up the new Soviet position on Israel: Tel Aviv was now a haven of "international Jewish bourgeois-nationalists," more dangerous even than "backward Arabs." From now on, Arab aggression against Israel would be justified by Soviet theorists as "revolutionary, proletarian, *just* war" against "Western imperialism" and its "Zionist vestige."[96] The sharp smell of anti-Semitism in Soviet policy—cunning Israel had been "minted on Wall Street"—helped to rally the Arabs. Khrushchev was less of a Jew-baiter than Stalin, but still insisted that "spying and provocation [by Russian Jews] would be channeled through Israel," which lay "under the thumb of American reactionaries."[97]

Gamal Nasser presented Khrushchev with a golden opportunity to step out of the shadow of Stalin—"no foreign aid to non-communist states"—and try out his own, more flexible theories about ex-colonies. According to Khrushchev, decolonized countries fell into three categories: prodigies like China, North Korea and North Vietnam that had bloomed into communist states; "progressive," *potentially* pro-Soviet ones like India, Syria and Egypt that had broken with the old imperial powers; and "reactionary" pro-Western ones like Iran and the Philippines that were nominally independent but still bound by "unequal treaties" with the old imperialists. As the Cold War moved into its second decade, Khrushchev wanted to push Soviet influence into the second category of states, and he pinned his hopes on Nasser. The charismatic Egyptian colonel seemed the perfect vehicle for Moscow's new strategy, which would use the pent-up nationalism and resentments of otherwise backward societies like Egypt as a substitute for "revolutionary proletariats" in the global struggle against the Western powers.[98]

"A HEAD FOR AN EYE . . ."

That pent-up Egyptian nationalism got a terrific jolt in February 1955, when the Israeli army—hewing to its new "doctrine of retaliatory action"—attacked Gaza and killed and wounded seventy Egyptian troops in reprisal for the murder, by Palestinian fedayeen based in the Egyptian-administered Gaza Strip, of an Israeli man who had been bicycling to the Jewish settlement at Rehovot.[99] Nasser, who had made much of his invigorating renaissance, felt humiliated by the swift, bloody action. He had made the hajj to Mecca in 1954 and pledged to end "the foreign occupation of Muslim territories."[100] Now it appeared that the "foreigners"—in this case the Israelis, led into Gaza by a beefy, twenty-seven-year-old major named Ariel Sharon—were thrashing Nasser instead. When one of Nasser's officers arrived in Damascus just after the raid to confer with the Syrians, they laughed at him and his depreciated inventory of tanks, trucks and artillery—60 percent of which were under repair—and his small mound of ammunition, which was estimated to be sufficient for no more than one hour of modern combat. "You have come to help *Syria* defend herself? Perhaps you had better see to your *own* defense needs."[101]

Those Syrian jibes were on target, for the Israeli swipe at Gaza had been entirely predictable. Ever since 1948, when the victorious Israelis had drawn borders in the sand around their new state, Palestinian fedayeen and refugees had been breaking back into Israel to farm, seek water and rejoin their broken families, but also to steal, vandalize, murder and kidnap. Since the war of 1948 had not been capped with a peace treaty, the Arabs felt free to come and go on land they considered their own and to attack any Jewish "settlers" they might find there. The Israelis defended their new country no less severely; they launched reprisal raids into the neighboring Arab states—killing hundreds of innocent civilians—and in 1952 alone the Israeli border police shot 620 Arabs trying to slip in and out of Israel. The Israelis permitted Arab families broken by the 1948 fighting to reunite in Israel if they could prove that at least one family member had remained in Palestine despite the fighting. Many Palestinian refugees tried to beat the system by sneaking back into Israel from the West Bank, Gaza or Lebanon, and the Israelis—trying to keep their Arab minority to a bare minimum—greeted them with bullets and left their unburied corpses rotting in the fields to deter other interlopers.[102]

Under nibbling, chronic attack—not unlike the situation today—the Israel Defense Forces (IDF) laid out its "doctrine of retaliatory action," which asserted that Israel would *always* counterattack with disproportionate force to deter future aggressors. That doctrine of the 1950s lay behind Israel's demolition of Lebanon's airports, roads, bridges, electrical stations and harbors in 2006 after Hezbollah had kidnapped two Israeli soldiers and fired missiles into Haifa. In October 1953—angered by an Arab grenade attack on an Israeli settlement that killed a mother and her two children—Major Ariel Sharon's elite Unit 101 crossed into the West Bank, surrounded the village of Kibya and killed every man, woman and child there. Reserve officer Sharon, who had been studying history at Hebrew University when the orders came to form a counterterrorist unit, then butchered Kibya's livestock and dynamited the houses, school and mosque. Sixty-six corpses were found in the village after Sharon's withdrawal. A stupefied President Eisenhower—still theoretically committed to "impartiality" in the Middle East—initially criticized the "merciless severity" of the Israelis and deemed their tactics "more like a head for an eye than an eye for an eye." Israeli prime minister David Ben-Gurion lied that

Israeli troops had not been involved, then coldly dropped the charade: "Our future depends not on what the *goyim* say, but on what the Jews do." Spilled Jewish blood needed to be avenged to reassure Israeli citizens (and prospective immigrants) and deter the encircling Arabs. "Yes," Israel's foreign minister shot back, "but it is also important what the *goyim* say."[103]

THE BIRTH OF AIPAC

Not that important: although Eisenhower and Dulles resolved to punish Israel for its savagery by cutting $26 million of aid, that proposed cut was immediately restored after intense lobbying from New York's congressional delegation, B'nai B'rith, Hadassah, the United Synagogue of America, the American Jewish Committee, the United Jewish Appeal and a potent new lobbying group formed in 1954 called AIPAC—the American Israel Public Affairs Committee. Interestingly, Ike and Dulles also restored aid to the Israelis so that a Republican censure of Israel would not entrench Democrat Robert Wagner in the New York mayor's mansion. Secretary of State Dulles protested that domestic political pressures were shoehorning him into "the policy of the previous administration, which had brought no peace but only trouble." The British, who had spent the 1930s and 1940s trying to wriggle out of their own commitment to a Jewish national home in Palestine, now urged the Americans to cut their losses too: Israel was a lost cause "surrounded by 40 million implacably hostile Arabs, devoid of natural resources, inhabited by a semi-Oriental population with negligible competitive skills, and utterly dependent on the whims of foreign governments and the good will of Jews abroad."[104] Whims and goodwill— chiefly from the United States—supplied 75 to 80 percent of Israeli government revenues in the 1950s and covered the outflow of dollars needed to finance Israel's chronic trade deficits. Those American donations were an obvious lever to shift Israeli policy away from retaliatory action like Sharon's and toward a final settlement of the land and refugee questions, but Dulles—like his predecessors—simply refused to pull the lever. Nor did he threaten to scale back America's guarantee of Israel's security. Military aid—or the promise of it in extremis—"is the one positive inducement we have to offer Israel to induce her to make concessions," a British diplomat remarked in 1955.[105] But the Israelis were shrewder; they were beginning to grasp that they could have the American security guarantee for free. The U.S.

ambassador to the United Nations, Henry Cabot Lodge, Jr., regretted this obeisance to the pro-Israel lobby but consoled himself thus: "It is not possible to please the Arabs anyway; they are childish; all we can do is set a standard for international peace and justice."[106]

In the wake of the Gaza raid, Cairo appealed for that American-administered "international standard." Nasser certainly distrusted the Soviet Union, whose "bloc policy" and calls for a Russian-led "world revolution" struck many Arabs as just another form of imperialism.[107] But the Egyptians interpreted Washington's failure to punish Israeli aggression in the 1950s as proof that *Egypt* was being "punished" for its nonalignment as well as its efforts to block Lebanese and Jordanian adhesion to the British-run Baghdad Pact. Sadat called the Israeli raid "a turning point in the history of Egypt" because it drove Nasser into the Soviet camp to fight "the colonial hegemony of Israel and the West."[108] Studying the raid in 1955, British analysts were left with the sneaking suspicion that the Israelis had launched it, on the very day that the Iraqis were joining the Baghdad Pact, to sow chaos and freeze any warming in American-Arab relations.[109] By hitting the Egyptians and provoking an international outcry, the Israelis forced the United States to take a position in favor of Israel, which drove a knife into Washington's relations with the wider Arab world.

Already in the 1950s the Americans were finding that their Israeli alliance left them scant room for maneuver in the Middle East. The Israeli government and IDF were fine-tuning a process they called "escalation dominance." By hitting back at fedayeen attacks with disproportionate force, they were actually aggressing without appearing to be the aggressor.[110] And when they wanted war to fine-tune their borders, they could bring one on by launching reprisal raids so big as to make Syrian, Jordanian or Egyptian intervention inevitable. No wonder Israeli prime minister David Ben-Gurion refused to trade land for peace and refused to let Palestinian refugees back into Israel. Permanent tension proved useful.[111] When lobbying, stonewalling and "escalation management" didn't work, the Israelis resorted to sabotage. Worried by America's friendly relationship with Nasser and the RCC as well as Britain's pending withdrawal from the Suez base, Israeli defense minister Pinhas Lavon activated several Israeli agents inside Egypt to bomb U.S. facilities and simulate *Arab* terrorist attacks in 1954. Israeli operatives attacked the U.S. consulate in Alexandria and the American-owned Cinema Metro in Cairo. The deception was discovered only when an Israeli operative caught fire when his bomb detonated as he looked for a seat in a movie theater in Alexandria. (Israeli agents had launched similar attacks in Iraq in 1950, where, posing as Arab terrorists, they threw hand grenades into Baghdad cafés frequented by Iraqi Jews and bombed the U.S. Information Center, to goad the Iraqis into expelling Iraq's hundred thousand Jews and to sour Baghdad's relations with Washington.)[112] In 1954, the Egyptian Mukhabarat tortured their Israeli captives till they coughed up the names in Lavon's terrorist network. Lavon resigned in disgrace, the bungled plot having arisen from disastrous competition between the Mossad and Israeli military intelligence. Prime Minister Ben-Gurion retired from public life to live on a remote kibbutz in the Negev Desert, and Israel's American benefactors may have wished that they could too.[113]

There was another problem. American strategy for the Middle East under Eisenhower envisioned Egypt in much the same light as President George W. Bush and Vice President Dick Cheney would later view Iraq: as a client state that would provide bases and "access" for Western ground, air and naval forces. Egypt would bury the hatchet with Israel and become an American-backed front in the Cold War against the Soviet Union. Yet such a view of Egypt as an American client and a good neighbor to Israel contradicted the very nationalism and anti-Zionism that had inspired the free officers to rebel against Farouk and his British masters in the first place.[114] Moreover, for an Egyptian alliance to work, Cairo needed to be accepted as a primary partner, not a secondary one subject to behind-the-scenes Israeli vetting. Compounding the problem, the Soviets had successfully staked their future in the Middle East on anti-Israel policies. To lure key states like Egypt away from the Western allies, the Soviet Union had broken diplomatic relations with Israel in 1953 and vetoed U.S. efforts to open the Straits of Tiran, the narrow sea passage between the Sinai and Arabian Peninsulas, to free navigation, which would have given the Israelis unfettered access to the Red Sea, the Indian Ocean and their rising daily oil imports. Those early Soviet moves drew an unmistakable line in the sand: the Americans and the Israelis on one side, the Soviets and the Arabs on the other. Under such conditions, American talk of "impartiality" seemed increasingly meaningless.

The election of Eisenhower and the Republicans in 1952 had raised hopes in Egypt and the Arab world that American policy would tilt away from the pro-Israel policies pursued by the Democrats toward a pro-Arab policy. Like secretaries Forrestal and Marshall in the Truman administration, Ike and his secretary of state, John Foster Dulles, initially viewed Israel as a net liability in the global struggle against the Soviet Union and vowed to inaugurate a policy of "friendly impartiality" in the Arab-Israeli conflict. Ike blurted out that he had *never* supported the creation

of Israel, "but now that it is done, we'll have to live with it."[115] That Republican cool-
ness toward Israel was summed up in the keynote address that General Douglas
MacArthur delivered to the Republican Convention which nominated Eisenhower.
MacArthur charged that the pro-Israel policies of the Democrats had cost the
United States valuable friends in the Middle East. Such candor was ill-advised on
the American political scene, and MacArthur and the Republicans were roundly
punished: 75 percent of American Jews voted for Adlai Stevenson in the 1952
elections.

Still, Ike's abandonment by Jewish voters did leave the president-elect with little
to lose if he were to shift to a pro-Arab foreign policy. And there was little disso-
nance in his administration. Unlike Truman, who routinely opposed the "striped-
pants boys of the State Department," Eisenhower and Dulles—as a White House
speechwriter put it—"were two men who thought like one." Entering office in 1953,
they agreed to ignore the cajolery of Jewish pressure groups and act only in the
broad strategic interests of the United States. That clear Republican change of course
was picked up by Abba Eban, Israel's ambassador to the United States, who alerted
Tel Aviv that the "strong Israel" policies of Harry Truman were nothing more "than
a fleeting and accidental circumstance of history." Eban warned that the Republicans would almost certainly "upgrade the Arab interest" and "downgrade" Israel's
in Washington.[116] Much more important than Israel in the Cold War, Ike and Dulles
reasoned, was the arc of Arab states that enclosed the southern flank of the Soviet
Union and the pools of Arab oil (and pipelines and tanker routes) that powered the
United States, Western Europe and Japan. With Eisenhower committed to a "peace
dividend" after World War II and Korea, his "New Look" defense policy also skimped
on conventional forces and relied on regional defense systems like the Baghdad
Pact.[117] From the Israeli perspective, these were dangerous, potentially fatal omens.

In May 1953, Secretary of State Dulles embarked on a "listening tour" of the
Middle East and South Asia to assess the prospects for an American-coordinated
security system. As a member of the Baghdad Pact's military committee—but not
of the pact itself—the United States now considered becoming a full political participant as well. But Dulles's "listening tour" went badly. None of the Arab governments on Dulles's itinerary would agree to join a pact that included the British, and
none were reconciled to the existence of a Jewish state in Palestine largely populated
by European settlers. In Jordan, Dulles was astonished to learn that Palestinian
refugees driven from their homes in 1948 comprised 50 percent of the Jordanian

population. This brooding mass of fugitives more than the political attitude of the Hashemite king or the meddling of Colonel Nasser shaped Jordan's decision *not* to join the Baghdad Pact. So long as the Israelis occupied the broad borders of the General Armistice Agreements of 1949 instead of the more modest borders of the UN Partition Plan of 1947, Jordan's horde of Palestinians wanted nothing to do with Israel or the Western powers, and King Hussein had little choice but to go along with them.[118] Normal relations with Israel would be political suicide. In Lebanon, where Palestinian refugees comprised 11 percent of the population, the prime minister scolded Dulles at their Beirut meeting for his assertion of "friendly impartiality," when America was all too obviously winking at Israeli reprisal raids and even defending them at the UN: "You must show us acts, not words."

Dining with General Naguib and Colonel Nasser in Cairo, Secretary of State Dulles learned that the Egyptians feared the British and Israelis far more than "international communism."[119] In Jerusalem, the American secretary of state found the Israelis more comforting. Prime Minister Ben-Gurion—delighted that Dulles had permitted himself to be lured to "official" meetings in disputed Jerusalem, not Tel Aviv—reassured Dulles that Israel was "geographically in the Levant, but culturally a Western nation" that would loyally battle communism. Having resolved to implant a "good attitude" and "wide philosophical grasp" in the new Republican administration, the Israelis succeeded stunningly. In Israel in 1953, they played Dulles like a harp. Meeting with Foreign Minister Moshe Sharett, Dulles gushed that Israel—unlike Egypt—"had a sense of history" and grasped the serious nature of the struggle against communism. The Arabs, he confided, just did not get it. They were too narrow-minded and spiteful.[120]

Still, Dulles was torn. Before the trip, Dulles had oscillated between the positions of his Near Eastern and European desks, between pro-Arab and pro-British-French-Israeli policies. After the trip, Dulles acknowledged that close association with London—led by an increasingly cantankerous Churchill and Eden—could only injure American interests in the Middle East. "The United States suffers from being linked to British and French imperialism," Dulles told Ike's National Security Council. "The days when the Middle East used to *relax* under the presence of British protection are gone."[121] Dulles now inclined to the view of his assistant secretary of state for Near Eastern affairs, Hank Byroade, that Egypt be "used as an opening wedge to reestablish our position in the Arab world." But "a *real* effort was needed," Dulles exhorted in June 1953.[122] In his last meetings with the Israelis in May, he had complained that the Israel lobby's efforts in Washington had led to "U.S. policy in the Middle East not always in the best interests of the *total* situation" and had promised to regain control of that "total situation" by treating the Arab regimes more equitably. In Baghdad, the last stop on the trip, he had wired Eisenhower that "time is short before loss [of Arab goodwill] becomes irretrievable," owing to "basic skepticism as to whether any United States administration can follow any policy not approved by Zionists."[123]

But Dulles's every effort to retrieve Arab goodwill was blunted by the Israel lobby, which stoutly resisted American proposals to aid the economies and arsenals of the Arab states. Pro-Arab in 1952, Dulles had become pro-Israel by 1953. Really that came as no surprise. Dulles had advised the Dewey presidential campaigns in 1944 and 1948 and competed vigorously for Jewish votes with the Democrats, applauding the "character and resolution" of the Zionists, urging early aid and recognition for Israel after World War II and attacking President Truman's secretary of state George Marshall for his attempts to rein in the Jewish state in 1948.[124]

Eisenhower came around to the Israeli position more slowly than Dulles, but pressure to win votes in November 1952 followed by lunches and parleys with Jewish lobby groups in New York and Washington, as well as Eisenhower's warm relationship with Rabbi Abba Hillel Silver—who liked Ike, not Stevenson, in 1952—served eventually to convert the president too. In October 1952, Ike had sent a message to a Republican fund-raising dinner in New York extolling "the valiant state of Israel, democracy's outpost in the Middle East." He enjoined "every American who loves liberty to join the effort to make secure forever the future of this newest member in the family of nations." Eisenhower suggested that the eight hundred thousand Palestinian refugees trapped in the ghastly camps of 1948 might be better suited to a desert life anyway than to Israel's modern economy.[125] So much for "friendly impartiality": although Dulles professed to loathe the Israeli pressure in Washington— "the paid advertisements, the mass meetings, the resolutions, the demands of Zionist organizations, the veiled threats of domestic political reprisals"—he was ultimately as vulnerable to such pressure as Marshall and Acheson had been.[126] The Israeli embassy in Washington delightedly reported in 1953 that the Republicans were finally learning that with national elections every two years they too needed always to "prefer the future over the past." The GOP had polled poorly among American Jews in 1952, but could do much better in 1954 and 1956. "There are 5 million Jewish voters in the U.S. and very few Arabs," Eisenhower reflected.[127]

THE BAGHDAD PACT

Ike's internally driven change of line left Dulles with fewer external options, and the anticommunist Middle East defense organization he helped create in February 1955 included only the non-Arab states of the region: Turkey, Iran and Pakistan. It was named the "Baghdad Pact" in the expectation that the Iraqis might be induced to join and give it an Arab member, and it was pessimistically based on the old British imperial model of using the limitless, cheap manpower of the Indian subcontinent—Pakistanis, in this case—to defend the Arabs and the Persians.[128] The Iraqis did eventually join, but were instantly set upon by Nasser's propagandists as "British pawns" until Iraq's own Arab nationalist coup of 1958 forced Iraq's withdrawal from the pact.

The controversy surrounding the Baghdad Pact of the 1950s held important lessons for British and American strategists. The pact seemed harmless enough—a Western-led anticommunist defense community—but Nasser struck a chord in the Arab capitals with his argument that adhesion to the pact would subvert Arab neutrality and bind the Arabs to "Western imperialism." Nasser's real thoughts and motives were cloudier: he did believe in neutrality—a free hand between the superpower blocs—but he also believed in Egyptian primacy and feared that an oil-rich, Western-armed Iraq would supplant Egypt as the dominant Arab power. With its British air bases, Anglophile elites (just like Farouk's effendis) and an unashamedly pro-Western king—Faisal II—and prime minister—General Nuri as-Said—Iraq, joined to the abundant manpower of Pakistan and Turkey—a NATO and Council of Europe member—might make a far more practical nucleus for Middle Eastern defense efforts than Egypt.[129]

In London, Churchill and Eden wanted to *use* this Iraqi-Egyptian rivalry to rip the Arab nationalist movement apart. They wanted to pull the United States, Iraq and Jordan into the Baghdad Pact to show Nasser that Egypt was *not* indispensable and to harden the Middle East against Soviet encroachment. In Washington, Ike and Dulles—still viewing themselves as virtuous anti-imperialists—shrank from such manipulation and dumbly accepted Nasser's (nervous) argument that the Baghdad Pact was just "an instrument of British policy" aimed at "breaking the Arab necklace and scattering its beads." The Americans also heeded Saudi and Israeli admonitions *not* to join the pact because it would strengthen Iraq—which sought leadership of the Arab world through control of the Fertile Crescent—at Egypt's expense, but also their own.[130]

Whereas Truman had tacked away from Roosevelt's anti-European policies because of the global demands of the Cold War (and the need for European allies), Eisenhower and Dulles now tacked back in the opposite direction. This was startling, inasmuch as Ike had entered the presidential race in 1952 in large part to deny the Republican nomination to isolationist senator Robert Taft and to buttress "the basic Truman strategy of cooperation with allies and collective security for containing the Soviet Union."[131] Truman had actually slowed the retraction of British power around the globe; Eisenhower now tried to accelerate it. On the eve of the Suez Crisis—the tumultuous Anglo-Egyptian showdown of 1956—Eden blasted Eisenhower's "uncertain diplomacy" and regretted Washington's deepening dependence on Saudi Arabia, "the most backward and greedy of states."

America, Eden sensibly concluded, needed to do three things. First, if it truly wanted to manage the defense of the Middle East and play a constructive role, it needed to resolve the inherent contradiction of *any* Middle Eastern defense organization in which Arab members would "not be a promising nucleus because they would direct themselves against Israel, not against external dangers."[132] To remove this fatal contradiction, Eisenhower would have to take on the Israel lobby in Washington and actually enact a policy of "evenhandedness," extracting major, painful concessions from Israel. Second, America needed to "accept the split in the Arab world between Iraq and Egypt," embrace it as a useful point of attack on the more mischievous aspects of Arab nationalism and neutralism, and stop trying to ingratiate itself with *both* nations, which merely empowered the Arabs, not the West. Third, America needed to drop its unilateral methods—its affectation of virtue and clean hands—and take a side. Throw your weight into the Baghdad Pact, Eden urged. "An ounce of membership will be worth all the havering, and save a ton of trouble later on."[133]

Unfortunately, "havering"—Scottish for wandering aimlessly—became American policy in the Middle East. When Nasser purchased arms and took in advisers from the Soviet Union in 1955, Dulles was approached by Iraq's pro-American prime minister, Nuri as-Said. "Will you *now* divert aid previously intended for Egypt to us?" Nuri eagerly inquired. "No," Dulles replied, for such a move might cause "serious trouble throughout the Middle East" and might disturb Washington's relations with Egypt, Saudi Arabia and Israel. Prime Minister Nuri was puzzled by this American timidity—so unexpected from a superpower—and the CIA reported that the

Iraqi army chief of staff was also confused: "But we joined the Baghdad Pact to *replace* Egypt as the leader of the Arab world." Iraqis, he sputtered, are "seething at these intricacies of American policy."[134] If Nasser was wooing the Soviets and Nuri the Americans, why shouldn't Iraq get American aid and arms?

Those "American intricacies" were unintentional; Dulles was muddling through, and ignoring British advice to use Iraq to pry concessions out of Egypt was just one symptom of a larger muddle. Even had Eisenhower decided to tilt away from Cairo in favor of Baghdad, he would have been torpedoed by the Israel lobby on Capitol Hill, which actually blocked American aid to Iraq in 1955 on the grounds that it would "create a more intimate relationship between Iraq and the United States than that which existed between Israel and the United States."[135] Here was more evidence of the informal control that Israel exercised over American foreign policy. In view of Dulles's muddling—he denigrated Iraqi efforts "to build up influence in the Arab world and challenge Egyptian leadership" when the Iraqis were pro-American and the Egyptians anti-American—it is easy to see why Eden and the French would completely misjudge American conduct during the upcoming Suez Crisis.[136] There did not seem to *be* a coherent American policy, so the British and French felt confident that Washington—"weak and irresolute . . . , tepid about taking any vigorous action," in the judgment of the British ambassador; "rambling and not very definite" in the judgment of Harold Macmillan after meetings with Ike in September 1956—would accept their thesis that Nasser was a troublemaker and a tool of international communism.[137]

BRITAIN LEAVES EGYPT

The last British soldier left Egyptian soil on June 19, 1956, in accordance with the evacuation agreement signed two years earlier. Egypt, Nasser exulted, was finally "liberated from imperialist control." Crowds cheered and whistled as signs on Cairo's English Bridge were ripped off and replaced with new ones that read "Evacuation Bridge." Four days later Nasser accepted full domestic, foreign and military powers from the RCC.[138] He was now a dictator. Until that moment, Dulles, the State Department "Arabists" and the British Foreign Office had hopefully encouraged Cairo with a program of economic and political incentives they code-named "Alpha." The Alpha program relied on economic "carrots" to bring Egypt into the anticommunist camp and to coax Cairo into "leading rather than following public opinion." Washington expected that, granted Alpha aid, Nasser would agree to negotiate a "final settlement" with Israel, which would have the salutary effect of weakening Soviet influence in the Middle East by solving, once and for all, the "Palestinian question."[139] Alpha's centerpiece was Eisenhower's pledge of $400 million to build the 365-foot-tall Aswan High Dam, which would control Nile flooding, improve navigation, generate half of Egypt's electricity, irrigate seven hundred thousand acres of desert, create a vast new freshwater lake and give concrete proof of America's willingness to give economic aid to developing noncommunist countries.[140]

To lock in a return on this American investment, Ike dispatched his navy secretary, Texas banker Robert Anderson, to Cairo. In secret meetings with Nasser, Anderson asked the colonel to recognize Israel, accept its frontiers as permanent and push for peace in the region.[141] Nasser refused: "You know I couldn't do anything like that! I'd be assassinated!" Anderson recalled that Nasser mentioned four times during their meeting the assassination of Jordanian king Abdullah I in 1951 by an Arab tailor's apprentice, who had shot the king in Jerusalem to stop him from signing a peace treaty with Israel. Nasser was confessing his greatest fear: were he ever to recognize Israel, he too would be murdered.[142]

"NASSER IS A COMPLETE STUMBLING BLOCK . . ."

Eisenhower writhed in frustration. He was seeking a path across the sucking quicksand of the Middle East and considered Nasser useless as an ally. "Nasser proved to be a complete stumbling block," Ike fumed to his diary in March 1956. "He just made speeches, all of which must breathe defiance of Israel." The Israelis were just as bad—their slogan "is not one inch of ground and their incessant demand is for arms"—but at least the Israelis were usually pro-American.[143] The Egyptian colonel's intransigence on Israel, his subversive activities in Saudi Arabia, Iraq, Jordan and Libya aimed at annexing the monarchies there to a "United Arab Republic," his prompt recognition of Mao Zedong's People's Republic of China and his turn to the Soviet Union for arms persuaded Eisenhower that Nasser was incorrigible and Alpha unworkable.[144]

Egged on by conservative Republicans like Senator William Knowland of California, Ike abruptly cancelled Alpha and replaced it with "Omega": a program of "sticks," designed, as Dulles put it, "to let Colonel Nasser realize that he cannot cooperate as he is doing with the Soviet Union and at the same time enjoy most-favored-nation treatment from the United States." Omega would prick Nasser's bubble by stopping all arms shipments to Egypt and suspending financial and economic aid, leaving him wholly dependent on the more penurious Soviets.[145] To launch Omega with a bang, Dulles withdrew the $400 million financing for the Aswan High Dam, which Ike had pledged in July 1956. Nasser's behavior, Dulles declared, "had not been such as to generate goodwill toward Egypt on the part of the American people." His embrace of the Soviets was "the most dangerous development since Korea."[146] The American secretary of state delighted in the change of line, from cooperation to coercion. "Okay," Dulles sneered to the Egyptian ambassador, "now you can go to *Moscow* for your money." Many later attributed the entire Suez Crisis to this misplaced American truculence. Dulles, an onlooker noted, "kicked Nasser in the teeth, with a missionary twist."[147]

The French ambassador in Washington immediately divined the next move. "What can the Egyptians do? They will do *something* about Suez. That's the only way they can touch the Western countries."[148] In a fiery speech carried on Voice of the Arabs radio from Alexandria's Al-Manshiah Square on July 26, 1956, Nasser reached out and touched the West, just exactly as French ambassador Maurice Couve de Murville had predicted. The colonel announced that the shares of the Suez Canal Company, which had been in British and French hands since 1875, would be confiscated and nationalized forthwith to compensate Egypt for decades of exploitation as well as Dulles's termination of the Aswan Dam loans. Anticipating an angry Western reaction, Nasser mocked Britain, France and America: "May you choke to death on your fury!"[149]

THE SUEZ CRISIS

Eisenhower appeared oddly unfazed by Cairo's expropriation of Western assets. "Egypt is within its rights," he declared, "and there is nothing to do."[150] Dulles also downplayed what was being called the "Suez Crisis" as "fundamentally a business dispute." U.S. secretary of defense Charles Wilson scoffed that "the Suez Canal thing is just a ripple."[151] But it was anything but a "ripple" to the British and the French. If Nasser confiscated the canal and used it to manipulate Europe's energy supply, he would convulse the Western economies and weaken the Western powers in Europe *and* the Middle East, where Western influence would gradually be replaced by "neutralist" national movements or Soviet ones.[152] "Hit Nasser hard, and quickly," Iraq's King Faisal II urgently advised Anthony Eden, who had succeeded Churchill as prime minister in 1955.[153] If Nasser survived the crisis, he would move against all the monarchical Middle Eastern regimes that were mainstays of Western influence and the chief source of Europe's oil. Eden wrote Eisenhower in September 1956 (accurately) forecasting "that Nasser believes that if he can get away with *this* . . . his prestige in Arabia will be so great that he will be able to mount revolutions of young officers in Saudi Arabia, Jordan, Syria and Iraq."[154] Hoping to touch an anticommunist nerve in Washington, Eden then declared that "Nasser . . . is now effectively in Russian hands, just as Mussolini was in Hitler's."[155]

Dulles now swerved back to the Franco-British position. He told the French that Egyptian control of the canal "would not be tolerated" and he told the British that Nasser must be forced "to disgorge what he was attempting to swallow." From those meetings, the French and British emerged convinced that the Americans were really on *their* side. Although Eisenhower chided the British for "making of Nasser a much more important figure than he is," Ike allowed in secret meetings that he "did not rule out the use of force." That seemed like a signal to Eden, who had vowed to Ike that he would go all the way on this issue: "I would rather have the British Empire fall in one crash than have it nibbled away." Sensing Eden's resolve, Dulles had reassured him that the United States was in his corner. Indeed, he had pointedly used the d-word: "'To *disgorge*,'" Eden later wrote. "These were forthright words. They rang in my ears for months."[156]

ANTHONY EDEN'S MOMENT

To Eden, Suez was the Rhineland and Munich crises of the 1930s rolled into one. Upstarts like Nasser and Mosaddeq needed to be reined in as aggressively as Hitler or Mussolini. Real threats—like Khrushchev and Mao Zedong—were subordinated to the emotionally satisfying but relatively unimportant Middle Eastern rogues. "Feeble impulses" toward "drift and surrender" in press, Parliament and public opinion needed to be decisively corrected. Sadly for Eden, a capable Old Etonian who had won a Military Cross in World War I and taken firsts in Farsi and Arabic at Oxford, his supreme political test coincided with supreme health and emotional problems, all of which the CIA—striving to supplant the British in Egypt—unhelpfully relayed to Nasser. Eden had lost his eldest son in World War II—he had also lost two brothers in World War I—and he had divorced his wife in 1950 after several messy affairs on both sides. Eden's appendicitis and duodenal ulcers—first diagnosed and treated in 1948—were followed by jaundice, gallstones and a sequence of mutilating operations in the 1950s. These ailments left the foreign secretary wrung out, anxious—"I work for a great historical figure, you work for a great hysterical one," Churchill's secretary told Eden's in 1954—and dependent on morphine to dull the pain and fistfuls of Benzedrine to get him going at moments when energy was required. The amphetamines made him jumpy—Eden often complained of his "largely artificial inside"—and cabinet colleagues, like R. A. "Rab" Butler, learned to dread the jangle of their telephones: "those innumerable telephone calls, on every day of the week and at every hour of the day, which characterized his conscientious but highly strung supervision of our affairs." Aides complained that Eden's private outbursts of anger were vicious, his tardy apologies even worse.[157]

Eden's medical and mental problems were aggravated by American duplicity—Washington had tipped off the Egyptian free officers about pending British moves—and by a shaky backbench in Westminster.[158] Conservative "Victorians," or hard-liners, who had decried Eden's decision to turn the Suez military bases over to the Egyptians in stages between 1951 and 1956, now drove Eden toward a clash with Nasser to protect "British honor" and grab back the bases. Harold Macmillan, a leading hard-liner whom another prominent Tory found disturbingly pugnacious—"[he] wanted to tear Nasser's scalp off with his own fingernails"—argued that it was not enough merely to roll Nasser back and restore international control of the canal. No, Nasser needed to be ousted and Egypt crushed. Macmillan was no less committed than George W. Bush's neocons to a thoroughgoing Middle East transformation. Britain's eventual counterattack in Egypt "must not be like Louis XVIII creeping back to France, but like Napoleon bursting upon the plains of Italy" to reshape the map and institutions of an entire region.[159] Moderation came from the most unlikely quarters. Sixty-eight-year-old field marshal Bernard Montgomery met with Eden a month before the British attacked Egypt and asked the prime minister what the political object of the looming war was. "To knock Nasser off his perch," Eden answered. "If I were your military adviser—and I am not," Montgomery admonished, "then I would make it very clear that *that* object would not do." Eden, Montgomery pointed out, needed to know what the political object would be *after* Nasser was knocked off his perch.[160] Knocking Nasser off his perch in 1956 would be as easy as knocking off Saddam in 2003. The hard part would be finding someone viable to replace Nasser (like Saddam) on the perch.

Even Eden's generally pacific Labour opposition was aroused. Michael Foot lamented in the *Tribune* that the brows of most of the leading Labourites were moist (for a few months) with an Eden-induced panic. Britain owned 44 percent of Suez Canal Company stock, and one-third of Britain's imports and two-thirds of Britain's oil supplies transited through the canal every year. "Hit back *hard* if Nasser nationalizes," Labour leader Hugh Gaitskell advised Eden. Another MP warned that Nasser was positioning himself to "strangle the whole industry of Europe," for "there does not exist in the world today sufficient tankers to move the oil required by Europe without using the Suez Canal." (European tankers sailing by way of South Africa would have had to cover five times the distance from the Gulf oil fields to European markets.)[161] The general hysteria in the UK suggested America after 9/11: "Weakness or faintheartedness now can mean carnage for our children within years," a Tory MP shouted to his colleagues on September 12. The Labour Party, like some Democrats in 2003, demanded that force be used only with the backing of the UN. Like Bush, Eden threw over the UN and groped after a "coalition of the willing." His efforts in that direction proved as incomplete as Bush's a half century later. "You know, sir, it's going to look awfully difficult if we are only supported by France and Portugal," one cabinet minister ventured. Another agreed, remarking that the coalition was even thinner than that. Like Bush's, sustained by the hurrahs of the Fox News Channel and the *National Review*, Eden's was really "only supported by the *Daily Express* and the *Yorkshire Post*."[162] If the war went badly, there'd be hell to pay.

Eden was trying to expunge the appeasements of the 1930s, but was also seeking, as he put it, to avoid "becoming a permanent pensioner of the United States." Britain, he insisted, still had "a role to play at the heart and center of a great empire" and needed to emphasize that fact, in blood and fire if need be.[163] Eden was also pushed by the French, who—in a sequence of grim meetings in the dank war rooms under Westminster—convinced him in October 1956 to rope in the Israelis and go to war.[164] The French saw a strike against Nasser as central to their own war against Algerian nationalists, which had begun in 1954 and intensified in 1956, when the Front de Libération Nationale (FLN) began planting bombs in French clubs, cafés and restaurants in Algiers. "One successful battle in Egypt is worth ten in North Africa," French foreign minister Christian Pineau scowled to an American envoy as the Suez Crisis heated up. Nasser was working to dethrone the sultan of Morocco and king of Libya and insert Arab nationalists into Tunisia, and he was the mentor of the Algerian FLN. The Egyptian leader warehoused many of the FLN's weapons at Sollum—a coastal village near Egypt's western border—beyond the reach of the French, and needed to be slapped down decisively.[165]

The chief of the French naval staff argued that "the whole French position in Algeria will collapse if counter-measures [against Nasser] are not taken immediately. Nasser must be made to yield—and in such a way as not to save his face in any substantial degree."[166] The "target was Nasser," French general André Beaufre concurred. "His was the revolution which was setting alight and unifying the Arab world." France needed to take Port Said, grab back the canal, then "turn right" to Cairo and "take over the reins of government in Egypt" in order to break or overthrow Nasser, unplug his radio campaigns and stop cold the "guerrilla resistance movement" that Nasser was planning along the lines of Saddam Hussein's fedayeen attacks of 2003.[167] "*Il faut coloniser le canal ou canaliser le colonel*," a French official tartly put it. "We must colonize the canal or canalize the colonel."[168]

Hitting Cairo would also stop Egyptian support for the FLN and buttress Israel as a French proxy in the Middle East.[169] French prime minister Guy Mollet had absorbed his mentor Leon Blum's affection for Israel, and former French defense minister General Pierre Koenig—whose Syrian Free French units had fought alongside Jewish volunteer battalions in World War II—was an ardent Zionist who eagerly agreed in 1956 to cooperate in an Israeli attack on Egypt, write off French loans to Israel and upgrade the Israeli military with an $80 million arms package: 72 Mystère IV fighters, 200 AMX tanks, 200 six-by-six Panhard trucks, dozens of 155 mm howitzers and 10,000 antitank missiles. Excluded from the Baghdad Pact and with its overseas empire crumbling, France until 1967 viewed Israel as its chief portal to the Middle East. From July to October 1956, French convoys secretly delivered weapons to the Israelis at night, landing such an impressive quantity of matériel that Israel's most celebrated poet, Nathan Alterman, was moved to write a poem about it, which Ben-Gurion, to the great annoyance of the French, read aloud in the Knesset. The poem described "steel, much steel, new steel," arriving from afar, thundering onto Israel's beaches, "and on its first contact with the soil becoming Jewish power."

To augment that steely Jewish power, French scientists covertly went to work on the Israeli nuclear weapons program at Dimona, which would yield two plutonium bombs in 1967.[170]

In Washington, President Eisenhower, who provided the Israelis with nothing more than scrap metal, .22 caliber training rounds and used half-tracks, applauded this French assistance because it untied America's hands in the Middle East. The Israelis "want the arms from the United States to make us a virtual ally in any trouble they might get in the region," Ike grumbled. From Ike's perspective, France was a better partner in trouble for Israel, although the American president would certainly have had second thoughts had he known the extent of the trouble France had in mind.[171] Eden discerned the dangers in France's war policy—ugly scenes with the Americans, a cutoff of Middle Eastern oil and a rapid depletion of Britain's sterling reserves—but charged ahead anyway, agreeing that "we cannot possibly risk allowing Nasser to get away with this."[172]

In Tel Aviv, sixty-nine-year-old prime minister David Ben-Gurion was only too willing to play his part in the unfolding conflict. He had returned refreshed from a two-year retirement in 1955 to take up the defense portfolio and reinvigorate Israeli policy after the demoralizing Lavon scandal. The Suez Crisis, Ben-Gurion reasoned, was the perfect opportunity for Israel to get back on its feet. The country had continued to grow rapidly after 1948 with the addition of nearly a million new immigrants from Eastern Europe. Ben-Gurion, who now doubled as prime minister and defense minister, took for granted a permanent state of war with Israel's neighbors: thirty million Arabs would never forgive their "humiliation" by seven hundred thousand Jews.

THE RISE OF THE IDF

In 1949, Ben-Gurion had created a file at the defense ministry titled "Renewal of War."[173] Into it, Ben-Gurion and his generals had poured plans for a second round of fighting. In the early 1950s, they conducted maneuvers with mechanized armies of a hundred thousand, tested secret and public mobilizations—in the secret ones, Israeli officers called their troops individually on the telephone—and drafted plans for defensive campaigns against Arab coalitions as well as preemptive strikes. What made the Israeli army stand out in comparison with its Arab adversaries, even in the early days, was the sophistication of its planning and its holistic conception of war and society. It was not enough to equip a potent military; society itself had to be educated, shaped and indoctrinated for a lifetime of struggle. Starting in 1949,

Israel laid down the system it retains to this day, and which emitted its first major hiccup in the Yom Kippur War of 1973, and then again in the Lebanon War of 2006. Israel's wars would be fought not by a standing force, but by civilian reserves who would be trained, furloughed and then called back to the colors at the first sign of trouble. All Jewish men and women—Israel's Arabs were exempted as a possible fifth column—served briefly in the active military upon turning eighteen and then passed into the reserves. Intelligence collection was improved by the admission of Bedouin volunteers and Arab Christians to the IDF.[174]

Technologically, the Israeli military strengthened its formidable human resources with quality matériel in the 1950s. The Israeli defense budget—fueled by charitable donations and American aid—rose from 23 percent of government spending in 1952 to 35 percent in 1956. It replaced its World War II air force—Spitfires, Mustangs, Mosquitoes and B-17s—with swept-wing Mystère jets, and its Sherman and Cromwell tanks were upgraded to faster, more maneuverable AMX-13s. The IDF in 1956 deployed three armored brigades, six infantry brigades and a paratroop brigade, all well equipped, agile and well trained. Israel, the British reminded their French ally, was now sufficiently armed "to annihilate the *entire* Arab League." Whitehall analysts agreed. Compared with Egypt, "the Israelis now have more of everything and *much* more of some things": more and better planes and tanks and five times as much field and antitank artillery.[175]

The CIA came to similar conclusions and warned that Ben-Gurion and army chief of staff General Moshe Dayan were actively *seeking* an opportunity to strike the Egyptians before they reequipped and retrained with the new Czech and Russian weapons that were just beginning to arrive in Egypt. Even Israel's chief advocates—the French—began to have doubts on the eve of war: "The attractive young nation was more artful than our people had realized," French general André Beaufre grumbled. Tel Aviv had exaggerated its own capabilities and underestimated the Egyptians in order to lock in the allied pledge of preemptive air strikes against Egypt's MiGs and Ilyushins and air cover for the Israeli coast, cities and tank columns, which would never have been able to cross the Sinai without French and British top cover.[176]

Shored up by the French and British—who conveniently freed Israel from the restrictions of the 1948 armistices by themselves invading Egypt and shattering the status quo guaranteed by the agreements—Ben-Gurion wanted to leap through that window of opportunity to punish the Egyptians for the random blockades they had been clamping on the Israeli port of Eilat since 1953. He also wanted to punish Menachem Begin's hard-line Herut Party—forerunner of today's Likud—at the polls. Begin had been scoring easy points off Ben-Gurion's alleged "coddling" of Nasser, and Herut was winning adherents with its demand for an aggressive improvement of Israel's territorial vulnerability: six hundred miles of land frontiers commanded by Arab artillery—a "ridge of steel"—and backed by no "strategic depth." Eilat, a gateway for Israeli oil imports, could be—and was occasionally—closed by Egyptian artillery at Sharm el-Sheikh and Egyptian patrol boats in the Straits of Tiran.[177] To quiet Israel's right-wing parties, which took "Eilat is our Suez" as their motto, Ben-Gurion fired his old friend and moderate foreign minister Moshe Sharett in July 1956 and replaced him with the alarmingly hawkish Golda Meir—Israel's fifty-eight-year-old Russian-born, Milwaukee-raised labor minister.[178]

Golda Meir wanted war in 1956 no less than Dayan and Ben-Gurion: to defeat the Egyptians, to banish even the thought of the UN peacekeepers Secretary General Dag Hammarskjöld wanted to place along Israel's borders, to steal the thunder of Begin's Herut, to uproot the fedayeen bases in the Gaza Strip and to advance into the Sinai to lift the Egyptian blockade of Eilat and the Straits of Tiran, which cut Israel off from the Red Sea and Indian Ocean.[179] "If I were an Arab leader," a British diplomat in Tel Aviv had written in 1953, "I would decide that the interests of the Arab world lie in getting Israel thoroughly tied up with international guarantees behind her *present* frontiers." That's why the Arab states liked having UN blue helmets on Israel's borders and Israel didn't: UN peacekeepers gave the impression that everything was provisional, negotiable and in flux. Ben-Gurion, in contrast, wanted to make the borders of 1949 permanent and nonnegotiable by embarking on "a course of dynamic expansion" that would give Israel strategic depth. For this, the Israelis needed flank protection against a world community that would react coldly to any new Israeli offensives.[180]

OPERATION MUSKETEER

In October 1956, the British and the French rather miraculously—from Israel's perspective—dropped in on Ben-Gurion's flanks and presented him with the chance to solve all his problems. Reading the French draft of Operation Musketeer—

the contemplated Anglo-French strike into Suez and Cairo to depose Nasser and take back the canal—Moshe Dayan's pulse quickened: "Here was an opportunity unlikely to recur, for action against Egypt in cooperation with France and possibly Britain as well. We will not be alone. I thought this called for a supreme effort on our part and in our interest not to miss a historic chance." Flattered by France's attention and leery of the wavering Americans, Ben-Gurion declared that "this was our first opportunity to find an ally . . . a Western power, and under no circumstances must we decline it." In such a war as this, Dayan added, Israel "should behave like the cyclist who is riding uphill when a truck chances by and he grabs hold." To grab the truck before it rumbled past, Ben-Gurion flew to Paris (on a DC-9 that had been a gift from Truman to de Gaulle) in the company of Dayan, Shimon Peres and Golda Meir.[181]

At secret meetings in Sèvres—where the Turkish Empire had been dismantled in 1920—the French and Israelis concerted their military plans and agreed on a redivision of the Middle East no less radical than the one that had been handed down from Sèvres thirty-six years earlier. If Nasser was beaten, Jordan would be liquidated: the territory east of the river would go to Iraq; the West Bank would be annexed by Israel. Lebanon would meet the same fate: the northern third would go to Syria, the central third would become a Christian state, and the southern third would be fashioned into an Israeli buffer zone. Though charity for Syria and Iraq was not the Israeli style, it was conditioned in this case on their willingness formally to recognize Israel's existence and borders and settle all the Palestinian refugees on Arab territory. Worried that the Americans might reject these broad aims and impose sanctions or even intervene militarily in the crisis to curry favor with the Arabs, Golda Meir insisted that the war be launched *before* U.S. elections in November. Eisenhower would probably do nothing "because of the Jewish vote."[182] At NATO headquarters, French general Maurice Challe observed that since the Americans were making no difficulties about the release of alliance equipment for use by the French and British contingents, they were probably (discreetly) assenting to Musketeer. With the allied forces gathering, Franco's paper, *Arriba*, snorted that the Western democracies were cynically grooming the Israelis for the role of "British sepoys" in Egypt. But it was arguably the other way around. The Israelis were grooming the British and the French.[183]

Anthony Eden was stunned by the extent of Franco-Israeli plotting, which was tardily discovered by his foreign secretary. Selwyn Lloyd had sat in on some of the planning meetings in Sèvres and, one of the Israeli planners recalled, gave the impression throughout of a man "with a dirty smell under his nose," a man "trying to hold something that was not quite clean and wanting to wash his hands afterwards." Eden and Lloyd worried that they were being used for Israeli ends and actually pondered loaning fifty British bombers (repainted in French colors) to the French so that they, not the British, could do most of the dirty work.[184] Anthony Eden's Guildhall speech in 1955—the major British foreign policy address of the year—had called for big Israeli *concessions* in Palestine, not further expansion. "The position today is that the Arabs take their stand on the 1947 Resolution. The Israelis, on the other hand, find themselves on the Armistice Agreement of 1949 and on the present territory they occupy." Eden wanted the Israelis to yield most of what they had conquered and cleared in 1948 as an essential first step toward peace, which made him no friends in Tel Aviv, where Ben-Gurion inveighed against this "plot hatched in the Guildhall for the tearing up of Israel," and provoked a worried and typically muddled outburst from Washington.

Eisenhower in July 1956 expressed disbelief at Eden's plans to invade Egypt. Mideast oil supplies—through the canal and the Syrian pipelines—would be disrupted, sending shocks through the Western economies. The UN—"formed to prevent this very thing"—would be undermined, and the "emotional needs" of the whole Muslim world would be aroused, "from Dakar to the Philippine Islands."[185] Militarily, European plans for a lightning strike into Egypt by a light airborne force looked hopelessly optimistic. They would "probably have to occupy the country and possibly never get out," Eisenhower fretted. That was also Ben-Gurion's concern; like the Israeli realists of 2003 who heaped derision on Bush's plan to "transform the Middle East" by shocking Iraq into democracy, Ben-Gurion criticized the wishful thinking of Operation Musketeer. Even if the British and French took Cairo, which one Arab paper vowed would become "a second Stalingrad," Nasser would simply retreat into the suburbs, villages and desert to wage a guerrilla war.[186] So confident was Nasser that the British and French would not dare attack him that he made no concessions.[187] Buttressed by a Soviet veto of French and British efforts to have their rights to the canal examined by the UN Security Council, Nasser agreed only to let the British and French come to Cairo to discuss the matter with his foreign ministry. He would not even condescend to meet them himself.

CHAPTER 6

· 🦀 ·

SUEZ

ON OCTOBER 29, 1956, the date that London and Paris had accepted for meetings with the Egyptians to settle the Suez Crisis peacefully, the British and French militaries launched Operation Musketeer instead. Israel's Operation Kadesh, named for the biblical place in the Sinai wilderness where the Israelites gathered to reach the Promised Land, jumped off at the same time to provide the pretext for the French and British "intervention." Those allied attacks into Egypt startled the Americans, who may still have been under the influence of Churchill's surprising confession on the eve of his 1955 retirement that "Suez no longer justifies the expense and diversion of our troops."[1]

Still, Eden and Macmillan had made plain to presidential envoy Robert Murphy in August that they would *fight* to assert their rights to the Suez Canal. At meetings in London, Macmillan and Field Marshal Harold Alexander had told Murphy that they would sooner "be destroyed by Russian bombs than be reduced to impotence by the disintegration of our entire position abroad." Macmillan recalled that he had left Murphy "in no doubt of our determination."[2] America's NATO commander in Europe had reported to Eisenhower in August 1956 that there was "no question" that the British and French would use force at Suez.[3] American U-2 flights—a brilliant new surveillance technology introduced in May 1956 and successfully kept secret until the Soviet shoot-down of Francis Gary Powers in 1960—had detected

large Israeli troop concentrations on the Egyptian border, as well as the hasty delivery of swept-wing French Mystère fighter-bombers to Israeli air bases. Yet Washington still failed to connect the dots. Ike merely noted in his diary that the Israeli
Mystères were exhibiting a "rabbitlike capacity for multiplication." There were now
sixty of them parked where there were supposed to be twenty-four.

With Iraqi troops entering Jordan to help police the restive Palestinians during
parliamentary elections in Amman, the Americans accepted Israel's explanation
that the IDF's mobilization around Egypt was a purely defensive move aimed at
Iraq. The Iraqi prime minister, Nuri as-Said, had given an interview to the London
Times in which he called for the recognition of Israel by the Arab states if Israel
would return to the borders of 1947. Golda Meir explained to Edward Lawson, the
American ambassador in Tel Aviv, that Israeli troops were deploying to stymie
Nuri's efforts "to truncate the State of Israel."[4] Even when the Israelis announced
full mobilization in the third week of October, Lawson accepted Ben-Gurion's ex-
planation that it was merely "a defensive precaution" against the Iraqi troops filtering into Jordan.[5] The Israeli ambassador in Washington, Abba Eban, recalled the
deep anxiety he felt when he received an urgent summons from Secretary of State
Dulles while playing golf at the Woodmont Country Club on Saturday, October 27.
Eban put down his clubs and arrived at the State Department to find Dulles and his
deputies hunkered around a map of the Israeli-Jordanian border region. Egypt,
Eban happily observed, was not even on their map.[6]

With Eisenhower and Dulles chasing up a blind alley, the British and French
clapped a "news blockade" on the Americans and plotted with the Israelis. Israel
would attack toward the canal on October 29, with Britain and France providing air
and naval cover.[7] Prodded by the French and his own loathing of Nasser, Prime
Minister Eden had dropped his qualms about Israel's borders and agreed to yet
more Israeli annexations.[8] Once Israel had driven most of the way to Suez—
threatening the "proper functioning of the Canal" and thus providing the "juridical
pretext" for Western intervention—the British and French would swoop in with
eighty thousand troops "to separate the combatants" and order both Israel and
Egypt to pull their lines back ten miles from the canal and restore it to Anglo-French
control. It was assumed that Nasser would reject the ultimatum; acceptance of it
would truckle to the "imperialists" and yield Egypt east of the canal to the IDF. That
certain Egyptian refusal would give the British and French the excuse they needed
to move in as "neutral" peacekeepers to secure the canal against "Egyptian interference" and deal Nasser's armed forces such a stinging blow that the colonel would

fall and release his "pan-Arab" grip on British and French interests across the Middle East.

MOUNTING "THE ROSTRUM OF SHAME"

The Israelis resented their role as what Christian Pineau, the French foreign minister, called "the detonator for Musketeer." Presented with the Anglo-French plan—carefully timed for the week before American elections so that Eisenhower would find it inexpedient to rein in the Israelis—Ben-Gurion asked, "Is this an ultimatum?" The French envoy looked him up and down and sniffed: "*Si vous voulez*"—"If that's what you want to call it."[9] Ben-Gurion pondered for a moment, and then agreed. "Israel," he grumbled, "would fill the role of aggressor, while the British and French appeared as angels of peace to bring tranquility to the area." Britain was nothing more than an "old whore" who needed to be paid off. Ben-Gurion would "mount the rostrum of shame" and leave the British and French to "dip their hands in the waters of purity" in return for new territory—the Sinai Peninsula and Gaza Strip—and "admission to the Suez campaign club," which would place Israel on an equal footing with Europe's great powers.[10]

On October 29, much of the newly purchased, Soviet-built Egyptian air force was destroyed on the ground by British and French air strikes. Like Saddam Hussein in 1991, Nasser dispersed the rest of his jets to neighboring countries for safekeeping, which left his tanks and infantry exposed to unimpeded French, British and Israeli air strikes.[11] Ben-Gurion went to the Knesset and explained that he was invading Sinai and the Gaza Strip not to enlarge Israel, but merely to preempt inevitable future attacks from that "Egyptian fascist dictator."[12] Four hundred Israeli paratroopers jumped from their Dakota transports onto the Mitla Pass—thirty miles east of the Suez Canal—and provided the excuse for a broad, "protective" Anglo-French invasion to secure the "threatened Canal Zone." Pausing to swipe at Egyptian fedayeen bases on the Israeli border—the pretext for the Israeli invasion—twenty-eight-year-old general Ariel Sharon then got down to his *real* business and charged with an Israeli armored brigade 190 miles across the Sinai to reinforce the isolated paratroops in the Mitla Pass.

Sharon's motorized infantry were slowed by France's failure to provide tire irons for the lug nuts on the new French six-by-six Panhard trucks. Each time one of the new trucks punctured a tire, it had to be abandoned, and the infantry or gear inside crammed onto the surviving vehicles.[13] Leaving a trail of abandoned Panhards in their wake, the Israeli tanks drove haltingly into the Sinai from the east, while French and British troops trickled into Egypt from the west and the 10th Hussars assembled near Eilat to block any Jordanian attacks on Israel's flank and rear.[14] To avoid the appearance of "collusion with Israel," the British had refused even to load their transports on Cyprus and Malta until *after* the "hooknosed boys"—as one British commander dubbed the Israelis—launched their "surprise aggression."[15] Nasser, who had been running the canal with Soviet managers, angrily implemented the threat that the French and British had been attributing to him. He scuttled forty-seven cement-filled ships in the Suez Canal to block it and began a precipitate retreat away from the onrushing Israeli spearheads.

Ex-Wehrmacht general Wilhelm Frambecher and eighty of his German colleagues had been reorganizing the Egyptian army since 1951—with a careless disregard for Israeli sensitivity on the subject of ex-Nazis in Arab uniform—and the Germans had based Nasser's Sinai forces in a chain of fortifications that ran from the Gaza Strip along the Mediterranean coast to al-Arish. Those troops were swiftly outflanked and cut off by the Israeli advance through the desert. The Egyptian MiGs and Ilyushins should have made short work of the Israeli tank and truck columns, but the Egyptian aircraft that had survived the French and British air raids (and not flown off to safety in Syria or Saudi Arabia) were poorly handled. The Russians had provided more than two hundred planes but only forty flight instructors, and the Egyptian pilots, with no hours in the new fighters and bombers, were thrashed in every engagement with the Israelis. Only one Egyptian bomber penetrated Israeli airspace, and it ended up dropping its bombs harmlessly on a hillside south of Jerusalem.[16] Drinking cocktails on the roof of his house with the Indonesian ambassador on October 31, Nasser watched the French and British jets striking Cairo's international airport and immediately telephoned orders to his army in the Sinai to withdraw toward Cairo. If the French and British were going to attack along the canal and the Israelis continued their advance, his divisions in the Sinai would be surrounded and lost.

Sadat called that snap decision of Nasser's to evacuate the Sinai a "stroke of genius," because the colonel evaded the trap set by the British, French and Israelis and saved two-thirds of the Egyptian army, which British and French planners had aimed to envelop and destroy once Nasser refused their ultimatum.[17] (Even as Nasser's troops reeled out of the Sinai, Sadat was scribbling a prevaricating piece for *Al-Gumhuriya* which assured Egyptian readers that, far from retreating in the face of the IDF, Nasser had "annihilated the Israeli spearhead.") Nasser's generals had actually wanted to *try* annihilating the Israelis, and Nasser had been forced to threaten resignation to get them to agree to a retreat. Once the troops had been pulled back to Cairo—after a bitter seven-hour battle in the Mitla Pass—Nasser furloughed the workers in the canal zone, paid them a month's salary in advance and ordered them to prepare for guerrilla war against the "Jews and imperialists." Nasser then closed Egypt's high schools and universities and herded the students into a National Liberation Army. Had the allies "turned right to Cairo" after securing the Suez Canal—as the French desired—they would probably have triggered a massive intifada.[18]

The Anglo-French demand that Nasser relinquish control of the Suez Canal within twelve hours dismayed the world. This was 1956 after all, not 1882—the year Prime Minister William Gladstone had also claimed that his occupation of the canal was only "temporary"—and the Soviets gleefully argued that the government of Israel had become "a tool of imperialist circles bent on restoring colonial oppression in the East."[19] Eisenhower was furious at the lack of consultation or even subtlety from his allies; he swore "like General Grant," *New York Times* columnist James Reston recalled, and deplored the "pretty rough" ultimatum. Eden later explained that he considered his letters to Ike in September and October 1956 describing Nasser's threat to British interests sufficient warning. Dulles—who had no qualms about crushing Iranian or Guatemalan governments that advanced dangerous policies—now pronounced the Anglo-French note "unacceptable, as crude and brutal as anything he had ever seen."[20] Churchill—who was resting from a stroke in the south of France—would never have launched the operation without American approval, but, one British official recalled, Eden and Mollet plunged ahead out of frustration with Dulles. "That sanctimonious voice would once again have sounded on the telephone, morally insistent, boring, confused but, no doubt, as the Cabinet feared, successful." By late October, Guy Mollet feared that his hammer—the Israelis—"would risk disappearing" if the allied task force did not strike. The British, with the interlocking plans and timetables for Musketeer now having swelled to the length of the London phone book, feared that the whole plan would collapse if not speedily launched. Streams of men and matériel were inbound from Southampton, Algiers, Malta and Cyprus, and could no longer be held up.[21]

Dulles's Most Agonizing Day

European haste and secrecy created a monumental headache for the U.S. government, which was completely absorbed by imminent presidential elections (just a week away) and the anti-Soviet risings in Poland and Hungary. Aides recalled that October 30, 1956, might have been Dulles's "most agonizing day as Secretary of State." Just back from Dallas, where he had delivered campaign speeches vaunting the Eisenhower administration's maintenance of world peace "with intensity and imagination," he now worked with unwonted intensity in his State Department office beneath the glowering portraits of his grandfather (secretary of state to Benjamin Harrison) and his uncle (secretary of state to Woodrow Wilson). One of Dulles's elbows rested beside the white telephone that was his hotline to the Oval Office. The other nestled beside his dog-eared family Bible, his copy of Stalin's *Problems of Leninism* and the stack of government-printed *Federalist Papers* he liked to give visiting dignitaries as proof of American democracy. Dulles read with mounting disbelief of the audacity of the French, British and Israelis. He had little real-time intelligence and relied for news on radio reports and the morning and afternoon papers, which only increased his rage at his allies and their "information blockade." He looked drained and haggard and kept asking his aides, "*What* can we do about it?" He was, a deputy recalled, "sore as hell." His light tweed Brooks Brothers suit and silk shirt began to sag as day turned to night. He poured himself a glass of his favorite Old Overholt rye whiskey. "How could people do this to *me*?" he spat out. "They have *betrayed* us."[22]

Unbeknownst to the British, French and Israelis, who assumed that the Americans would accept their fake narrative of the war—that it was an Anglo-French "stability operation" amid an Arab-Israeli war—Eisenhower and Dulles now reexamined their U-2 photographs snapped from eighty-five thousand feet and saw conclusive evidence of Anglo-French—not Israeli—bombing runs against Egyptian airfields. Operating from carriers as well as bases in Malta, Cyprus and Israel, two hundred British bombers and forty French Thunderstreaks had knocked out a dozen Egyptian airfields around the delta and canal. Meanwhile, HMS *Newfoundland* had sent an Egyptian frigate to the bottom of the Gulf of Suez.[23] "Nothing justifies double crossing us," Eisenhower barked to Dulles. The world must not be permitted to think that "we are a nation without honor."[24]

To salvage American honor, Ike instructed Dulles and Lodge to protest the allied attacks in the UN Security Council and demand an immediate cease-fire and Israeli withdrawal. "We'll handle our affairs exactly as though we don't have a Jew in America," Ike vowed to Dulles. The president assumed that the Israelis had launched the invasion on the eve of America's November elections to paralyze and manipulate the Republican incumbent: "Well, it looks like we're in trouble. If the Israelis keep going . . . I may have to use force to stop them . . . Then I'd lose the election. There would go New York, New Jersey, Pennsylvania and Connecticut, at least."[25] Britain and France seemed easier nuts to crack, but they brashly vetoed Ike's cease-fire demand, and the French even widened the war. Mollet dispatched Israel-based F-84 Thunderstreaks to Luxor to blow up twenty Egyptian Il-28 bombers that had been flown there for safekeeping and ordered the light cruiser *Georges Leygues* to prowl up to Rafah and shell the city with its six-inch guns.[26] To Eisenhower and Dulles, this Anglo-French freelancing was more dangerous than any mischief Colonel Nasser might concoct. But Ike and Dulles should have paused to consider the helpful effects of Musketeer inside Egypt. Some of Cairo's old-guard politicians—reared on Farouk's defeatism and impressed by the plucky British and French vetoes—were imploring Nasser to *accept* the Anglo-French terms. The colonel indignantly mustered a firing squad outside his office and threatened to march anyone before it who persisted in arguing for acceptance of the ultimatum. No one persisted. Nasser then rejected the ultimatum in a speech carried on the radio from al-Azhar Mosque on November 2, 1956. He summoned U.S. ambassador Raymond Hare and gave him a message for President Eisenhower: "Will you please deal with your allies—Britain and France—and leave us Israel to deal with?"[27]

The British felt certain that Washington would look the other way and let them finish the job. Although Chancellor of the Exchequer Harold Macmillan sounded an early financial alarm—"reserves of gold and dollars [are] falling at a dangerously rapid rate . . . [We cannot] afford to alienate the U.S. Government more than . . . absolutely necessary"—Prime Minister Eden recalled that optimism still reigned.

> We were ashore with a sufficient force to hold Port Said. We held a gage. Nasser had received a humiliating defeat in the field and most of his Russian equipment had been captured or destroyed by the Israelis or ourselves. His position was badly shaken. Out of this situation intelligent international statesmanship should, we thought, be able to shape a lasting settlement for

the Arab-Israeli conflict and for the future of the Canal. *We had not under-stood that, so far from doing this, the United Nations, and in particular the United States, would insist that all the advantages must be thrown away before serious negotiation began.* This was the most calamitous of all errors.[28]

In Paris, Guy Mollet had the same reaction. The French and British landings had succeeded everywhere; the Israelis were ten miles from the canal, and French paratroopers were poised to take Suez City.[29] Eden felt confident that the Americans were sufficiently disillusioned with Nasser to back their effort at Suez to rupture what Eden was calling "the Moscow-Cairo axis."[30] Macmillan agreed. "I know Ike," the Tory hard-liner confidently assured his colleagues. "He will lie doggo."

"THE SHOCKING RECORD OF NASSER, NIXON AND DULLES"

But Dulles had warned Eden *not* to act before U.S. presidential elections in November 1956. To win Jewish votes, Adlai Stevenson and the Democrats were running against "the shocking record of Nasser, Nixon and Dulles." On November 2, Stevenson in Detroit lashed out at the "inconsistency and irresolution" of Ike's policy. "The Administration first offered and then refused to help Egypt with the Aswan Dam. It refused to send Israel defense arms, but then encouraged others to do so . . . in the dispute over the Suez Canal [it] never really committed itself to stand firm on anything." Ike, Stevenson concluded, had acquired nothing "but a reputation for unreliability" and had not "really been in charge of our foreign policy."[31] By complicating Ike's expected reelection, Eden may have ignited Ike's wrath in a way that a better-timed attack on Nasser would not have.[32] In fact, there appeared to be no reason for presidential wrath: consenting to an attack on Nasser was the *best* way for an American candidate to win Jewish votes in 1956, and polls showed that Ike was probably going to win his second term by a landslide anyway. Moreover, as the Suez Crisis climaxed in October 1956, Dulles wrote the U.S. ambassador in Paris that the American public had eyes and ears only for the epic World Series between the New York Yankees and the Brooklyn Dodgers, which conveniently went to seven games.[33]

To sidestep British and French vetoes in the Security Council, Dulles took the hugely irregular step of bypassing the Security Council altogether and appealing directly to the General Assembly to end "this tormenting problem . . . this raging war in the Middle East." Eden was infuriated by this U.S. effort at "retrogression and imposition." Once handed off to the UN General Assembly, Suez became the province of the more numerous states of the Third World—whose pro-Nasser sympathies were never in doubt—and of the American ambassador to the UN, Henry Cabot Lodge, Jr., whose grandfather had effectively killed U.S. participation in the League of Nations in 1919. Lodge, Jr., was determined to undo the sin of Lodge, Sr., by rallying the large "anti-colonialist Afro-Asian bloc" to condemn Britain and France and restore the authority of the United Nations.[34]

Like George W. Bush years later, Eden and his foreign secretary, Selwyn Lloyd, deplored the "wilderness of debate" in New York and felt certain that it all just played into Nasser's hands, as it would later into Saddam's. "Nasser will go on saying 'no' until he has got unconditional surrender," Lloyd growled.[35] But Ambassador Lodge was deaf to British and French complaints. On November 10, while Dulles lay in a Washington hospital room hearing a dreadful diagnosis of cancer and distractedly watching the Princeton-Harvard football game on television, Lodge in New York—with scalding effrontery—characterized the Security Council, with its villainous British and French permanent members, as "an abdomen [in which] gangrene has set in," and asked the General Assembly to perform the "clean, quick operation." Eisenhower piously demanded that the "opinion of the world" be heard and heeded through "the General Assembly, with no veto operating."[36]

Meanwhile, Moshe Dayan's tanks and paratroopers had knifed deep into Egypt. With the Americans, the Soviets and the UN arrayed against them, the Israelis were fighting a deliberate blitzkrieg, enveloping and cutting Egyptian communications to collapse the forces in the field instead of seeking time-consuming battles of annihilation. As a result, Egypt's casualties were low—an estimated five thousand killed and wounded, another five thousand captured—but the loss of face for an Egyptian regime that had vowed to annihilate Israel was scarring. In just a week of combat, the Egyptians had lost ten thousand troops and mountains of costly matériel: seven thousand tons of ammunition, five hundred thousand gallons of fuel, two hundred armored vehicles, two hundred guns and a thousand trucks. Israeli casualties were light by comparison: one thousand killed and wounded, twenty planes and two thousand vehicles.[37]

The IDF's mechanized swoops through the Sinai bagged whole Egyptian units with their supplies and seized Sharm el-Sheikh as well, which the Israelis promptly renamed "Mifratz Shlomo." Noting the proximity of Sharm el-Sheikh to the ancient Hebrew port of Yotvat, Ben-Gurion proudly informed the Knesset that he had expanded the "Third Kingdom of Israel, from Yotvat to the foothills of Lebanon."[38] Ben-Gurion's triumphalism—he read aloud from Procopius and the Old Testament ("in that day shall Egypt tremble and be afraid") and cast himself as a new King Solomon making good the losses of three thousand years—embarrassed the British, who privately assured their Iraqi and Jordanian allies that they were merely temporary "associates," not long-term "partners" of Israel. They were fighting around Suez not to destroy Nasser, but to contain Israel's attack on Egypt and limit annexations like "Mifratz Shlomo." To the Baghdad Pact—whose Iranian, Turkish, Pakistani and Iraqi members worriedly convened in Tehran during the Suez Crisis—the British declared that their principal purpose at Suez was to smash Egypt militarily in order to establish Iraq "as the major Arab Power, to which, if the other Arab states are worried about Israel, they will have to look for protection."[39]

Those were creative and perfidious ways to evade the odium of an Israeli alliance—"It was preferable that we should be seen to be holding the balance between Israel and Egypt rather than appear to be accepting Israeli cooperation in an attack on Egypt alone," Eden told his cabinet on October 25—but no one was fooled. In Karachi, the newspapers were already calling Eden—not Nasser—"Hitler Reborn."[40] The French foreign minister concluded that this "British desire to appear virtuous while being Machiavellian" was "one of the main mistakes in the whole project," for it undercut the allied military effort while paying no appreciable political dividends in the Arab world. The Arab states were in no doubt as to the *real* reason for British troops at Suez, and Syria's President Kuwatli now demanded with increasing stridency that the Soviets *do* something for the Egyptians.

Doing something for the Egyptians even at this late date was still possible because of the slow, light-hitting, poorly coordinated pace of the Anglo-French invasion. Having planned for months to strike into Egypt by way of Alexandria with its modern port, its deepwater quays and cranes and its good routes down to Cairo, the allies decided just a week before their invasion to assault Port Said instead and merely hold it as a "bargaining chip" to extort better behavior from Nasser, or whatever regime might succeed him after his disgrace. For political reasons—London and Paris feared damaging Alexandria and outraging the UN, the Americans and the Soviets—Musketeer was redirected into a port that was two hundred miles farther from Britain's Malta base, one-third the size of Alexandria and easily cut off and isolated by the Egyptians.

"WHO'S THE ENEMY?"

British ground force commander General Hugh Stockwell called Port Said—perched at the end of a skinny causeway—"a cork in a bottle with a very long neck."[41] If Nasser's engineers blew up the causeway that connected Port Said to the mainland, then the Anglo-French force would be marooned on an island. Jacques Baeyens, the French political adviser to the expedition, noted the impact of this scenario on Stockwell: "He passes in an instant from the most cheerfully expressed optimism to a dejection that amounts to nervous depression."[42] Allied logistics were also depressing: the Anglo-French task force arrived with a large air force including medium and light bombing squadrons and ground attack planes, 7 aircraft carriers, 130 warships, hundreds of landing craft and 80 merchant ships carrying stores and baggage. From the holds of those ships and landing craft swarmed a force as big as had been unleashed on Anzio in 1944: 50,000 British troops, 30,000 French and 20,000 vehicles. They all had to be put ashore around Port Said, but were slow to arrive because of British inefficiency—"Gilbertian situations arose in the loading of guns and equipment when the Port authorities, Board of Trade, and Ministry of Transport continued to follow peacetime regulations"—sketchy Egyptian facilities and the impassable bulk of the U.S. Sixth Fleet, which loitered with its lights on in the path of the Anglo-French landings and in the middle of the British carrier zone to harass the allies by picking out their hulls with searchlights and launching and recovering noisy American aircraft at all hours. "*Whose* side am I on?" American admiral Charles Brown telegraphed Washington. "*Who's* the enemy?"

Having counted on American support, the British felt increasingly naked. "This is the same kind of damn nonsense that happened at Dieppe," British admiral Guy Grantham sputtered from his office in Malta, and he was right. By pulling on "woolen gloves" before striking (as Grantham put it), the Western allies were letting Nasser off the hook.[43] The French wanted to brush past the balky Americans and arrive in Cairo violently and in force by D+14 (for what they were grandly calling "the New Battle of the Pyramids"), but estimated that Egyptian unloading facilities were so deficient that the operation would probably take seven *weeks*, which would be more than enough time for Nasser to organize the international community against the Anglo-French task force and its Israeli ally. General André Beaufre argued that the damage that French collusion with Israel would do to France's interests in the Middle East and North Africa was so great that nothing less than the conquest of Cairo and the replacement of Nasser with a pro-Western regime was acceptable, or even thinkable.[44]

So as not to alarm the superpowers, the UN and the already alarmed Arab world, the allied air forces surgically bombed oil depots, bridges, airfields and railway stations with light ordnance when they were not restricting themselves to "aero-psychological" sorties that dropped only leaflets (poorly) composed to "break the Egyptian will to fight." Musketeer anticipated the wars of the future in that the British and French shrank from annihilating violence—dropping only 1,962 bombs on a broad array of scattered targets—and formed a "targeting committee" to vet (and usually discard) the best targets, like Cairo Radio, which successfully carried on throughout the crisis because of British reluctance to hit its transmitters. The British even fired theatrical warning bursts at Israeli troops who went to help downed British pilots, to demonstrate their "impartiality."[45]

The Suez War, a French planner noted, was really a harmless "hesitation waltz," a "cloud cuckoo-land" infused with rules of engagement that were restrictive even by twenty-first-century standards.[46] The Royal Navy off Port Said was not allowed to fire guns of greater caliber than 4.5 inches, which eliminated all cruisers from the fire missions. Egypt's Soviet-supplied Ilyushin-28 bombers were parked at Cairo West airport, but neither the British nor the French dared strike them lest they hit civilians in the terminals, or the Soviet "volunteer pilots," who were presumed to be on hand as well.[47] Naturally, the allies also declined to invite Israeli troops to cross the canal to reinforce the small numbers of French and British troops on the west bank. Such a junction would have inflamed the Arab world and ruptured the Baghdad Pact, so the French and British waited impatiently for their armor and supports to arrive at Port Said in landing craft from Malta (936 miles away), while *Paris-Match* unhelpfully published maps and diagrams of the Anglo-French plan and landing zones.[48]

THE KHRUSHCHEV-BULGANIN ULTIMATUM

Tied down by the Hungarian revolt, the Soviets refused to intervene in Egypt, despite the excellent prospects for success. In their radio and leaflet appeals to the Egyptians over Nasser's head, the British were getting nowhere. They had set up an

Arabic radio station on Cyprus designed to demoralize the Egyptians with psychological operations, but all the Arab employees went on strike after broadcasting a collective statement to Egypt that they were on the side of Nasser, not their British employers. When the British were finally able to transmit into Egypt—via Voice of Britain radio—their message was juiceless: "Oh, Egyptian people, Abdel Nasser has gone mad and seized the Suez Canal. Oh, Egyptians, accept the proposal of the Allied States." When no one rallied to the allied proposals, London tried bluster: "We shall have to come and bomb you in your villages. You have nothing to protect you—nothing—no air force—nothing."[49] Presented with these proofs of Western stupidity, the Russian bear remained seated on its paws. That puzzling Russian reticence made Sadat—who would eventually boot the Russians out of Egypt himself and return to the American camp—"believe that it was always futile to depend on the Soviet Union."[50]

France and Britain still hoped that they might win over Eisenhower, who continued to wobble uncertainly and express deep confusion to his director of defense mobilization, Arthur Flemming: "Good Lands! I'm a *friend* of theirs. I'm not going to make life *too* complicated for them."[51] But that same day—November 5, 1956—Ike did decide to make life exceedingly complicated for them. With British and French paratroopers and marines finally—and miraculously, in view of their small, lightly armed numbers—in control of Port Said, Port Fuad and El Cap and pushing toward Suez City, Eisenhower ordered the British and French to cease fire, release pressure on the Egyptian military and evacuate Egypt. Only then—once assured of American credulity, Vice President Richard Nixon actually trumpeted this "second declaration of independence, from Anglo-French colonial policies" and Dulles vowed "not to be dragged along at the heels of Britain and France"—did an amazed Moscow issue the blustering Khrushchev-Bulganin Ultimatum, which threatened to rain nuclear bombs on Britain and France if they did not halt their "piratical war." Khrushchev also hinted that Israel might be wiped off the map. ("It is hard to see how an official communication from one government to another could be *more* ominous in tone," the *Washington Post* commented the next morning.)[52] Sadat called Moscow's last-minute truculence "an attempt to appear as though the Soviet Union had saved the situation. This was not, of course, the case. It was Eisenhower who did so." But it was Eisenhower's wavering between loyalty to Eden and sympathy for Nasser that finally persuaded the Soviets that it was safe to intervene and stake their own claim to Egypt. If Eisenhower did not know his mind, they at least knew theirs.[53]

For Eisenhower, who trounced Adlai Stevenson by nearly ten million votes on November 6, it proved just as easy to trounce the British and French. "[The Americans] like to give orders, and if they are not at once obeyed they become huffy. That is their conception of an alliance—or Dulles' anyway," Eden spat.[54] Dulles shortly became huffy in an unmistakable way. First, he asked Admiral Arleigh Burke if the Sixth Fleet could stop the allies militarily, and Burke assured him that it could: "We can defeat them—the British and the French and the Egyptians and the Israelis—the whole goddamn works of them we can knock off, if you want."[55] But with the Soviets busy knocking off the Hungarians and the Poles, Dulles shrank from knocking off his staunchest Cold War allies. Instead, he and Ike ordered the U.S. Federal Reserve to begin selling $3 million blocks of sterling on November 5 to induce a devaluation of the British pound. To prevent devaluation, the British bought the pounds as fast as the Americans dumped them, but this merely drained the cash out of an already faltering war effort that had been laughingly characterized by Dulles as "spending $10,000 to inflict $1 worth of harm on the Egyptians."[56]

THE RUN ON THE POUND

The pound and the dollar were both "world currencies," but the British were forever scrambling to shore theirs up with sufficient reserves. Any major crisis could provoke a run from the pound to the dollar, and Suez was just such a crisis. The pound fell in September and October and then plummeted in November as the U.S. Federal Reserve began dumping sterling to increase the pressure on Great Britain. Treasury Secretary George Humphrey warned Rab Butler that Washington would "save the pound" only when the British left Suez. "The Americans seem determined to treat us as naughty boys who have got to be taught that they cannot go off and act on their own without asking Nanny's permission first," the British embassy in Washington furiously commented.[57]

In the first days of November alone, the British spent $300 million shoring up the pound against heavy American selling. Harold Macmillan, Eden's chancellor of the exchequer, turned to the International Monetary Fund (IMF) for a $1.3 billion bridge loan but was icily rebuffed by George Humphrey, who effectively controlled the IMF board of directors owing to the size of America's deposits in the fund and now informed the British ambassador: "You will not get a dime from the United States government until you have gotten out of Suez."[58] Humphrey made Nasser out to be a helpless victim of diabolical intrigues. "The U.K. is a burglar who has climbed through the window," Humphrey lectured. "Nasser is the householder in his nightshirt appealing to the world for protection." Macmillan expressed surprise at the emotional way in which Washington was framing the crisis. After appealing to Humphrey's anticommunism—"the forces of communism have always asserted that capitalism carried within itself the seeds of its own destruction; here would be the proof"—Macmillan threw in the towel. A friend reported that he returned from his meetings with the Americans "a chastened man. He does not appear to have thought of this possibility beforehand."[59]

Oil was another American lever against the British and the French. Having attacked along the banks of the canal and provoked Saudi and Kuwaiti oil embargoes, the British and the French needed American supplies of fuel at least as much as they needed American money.[60] Eisenhower had only—as he put it—to leave them "to boil in their own oil." Boil they did, to the immense satisfaction of America's oil companies. As in the aftermath of the Iraq invasion of 2003, Exxon and its "sisters" reaped windfall profits from the Suez Crisis, which drove the oil price from thirty-five to forty cents a barrel. Rationing had to be introduced in Britain and France, which quickly shattered the multiparty coalitions that had engineered the war, and public opinion as well.[61] Cab fares went up, Sunday driving was restricted, and taxes on rationed fuel oil and gasoline increased sharply. Only the fact that Europe was still primarily a coal economy—petroleum accounted for just 20 percent of energy consumption in 1956—saved the British and French from a frigid winter and an economic nosedive. The American oil companies did well out of the crisis by unloading East Coast stocks of (Saudi) oil at premium prices, diverting Venezuelan oil to Europe and then ramping up production in Texas to supply the American market as well as an additional five hundred thousand barrels a day to the British and French. Although their supplies rose quicker than demand thanks to U.S. production and European rationing, the oil "majors" used the Suez Crisis as an excuse to raise prices anyway.[62]

In scenes redolent of George W. Bush's America, pundits and politicians like Democratic senator Estes Kefauver protested the price hikes, which plucked more than $1 billion out of the pockets of American consumers in the fall of 1956. Eisenhower stolidly declined to interfere "in the free market mechanism." And "stolid" is the word; whereas Bush in the early 2000s would feel compelled to make occasional releases from the national petroleum reserve to depress gas prices at a time when Exxon was reporting quarterly income of $10 billion, Eisenhower directed his assistant secretary of the interior, Felix Wormser, to leave domestic reserves intact and show no mercy. "What if [the oil companies] raise the price ten cents a gallon? Would you do anything about that?" Kefauver asked Wormser at Senate hearings. Though a gallon of regular cost just nineteen cents at the time, Wormser shrugged: "Nothing at all."

> KEFAUVER: Fifty cents a gallon?
> WORMSER: It is entirely up to them whether they raise it.
> KEFAUVER: That is the most outrageous statement that I have ever heard.
> WORMSER: I cannot help it.[63]

MACMILLAN'S REVOLT

Eisenhower accompanied his financial and economic sanctions with harsh criticism of Eden intended to wreak regime change in Westminster. "I will *never* forgive Eden for what he has done," Ike told George Humphrey, who told the British ambassador, who told Harold Macmillan, who duly organized a revolt of the backbenchers against Eden.[64] Macmillan's treachery was particularly poignant. He had been among Eden's most bellicose backers in the early days, growling to Eden "that Britain must not become another Netherlands" and that "the lawns of England had to be kept green for their grandchildren." Macmillan had deprecated Musketeer and called for a much bigger, Desert Storm–type operation that would base itself in Libya and Malta, take Nasser between two fires, and "seek out and destroy the Egyptian forces and government." The future prime minister now unctuously complained that Eden was "playing ducks and drakes" with the British future, and retreated into the American camp to secure his own.[65]

Alone at the top, Prime Minister Eden agreed to a cease-fire on November 6, which the Americans set as the minimum price for a desperately needed $1.5 billion IMF loan. In a despairing phone call to Mollet, Eden said, "I can't hang on; I'm deserted by everybody." Summoned to Parliament to explain how Operation Musketeer could have produced such nugatory results, Eden seemed dumbfounded. Eden in Egypt had operated in a dark secrecy that facilitated the big troop and naval buildups on Malta and Cyprus—Labour was never even briefed on Musketeer—but triggered outrage and collapse when the operation faltered. Britons in 1956, Eden sighed, "were quite pleased to see the Government flex its muscles, provided it was a success." When it was not a success, support evaporated. This was what British strategic thinker Basil Liddell Hart meant when he talked in the 1950s and 1960s about the *new* Western way of war, which, in a democratic, media-saturated age, was nervous, excitable and intolerant of long, attritional struggles. Liddell Hart cautioned against the "Napoleonic fallacy" of believing that military campaigns achieved great and lasting results. So did the British public. A British poll on November 2—when the war was still going *well*—revealed that only 37 percent supported the Suez War, 44 percent opposed it and 19 percent remained undecided.[66]

The French were even more secretive than the British, but had fewer problems with public opinion because the citizenry was accustomed to a "strong" foreign policy and was heavily invested in Algeria and Israel. Also, Mollet's government was staffed with a number of ex-Resistance leaders who planned and launched Musketeer using their old clandestine methods and even nicknames—army chief of staff General Paul Ely became "Algèbre" again; Defense Minister Maurice Bourgès-Maunoury, "Polygone"—to evade parliamentary and ministerial oversight.[67] Labour leader Hugh Gaitskell was much less permissive than the French, who hid and burned papers and confused even themselves as to what they were doing. When Gaitskell learned of Eden's war planning not from the prime minister but from the editors of the *Daily Mirror*, he objected that Eden must be "either a tyro or a drunkard"; there could be no other explanation for an operation as poorly conceived and implemented as Musketeer.[68] Lady Eden happened to be sitting in the gallery of the Commons during the exchange. "Can you stand it?" she muttered. "The boys must express themselves," Mrs. Gaitskell replied.[69]

"THE WEASELS [WERE] AT WORK AGAIN"

Eden did not withstand Gaitskell's expressions, or anyone else's. By now, Tory whip Edward Heath was working overtime just trying to keep Eden's fellow Conservatives in line, and, as Eden's press secretary put it, the "first fine careless rapture in the press [had] died away, and the weasels [were] at work" again, criticizing and questioning everything.[70] Labour was organizing street rallies to "Stop Eden's War" and demand to know "why the machinery of the UN had not been used." Like the Democrats (and Republicans) who uncritically seconded Bush in 2003, initially bellicose Labourites like Gaitskell now repented and, as Michael Foot jotted in the *Tribune*, "soothed [their] moist brow[s]" and coldly withdrew their support of "Eden's panic measures."[71]

Hugh Gaitskell insisted in November 1956 that Parliament must belatedly be "allowed to take charge of the situation, to keep peace in the country," Eden and the Conservatives having made such a hash of the war.[72] Although the right-wing tabloids continued to defend the Suez War in panic-stricken tones—"if we had remained quiescent, Britain and the whole world would have suffered irreparable damage"—no one else did. Even the patriotic, middle-class *Observer* broke ranks: "We wish to make an apology . . . We had not realised that our government was capable of such folly and crookedness." Just as Bush's Iraq War deeply wounded the GOP, the *Observer* predicted that Britain's Conservative Party would be "obliterated for a generation" by Eden's conduct in the Suez Crisis unless it promptly purged itself through a "party rebellion."[73] Nye Bevan—the charismatic Welsh leader of the Labour left—began to lampoon the prime minister. "If Sir Anthony is sincere in what he says—and he may be—then he is too stupid to be Prime Minister," Bevan told a mass rally in Trafalgar Square on November 4.[74]

Eden appeared stiff, defiant and painfully uninformed. The editors of the *Economist* wrung their hands over the prime minister's "splenetic isolation." Eden was as worryingly unable to account for the spiraling costs of the conflict, which, like the Republicans in Iraq, the Tories minimized ($15 million) by counting only the most direct military costs while Labour maximized ($1 billion) by factoring in lost exports, pricier imports (like oil) and other side effects and opportunity costs. Whatever the true price, the Suez War devastated Eden. The visiting French foreign minister was struck by Eden's listlessness—he was shivering through bouts of 106-degree fevers—and an MP in the Commons noted that "the Prime Minister sprawled on the front bench, head thrown back, and mouth agape. His eyes, inflamed with sleeplessness, stared into vacancies beyond the roof except when they twitched with meaningless intensity to the face of the clock."[75] Eden may also have been suffering from rumors of American treachery in the crisis. Nasser's confidant and editor of Cairo's *Al-Ahram*, Muhammed Heikal, divulged that American agents had tipped the Egyptians off about British plans, paid General Naguib a $3 million bribe to gain access to formerly British communications facilities and passed on details of Eden's deteriorating physical and mental condition to Nasser's RCC.[76] Revelations like these may have pushed Eden over the edge; he suffered a nervous breakdown and withdrew to Ian Fleming's Jamaican retreat Goldeneye to recuperate. "I seem for months to have had the Suez Canal flowing through my drawing-room," his young wife bitterly reflected.[77]

Although Britons would pitilessly vote Eden the "worst prime minister of the twentieth century" in 1999, he did not appear to have very many good options in 1956.[78] Ike had threatened to cut Eden off and once the American president withdrew support, so did the Commonwealth, Europe, the oil companies, the archbishop of Canterbury, the Labour Party and even Eden's fellow Conservatives. To Eden's insistence that Egypt was "threatening" British nationals, Archbishop of Canterbury Geoffrey Fisher replied, "But *who* is the attacking power?"—"*Who* is making the attack?" The Eden government did not dare answer the questions frankly—or Nye Bevan's demand that "the Government stop lying to the House of Commons"— which further eroded public and parliamentary support.[79] France, whose military contingent in Musketeer was commanded by British officers, also laid down its arms. Onlookers with a good grasp of the military situation on the ground—the British and French advancing easily, the Israelis trouncing the Egyptians in Gaza and Sinai—were stunned by Eden's capitulation. "I cannot understand why our troops were halted," Churchill complained. The whole operation had been designed to discredit Nasser; now that he was nearly discredited, the allies were releasing pressure. "To go so far and not go on was madness."[80]

In Washington, Eisenhower and Vice President Nixon heaved sighs of relief. They had wanted the French and British to capitulate quickly so as not to give the opposition Radical Socialists and Labourites a hot issue to run on in the next general election. "If they throw [Eden] out, then we have these Socialists to lick," the U.S. embassy in London reminded Secretary of State Dulles in November 1956. Nixon concurred, confiding to the NSC that he "was scared to death at the prospect of Nye Bevan [the great exponent of socialized medicine, neutralism and nuclear disarmament] in a position of power in a future British government."[81] The Eisenhower administration also worried that a protracted war in Egypt might bring Pierre Mendès-France—the man who had surrendered North Vietnam to the communists in 1954—back to power in Paris.

"The Death Knell of Great Britain and France"

It is easy to understand why the Americans did not overtly support their Western European allies or Israel in 1956, but it is hard to understand why Washington pulled out all the stops to support *Nasser*. By 1956, it was clear that the Egyptian colonel with his cult of personality would be more of a hindrance than a help to Western interests. Eden was correct when he warned Eisenhower during the Suez Crisis that Nasser was "a Muslim Mussolini"—not quite a Hitler, but certainly a Mussolini—who menaced "our friends in Israel, Jordan, Saudi Arabia and even Iran." Eden scored Ike for not backing "the removal of Nasser and the installation in Egypt of a regime less hostile to the West."[82] Once the removal was in train, why did Ike *oppose* it so staunchly? In a crucial NSC meeting on November 1, 1956, Dulles—who just the night before had told the *Washington Post* that Nasser needed to be "dumped"—angrily called the crisis not the end of Nasser, but "the death knell of Great Britain and France." White House adviser Harold Stassen couldn't believe his ears, and took on the president and Dulles. The Soviets, Stassen argued, were as much to blame as the Western allies, for they were arming and inciting the Egyptians. (Ike worried throughout the crisis that the Soviets might have "slipped Nasser" a half dozen atom bombs.) The canal was a vital lifeline of the British Commonwealth—so Britain's defense of it was understandable—but why strike politically, financially and perhaps militarily at the French, British and Israelis anyway? They were America's *allies*. The United States, Stassen concluded, should support a simple cease-fire, and nothing more.[83]

But Dulles, not Stassen, carried the day, and all British and French forces were out of Egypt by December 22, 1956. The French had weighed various stratagems to defy the American rollback and continue the war—including dressing Israeli troops in French uniforms to attack across the canal toward Cairo—but had agreed to withdraw.[84] Eisenhower approvingly took his foot off the hose and five hundred thousand barrels of American oil gushed back into European gas tanks every day. That was an essential measure because the Israelis—demanding concessions that Nasser refused to grant—would not complete their withdrawal from Egyptian territory until March 1957. With Israeli tanks still parked on the Sinai Peninsula,

Nasser blocked all efforts to clear the Suez Canal and no European oil tankers passed through it in the winter of 1956–57. The IPC pipeline from Kirkuk across Syria to Tripoli would not pump a drop of oil until the spring of 1957.[85] This was the nightmare scenario that Eden and Mollet had invaded Egypt to prevent: a Third World assault on the "energy security" of Western Europe. Pressed hard by the Europeans, Dulles pressed Ben-Gurion to trade his territorial demands for American and UN security guarantees for Eilat and Gaza, and a deal was quietly struck. Eisenhower insisted that "the Israelites," as he still quaintly called the Israelis, "return to their national territory." In a sign of the power of the Israel lobby, Ike met more resistance from Senate Majority Leader Lyndon Johnson than he did from Tel Aviv. If the Soviets get to keep Hungary, LBJ wheedled, why can't the Israelis keep the Sinai?[86] But Ike went on national television, rallied the American people and silenced Johnson. Shortly after Foreign Minister Golda Meir had triumphantly told the Knesset that the Sinai was annexed to Israel, Israel gave the peninsula back to Egypt. Meir's embarrassing climbdown was the occasion for Prime Minister Ben-Gurion's famous line: "What must be feared, must be feared."[87] With few friends in the world, Israel had to fear the loss of its American mentor above all things, and by March 1957 had exhausted the patience of everyone, including Dulles and Eisenhower.

With American fuel rushing back into their empty tanks, the Europeans were not exactly grateful. Before the crisis, Ike had reminded his NSC of America's undiminished need for "allies and associates." Without them, "the leader is just another adventurer, like Genghis Khan."[88] In Britain and France, Americans were now about as welcome as Mongols. In the House of Commons, 126 Tories voted to censure the U.S. government for "gravely endangering the Atlantic Alliance." Britain's chancellor of the exchequer warned that exasperated British voters might demand withdrawal from the UN and closure of all American bases on British soil. Some London cabbies refused to pick up American tourists, and some British filling stations refused to sell gas to American drivers. The CIA lamented that its "estrangement [from British intelligence sources] was becoming dangerously acute."[89] In France, U.S. ambassador Douglas Dillon noted that the Suez Crisis had "bitten deeply into French pride." Rising anti-Americanism and distrust of the UN eroded faith in President Eisenhower, who was believed to have sabotaged the French position in North Africa and "irretrievably established the Soviets" there. Churchill warned Eisenhower that the American president and Eden had, through their various misunderstandings, "opened a gulf on which our whole civilization may founder." Dillon wrote from Paris in a similar vein: the French believed that the United States had foolishly abandoned its "oldest and staunchest allies in pursuit of popularity with the Afro-Asian states." Eisenhower admitted as much in his reply to Churchill: the United States *had* to oppose the invasion because the Anglo-French-Israeli use of force "would only turn Arab opinion against the West."[90]

France broke with the United States after Suez, which, as Vice President Nixon succinctly put it, "decreased French prestige and influence in North Africa at an alarming rate."[91] Embroiled in the Algerian War, which sapped the French treasury as well as French troop levels in Europe, the tottering Fourth Republic resented American interference in the Middle East at least as much as did the British. The discovery of oil reserves in the Sahara intensified French resentment. Early, frothy estimates had those Algerian wells producing enough oil to make France self-sufficient by 1980. Naturally the French took American criticism of their "colonial war" in Algeria as little more than political cover for American oil companies, who would surely file into the Sahara as soon as the French had filed out.[92] On the day French troops began to pull out of Egypt, France's ambassador to the United States reported a surreal meeting with President Eisenhower, who assured the Frenchman that France was doing the right thing, and America too: "Mr. Ambassador, life is a grand staircase, which rises to Heaven. I shall arrive at the top of that staircase and I wish to present myself before the Creator with a pure conscience."[93] When CIA director Allen Dulles called for U-2 flights over Soviet territory during the crisis, Ike refused the request: "Policies," he insisted, "must be correct and moral."[94]

Secretary of State Dulles, Harold Macmillan muttered, did not supply much of a corrective. He was a "Gladstonian Liberal, who disliked the nakedness of facts." Allen Dulles was less Gladstonian than his brother, lamenting to his Intelligence Advisory Committee in January 1957 that "the adverse effects of the Suez situation" had weakened the French army, strengthened the Algerian nationalists, "led to an upswing in terrorist activity" and raised the distinct possibility of a "military coup in France."[95] Even if "correct and moral," none of those developments would serve American interests. The costs of that Algerian War—coming hot on the heels of the war in Indochina—killed off the Fourth Republic, but Charles de Gaulle's Fifth Republic, which followed in 1958, was no friend of the United States either. Indeed, the defiant, uncooperative course dubbed "Gaullism" leaked from the wounds opened at Suez, as did the French determination to build an independent nuclear capability so that they would never again find themselves subject to nuclear black-mail as they had been at Suez, where Eisenhower had threatened to withhold American support and Khrushchev had threatened to "rain" atom bombs on Paris and London.

Suez gave birth to the modern French conviction that Americans are pharisees who say one thing and do another and—unlike the French and British at Suez— generally get away with it only because they *can*. Having stood with the United States through the first decade of the Cold War, the French were perplexed by America's haste to supplant them in North Africa. "The Suez action was quashed," Pierre Mendès-France said in December 1956, because "the political constellation was not characterized by the old opposition of the three (America, France and Britain) against one (Russia), but by a new formula . . . the two biggest (America and Russia) against the two less big."[96] De Gaulle certainly agreed with that assessment, and would even have given the advantage to the Soviets, for at least knowing what they wanted. De Gaulle and his successors made it a matter of principle not to trust the Americans with French security. They resented Suez as well as America's opportunistic and hostile takeover of the French presence in Tunisia and Morocco after the crisis, and they bewailed France's pointed exclusion from the 1958 Lebanese intervention, which would be the first application of what would shortly be called the Eisenhower Doctrine. ("It only remains to say a mass for their souls," Lebanese president Camille Chamoun said of the fading French presence in the Middle East.)[97] In response to those American snubs, de Gaulle pointedly identified France with the "Arab Revolution," spurned Israel, contrasted "progressive" French Middle Eastern policies with "reactionary" Anglo-Saxon ones, withdrew French forces from NATO's command structure, questioned America's right to deploy nuclear weapons in Europe, went to Moscow and began building the European Union as an alternative to American primacy in Western Europe. "Europe will be your revenge," German chancellor Konrad Adenauer had consoled Mollet after Suez.[98] Those were the aftershocks of American Middle East policy in 1956—"a bitter harvest of Allied anger and ill will," as Joseph and Stewart Alsop put it in the *New York Herald Tribune*—and regular EU opposition today to American policy initiatives is one facet of the "revenge" described by Adenauer.

The impact of the Suez Crisis on American-Israeli relations was complex. Israel would always pose unique problems for American foreign policy because of its entrenched lobbyists in Washington, its reprisal policy against all terrorists and their havens—which made foreign invasions easy to foment and justify—and the fact that Israel was generally allied with Western interests but followed an independent foreign policy. Although the Soviets chortled that Israel was just a "Levantine province of the United States," an "American colony," a "property of Wall Street," it was anything but those things.[99] Indeed, Israel's ability to act independently—within limits—was driven home by Tel Aviv's deceitful comportment toward Washington during the Suez War. Tel Aviv deceived Washington in the days before the attack, which led to some excruciating moments for Ambassador Abba Eban. "I am certain, Mr. Ambassador, that you will want to get back to your embassy to find out just exactly what is happening in your country," a State Department official snarled at Eban upon hearing reports of the Israeli invasion. Ike, campaigning in Miami when the news broke, was even blunter in his first call to Dulles: "Foster, you tell them, goddamn it, we are going to apply sanctions, we are going to the United Nations, we are going to do everything that there is so we can stop this thing."[100] Acting Secretary of State Herbert Hoover, Jr., was even more adamant. When it was rumored on November 8 that the Soviets would "flatten" Israel or, at the very least, send 250,000 "volunteers" to roll back the IDF, Hoover threatened to cut off American aid to Israel and expel the Jewish state from the UN if it did not immediately give ground.[101]

Forced to relinquish their conquests in 1956, the Israelis nevertheless achieved their *real* agenda, which was to solidify the borders of 1949. Just before the war, the British embassy in Tel Aviv had noted "a mood of defiance and desperation" in Israel. "The Israelis are deeply suspicious that we shall subject them to intolerable pressure to accept an intolerable settlement." What the Israelis particularly feared was American and British pressure to cede a broad strip of the Negev, including possibly Eilat, to Egypt and Jordan. Dulles by 1955 was insisting (as part of the Alpha Program) that Israel grant a dramatic "revision of boundaries" in Gaza and the Negev to purchase peace with Egypt and Jordan. The U.S. ambassador to Egypt, Henry Byroade, was in close contact with Egyptian foreign minister Mahmoud Fawzi, who assured Byroade that "the iron is now hot" and that peace could be achieved if only the Israelis would compensate the Palestinian refugees, open up Jerusalem and cede "a big chunk of the Negev" to Egypt.[102] Britain's ambassador in Washington wryly observed that this outbreak of American-Egyptian amity was a *disaster* for the Israelis, for it "increased Israel's sense of insecurity and isolation" and revealed "the true precariousness of Israel's position."[103] The Israelis could cling to the territorial gains of 1948–49 as well as their intransigent position on Palestinian refugees only because America backed them unconditionally. But what if America swung into the Egyptian camp, as Byroade was attempting to do?

From the Israeli perspective, the prospect of a real American-Egyptian entente was terrifying; hence the British actually predicted in late 1955 that the Israelis would soon launch "a large scale reprisal raid" against Egypt to derail further parleys between Byroade, Fawzi and Nasser.[104] Operation Kadesh in October 1956 was that anticipated "reprisal raid," and one of the first things Ben-Gurion did once the Israeli invasion was rolling forward was to pronounce the 1949 "armistice agreement with Egypt . . . dead and buried." That cease-fire, which had been laboriously brokered by American Ralph Bunche, would have to be traded for something more advantageous to Israel "without prior conditions."[105] Despite their loud lamentations, the Israelis got what they *really* wanted in 1956: the Big Israel of 1949, as opposed to the Little Israel of 1947.

ISRAEL WINS

Before the Suez War, John Foster Dulles had warned his Israeli counterpart Moshe Sharett that "the safety and continued existence of the free world" depended on substantial Israeli concessions on territory ("a land bridge across the Negev"), good behavior (no more "exploiting frontier incidents" to launch reprisals) and the repatriation or compensation of refugees. The United States would not continue "sticking to Israel" without such concessions, Dulles warned.[106] Here was the *beauty* of Israel's diplomatic defeat in 1956: it permitted Sharett to concede the new conquests in Gaza and the Sinai without making *any* concessions on the 1948 conquests and refugees. And the groans Israel and its lobbyists emitted in 1956 over their superficial losses served to foreclose all talk of deeper concessions. Before the Suez War, Secretary of State Dulles pressed the Israelis to retreat from the "armistice lines" of 1949; after the war—pressured by powerful senators like J. William Fulbright, Lyndon Johnson, Hubert Humphrey and William Knowland, who decried the "Lodge-Dulles-Eisenhower policy" of squeezing Israel and appeasing Nasser—Dulles dropped the matter altogether.[107] The British ambassador in Washington, Harold Caccia, was flabbergasted. Eisenhower, he recorded, craved Arab oil and "strategic space" but would not force the concessions from the Israelis that would have lodged him more securely in that space. Tel Aviv, meanwhile, "demanded an American guarantee of their frontiers *without any sacrifice at all.*" Caccia advised Dulles to *sell* the guarantee for some usable price—land or refugees—but Dulles's heart had gone out of the whole policy of "evenhandedness." He would now tilt heavily toward Israel. "With Israeli pressure what it is and U.S. elections coming on," he said, "I cannot any longer refrain from offering guarantees, arms and even a defense pact."[108] One night, Dulles reread his Bible and declared, "It does not make sense that I can solve problems which Moses and Joshua with Divine guidance could not solve."[109]

"Knowland is running for the Presidency," Dulles muttered. "The pressure of the Jews largely accounts for his attitude." To Henry Cabot Lodge, Jr., Dulles complained of "the terrific control the Jews have over the news media and the barrage the Jews have built up on Congressmen."[110] Under cover of that barrage, Israel had actually done well out of the Suez War, though it was not easy to perceive that fact through the palls of smoke. "How irritating the Israelis can be," a British official complained. "They seem unable to rid themselves of cant." That habitual cant made all negotiations with them uniquely difficult: "Years of seeking sympathy from the world, of pleading a case, have produced this truly formidable disingenuousness." Their statesmen "preferred ingenuity and smoke-screens to candor." They "filled the air with propaganda, yet censored the dissemination of honest news."[111] An example of this was Ben-Gurion's insistence in 1956 that even though Tel Aviv had started the war—dropping paratroops at the Mitla Pass and thrusting tanks into the Sinai—Egypt was the *real* aggressor: the armistice of 1949 had "expired because the Egyptian dictator had for years been attacking it."[112]

When Eisenhower threatened to impose $200 million worth of sanctions—the Syrians were refusing to let the Iraqis ship oil up their pipelines so long as the Israelis held Gaza and Sinai—the Israelis discreetly climbed down.[113] Removing oil from the market was one sure way to get America's attention. Nevertheless, even in defeat, the Israelis showed great suppleness, recasting Operation Kadesh—originally designed to annex the Sinai, administer the Gaza Strip (Ben-Gurion had no desire to *annex* its three hundred thousand Palestinian refugees, who "would be like a cancer") and prepare a vast redivision of the entire region—as mere "self-defense," a hop across the border to eradicate fedayeen bases. Permitted only a symbolic victory, Ben-Gurion made a meal of it: "Israel after the Sinai Campaign would never be the Israel that existed before it."[114] The Israelis gave back all the land they had conquered but unlocked the Gulf of Eilat and evicted the fedayeen—for a while— from Gaza. That was brilliant, for it allowed Israel to disassociate itself from Operation Musketeer and duck Eisenhower's heaviest punches, which landed squarely on Britain and France. Ben-Gurion must have enjoyed the immense irony of it all: denied the "waters of purity" at Suez, the British and French instead mounted the "rostrum of shame" that they had erected for Israel. The Israelis then had a go at the waters of purity themselves, assuring the UN that they would run the Gaza Strip as a "pilot plan of general cooperation with the Arab world."[115]

Strong bipartisan intervention in Washington on Israel's behalf—a bloc of 26 pro-Israel senators and 116 representatives plus elder statesmen like Harry Truman and Eleanor Roosevelt—got Israel a much better deal in 1956 than it would otherwise have received: free passage in the Gulf of Eilat, which was critical for the supply of Iranian oil to Israel, and the transfer of Gaza from Egypt to the UN.[116] When Senate Minority Leader William Knowland leaned on Dulles to stop pressuring Ben-Gurion to restore Gaza to Egypt in February 1957, Dulles complained, "We cannot have *all* our policies made in Jerusalem." Eisenhower joined Dulles in lamenting the "pettiness" of Congress's criteria: "I found it dismaying that partisan considerations could enter so much into life or death, peace or war decisions." But Eisenhower himself had shown no appetite for a showdown with Israel in this crisis or any other. Ultimately, Knowland, Johnson and their congressional allies prevailed in the struggle to strengthen Israel, and Ike and Dulles—meekly protesting that "we will lose the Middle East"—gave way despite the fact that just 19 percent of Americans supported Israeli actions in the Suez War.[117]

The Soviets reaped huge dividends from Suez with no investment. Committed to the repression in Hungary, Khrushchev wrote Nasser off until the colonel was rescued by Ike. The Soviets then took credit for the American rescue. So did Nasser, who gleefully posed as "the hero who had defeated the armies of two great empires, the British and the French." He had single-handedly withstood the "triple aggression" of Israel and the "imperialist powers" and carried the day. He was the invincible *rais*, or leader. Ignoring the pivotal intervention of Ike, Nasser insisted that he had won, when he had actually been defeated.[118] Nasser's *Philosophy of the Revolution*, published in 1955 and triumphantly reissued after the Suez Crisis, grandly placed Egypt at the center of three concentric circles encompassing the Arab, Islamic and African worlds. It was his historical task, Nasser believed, to rid all three circles of imperialism, nudge them toward neutralism, demolish Israel and embark on fruitful cooperation with the Soviet Union and the socialist camp.[119]

Predictably, the American protégé of 1956 became increasingly unmanageable. In July 1957, Nasser addressed a crowd of eighty thousand in Alexandria and declaimed that alliance with the United States was "a partnership of the wolf with the lamb" and that states that partnered with the wolf—Lebanon, Saudi Arabia, Jordan, Iraq, Libya, Tunisia and Morocco—were "traitors, Arab deviationists, who had sold their countries to imperialism." As for Eisenhower—Nasser's savior—the American president was "engaged in imperialistic maneuvers, seeking to attain the objectives which Britain and France failed to get by aggression." How? "With starvation and economic pressure, orchestrated by World Zionism." Paid cheering sections amplified by microphones roared their approval, and in the stillness between the colonel's exclamations it dawned on an American onlooker that Nasser was never going to repay the lifesaving commitment that Ike had made to him at Suez.[120]

"PERPETUATING FEUDAL DESPOTISM"

Having failed in their Nasser gambit, Eisenhower and Dulles then tried "to create a hero out of King Saud, to elevate him to the position of leader of the entire Arab world, so as to destroy Nasser [and] isolate Egypt." The Saudis, for want of anything better, became a central strut of the Omega Program and the Eisenhower Doctrine. Appeasing them became the new American policy when Dulles was released from the hospital in December 1956.[121] "King Saud," Eisenhower improbably announced, must be made into "a figure with sufficient prestige to offset Nasser." After 9/11, Americans struggled to understand how their government could have winked at the fanaticism and backwardness of the Saudi regime over the years. The process began with the oil strikes of the 1930s, but quickened after the Suez Crisis, when Ike resolved to make Saud "the great gookety gook of the Muslim world." Dulles enlisted the king and his clerics against "the atheistic creed of Communism," and a rather desperate State Department communiqué announced that—Egypt being "lost"—Saudi Arabia, "by virtue of its spiritual, geographical and economic position, is now of vital importance in the Middle East." Riyadh would have to be "strengthened," "maintained" and "safeguarded" in—and here was a tremendous irony—"the interests of world peace." Saudi Arabia would do a great deal of damage to world peace in the years ahead, but even in 1956—in spite of its American sponsorship—it had given $10 million to Nasser's war chest and urged the annihilation of Israel.[122]

In 1957, Riyadh flunked its first test as an American ally. When Washington brokered a deal in which the Israelis would return Sharm el-Sheikh and the Gaza Strip to the Egyptians in return for guaranteed maritime access to their port of Eilat, King Saud embarrassingly declared that it was the "sacred duty of Muslims" and a "matter of life and death" to keep the Jews out of Eilat.[123] Washington eventually persuaded King Saud to shut up and (sourly) pocket $20 million in Eisenhower Doctrine aid. Still, Saud refused to endorse the doctrine, complained of American-led "economic war" in the Middle East—an especially hypocritical sop to Nasser given all the petrodollars that were welling up from American oil investments in Saudi Arabia—and obliquely noted, even as he accepted the American cash, that "other forms of imperialism"—Zionist and American—were as dangerous as the Soviet variety.[124]

The whole concept of frog-marching Riyadh into the breach to replace Cairo should have been acknowledged as absurd from the outset, for even turning to the archaic Saudis represented a crushing defeat for American policy. By taking Nasser's side in the Suez War—despite the colonel's Soviet arms purchases and recognition of Red China—Washington had naively assumed that it could co-opt the Arab radical regimes and win them over to free markets and containment. The smoke had barely cleared over Suez when Washington circled morosely back to a reliance on the monarchies.[125] Ike met the Saudi king for the first time in 1957 and was crestfallen. Saud was nothing like Ike had imagined: "introspective and shy," and not even "master of his own house." He was locked in a struggle for power with his brother Faisal, who would seize control of foreign and domestic policy the following year.[126] The Democrats, lining up to contest the White House in 1960, had a field day with Saud's obsolescence: "Do we build strength against Communism by contributing American tax dollars to perpetuate this kind of feudal despotism?" Representative George McGovern burst out.[127] Ike fretted to Republican congressional leaders that he could "see nothing to show that [Saud's] the person we should tie to." Still, American propagandists would just have to stress Saud's "spiritual leadership" of the Muslim world, and then gradually argue for his political leadership as well. "He's the only 'stone' on which to build," Ike admitted to British defense minister Duncan Sandys in February 1957.[128] The CIA recommended using Wahhabism to roll back Nasser; Langley advised an "all out propaganda campaign by the Hashemite and Saudi families, with overtones of Wahhabi theology."[129] It was a losing, ill-advised battle from the outset. A secret CIA report on ideological warfare reminded the White House that "human activity follows this sequence: emotion, ideas, organization and action."[130] The Saudis lacked three of the four processes, and the only one they were (occasionally) capable of mustering—emotion—was reckless and uncontrollable.

This placed the United States in an impossible predicament. It could not intervene against Nasser without making itself hateful, but it could not back him either, for Nasser's ambition to be the regional policeman overlapped with Washington's identical ambition.[131] Arguably unavoidable, the clash was needlessly sharpened by Washington. Even in the 1950s, the British cabinet protested the American shift in favor of Saudi "feudal authority." In trying to "build up King Saud as the leader of the Arab world, the Americans [were backing] the losing horse, a certain loser."[132] A 1956 CIA study found Saudi Arabia "too small and insignificant on the world stage and too backward to command much respect."[133] That very backwardness made troublemakers of the Saudis, who succumbed over and over to regional bullying and peer pressure. The kingdom was riddled with Nasser sympathizers. In 1955 and 1956, there had been pro-Nasser uprisings among the Saudi garrisons at Taif and Dhahran; both were brutally repressed and the officers beheaded, but the king often discreetly supported Nasser to mollify the colonel's many Saudi supporters. Nasser's support of the Algerian War against the French, for example, was "long on propaganda and short on arms," but the arms were paid for—and the French security forces killed—by Saudi "charitable donations."[134] This would not be the last time that the Saudis would try to buy their way into more dynamic Muslim circles by funding murder and mayhem with petrodollars.

EATING DIRT IN BERMUDA

No mayhem was on display at the Bermuda Conference in March 1957, where Ike and the new British prime minister, Harold Macmillan, patched up the Anglo-American "special relationship" as if the bruising Suez Crisis had never happened. Eden had returned from Jamaica in December 1956 determined to resume his responsibilities, but found himself so undercut by his falling out with the Americans as well as the "half-truths" he had told Parliament about the nature of the Suez operation that he had little choice but to give way to Macmillan. "The moral for British Governments is clear," A. J. P. Taylor sallied. "Like most respectable people they will make poor criminals and had better stick to respectability. They will not be much good at anything else." In weirdly convivial meetings at the Mid-Ocean Club, Prime Minister Macmillan and his ministers proved far more respectable (and agreeable) than Eden, and turned their backs on the French. "They have tossed their partner in the Suez adventure to the wolves with a cynicism which I doubt the French will easily or quickly forget," a State Department analyst observed.[135]

In Bermuda, Macmillan agreed to "eat dirt" in the Middle East; in return, Eisenhower did a number of favors for the British. He agreed to reduced British troop levels in Germany; he shared expensive missile technology with the British; he joined the military committee of the Baghdad Pact and he gave Britain "freedom of action" in its Persian Gulf outposts, including the hotly contested oasis of Buraimi, which the Saudis would not formally relinquish claim to until 1974. Macmillan, maligned in the conservative newspapers as the "leader of the bolters," took Churchill's post-Suez dictum to heart: "We must never get out of step with the Americans—never."[136] Like Tony Blair years later, Macmillan came to view himself as an American lieutenant. Ike's concessions to Macmillan were accompanied by a vast expansion of American responsibility all across the Middle East. The Eisenhower Doctrine, Macmillan chuckled, was nothing but "Suez in reverse." Ike would now have to take up the cudgels himself against Nasser.[137] In 1957, America even stepped into the old British protectorate of Jordan, where the Anglophile King Hussein, continually attacked as a "British puppet" by Nasser and the Palestinians, finally decided to void his British security pact—as a sop to the Arab nationalists—and accept more discreet American support against "international communism" and, of course, Nasser.[138] Harold Macmillan bore all these insults with a brave face. Suez, he explained to Dulles, "was the last gasp of a declining power. Perhaps in two hundred years the United States will know how we felt."[139]

CHAPTER 7

·❧❧·

THE EISENHOWER
DOCTRINE

EISENHOWER EMERGED FROM THE SUEZ Crisis profoundly conflicted. Having rescued Nasser from the British, French and Israelis, he regarded his new protégé warily. In March 1957, Ike signed the "America Doctrine," which congressional Democrats—sensing a sure loser and worn out by what Senator Richard Russell called "the horrible example of Korea"—defiantly renamed after its author.[1] The Eisenhower Doctrine pledged $200 million to combat Soviet expansion in the Middle East—communists had entered the Syrian government in 1955—but also, a puzzling reference to Nasser, "any nation controlled by International Communism." Still smarting from Suez, the new British prime minister, Harold Macmillan, dubbed the Eisenhower Doctrine "this gallant effort to shut the stable door after the horse had bolted."[2]

The horse immediately began to buck and kick. Flush with victory at Suez, Nasser used his soaring postcrisis prestige and popularity to merge with Syria. The fact that the United Arab Republic (UAR) proclaimed in February 1958 was a desperate, defensive play by Nasser to undercut the communists and Baath "revivalists" who had entered the Syrian government in 1954 was not understood in Dulles's State Department. The UAR was seen as a mortal threat to American interests, even more so after July 1958, when Iraqi officers led by General Abdul Karim Kasim ousted the pro-Western Hashemite dynasty in Iraq.[3]

THE IRAQ COUP

The fall of the twenty-three-year-old "boy king" Faisal II and his prime minister Nuri as-Said hit Washington like a bombshell. Faisal and Nuri had backed the Western powers during the Suez Crisis and had given the Baghdad Pact its only Arab member state. Now they were gone in a cyclone of violence. General Kasim bragged that he had personally strangled the king with his bare hands, torn him up and then mutilated the corpses of Nuri and Crown Prince Abdullah for good measure. Mobs in Baghdad found the graves of the king, crown prince and prime minister, dug them up and danced on the body parts. "Iraq is now the most dangerous spot on earth," CIA director Allen Dulles direly noted.[4] It may well have been. Like the Syrians, General Kasim eagerly accepted Soviet aid and brought communists into his government. Communist militias took control of the streets, sacked Faisal's palace, torched the British embassy and killed hundreds of political prisoners. "Not even the invasion of Korea posed so grave a threat to the security and strategy of the West," the *New York Herald Tribune* warned. The *New York Times* called Kasim's coup "a stunning blow to the Western democracies," and the *Washington Post* cited it as yet more evidence of "the failure of American policy in this vital part of the world."[5] Just as George W. Bush feared that Iraq's oil revenues would be plowed into nuclear weapons and terrorism, President Eisenhower worried that they would be used to power communist expansion. "The Iraq Communists are getting a prosperous oil industry *free*, with access to European markets, and we must be prepared to shut down those operations . . . Relevant plans should be made *now*," a Harvard University consultant wrote CIA director Allen Dulles.[6]

Amid this deteriorating situation, even the Saudis prepared to bolt. Fearing that the Iraq coup might spread to Saudi Arabia, King Saud demanded an American invasion of Iraq. "What is the use of all these pacts?" he scoffed to the American ambassador. "Do something," he threatened, or the Saudi kingdom would have no choice but to "go along with UAR foreign policy."[7] With the Soviets launching Sputnik, American rockets blowing up in their gantries and the U.S. government trying to desegregate the schools in Little Rock, Arkansas, against white backlash, Ike— who suffered a stroke in November 1957—appeared flummoxed. "American cocksureness is shaken," the British ambassador reported from Washington. Ike and

Dulles expressed surprise that their intervention at Suez on behalf of Nasser had brought them no tangible benefits.[8]

CRISIS IN LEBANON

Nasser had been instrumental in whipping up the Iraqi street against the Hashemites. Cairo Radio had conducted a vitriolic campaign against Nuri for years ("Kill Nuri and throw his carcass to the jackals") as well as the royal family.[9] Although Nasser exerted even less control over Baghdad than he did over Damascus, the colonel now took aim at Beirut. Carved by the French from formerly Ottoman Syria in 1920, Lebanon was an entirely artificial creation rife with sectarian tensions. The Maronites—a Byzantine Christian sect that had once insisted that Jesus had one nature, not two (divine and human)—now pressed political claims more urgently than theological ones. After World War I—with the British forging what appeared to be a client state in Palestine—French strategists had done the same, expanding the useful little haven for Maronite Christians on Mount Lebanon that had been established by French emperor Napoleon III in the 1860s to include the largely Muslim seacoast around Tripoli and the largely Muslim Bekaa Valley. Grand Liban—the country we now call Lebanon—was created in that creeping way by French and Maronite collusion, and further Islamicized by the addition of tens of thousands of Palestinian refugees in 1948 (and the subtraction of thousands of Christians, who emigrated in this period to North and South America, Europe and Africa).[10] By the 1950s, Lebanon was bursting with sectarian disputes, which welled up around the crisis of Christian president Camille Chamoun's support for the Eisenhower Doctrine and his pursuit of a second presidential term, which would have violated the one-term limit in the Lebanese constitution that had been delicately brokered by the French in 1926.

Excoriated by Nasser on Cairo Radio and attacked at home by a United National Front (UNF) of all Lebanese Muslim parties—which wanted more offices, a new census (the last one had been taken in 1932) and a shot at the presidency (reserved for Christians)—Chamoun was the first Arab leader to seek American aid. His motives were obvious: Chamoun was milking American anxieties about Egypt, Syria and Iraq to win U.S. intervention against the UNF, whose spokesman, Sheikh Nadim el-Jisr, a Muslim leader from Tripoli, complained that "ever since the end of the Ottoman Empire, Christians have been enjoying first-class citizenship and treating their Muslim compatriots as second-class citizens."[11] Even growing numbers of Lebanese *Christians* viewed Lebanon as unviable—and desired a retreat to the more manageable borders of Petit Liban—shorn of Tripoli and the Bekaa. Many Lebanese Muslims viewed Lebanon—*grand* or *petit*—as nothing more "than a temporary expedient until a broad, secular Arab state should be ready to absorb it. "Taking it all in," the British embassy in Beirut warned that the 1958 crisis could well be "a genuine manifestation of the popular will of the Lebanese people," not the "partisan, factional disturbances" deplored by Chamoun and a noticeably confused but still adamant Eisenhower.[12]

Distracted by Nasser's UAR and Dulles's warnings about the spread of "international communism," Eisenhower plunged into Lebanon. Like the George W. Bush administration years later, Eisenhower clung hard to Lebanon as the most likely "success story" in the region. It was a beautiful green country of soaring, snowcapped peaks with the highest literacy rate in the Arab world (85 percent). Lebanon educated more girls than boys (thanks to its Christian convent schools) and freely tolerated political and cultural dissidents. Hundreds of Middle Eastern political exiles called Beirut home, as did the American University and several good French, American and English schools, and Lebanon was a real, functioning democracy.[13]

Fearing that Kasim's coup in Iraq and Nasser's UAR portended similar trouble in Lebanon—"Nasser is only 50 kilometers from Beirut; he will come to *our* rescue," the Lebanese paper *Beirut al-Masa* promised its readers in late 1957—Lebanese president Camille Chamoun appealed to Washington for military support to repulse the UAR.[14] Chamoun, a fifty-seven-year-old French-educated Maronite, had been in deep trouble since the Suez Crisis, when, alone among the Arab states, he had refused to break ranks with France and Britain. Nasser had never stopped attacking him as a "scab," "stooge" and "traitor," but neither had Chamoun's Sunni Muslim prime minister, Rashid Karami, who, after Suez, began to push for Lebanese union with Nasser's UAR as perhaps the only way to break the Christian hold on jobs in Lebanon's administration, army, gendarmerie and police. Although Cairo had little hope of controlling—let alone annexing—powerful Lebanese Muslim and Druze enemies of Chamoun like Sabri Hamadi of the Bekaa Valley, Rashid Karami of Tripoli and Kamal Jumblat of the Chouf Mountains, Nasser did build up the "Beirut Four"—Saeb Salaam, Abdallah Yafi, Adnan Hakim and Abdullah Mashnuq—as clients. They relied entirely on Egyptian aid and could be relied on to press a pro-Cairo line in Lebanon. The Egyptians poured in millions of dollars of aid (and bribes) to pull Lebanon into the UAR. The money financed "mobs" and votes—one of the "Beirut Four" received $7 million in cash from Cairo—and Egypt's Mukhabarat ran a very effective anti-Chamoun operation out of the UAR embassy in Beirut.[15] That explained Chamoun's eager adhesion to the Eisenhower Doctrine in 1957. He wanted American weapons and aid dollars, but he also needed protection against Lebanon's increasingly assertive and well-funded Muslims.[16]

Chamoun, the leading Lebanese Maronite, was a controversial figure because of his unconstitutional quest for a second term, but Eisenhower backed Chamoun out of desperation. Ike feared that free and fair elections and a too strict observance of the constitution would merely return "Arab-oriented"—as opposed to Western-oriented—politicians. In that extrapolation, he was correct. France's Lebanese electoral law used proportional representation based on religion, not parties, which meant that Lebanon's surging Muslim population was about to wash away Christian rule.[17] The future in the 1950s was clear and terrifying to old-guard Maronite politicians like Alfred Naccache, who warned an American visitor that Lebanon was about to be "drowned in a Muslim sea."[18]

With Egypt and Syria pouring money, advice and propaganda into the UNF, Eisenhower stoically provided jeeps and guns to Chamoun—to police the streets—and authorized his envoy Wilbur "Bill" Eveland to hand suitcases of U.S. dollars to pro-Chamoun candidates. If the Lebanese parliament could be packed with pro-Chamoun deputies, the president might successfully amend the constitution. This exercise in vote-rigging would be an American show, to exhibit the strength of the Eisenhower Doctrine, "restore Western influence in the Middle East" and "oppose Nasser's hegemony."[19] When quizzed by Congress as to why the French and British weren't involved in the rather sordid operation, Dulles replied, "I cannot think of anything that would more surely turn the area over to international communism than to go there hand in hand with the British and the French."[20] Henry Cabot Lodge, Jr., at the UN, agreed: "Suez is still too fresh in the minds of the world's leaders and peoples." Washington, the honest broker, would have to carry the ball.[21]

CHAMOUN STEALS THE ELECTION OF 1957

American brokerage suited Camille Chamoun perfectly. Although Dulles insisted that "more important than Chamoun's second term is the continuous existence of a genuinely independent Lebanon with pro-Western policies," Chamoun considered the second term more important.[22] Funded with American cash and assisted by massive vote fraud, Chamoun's candidates won two-thirds of the seats in parliament. This was a patently fraudulent outcome—not unlike Hamid Karzai's in 2009—and an abashed President Eisenhower professed his disgust with Chamoun's methods. "This has turned into a battle between Nasser's goons on the one side and Chamoun's goons on the other," a presidential adviser groused. "Chamoun's goons just have the advantage of official status."[23] The Lebanese president—a former interior minister with a specialist's knowledge of Lebanon's electoral machine—did *too* well in the elections, manufacturing an impossibly large majority and flushing out even the most beloved and respected Lebanese moderates to replace them with Maronite creatures. In Cairo, Nasser had a field day with the results: "The greatest mistake of the U.S. government in the Middle East is that it fails to understand that the basic fact of life in the area is that people are tired of being exploited."[24] To tamp down pro-UAR agitation, Chamoun expelled all Syrians and Egyptians living in Lebanon. U.S. ambassador Robert McClintock wrote from Beirut that Lebanese Muslims were "bitter against the U.S. government for supplying arms to the Lebanese army and police," which were presumed to be Christian militias. "They interpret this as an attack on Muslims personally."[25]

Even prominent Maronites turned on President Chamoun in the crisis. The Maronite patriarch and the Lebanese army's Christian commandant—General Fuad Chehab—agreed that Chamoun was too "extravagantly pro-Western and despotic." The streets filled with UNF protesters, who—seeing division in the Christian ranks—now redoubled their denunciations of Chamoun and their appeals to Nasser. Even Phalange Party leader Pierre Gemayel, a great exponent of Chamoun's dictatorial methods, whose son would become Ronald Reagan's great Christian hope for Lebanon in the 1980s, had to admit that the jury-rigged parliament that Chamoun concocted in 1957 "represents, in my opinion, only ten percent of the population of the country—at the moment the real parliament is in the streets."[26]

All of this was a horrific embarrassment for Eisenhower, who was striving to put a smiling American face on the Chamoun regime. Now, in its first vigorous application, Chamoun was manipulating the Eisenhower Doctrine to steal an election and fabricate a parliamentary majority that would amend the Lebanese constitution in such a way that Chamoun could extend his presidency indefinitely. "The Arab world of [today] is not that of Lawrence of Arabia," a State Department official testily reminded the White House. There were laws that needed to be observed.[27] In May 1958, things sagged further when pro-Chamoun gunmen shot and killed the investigative reporter Nesib Metni, who had been among Chamoun's most dogged Christian critics. Eisenhower should have backed off; instead, he dug in, believing that *something* needed to be done to arrest Soviet and Nasserist expansion into Lebanon.

OPERATION BLUE BAT

Ike, who had considered invoking the Eisenhower Doctrine to block Soviet arms deliveries to Syria in 1957 and even weighed mad suggestions to unleash the Israelis against Egypt and the Ugandans against the Nile headwaters in Sudan to slow the spread of "Nasserism" and "international communism" that same year, considered action in Lebanon in 1958 a much safer bet.[28] Warning that the spread of communism and Nasserism "could, without vigorous response on our part, result in a complete elimination of Western influence in the Middle East," Ike vowed to fight to "keep Lebanon in the Western orbit." Losing the Middle East would be worse even than "the loss of China."[29] Dulles had snickered at Eden's characterization of Nasser as a "Hitler." He now, a year after the Suez Crisis, defined Nasser as an "expansionist dictator somewhat of the Hitler type" who had to be thrown back. Lebanon was the obvious place to make a stand: "This is our last chance to make a move. We cannot ignore this one. We have to act in the Middle East or get out," Ike grimly told his National Security Council on July 14, 1958.[30]

Although the CIA in 1958 predicted a future of continual civil war in Lebanon because of "the basic incompatibility of the country's religious groupings"— sect-ridden Christians against sect-ridden Muslims—and the ease with which outside powers like Syria, Egypt, Israel and Iran could intervene there, Ike sent in the marines anyway.[31] The Sixth Fleet gathered in the eastern Mediterranean and fourteen thousand U.S. troops—"wave after wave of grim-faced Marines, rifles poised for action, greeted by startled bathers sunning themselves and hordes of little boys selling chewing gum"—tramped across the beaches south of Beirut, hopped the seawall and entered the capital in July 1958. Ike worried to Macmillan that he might be "opening a Pandora's box."[32]

Eisenhower's objectives in Lebanon were unclear from the start. "Make clear to Chamoun that he does *not* have a blank check," Dulles cabled the U.S. ambassador in Beirut, Robert McClintock, in May 1958. "He must take decisive action to dissolve the country's political problems and must not count upon foreign forces to back him against domestic opposition."[33] Even as Dulles dictated those instructions, U.S. forces were readying to back Chamoun against swelling domestic opposition. Muslim towns rose against the Christian government, and so did the tribal leaders in the countryside: Karami in Tripoli, Hamade in the Terbol and Maarouf Saad in Saida.[34] In the Chouf Mountains, the wooded peaks that ran parallel to the coast and soared to ten thousand feet, Lebanon's Druze community attacked government posts and drove Chamoun's troops and police out of the hills. The Druze—a clannish sect of Muslim heretics who worship an eleventh-century Egyptian caliph, not Allah—proved as intractable in 1958 as they would twenty-five years later, when Ronald Reagan would unsuccessfully try his hand at pacifying Lebanon and steering it into the Western camp.

While Chamoun tried to bring Tripoli and Beirut under control, Druze leader Kamal Jumblat (the father of Walid, who would torment Reagan's marines in 1982–83) opened another front in the Chouf, driving out Lebanese army units and pulling in Syrian "volunteers." Another front flared up in the Bekaa Valley, where armed tribesmen attacked Lebanese gendarmes in Baalbek and drove them away. Counterattacks rolled back and forth across the valley, while Syrian army trucks rolled unperturbed into Lebanon to dump caches of arms for antigovernment rebels.[35] "Lebano-Syrian mobsters"—the term was invented by the U.S. embassy— slipped over the border to terrorize Americans. They bombed an American apartment block in May, and Sweden's ambassador reported that grim-looking Arab men in suits were scouring upscale neighborhoods in search of U.S. citizens to kidnap.[36] The thrill of the Iraq coup in July intensified the threats and violence. The Lebanese army worried that Arab nationalist "exuberance" would "cause more defections" from its ranks. Lebanese rebels attempted to blow up the Trans-Arabian Pipeline terminal at Sidon. Now *that* was hitting close to home. Tapline, which conveyed half a million barrels of Saudi oil across Jordan, Syria and Lebanon to the

Mediterranean coast every day, was a vital free-world energy artery. Any doubts that Dulles and Eisenhower still entertained about their Lebanese intervention evaporated.[37]

Prime Minister Harold Macmillan—still nursing the humiliation of 1956—darkly joked to Ike that "you are doing a Suez on me."[38] President Chamoun had appealed to the Security Council for UN help against "massive, illegal UAR intervention" in the internal affairs of Lebanon in the hope that the Soviets—Nasser's new patron—would veto his appeal and justify a request for American peacekeepers. The Soviets dashed Chamoun's hopes by merely abstaining, and permitting a little UN peacekeeping force under the Norwegian general Odd Bull to set sail for Beirut. Had Eisenhower applied the same standards to himself as he had two years earlier to Eden and Mollet, he would have had to stand down and give Odd Bull time to secure Lebanon's borders and disarm the various militias.[39] Only thus would Washington have upheld the "one law" of the UN.

Instead, like the British, French and Israelis in 1956, Ike applied his own law. "We had come to the crossroads," he reminded Vice President Nixon. Nasser was trying to get control of the world's oil supplies, first through Suez and now through the Syrian and Lebanese pipelines. He needed to be defeated so that he would not "get the income and power to destroy the Western world." The rhetoric of mortal threat and destruction anticipated Operation Iraqi Freedom fifty years later. Dick Nixon, unlike Dick Cheney, at least had the good sense to entertain a few doubts about the adventure: "If it works we are heroes and if not we are bums."[40] Eisenhower and Chamoun banked on the first outcome. U.S. Marines, Chamoun argued, were indispensable, for the UN blue helmets were no good at all at flushing out insurgents and arms caches: "They spend their time in social clubs at night."[41] Eisenhower justified the unilateral move with other arguments: the pro-Western regime in Iraq had just been swept away. Lebanon was the next domino in line poised to fall, and "the Soviet Union is undoubtedly behind the whole operation."[42]

Prime Minister Macmillan knew that Moscow had little to do with events in Lebanon, but he did worry about Egyptian subversion. The Lebanese airwaves in 1958 rang with scurrilous attacks on Chamoun by Cairo and Damascus Radio. Weapons and "volunteers" easily crossed the Syrian border into Lebanon, or rode in Egyptian boats from Gaza to beaches on the Lebanese coast. The CIA—briefed by Chamoun, a not entirely disinterested source—reported Egyptian plots to blow up the Iraq Petroleum Company pipeline, the British School, the St. George Club, the British Bank of the Middle East and the French Banque de Syrie et Liban, as well as eighteen documented acts of Syrian sabotage against Lebanese schools, newspapers, bridges, electrical stations, railway lines, water pipes, homes and the Jordanian embassy.[43] But having observed Ike's refusal to support military intervention against Egyptian subversion during the Suez Crisis, Macmillan must have wondered why armed force was suddenly so acceptable. A loyal ally locked in a "special relationship," Macmillan swallowed his objections and agreed to support Ike by sending British troops into Jordan, where radical Palestinian "West Bankers," marooned in Jordan since their expulsion from Israel in 1948, were rising against twenty-two-year-old King Hussein and his pro-British "East Bankers" and demanding that Jordan—the "land bridge connecting Syria and Egypt"—also dissolve itself and join the UAR.[44]

Although Dulles belittled poor Jordan with its tiny native population and swollen mass of Palestinian refugees—"the brutal fact is that Jordan has no justification as a state"—he thought it better to support King Hussein and his independence-minded Bedouin officers against non-Bedouin Arab nationalists, even if their Arab nationalism flowed more from resentment at their slow rate of promotion compared with the king's favored Bedouin than from any love for Nasser.[45] Dulles also believed that a hard line in Lebanon—even on behalf of Chamoun—was necessary to halt a Middle Eastern domino effect in other "peripheral countries," like Yemen, Libya and Sudan: "If we were to adopt the doctrine that Nasser can whip up a civil war without our intervention, our friends will go down to defeat."[46]

Lebanon's French community goggled at America's innocence.[47] "The French are very critical of U.S. policy in the Middle East," one analyst reported. "The Americans make far too much of communism, which has no traction in Arab societies, and think in terms that are too black and white." The "main threat in the Arab states," the French wisely concluded, "is not communism; it is the direct appeal of charismatic leaders like Nasser"—or Saddam or bin Laden—"to the Arab peoples over the heads of their kings and presidents." Their appeals were generally made sharper, not duller, by the arrival of U.S. troops. In a moment of clarity, Eisenhower admitted as much to Vice President Nixon: "The trouble is that we have a campaign of hatred against us, not by the governments but by the people. The people are on Nasser's side."[48]

For the moment, Operation Blue Bat succeeded. President Chamoun was buttressed. King Hussein was rescued. The Jordanian king bravely took the wheel of his favorite Chevrolet and drove out to the Bedouin army post at Zarqa—future birthplace of al-Qaeda-in-Iraq leader Abu Musab al-Zarqawi—to rally loyal troops and defeat efforts by his Arab nationalist prime minister to overthrow the Hash-emite monarchy and join the UAR. Peace descended for a moment, but Eisenhower had *solved* nothing. In Jordan, he had reversed everything he had wrought at Suez by giving Prime Minister Macmillan a "blank check" to restore British influence and drag Amman back into "the Western orbit."[49] At least one pro-American Arab states-man thought that the United States had fundamentally erred in propping up the Kingdom of Jordan: "Nasser must now hope that King Hussein *retains* his throne, because if he loses it, Nasser will find the Jordanians, the latest poor relations, clam-oring to enter his family circle, with implications of imminent bankruptcy should that take place."[50]

In Lebanon, the results of American intervention were meager. "Local political result is dubious," presidential envoy Robert Murphy cabled from Beirut in July 1958 after the landing of U.S. Marines. "The mere presence of our forces in a small coastal portion of the country seems to have brought no fundamental change in the local political climate." A British diplomat who met with Murphy noted that "Mr. Murphy, after twenty-four hours here, is beginning to hold his head in his hands at the intricacies of the Lebanese situation."[51] Miles Copeland, the old OSS Middle East specialist who had worked with Nasser and facilitated the coup against Mosad-deq and now served as a Booz Allen consultant and nonofficial cover operative for the CIA in Beirut, dismissed Murphy as a Washington insider unversed in Lebanese history and politics. Murphy was "the standard solution: send out a Great White Father" who, at the time of his appointment, was "working a twelve-hour day at a wide miscellany of problems, none of which had any connection with the Mid-dle East."[52]

The Lebanon crisis flared through the winter of 1958–59—long after the last U.S. Marines had packed their duffel bags and left—before finally sputtering out. The largely Muslim UNF exploited the retreat of Chamoun to grab offices, demote Christians—"They've taken Jacksonian strides through the army and civil service," McClintock observed from Beirut—and expose Chamoun's corruption. The Ma-ronite president had accepted bribes from Iraq's Nuri as-Said to join the Baghdad Pact. Lebanon's fifteen Palestinian refugee camps exploded into open rebellion against Lebanon's pro-Western orientation, but mainly against the United Nations Relief and Works Agency (UNRWA), which ran the camps through a Belgian direc-tor and two French deputies. UNRWA, Palestinian activists charged, was really "an Extermination Agency that implements imperialistic conspiracies" by "spreading disease and illiteracy" and seeding the camps with "Zionist spies." If this was the

Arab response to Western charity, what could possibly be expected of Western military occupations, in Lebanon or anywhere?

In Washington, Senator John F. Kennedy argued that "doing business with Nasser" would avail more than random deployments of U.S. Marines across the Middle East. "It is sheer delusion," he said, "to underestimate the cutting force of Arab nationalism." Girding for a run at the presidency in 1960, Kennedy accused Ike and Dulles of handling the Middle East "almost exclusively in the context of the East-West struggle." Feckless Republican policies needed to be "junked, for the sake of the Arabs, and for our own sake as well."[53] In Beirut, Miles Copeland reacted disgustedly to Ike's foreign policy. As in Egypt during the Suez Crisis, the problem was not that Ike chose the wrong side, it was that Ike chose a side at all, when the problem would have been best left to the warring parties, who would have arrived at their own solution without American mediation, which, experience told, would be taken in the wrong spirit by virtually everyone. "The outcome was exactly what Gamal Abdel Nasser was seeking. It was as though the Marines had been brought in to achieve Nasser's objectives for him." General Fuad Chehab and Prime Minster Rashid Karami emerged victorious from the squabble, and they were just "the two whom Nasser *wanted* to see in office." Moreover, with its bombs, shootings and kidnappings, the crisis had "established terrorism as an effective—even respectable—weapon."

"The Eisenhower Doctrine Is Dead"

According to Copeland, who was in Beirut throughout the crisis, the compromise arranged by Robert Murphy meant that "the Eisenhower Doctrine is dead." Lebanese independence had been upheld as a mere fig leaf. "Chehab," it was whispered in the U.S. embassy, "is a Naguib without a Nasser," a nobody who would easily be manipulated or knocked over by the Egyptians or the Syrians.[54] "No Lebanese government was likely to make a deal with the West" now. Even loyal Christians had soured on American protection. To assert their power, Pierre Gemayel's Christian Phalange orchestrated a strike of all Christian-run businesses, which paralyzed the country and forced the Americans into busy rounds of sectarian diplomacy to get Lebanon back to work. "American influence in Lebanon is now reduced to the Basta [the Muslim quarter of Beirut]," the French quipped with malicious irony. Of course, America exerted little influence over Lebanon's Muslims, even less over the thirty thousand Palestinian refugees, who used the turmoil of the Lebanese crisis to escape squalid, poorly guarded camps like Shatila and Dekwaneh to take up residency in Lebanon proper.[55] Eventually, after tedious negotiations—"Both sides were so groggy with fatigue that they would eventually stumble to some sort of a live-and-let-live solution," General Chehab assured the U.S. ambassador in early October—all parties *did* come together to agree upon a "no victor, no vanquished" formula.[56]

The Maronite general Fuad Chehab was confirmed as president—sensibly agreeing to "appease Muslim leaders to avoid open rebellion and reliance on the UAR"—and also agreeing to accept a "quadrumvirate" of advisers that included Christians Pierre Gemayel and Raymond Edde and two leading Muslims, Rashid Karami and Hussein Aoueni. Gemayel's strike ended and everything went back to normal, "so long as one accepts factional and feudal wrangling and even assassination as part of the normal picture in Lebanon," McClintock smiled. Eisenhower smiled at his own dumb luck. Lebanon could as easily have become a quagmire, but happily settled its differences. "I don't care if Muslim kills Muslim or Armenian kills Armenian; it is only dangerous when Muslim kills Christian or Christian kills Muslim," Edde, the new Maronite interior minister, pragmatically summed up.[57]

Lebanon settled down in 1958 because the army did not fracture along religious lines (as it would in 1975–76) and because Chamoun was persuaded—by General Chehab and Ambassador McClintock—*not* to push for a second term. Perhaps only a happy accident—presidential envoy Robert Murphy had earlier urged Chamoun to break with Chehab and attack rebel troops—permitted Eisenhower to "declare victory" and extricate himself from Lebanon.[58] As for Jordan, Secretary of State Dulles applauded King Hussein's hard line against the country's Arab nationalists: his dissolution of parliament, his ban on political parties and his proclamation of martial law. "It's a good tough program and if it works it will be wonderful for us," Dulles said. Eisenhower agreed: "It's a gallant fight to eject subversive elements." King Hussein gratefully characterized the Americans as purveyors of "right and justice."

Ike and Dulles were at least more incisive than George W. Bush, who would naively seek to solve the Middle East's problems with a "freedom agenda." The 1950s Republicans were realists by comparison. "Popular rule in Jordan is mostly an illusory hope," the American ambassador cabled from Amman in November 1957. "The West cannot afford at this time to assist the free exercise of democratic processes, as such freedom now could lead only to the complete loss of Jordan to

[the] Western cause."[59] They were also better historians. Dulles, who threw around Hitler analogies as casually as Bush, Cheney and Wolfowitz, nevertheless understood that Hitler and his imitators were ultimately weak. Like Hitler, Dulles observed in 1958, Nasser "goes from conquest to conquest without consolidating his gains" and would "not be a lasting phenomenon." Allen Dulles agreed: Nasser was a charismatic fad who would eventually be erased by resurgent "local forces" in every corner of the Middle East. America needed only to wait patiently and "buy time." Fortunately, the Republicans of 1958 knew their limits. "I would not want to go further [than Lebanon]," Ike concluded. "A big operation that could run all the way through Syria and Iraq [would be] far beyond anything I have [the] power to do constitutionally."[60] The *Washington Post* shared the president's doubts: "Sending Marines to Lebanon does not constitute a policy—rather it makes the formulation of a policy imperative."[61]

NASSER REHABILITATED

Ike had a stab at a new policy in October 1958. Having dispatched troops to Lebanon to defeat Nasser, Eisenhower swerved back into alliance with the colonel after the crisis. Eisenhower's NSC directive 5820/1 of November 1958—"U.S. Policy toward the Near East"—startlingly rehabilitated Nasser as "an essential element in the prevention of the extension of Soviet influence." Nasser's Arab nationalism might "muster ideological weapons far more powerful than anything the United States or its allies could bring to bear."[62] The incoming Kennedy administration resisted the temptation to damn Ike's vacillation—first supporting, then opposing, then supporting Nasser—and decided merely to embrace Eisenhower's latest change of line.

"Peace in the Middle East is not one step nearer reality today than it was eight years ago," JFK remarked on the campaign trail in August 1960.[63] Kennedy hoped to charm leaders like Nasser with friendly new initiatives. He named an "ambassador-at-large for the Third World," promised $500 million of "Food for Peace" aid to Cairo, sent his old Harvard economics professor Edward Mason on a goodwill mission to Egypt and told aide Richard Goodwin that the Kennedy administration would mend fences with Nasser. "Impartial but firm, deliberate but bold" was how JFK characterized his policy for the Middle East. Sounding a lot like Barack Obama on the subject of Iran in the 2008 presidential campaign, Kennedy said, "Nasser's got his problems; I've got my problems . . . , but it can't hurt down the line if we understand each other a little better."[64]

To Kennedy as to Eisenhower, Nasser proved a massive disappointment. No sooner had Kennedy moved into the White House than Nasser was on the move again. The breakup of the UAR in 1961 embarrassed Nasser. His vision of the United Arab Republic had been simply to transfer the most imposing Syrian politicians to new UAR ministries in Cairo, where they would be drowned in paperwork. That realization, not long in coming, persuaded the Syrian leadership to back out of the UAR just three years after its creation. In 1962, Nasser fixed his sights on Yemen. A threadbare little country—"The human race would not be seriously inconvenienced if Yemen were to slide quietly into the Indian Ocean," Nasser himself allowed— Yemen had great strategic importance to the United States, Soviets and Egyptians because of its proximity to the Saudi oil fields and the Red Sea portal to Suez.[65]

"NASSER'S VIETNAM"

Nasser called Persian Gulf oil "the sinew of modern civilization," and he resolved to use Yemen as a foothold to bring the oil fields under his control and make the world forget the fizzle of the UAR.[66] Pro-Nasser forces under General Abdullah Sallal ousted the pro-Saudi imam Muhammed al-Badr in Yemen in September 1962 and proclaimed a Yemeni Arab Republic (YAR). President Kennedy was sucked into the dispute. If Yemen fell into Nasser's camp, it could be used to pressure the Saudis, who already had their hands full fending off conspirators based in Cairo—Nasser's "Union of the Sons of the Arabian Peninsula"—and in Baghdad. Seven Saudi air force pilots had defected to Egypt with their jets, which demonstrated Nasser's appeal even to coddled protégés of the Saud family.[67] A Nasserist regime in Sana'a would also enclose the British port, air base and protectorate of Aden, which the U.S. and British governments considered a key Cold War asset. Prodded by the Saudis, JFK held his nose and gave grudging support to Imam Muhammed al-Badr. The State Department had characterized al-Badr as "a weakling" whose medieval policies had produced "severe internal disturbances." But he was the only horse in the stall.[68] Nasser knew that he was playing with fire; by pushing aggressively into Yemen—even against al-Badr—he was provoking two of the most powerful lobbies in Washington, Big Oil and AIPAC, which "agreed on very little, but they agreed on Nasser." The colonel was "a menace to the region and a sinkhole for U.S. aid dollars," and he needed to be stopped.[69]

But Nasser's reputation as Arab nationalist leader was at stake, so he waded in and gave General Sallal and the other YAR "free officers" money, troops, tanks and jets. Forty thousand Egyptian troops became seventy thousand, and, before long, Nasser—who was spending a million dollars a day in Yemen—was calling the blighted country "my Vietnam."[70] With the Saudis and Jordanians supporting royalist, countercoup forces and the shah of Iran fending off revolutionary riots in 1961, Kennedy and then Lyndon Johnson were placed on the horns of a dilemma. Support reliable if vulnerable monarchies—Kennedy poured $90 million of development aid into Iran in 1961–62—or try to ride the new wave of Arab republics and nationalism. Rodger Davies at the State Department thought America had little choice but to ride the wave and welcome the coup. Royal Yemen "was one of the most primitive countries in the world, a theocratic state, and an anachronism even in the Arab world"; Abdullah Sallal's Yemeni "republic" was modern and progressive by comparison. Over the objections of the British and the Pentagon, JFK dumped al-Badr and recognized the YAR in December 1962—not from love of republics, rather from the need to "curtail the influence of Egyptian, Soviet and Chinese influence over it." *That* explanation completely baffled Nasser: "To his way of thinking, reasons which should have militated *against* our recognizing the republican regime [the likelihood of Egyptian, Soviet and Chinese influence] were being advanced in *support* of recognition, and vice versa."[71] Shortly, Kennedy swung back the other way, grousing that he was being forced to choose "yesterday over tomorrow." Pressured by Riyadh and the oil lobby, he withdrew support for Sallal and restored it to al-Badr. Washington found itself, Dean Rusk ruefully observed, supporting a backward "imamate" against a secular republic.[72]

Nasser—described by the CIA in 1960 as man needing quiet to tend "Egyptian domestic affairs"—simply could not contain himself.[73] "Nasser is trapped in Yemen," Bob Komer observed in 1963. "It's bleeding him," but the colonel feared "the sharp loss of face in letting go" more than the consequences of hanging on. "What *else* can we do but keep going on?" Nasser asked a puzzled U.S. ambassador.[74] Just stop, was Miles Copeland's advice. "Why is it so important for Gamal to appear a Big Wheel to a lot of losers?" Copeland asked a Nasser adviser. The "losers" in question were the Arab and African states that Nasser was forever trying to impress with his grandeur. "I wish we knew," the adviser gloomily replied. No one knew. Nasser puffed his way nervously through four packs of L&M cigarettes a day, tugged in every direction by threats to his power and reach. Internally, he maintained five separate intelligence agencies employing fifty thousand agents; each agency reported separately and directly to Nasser and spied on its brothers to prevent coups and other conspiracies.[75] Externally, Nasser *needed* to strike a gallant pose everywhere, even in poor, rather hopeless Yemen. Despite massive Egyptian sacrifices, the Nasserist YAR never took root. It fractured into hard- and soft-line factions, which fell to fighting with each other. The hard-liners embarked on a futile effort to introduce socialism all across the sheikhdoms and sultanates of the old British protectorate. Their writ never extended beyond Aden, where they propounded a cult of Che Guevara to an uncomprehending citizenry. In the provinces, the hard-liners were driven back by the qat-smoking sheikhs and their holy men, or *walis*, who laughed at presidential threats, issued from the former sultan's palace, "to crush our enemies to the bone" and "defeat the forces of reaction and imperialism."[76]

And Yemen was just the tip of Nasser's heaving iceberg. He poured funds into missile and jet engine programs—coordinated by retired Nazi rocket and electronics experts—to deter Israel and its veiled nuclear weapons program begun in 1957.[77] Nasser provided tanks, planes and advisers to Algeria's Ahmed Ben Bella in his border war with Morocco, and he backed Oman against British-controlled Muscat, the Muslim Sudanese against the British and non-Muslims, the Indonesians against the Dutch and Soviet-backed rebels against American-backed government troops in the Congo.[78] He needlessly bought trouble with the rich, well-armed Iranian Empire by attacking Shah Muhammed Reza's "backwardness." He railed against the Iraqi and Syrian Baath regimes and tried to cram them into a revived three-nation UAR.[79] When Nasser proposed a plebiscite of Egypt, Iraq and Syria on the question of whether the three countries should merge under a federal union and a single presidency (his, naturally), the Baath regimes in Iraq and Syria cracked down viciously on democracy *and* unity to maintain their slipping hold on power.[80] "Egyptians cannot even *live* with such regimes in peace," Nasser wailed from Cairo.

For their part, the Syrians and Iraqis now dismissed Nasser as an "old reactionary." The Iraqi Baathists took no prisoners, literally. General Kasim was murdered and hundreds of Iraqi communists were rounded up and killed. A twenty-nine-year-old rising Baathist named Saddam Hussein boasted that he had personally strangled Kasim, no doubt recognizing that Kasim had established *his* credentials for leadership in 1958 by strangling King Faisal II. Insisting that *they*, not the Egyptians, stood for "democracy and Arab unity," the Iraqi Baathists took an immediate stand for a particular kind of Arab unity in 1963, when they launched a savage invasion of their Kurdish provinces and renewed General Kasim's claim to Kuwait—the "lost *vilayet*" of Iraq that had been given a seat in the Arab League over Baghdad's violent objections in 1961.[81] The Iraqi Baathists then shut all opposition media, banned all political parties (except the Baath) and muzzled Nasser's efforts to deepen the "tripartite union" of Egypt, Syria and Iraq.[82] Naturally, Nasser's increasingly futile efforts to rein in rivals like Assad of Syria or Saddam Hussein in Iraq came at the expense of the Egyptian people, who watched their standard of living plummet under a sequence of austerity programs implemented to pay for Nasser's turns on the world stage. Nasser took on high-interest, short-term loans to finance his activism and, as the CIA noted, allowed "political requirements to overrule sound economic practice."[83] "His doctrine," a British analyst wrote, "*requires* an enemy. The fact that belief in such myths is sincere only aggravates the situation."[84]

Optimistic right up to his death in Dallas in 1963, President Kennedy increased economic aid to Egypt and generously furnished the heavily populated nation with one-third of its wheat supply. Kennedy looked the other way when Nasser denounced American behavior in Vietnam, Cuba and the Congo, and he welcomed Nasser's deployment of troops to Kuwait in 1961 to defend the emirate against Iraqi efforts to "reincorporate" the "lost province," which possessed a long coastline— useful for exporting oil—and sat atop the Burgan oil field, one of the world's biggest.[85] Kennedy hoped that Nasser might be rehabilitated to ward off the Iraqi threat and others. McGeorge Bundy advised Kennedy "to see a little more of Nasser's money" before conceding so much in their diplomatic poker games, but Kennedy persisted. He believed that he was on the verge of solving the Israeli-Palestinian question, and thought that Nasser had a vital role to play.[86]

SOLVING THE ISRAELI-PALESTINIAN QUESTION?

Straining to solve the Palestinian refugee crisis once and for all, Kennedy, who had visited Palestine and absorbed its complexities during the British Mandate years, eagerly backed the Carnegie Endowment's Johnson Plan in 1962. Named for Joseph Johnson, the endowment's president, the plan gave the Palestinian refugees—whose number had now swelled to 1.3 million—the choice of returning to their homes in Palestine—now Israel—or resettling with cash compensation in other Arab states. Israel opposed the plan—as well as Johnson's call for a "Palestine entity" (forerunner of the Palestinian National Authority) and a UN trustee for confiscated Arab properties in Israel—and ultimately agreed to accept no more than twenty thousand refugees, less than 2 percent of the total, which was tantamount to rejection.[87] Kennedy, who had named Myer Feldman White House "desk officer for Israel"—a new position that reflected the power of the Israel lobby—heard arguments from both sides. "The faster you disengage from this plan the better," Feldman warned him. "Otherwise . . . there will be a violent eruption both domestically and in our relations with Israel." But Secretary of State Dean Rusk warned of "political repercussions" in the Arab world if Kennedy did not begin to lean hard on the Israelis.[88]

To regain the upper hand in America's relationship with Israel, to score points with the UN's eternally frustrated Palestine Conciliation Commission, which had been formed in December 1948 to insure that the Israelis compensated or repatriated all refugees, and to impose *American* needs on the Israelis, Kennedy tried to link the Johnson Plan to arms sales.[89] With the Soviets selling Il-28 and Tu-16 bombers and MiG-21 fighters to the Egyptians, the Israelis wanted Hawk surface-to-air missiles to counter them. The Hawk (Homing All the Way Killer) missiles were the most advanced surface-to-air missiles (SAMs) in the American arsenal, and Israel would be the first non-NATO nation to receive them; the sale would also punch a hole in the American embargo on "major armaments" to the Middle East.[90] With trade bait in hand—Ike had denied Hawks to Israel in 1960 on the grounds that "the United States does not want to establish itself as a partisan supporter of any nation in the Middle East"—Kennedy now tried to trade the SAMs for Israeli compensation of the Palestinian refugees still camped in Lebanon, Syria, Jordan and the Gaza Strip.

"We know that Israel faces enormous security problems," JFK told Israeli foreign minister Golda Meir, "but *we* do too."[91] Old problems from the aggrieved Arab states were compounded by new ones. The Syrians had given sanctuary and support to Yasser Arafat's Palestinian guerrillas, or al-Fatah, which, in turn, prompted Nasser to stand up a rival guerrilla force called the Palestine Liberation Organization, or PLO. Nasser and the other Arab nationalists had traditionally subordinated the "Palestinian question" to missions like the UAR or the war for Yemen, but, by the early 1960s, that calculated restraint was no longer possible. There was too much pressure in the refugee camps from spokesmen like Arafat and Ahmed Shuqairi— "our place should not be in Jordan, but in Jaffa, Acre, Haifa and Nazareth"—too much pressure from other Arab states to "do something" for the refugees and too much "charitable" money flowing to the PLO from Kuwait and Saudi Arabia, which required violent employment.[92]

Washington now found itself arrayed against the Arab states and an increasingly well-organized, well-funded and popular "liberation movement" that was pulling weapons and explosives in over the Egyptian, Syrian, Jordanian and Lebanese borders and was airing virulent propaganda on Cairo's Voice of the Arabs, Radio Mecca and Damascus Radio, which were the Al Jazeera of their day.[93] Moreover, as a French diplomat noted, the grinding, insoluble "Palestinian affair created a psychological tension in the Middle East that increased, not decreased, with each passing year, and became the touchstone—*pierre de touche*—of all Arabs."[94] Like FDR, Truman and Eisenhower before him, Kennedy was confronted by different "touchstones"— Jewish pressure groups and their congressional advocates—who mocked the State Department's warning that "the Arabs sincerely believe that Israel is the chosen instrument of the U.S. Government."[95] Jewish votes had been critical in Kennedy's razor-thin victory over Nixon in 1960, and Kennedy, no less than his predecessors, was an expedient politician. He nervously watched Congress, where the Israel lobby worked the aisles and, as John Badeau recalled, withheld its campaign contributions for the fall elections through the summer and bluntly told members of Congress, "You don't get this until we know what you are going to do for Israel."[96] The idealistic president who had campaigned on the slogan "the Middle East needs water, not war, tractors, not tanks, bread, not bombs," now disconsolately began sending bombs and tanks.[97]

ISRAEL'S BREAKTHROUGH TO MILITARY PREDOMINANCE

Although Kennedy balked at a formal security guarantee for Israel—fearing that it might prompt an equivalent guarantee from the Soviets for the Arab states and lead to World War III—Israel did receive critical hardware, without major concessions, including early-warning radars in 1960, Hawks in 1962, Skyhawk fighter-bombers in 1966 and F-4 Phantoms in 1968. For the Israelis, the 1962 Hawk sale was a turning point: "one of the most significant acts in the Israeli-American relationship."[98] In an act of breathtaking chutzpah, the first Hawks were installed around Israel's nuclear weapons facility at Dimona, which the Kennedy administration staunchly opposed.[99] The IDF would no longer have to rely on secondhand Western weapons; it now had a direct pipeline into the high-tech American arsenal. The Hawk sale, one historian recently observed, "set the precedent that ultimately created the U.S.-Israel strategic relationship: a multimillion-dollar annual business in cutting-edge weaponry, supplemented by extensive military-to-military dialogues, security consultations, extensive joint training exercises, and cooperative research-and-development ventures." The turn was effected by thirty-nine-year-old Shimon Peres, who made a series of visits to Washington in the early 1960s, where he drove a wedge between the State Department and the Pentagon, persuading senior Defense Department officials that a security relationship with Israel was indispensable, and undermined by Rusk's worrywart "Arabists."

Pressured by Congress, the White House and the Pentagon, the State Department vented frustration—"a military alliance with Israel would destroy the delicate balance we have so carefully maintained in our Near East relations"—but ultimately accepted the sale of Hawks and other advanced weapons.[100] Nasser of course resented the deepening Israeli-American security relationship. "The cost of every bullet aimed to kill an Arab," he told a rally at Port Said, "is paid by America and Western imperialism."[101] Nasser would have been even more resentful had he overheard the conversations between President Kennedy and Golda Meir in Palm Beach, Florida, in December 1962. Kennedy assured Meir that the United States *would* in fact "come to the support of Israel . . . in case of an invasion," which amounted to a security guarantee. Meir must have glowed when Kennedy characterized the American-Israeli alliance as no less intimate than the "special relationship . . . with Britain over a wide range of world affairs."[102]

After Kennedy's assassination, the Lyndon Johnson administration found little time to strategize on the Middle East. A British official in Washington noted after meetings with George Ball in January 1965 that "the Government here is conscious that they are overextended."[103] A few weeks later, Secretary of State Dean Rusk admitted as much to the British embassy: "Everything to do with [the Middle East] must be subject to events in Southeast Asia."[104] Not surprisingly, no coherent Johnson policy emerged to replace Kennedy's, which had really not been all that coherent itself, "making an understanding with Nasser the keystone of U.S. policy" but cozying up to the Israel lobby as well. Johnson was less devoted to Nasser and far cozier with Israel: "I've got three Cohens in my cabinet," he boasted to the Israeli ambassador after Kennedy's death. No president had done more for the Jews than he would.[105]

Lyndon Johnson's patience with Nasser snapped in 1965, when the Egyptian air force mistakenly shot down the private jet of Dallas oilman (and Johnson friend and donor) John Mecom and Egyptian rioters sacked the Kennedy Memorial Library in Cairo at a cost to American taxpayers of $400,000.[106] When LBJ sought apologies and restitution from Nasser, the colonel furiously protested—"If the Americans don't like my behavior, they can go drink the Mediterranean!" He haggled over the sum of damages—refused to pay them—and then brazenly put in a request for $450 million in American food aid, which Johnson initially refused. "How can I ask Congress for wheat when you burn our library?" the president prodded Egyptian ambassador Mustafa Kamel. Walt Rostow, Johnson's national security adviser, pointed to the wider damage Nasser was wreaking on American interests: "He has lambasted us on Vietnam and he continues to stir things up for us in Yemen and Saudi Arabia." Johnson eventually sent Averell Harriman to sit down with Nasser and disburse $55 million of aid "to prevent Nasser getting too close to the Communists." LBJ did all of this with extreme reluctance, viewing Nasser as just another "tin-pot colonel," who, as George Ball would put it in 1965, "gave no cause for hope" other than a vague promise to help secure the release of American POWs in Vietnam.[107]

LBJ, while continuing to supply the ingredients for 80 percent of the bread consumed in Egypt, never really endorsed Kennedy's idea of trying to see things Nasser's way.[108] Indeed, the early 1960s had something in common with the early 2000s, when Princeton historian Bernard Lewis made a roaring comeback in the corridors of the George W. Bush administration with his argument that the Arab states were incorrigible and in need of transformation. Lewis, in his late eighties in the early 2000s, had conceived that argument as a forty-eight-year-old in 1964. Rostow and others in the Johnson administration were receptive to Lewis's argument that what was happening in the Middle East was not a rational clash of states, but an irrational "clash of civilizations," between Islam, Judaism and Christendom. Unlike the Turks or Iranians, who had learned to negotiate and compromise as sovereign states, the new Arab countries had grown up as Ottoman vassals and colonial dependencies of Christian great powers and had learned only to blame and complain: "They [were] still at the mercy of a mood of ethnic and communal collectivism, which treats the West as a collective enemy."[109]

LBJ was friendly with Israel—he had been one of the Jewish state's doughtiest supporters in the Senate—and increasingly impatient with Nasser, who, Johnson complained, spent too much time appealing to the mood of ethnic and communal collectivism described by Bernard Lewis and too little time thinking of good ways to spend his $600 million of American aid to "improve the lot of his own people."[110] LBJ left the American embassy in Cairo vacant for almost four months—a pointed snub—then named a combative new ambassador, Lucius Battle, who loathed Nasser's "Messianic complex" and—as the British put it—"went for the Egyptians bald-headed without playing himself in ... When calling on [the foreign minister] Battle refused a seat and stamped around the room breathing fire and slaughter."[111] LBJ cut Nasser's American aid in 1966—heeding British advice to "let the economic shoe *really* pinch"—and invited King Faisal of Saudi Arabia to Washington for a full-blown state visit in June. The contrast was deliberate. The Saudis would be rewarded for their friendship, the Egyptians punished for their surliness.[112]

Nasser was told that American aid to Egypt would be restored if he followed IMF-approved economic policies, "avoided extreme statements about U.S. policies" and proved more "responsive to U.S. interests."[113] The strains of Vietnam made LBJ and Congress more impatient than ever with Nasser's shades of meaning: the colonel would no longer be allowed to have his cake and eat it too at a time when the United States was "absorbed by pressure on its finances and the realization that resources are finite."[114] In 1967, LBJ promoted Luke Battle from the Cairo embassy to assistant secretary of state for Near Eastern and South Asian affairs, with the special brief of "changing opinion in the State Department below the Seventh Floor": from "moderation and conciliation" in America's dealings with the Arabs to a hard line. He was successful, the British remarking "more pragmatism and less ideology" in the State Department on the eve of the Six-Day War. Even "Arabist" special-pleaders had been "converted from their old Nasserist views" by LBJ and Luke Battle.[115] Contrasting the Johnson approach to the Middle East with Kennedy's, McGeorge Bundy found that "U.S. foreign policy is now a little more hard-nosed and a little more realistic." The Johnson administration was insisting on "direct results and immediate bilateral relations with the USA," not mere hopes for the future.[116] The contrast between Kennedy and Johnson was like that between Clinton and George W. Bush. Like Bush, who would swallow the prescriptions of Ariel Sharon and the Likud without chewing, Johnson veered tamely down the Israeli line that the Palestinians were Middle Eastern Vietcong—unappeasable terrorists—and that Nasser's "Arab revolution" was subversive, not positive, and was squarely aimed at "major American oil interests."[117] Congress did not contest these impressions; its exasperated view, the British embassy reported in 1967, was "a plague on all their houses," revolutionary or counterrevolutionary, Arab or Israeli.[118]

Politically, the Arab world stagnated in the dynamic 1960s. Nasser's Arab Socialist Union, the only legal party in Egypt, was nothing more than a "rubber stamp for presidential decisions." The twelve-man RCC of 1952 had withered to just three survivors: Sadat, Hussein el-Shafei and Nasser, who had put on weight and contracted diabetes.[119] Algeria's colonel Houari Boumedienne—who called himself an Arab nationalist—was grimly fighting the spread of "Nasserism" into his precincts lest he be overshadowed by Cairo's "Big Man." In Syria, Nasser had faced facts even before the UAR broke up in 1961, had thrown over his ideological Baathist allies and had embraced the old conservatives, who had never lost power in Syria, just briefly submerged themselves. Under those resurgent elites—landowners, merchants and old-guard politicians—Syria remained stagnant, a stagnation that most traced to the failed union with Egypt. "Three successive years of drought have been popularly blamed on the Egyptians," the CIA approvingly noted.[120] Iraq's government was regarded as effectively "disintegrated" by fights between the parties and sects, and the economy—drained by heavy military expenditures and civil war with the Kurds—limped along only because of oil revenues, not Baath economics. "When the government flops, everything else flops with it," an Englishman wrote from Baghdad. In 1967, just before the Six-Day War, a British analyst compared the perception of Egypt in the Arab world between 1956 and 1967 to that of France in Europe between the Great Revolution and the Napoleonic Empire: "The Egyptian image has changed from liberating force to imperialist." Nasser himself, like Napoleon to the end of his days, still retained some "magic," but the Egyptian regime was recognized to be clumsy and prone to "subversion and conspiracy."

Egypt's vaunted economic model—"Arab socialism"—was proving a disaster. With the population of countries like Egypt, Syria and Iraq increasing 3 percent annually in the 1960s, the Arab socialists were unable to create jobs fast enough, unable, as the *Economist* put it, "to keep up with the patter of little feet."[121] They also suffered predictable brain drains and capital flight as smart young people and investors fled from their clumsy nationalization and land reform programs. Egyptian economist Charles Issawi wrote in 1963 that "the ill-conceived nationalizations and sequestrations and the general political climate have broken the spring which made the old order work, however imperfectly, yet put no adequate motive power in its place." Four years later, a British official observed that the resource-starved but capitalist and discreetly pro-American desert kingdom of Jordan was attracting three times as much foreign aid per capita as socialist Egypt.[122] Having failed to exert economic or political leadership, would Egypt now try war?

CHAPTER 8

·🙪·

A SIX-DAY WAR

DESPITE INFUSIONS OF SOVIET WEAPONS, money and advisers, the military power of Egypt and the other Arab states wilted along with their economies. Israel continued to arm itself to the highest regional standard to deter its enemies, and—in the aftermath of the 1948 and 1956 wars—developed an offensive doctrine that would carry the war immediately into enemy territory with preemptive air strikes and armored spearheads. In October 1955, the first hints of an Israeli nuclear bomb project surfaced, and the Israelis successfully tested their first nuclear bomb in 1967.[1] The IDF, which acquired increasingly sophisticated weapons from the French and the Americans, trained with an increased, Western-style emphasis on armor, speed and high technology.[2] A CIA analysis of the Arab-Israeli military balance in the early 1960s found that despite their menacing rhetoric—"to accept Israel as a fact would be to permit a thief to keep what he has stolen"—the big Arab states surrounding Israel were not very menacing at all.[3]

The Egyptians, by far the most lethally equipped Arab military, had "low combat efficiency" because of "weak senior leadership and poor troop morale" and a tendency to rotate and transfer men and officers between units and around the country too frequently "as a security precaution" against coups and uprisings. A week before the outbreak of the Six-Day War in 1967, Nasser fumed to Field Marshal Abdel Hakim Amer that the army was "ten years behind the times" and incapable of beating even the Yemenis, let alone a modern army like Israel's.[4] Despite their Soviet trainers and doctrine, the Egyptians had no capability for "sustained offensive ground operations." At best, they might manage small attacks of short duration by one or two divisions. Egypt's air defenses were vulnerable to preemptive Israeli attacks because the Egyptians lacked countermeasures against radar jamming, were slow to scramble their excellent Soviet fighters and light bombers and "had inferior personnel." The Egyptian navy was feckless, sporting poor, deteriorated ships, haphazard logistics and inefficient crews and administration. (The cause of the 1967 Six-Day War would be Nasser's announced blockade of the Straits of Tiran, which the Egyptian navy would fail to execute.) After the Six-Day War, Soviet analysts discovered that whereas 80 percent of Israeli military personnel had been to university or technical school, 70 percent of the Egyptian military were illiterate, an alarming statistic that would be reduced to only 50 percent by 1973.[5] And Egypt was the gold standard among Arab armies.

From the heights of the well-equipped, relatively well-trained Egyptians, it was a steep drop down to the lesser Arab armies. The Syrians, who possessed a $250 million Soviet arsenal, were led by "a weak, inexperienced and politically factioned officer corps" entirely lacking in "sophisticated military skills." The CIA judged the Syrian navy "incapable of defending even the national coastline." The air defenses around Damascus—Soviet and Polish radars, jets and antiaircraft artillery—would not withstand an attack by Israeli light bombers flying from bases less than a hundred miles away. In April 1967, Israeli planes effortlessly shot down six Syrian MiGs during a border skirmish. The Israelis downed two of the MiGs near the border—the Syrians had been strafing Israeli tractors, "easy targets, this being the only kind they can hit"—and then pursued the surviving MiGs all the way to Damascus, where, untroubled by Syria's air defenses, they shot the MiGs out of the sky on the outskirts of the capital. While the Syrian government boasted to its disbelieving citizenry, who actually watched the defeat of their air force, that their "heroic eagles" had vanquished the IAF, the Israeli Mirages lit their afterburners, flew an impudent victory loop around Damascus and then roared back to Israel.[6]

According to the CIA, the Jordanians had "virtually no combat capability with respect to Israel" and if attacked would crumple within a week. The big, Soviet-equipped Iraqi army—full of bluster—was really good only for "internal security" against Iraq's restive Kurds and Shiites and "minor harassing actions" beyond Iraq's borders. "No effective defense" was possible against a determined Israeli air offensive. The Iraqi navy's combat capabilities were "negligible." The Lebanese military was designed to quell internal disturbances and "had no capability to engage a foreign aggressor." The Yemenis had "no technical competence." The Saudis "would be incapable of organized resistance against a modern army."[7] A British analysis in 1965 found that the Arab states were doubly damned because their largely ineffective military spending was at the expense of internal development projects that might have propelled them toward a brighter future: "The Arabs will always find a good excuse for not spending their own money on long-term development projects. How much easier it is to parade a modern tank or fly past a flight of MiGs for face value and as a sign of achievement."[8]

Israel's particular genius was to take these minor threats and transform them into major ones. An example of this was Foreign Minister Golda Meir's denunciation in 1963 of Egypt's employment of German scientists to build "weapons of mass destruction" to destroy Israel. Presidential adviser George Ball convened a special panel in April 1963 to weigh the Israeli fears and concluded that "Israel's fears [were] exaggerated" and "based on speculation not intelligence." The Egyptian program was working on missiles, engines and airframes, but had no nuclear capability and was years away from even a limited *conventional* missile capability with small, 500-pound payloads.[9] The CIA regarded the two Egyptian missiles in production as little better than Germany's World War II V-2s. No matter: from his retirement in a Negev Desert kibbutz, David Ben-Gurion rumbled that Israel would have no choice but to develop nuclear weapons at the nearby Dimona reactor to deter the Egyptian missiles. Ben-Gurion accused Nasser of developing "death rays" to resume Hitler's Holocaust, and the CIA warned that the net effect of Israeli nuclear weapons would be to make Israel "more rather than less tough" on its neighbors, and the United States. A nuclear-armed Israel would fear nothing and would not hesitate to throw its weight around the region.[10] There was also an Israeli internal political dynamic at work. In 1967, Prime Minister Levi Eshkol, Defense Minister Moshe Dayan, and IDF chief of staff General Yitzhak Rabin—all ambitious politicians angling for national leadership—attempted "to outdo the other and impress upon the Israeli people that they were tough on the Arabs."[11]

There was little real need to "outdo and impress," because the IDF was steadily pulling away from its Arab rivals in the 1960s. American foreign aid permitted massive Israeli expenditures on defense: 9.5 percent of GDP in 1965, 10.4 percent in 1966, 17.7 percent in 1967 and 26.3 percent by 1971.[12] A CIA report prepared in May 1967 noted that appearances of surging Arab power deceived. True, the Soviets had recently shipped Egypt 1,200 tanks and self-propelled guns, 500 advanced aircraft,

9 submarines, "numerous" surface-to-air missiles and several dozen batteries of radar-controlled 85 mm antiaircraft guns. The Syrians had received 400 tanks and 150 fighter aircraft. But arms did not make the man. The Syrian air force in 1967 rated only 45 percent of its pilots "good," 32 percent "average" and the rest "below average."[13] The Arabs never adapted their Russian all-climate equipment to the desert environment. Israel meanwhile had improved fuel efficiency, widened caterpillar tracks and raised suspensions on their tanks and trucks to make them run better in the desert. The IDF routinely "up-gunned" its armored vehicles—replacing 75 mm or 90 mm cannon with 105 mm guns—scraped out more space for the crews and ammunition-carrying capacity, and retrofitted the latest fire control systems.[14] In startling contrast, half of the "new" Egyptian and Syrian tanks were unimproved Soviet World War II models manufactured between 1942 and 1947. The CIA attributed the inability of the Arabs to keep such tanks in action to their old age and Moscow's inexplicable provision of maintenance manuals in English—"a language foreign to Russian instructors and Arab trainees alike"—which no one bothered even to look at.[15]

"ISRAEL MUST BE STOPPED . . ."

Not only were Israel's equipment, training and personnel better and unaffected by linguistic difficulties, but the country's flanks were secured by an informal American security guarantee. "The UAR cannot attack Israel because to do so would mean taking on the Sixth Fleet," a British diplomat wrote the Foreign Office's Eastern Department in May 1965. The way the Americans fashioned the security guarantee was clever. "It is the American intention," U.S. ambassador Wally Barbour said in 1965, "to stop *any* massive aggression across the Israeli-Arab frontiers in *either* direction." Such a formulation favored Israel, because the Israelis had achieved the frontiers they desired—the armistice borders of 1949—in the aftermath of the Suez War. Anything else—such as the territory acquired in 1967—would be icing on the cake. That explained Barbour's warning in 1965 that "Israel must be stopped from forcible action in the area since this might cause incalculable damage to Western interests owing to Arab reaction." Barbour predicted that the long-term damage to *American* interests of further Israeli annexations would be so great that he advised merciless American punishment of Israel if the Israelis struck again offensively: "We must stop the Israelis by threat of total economic sanctions at the very first sign that Israel contemplates war against *any* neighbor." Israel certainly had the right to defend itself, but Washington needed to make clear to Tel Aviv that there could be no Israeli *offensives*, for they would only increase Arab fury and intractability. "The U.S. has to contain *both* sides."[16]

Barbour's warning fell on deaf ears in Washington. The Arab-Israeli War of 1967, commonly known as the Six-Day War, burst upon this atmosphere of Israeli strength, Arab bellicosity, Palestinian despair, American preoccupation with Vietnam, and Russian opportunism. With even moderates in the Middle East stiffened up for war, President Lyndon Johnson's State of the Union address in January 1967 made a single despairing reference to the region: "In the Middle East, the spirit of goodwill toward all unfortunately has not yet taken hold. An already tortured peace seems to be constantly threatened."[17] Psychic and astrologer Jeane Dixon—who had predicted Kennedy's assassination and would go on to advise the Reagan White House—foretold in her 1967 New Year's Day predictions that the United States was heading for a severe crisis in the Middle East that would confront LBJ with "the most momentous decision of his life."[18] The British Foreign Office also felt the pressure and threw up its hands in frustration. "It is well worth giving serious consideration to how to rid ourselves of the albatross of Israel and the dead dog of Arab rancor," the UK ambassador in Tel Aviv wrote London in May 1967.[19]

As leader of the free world, the United States could not simply walk away from Middle Eastern albatrosses and dead dogs. It had to work with them, yet the Six-Day War of 1967 erupted at a moment of great strategic anxiety for the United States. A 1966 British white paper had announced the decision of Prime Minister Harold Wilson's Labour government to "readjust" the "British defense posture East of Suez" and "lighten the British presence in the [Persian] Gulf." Focused on Vietnam—where American troop levels climbed from 385,000 to 486,000 in 1966–67—the Johnson administration greeted Wilson's decision with dismay. "For God's sake, be *Britain*," Dean Rusk exclaimed to Foreign Secretary George Brown when they met to discuss the details of what was now being called the British "scuttle" from the crucial strategic space between Bahrain and Singapore. But the new Britain of deficits could not be made into the old Britain of surpluses, and Prime Minister Wilson replied to President Johnson's personal appeal that he postpone the British scuttle with words that Americans in the early 2000s—fighting Middle Eastern wars on borrowed Japanese and Chinese money—might study with interest: "The British people were sick and tired of being thought willing to eke out a comfortable existence on borrowed money."[20] The Americans, then as now, were only too willing.

By 1967, Johnson was borrowing heavily—not thinking it prudent to raise taxes to fund an unpopular war. But even with mounting federal debt—nearly $400 billion in the late 1960s—there was nothing left over for new Middle Eastern commitments. Besides agreeing to establish an American air and naval base on the British island of Diego Garcia, twenty-five hundred miles south of the Straits of Hormuz, LBJ spent next to nothing on what CIA and State Department analysts were calling "over the horizon threats to the oil-rich Persian Gulf."[21]

U.S. VULNERABILITY IN THE MIDDLE EAST

A secret interdepartmental report on "tomorrow's crises" that was prepared by teams from State, the Pentagon and the intelligence agencies under the overall direction of career soldier and diplomat Julius Holmes for President Lyndon Johnson in April 1967 expressed the keenness with which this sudden American vulnerability in the Middle East was felt at the highest levels of government. Sixty-eight-year-old Julius Holmes had been U.S. ambassador to Iran from 1961 to 1965. The "Holmes Report"—which was almost immediately leaked to the press—warned that the United States was at considerable risk in the "strategic triangle stretching from Iran in the Middle East to Morocco on the Atlantic and south into Black Africa" because of a mischievous Egyptian policy that fanned up local resentments, and a growing Soviet presence. In the crucial Red Sea basin—where so much Gulf oil transited to Europe—Nasser and the Soviets were "burning away the last vestiges of a century of Western control." Nasser had already seized the Suez Canal and was extending his influence in Yemen and Eritrea, which placed him on both shores of the Red Sea. The Soviets had invested $140 million in Yemen, building a port at Hodeida and an airfield at Sana'a, and had constructed a port at Berbera in Somalia, where they invested an additional $135 million to wean the regime from its old colonial overseers in Britain and Italy. In Ethiopia, Nasser had sent guns and advisers to Eritrean guerrillas—to create a breakaway client state on the Red Sea littoral—and the Soviets had built an oil refinery at Assab and a meat-freezing plant in Massawa. Like Mussolini in the 1930s, the Russians and Egyptians in the 1960s looked to be maneuvering for control of the critical choke points to the Red Sea, Suez and the Mediterranean.

Holmes and Secretary of Defense Robert McNamara—in testimony to the Senate Armed Services Committee in January 1967—worried that the Soviet push from Yemen across to Ethiopia effectively "outflanked" the anticommunist "Northern Tier" defense barrier—Turkey, Iran and Pakistan—that the United States had relied on since the 1950s. Now the Soviets, alone or in league with Egypt, Syria and Iraq, were poised to seize "the warm water ports and resources of the Middle East."[22] Generally scornful of de Gaulle and the French, the Americans in 1967 found themselves thrown back on the little French enclave of Djibouti—where the locals had voted against independence and for French Union—for continued access to the Horn of Africa. "The U.S. enjoyed the riots against de Gaulle [in August 1966]," the Holmes Report abashedly noted, "but now gives full-fledged support to French rule in this tiny barren country."[23]

Ethiopia was a concern because of its strategic location (and American listening posts) athwart the routes from the Red Sea to the Persian Gulf, but also because the Americans viewed Soviet and Egyptian pressure on Emperor Haile Selassie as "the climax of the battle for the Red Sea basin." Islam covered half the land mass of Africa—North Africa plus eighteen sub-Saharan countries—and Nasser was still striving to make Cairo the focal point of Arab *and* African politics. Soviet and Egyptian pressure on Haile Selassie was "just one small cloud in the broader storm against all the vulnerable pro-Western kings in the Muslim world: Faisal in Saudi Arabia, Hussein in Jordan, Idris in Libya, and Hassan of Morocco." The *Washington Post* reported that Julius Holmes's list of vulnerable Middle Eastern monarchs made American strategists—with their fresh, unhappy experiences with the "analogous regimes of Syngman Rhee and Ngo Dinh Diem" in South Korea and South Vietnam—"shudder" with fright. At the Senate hearings in January 1967, Secretary of Defense McNamara declared that the Soviet-penetrated Red Sea basin was "the area of most immediate concern to us," but with the Vietnam War raging, McNamara confessed that he had nothing to spare for the defense of American interests in Yemen, Somalia or Ethiopia.[24]

"THERE *HAS* TO BE A POLICY" FOR THE MIDDLE EAST

With war in sight between Israel and its Arab neighbors, the Holmes study group expressed dismay at the parochial nature of American strategy. The major threats detected by Holmes found "few echoes in Washington, where the views expressed by American officials tended to reflect the special interests on which they focused." That was a delicate way of saying that key strategic decisions were filtered through the Israeli and Saudi lobbies.[25] "There *has* to be a policy" for the Middle East, Senator Everett Dirksen complained during a secret briefing at the State Department in 1967, "but precisely *what* it is I can't say."[26]

In fact there was a policy. With the British "scuttling" from the entire space "east of Suez" and headed home to their "thatched cottages and Beefeaters, [their] miniskirts and Beatles"—as one critic snarled—President Johnson and Secretary of Defense McNamara were already inclining toward the "twin pillars" concept that would later be enshrined in the Nixon Doctrine. "Don't mourn, organize," LBJ's national security adviser Walt Rostow enjoined the administration. Use the nations of the Near and Far East "to fill the gap left by the British."[27] With no other cards to play—America was fully invested in Vietnam—Johnson took Rostow's advice. Australia, Indonesia and Japan would guard American interests in East Asia, while Israel, Iran and Saudi Arabia would defend the Middle East. In June 1966, Johnson asked Saudi king Faisal to "help fill the gap the British will leave in South Arabia and the Persian Gulf." He offered to sell Faisal $100 million in "nonlethal" military hardware—trucks and jeeps—to improve the Saudi army's mobility. With the shah of Iran—the sturdier pillar, who did not suffer Faisal's Israel complex—LBJ was more lethal. He agreed to sell the shah F-4 Phantoms and approved a $200 million loan to finance Iranian purchases of other American weapons.[28]

CLOUDS OF WAR

American efforts to mollify Arab loathing of Israel were dropped, from lack of interest and distraction with Vietnam. Although Americans (and Israelis) complained of Arab intransigence, the Suez War had so inflamed Arab opinion that real negotiations with Israel were all but impossible in its aftermath. Any Arab leader who treated with Israel would be denounced as a traitor by other Arab leaders and by his own citizens. Nasser told the U.S. ambassador in Cairo that he could not make peace with Israel, for to do so would merely shift the mantle of Arab nationalism from Egypt to Iraq. The Syrians, a Syrian diplomat told an American colleague, would never make peace with Israel. To do so would make Damascus "a traitor" in the eyes of its Arab rivals and its own public.[29]

Nasser was not an immediate problem. His rhetoric had not cooled over the years, but he was distracted by the ongoing war in Yemen, where eight brigades of the Egyptian army were bogged down trying to implant an Arab nationalist regime and defeat Saudi efforts to pursue what the State Department called "Saudi Monroe Doctrinism"—"extending Saudi influence to the water's edge"—on the rim of the Arabian Peninsula.[30] Syria was a more pressing problem. The Israelis and Syrians had been fighting since 1949 over the Golan Heights and other supposedly "demilitarized zones" that Syria clung to and Israel coveted. General Moshe Dayan frankly admitted that Israel caused "at least 80 percent" of the frontier clashes in the hope that they would enable the Israelis to evict the Syrians. Israel's efforts to divert water from the Sea of Galilee to the expanding kibbutzes of the Negev—an effort intended to populate the Negev with Jewish settlers and thwart Egyptian demands for a land corridor to Jordan—had been repulsed by Syrian tractors and bulldozers, which trumped the Israelis by diverting the sources of the Sea of Galilee inside Syria. Israeli planes and tanks attacked the Syrian tractors, which called up Syrian troops and planes for their own defense. Regular "water skirmishes" like these always threatened to explode into a wider regional war.

There was also the problem of Syrian support for Palestinian guerrillas. The Alawite clique around Hafez al-Assad, which had seized power in Damascus in 1966, was looking for ways to widen its base among Syria's Sunnis and Shiites and all across the Arab world, where Nasser was belaboring the Syrian regime for its lack of Arab nationalist zeal. Syrian attacks on Israel seemed the perfect way to assert the pan-Arab credentials of the Alawite regime. "In Syria," IDF chief of staff General Yitzhak Rabin growled in May 1967, "the authorities themselves activate the terrorists."[31] Before war broke out in 1967, the Israelis were planning heavy reprisals against Syria, and the U.S. government, which had squirmed helplessly while the Soviets vetoed every UN effort to punish Arab-sponsored terrorism, raised few objections. "The Syrians are sons of bitches," a senior Pentagon official confided to the Israeli foreign ministry in March 1967. As they would after 9/11, the Americans in 1967 agreed, as Eugene Rostow put it, that "an attack *from* a state is an attack *by* a state."[32] President Johnson deplored the "new radical government in Syria [that] increased terrorist raids against Israel."[33] If Palestinian guerrillas armed or based themselves in Syria, then Syria—according to the Israelis—was a legitimate target.

Israeli attacks on Syria, though, would almost certainly bring Egypt into the war, for Nasser and the Syrians had signed a mutual defense alliance in November 1966 that obliged each country to help the other if it was attacked by Israel.

Enter the Soviet Union. With Israel finally "weaponizing" its nuclear program at Dimona, the IDF unbeatably strong, the Americans insisting on peace and good behavior, the Egyptians distracted by the quagmire in Yemen and the Syrians struggling with everything, there may not have been a war in 1967 at all had the Russians not sparked one.[34] The Soviets had been heavily invested in Egypt, Syria and Iraq since the 1950s but felt stymied by Nasser's "third force neutralism" and aversion to pro-Moscow "bloc politics." To jerk the Arab states into the Soviet bloc and demonstrate the efficacy of Soviet armaments, Moscow decided to force a war on the Middle East in May 1967.[35] "Even if the war was not won by our [Arab] side," Evgeny Pyrlin, head of the Soviet foreign ministry's Egypt department, recently confessed, "a war would be to our political advantage because our side would demonstrate its ability to fight with Soviet weapons and with Soviet military and political support." An Arab-Israeli war would also "create another trouble spot for the United States in addition to . . . Vietnam" and force the Americans to back Israel, ruining their already tenuous relations with the Arab states.[36]

During a routine visit to Moscow, Anwar Sadat, a Nasser aide and speaker of the Egyptian National Assembly in 1967, was warned by the Soviets that "ten Israeli brigades had concentrated on the Syrian border." In Cairo and Damascus, the Soviet ambassadors delivered the same (false) intelligence to Nasser and to the Syrian junta. Although the Egyptian and Syrian general staff chiefs scoured the Israeli-Syrian border for evidence of the Israeli deployment and found none, Nasser swallowed the Soviet bait and pushed an armored division and three infantry brigades across the Suez Canal, into the Sinai and toward the Israeli border. Seeking to take pressure off the Syrians, Nasser was also positioning Egyptian troops to smash open a land corridor to Jordan and take the port of Eilat, which the Israelis had seized in violation of the 1949 armistice agreements.

NASSER'S GAMBLE

Nasser had more than a strategic interest in the war. He viewed a great victory over Israel as essential to his political survival. Since he'd fallen deeper into the Soviet pocket, his American aid—$500 million since the Lebanon crisis—had dwindled, and his financial position had become desperate. In the spring of 1967, Egypt was running a $400 million trade deficit and was down to its gold reserves and about $3 million of hard currency. Factories had been shut down for want of spare parts and Egypt Air had canceled all of its flights. The country had always managed to scrape along somehow, but this time, an old Egypt hand noted, "it was clear that the UAR had hit bottom." Some of the bolder free officers were muttering that it might be time to "Sukarnoize" Nasser—kick him upstairs to a figurehead presidency and then turn the affairs of the country over to more capable men. Washington lawyer Ward Elliott wrote in *Public Policy* that Nasser's efforts over the years to "piece his opulent throne with kingdoms"—in Yemen, Sudan, Algeria, Jordan, Lebanon and Syria—had emptied the Egyptian treasury.[37]

Instead of retrenching, Nasser rolled the dice. On May 22, he stationed a garrison at Sharm el-Sheikh and announced a blockade of the Straits of Tiran, which—if actually enforced by actual ships—would have closed the Israeli port of Eilat to trade and the seventy thousand barrels of Iranian oil that arrived there daily.[38] President Johnson was staggered by the Egyptian move, which handed the Israelis an incontestable pretext for war, if they wanted one. "If any single act of folly was more responsible for this explosion than any other it was the [Egyptian] decision that the Strait of Tiran would be closed."[39] Nasser seemed unaware of the danger he was in. "The Jews have threatened war," Nasser rumbled, "we tell them 'you are welcome, we are ready for war.'"[40] So, apparently, was the rest of the Arab world. In the last week of May 1967, Jordan placed its army under Egyptian command, the Saudis mobilized, Iraqi troops marched west into Jordan, and Algerian units began arriving in Egypt. All of those moves—but especially the threatened blockade of the Straits of Tiran and the arrival of an Iraqi infantry division in Jordan—represented a casus belli for Israel.

Where was America during this headlong pitch toward war? Angry with Nasser, LBJ had summoned Ambassador Luke Battle home to Washington in March 1967 and neglected to replace him. Middle East expert Harold Saunders posted through Cairo as Battle was leaving and emphasized the critical importance of Egypt: "Its 30 million people, its economic inheritance, its drive to lead, its pride of achievement and its military power make... it unquestionably *the* Arab power."[41] Unfortunately, as war clouds gathered, American relations with Egypt were carried on by the Spanish embassy. Richard Nolte was belatedly dispatched from Westport, Connecticut, to Cairo in May 1967 to replace Luke Battle, but arrived only as Egyptian troops were crossing the canal and heading toward Israel in late May. Asked for the U.S. position on the crisis, Nolte answered, "What crisis?"[42] Nolte had his hands full transferring the functions of American diplomacy in Cairo from the Spanish embassy back to the U.S. embassy, which came under immediate attack from anti-American rioters. Nolte would leave his post in September and give way to another ambassador. Congress was in summer recess when the war broke out, but when it returned, Republican senator Chuck Percy demanded answers to the "grave questions raised about the quality of [America's] advance planning" and Democratic congressman Wayne Hays, not yet in the negligent clutches of Elizabeth Ray, blasted the "contributory negligence" of American policy.[43]

Ensconced in Cairo on May 21, Ambassador Nolte quickly found his stride. Nasser, he wrote Rusk, is merely doing to Israel—"a nation established by force"— what Israel had done to Egypt in 1956. It was a case of "tit for tat," and the United States would be wise to sit this one out. To intervene or back Israel would inflame the Arabs against America and unleash what Harold Saunders called, in a meeting of LBJ's National Security Council, a "parade of horribles." Assessing the uproar in Israel and Washington over the still nonexistent Egyptian blockade of the Straits of Tiran, the American ambassador in Beirut queried: "Would the United States be as concerned over the issue if it were a blockade of Jordan's port of Aqaba?" Certainly not, and backing Israel to secure Eilat—a port the Israelis had seized in violation of the armistice agreements of 1949—would, U.S. ambassador Findley Burns in Amman wrote, "wreck every interest we have in North Africa and the Middle East for years to come." American diplomats in the Middle East were plainly worried that LBJ, challenged by New York senator Robert F. Kennedy and Minnesota senator Eugene McCarthy for the 1968 Democratic presidential nomination, would tilt aggressively toward Israel to win votes and campaign contributions. Secretary of State Dean Rusk was worried too. Johnson's Democratic rivals were playing the Israel card, and so was Walt Rostow's NSC: "[Will] the U.S. . . . stand up for its friends, the moderates, or back down as a major power in the Near East?"[44] Rusk had a different take on Israeli "moderation." He read the reports from his embassies and agreed that the Israelis needed to be prevented "from taking the law into their own hands." If they attacked, they would further constrict the already constricted American "flexibility" in the region, or even drag America into a war.[45]

Israel Mobilizes

The Israelis, of course, had every intention of attacking and taking the law into their own hands. "We must be honest with ourselves," Menachem Begin chuckled. "*We* decided to attack [Nasser]."[46] Israel's "one chance for winning this war is in taking the initiative and fighting according to our own designs," Defense Minister Moshe Dayan told his colleagues. "God help us if they hit us first." IDF chief of staff General Yitzhak Rabin proposed a strategy like that of 1956: "Give Nasser a knockout punch [and] change the entire order of the Middle East."[47] The Israelis had still not learned that clobbering the Nassers of the Middle East paradoxically *strengthened* them, by martyring them. In June 1967, Israel mobilized eight divisions, or 275,000 troops, 1,100 tanks, 200 guns, 260 combat aircraft and 22 ships against a 410,000-man Arab coalition (twenty-three divisions) with 2,500 tanks, 1,500 guns, 650 combat aircraft and 90 ships. The Egyptians alone equaled the Israelis—with 200,000 men, 1,200 tanks, 600 guns and 431 combat jets—and the addition of thirteen Syrian, Iraqi and Jordanian divisions with tanks and air cover made for a colossal imbalance in numbers. That imbalance explained Nasser's bubbling optimism. When he called for the blockade of Eilat, he exulted to his colleagues: "Now, war will be 100 percent certain." Sadat fretted that "Nasser was carried away by his own impetuosity."[48] The colonel never even bothered to inform the Syrians and the Jordanians that he was bringing on a war. David Nes, the chargé d'affaires at the American embassy in Cairo, worried that Nasser by 1967 had reached "a degree of irrationality bordering on madness."[49] In conversations with more prudent colleagues, Nasser explained that the Israelis would not dare move without American support and that the Americans would never give it because they were frozen by Soviet pressure and Vietnam.[50]

"Our basic objective," Nasser confidently announced in a speech on May 26, "will be to destroy Israel." Such cataclysmic rhetoric reopened the wounds of the Holocaust in Israel. "Auschwitz came up," Israeli general Uzi Narkiss recalled. Israelis said, "We are surrounded and if the Arab armies invade, they'll kill us."[51] The Arabs *wanted* to invade and kill but, in a queer twist of events, were reined in at the last minute by the Soviets. Having instigated the war with their lies about Israeli deployments, the Soviets abruptly changed course. Fearing a wider war with the

Americans, Prime Minister Alexei Kosygin warned the Egyptians that they must not rely on Soviet support or even a Soviet promise to replace Egyptian weapons and ammunition consumed in a war with Israel if the Egyptians struck first.[52]

UNLEASH THE ISRAELIS "LIKE A SHERIFF IN *HIGH NOON*"

That Soviet warning—heeded by Nasser—handed the initiative back to the Israelis, who opted for preemption. First they had to sell preemption to the Americans, who breezily authorized it. Although President Johnson had warned Ambassador Abba Eban that "Israel will not be alone unless it decides to go alone," the Israelis persuaded the Americans to authorize going it alone. General Meir Amit flew to Washington on May 31 and met with Rusk, McNamara and the CIA's Mossad liaison, James Angleton. Rusk was supportive; Angleton actively encouraged a shattering attack on Egypt; and McNamara, briefed on Israel's plans for a blitzkrieg down to Sharm el-Sheikh and across to Suez, gave his approval too. "I read you loud and clear," he smiled to Amit.[53] Walt Rostow described the tension in Israel to President Johnson—"these boys are going to be hard to hold a week from now"—and advised LBJ to unleash the Israelis "like a sheriff in *High Noon*." If Johnson reined them in instead, he would be "back[ing] down as a major power in the Near East."[54] Rostow successfully advanced a line of argument that the neocons would revive in 2003: if Nasser was removed from the equation, then everything would magically improve. Sounding a lot like Dick Cheney in the run-up to the Iraq War, Rostow urged Johnson to *use* Nasser's blockade of the Straits of Tiran as the cause of a war to remove the Egyptian leader. "Just beneath the surface is the potentiality for a new phase in the Middle East of moderation," Rostow assured LBJ a day before the shooting started. If Nasser fell, a new era would surely dawn: "of economic development, regional collaboration, and an acceptance of Israel as a part of the Middle East. But all this depends on Nasser being cut down to size."[55]

Besieged by "cussers and doubters" and trying to win support for an additional hundred thousand troops for Vietnam, Johnson was not focused on Israel and the Arabs when 183 Israeli strike fighters finally had a go at creating Walt Rostow's imagined New Middle East on June 5, 1967.[56] The IAF—composed of French-made Ouragans, Mystères and Mirages—looped low over the Mediterranean toward

Libya—sometimes as low as fifteen meters—and then doubled back from west to east, hitting every Egyptian air base in a stunning surprise attack that wiped out Nasser's inventory of Soviet aircraft while the Egyptian pilots were eating breakfast. Two hundred and ninety-eight Egyptian planes were destroyed on the ground. The chief of Egypt's Soviet military mission complained that Israeli intelligence had better knowledge of Egypt's airports and hangar locations than the Soviets, or even the Egyptians themselves.[57]

The Egyptians received no warning of the attack. Modeled on the Soviet Central European network, Egypt's radars were trained on the land approaches from Israel and left wide gaps along the Mediterranean, which the Israelis flew through.[58] Even if Egypt's radar net had been more complete, it wouldn't have mattered on June 5. The entire system had been shut down that morning while the Egyptian army commanders flew into the Sinai to inspect the troops there. Egyptian air traffic controllers, radar operators and antiaircraft gunners were so unreliable—it was they who had mistakenly ordered the shoot-down of Texas oilman John Mecom's private jet— that the Egyptians worried that sending friendly commanders through their own airspace might also end in tragedy. So they switched the radars off as the Israeli jets screamed in from the west and north. The Israelis bombed and strafed against little resistance. It was a cruel irony that the Israelis had pressed the Americans for Hawk missiles in 1962 in order to deter an Egyptian first strike with their Il-28s and Tu-16s. In the event, it was the Israelis who struck first and devastatingly. In Cairo, Nasser damned the Israelis for their treachery: "They came from the *west*," he fulminated. "We expected them from the *east*." He then phoned Colonel Houari Boumedienne in Algiers and asked him—while Mossad operators eagerly listened in—if he could lend him Algeria's air force. Boumedienne couldn't, but he did encourage Nasser to "destroy the Zionist entity and expel the British and Americans from the region." After hanging up with Boumedienne, Nasser phoned a nervous King Hussein in Jordan and tried to buck him up: "We have sent all our airplanes against Israel. Since early this morning we've been bombing the Israeli air force."[59]

NASSER'S "BIG LIE"

Other IAF squadrons hit the Syrians, Jordanians and even the Iraqi air force in its distant base at Mosul. Jordan's Prince Abdullah, today King Abdullah, was a little boy in 1967; he leaped and shrieked delightedly as the Israeli light bombers passed over his house, hit the royal palace, cratered every runway in the country and pulverized the Jordanian air force.[60] The instant destruction of the Arab air forces placed the Arab leaders—Nasser in particular—in an embarrassing position. Nasser had told his populace on June 5 that UAR squadrons had shot down "more than 100 Israeli planes" and lost only two of their own. "Pack your bags!" he had crowed in broadcasts to the Palestinian refugee camps. "We will be in Tel Aviv by tomorrow night." Posters were hung around Cairo showing scrawny Jews with nooses around their necks being booted out of Israel by brawny Arab infantrymen.[61] The reversal of fortune had to be explained *somehow*. The CIA had predicted in May that "Nasser would politically survive a military misadventure if he could make it appear to his own people that the great powers had conspired against him."[62] Now Nasser concocted the face-saving conspiracy. Jordan's King Hussein was caught by Israeli surveillance on the telephone with Nasser—an unsecured civilian line—plotting to blame the whole disaster on the United States. To admit that the Arabs had been knocked out by Israel alone was too humiliating. "Will we say that the U.S. and Britain [are attacking], or just the United States?" Nasser asked Hussein. "Do the British even have aircraft carriers?" Nasser wondered, not apparently recalling that two of Britain's four light fleet carriers had attacked Egypt during the Suez War. Yes, they do, Hussein reminded him, so let's blame it on "the United States *and* England." The Jordanian king agreed to issue a joint statement with Cairo condemning the fictitious Anglo-American onslaught. Israeli tape recorders captured the whole conversation, which Lyndon Johnson later dubbed "the Big Lie." When the Israelis played the tape back to Hussein, he sheepishly opted out of the charade.[63]

Nasser didn't. He went to see the commander of the Egyptian forces in the field—Field Marshal Amer—who swore to Nasser that one of his pilots—a young squadron leader by the name of Hosni Mubarak—had observed American jets attacking Egyptian targets with his own eyes. Enraged, Nasser had a bulletin read on Voice of the Arabs radio: "The United States is the enemy. The United States is the hostile force behind Israel. The United States, O Arabs, is the enemy of all peoples, the killer of life, the shedder of blood, who is preventing you from liquidating Israel."[64] Even as the BBC and other world services broadcast the news of Egypt's collapse, Nasser's radio towers on the hills west of Cairo continued to send out reports of Arab victory—a fifteen-year-old boy in Alexandria was congratulated for apprehending "six Israeli frogmen"—and scurrilous accusations that "American planes [were] killing Egyptian children" and that American reporters were lighting cigarettes on their hotel balconies to guide "imperialist" bombers onto their targets. Nasser, taking Johnson's offhand remark to his wife, Lady Bird, that "we have a war on our hands" as proof that "we" signified American and Israeli collusion, broke diplomatic relations with the United States, awarded the Alexandrian teenager twenty dollars and the promise of a "well-paying government job," confined American journalists to the interior of the dingy Nile Hotel, rounded up startled American tourists (some of whom were plucked from Nile cruise ships and the ruins of Luxor) and went ahead with the "Big Lie" on Cairo Radio on Tuesday, June 6.

"America Is Now the Number One Enemy of the Arabs"

In Cairo and Alexandria, furious demonstrators torched American facilities, including the USIS library and the consulate in Alexandria. Ambassador Nolte, newly arrived from Westport, began burning files in the Cairo embassy. Arab rage spread like fire across the region. Nasser used the radio to order "the Arab masses to destroy all imperialist interests," and within hours mobs were hurling stones, trash and firebombs at American embassies and consulates in Baghdad, Basra, Aleppo, Algiers, Tunis and Benghazi. "America is now the number one enemy of the Arabs," Algiers Radio shouted. "The American presence must be exterminated from the Arab homeland."[65] To tamp down the Arab rage, President Johnson initially expressed neutrality in the war, "in thought, word and deed." His friend David Ginsburg immediately phoned the president to advise him that invocation of the Neutrality Act would bar Israel from fund-raising in the United States. Johnson bridled at first. Pressed by White House aides Lawrence Levinson and Ben Wattenberg to replace his declaration of neutrality with one of support for Israel, LBJ wheeled on them and shook his fist in their faces: "You Zionist dupes! You're Zionist dupes in the White House!" But Johnson's rage melted away under the flood of calls and letters pouring into the White House from American Jews, demanding support for Israel's preemptive war and annexations. When it came to Israel, Johnson ruefully reflected, there was no distinction between foreign and domestic policy.[66]

With Washington tilting toward the Israelis despite their aggression, the Jordanians held back. King Hussein knew that the Israelis coveted the West Bank, which bulged inconveniently into Israeli territory and provided convenient bases for cross-border fedayeen attacks; there were 270 attacks over the Jordanian border into Israel in the first six months of 1967 alone.[67] Guilt and vulnerability explained Jordan's halfhearted approach to the war; the king refused to send ground troops into Israel but, pressured by Arab opinion and his own population—half of whom were Palestinians—did authorize bombardments of Tel Aviv and the Israeli air base of Ramot David. Desperate to drag King Hussein into the war, Nasser assured the king—and his own citizenry—that he had destroyed the IAF on the ground and that Egyptian armored columns were rolling up the Israeli army. Hussein shortly discovered the truth. The Israelis saw the 1967 war as "a miraculous second chance" to do what they had failed to do in 1948: seize the Old City of (East) Jerusalem, with all its Muslim, Christian and Jewish holy places, which still lay in Jordanian territory.[68] On June 6 and 7, three Israeli divisions crossed the border and seized Jenin, Nablus, Ramallah and East Jerusalem from the Jordanians, who fought stubbornly with their two hundred Patton tanks and British-trained infantry for three days.

Inside Israeli headquarters, a battle raged over the issue of East Jerusalem. Prime Minister Levi Eshkol feared Soviet intervention, blowback in the Muslim world and even sanctions from the Western powers, but hard-liners like Menachem Begin carried the day: "This is the hour of our political test. We must attack the Old City." Eshkol's reply was farseeing: "Even if we take the West Bank and the Old City, we will eventually be forced to leave them."[69] Their own air cover having been destroyed by fifty-one Israeli sorties, the Jordanians appealed to the Syrians for help. Damascus improbably replied that "all of our aircraft are on training missions and not a single aircraft is available."[70] Under clear skies, the Tel Aviv–Jerusalem highway opened to Israeli traffic for the first time since 1948.

With command of the air, four Israeli mechanized divisions knifed into the Gaza Strip and the Sinai. Deployed defensively to stop a thrust by a hundred thousand Egyptian troops toward Eilat, the Israelis—noting the torpor of the seven Egyptian divisions and the destruction of Nasser's air force—quickly swung over to the offensive. Ariel Sharon's division held the southern edge of the envelopment, rolling through An Nakhl with its guns and armored brigade and leapfrogging ahead to the Mitla Pass with two paratroop battalions, while generals Israel Tal and Avraham Yoffe and Colonel Yehuda Resheff struck through Gaza, Rafah and al-

Arish on the northern edge of the great sack that the Israelis were casting over the Egyptian army. Some Israeli ministers advocated a halt at Gaza to trade the strip for a cease-fire and an end to Nasser's blockade of Eilat, but, eyeing the 250,000 Palestinian refugees there, Defense Minister Moshe Dayan prudently declined: "What will we *then* do with all those Arabs?"[71] Kick them out, Labour Minister Yigal Allon suggested. "Take the Gaza Strip and plan the transfer of its Palestinian refugees to Egypt." In the end, the Israelis would take the strip but shrink from expelling the refugees, leaving the Israelis stuck—until they relinquished the Gaza Strip in 2005—with what Dayan was already calling in 1967 "a nest of wasps."[72]

The IDF surged past Gaza, pausing only to note worriedly that the Palestinian fedayeen were "more willing to make sacrifices" in battle than regular Arab troops like the Egyptians.[73] The Egyptians were not valiant, providing a generation of Soviet advisers with jokes about "Egyptian officers who draw their swords and cut down side streets." The Red Army chief of staff worriedly informed Soviet leader Leonid Brezhnev that Egyptian officers had deserted their units en masse, commandeering jeeps, trucks, sedans and even ambulances to get across the Suez Canal to safety.[74] While the Israelis mopped up the Gaza Strip, American president Lyndon Johnson and Soviet premier Alexei Kosygin used the "hotline" between Washington and Moscow for the first time in anger. When the red telephone was handed to him in the White House Situation Room early on June 5, LBJ's first utterance was not magnificent: "My God, *what* should we say?" The president had been placed in great peril by the Israelis, who had learned that Egyptian vice president Zakaria Mohieddin was headed to New York to announce a crisis-dissolving end to the still ineffectual blockade of the Straits of Tiran and had launched their surprise attack on the morning of his departure to kill Nasser's attempt at conciliation. "After all," a CIA operative in Cairo observed, "the Israelis had been rehearsing their assault for years, and never again would they get such favorable circumstances in which to launch it."[75] Kosygin saved Johnson the trouble of thinking of something to say by thundering from Moscow that the conflict had to end at once. "We moved very close to the precipice," a White House aide recalled.[76] To buy time for the Israelis to smash the Arabs, Johnson's advisers, led by Walt Rostow's brother Eugene, persuaded LBJ to stall Kosygin: "Let us not forget that a crisis is also an opportunity. Many patterns become loosened, and doors open. Let your minds rove over the horizon." Harold Saunders concurred: "Delay your response long enough to allow a clear Israeli victory."[77]

"A CONTINUOUS UNFOLDING OF SURPRISES"

On Wednesday, June 7, the third day of war, Johnson told his NSC that he didn't share their optimism. America, LBJ averred, was "going to wish this war hadn't happened."[78] Egypt had begun to wish it hadn't happened either. Nasser's propagandists emitted the first hint that they were losing. "Our valiant forces have withdrawn and regrouped at the second line of defense, fighting with unparalleled ferocity and heroism."[79] The "regrouping" was not entirely the fault of Nasser or Field Marshal Amer; it was also owed to Egypt's "woefully inadequate and even misleading" Soviet training. Centralized, top-down command marooned Egyptian officers without orders as the decentralized Israelis swooped in and enveloped them. Soviet trainers deployed their Egyptian charges as if they were fighting in the mud of Russia against a depleted Wehrmacht and Luftwaffe, not in the desert against fleet Israeli tanks and jets. At Gaza and in the Sinai, the Egyptians—like the Iraqis in 1990—entrenched their T-54 tanks in the manner of "Soviet films of World War II." The Israeli tanks simply bypassed the sitting ducks—unhampered by harmless Egyptian minefields, where only 5 percent of the mines were properly fused—and the Israeli air force destroyed the T-54s from the air.[80] "It was like watching a snake of fire uncoiling," an Egyptian officer remembered. Egyptian veterans joked darkly about their defeat: "It was the Russian weapons," one complained. "No, they worked just fine," replied another. "It was the Russian military strategy manual: first, draw the enemy onto your own territory. Second, wait for winter."[81] Tal rolled through fine summer weather from Gaza to al-Arish and Rafah, taking command of the coast road between the dunes and the sea that the British had used—in the opposite direction—to crush the Turkish army in 1918. With Tal driving the Egyptians back on Port Said, Sharon hit from the south at Abu Ageila and Kuseima, and Yoffe's two brigades of Centurion tanks jounced into the sandy, nearly impassable gap between generals Tal and Sharon to outrun the Egyptians to the Mitla and Giddi passes and tie off the mouth of the sack. The Israeli approach was what Sharon called "a continuous unfolding of surprises" that panicked and unhinged the unwieldy Egyptian army. "Good Lord, what are we going to do with them?" an Israeli general jotted in his diary; there were more Egyptian prisoners than the Israelis could handle. They simply bypassed most of them, including scores of barefoot desperadoes lying underneath abandoned vehicles licking the last drops of water from their empty radiators. After visiting the Israeli troops in the field, U.S. presidential adviser Harry McPherson hastened home to assure LBJ that "Israel at war destroys the prototype of the pale, scrawny Jew . . . the soldiers I saw were tough, muscular and sun-burned."[82]

Attack on the USS *Liberty*

Feeling the tough Israelis all around them, the Egyptians fell apart. Their Russian tanks broke down or retreated and their air cover vanished. Egypt's air force had been destroyed on the ground, and Cairo's Soviet-supplied SAMs scarcely functioned. An Israeli tank column seized a SAM battery in the Sinai still in its packing crates and shared the following telling anecdote with the Americans: "The missiles had written on them in English, these words: 'By operating with plunger the drive should be engaged to reduction gear. It is not allowed to operate with plunger at accelerated gear.' Would any two people interpret these instructions in the same way?"[83] In its confused retreat back to the safety of the Suez Canal, the Egyptian army lost five times as many men (ten thousand) to desertion and malingering as it did to enemy action.[84] Nosing in to follow the rout on June 8, the USS *Liberty*, an American electronic surveillance ship, approached the coast near al-Arish and was pounced upon by Israeli fighter-bombers. "What's this? Americans?" an IAF controller blurted out as the Israeli Mirages plunged onto the target. He was too late—the Mirages bored eight hundred holes into *Liberty*'s hull in three passes—and was ignored anyway, as the Mirages returned to base only to be replaced by several Mystères, which dived down on the smoking *Liberty* and dropped napalm and high explosive, killing 34 American sailors and wounding 171. The Israelis apologized for the "mistaken action," and LBJ expressed "strong dismay." In one briefing, LBJ alluded to Israel's "deliberate attack" on the *Liberty*, presumably because the American spy ship had overheard talk of the imminent Israeli attack on Syria or the mass execution of Egyptian prisoners in the Sinai. Walt Rostow, usually a stalwart friend of the Israelis, had to admit in this case that the IDF's explanations for the attack—repeated passes by two waves of strike fighters, both of which ignored American flags, hull numbers and distress calls—"made no goddamn sense at all." Rusk called the attack "a genuine outrage." Iowa senator Bourke Hickenlooper accused Secretary of Defense McNamara of whitewashing his after-action inquiry and "carrying a torch for the

Israelis." Hickenlooper wondered why the United States had gone to war with North Vietnam over a trivial attack on a U.S. destroyer in the Tonkin Gulf in which no one had died and was now doing *nothing* to avenge the Israeli destruction of the *Liberty*, in which 205 Americans had been killed or wounded. Only when the Israelis submitted abject apologies—"this behavior is not appropriate conduct for a well-organized army like ours"—and agreed to pay almost $7 million to the families of the killed crew members did the scandal and cover-up finally burn out.[85]

Dayan had instructed his commanders *not* to drive as far as the canal, for to install themselves there, just 180 yards from the Egyptian troops on the other side of the waterway, might cause Nasser to shut down the canal, alienate the oil-hungry Western powers and prolong the war. But, as in the case of the Gaza Strip, where IDF units seized the "nest of wasps" to silence guns firing at nearby Israeli settlements, military necessity won out and the IDF drove right up to the east bank of the Suez Canal to envelop the Egyptian army and close off its last escape route. That was a fateful decision. Although Nasser surrendered his troops east of the canal, he refused to sign an armistice with the Israelis, who bunkered up against the canal in temporary fortifications that were eventually made permanent with the Bar-Lev Line. Heavily supplied and funded by Moscow—which took over Egypt's air defenses and beefed up the Egyptian air force, armor and artillery—Nasser decided to initiate his own Battle of Verdun.[86] Unable to beat the Israelis in open warfare, he would grind them up in a "war of attrition," prolonging the conflict and shelling and bombing the Israeli troops in the Bar-Lev Line until an armistice was wearily agreed to three years later, in August 1970, by which time another twenty-four hundred Israeli troops had been killed or wounded in their sand forts along the Suez Canal.

The guns on the Syrian front were quiet until the fifth day of the Six-Day War, when the collapse of Jordanian resistance in Jenin and Nablus gave the Israelis the opening they needed to outflank the Syrian defenses on the Golan Heights. Dayan hesitated. He worried that an attack on Syria after thrashing Egypt would finally bring in the Soviets on the Arab side. He also worried, with good reason, that the Golan Heights, once seized by Israel, would be impossible to relinquish and would irretrievably poison relations with Syria. As in the case of the Gaza Strip, however, Dayan was talked around by the "now or never" mood of the Israeli press—"Finish the job," *Haaretz* blared, and "create borders appropriate for our needs"—as well as his more aggressive colleagues, one of whom asserted that Israel would "weep for generations" if the opportunity was lost to seize the Golan.[87] With the UN insisting that all armies stop fighting on June 9, Dayan himself picked up the phone and telephoned orders to General David Elazar: strike with three divisions east from Mount Hermon and north from the Sea of Galilee to envelop the twelve Syrian brigades holding the heights. Dayan had just told Elazar that nothing much would happen on his front: "Get used to the idea: this is a war with Egypt."[88] With no air cover, the Syrian infantry, artillery and armor on the heights—pinpointed by Israeli spy Elie Cohen in his four visits to the heights in 1966–67—absorbed a punishing aerial bombardment. "In two days we dropped more [bombs] than we had dropped on all Egyptian airfields throughout the war," an IAF commander reminisced.

The Syrians panicked and broke, like the Egyptians in the Sinai. The Syrians yielded their formidable defensive positions on the Golan Heights on June 10 and the Israelis swarmed in gratefully behind them. "We must ensure that if war breaks out it doesn't end on the Green [armistice] Line," General Elazar had told Dayan in May. It didn't: the Israelis used the Six-Day War to install themselves on the thousand-foot heights and in control of the Jordan headwaters.[89] General Abdel Razzak al-Dardari, who commanded four Syrian brigades, observed that his men deserted and ran away without their weapons "in total chaos . . . even before the Israeli soldiers had come anywhere near their positions."[90] Had the Israelis pursued to Damascus—just sixty kilometers away—the Soviet Union would almost certainly have struck Israel. The Russians were already pouring tons of weapons and ammunition into Syria and Egypt—forty-eight thousand tons in the first week of June 1967—and now Soviet attack aircraft were readied in Ukraine with Israeli target sets, and Soviet submarines drove into position off the coast of Israel.[91]

The war had lasted just six days. In all, 800 Israelis fell, 2,440 were wounded, 100 Israeli tanks were destroyed, and 40 Israeli planes were shot down. Arab losses were much heavier, and bred the complacency that afflicted the Israelis in 1973, when they were surprised and thrown back by a rebuilt Arab coalition. Egypt lost 11,500 killed and 15,000 wounded, 5,500 prisoners and missing, 700 tanks and 264 planes. Syria had 4,700 casualties and lost 105 tanks and 58 aircraft. The Jordanian army melted away. More than a third of its 11,000 casualties were unwounded prisoners and "missing": troops who had dropped their weapons, stripped off their uniforms and melted into the West Bank towns and villages. "O Lord, we have erred and strayed from Thy ways like lost sheep," Morocco's King Hassan wailed to his disbelieving subjects.[92]

"NONE OF THE OCCUPIED TERRITORIES
WILL BE GIVEN BACK EVER"

The political results of the Six-Day War were stunning. They did indeed, as Michael Oren has recently argued, "make the modern Middle East" in the sense that Israel grew from a still vulnerable sliver of a country to a regional superpower. Because of the 1967 annexations, Israel's territory more than quadrupled, from 20,250 square kilometers to 88,000 square kilometers. This bulked-up Israel was eighteen times bigger than the Jewish state that had been proposed by Lord Peel in 1937 and four times bigger than it had been on June 4, 1967. The conquest of the Golan Heights, the West Bank, East Jerusalem, the Gaza Strip and the Sinai desert gave Israel "strategic depth": the ability to absorb an enemy attack and then repulse it.[93] The annexations also limited the options available to Israel's enemies by shortening the frontier with Jordan by 50 percent and with Egypt by 25 percent. Moshe Dayan told CBS's *Face the Nation* that *none* of the occupied territories would ever be given back.[94]

The startled world looked to the White House for a reaction. "The situation in the Middle East is more fluid and presents wider possibilities and graver dangers than at any time since 1948," the British Foreign Office advised its embassies as the war wound down. The Soviets and the Chinese would use this crisis to "divide the Arabs irrevocably from the U.S. and the U.K. by identifying them with the Israeli annexations."[95] Mao Zedong had just secretly sent Nasser a "military plan of action" that called for dissolving the Egyptian army into fedayeen bands that could hide amongst the civilian population. Nasser declined that option—unlike Saddam in 2003—but thrilled to Chou En-lai's description of what the Chinese were doing to weaken the U.S. Army in Southeast Asia: "We are planting the best kinds of opium especially for the American soldiers in Vietnam . . . The effect of this demoralization . . . will be far greater than anyone realizes."[96] Johnson was already sounding a bit demoralized by events in the Middle East. At a press conference on June 15, LBJ sounded, alarmingly, remarkably like the next president from Texas: "The best thing for us to do is to let things clear up and let the people of the world realize just what has happened." The White House press corps *knew* what had happened and pressed Johnson for his reaction. Eisenhower had forced the Israelis to give back their annexations in 1956. Would Johnson do the same, or would he, as CIA director Richard Helms put it, permit "America to be fully black-balled in the Arab world, as Israel's supporter?" Well, Johnson hazarded, "the U.S. remains committed to the territorial and political integrity of all the nations of the Middle East, *but* this depends a good deal on the nations themselves and what they have to say, and what their views and proposals are."⁹⁷

"WE'VE BEEN GIVEN A GOOD DOWRY, BUT IT COMES WITH A BRIDE WE DON'T LIKE"

Moshe Dayan and Golda Meir were ready with their views and proposals. "Never before has our situation been better," Golda Meir exulted, but strategic depth and a fourfold increase in territory brought a host of problems too.⁹⁸ The Egyptians would not reconcile themselves to the loss of the Sinai Peninsula, the Syrians would not accept the amputation of the Golan Heights and Israel's internal arrangements would be vastly complicated by the addition of "occupied territories" like the West Bank, East Jerusalem and Gaza, which put the bulk of Palestinian refugees right back under Israeli control. They had been expelled in 1948 to ease the creation of a Jewish state; now they had been freshly annexed. "We've been given a good dowry," Eshkol joked, "but it comes with a bride we don't like." As in 1948, the IDF moved quickly to evict the Palestinians and clear the occupied territories for Jewish settlement. Loudspeaker trucks drove through towns and villages ordering the Arabs to leave and Israeli buses carried refugees to the Jordanian border while Israeli tanks and bulldozers flattened their houses and shops. Many Palestinians, terrified by Israeli fire, which Dayan ordered trained on civilian areas to induce flight, simply trekked, littering the roads east with cast-off belongings. About 300,000 Palestinians and Syrians were evicted from their homes in 1967 and forced to flee, which handed a powerful propaganda weapon to the enemies of Israel.⁹⁹ The *Times* of London ran a full-page advertisement that waggishly asked Earl Balfour to find a home for 2 million wandering Arabs—the 300,000 "new refugees," and the 1.7 million "old" ones.¹⁰⁰ Most Palestinians stayed put, effectively quintupling Israel's Arab population, from 200,000 to 1 million. Israeli economists estimated that it would cost at least $50 million a year to police and maintain this sullen mass.¹⁰¹ French president Charles de

Gaulle had surrendered Algeria in 1962 to avoid just such a demographic overhang; the Israelis walked right into it, and have been struggling to hold it off ever since.[102]

The Six-Day War and the Israeli annexations placed America on the hot seat. To do nothing was to invite the odium of the Muslim world and hand the Soviets an easy propaganda victory. "The Israeli attack," Brezhnev droned in a July 1967 speech, "was an American-British imperialist strike at the National Liberation Movement in the Middle East."[103] *Pravda* echoed Brezhnev's line: "The U.S. supported Israel fully in the June War in the hope of overthrowing the progressive Arab regimes; the Arabs have been shown again that their mortal enemy is imperialism."[104] Yet to roll back Israeli "imperialism" was to invite the wrath of America's powerful Israel lobby. Just after the war, Florida congressman Claude Pepper showed which way the wind was blowing when he requested and received permission to insert James Michener's paean to Israel—"A Nation Too Young to Die"—in the *Congressional Record*. The Michener piece asserted that "to understand the problem of Israel, the outsider must imagine himself living in Washington, D.C., and reading each morning that neighbors in Baltimore and Alexandria threatened to blow Washington off the face of the earth and push all Washingtonians into the Potomac." Overlooked was the fact that many of those neighbors in "Baltimore" and "Alexandria" were really "Washingtonians" who had recently been chased out of their homes, businesses and farms. Such Washingtonians perusing their papers might feel unsettled by the threats of Baltimore and Alexandria, but not indignant or even righteous.[105]

The Arab world did react indignantly to the Israeli victory and annexations. Though he had lost spectacularly, Nasser was applauded as a martyr to the Arab cause and a blameless victim of incompetent subordinates. *Newsweek* put Nasser on its cover after the defeat, with the caption "Hail the Conquered!" Like Saddam after the Persian Gulf War, Nasser appeared stronger in defeat than he would have been had he chosen to avert the war.[106] In Egypt, an American journalist nosed around in late 1967 and wonderingly reported: "Ask a peasant in a Nile Valley village if he blames Nasser for last June's defeat and the *galabia*-clad *fellah* shakes his head. He blames 'the bad people whom Nasser has since removed from the government.'" With his usual wiliness, Nasser used the defeat to purge disloyal bureaucrats and officers as well as emerging rivals like Field Marshal Amer, who briefly pondered a coup in June 1967 before succumbing to a suspicious and untimely death that was officially termed a "suicide."[107]

Nasser Is "Part of a Dream-World of Arab Greatness"

Outside Egypt, Nasser's aura was even more impressive. "It's not just Nasser who's your enemy," the colonel called to the foreign press, "it's the whole Arab nation." Nasser's attempted resignation on June 9, when the Egyptian army collapsed, fired panic all across the Arab world. In Cairo, all Americans were rounded up, placed on a special train to Alexandria and then rudely bundled onto an overcrowded Greek ferry. As the Americans rolled north from Cairo, "small crowds of Arabs gathered in the early dawn, took off their shoes and waved the soles at the passing train." That was the Arabs' maximum insult—"the object of their scorn is lower than the soles of their shoes."[108] From Tripoli, diplomats reported that "many Libyans were admitted to hospital showing the symptoms of advanced hypnotic hysteria."[109] In Beirut, the British reported that in a "typically Lebanese paradox" Nasser's stock had *risen* on news of his shattering defeat. "Nasser's personal standing has seldom been so fiercely asserted than it currently is." Muslims spoke of "him sorrowfully, almost desperately, as though he were the sheet anchor of their political environment." His defeat had aggravated sectarian tensions, with Beirut's Sunnis forming into angry militias and reminding Christians that "the only 'good Arabs' are Muslims."[110] Overall, the defeat in 1967 had cost Nasser only his health, which deteriorated noticeably after the debacle. Politically and strategically, "Nasser can make future mistakes and suffer more setbacks without risking rejection by the Egyptians or the Arabs as a whole," a British analyst wrote. "For Arabs, he is established as part of a dream-world of Arab greatness."[111] In Washington, Dean Rusk solemnly concurred: "Nasser will be with us for a long time yet," he sighed to the British ambassador in December 1967.[112]

Inside the Johnson administration, pro-Israel hawks like Walt and Eugene Rostow clashed with career State Department officers, who recoiled from the new American liabilities created by the Six-Day War. In July 1967, a British diplomat who met with Eugene Rostow, the number three man in the State Department, recorded his astonishment at Rostow's casual acceptance of the Israeli annexations, which were euphemistically called "occupations." Rostow, who uncritically embraced the "old Israeli ploy" of demanding that moderate Arab states initiate a settlement, had endorsed an Israeli proposal that other governments besides Israel should pay for the resettlement of Arab refugees outside of Israel, and had just assured the governor of the Bank of Israel that the United States would help finance an Israeli program to improve agriculture and create small handicraft industries in the occupied West Bank. Such investment, based on Jewish settlers, would violate the Geneva Convention, which forbade occupying powers from settling their citizens in occupied territories. "Clearly, Rostow has not thought through the full consequences; at desk level, the State Department is doing what it can to preserve *Jordan's* claim to the West Bank." Rostow seemed to be delivering the West Bank (as well as East Jerusalem, Gaza and the Golan Heights) to the Israelis, with no strings attached.[113]

In Congress, Senator Jacob Javits successfully demanded that the United States not merely accept the Israeli annexations, but fortify them, by "shifting from a supplementary source [of weapons for Israel] to the prime source." France, the prime source till June 1967, had pulled the plug just before the war, when President de Gaulle concluded that continued arms sales to Israel would drag France into the same hole in which the United States found itself. Hard as it was to contemplate, de Gaulle stopped a $60 million sale of fifty Mirage Vs to Israel on the grounds that Israel would undoubtedly use them for offensive operations against the Arabs. When the Israeli ambassador protested that de Gaulle had no right to cancel the order without knowing what the Israeli government planned to do, de Gaulle grandly replied: "My dear sir, I know only one thing: that you also don't know what your government will decide."[114] ("The French have written off the Israelis as definitively as the Israelis have written off the French," the U.S. embassy in Tel Aviv concluded. "The Israelis will use [this] to get more arms from the USA.")[115] Dubiously equating de Gaulle's pragmatism with anti-Semitism, Senator Javits deplored France's "extraordinary attack on people of Jewish faith in general and Israel in particular" and demanded that the United States step in with swept-wing F-4 Phantoms. "This is not just Israel's security, it is *our* security . . . We must keep Israel strong so that the Arabs are not tempted back to the disastrous path of total belligerency. It would be a pure case of irresponsibility if we did not do so."[116]

McGeorge Bundy, a Republican still in Democratic harness, pushed back against the pressure from the Rostow brothers, Javits and AIPAC. Bundy's view of American responsibility was different from theirs. He was leery of arms sales to Israel and told President Johnson that "we must not leave behind a truncated and bitter Jordan and an area of irredentism." Since America, not Israel, "would receive all of the blame," America needed to hold the line against Israeli chauvinism. This, however, was unlikely. "U.S. power and influence to effect a general withdrawal," Bundy confided to the British ambassador in July 1967, "is severely limited by domestic political pressures." It was certainly desirable to forbid Israeli annexations—"Eshkol should be held to his statement that Israel desires no territorial aggrandizement"— but unlikely that such bans would ever be enforced. The Johnson administration was buying into the Israeli argument that the gains of 1967 made possible a "transformational strategy." The Arabs had been thrashed, fair and square, and could now be safely put through the wringer.

Prime Minister Levi Eshkol had already launched the transformation; he was busy expelling Palestinians from the occupied territories and demanding that they "take up residence in the Arab states." Shimon Peres was suggesting that Israel might not stop on the West Bank; it might like the East Bank as well: "Israel is trying to keep the Jordan River open for emigration to the east."[117] After studying the legal status of the occupied territories in September 1967, the Eshkol government secretly concluded that it did *not* have the right to place settlers in the territories, but went ahead and settled them anyway. This created the intractable situation that exists today: 250,000 Israeli settlers living on the West Bank with all the rights of Israeli citizens, surrounded by 2.5 million Palestinians without rights, living under military occupation.[118] Bundy also regretted the rift in Tel Aviv itself—"the complete polarization between Dayan and Abba Eban" (Eban was disparaged in Israeli government circles as "the learned fool")—which Bundy compared to "trying to run the Vietnam War with Senator Fulbright as Secretary of State." There were, in short, "no candid relations" between the two governments at a crucial moment.[119]

Bundy's duel with Eugene Rostow revealed a similar lack of candor in Washington. Struggling to understand how the Americans could possibly consent to the vast, complicating Israeli annexations in 1967—which caused the "forever war" still sputtering in Israel and the Palestinian Authority today—the British deconstructed American decision making in the summer of 1967. They found a structure remarkably like the neocon "shadow government" of Dick Cheney and Donald Rumsfeld that would sprout under George W. Bush. American Middle East policy, the British concluded in July 1967, was defined at three levels: it originated in the State Department and in reports from American ambassadors, but was then filtered through Eugene Rostow, "who read and radically altered their papers" before delivering them to Bundy, who advised the White House and secretary of state working from "Rostow's consideration of the [State Department] papers," which Rostow had largely rewritten. This, of course, would become the neocon tactic under George W. Bush: distorting evidence to justify radical policy changes.

"THE FILLING IN THE SANDWICH IS PURE KOSHER"

Eugene Rostow did what pro-Israel hawks in Feith's Office of Special Plans would do in 2003: he intercepted and reshaped intelligence bound for the White House, and created a bunker mentality of fear, menace and unilateralism. "All of us would prefer to escape into the past and leave the task of security to someone else. But there is no one else," Rostow told an audience of law students in 1967. Still, America lacked the "wealth, power, wisdom and imperial will to build a world after the manner of the Romans." It would have to "make the Third World take principal responsibility for itself," which, to Rostow's mind, involved letting out the reins in 1967 so that the Israelis could impress upon the Arab world the futility of continued resistance.[120] Frustrated with the way Rostow wedged in between the State Department and the White House to shape policy, the British Foreign Office acidly observed that "the filling in the sandwich is pure kosher." At the lower levels, "Israel takes its place in a general assessment, but almost every report of Rostow's thoughts reproduces in pretty undigested form the policies which the Israeli government are trying to put across to the Americans."[121]

Johnson strode right into Rostow's snare. Disgusted by Nasser's "Big Lie" and irked by Kosygin's threats, LBJ came around to the hard-line position that Rusk too embraced. Israel would not be forced to "accept a puny settlement." America would let Tel Aviv trade land for peace. As presidential adviser John Roche put it, there'd be no more "sweet-talk," no more "kissing Arab backsides," which would only "alienate Jewish support in the U.S."[122] Walt Rostow went further: the war would not be settled on the basis of armistice agreements like 1949 or 1956, "which leave the Arabs in the posture of hostilities toward Israel." *This* time, if the Arabs wanted their land back they would have to "accept Israel as a Middle Eastern state with rights of passage through the Suez Canal." Bundy too went along: the war "changes the landscape" and enables "a strong and secure Israel in a prosperous and stable Middle East." Bundy at least recognized that there needed to be some give with the take. "Put us on record in favor of a real attack on the refugee problem. . . . This is good LBJ doctrine and good Israeli doctrine." Rusk agreed: "If we do not make ourselves attorneys for Israel"—trading Israeli concessions for diplomatic recognition and security—"we cannot recoup our losses in the Arab world."[123]

Some, like I. F. Stone in *Ramparts*, argued that Israel's victory in the Six-Day

War "made sense only if it led to a new era of reconciliation with her Arab neighbors." With its $2.5 billion stake in Middle Eastern oil—"the Arabian deserts are the holiest places of the Middle East for the world's oil cartels"—and its global commitments, the United States would hesitate to throw its entire support behind Israel—"2 million Jews in a sea of 50 million Arabs"—and would inevitably "bring strong pressure on Israel to give up her territorial gains in return for new international guarantees." That being the case, Stone pressed Israel to scale "the other side of the ravine"—not war, reprisal and expansion, but reconciliation with Tel Aviv's Arab neighbors: a binational state along Swiss lines, with Jewish and Arab cantons. If Israel continued to pummel Nasser and the other Arab leaders and to cling to the Golan Heights, West Bank, East Jerusalem and the twenty-three thousand square miles of Egyptian territory seized in the Six-Day War, it would only open the door to much worse: "some far more fanatical and less constructive force, like the Muslim Brotherhood." Only concessions and peace, Stone said, "can make Israel secure." Continued reliance on blitzkrieg, buffers and espionage would merely make Israel "a minuscule Prussia, a new Wild West, where Israel can only rely on a quick draw with a six-shooter."[124] The war transformed Israel from underdog to occupying power, and this pitched Tel Aviv off the moral high ground that it had enjoyed for years after the Holocaust. No country recognized the Israeli annexation of East Jerusalem in 1967 and its creation of a new wave of Palestinian refugees, and Tel Aviv's increased isolation made it almost totally dependent on the United States for diplomatic support. That, in turn, deeply eroded America's power to operate as an "honest broker" in the Middle East.[125]

"We Have Turned Away from God and God Has Turned Away from Us"

The unending tragedy of the Arab-Israeli dispute was that even if Israel had been in a mind to negotiate, the Arabs probably were not. "You can take your Arab horse to water," a British diplomat wrote in July 1967, "but far from drinking, he will probably shy." The Saudis professed outrage at Israel's annexation of the Muslim holy places in East Jerusalem. Morocco's King Hassan argued that the war made necessary a religious revival: "Defeat had come to the 70 million Arabs in 1967 because they had not been faithful to the precepts of their religion, which should have been their unifying force . . . We have turned away from God and God has turned away from us." The Arab world's "only hope" was not technology, education or negotiations, but "a return to the eternal verities: the faith of Allah and the religion of his Prophet."[126] Nasser's concern with his standing in the Arab world meant that he would "never allow himself to be outflanked on the left as a 'nationalist,' " even when "economic realism" demanded it.[127] Miles Copeland detected and noted in 1969 a fundamental misunderstanding—that certainly survives to this day—between American "High Roaders" and Arab "Low Roaders."

> The High Roader can only look on in bewilderment when he sees a mob of Palestinian refugees, on the coldest night of the year, pile up the blankets given them by Western charities and set fire to them—or when he sees the Egyptians, after a catastrophic defeat at the hands of the Israelis, sit down with the Syrians and Algerians to work out how they can go through the same exercise again, at the same time doing as much damage as possible to alienate the Western powers whose help they need.

For the Low Roaders, Copeland discovered that such behavior was natural and not the least bit "bewildering." They felt themselves "dropouts from a system to which they can never belong except as second-class citizens," politically and economically condemned to remain several steps behind the Western powers and Israel: "No matter how fast they advance, the Western countries are going to advance that much faster . . . [Out of] frustration, they reject Western logic and Western values even when they have nothing better to turn to."[128]

The United States accepted and even embraced the results of the Six-Day War. To Israel's relief, there was no reprise of 1956–57, when Ike and Dulles had ordered Israel out of its occupied territories. Far from pressuring Israel, LBJ and Rusk merely called for "justice for the refugees," a peace based on "recognized boundaries" and no more threats to the existence of any nation.[129] In May 1968, in his run for the presidency, Vice President Hubert Humphrey tried to outbid his Democratic rivals and Republican Richard Nixon in his support for Israel. "The U.S. will not permit Israel to stand defenseless against *any* who would destroy her!" he told an audience of fifteen thousand that had gathered in Chicago to celebrate the twentieth anniversary of Israeli statehood. The Republicans raised the stakes; they flailed the Johnson-Humphrey administration for its "precarious policy" in the Middle East and demanded that it outline to the "the State of Israel and the American people"—in that order—its plans to "expose and isolate militant troublemakers" in the region. Republican leaders Senator Everett Dirksen and Congressman Gerald Ford went beyond mere exposure and isolation to demand that LBJ sell F-4 Phantoms to Israel "to maintain the balance of power in the Middle East."

"Are You Building a Democracy or an Armed Empire?"

The F-4 dispute in 1968 revealed again the power of the Israel lobby in America. Johnson and Rusk did *not* want to sell the Israelis F-4s because they wanted to "maintain a position of being able to exert pressure on Israel." Johnson invited Eshkol to his Texas ranch and bluntly told him that "the U.S. will resist aggression, whether it be Hitler, Nasser or Israel." "What kind of Israel" are you building, LBJ asked Eshkol, "a democracy or an armed empire?"[130] The president and Rusk recognized that better weapons merely emboldened the Israelis and enabled them to goad and smash their neighbors with a doctrine called "limited use of military force," which—thanks to overpowering American weaponry—was really "unlimited use of limited military force." That was no small distinction: unlimited use of high-tech platforms, even in a limited way, could achieve stunning, scarring results—like the destruction of the Arab air forces on the ground in June 1967.[131] But both presidential candidates, Humphrey and Nixon, needed Jewish votes and donations and thus barnstormed for the immediate sale of fifty F-4s to Israel. "If Mr. Humphrey really favors providing Phantom jets to Israel," House Republican leader Gerald Ford told the B'nai B'rith Convention in 1968, "then he should argue his case at the White House . . . He is President Johnson's political protégé after all." Both parties had military-sales-to-Israel planks—proffered by AIPAC—nailed into their presidential platforms.[132] With every Phantom earmarked for Vietnam, Johnson initially offered only A-4 Skyhawks, but he authorized IAF pilots to train on the Phantom—for the day when they would get them—and had a menacing statement read into the *Congressional Record*. LBJ warned "every one of Israel's warring neighbors, who would destroy this tiny citadel of human dignity," that America would not allow it.[133]

Congress had other citadels to protect besides the one of human dignity: like the McDonnell Douglas citadel in St. Louis. Missouri senator Stuart Symington threatened to kill Johnson's Foreign Military Sales Bill—which sustained South

Vietnam—if Johnson continued to deny Israel Phantoms (and Missouri the chance to build them). Pressured by Humphrey, Nixon, AIPAC and Congress, Johnson keeled over and approved the $285 million Phantom sale in December 1968. So much for Rusk's desire to "exert pressure on Israel": the Phantom sale would double the combat power of the IAF and hand Tel Aviv a miracle weapon—a strike fighter that could lug seven tons of bombs and missiles and still maneuver as crisply as an interceptor. Johnson, normally the supplest of politicians, felt especially bitter about this particular ruckus. American Jews, he complained, were interventionists in Israel and noninterventionists everywhere else. They wanted LBJ "to send the Sixth Fleet to the Gulf of Aqaba, but wouldn't send a screwdriver to Vietnam," where twenty-six Americans were dying every day in 1967 and the Pentagon was spending $38,052 a minute.[134]

Given the domestic political benefits of a "strong Israel" policy and the euphoria that swept Israel and America—where exultant Jewish groups effortlessly raised $1.5 billion in private gifts to Israel—after the stunning Israeli victory in 1967, it was understandable that both Republicans and Democrats took this line, but not wise. David Nes, the American diplomat in Cairo who had warned of Nasser's encroaching "madness" in early 1967, considered the deepening American security relationship with Israel after the Six-Day War disastrous. Cairo Radio now called America and Israel "the pirate and the lackey, the speckled snake and its tail."[135] Noting the State Department's discomfort with the war but its loyal silence, Nes raised his voice; he resigned in protest from the Foreign Service in January 1968 and then went public—in the *Baltimore Sun*—with a critique of American policy in the Middle East. "Washington's policy," Nes argued, "forestalls the peace it professes through its indifference to the Arabs and its partiality toward Israel."[136] According to Nes, U.S. "prestige and credibility in the Middle East [had] sunk to the lowest point since [America's] sponsorship of Israeli independence twenty years ago." Truman's policy—coordinated in the White House by Max Lowenthal and David Niles—had been laughably one-sided, Ike's and Kennedy's "more balanced," but Johnson's was awful. "Caught napping"—as Congressman Gerald Ford put it—when war broke out in June, LBJ neglected to force Israel to implement the November 22, 1967, UN resolution calling for an Israeli withdrawal from the occupied territories and a political settlement. That deliberate neglect constituted "a basic change in the attitude of the U.S. government toward the Arab-Israeli problem from one of balance and fairness to one of total support for the development through force of an Israeli empire." Johnson's change of line in the war was breathtaking, and generally ascribed to the Israel lobby. As Nicholas Katzenbach at the State Department wrote: "If the Israelis screw up the relations [with Washington], then the Jewish groups are going to bail out the Israelis."[137]

Like George W. Bush in the early 2000s, LBJ failed to grasp the intricacy of policy in the Middle East. The Arab leaders had convened in Khartoum after the Six-Day War and hardened, not softened, in their position on Israel. The new "triple-no" policy" was adamantine: "No peace with Israel, no recognition of Israel, and no negotiation with it." No Arab leader would consent even to meet with an Israeli.[138] Two months later, the UN passed Security Council Resolution 242, which called for recognition and acceptance of "every state in the area"—including Israel—in return for a "just settlement of the refugee problem" and a "withdrawal of Israeli armed forces from territories occupied in the recent conflict."[139] This seemed like a good basis for a "final settlement," but Johnson demurred. Lunching with a half dozen Arab ambassadors in the White House, Johnson heard their criticism of his hands-off approach to the war and the Israeli annexations, then turned to his beagle, seized it by the muzzle, looked into its eyes and—to the astonishment of his Arab visitors—explained American policy: "What can I do? One man was so nasty to his neighbor that his neighbor was not able to stand it any more, so his neighbor took hold of him and gave him a good beating. What can I do to him?"[140]

No wonder Nes resigned: Johnson's indulgent position on Israel's massive June 1967 annexations, Nes argued, "terminated the U.S. politico-military position in the Middle East"; it had a more dramatic impact "than any single event since 1948," and, naturally, "the Soviets [took] quick advantage of the psychological environment engendered." Johnson had focused everything on Southeast Asia—"an area far less important to Western interests than the Middle East"—and America would pay the price for his inattention, and his subcontracting of the region to Israeli chauvinists like Menachem Begin, Golda Meir and Moshe Dayan. "American credibility was at a vanishing point"; Washington had thrown away the support of a hundred million Arabs, had put its enormous private investments in the region at risk and had imperiled the "long range viability of Israel" by its one-sided policy. Nes held out no hope for the Johnson administration, or a Humphrey one. HHH was as discredited as LBJ. "Only a new Administration dissociated from the indifference to the Arabs and the seeming partiality to Israel can accomplish this goal."[141] But was Nixon the one?

CHAPTER 9

THE NIXON DOCTRINE

RICHARD NIXON ENTERED OFFICE after the bitterly contested 1968 elections with the smallest plurality enjoyed by any American president since 1912. He had squeaked past Hubert Humphrey by half a million votes and assumed leadership of a country that was demoralized by its performance in Vietnam and disillusioned with foreign entanglements. To American voters, world power looked increasingly thankless and expensive. Determined to maintain American power without breaking the bank, Nixon attempted to modify U.S. foreign policy by handing the State Department off to a capable administrator, William P. Rogers—and vesting the real power to craft strategy and policy in the NSC (established by Truman in 1947) and his handpicked national security adviser—Henry Kissinger. Rogers, who had been Ike's attorney general, was supposed to keep a lid on a State Department that Nixon viewed as a mischievous liberal hotbed.[1] Since Kissinger was not subject to Senate confirmation and held no cabinet portfolio, he was Nixon's man—"the creature of the President"—who would facilitate a personal, creative foreign policy.[2] Nixon was the first American president in 120 years to confront opposition control of *both* houses of Congress, which made a personal, even secretive foreign policy all the more desirable.

America's fears in the Middle East under Nixon were the same as they had been under Eisenhower, Kennedy and Johnson. Admiral Charles Griffin, commander of

NATO's southern forces, summarized those fears in January 1968. The Soviets had begun a "concerted effort to alter the strategic balance in the Arab world." They were building "strong client states" in the Middle East and Mediterranean, pouring in $2 billion of military aid, seeking warm-water outlets and sacrificing everything— "even local communist parties"—to gain control of Middle Eastern oil, which furnished 70 to 80 percent of Western Europe's needs, 43 percent of Japan's and 6 percent of America's.[3] Soviet analysts underscored the energy insecurity of the free world: "The 'energy crisis' in the U.S. will only get worse; the U.S. will need to import 50 percent of its needs by 1975." Western Europe and Japan were already entirely dependent on Middle Eastern oil, and would become more so in view of the high price of extraction in Alaska and the North Sea, which was "six times more expensive than in the Persian Gulf." *Pravda* drew the obvious conclusion: "In the current situation the stoppage of the flow of oil from the Persian Gulf would threaten the entire capitalist economy with economic shocks."[4] Thus, Soviet propagandists encouraged what they called "the politicization of oil"—tagging the oil countries as "proletarian nations" and Western producers as "imperialists"—and Soviet strategists dangled a mailed fist over the Middle Eastern arteries. In the 1960s, $2 billion bought a lot of Soviet hardware: the Soviets increased Egypt's armored divisions from 350 tanks to 1,600 between 1967 and 1970, Syria's from 300 to 1,000. Egypt's Soviet-built artillery establishment increased from 400 guns to 1,600, Syria's from 350 to 1,000. The Egyptian and Syrian air forces swelled just as alarmingly, from 100 to 600 planes and from 55 to 260, respectively.[5] Both air forces included the latest supersonic MiG-21s and Sukhoi bombers and gave a hard edge to the revamped Soviet strategy: not conquest, but the more achievable "control of the terms on which [Arab] oil was sold to the West" in order to bend the United States and Western Europe to Moscow's will without resort to war. In the Arab-Israeli conflict, the Russians much preferred "continued ferment" to a "permanent settlement." "Keeping up the animosity" suited Moscow's book because it "kept the area polarized and put the U.S. permanently on the defensive."[6]

Nixon, like his predecessors, struggled to hit upon the right strategy to counter this Soviet threat. The United States had planned a strategic shift since Eisenhower. Ike's rapprochement with Nasser in November 1958 via NSC-5820 had been conceived to mend fences with Arab nationalism as British power evaporated in the Middle East. When Nasser spurned Ike's advances, the president had then turned to Iran as an even better substitute for British power. Ike's NSC-6010, drafted in July 1960, posited Iran as "the logical heir to present British influence in the area." Shah

Muhammed Reza Pahlavi was "deeply disturbed by Pan-Arabism," which might become "a barrier to Iranian aspirations in the Persian Gulf." The shah also sup-ported the existence of Israel because it meant that Persian Iran would not "be the only outsider in the [Arab] Middle East." Nixon, like Ike, resolved to enlist Iran as an American policeman.[7]

The British decision to withdraw from "east of Suez" in 1966—when America was pinned down in Vietnam—tightened Washington's focus on the "twin pillars" of Iran and Saudi Arabia. The Saudi pillar was thin, but coated in oil. The Iranian one was thick *and* oily; moreover, the Pahlavis showed a real eagerness to please. They recognized Israel—"Israel has the same qualities that Iran would like to have, a determination to defend one's own country because no one else will"—and were unabashedly pro-Western. Statecraft "requires farsightedness more than emotions or blindfolded zeal; we will not go to war against the world with talk."[8] Nixon liked what he was hearing from Tehran. The Saudis were less helpful, always "roasting" their American ambassadors "about the inadequacy of their efforts on the Arab-Israeli question."[9] Nixon inferred from America's shocked reaction to the Vietcong Tet Offensive in January 1968 and his own narrow victory over Humphrey in No-vember that America was weary of world leadership. He pondered an opening to communist China and strategic arms limitation talks (SALT I) with the Soviets. "Vietnamization," begun in 1969, would gradually turn the Vietcong problem over to the South Vietnamese government and military. Elsewhere, Nixon would replace American "presence" with pro-American proxies, who would be armed and advised by Washington to a level where they would be able, as Nixon put it in July 1969, to repel any threat short of "a major power involving nuclear weapons." In July 1969, he formalized the Johnson practice of relying on Israel, Iran and Saudi Arabia as America's regional sentinels and called it the Nixon Doctrine.[10] "We will not give up friends or let down allies," Nixon explained to Congress, "but we are not in a posi-tion to carry the entire burden alone."[11]

AMERICAN WORRIES ABOUT SAUDI ARABIA

In 1971, Nixon sent Secretary of State William P. Rogers and then Vice President Spiro Agnew to Saudi Arabia. Their mission was to cinch up the relationship and share out the security burden. Six American administrations had committed to the defense of Saudi Arabia since 1932, and the British had patrolled the Gulf for decades, but the British were leaving and the Americans were overstretched. "Time is running out for the establishment of a stable political structure after the withdrawal of British forces and protection," Agnew declared on arrival in Riyadh. Saudi Arabia remained the foundation of the American position in the eastern Arab world, what the CIA dubbed "an oasis of stability in the otherwise volatile Middle East."[12] The "oasis" dripped with oil—150 billion barrels of proven reserves (about a third of the world's oil), four refineries and $700 million a year of repatriated U.S. profits that helped soften America's trade deficit—but it also held key strategic positions.

Located at the junction of southwest Asia and East Africa, Saudi Arabia flanked the shortest sea route between Europe and East Asia and provided the United States with critical military overflight rights as well as an American-equipped joint air defense command.[13] But there was much to be worried about in Riyadh. In 1972, the CIA warned that four decades after national unification, Saudi Arabia's people "still lacked a sense of common nationality"; family and tribe were still the primary loyalties.[14] No one even new how *many* Saudis there were. The census of 1969, which counted 5.5 million, had been secretly doubled by the king to give the appearance of strength. By 1990, the Saudi kings were claiming 14 million subjects, when there were really only about 5 million.[15] In 1971, the U.S. embassy identified the "essential weakness of the U.S./Saudi relationship: it lies on a narrow governmental base on both sides. There is no strong public support in the United States for a regime ruled by a king who is a compulsive and conspicuous spender and who strongly disagrees with U.S. support for Israel." Worse were the kingdom's "religious-oriented conservatives, who oppose American influence as foreign and materialistic." Even "liberal, Western educated Saudis were affected by the anti-American aspects of Arab nationalism and by Palestine." Unlike the Iranians, who were "moving forward to modernize the monarchy" with a "White Revolution," Saudi Arabia showed "no energy, no urgency. Tradition, religion, and tribal consultation still reigned."[16] There was no parliament in Saudi Arabia, just a tight circle of royal advisers and princely ministers, several thousand princes and a vast, politically neutered bureaucracy. The civil service and armed forces were "saturated" with officers and employees, who exhibited the "Saudi's disdain for manual labor" and bound everything in red tape.[17] The Wahhabi clergy were arrogant and repressive. When Sheikh Muhammed bin Ibrahim al-Shaikh, the grand mufti and chief *qadi*, or judge, of Saudi Arabia, died in 1969, the whole kingdom sighed with a relief that was tempered only by the awareness that the mufti would assuredly be replaced by someone just as severe, and corrupt.[18]

Willie Morris, Britain's chief Middle Eastern hand in the sixties and seventies, complained of Saudi Arabia's perennial "unheroic role." As they would in the years before and after 9/11, "the Saudis tried to keep trouble away from themselves by privately paying for and discreetly assisting the frustration of extremists," first the Palestinian fedayeen and later the jihadis in Kashmir, Somalia, Chechnya, Afghanistan, Pakistan and Iraq. Inside the Arab world, Riyadh opposed the nationalism of Egypt, Syria and Iraq with calls for a "broad Islamic front"—a "Muslim World League"—extending from Morocco to Indonesia coordinated by a "permanent Islamic secretariat" in Mecca.[19] The World League channeled funds to schools and mosques and paid for Voice of Islam radio broadcasts in multiple languages. In the World League's assembly, Riyadh's "choice of delegates," a British analyst noted, "was not always happy." Even in the 1960s, the Saudis selected "religious fanatics to sharpen the weapon of Saudi diplomacy." The influence of such men might not "set the world on fire," but it "would not die out at an early date" either.[20]

Fearing that "others might steal their Islamic clothes"—Farouk, Nasser, Sukarno or the Pakistanis—the Saudis also belabored the "Zionists and Imperialists," who were "continually dividing the Islamic world with foreign and ideological domination." Saudi organs regularly issued bulletins asserting that "the long-range aim of the Zionist plot was not limited to the capture of Palestine, but included the destruction of the Muslim religion." In public addresses, King Faisal called Israel "a cancer in the body of the Arab states."[21] That Saudi royal paranoia—trumped up to satisfy the Wahhabi clergy and "weaken the appeal of the Arab socialism"—contained the seeds of Osama bin Laden's al-Qaeda caliphate.[22] It was a Saudi royal official after all, not a terrorist, who declaimed from Mecca in 1967 that "Islamic solidarity and the spirit of jihad and sacrifice" were the duties of all Muslims until Jerusalem, its holy places and all other "usurped land in Palestine" had been restored to their rightful Muslim owners. King Faisal encouraged all Saudi public employees to contribute 1 percent of their monthly salaries to the "Popular Committee for the Welfare of the Families of Palestinian Warriors and Martyrs," much of which went not to families, but to the fedayeen.[23] The Saudis, of course, were the chief drivers of this line, which would become a signature line on 9/11, when fifteen of nineteen hijackers proved to be Saudis. A Saudi businessman speaking with the American consul in Dhahran in 1972 warned of this trend: "The arrogant U.S. practice of exploiting Arab weakness is sowing a whirlwind. The older generation is tired and ashamed, but their sons in college will obtain justice. They seethe with hatred of America and its policy toward Arabs. One day they will destroy everything American in the Middle East—wreck every oil well if that is required—and their fathers will be proud of them."[24] The British detected the simmering radicalism, but also the hypocrisy behind it: "In the commercial exploitation of piety, this country has been expert ever since Mecca became a place of pilgrimage in pre-Islamic times."[25]

Nixon and Kissinger understood that the Saudis stoked international crises because they had so little legitimacy themselves. The Saudis played the role of Puritans while they kept $30 billion of "walking around money" on deposit in U.S. banks. "Abdul Aziz, Saud and Faisal fought as desert warriors, but since the 1930s, there has been no stress on the military character of the Royal Family. It is even debatable whether they should be termed 'Bedouin' or 'civilian,' " an American diplomat wrote in 1965. "Unlike the Shah or King Hussein of Jordan, who delight in flying military aircraft, the Saudi royals are always in robes, not uniforms."[26] Their kingdom was stultifying; the system of "horizontal succession" among the sons of Ibn Saud gave the Saudi monarchy an eternally geriatric appearance. The five thousand members of the Saud family required expensive care and feeding, and were themselves riven into competitive factions, like the "Sudayri Seven," half brothers of Faisal led by Prince Fahd, or Crown Prince Khalid's faction of princes, which included the national guard commander, Prince Abdullah. Oil kept the five thousand princes in sports cars, private jets and palaces, but Saudi Arabia's efforts to buy acceptance in the Arab world were a worrisome drain on the treasury. To buy their way out of the war with Nasser's proxies in Yemen (and to silence Nasser's vituperative propagandists), the Saudis agreed to pay an annual subsidy to Egypt of $100 million. The Saudis paid $40 million per year to the Jordanians to keep the Palestinians *there* and mitigate "the effects of the Israeli aggression." Pakistan was another Saudi client; Riyadh wanted to buy Pakistani friendship as a hedge against the Arab nationalists, but also as an added force against Israel. Defense cost the Saudis an additional $800 million a year—one-third of the national budget—which drew down funds available for education and development.[27]

The kingdom was synonymous with sloth, corruption and bureaucratic drift. Throughout the 1970s, Washington worried that Saudi Arabia might go the way "of that other *bedu*-oil state, Libya" and succumb to an anti-Western Arab nationalist coup, as Libya did in 1969, when Colonel Muammar Qaddafi overthrew King Idris.[28] A 1971 American report on Saudi problems enjoined Washington to help the Saudis curb corruption. When the report landed in the State Department, someone scrawled "How?" in the margin.[29] Meeting with the senior Saudi princes and their minister of economic planning in 1973, Henry Kissinger told them, "Most countries have the problem of finding resources to meet their ambitions; you have the problem of finding ambitions to meet your resources."[30] There was little ambition on display in Saudi government offices. When the editor of Bahrain's *Sada al-Usbou* newspaper arrived for a nine a.m. meeting at Riyadh's ministry of information, "no one was there, not even the coffee boys." At ten thirty, "the minister and a few officials drifted in." The editor had his meeting, two hours late, then sourly observed that most of the officials went home (for good) at twelve thirty.[31]

Not only were the royals and their ministers thieves of time, they were bounded by the notorious "five-percenters": high-pressure agents who had access to the royal family and government procurement contracts. "The money-grubbing habits of SAG [Saudi Arabian Government] officials are a well-entrenched system," the American embassy lamented in 1970.[32] To curb opposition, the Saudi kings controlled the press through a ministry of information that edited all the newspapers in Saudi Arabia, and employed two vast domestic intelligence services—Intelligence and Investigations—which were so large and entrepreneurial (their agents were required to be "successful") that no one dared utter a critical word. Innocents were routinely hauled in for interrogation by a "bad quality personnel" bloated with large numbers of retired military officers. According to the U.S. embassy, they "used blackmail tactics to gain access to 'sex and money.' "[33]

Successful Saudi military officers in the armed services were even less fit to stabilize the region than the unsuccessful ones in the intelligence services. U.S. Army advisers reported an alarming lack of intelligence and literacy.[34] Studying the Saudi army in 1968, a British advisory mission reported that it was unfortunate that the Saudi division promised to the Jordanians in 1967 never arrived in time to fight the Israelis, "for the annihilation of a division might have done much to disabuse those who are still convinced that a thousand men charging across the desert screaming '*Allah al Akbar!*' and with green banners flying will strike terror into the hearts of well-trained opponents with tanks, artillery and aircraft." The Saudi army had no antiaircraft guns, mines or engineering capability despite constant threats of invasion from Nasser—"only sandbags, which are just sugar sacks cut down and re-sewn by a local tailor." When British advisers tried to teach the Saudi infantry how to dig field fortifications in the Jizan area—siting, digging and revetting weapon pits—they could not induce the Saudis—enlisted men or officers—to pick up a shovel: "They were interested and admiring spectators."

The American Military Training Mission, which had been working in Saudi Arabia since 1953, observed dolefully in the 1960s and 1970s that "the Saudi armed forces," despite millions in investment, "are far from possessing combat capability." There was "little trainable manpower"—only 54 percent of Saudi males between fifteen and forty-nine were deemed fit for military service—and what there was had poor training, poor discipline, poor logistics and a dismaying reliance on foreigners (Americans, British, French and Pakistanis) for maintenance, training and operational functions.[35] The Saudis evidenced a total "lack of motivation manifested in lethargy, weak discipline, poor morale, and flaccid leadership." How could it be otherwise? There was a deep gulf between the 90 percent illiterate Bedouin enlisted ranks and their educated officers, 80 percent of whom came from the kingdom's cities. Saudi officers "scorned the low cultural level of the troops, who came straight from the desert to the ranks." The troops scorned the officers, who descended from shop owners and clerks and "had never exchanged fire with an enemy."

Instead of educating their rustic troopers, Saudi Arabia's urbane officers as often as not turned their education to nonmilitary ends, seeking "financial security, steady promotion, higher pay and benefits than were available in the civil service and early retirement." Many officers joined the military for the free housing, which permitted them to plow the savings into "land and real estate." That practice became a distracting "small business" for every Saudi officer. The Americans rued the "strongly materialistic outlook" and "tribal behavior" of Saudi soldiers and officers, who "argued brusquely with their superiors, waving fingers in their faces." That "traditional egalitarianism of the tribes would pose serious difficulties in military operations." All the Saudi services were permeated by dual hierarchies that queered the chain of command. "There seems to be a secondary hierarchy of ranks in existence," an American diplomat wrote from Jedda in 1965. "The enlisted men feel a tribal sense of superiority to their urbanized officers . . . or an officer may be from a tribe rated socially inferior to that of his corporal." Hejazis predominated in the senior echelons, which led to cliquishness and bureaucracy. "As in the ministries, most of the officers freeload," a U.S. adviser wrote. "They drink tea, socialize and counter-sign documents. A recent authorization to release a bucket of paint from the Taif supply depot required thirty-six signatures." No wonder American trainers remarked a "dismaying degree of shirking, a lack of purpose." There was so much red tape and no concept of "public service . . . Tribal and regional interests superseded national ones." The predictable result was "pervasive poor discipline and morale . . . curiosity and alertness fade quickly." More difficulties were caused by the apparently incurable impulse toward desertion among the Bedouin, who comprised 98 percent of conscripts. Twenty-five percent of them routinely deserted and went back to their villages; the military police did not even bother to pursue them, merely shrugging: "What can be expected from Bedouins?"[36]

The thirty-two-thousand-man Saudi national guard, created to backstop and "coup-proof" the army, was not fearsome. Its very origins were curious. A successor to Ibn Saud's old Ikhwan army, the Saudi national guard had been revived in the 1960s by Minister of Defense Prince Sultan as a countercoup force—a "White Army"—because, as a Saudi officer confided to an American, "the king and the royal family do not trust the regular army, whose senior officers had been bought off and were unfit to lead" and whose more dynamic junior officers spent their time pondering how to implant a "harsh military regime that would shape the Saudis into a *true* nation."[37] The U.S. embassy warned that the regular army contained 137 American-trained majors who were "capable and frustrated, a source of active dissidence. They naturally feel superior to their generals."[38] Drawn exclusively from Bedouin tribal elements (20 percent of the Saudi population), the national guard was described by the Saudi royals themselves as a "blocking force between the army and the government," dissident army officers—"the old brigade"—having actually tried and failed to assassinate King Faisal on the road between Riyadh and Taif in 1969.[39]

Unfortunately, like the thirty-seven-thousand-man regular army, the national guard's fighting units were weighed down by a "grossly underemployed civilian staff," whose signatures were required for everything but who worked even less than other Saudi bureaucrats. An astonished Ford Foundation survey discovered that the average workday in the Saudi civil service was just forty-five minutes. In the national guard, functionaries worked just thirty minutes a day, and much of that was taken up restricting the supply of ammunition, vehicles, fuel and training programs to the frontier-based regular army. Taken to meet the Saudi national guard's new director of operations in March 1968, British general H. E. R. Watson remarked his fecklessness: "He offers little beyond a large staff, numerous offices and office equipment, and a large glass-topped and brass-studded conference table in green leather with chairs to match: all outward and visible signs of increasing personal importance." The Saudi director of training was even less formidable: "He is immersed in a sea of irrelevant detail; most of his work is done by the British military mission." The commander of the Saudi national guard—Prince Abdullah—foolishly "insisted on sending only sons of sheikhs and emirs for training overseas in the belief that leadership is hereditary and breeding will tell. Results," General Watson sniffed, "so far have not borne out this belief." The American military mission reported that the separation rate in the Saudi civil and military services was alarmingly low, just one-tenth of 1 percent, as compared with 5 to 10 percent in more normally constituted countries. Who would separate himself from a job that required just thirty minutes of work a day and permitted retirement at age forty-seven on a rich pension?[40] With "chairborne progress" the preferred means of ascent in the Saudi military, there were few "suitable serving soldiers" to be found. Instead, the national guard was run by an "aged collection of emirs," who turned up at exercises in "widely varied dress—army boots, desert boots, white tennis shoes, gaudy nylon socks with no shoes, some even barefoot."[41]

"Protect Me"

Unimpressed by the Saudis, Nixon and Kissinger visited Tehran in May 1972. At a meeting with the shah, Nixon looked the "king of kings" in the eye and humbly entreated him to "protect me." The shah, a prickly, insecure man who had resented the U.S. assumption of the old British naval base at Bahrain (a largely Shiite country) four months earlier, was immensely flattered by Nixon's suggestion that Iran could protect the United States, and immediately agreed to do so. Iran would provide America with intelligence facilities, a secure air corridor from Europe to Southeast Asia and a reliable source of oil. In return, the shah demanded the latest American weapons systems, which Iran would buy with oil revenues. "Advanced military technology and supersonic jet fighters will function like the mosques and monuments of the past Persian dynasties . . . to dazzle Iran's neighbors with the prestige of the Pahlavi line," an American diplomat jotted in 1973. The shah requested access to America's entire nonnuclear arsenal, including the latest fighters—F-14 Tomcats and F-15 Eagles—and Nixon eagerly agreed. In underwriting the shah's Great Civilization, he was deepening the commitment made at the time of Operation Ajax, a decision that would have vast consequences for America's position in the Middle East.[42]

Preoccupied with exiting Vietnam, Nixon and Kissinger handed the Middle East off to Secretary of State William Rogers in Nixon's first term. Besides bolstering Saudi Arabia and Iran, Rogers was given the unenviable task of trying to wring concessions from Israel's new prime minister—seventy-year-old Golda Meir, who succeeded Levi Eshkol in March 1969. Locked in an external war of attrition with the Egyptians along the Suez Canal as well as an internal war with rivals Moshe Dayan and Yigal Allon, Meir, the American embassy in Tel Aviv noted, began to use "external policy as a means of [asserting] her status, and as a scoreboard of her victories." Whereas the Egyptians impatiently demanded Israeli withdrawal from the occupied territories—particularly the Egyptian ones—Meir became flagrantly "uncompromising" to fend off Dayan and Allon and to rope in little coalition partners like the National Religious Party, which partnered with her Labor Party in return for Meir's pledge to hold the Sinai and Gaza Strip and "retain the West Bank permanently."

Meir also had to keep ultranationalists like Menachem Begin at bay. The leader of the Herut Party—forerunner of today's Likud—Begin had already mentally annexed the occupied territories, which he called "Greater Israel." Begin and the Herut orchestrated a pressure group called the "National Resistance to Withdrawal," whose brief was to prevent any backsliding on the issues of refugees, settlements or occupied territory.[43] Israel's right-wing and religious parties—as well as the Labor hawks—refused even to contemplate a restoration of the West Bank to Jordan. Hebron was Judaism's second holiest city and the surrounding territory—"Judea and Samaria" to Jews—was considered an inalienable part of Israel.[44] The American embassy in Tel Aviv worriedly reported on the spread of Jewish Jerusalem between 1967 and 1973. By doubling the municipal borders of Jerusalem, the Israelis effectively annexed a big chunk of the West Bank, a ruse that was not lost on the furious Palestinians.[45] A moderate politician like Moshe Sapir, the secretary general of the Israeli Labor Party, saw his chances for the prime minister's job dashed when he quite reasonably argued that the West Bank should not be absorbed because the "large numbers of Arabs there would put Jews in the minority."[46]

Redeeming "Israel's Narrow Hips"—
Settlement Policy

Bounded by hawks and hawkish sentiment—Israel's chief rabbi threatened to excommunicate any government minister who even considered surrendering the West Bank—Meir chose to ignore the State Department's worrying about tough Israeli policies—"no Arab government can make peace with Israel by transferring substantial territory to Israel"—and persuaded Nixon that Russia and the Arabs simply needed to be told that America would never accept the destruction of Israel and *would* accept settlements. Israeli settlements, underwritten by American aid and characterized by Israel as "the creation of facts on the ground," spread across the occupied territories after 1967. Israel spent $35 million a year in the late sixties and early 'seventies on Jewish settlements: nineteen in the Golan, sixteen in the West Bank, eight in the Sinai and four in the Gaza Strip. Meir gradually made a strong Israel—with an indefinite lease on the occupied territories—a key plank in Nixon's strategic platform. Yitzhak Rabin called settlements the only available "redemption from Israel's narrow hips."[47] Joseph Sisco at the State Department liked Israel's hips just the way they were, but, like a nervous suitor, did not dare say so: "We disagree with this policy, but we say nothing, so the Israelis assume our acquiescence, if not our approval."[48]

Unaware of the depth of Nixon's commitment to Tel Aviv, Rogers innocently spent his time as secretary of state—he would be ousted by Kissinger in 1973—trying to extract concessions from Israel. The State Department tended to agree with the assessment of a Syrian diplomat that a "lack of U.S. action in the Middle East was causing despair in the Arab world and creating the appearance of Israel dictating U.S. policy." In a meeting with the U.S. deputy secretary of state for Near Eastern affairs in February 1973, Rabbi Arthur Herzburg, the president of the American Jewish Congress, confided that Israel felt no pressure whatsoever from Washington. "The Soviets realize that the U.S. is fully committed to the security of Israel. Israel is stronger than it has ever been in its history thanks to U.S. assistance, and won't 'budge an inch' in any settlement with the Arabs."[49]

The CIA worried that Israeli intransigence would spark a coup in Cairo or push the new Sadat regime in Egypt into a face-saving renewal of war with Israel: "Military officers are said to be increasingly frustrated with Sadat's inability to obtain Israeli agreement on the vital issue of withdrawal."[50] The pressures on Sadat were already enormous. Externally, Sadat was mistrusted by the Arab monarchies, which still equated him with his old boss Nasser. But he was also despised as too moderate by the new radicals, Muammar Qaddafi, who had seized power in Libya in 1969, and Hafez al-Assad, who had taken over Syria in 1970. Internally, Sadat took heat from the Muslim Brotherhood, who heaped scorn on his pandering efforts to call himself "the believer president" and "the first man of Islam."[51] Sadat's efforts to invigorate Egypt's economy foundered on the unhelpful legacy of Nasser: a bloated "state industrial bureaucracy" that equated foreign direct investment with "imperialistic exploitation" and "subservience to the U.S." That left Sadat struggling with chronic stagflation and poverty, and vulnerable to mounting calls for "tangible results from Israel."[52]

The Syrian government faced identical problems. U.S. embassy officials in Beirut reported that Assad was "taking the wraps off the *fedayeen* and directing attacks [on Israel] from Damascus" to "rally unhappy Baathists, Nasserists and Communists and create a tense situation in which unhappy Army elements must stick to military business" and avoid politics. Syria's was an unmistakably "aggressive policy" keyed to release domestic political pressure.[53] To relieve some of that pressure, Rogers became the first American secretary of state to use the term "Palestinian" (instead of "refugee") and bluntly told the Israelis that America would "not support expansionism," would insist on a Jordanian role in East Jerusalem and would regard the occupied territories as "armistice lines," not conquered provinces of Israel.[54] The American ambassador in Tel Aviv warned that Israel's security demands—"the Jordan River as her eastern defense border," the Sinai and Gaza as buffers in the south and the Golan in the north—had to be weighed against Arab needs, as well as Israel's own precarious demography. "What about those Arabs? There are 700,000 now on the West Bank, and 300,000 more would return after a peace agreement, and there are 350,000 more in the Gaza Strip." How would Israel possibly absorb them?

It wouldn't. Meir coldly informed the Knesset in 1972 that "when the time comes to define Israel's new borders, the fundamental consideration will be *not* to include too many Arabs in the framework of any final settlement." This portended a new round of 1967-style ethnic cleansing and a flood of controversial new immigration from Soviet Russia. "The land belongs to the people who live on it; the territories will be ours if Jews settle there," Deputy Prime Minister Yigal Allon declared in 1970. This explained the fervor of American pro-Israel hawks like Senator Henry "Scoop" Jackson and Congressman Charles Vanik, who relentlessly pressed the Russians (and Nixon) to permit Jewish emigration from the Soviet Union to Israel. If Moscow could be persuaded to let loose thirty thousand to forty thousand Soviet Jews per year, the Jewish settlements in the occupied territories would fill up quickly. Here was the root of the settlement policy that has confounded peacemakers ever since, for the Soviet Jews of the late twentieth century were as loathsome to the Palestinians as the Russian and Balkan Jews of the late nineteenth century. The Israelis scoffed at the Palestinian objections: "There is no 'Palestinian' nation," Abba Eban assured *Le Figaro* in January 1970. The Israeli expulsions of 1948 had given these "so-called Palestinians" a perfectly good country of their own—Jordan—

and "the Palestinian and non-Palestinians Arabs there could now decide amongst themselves what name and what government structures to have."[55]

Needless to say, Secretary of State Rogers had his work cut out for him. Before a Nixon Doctrine or any other U.S. strategy could be lowered over the Middle East, some territorial compromise had to be hammered out between the Jews and the Arabs. Although the *New York Times* applauded Rogers's "call to reason in the Middle East" and his efforts to rein in Israeli ambitions, the Israeli government reacted furiously. Golda Meir declared herself "incensed" by Rogers's cavils and pointedly distinguished between the friendly views of Nixon's "U.S. government" and the hostile treatment of Rogers's "State Department." J. Owen Zurhellen, the deputy chief of mission at the U.S. embassy in Tel Aviv, recorded a very deliberate attempt by the Israelis "to attack the Administration through the State Department so as to preserve its purer relationship with the President." (This was the exact same strategy that Prime Minister Ariel Sharon would adopt during the George W. Bush years—squeezing in between the White House neocons and Colin Powell's State Department to split the administration.) Meir in the early 1970s, Zurhellen reported, was trying to dilute or destroy "the hard facts of U.S. policy by concentrating her fire on Rogers and the State Department to discredit their mediation efforts."[56] Foreign Minister Abba Eban accused Rogers of trying to improve relations with the Soviet Union at Israel's expense, as if such routine diplomacy were a crime. Over American objections, Deputy Prime Minister Allon defiantly invited Israelis and new immigrants to settle in East Jerusalem. The government promptly seized four thousand acres of Arab land and threw up twenty-five thousand apartments to create a "new reality"—Jewish East Jerusalem—that would supersede the old Palestinian one. When Senator Eugene McCarthy tried to visit Hebron to speak with Mayor Muhammed Ali Jaabari, he was turned away by Israeli troops, who announced that McCarthy could visit only if escorted everywhere by an IDF officer. McCarthy declined, but noted a "flood of Jewish settlers—250 families—flowing into Hebron."[57]

The problem, an American diplomat wrote from Tel Aviv, is that "the West Bank contains in acute form all the strands which tangle Israel's approach to the territory issue: security needs, too many Arabs (the demographic problem), and religious-historic affinity."[58] Rogers bravely plunged ahead anyway, urging the Israelis to retire behind the pre-1967 lines. He was slapped back by Congress. Intensively lobbied by AIPAC—which organized a fourteen-thousand-man "mass lobby" on Capitol Hill to defend Israel's conquests in January 1970—the House and Senate passed resolutions urging direct negotiations between the Arabs and Israelis (so that Israel could insist on diplomatic recognition and trade its conquests for something tangible) and a relaxation of U.S. government pressure on Tel Aviv. In Tel Aviv, the American embassy reported that Israeli national strategy was to use all available levers—"war, diplomacy and the manipulation of public opinion"—to assure that there would be no reprise of 1956, when Washington had forced Israel to give back its conquests. "Every effort is bent to assure that a similar constellation of forces is not allowed to form again."⁵⁹ A good example of Israeli efforts was provided by the visit of Golda Meir and Yitzhak Rabin to the Pentagon in February 1973. In meetings with Secretary of Defense Elliot Richardson, Meir told him that she needed more and better weapons. "The Soviet Union is pouring billions of dollars into the Arab world, yet [Arabs] consider it unfair if the U.S. provides some military equipment to the Israelis." Meir and Rabin asked for thirty-six Phantoms and thirty Skyhawks and brushed off Richardson's objection that "Israel's relative strength" continued to increase, not decrease—thanks to American high-tech deliveries—and that the United States "must not be seen to be feeding the arms race." Meir laughed: "What is the danger if Israel has a few planes more than we ought to have? Will a few extra planes turn Israel into a 'wild man'? Who is little Israel endangering?"⁶⁰

"WEAPONS SUPPLY IS THE GUTS OF THE U.S.-ISRAELI RELATIONSHIP"

Privately, the State Department worried that little Israel had indeed become a wild man and that American policy could no longer contain him. The British had the same worry. Having decided in 1970 not to sell the Israelis Chieftain tanks—"too offensive"—they watched in wonderment at the array of high-tech equipment proffered by the Americans. "Israeli military superiority over all her neighbors has rarely been more obvious, yet this decision to send more aircraft to Israel reveals the U.S. to be insincere on *any* settlement. The Americans are throwing away their highest card, and weakening their ability to influence the Israelis."⁶¹ Indeed, American policy in the Middle East had changed fundamentally since Ike and Dulles had intervened at Suez. Kennedy, Johnson and Nixon had all bought into an "Israeli siege mentality" that had drastically reduced Washington's freedom of maneuver in the region. The Israelis argued (disingenuously) that more and better weapons would permit them "to take bigger chances for peace," and the Americans meekly bought the argument. A senior Israeli official meeting with a young Richard Perle in Tel Aviv in December 1972 declared that "weapons supply is the guts of the U.S.-Israeli relationship." Perle—the future neocon maestro and a staff assistant to Scoop Jackson in the 1970s—heartily agreed, and pressed the argument on the U.S. embassy, deploring the fact that "some elements in the U.S. government are filibustering and questioning Israel to death, asking scores of pointless questions." Perle was for making Israel militarily self-sufficient in one fell swoop, with massive transfers of high-tech armaments and proprietary technology that would "decrease Israel's identification with U.S. weapons" and—it was Perle's turn to be disingenuous—"work to the U.S. advantage in the Arab world."[62]

Little by little, deliveries of American weapons and Washington's tolerance of Israel's nuclear program, fortified settlements, "deep penetration" raids—Israeli jets had bombed the suburbs of Cairo in January 1970—and other so-called spectaculars—like the Israeli shoot-down of a Libyan airliner and its 104 passengers over the Sinai—had diluted the effect of the Nixon Doctrine, which required Arab as well as Israeli and Iranian defense of the region against communism. The Meir government, backed by its lobbyists, members of Congress and other partisans in Washington, successfully lumped the Arabs into the Soviet threat, asserting that "only iron resolution stands against the eventual Arab flood; if the Arabs and Soviets taste blood, they'll move in for the kill."[63] A State Department analyst warned that "the Israelis used to want the U.S. to have good relations with the Arab governments . . . Now they're suspicious of *any* U.S. dealings with the Arabs and the Soviets in which Washington might give away Tel Aviv's 'trump cards,' " which were the occupied territories, settlements and American arms sales and security guarantees.

Israeli policy and lobbying in the 1970s boiled down to driving a wedge between Washington and the Arabs. The State Department noted the tremendous "paradox" that "Israeli military initiatives" like the Six-Day War or the reprisal raids into Egypt and Jordan had begun to "function as the catalyst and arbiter of American actions in the region": a classic case of the tail wagging the dog. Just as they would belabor the threat of terrorism in the 2000s, the Israelis nurtured a red scare in the 1970s and suggested the same response to both threats: brute force. "Tel Aviv needs 100 percent American backing in all fields, and such backing can best be assured if Washington is bereft of options, if the Middle East is effectively polarized between the Arabs-Soviet Union and the Israelis-U.S."[64]

Nixon, no less than his predecessors, was vulnerable to such arguments, as well as the push in Washington from AIPAC and pro-Israel rallies and politicians. When French president Georges Pompidou visited the United States, he was heckled and harassed in Chicago by a Jewish veterans group for having sold French arms to Libya. In New York, Pompidou was spurned by Mayor John Lindsay and Governor Nelson Rockefeller. Nixon, who privately lamented the "unyielding and short-sighted" pro-Israel sentiment in the United States, nevertheless assured the Israelis that he would not press them too hard publicly.[65] Although he, Rogers and Kissinger disputed Golda Meir's view that "real peace with the Arabs is not to be had at *any* price," the advanced weapons that LBJ and Nixon had been selling into Israel since 1965 had created a new dynamic there. "The Israelis are less and less worried about international opinion," the American embassy in Tel Aviv complained in April 1972. "They believe that the U.S. sees things in the Middle East their way, and their con-fidence is enhanced by the strength of the IDF, which has received more advanced equipment [since 1967] than *ever* in its history." Nixon, the American diplomats in Israel went on, had removed "another brake on Israel's freedom of action, or free-dom *not* to act" by quietly abandoning the Rogers Plan to settle the fate of the oc-cupied territories and resettle the refugees. He let the plan wither on the vine even as he was beefing up the IDF with $500 million annual military aid packages.[66]

Just how complicit Washington had become in Israeli policy became clear dur-ing an awkward, hour-long Oval Office meeting in December 1970 involving Pres-ident Nixon, Secretary of Defense Melvin Laird, Deputy National Security Adviser Alexander Haig, Israeli defense minister Moshe Dayan and Israeli ambassador Yitz-hak Rabin. Nixon tried repeatedly to tie military aid to Israel to Israeli concessions on the occupied territories and refugees. "We expect Israel to move to the confer-ence table," Nixon told Dayan and Rabin. "We expect this because Congress will shortly approve a $500 million aid package and the international environment dic-tates negotiations, and all responsible U.S. officials are of one mind on this." Dayan bobbed and weaved. "Israel *wants* to negotiate," he said, but was prevented by "Arab violations": Egyptian shelling across the canal and fedayeen attacks. Dayan then attempted to sell even the distant *consideration* of negotiations for something immediate: "If the U.S. would commit to a flow of six Phantoms and six Skyhawks per month starting in January 1971, I'm sure that talks [with the Arabs] could pro-ceed." Like Ike, Nixon had intended to "get tough" with the Israelis, and, like Ike, he ended up beating a retreat instead. "This poses complex problems for us," he pleaded. "Israel must understand that the U.S., on occasion, cannot meet *all* of

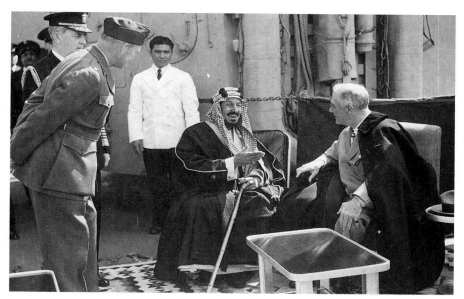

ABOVE: Returning from Yalta in 1945, FDR met with King Ibn Saud of Saudi Arabia aboard the U.S.S. *Quincy* in the Suez Canal. FDR was struck by the Saudi's obsession with Palestine. Each time FDR tried to shift the subject away from the Holy Land, the king swerved back "to expound the case of the Arabs and their legitimate rights." *(Franklin D. Roosevelt Library and Museum)*

BELOW: Truman—shown accepting the gift of a menorah from Israeli prime minister Ben-Gurion (center)—rebuffed counsels to adopt an even-handed policy in Palestine: "I am sorry, gentlemen, but I have to answer to hundreds of thousands who are anxious for the success of Zionism; I do not have hundreds of thousands of Arabs among my constituents." *(National Park Service, Abbie Rowe, Courtesy of Harry S. Truman Library)*

ABOVE: Iranian prime minister Muhammed Mosaddeq traveled to America to appeal for relief from a British-led boycott of Iranian oil in 1951: "I am speaking for a poor country—a country all desert, just sand, a few camels, a few sheep." Acheson interrupted Mosaddeq: "With its sand *and* oil Iran is not a very poor country; it is more like Texas." *(National Park Service, Abbie Rowe, Courtesy of Harry S. Truman Library and Museum)*

BELOW: In the Suez Crisis of 1956, Ike and Dulles were thunderstruck by the British, French and Israeli invasion of Egypt. The White House received no advance warning and relied for intelligence on radio reports and newspapers. "How could people do this to me?" Dulles spat. "They have betrayed us." *(Dwight D. Eisenhower Presidential Library)*

LEFT: JFK campaigned on the slogan "the Middle East needs bread, not bombs," but almost immediately began sending the Israelis bombs. He succumbed to pressure from Israel's bumptious foreign minister, Golda Meir, who visited Kennedy in Palm Beach, Florida, in December 1962 to secure direct U.S. arms sales to Israel. *(Cecil Stoughton, White House/ John F. Kennedy Presidential Library and Museum)*

BELOW: Preoccupied with Vietnam in 1967, LBJ, Rusk and McNamara winked at Israel's preemptive attacks and massive annexations in the Six-Day War. Pressed by a delegation of Arabs to roll back the Israeli gains, Johnson explained U.S. policy to his visitors: "What can I do? One man was so nasty to his neighbor that his neighbor could not stand it anymore, so his neighbor took hold of him and gave him a good beating." *(Lyndon Baines Johnson Library and Museum, photo by Yoichi R. Okamoto)*

ABOVE: "The filling in the sandwich is pure kosher" was how the British Foreign Office described the influence of the Rostow brothers, Walt (shown here) and Eugene on LBJ. Unleash the Israelis, the Rostows argued in 1967, to teach the Arabs that they would never win by war. *(Lyndon Baines Johnson Library and Museum, photo by Yoichi R. Okamoto)*

BELOW: With one third of the world's oil and seven million barrels per day of production, King Faisal's Saudi Arabia was the Nixon Doctrine's power plant. But Faisal was a reluctant ally. In 1973, he demanded a U.S. "disavowal of Israeli actions and policies" and then provoked a global energy crisis when Nixon refused to pressure Israel. *(Richard Nixon Library and Birthplace Foundation)*

Nixon desperately wanted to broker a lasting peace between the Israelis and Palestinians, but was put off by Moshe Dayan's cavils and contacts with the Israel lobby. Nixon, like his predecessors, wearily surrendered to that pressure. *(Richard Nixon Library and Birthplace Foundation)*

Committed to exiting Vietnam, Nixon devolved Persian Gulf security to the shah, who was a gluttonous consumer of U.S. military hardware. British diplomats warned that Nixon's arms sales were pushing Iran down the road to ruin. *(Richard Nixon Library and Birthplace Foundation)*

ABOVE: Israeli prime minister Golda Meir (raised in Milwaukee as Golda Meyerson) with Nixon and Kissinger in 1973. Nixon reacted nervously to Meir's devastating counterattacks in the Yom Kippur War. As the tide turned, Nixon understood that Meir might try to annex even more Arab territory or cling stubbornly to the already occupied territories: "When they finish clobbering the Egyptians and the Syrians, [the Israelis] will be even more impossible to deal with than before. They can't do this, Henry. They can't do this to us again. They've done it to us for four years, but no more." *(Richard Nixon Library and Birthplace Foundation)*

BELOW: "No more war." Israeli prime minister Menachem Begin and Egyptian president Anwar Sadat make peace at Camp David in September 1978. *(Jimmy Carter Library and Museum)*

Vance's State Department gave up on the shah—"a defective personality"—and argued for contacts with "moderate elements" among the Ayatollah Khomeini's followers. Brzezinski still pressed for a crackdown using Iran's four-hundred-thousand-man military. Vice President Mondale, like Carter, found Zbig's coup idea "morally troublesome." *(Jimmy Carter Library and Museum)*

"Draw the Soviets into the Afghan trap; give them their Vietnam War," National Security Adviser Zbigniew Brzezinski advised President Carter in 1979. *(Jimmy Carter Library and Museum)*

In 1982, Reagan naively blessed an Israeli plan to invade Lebanon and flush out the Syrians and PLO. The operation caused such chaos that Reagan was forced to deploy marines as a peacekeeping force, only to see 241 of them exterminated in their bunks by Hezbollah bombings of the U.S. embassy and marine barracks in Beirut. *(Armed Forces Information Services)*

After Iraq's takeover of Kuwait in 1990, the Bush 41 administration weighed sanctions and a blockade of Iraq, but Secretary of Defense Cheney—shown here arriving in Saudi Arabia with Powell and Wolfowitz—wanted more than just sanctions or a quarantine: Saddam was angling to "dominate OPEC and the Arab world. . . . The problem would get worse, not better." *(Armed Forces Information Services)*

LEFT: George H. W. Bush met in Aspen with British prime minister Margaret Thatcher, who urged him to take a hard line with Saddam. "If Iraq wins, no small state is safe. They won't stop here. They see a chance to take a major share of oil. It's got to be stopped. We must do everything possible." *(George Bush Presidential Library and Museum)*

BELOW: Under fire throughout Desert Shield from critics such as Senator Ted Kennedy, who declared that "this war's cruelty will be exceeded only by the lack of any rational necessity for waging it," President Bush joined Centcom commander General Schwarzkopf for a Thanksgiving visit to the troops in Saudi Arabia, November 1990. *(George Bush Presidential Library and Museum.)*

Schwarzkopf agonized over the massive U.S. military presence in Saudi Arabia, which made inviting targets for Iraqi Scuds: "Every dock and airfield in the kingdom was overflowing with American equipment, ammunition and supplies. . . . The Riyadh air base looked like the deck of an aircraft carrier." *(Armed Forces Information Services)*

Schwarzkopf's decision in 1991 to grant the Iraqis an immediate cease-fire was hugely controversial. "You've got to be shitting me. Why a cease-fire now?" Schwarzkopf's deputy asked. "*You* go argue with them," Schwarzkopf shot back. Schwarzkopf had never squared off against Powell and was not about to begin now. *(Armed Forces Information Services)*

Israeli prime minister Ariel Sharon had fought in every Israeli war since 1948. Bush and Rumsfeld (shown here with Sharon in 2001) embraced the pugnacious prime minister as a key ally against terrorism. One Washington think tank observed that "this is the best administration for Israel since Harry Truman." *(Armed Forces Information Services)*

Special forces on the ground pinpointed Taliban units for destruction by American air strikes. The 2001 Afghan invasion, which tyros like bin Laden had insisted would become a U.S. "quagmire" and "graveyard," proved astonishingly fast and cheap: just $3.8 billion for the "major combat operations" concluded in December. *(Armed Forces Information Services)*

Condi Rice declared that the apparent U.S. victory in Afghanistan had "a useful demonstrative effect" and that the same medicine would be administered to Saddam if he didn't toe the line. When Powell warned Rice that an Iraq invasion would divert attention from the hunt for bin Laden, she replied: "Don't waste your breath; that decision's been made." *(Armed Forces Information Services)*

General Tommy Franks devised a wildly optimistic "new paradigm" to fit the small troop numbers destined for Iraq in 2003. "You know, the doctrines that existed for our armed forces several years ago really don't apply to the first war of the twenty-first century," Franks hazarded. *(Armed Forces Information Services)*

Coalition Provisional Authority chief Jerry Bremer—shown here with Miss New York during her visit to Baghdad in 2004—sidelined regional experts assigned to him as advisers and relied instead on "a coterie of sycophantic young aides, whose only loyalty was to the viceroy." *(Armed Forces Information Services)*

Having predicted a bloodless victory in Iraq, Wolfowitz was shocked by the bitter sectarian divisions and the furious insurgency. Visiting Iraq in 2004, Wolfowitz still blamed cussers and doubters, not his own feckless strategy. *(Armed Forces Information Services)*

ABOVE: The 9/11 Commission Report in 2004 concluded that there had been no "operational relationship" between Iraq and al-Qaeda. Rumsfeld and Wolfowitz, shown here before the commission, daringly reinvented the Iraq War. No longer about WMD or Saddam's fictive ties to al-Qaeda, it was now about "taking the fight to the enemy, dealing with terrorists in Iraq rather than in the United States." *(Armed Forces Information Services)*

LEFT: Petraeus, who had gloomily projected an eight-year struggle in March 2003, was halfway there when he assumed Casey's command in 2007. With Princeton doctoral work on Vietnam under his belt and a keen interest in counterinsurgency, Petraeus advocated a twenty-thousand-troop "surge" to defeat the spreading insurgent attacks and establish security in key Iraqi towns and neighborhoods. *(Armed Forces Information Services)*

RIGHT: Petraeus's surge drove down violence in Baghdad but at the cost of higher U.S. combat deaths. Republican senator Chuck Hagel blasted the very idea of the surge. "What is the point of bringing the violence down?" he asked, when Iraq's Kurds, Sunnis and Shiites were making no serious effort to reconcile. Hagel warned that civil war might break out the moment Petraeus relaxed the surge, or even if he didn't. *(Armed Forces Information Services)*

ABOVE: Petraeus organized the "Anbar Awakening," which was the conversion of Iraq's formerly anti-American Sunni tribes to the American cause. By arming, paying and schooling the Anbar sheikhs—Petraeus hired one hundred thousand "sons of Iraq" at a monthly rate of three hundred dollars per son (here several of them wait in line to be paid)—the general turned the tribes against al-Qaeda in Iraq. *(Armed Forces Information Services)*

BELOW: "You've allowed the Persians to take over Iraq," Saudi King Abdullah (shown here with Defense Secretary Gates) sputtered to the Bush administration in April 2007. The U.S. invasion had converted Iraq into "the first modern Arab Shiite–dominated state," and the Iraq insurgency was fueled by the conservative Sunni states around Iraq, which were willing to try anything, even Sunni terrorism that killed U.S. troops, to stop the spread of militant Shiism under the banner of Iran. *(Armed Forces Information Services)*

President Obama doubled U.S. troop strength in Afghanistan in 2009, hoping to secure the population against Taliban inroads and slow the spreading and hugely profitable traffic in opium. Here a U.S. soldier scans for suspicious activity along Afghanistan's border with Pakistan. *(Armed Forces Information Services)*

As the Bush administration wound down, the army changed its doctrine to "stability operations" and the resuscitation of "fragile states" like Iraq and Afghanistan. An administration that had mocked Clinton's use of U.S. troops to "walk kids to school"—Condi Rice's infelicitous phrase—now unashamedly measured progress by the number of kids in school. *(Armed Forces Information Services)*

Israel's requirements." Trust in our good faith, Nixon begged Dayan. No, Dayan answered; good faith is never enough: "We need a steady pipeline of matériel." Nixon ran up the white flag. He knew that he'd be pressured into supplying the aid and weapons anyway, so he'd better take credit for it up front. "I have no intention of permitting Israel to fall—I am personally committed to Israel's survival."[67]

That combination of unflinching support for Israel and flinching abandonment of the peace process sucked the energy out of the Nixon Doctrine and left Nixon exposed to the full weight of Palestinian anger. Nixon told an NSC meeting in June 1970 that failure to solve the Palestinian refugee question was one of the "major lapses" of the post–World War II era.[68] The British Foreign Office agreed, observing in 1970 that "the growth of Palestinian Nationalism has been one of the most significant recent developments . . . We shall have to take increasing account of this phenomenon, which is the main political dynamic in much of the Arab world today." Not only were the Palestinians more assertive, they made leaders like Qaddafi, Sadat, Assad and King Hussein more aggressive to hedge themselves "against the militant approach of the Palestinian organizations."[69]

The new Palestinian dynamic began immediately to exact a price: first a rash of hijackings (of American, Swiss and British airliners) by the Popular Front for the Liberation of Palestine, and then an uprising of Palestinian guerrillas inside Jordan, which King Hussein moved to crush in September 1970. Drowning in fast-multiplying Palestinian refugees, the king wanted to stop PLO recruitment inside Jordan and reassert Hashemite and Bedouin authority against the radical Palestinian challenge that had threatened since 1948 to swallow his kingdom.[70] When Syrian armored columns crossed Jordan's northern border to rescue the Palestinians and create a client state on Israel's eastern border, Nixon was faced with the same threat that Ike had confronted in 1958, when American and British forces had helped suppress pro-Nasser risings in Jordan and Lebanon. If Jordan fell to the Palestinians or Syrians, a regional war might break out, drawing in the superpowers. If Syria continued to intervene in Lebanese politics—"supporting Sunni elements in Lebanon to get the support of other elements in Syrian society"—then Nixon might be forced to send the marines back to Beirut when they were more urgently needed in Da Nang.[71] Thus, Nixon increased the Sixth Fleet from two to five carriers, and pushed them into the eastern Mediterranean to menace the Syrian units invading Jordan and to deter the Soviets. Like Ike, Nixon viewed the Jordanian crisis through the lens of the Cold War: "Soviets must recognize that the U.S. must guarantee Israel's survival, and the moves of the U.S. Sixth Fleet were to convey this point."[72] He told the *Chicago Sun-Times* that "we will intervene if the situation is such that our intervention will make a difference," a clear warning to the difference-making Soviets.[73]

With Israeli armor, air and infantry also assembling to hit the Syrian flank, the Syrians pulled in their horns and withdrew, leaving seventy shattered tanks in their wake. The Jordanian army furiously punished Jordan's Palestinians, razing the camps around Amman and killing three thousand refugees.[74] The Syrians and the Palestinians called this "Black September," a month of humiliation that would have to be expunged through terrorism or better-organized conventional wars. Resentment in the Arab refugee camps and capitals over the annexations of 1967—and the retreat of 1970—welled up. In Syria, the new moderate regime of air force general Hafez al-Assad—who had criticized the foray into Jordan and discredited the civilian government by withholding air support—developed a harder edge. Mocked by the Damascus press in 1970 as an "agent of Western imperialism and the oil monopolies" and applauded by the U.S. State Department as a "moderate," Hafez Assad began nurturing fedayeen groups like al-Saiqa as "instruments of Syrian regional policy in Lebanon and Jordan."[75] Just as the Syrians recently inserted fedayeen into Iraq and Lebanon to destabilize pro-American regimes, they shuffled them around in the 1970s to broaden Syria's footprint, weaken pro-Western governments, and burnish Syria's Arab nationalist credentials. In Egypt, Nasser was succeeded in November 1970 by Anwar Sadat, who vowed to eject Israel from the Sinai.[76]

Despite Sadat's bluster and diplomatic acumen—he publicly "threw out the Russians" in July 1972 to curry favor with the Americans, while privately retaining thousands of Soviet advisers attached to Egyptian military units—the Israelis remained confident that they had little to fear from Arab armies that had fought so badly in 1967.[77] Though rebuilt by the Soviets with advanced tanks, aircraft and missiles, and with Russian ports, East German highways and Czech factories, the Syrians remained an object of derision. Assad's regime remained a narrow clique of Alawite tribesmen, who clung to an overwhelmingly Sunni country by backstairs deals and sleights of hand. Sadat struggled to assert himself in Cairo. "The Israelis believe that Sadat cannot afford to fight again," the U.S. embassy in Tel Aviv reported in April 1972. Another defeat would doom his young government. The Soviets had been "feeding the Egyptian armed forces through a cage" since 1967, delivering advanced platforms like the SAM-3, the MiG-23 and the Su-11, but rationing the all-important spare parts to control Egyptian behavior. For all its superficial gloss, the Egyptian military was threadbare and fundamentally weak, which was one reason that Sadat had expelled the Soviets.[78]

Some leading Israelis—like Ezer Weizman, the number two man behind Menachem Begin in the right-wing Gahal Party and a former IDF deputy chief of staff—were actually planning expansion, not defense, for 1973. The IDF would cross the Suez Canal to end the "war of attrition" that had been flaring on and off since 1967, and the occupied territories would be formally annexed. "Gaza is a part of the state of Israel," a Meir confidant told the Knesset in 1972. "The Jordan River should be the border with Jordan . . . Outsiders will *never* determine our borders."[79] This was hubris, for the Arabs had reformed deeply, and the Americans were increasingly anxious about the new Israeli "maximalism" expressed by Meir and "Ezer the Terrible." Of course the U.S. government was feeding that maximalism through its new, post–Black September stance. Middle East policy had been transferred from Rogers to Kissinger, who scrapped the conciliatory Rogers Plan and took a firmer line. Arab radicals, Kissinger believed, would not come to the peace table unless they were beaten and out of options.[80]

Even if the Americans failed to restrain Israeli maximalism, the Arab armies might. They *seemed* much better in the early 1970s than they had ever been. Deeply flawed, they were nevertheless greatly improved. The Egyptians had huddled with their Soviet advisers, worked out sophisticated new tactics, added 210 MiG-21s and laid in more surface-to-air missiles than the United States had in its entire arsenal: 135 SA-2 and SA-3 batteries, 20 to 40 SA-6s (so new that they had never been fired in combat) and 5,000 shoulder-launched SA-7s, all of which had a startling impact on the Israeli air force, shooting down their Skyhawks and Phantoms faster than the Vietnam-cumbered Americans could replace them during the "war of attrition" along the canal.[81] Although the Egyptians had never accepted Israel's occupation of the Sinai—one-fifth of Egypt's land mass—the IDF failed to detect the approach of the October 1973 Yom Kippur War.[82] The Israelis had become accustomed to Egyptian troop exercises along the canal—always training for a crossing. When Egyptian forces gathered there in October 1973, no one on the Israeli side thought that it was anything more than an exercise.[83] Likewise, the Israelis and Americans made nothing of intelligence that showed the Syrians requisitioning civilian taxis and privately owned trucks to haul troops and supplies. They would later regret that complacency, the CIA repenting its "excessive dependence" on plainly inadequate intelligence assets—whether satellites or Israelis (the actual culprit is blacked out in the declassified report)—and the Pentagon reminding itself that "you have to know the doctrines and procedures by which your opponents prepare for war."[84]

THE YOM KIPPUR WAR

While war clouds gathered over the Middle East, Prime Minister Golda Meir remained in Strasbourg, Foreign Minister Abba Eban in New York, and the Israeli defense chiefs and intelligence agencies completely misread Egyptian and Syrian intentions. Dismissing the Arab deployments near the Golan and the canal as defensive maneuvers, the IDF permitted much of the Israeli military to remain at home with their families for Yom Kippur. Washington later concluded that the Americans and the Israelis "were a victim of their own proliferation of sources"— human, satellite and electronic—and were also "overwhelmed by many other things that looked completely normal."[85] Only on October 5 did Meir's government weigh preemptive air strikes and full mobilization. Still, Meir worried that she would lose international support if Israel reprised the sneak attacks of 1967. The Israelis also failed to grasp the Syrian and Egyptian aim: not to destroy Israel, but merely to grab back the territory lost in 1967.[86]

On October 6, 1973, Syrian tanks and airborne infantry attacked the Golan Heights and Mount Hermon. A thousand Egyptian guns pounded the Bar-Lev Line along the Suez Canal, while two Egyptian armies—90,000 troops, 850 tanks and 11,000 other vehicles—threw bridges across the canal and safely crossed to the Israeli side. Having failed to preempt or even detect the Arab attacks, the Israelis appealed to Henry Kissinger—who was awakened in his New York hotel room two hours before the Arabs struck—to intervene in Moscow, Damascus and Cairo. When Kissinger finally got through to those governments, the war was already in full swing. Israeli jets that screamed in to bomb, rocket and strafe the Arab ground units were shot down by Soviet SAM-6s that were cleverly placed in a protective belt between the Israelis and the Egyptian and Syrian tanks and infantry.[87] Eighty Israeli strike aircraft—including thirty Skyhawks and fourteen F-4 Phantoms—were lost in the first days of the war. Driven from their preferred bombing altitudes by the Egyptians SAMs, the Israelis swooped low and either crashed or ran into barrages of antiaircraft artillery.[88] Even though IAF loss rates remained low—less than 1 percent per sortie, the Egyptians firing off 190 SAMs for every Israeli aircraft actually shot down—this was the first time the IAF had suffered *any* noticeable attrition in advanced aircraft and trained pilots.[89]

The aim of Sadat and Assad in the war was to damage the IDF, grab back occupied territory and compel the United States to "take a more active role in persuading Israel to make concessions." The Syrians argued that even a partial Arab victory would "increase Israel's incentives for making unpalatable concessions."[90] Assad was betting that a hot war in the eastern Mediterranean, the possibility of Russian involvement and the threat of a Saudi oil embargo would so alarm President Nixon that he would have no choice but to force Israel to conclude a final settlement with the frontline Arab states and the Palestinians.[91] Sadat believed that such a limited, achievable effort would break the impasse that had stalled every Arab effort to recover the occupied territories and force the Israelis to lend an ear, as well as "respect" and "dignity," to the Arab states, instead of the usual cold shoulder. Kissinger emerged from the war with a newfound respect for Sadat—"a statesman of the first order"—because of the way he discarded Nasser's delusional rhetoric of unlimited war and fought instead for limited aims that would improve Egypt's standing and security. Sadat explained to Kissinger that his aims were modest: an Israeli withdrawal from the occupied territories and a peace conference.[92]

Three days into the war, the Arab aim of wearing down the IDF (with militaries that had doubled in size and combat power since 1967) was well under way. Simcha Dinitz, Israel's ambassador in Washington, reported brutal, unanticipated losses: 500 tanks—400 on the Egyptian front alone—and 80 aircraft destroyed. Having studied the way that the Israelis had flung their tanks forward and used their air force as "flying artillery" in the Six-Day War, the Egyptians fought differently in 1973. Their forces were better educated and trained—60 percent of officers were university graduates in 1973 (versus 2 percent in 1967) and 51 percent of enlisted personnel were high school graduates (versus 25 percent in 1967)—and they fought to a carefully scripted plan that assigned every unit and every man specific tasks that were synchronized by Soviet military advisers embedded in every Egyptian battalion and company.[93]

Devastated in the opening hours of the Six-Day War, the Egyptians this time placed their aircraft in hardened bunkers and held their tanks and infantry behind a hedge of SAMs and wire-guided antitank missiles that tore apart every Israeli attempt to get at the armored vehicles or the bunkered planes. Israeli armored units that tried to envelop Arab infantry were set upon by well-trained Egyptian and Syrian antitank teams that hid themselves and then fired into the backs of the onrushing Israeli tanks—Centurions and M-60s—with antitank guns and the latest Soviet portable weapons: AT-3 Sagger antitank guided missiles and rocket-propelled grenades (RPGs). Like the SAMs, which made the Arab-Israeli air war in 1973 altogether different from the one in 1967, the wire-guided and shoulder-fired antitank missiles radically changed the face of the ground war. Reckless Israeli charges and flank attacks now had to be launched under smoke screens and behind creeping barrages of artillery fire intended to blind and suppress the Saggers and RPGs.[94] The heavy losses on the Egyptian front necessitated some shifting of Israeli forces from the Golan Heights, where the Syrians initially did as well as the Egyptians. They pushed across the Israeli antitank ditches on the Golan and hit the Israelis hard with artillery, air strikes and helicopter-borne infantry. They shot down thirty Israeli aircraft in the first day of fighting. "The doggoned Syrians surprised me," Nixon observed from Key Biscayne. "They're doing better than I ever thought."[95]

So were the Egyptians, though Kissinger and Secretary of Defense James Schlesinger had an interesting exchange in which Kissinger wondered why the Egyptians and Syrians were not "clinching their gain" they had made in the first hours of the war instead of pushing deeper into Israel and demanding the return of the entire Sinai, and perhaps more in a "phase two" offensive. "You're being logical. You can't ascribe that kind of logic to them," Schlesinger replied.[96] Prime Minister Meir was not yet ready to put her faith in Arab impetuosity; she appealed desperately for replacement weapons from the United States, but Nixon and Kissinger hesitated. Open intervention on Israel's side might drag in the Soviets and would certainly trigger an Arab oil embargo.[97]

THE "OIL WEAPON"

The threat of the "oil weapon" in 1973 was a powerful deterrent. Until the late 1960s, the big oil companies had always been more worried by the prospect of too much oil than too little. They had viewed the discovery of Alaskan, North Sea and Libyan oil as a two-edged sword that might glut the market and drive down prices. Everything changed around 1970, when "peak oil"—the moment in history when petroleum extraction shifted in a bell-shaped curve from its maximum level to eternally declining ones—arrived and American "energy security" evolved as a concept and a concern. Although only about 6 percent of U.S. oil imports came from the Middle East in 1973, nearly 80 percent of Europe's did, and 43 percent of Japan's. With Kuwait cutting back its daily production, Libya proving to be an unreliable supplier and U.S. domestic crude production declining, American oil imports shot up to 35 percent of consumption in 1973. With Alaskan production restricted by conservationists, that percentage was rising every year. Energy analysts projected that 40 percent of U.S. oil would have to come from the unstable Middle East by 1985, and the imports would explode America's balance of trade. The deficit on oil alone was projected to be $6 billion by 1975, $15 billion by 1980.[98] "This time the wolf is here," a State Department official gloomily reported to *Foreign Affairs* in April 1973. An "oil crisis" loomed.[99] Oil consumers, the chairman of Shell warned in October 1971, were "looking down the muzzle of a gun."[100]

The Yom Kippur War trained the gun muzzle on America's head. In the first week of October 1973, a barrel of oil cost $3.02. By the third week of October the same barrel cost $5.11, a jump of nearly 70 percent propelled by the profiteering shah of Iran and the dozen members of the Organization of Petroleum Exporting Countries (OPEC), who crimped supply to crimp U.S. support for Israel, driving the barrel price to $11.65 in December.[101] "The problem is not whether oil will find markets but whether markets will find oil," the *New York Times* observed. When an American reporter quipped that the Saudis would have to drink their oil if they did not sell it into Western markets, the Saudi foreign minister unexpectedly replied: "All right, we will." Egypt's Sadat, Iraqi vice president Saddam Hussein, and Libya's Muammar Qaddafi—who had doubled the price of Libyan oil in September—firmly pressed the oil back down King Faisal's gullet. Saddam called the Saudis "Arab reactionaries" and demanded that they nationalize Aramco and other American oil interests.[102] Like Saudi kings before and after, Faisal felt the heat. He had been granting Sadat $200 million a year since 1970 to pay for weapons, and now pondered use of the oil weapon on Egypt's behalf.[103] In interviews with the *New York Times* and the *Washington Post*, Faisal enraged Nixon by declaring that he would feel compelled to "provoke a major petroleum supply crisis" if Washington did not curtail its support for Israel and pursue a more "balanced policy" in the Middle East.

The Saudi king, an old man who yearned to pray in Arab Jerusalem before he died, had tested this menacing line on John Ehrlichman in January 1973 during the

White House adviser's visit to Riyadh: "We Saudis love you people, but your American policy is hurting us." Now it was Riyadh's turn to hurt the Americans. Faisal warned the American stakeholders in Aramco—Exxon, Mobil, Texaco and SoCal—that they "would lose everything" if Washington continued its muscular support for Israel. The Saudis considered themselves as important a pillar in the Nixon Doctrine as the Israelis or the Iranians. Faisal demanded that they be treated as such. At a minimum, Faisal wanted "a simple disavowal of Israeli policies and actions and policies."[104] Of course, in view of the power of the Israel lobby in Washington, there would be nothing "simple" about such a disavowal. Exxon panicked. Saudi Arabia's daily production of seven million barrels kept the world and the "Seven Sisters" running. Exxon, Mobil and SoCal all took out newspaper ads urging the Nixon administration to improve its relations with the Arab states and avoid a too close alignment with Israel.[105] They also paid for ads urging conservation of dwindling stocks—"Smart drivers make gasoline last," Mobil ads trumpeted in the fall of 1973. Former interior secretary Stewart Udall made the heretical argument that Americans should simply use less energy: "A lot of our energy problems will be solved if we stop doing what we're doing. The country should look at its *own* resources and play the hand it was dealt."[106] Such un-American scrimping did not suit the worried Big Oil CEOs, who shot off a collective letter to Nixon. Sadat had already met with Faisal and persuaded him to cut Aramco production. The CEOs, who had donated $2.7 million to Nixon's reelection campaign, seemed miffed that AIPAC was beating them at the lobbying game. One pundit compared Manhattan's Avenue of the Americas to the River Jordan: it coursed between the pro-Arab offices of Aramco and Exxon and the pro-Israel studios of ABC, CBS and NBC. From the West Bank of the avenue, Exxon remonstrated that "the whole position of the United States in the Middle East is on the way to being seriously impaired."

Seriously impaired himself by the Watergate scandal, the War Powers Resolution pending in Congress and Vice President Spiro Agnew's resignation amid charges of tax evasion, Nixon (still hunkering down in Key Biscayne) did not even bother to reply. He assumed that the Saudis were bluffing. Heavily dependent on the United States for their own defense—against the Soviets and Iraqis—could the Saudis really afford to alienate the Americans? There were six thousand U.S. military advisers in Saudi Arabia in 1973, and a state-of-the-art U.S. air defense system was under construction. Moreover, Faisal had lately begun to *depress* oil prices to head off a world recession and impoverish his rival, the shah of Iran. With a surging, needy population of fifty million and grandiose military ambitions, the Iranians desperately needed oil revenues, and the Saudis—whose oil revenues at any price sufficed for the kingdom's six million subjects—enjoyed using their power of the pump to constrict the shah.[107]

With the Nixon Doctrine in shambles, its chief "pillars" at war with each other, a seesaw struggle ensued in 1973–74, with the Saudis lowering prices and the shah raising them.[108] Vice President Saddam Hussein of Iraq looked on in frustration. He had a different take on the oil weapon, which foreshadowed his use of it years later, and explained the subsequent fears of the George W. Bush administration and Dick Cheney's Energy Task Force. In the councils of OPEC in 1973, Saddam argued that oil embargoes actually *strengthened* the United States—the Arab world's principal enemy—and weakened Western Europe, which was the Arab's best friend in the noncommunist world. "Since 80 percent of Arab [petroleum] output is under concession and 65 percent of that by U.S. companies, the rise in oil prices benefits the *Americans.*" And since Americans were the biggest refiners of oil—where the margins were higher than in the sale of crude—they were getting richer, not poorer. And because the United States relied far less than Europe and Japan on imported oil, Middle Eastern "oil cutbacks [gave] U.S. industry a big advantage over Europe and Japan." To hit at the United States—Israel's key ally—Saddam proposed a simple, devastating policy: nationalize all American oil interests all over the Middle East "to deprive the U.S. of the economic, financial and strategic value of the oil concessions." In October 1973, Saddam confiscated the American shares of the Basra Petroleum Company. Only such a predatory policy, he argued, would strike "at the core of U.S. interests" and permit a flowering of the more likable de Gaulle policy of "gradual independence from the U.S. attitude of absolute support to the Zionists."[109]

With the Iranians and Saudis jousting over oil prices and the Iraqis nationalizing Western oil companies and targeting the embargo more precisely on America, the pressure in Washington was tremendous. Kissinger, who assumed effective control of American policy during the Yom Kippur War because of Rogers's resignation and Nixon's various embarrassments, must have listened raptly when approached by Jack McCloy, the New York lawyer for the Seven Sisters, who warned Kissinger that "the Administration must not just think in terms of the next New York election."[110] Jewish votes were a pressing domestic concern, but Arab and Iranian oil fields were a no less urgent foreign one.

KISSINGER WALKS A TIGHTROPE

Throughout the Yom Kippur War, Kissinger was engaged in a struggle that his predecessors and successors would immediately recognize. He had to defend Israel yet also restrain its eventual counterattacks in order to preserve America's standing as a mediator. Even a close, generally pro-Israel ally like the shah of Iran needed to guard his flanks against "Iranian public opinion and educated elites and mullahs," who demanded a pro-Arab, anti-Israeli line.[111] Kissinger spoke with Mordechai Shalev, the deputy chief of mission at the Israeli embassy, during the afternoon of October 6. Kissinger told Shalev that the Egyptians were asking for an emergency meeting of the General Assembly to discuss the war but that he regarded the General Assembly—with its array of communist and developing nations—as "a bad forum for you—extremely bad." Debate on the war there would be "a brawl, a real donnybrook." The limited aims of Sadat and Assad—not to destroy Israel, but merely to restore the pre-1967 borders—would win easy approbation in the General Assembly. Kissinger struggled to place the war in the more manageable Security Council. Better would be a "Security Council Meeting . . . to make [our strategy] effective."[112] To White House chief of staff Alexander Haig—who lingered in Key Biscayne with Nixon—Kissinger complained that "Defense wants to turn against the Israelis." Indeed the Pentagon was husbanding weapons for Vietnam and feared escalating Israeli air attacks on Damascus and Cairo that might suck in an already overtaxed U.S. military.

With one eye on the Soviets and the other on the Israel lobby, Kissinger pledged that he and Nixon would not go wobbly. "We cannot be soft guys in this case." Haig agreed: "No, we can't be soft." When Israeli foreign minister Abba Eban pressed Kissinger to obstruct any planned meetings of the Security Council until after the Israelis had rolled back the Arab gains, Kissinger went along: "The Israelis will never forgive us for a straight cease-fire." At a minimum, Tel Aviv expected a "return to the status quo ante," and they expected Kissinger to buy the necessary time and "preempt" any Soviet attempts in the Security Council to propose a cease-fire in place that would have cemented the Arab conquests in the Sinai and the Golan. In secret meetings in Blair House with the Israeli ambassador, Kissinger proposed that Washington and Tel Aviv agree on a desirable outcome to the war in advance. "Then," Kissinger said, winking, "you can take an outrageous position and let us force you off it." The desired position would then seem like an Israeli concession, not a triumph. It would also increase American leverage with the Arabs. "I have convinced Egypt . . . that the Russians can give them arms," Kissinger said, "but only *we* can give them territory."[113]

Throughout the crisis, Kissinger hewed to one central concept: if the Arabs took ground, "they [would] become totally unmanageable" because of the thrill of victory and the goad of Soviet patronage. Conversely, if the Israelis got back to the prewar borders, or even "came out ahead," Kissinger assumed that they could be managed back down to acceptable limits by American pressure: "If [the Israelis] go beyond [the previous lines] . . . if you appeal to them to return, they *must* return," Kissinger assured Nixon on October 7. Kissinger paradoxically believed that strong support for Israel was the only way to be "evenhanded," because the Israelis would respond to U.S. pressure and the Arabs wouldn't because of their high emotions—"the Arabs will scream that they are being deprived of their birthright"—and their Soviet connections. "A defeat of Israel by Soviet arms would be a geopolitical disaster for the United States," Kissinger ventured. It would signal American weakness and "ratify Arab territorial gains" that Moscow would use to erode America's position in the Middle East.[114] In Kissinger's view, lifesaving support for the Israelis would also be "money in the bank . . . to draw on in later negotiations." Kissinger assumed that heavy backing for Israel in 1973 would pay off in Senate passage of most-favored-nation trade status for the Soviet Union—critical for détente—which pro-Israel hawks like Scoop Jackson had been holding up because of Soviet restrictions on Jewish emigration. The Arab states offered fewer domestic political boons and would not be so malleable in American hands, or grateful afterward. Thus, Kissinger pressed Nixon throughout the war to back Israel to the hilt. He understood that he was giving away things that he might more shrewdly have traded for substantial Israeli concessions, but felt that overt backing for Tel Aviv would leave America with good diplomatic options and big domestic political dividends as well.[115]

To buy time and arm Israel for the counterattacks required to recover the ground lost in the first hours of the war, the Americans ran a major airlift—bigger than the Berlin airlift of 1948–49—to resupply the IDF and prepare it for a desolating counterpunch. Since the Israelis appeared to have turned the tide in the war—Israeli ambassador Simcha Dinitz informed Kissinger on October 8 that "we have gone over from containment to attack both on the Sinai and Golan Heights"—the airlift was controversial.[116] With the Israelis describing their military situation as "considerably better," many in Washington felt that America's best course would be a studied neutrality. Resupplying Israel with ammunition, spares and even whole weapons systems—the Israelis wanted forty Phantoms immediately to replace their losses to Arab SAMs—would be interpreted as U.S. support not only for Israel but for its occupied territories as well. Moreover, Nixon worried that "massive open support for Israel . . . will just bring massive open support by the Russians" for the Arabs.[117] The president and Kissinger fended off intensive lobbying from the Israeli embassy for a week. Ambassador Dinitz threatened Kissinger that he was doing what he could to reassure important U.S. senators—Birch Bayh, Ted Kennedy and Alan Cranston were named to indicate just how important—that "the American government is . . . seeing things eye-to-eye" with Israel. Nixon got the message, angrily ordering Kissinger to "lean very hard on the Israeli ambassador" and his pet journalists to get them to stop "putting out the line that we are not supporting Israel . . . If we hear any more stuff like this, I will have no choice domestically except to turn on them."[118]

That, of course, would be easier said than done. Powerful members of Congress leaned hard on Kissinger, who complained of continual "harassment from the pro-Jewish senators" like Javits and Jackson. On October 13, while Kissinger weighed an American airlift to Israel, Jackson, who was organizing a run for the presidency in 1976, threatened that if Nixon didn't authorize the airlift, the Democrats would launch a congressional investigation into Nixon's "lousy management of the crisis" and demand "an overall review of the national security system."[119] Scoop Jackson—"the senator from Boeing"—planned to fill American airlifts to Israel with armaments from his home state. Weighing a presidential bid of his own, Idaho senator Frank Church sided with Jackson and asserted that the Israelis must *not* be prevented from "breaking these Egyptian and Syrian forces sufficiently to eliminate the threat for a long time to come."[120]

Determined not to break the Arabs too dramatically, or to implicate America too deeply in the Israeli resupply effort (lest he trigger a Saudi oil embargo and provoke Soviet intervention), Kissinger at first relied on seven El Al jets and twenty charter planes with limited quantities of ammunition, field artillery, antitank missiles, and tank and aircraft parts. To conserve his own stocks of fighters and USAF tankers, which had to escort the American Phantoms in flight from their bases in the United States and Europe to Israel, Secretary of Defense Schlesinger had at first tried to limit Israel to one and a half Phantoms per day, up to a maximum of sixteen. Prodded by Golda Meir's panic—"we are faced with a tremendous gap in quantity"—as well as loud complaints from Congress—"I'd like to see a number of [Phantoms] made available promptly," Minnesota senator Hubert Humphrey admonished Kissinger—Nixon finally consented to additional Phantoms and a full-blown American "airbridge" to Tel Aviv's Lod airport on October 13. Although willing to work with Javits as well as pro-Israel Democrats like Humphrey, Symington and Church, Kissinger drew the line at the orgiastic demands of Scoop Jackson and his neocon kindergarten. "Jackson wants fifty Phantoms within twenty-four hours," an astonished Schlesinger told Kissinger on October 12. "Tell him to go screw himself," Kissinger growled.[121]

Nixon wearily gave the thumbs-up to an airlift on October 14. He was now determined to reap as much domestic political benefit from the crisis as possible. "Don't spare the horses, just go gung ho," he phoned Kissinger, and flights of American C-5 and C-130 transports loaded with military equipment began touching down in Tel Aviv. Kissinger saw provision of American fighters (Skyhawk A-4s and Phantom F-4s), M-60 tanks and even the latest TOW (tube-launched, optically tracked, wire-guided) antitank missiles—"They have never appeared out there before so there'll be a certain dramatic effect," Schlesinger warned Kissinger—as the best way to *limit* the scope of Israel's looming counterattacks. "My profound conviction is that if we play this the hard way, it's the last time [the Israelis] are going to listen. If we kick them in the teeth, they have nothing to lose."[122] Kissinger foolishly reasoned that it would be better to give the Israelis everything they asked for in the hope that they would be grateful (and tractable) after the war. Schlesinger was wiser. "Is there a distinction between defending Israel and defending her 1967 conquests?" the secretary of defense queried in a White House meeting. If there was—and everyone agreed that there was—then America needed to rethink the airlift. Schlesinger proposed shipping only "consumables" like fuel and ammunition and holding back the planes and tanks until *after* the war, when they could be used as levers to pry the Israelis out of the occupied territories. But Kissinger, besieged by critics for his détente policy, was looking for a place to "get tough" with Moscow. The Middle East seemed the perfect place. He overruled Schlesinger's "fine-tuning" and insisted that the Israelis be given everything at once—consumables, missiles, and replacement tanks and aircraft.[123]

Resupplied and fine-tuned, the Israelis set about kicking the Egyptians in the teeth. Having been overrun on Yom Kippur, they now set out "to destroy as much as possible of the Egyptian army" to restore faith in Israeli arms and deterrence.[124] General Ariel Sharon crossed the Suez Canal north of Great Bitter Lake and knifed into the rear of the Egyptian Third Army. "Poor dumb Egyptians," Nixon muttered to Kissinger.[125] Golda Meir told Kissinger that the IDF's aim was deterrence: "It is our objective that the heavy blows we will strike at the invaders will deprive them of any appetite they will have for any future assault."[126] Having assumed that he could steer the Israelis, Kissinger expressed surprise at their aggressiveness. "It is all the more important for us to gain time to complete the job," Ambassador Dinitz told him. "We not only reject that which freezes the cease-fire but which calls for return." The IDF would not hesitate to cross the Suez Canal into Egyptian territory, and thought nothing of advancing past the "former cease-fire line of the Golan Heights in hot pursuit" of the retreating Syrians.[127]

"THEY CAN'T DO THAT, HENRY. THEY CAN'T DO THAT TO US AGAIN"

Kissinger deplored Israel's pugnacity. Meir had placed Israel's nuclear forces on alert, and Israeli columns had driven most of the way to Damascus by mid-October, where Soviet advisers took over the defense.[128] The Russians gaped at the ruins of the Syrian military, infrastructure and economy. In Syria, the IDF had overrun an additional 350 square miles of territory, blasted $225 million of roads, bridges, railways, and oil and industrial facilities, destroyed $400 million of advanced military hardware (including 400 tanks and 70 aircraft) and inflicted $350 million of indirect losses on the already straitened Syrian economy.[129] Nixon returned from Florida and vented his frustration with the way the Israelis seemed to be running away with a war that Kissinger had assured him would be directed in America's interest. "When they finish clobbering the Egyptians and the Syrians . . . [the Israelis] will be even more impossible to deal with than before . . . They can't do that, Henry. They can't do that to us again. They've done it to us for four years, but not more."[130] Nixon worried that the Israelis would treat the Yom Kippur War as an excuse to annex permanently the occupations of 1967. Conflating the Arab-Israeli conflict with Soviet adventurism, Kissinger had thrown away his best chance to pressure the Israelis into a final political settlement with the Arabs.

WORLD WAR III?

While Nixon raged at Israeli effrontery, Kissinger and Soviet ambassador to the United States Anatoly Dobrynin worried about World War III. If Sadat appealed for a Soviet "airbridge"—the Syrians had already established a limited one to bring in MiGs—the United States and the USSR might come to blows, and who knew how far that would go? Washington and Moscow had traditionally observed "parallelism," which held that "incidents in the Middle East should not mushroom into confrontations between the West and the Soviet Union," but *this* widening war had the potential to mushroom into something ghastly. The Soviets had eighty-eight ships (including twenty-three submarines) in the eastern Mediterranean, and the Russian Mediterranean squadron hewed to the "doctrine of the first salvo." Without aircraft carriers and without access to Egyptian airfields, the Soviets banked everything on an onrushing surprise attack with every gun, torpedo and missile afloat—"the first salvo"—before U.S. carriers could launch their strike aircraft. "We are kamikazes," a Russian naval officer cracked as the crisis intensified and Russian destroyers—missiles visible in their launcher rails—shadowed each of the Sixth Fleet's three carriers.[131] America's European allies were appalled by the threat of superpower war and a cutoff of Arab oil, and would certainly have been even more appalled had they known that Secretary of Defense Schlesinger was recommending an American military occupation of "part of Saudi Arabia" (undoubtedly the oily part) if the Saudis joined the war against Israel and continued to hike oil prices.[132]

Kissinger's assertion that he was acting as an honest broker in 1973 did not wash in Europe. Surely the Israelis would not *win* without American airlifts, so why not enforce a cease-fire and negotiations toward a "permanent settlement" instead of shipping twenty-two thousand tons of U.S. matériel into Israel? American resupply merely facilitated massive IDF counteroffensives and made the Israelis more powerful and intransigent than ever. "The Arabs have got some of their honor back, and we don't want the Israelis to take it away. It's time to settle," one U.S. official nervously advised. But in private conversations with Schlesinger, Kissinger made clear that, far from acting as an honest broker, Washington was actively encouraging the Israelis to undertake counteroffensives that would hammer the Arabs, humiliate the Soviets and win the gratitude of Scoop Jackson's pro-Israel bloc in the Senate. Kissinger told Schlesinger that "the scenario on diplomacy" would be geared to American resupply and Israeli offensives and assured Ambassador Dinitz that Israeli attacks and American peace talk would be "synchronized."[133] Although President Nixon insisted that American deliveries of munitions, parts and weapons were not meant "to fuel the war" but simply "to maintain the balance . . . and create the conditions [for] an equitable settlement," America's European allies, all fearing an Arab oil embargo, were not persuaded. France refused to assist the airlift, despite evidence that Soviet air- and sealifts were streaming into Egypt and Syria. In London, Edward Heath's Tory government denied American planes headed to Tel Aviv access to the British air base on Cyprus. West Germany, Spain, Greece and Turkey all refused to support the American airlift. Only the Netherlands and Portugal, with its critical base in the Azores, agreed to cooperate.[134]

As the U.S. airlift proceeded, the Saudis cut production 5 percent on October 18, 10 percent the next day, and then totally embargoed exports to the United States (and Portugal and the Netherlands) on October 20, the day after Nixon asked Congress for $2.2 billion in emergency aid for Israel.[135] The impact on Americans was dreadful. Having basked in the reassuring conclusions of George Shultz's task force on energy imports—that the United States would easily weather an Arab embargo—Nixon was stung by gas lines, skyrocketing prices, shortages and the blistering statements of détente critics that the oil shock was just one more symptom of U.S. weakness. Nixon ought to have pondered the words of Exxon's chief Middle East negotiator, who had warned in 1972 that "our economic policy was ensuring that we became increasingly dependent on Middle East oil, while our foreign policy was ensuring that the oil would be cut off." Too late, Nixon launched Project Independence, which challenged America to become self-sufficient in energy by 1980.[136] Awed by the sheer weight of the American airlift, Sadat, who had resisted Soviet calls for a cease-fire, began seriously to consider one when presented with Soviet satellite photos on October 16. They depicted Sharon's armored divisions coiled around the Egyptian Third Army, which was still marooned without a single functioning supply line on the east bank of the Suez Canal.

Egypt's awaited "phase two" offensive had jumped off on October 14 and been promptly mauled by Israeli counterattacks, which chewed up 465 Egyptian tanks and armored vehicles and shot down 100 Egyptian fighter jets. In the fifty-two major dogfights between Israeli and Egyptian pilots, the Egyptians lost 172 planes, the Israelis 6. A 1 to 7 aerial "kill ratio" that had seemed disastrous for the Arabs in 1967—they had shot down only one Israeli plane for every seven of theirs downed by the Israelis—soared to 1 to 29 in 1973.[137] Egyptian operations that had flowed smoothly in phase one—when the artillery had fired at preregistered targets and the tanks and infantry (shielded by SAMs and Saggers) had assaulted predetermined objectives—foundered in the more free-flowing phase two. Egyptian forces couldn't improvise in mobile operations; their tanks charged ahead blindly and their how- itzers fired wildly inaccurate artillery barrages that churned up vast tracts of desert without scratching an Israeli.[138] When a chastened Sadat requested a cease-fire—his Third Army was literally starving to death—it was Golda Meir's turn to object. She now wanted to prolong the war, to punish the Arabs and drive home the point that they would *never* get the occupied territories back by force.

General Brent Scowcroft, Nixon's deputy assistant for national security affairs, worried that the Israelis might do something "foolish, like bombing downtown Cairo," inflaming world opinion and provoking the Soviets, who were already plan- ning to insert a naval surface group into Port Said as well as fifty thousand combat troops along the Suez Canal.[139] Nixon and Kissinger were horrified by the prospect; they refused to be dragged into a war with the Russians to serve Israel's widening war aims.[140] Kissinger's objective had by this time boiled down to sustaining Israel "*without* a confrontation with the Soviets and without ripping our relations with the Arabs"—no mean feat.[141] With Nixon sidelined by the "Saturday Night Massacre"—the Watergate-induced firing of Special Prosecutor Archibald Cox and the resignations of Attorney General Elliot Richardson and Deputy Attorney Gen- eral and acting FBI director William Ruckelshaus on October 20—Kissinger flew to Moscow—"Tell them I'm coming on a B-52," he joked to Dobrynin—and ham- mered out Security Council Resolution 338, which he then forced Meir to accept. She accepted, with her usual lack of tact, remarking that it amounted to "Russian and Egyptian ultimatums, assented to by the United States."[142]

The Arabs and Israelis were to cease fire, hold their positions—including the menacing Israeli bridgehead on the Suez Canal and the armored brigades on the west side of Great Bitter Lake—and begin implementing Resolution 242 "in all of its parts" as well as direct Arab-Israeli negotiations for "a just and durable peace in the Middle East." There was something in this proposal for the Arabs—Resolution 242, with its promise of a return of "some" (but not "all") occupied territories—and something for the Israelis: the ability to retain some occupied territory and the right to hold direct negotiations with the Arab states, which implied legitimacy and diplomatic recognition.[143] With Israeli forces pointedly ignoring the cease-fire and consolidating their positions on the Gulf of Suez behind the Egyptian Third Army, the Soviets put seven airborne divisions on alert and threatened to intervene on the Suez Canal and on the road to Damascus. Supersonic Soviet MiG-25 Foxbats were already flying reconnaissance missions from Egyptian airfields to track the Israeli advance (and the collapse of the Arab armies).[144] Washington replied by placing its forces on America's highest level of peacetime war readiness—Defense Condition 3, or DefCon 3—on October 25. The Soviet Red Fleet increased its Mediterranean squadron to ninety-six ships while Antonov-22 transport planes prepared to lift five thousand Soviet troops a day into Egypt. The United States countered by preparing to move the 82nd Airborne Division and ordering three carrier battle groups with sixty ships—the *Franklin Delano Roosevelt*, the *John F. Kennedy* and the *Independence*—to rendezvous south of Crete.

With World War III in sight, three days of tense negotiations ensued until a new Arab-Israeli cease-fire was successfully brokered by Kissinger. The *New York Times* described the crisis as being directed on the American side by "an abbreviated National Security Council of Kissinger, Kissinger and Schlesinger"—Kissinger mentioned twice because he was now secretary of state and national security adviser. Agnew's chair was empty because he had resigned in disgrace and no successor had been found. Depressed and embarrassed by his predicament, Nixon refused to leave his living quarters on the upper floor of the White House. He kept in touch with the NSC by telephone.[145] Distracted by resolutions for his impeachment in Congress, Nixon did find time to remind Kissinger that "the Boss" was still in charge: "The Israelis will squeal like stuck pigs, [but] tell Dobrynin . . . that Brezhnev and Nixon will settle this damn thing." Although the Soviets wanted war even less than the Americans—they depended on American wheat and Western loans—they needed to "retain credit with the Arabs," even at the risk of war, or a skirmish.[146] Nixon recognized that the Israelis were trying to win "two or three weeks to . . . really start clobbering these people," and Kissinger agreed that further Israeli mopping-up operations would make "international pressures . . . unmanageable." Secretary of Defense Schlesinger warned the White House that continued supply of 175 mm artillery shells to the Israelis would expose the United States to the charge of "supplying ammo for the destruction of Damascus," and Al Haig told Kissinger that, unless the war ended at once, the Soviets really *would* insert "peacekeepers" to save their Arab allies.[147]

"My Job Is to Serve the Interests of *American* Foreign Policy"

Commenting that "we had not worked to reduce the Soviet military presence in Egypt for years only to cooperate in reintroducing it," Kissinger expressed frustration with Israel's demand for "a veto over all our decisions regardless of the merits of the issue, and a free hand to destroy the Egyptian Third Army," and he belatedly wrestled Golda Meir to the mat. "Our whole foreign policy position depends on our not being represented as having screwed up a crisis," he vented.[148] In a meeting with Golda Meir and Moshe Dayan, Kissinger, ever the Harvard historian, compared Israel to the Prussia of Frederick the Great and Bismarck. "Prussia started as Israel did and just expanded and filled the territory it expanded into. But there was no UN" in that bygone age. Nowadays, Kissinger reminded Meir, "the Arabs . . . have globalized the problem. They have created the conviction that *something must be done*."[149] America and Israel—great practitioners of hard power—could not stand forever against that kind of soft power without losing legitimacy and support. Moshe Dayan remarked that Kissinger had threatened a cutoff of American aid if the Israelis continued to block Red Cross and UN relief supplies to the Egyptian Third Army, and Golda Meir sniffed that Kissinger seemed more determined to preserve the appearance of Egyptian victory than to strengthen Israel. "Give me *something*," Kissinger coldly replied. "My job is to serve the interests of *American* foreign policy, not to act as psychiatrist to the Israeli government." He succeeded in implementing the new cease-fire on October 27, when Israeli and Egyptian generals finally began direct talks at Kilometer 101 on the Cairo-Suez road.[150]

By now the lamest of lame ducks, Nixon tried to extract some domestic political bounce from the crisis. Steered by Kissinger, the president had thrown away a golden opportunity in 1973 to coerce the Israelis into making the major territorial concessions that might have opened the door to a lasting peace. Not seeming to notice, Nixon instructed Kissinger to summon the heads of CBS, NBC, ABC, the *New York Times* and the *Washington Post* to the White House. "Get the whole bunch in a room" and make them understand that Nixon saved Israel. Would anybody else have saved it?" Nixon had "pushed in the chips" that won the bet.[151] Golda Meir too claimed victory—her forces were in "Africa," as she called Egypt—and the IDF had clawed back Mount Hermon and pushed to within fifteen miles of

Damascus. Still, Israeli losses were alarmingly high in comparison with 1956 or 1967: 2,412 dead and 115 aircraft and 800 tanks lost.[152] Both the Syrian and Egyptian armies had fought more competently than ever, and they had cracked Israel's invincible facade. Israel's American mentor had displayed its own Achilles' heel in a Middle Eastern fight—the Arab "oil weapon"—but had also established itself as the critical regional power broker. Kissinger had partnered with the splenetic Russians—without giving anything away—had reined in both the Arabs and the Israelis and had imposed a cease-fire that left some hope for a broader peace. "My strategy," he told Meir, "is to be in a position to make the Arabs *think* that they can get some progress from us. The Soviets only save Egypt from disasters; they offer nothing positive."[153]

Not everyone was happy. In Libya, President Muammar Qaddafi divined the deviousness that Kissinger expressed so openly to Prime Minister Meir and Ambassador Dinitz. Qaddafi angrily condemned Sadat's acceptance of the cease-fire and called for the war to be "continued by hand-to-hand fighting." He exhorted the Jordanians to overthrow their cautious king.[154] Radicalism welled up in Egypt as well. Al-Gam'a al-Islamiyya, or the Muslim Group, led by angry Muslim Brothers like twenty-two-year-old Ayman al-Zawahiri, who would become Osama bin Laden's right-hand man in the jihad against the West, began to dominate every major university and technical college, where, for the first time in modern Egyptian history, men stopped trimming their beards and women donned the veil.[155] The oil crisis dragged into the winter, with Arab production cuts removing 4.4 million barrels per day—10 percent of Western supply—between October and December 1973. The Saudis were delighted to leave oil in the ground, for two successive dollar devaluations under Nixon had devalued their petrodollars.[156] With supplies down, prices leaped again, from $3 a barrel in October to $17 a barrel in December. Kissinger was appalled: "It is a novel experience for the world that 50 million people in a handful of backward nations can drastically change the style of life of 800 million people in the most advanced nations of the globe."[157] A New York investment banker was blunter: "What the hell right do 6 million people in Saudi Arabia or 3 million people in Libya have to put *us* out of business?"

The European Economic Community (EEC), which had never seconded American support of Israel, took an appeasing line. They issued a pro-Arab communiqué in November, which had the desired effect of inducing Arab producers to restore normal supplies to all of Western Europe except Portugal and the Netherlands. To get *its* oil flowing again, Japan broke ranks with the United States for the first time since 1945, issuing its own pro-Arab proclamation. In Washington, a kind of strategic hysteria broke out. The Saudis were even denying oil to the U.S. Sixth Fleet, which was sputtering toward a confrontation with the Red Fleet. Andrew Tobias reported that senior American officials—including Kissinger and President Gerald Ford—were now pondering an invasion of Saudi Arabia. Because of "unmanageable prices, the U.S. should now seize the Saudi Arabian oil fields, or get someone else to do it for us." Some Americans wondered how so much could have been squandered in Vietnam, where so little was apparently at stake, when so little was being expended in the Middle East, where so much was obviously at stake. But sensible opinion—buoyed by the realization that OPEC's $100 billion windfall in 1973 amounted to just 2 percent of the world's $5 trillion GDP—held back. No one in the Western world was going to starve because of higher energy prices. An Operation Saudi Freedom might become a "mini-Algeria," and nobody wanted a presidency-destroying headache like that. Strategic theorist Herman Kahn was especially prescient when questioned on the subject in 1974: "It would be fairly easy to knock over any one of these [oil-producing] countries—but you've got to go in and kill people to do it. It's very difficult to kill people on an enterprise that's immoral, illegal, and long-lasting. Day after day those pictures would show up on television: two Arabs killed, ten Arabs killed . . . We haven't the stomach to mount such an enterprise now." An energy consultant tapped by President Ford didn't think it would be easy at all, if the basic objective was to get oil to market: "You don't produce oil sitting on bayonets. I don't know what you do when you take over a country by force. You have guerrilla movements, you have destruction of facilities and all these kinds of problems." And who would walk blindly into such a mess? Journalist Tad Szulc came to the depressing conclusion—affirmed in 2003—that "there is *always* someone who is foolish enough to open a can of worms like this."[158]

TAMING THE "MADMEN OF THE MIDDLE EAST"

During the war, Kissinger had assured the powerful chairman of the Senate Foreign Relations Committee, Arkansas senator J. William Fulbright, that he and Nixon would first buttress Israel with their airlift and then "put the whole prestige of the U.S. behind . . . a solution to the *causes* of the war." Kissinger wanted to nip the chronic problems of what he called "the madmen of the Middle East"—Arabs and Israelis—in the bud.[159] That was easier said than done. The smoke had barely cleared over the Sinai and Golan battlefields before Nixon, Kissinger and Schlesinger came under crushing pressure to rearm the Israelis *again* and "restore the military balance in the area." Nixon complied, granting an eye-popping $2.2 billion in November 1973 to replace damaged Israeli planes, vehicles and other equipment. Congress had applied the usual pressure, Hawaii senator Daniel Inouye writing Kissinger that "Israel only needs $1.1 billion, but the other billion is a cushion to deter neighbors from war." In the end, the embattled Nixon coughed up the extra money only too willingly, on political grounds. Representative Thomas Morgan recalled that "Congress wanted to grant no more than $1.5 billion, but Nixon and Kissinger twisted arms to increase it to $2.2 billion."[160] Kissinger sounded almost Israeli in his comments on the foreign aid: "If we are not going to let [the Israelis] use both territory and weapons to produce security, then we have to supply weapons."[161]

Kissinger and Israeli defense minister Moshe Dayan were articulating the new Israeli strategy that remains in force today. Instead of relying on land and territorial buffers—difficult because of Arab pressure on world opinion and the UN—the Israelis would rely on military superiority. As Joseph Sisco put it in a memo to Kissinger: "Dayan is not enamored of the tendency in Israel to equate security solely with borders; better: sophisticated weapons to meet specific challenges." Dayan's shopping list was alarming: Lance and Maverick missiles and glide bombs—the cream of the American arsenal.[162] Not surprisingly, Kissinger shortly found himself in a plane flying to Riyadh to reassure the Saudis that all was well, that the Israelis would not be bulked up too much and that the Arabs should trust America's commitment to a solution to the Palestinian problem. "The Europeans and the Japanese can say what you want to hear . . . as long as you give them oil. They can make promises, but they can't give you anything. Only *we* can give you progress." Only Nixon and Kissinger could dislodge the Israelis from the "West Bank of the Suez Canal, the Golan Heights, and the West Bank of the Jordan." But could they really? In the same meeting (with princes Saud and Turki, and King Faisal), Kissinger confessed that he and Nixon really had little leverage with the Israelis. "My most difficult stop will not be in Damascus, but in Tel Aviv . . . Israel has never withdrawn; Israel has always advanced . . . There are strong pressures directed against us in the U.S.; we do not want to fight theoretical battles with Israel." Kissinger would, however, take up the cudgels if the Saudis would end the oil embargo and push down prices: "Keep this in mind as you consider your policy on oil. The

American public will not understand if the first administration willing to disagree with Israel is being punished by the Arabs."[163]

Damascus, of course, was no cakewalk, even in comparison with Tel Aviv. There the Americans discovered a regime that, as the CIA put it, "was skeptical about Washington's ability to extract the necessary concessions from Israel" and determined to reduce American presence in the region by any means. Moscow rebuilt Syria's conventional military with MiG-23s, T-62 tanks and Scud missiles, and armed the fedayeen irregulars for raids into Israel. The Palestinian issue was the glue that held the fragile Syrian regime together. It bonded the pragmatists of the armed forces—like General Assad—with the ideologues of the Baath Party, and knitted up the sectarian tears between the country's Sunni majority and the small, politically dominant Alawite sect. A secret CIA memo of 1974 acknowledged that "no Syrian leader—however moderate and pragmatic—can afford to disregard the Palestinian cause any more than he can afford to demand less than a complete withdrawal of Israeli forces from the Golan Heights." To do so would be to invite a coup.[164]

The Egyptians went in an entirely different direction—the direction hoped for by Kissinger in 1973, but nonetheless surprising in the event. Sadat's army had fought just well enough to retrieve the honor lost in 1967, and Sadat felt comfortable pushing for peace with Israel. His experience with the Soviets—arguments over weapons, aid and the environmental damage wrought by the Aswan Dam—pushed him closer to the Americans, and Israel.[165] It was an astonishing transformation for a man who had emerged from Nasser's shadow in 1970 with a mediocre record. Egyptians had laughed him off for years as "Major Yes Sir!"—an obsequious subordinate of Nasser. "Sadat is quite lazy and obedient," the State Department's Near Eastern Affairs desk had informed Kissinger and Rogers at the time of Nasser's death. "He is anti-British, anti-American and anti-Israeli." But the State Department had detected another face of Sadat that gave cause for hope. He was "less Pan-Arab, more 'Egypt-first' in character."[166] He was a pragmatist who recognized that Egypt could not be whipsawed forever by the "poison of Arabism" and the Palestinian refugee question. Egypt needed to get down to business and, as Sadat declared in July 1971, "build a modern, technologically advanced state based equally on science and faith."[167] Before and after the Yom Kippur War, Sadat carried out purges to remove Nasserites from power and radically reorient Egyptian policy. The new course had three pillars: a deemphasizing of pan-Arabism ("de-Nasserization"), an acceptance of the need for peace with Israel and better relations with the United States.[168]

In November 1977, Sadat told an astonished Egyptian parliament that "I am prepared to go to the end of the earth, and Israel will be surprised to hear me say to you, I am ready to go to their home, to the Knesset itself, and to argue with them there." Ten days later, Sadat flew to Tel Aviv to meet with Prime Minister Menachem Begin. In his speech to the Knesset, he declared "no more war." Greeting General Ariel Sharon, Begin's agriculture minister, at Ben-Gurion airport, Sadat joked, "If you attempt to cross the Suez Canal again, I'll have you arrested."[169] Sadat was ready for *real* peace: normalization, diplomatic relations and trade. Egypt, he felt, could not withstand the strain and expense of an interminable cold war with Israel. In September 1978, Sadat, Begin and U.S. president Jimmy Carter would negotiate the Camp David Accords, which effectively removed Egypt from the struggle to destroy Israel. Ambassadors were exchanged, trade was begun, and Egypt began receiving $1.3 billion in U.S. aid annually; Israel $3 billion. Sadat had achieved his ambition—to set Egypt on an independent, sensible course where it fought for its own interests, not those of a few million Palestinian refugees or the dreams of Arab nationalism. Accolades rolled in from Washington and Tel Aviv, but also from Tehran, where Shah Muhammed Reza Pahlavi, the king of kings, greeted Sadat's new pragmatism with delight and eagerly restored diplomatic relations with Cairo.[170] Despite the near cataclysm of 1973, the Nixon Doctrine seemed to have achieved its purpose: powerful pro-American sentinels, from Egypt east to Iran.

CHAPTER 10

·✖✖·

GREAT CIVILIZATION

THE IRANIANS HELD THE EASTERN FLANK of Nixon's Middle Eastern security system. They were Persians, not Arabs, and were Shiites, not Sunnis. Shiites, including the millions of Arabs on Iran's border with Iraq, were not natural adherents of Arab nationalism, which was an ideology based on Sunni notions of Islam and Arabism.[1] Those differences made Iran a natural wedge in the region for American influence, as did the predilections of the shah himself, who was a technology-besotted Americanizer with oil money and soaring regional ambitions.

REZA KHAN

Nixon was greatly impressed by the nouveau riche Pahlavi dynasty in Iran. They were "new men," like Nixon himself, who had clawed their way to power. Shah Muhammed Reza, who had been seated on the throne by the British in 1941 at the age of twenty-one and buttressed by the Americans during the Mosaddeq coup in 1953, descended from a gruff, hard-riding father, Reza Khan, who had been a brigadier general in the Iranian Cossack Brigade before ousting Iran's last Qajar king in 1925. An ambitious commoner, Reza Khan had founded an "imperial" dynasty from scratch, and given it the ancient name Pahlavi to conceal its green roots. Although Muhammed Reza was notorious for his vacillation, his father, who ruled from 1925 to 1941, was decisive to a fault.

Reza Khan and the Pahlavis were inspired by developments in Turkey, where the "Gray Wolf"—Mustafa Kemal Atatürk—had ripped up the traditions, piety and exoticism of the Ottoman Empire and replaced them in the 1920s with a modern, Westernizing regime and society. Atatürk scrapped the Arabic script used by the Ottomans and ordered Turks to write in the Latin alphabet. He banned the fez and discouraged the veil in every Turkish town, slashed the powers of the clergy and introduced the forms of Western law and democracy with the stroke of a pen. He created an opposition party from scratch, put up Turkish women as candidates for parliament in 1935 and watched them get elected in impressive numbers.[2]

Reza Khan made no secret of his admiration for Atatürk, and all other political strongmen. A journalist visiting Iran in 1940 was surprised to find official government calendars on the walls of public offices portraying the "Greatest Men of All Time." Large portraits of Reza Khan and Napoleon Bonaparte took pride of place in the center. Off to one side were cameos of Mussolini, Atatürk and Hitler; off to the other, Teddy Roosevelt, Louis XIV, Julius Caesar and Alexander the Great.[3] Like Atatürk, Reza Khan banned tribal costumes and fezzes, unveiled Iran's women, introduced the Western-looking "Pahlavi hat," and then embarked on a pitiless campaign to bring the tribes and the Shiite clergy under state control and give Iran's cities a modern, Western appearance. He built roads, railroads and ports, founded the University of Tehran, recast Iran's historical provinces as numbered *ustans* that were placed under the control of loyal, modernizing prefects and abolished Iran's Islamic law courts. Reza Khan impatiently brushed aside the five hundred Koranic verses that are the basis of sharia Islamic law and replaced them with Western codes derived from the law books of France, Belgium, Switzerland and Italy.[4] Reza razed old walls and gates, tore up entire quarters, and laid down broad boulevards, apartment blocks and department stores. In the course of Reza Khan's urban renewal, he gave a glimpse of the wooden stubbornness that would characterize his son Muhammed Reza and exasperate the son's American patrons. Reza contracted with a German firm to build a sewer system in Tehran in the 1930s. The Germans submitted their bid, which called for a two-tiered system of water and waste pipes. Reza scolded their "extravagance." *One* set of pipes was enough, he insisted. It would carry clean water for washing and drinking into Tehran during the day, and carry wastewater and sewage out at night. The disgusted Germans refused to build such a system, and Reza—convinced that he was being swindled—refused to pay for the one that they wanted to build. So Tehran lived well into the 1950s with raw sewage slopping through the gutters of the city streets.[5]

Sewers were not the only flaw in the Pahlavi regime. Reza Khan proved more interested in creating a family despotism than a modern republic. He beefed up the Iranian military and increased its pay and perks to guarantee loyalty. His provincial *ustans* extended his patronage and cronies into every corner of Iran. He concluded a lucrative deal with the (Teapot Dome–besmirched) Sinclair Oil Company to fill the family coffers, and then quashed earnest Iranian efforts to emulate the example of Turkey and create a secular republic. Recognizing that the Shiite clergy based in Qom would rebel at such a change, Reza Khan in 1924 vested them with bigger budgets and some restored powers in return for their connivance in his imperial project. The mullahs connived away, and blessed the colonel's overthrow of the reigning Qajar shah in 1925 to seat himself on the throne. Reza Khan thus became Reza Shah, and Pahlavi Iran became the volatile hybrid state that would come spectacularly unglued in 1979: torn between its forward-looking pro-Western dynasty and its backward-looking anti-Western clergy, or ulema. Tactically, the Shiite clergy aligned with Reza. Strategically, they were unappeasable, for the ideology of Shiism is explicit: ever since Allah's removal of the messianic Twelfth Imam in the ninth century, no temporal power is considered legitimate. Every secular Iranian government is a usurper, fiendishly perpetuating the "great occultation"—the disappearance of the Twelfth Imam, or Mahdi—and substituting itself for that legitimate, hidden executor of the divine will. Every Pahlavi effort to open Iran to Western influence would be met by fusillades from Qom, where the ulemas, or doctors of Islamic law, would protest the dynasty's "perversion of Islam."[6]

Before his removal by the British in 1941, Reza Shah had always maintained that Iran would "remain a pawn of the great powers until it made itself a great power by its own efforts." That anxiety explained his nervous quest for modernization and his aggressive Westernization of Iran, which was all the more remarkable in view of the fact that Reza had never been further abroad than Iraq. When foreign statesmen persisted in calling his country "Persia," Reza Shah led a determined campaign in the League of Nations in the 1930s to have it called "Iran." The name Iran was significant because it was the name Iranians themselves used, not a quaint European derivation from fairy tales and classical literature.[7] Reza Shah's flirtation with Nazi Germany was part of his campaign to make Iran a regional great power. By offsetting Iran's traditional overlords—Russia and Britain—with the Germans, he aimed to secure real as opposed to merely nominal independence for Iran. Thus, he exchanged oil for German money, technicians, advisers, commercial airliners, ships and construction materials for the Trans-Iranian Railway. By 1939, Nazi Germany accounted for 50 percent of Iran's foreign trade.

Reza Shah was ousted by the British and the Soviets in 1941 because of those links to Berlin. His son, Muhammed Reza, grew up in a different age, and viewed the Americans as a more politically correct vehicle for what his father had been trying to accomplish with the Nazis. Muhammed Reza's complicity in the Mosaddeq coup had been founded in part on his desire to get himself into a special relationship with Washington. Unlike the British, the Americans would let Iran grow and run; their patronage would be remote and indirect. Washington would let Iran become a great power in its own right. Indeed Eisenhower's NSC-6010 of July 1960 designated Iran as "the logical heir to British influence in the area."

THE SHAH OF IRAN

Richard Nixon viewed Iran as just that—a sturdy fence post in the Persian Gulf. When Nixon took office in 1969, the Gulf contained two-thirds of the world's known oil reserves and supplied one-third of world production. Of the forty-five million people living along the shores of the Gulf, thirty million were Iranians, and they were the logical heirs of British influence. No one expected the little pro-Western states that the British left in the wake of their "scuttle"—Oman and the United Arab Emirates—to afford *any* protection to the vast Western oil concessions in the Gulf, 54 percent of which were controlled by the United States, 30 percent by the United Kingdom.[8] When a worried Nixon famously and humbly asked Muhammed Reza to "protect him" during a visit to Tehran in 1972, it must have seemed like poetic vindication for all the hopes and dreams of Reza Shah.

Although dismissed throughout his reign as a pale shadow of his hearty father, Shah Muhammed Reza had actually taken power with the sword. After conspiring with the British to remove Reza Shah during World War II, the Soviets had sedulously fostered Iran's "Party of the Masses"—Tudeh—which expanded under the leadership of a small group of Iranian communists, trade union leaders and intellectuals and attacked the corruption of the Pahlavi regime. In late 1944—with the British and Americans pinned down in Italy, France and the Pacific—the Soviets gruffly demanded the mineral rights to Iran's five northern provinces. To drive the point home, they dispatched Red Army units into Tehran to defend Tudeh demonstrations—in favor of the oil giveaway—against government repression. Iranian officials in the Soviet zone who defied Tudeh were purged. In early 1945, Moscow began a campaign to annex Iran's Kurdish and Azeri provinces to the Soviet Union, which seemed to herald a postwar partition of Iran along the lines of Germany or Korea. VE-day hardly registered in Iran. Tehran's war was just beginning.[9]

Shah Muhammed Reza, a twenty-seven-year-old stripling, rode into the red breach at the head of his imperial army in December 1946 to reclaim northern Iran. Amid savagery that surprised even Iranians, the shah's troops made the streets of Tabriz and Mahabad run with blood. Iran's Kurdish and Azeri minorities, who had listened raptly to Soviet promises of nationhood, were viciously purged. Tabriz and the surrounding country became the sole example of a territory that was seized by Stalin at the onset of the Cold War and then restored to its rightful owners.[10]

The shah spent the 1950s and 1960s buttressing his power. He made himself a central player in the Arab-Israeli peace process by opening an "office" in Tel Aviv in 1958 that was essentially an embassy. Iranian recognition of Israel permitted the shah to mediate between the key players—Egypt, Syria and Israel—and created a covert but effective Iranian-Israeli front against the Baathist, Soviet-backed regime in Iraq. Iran was a major buyer of Israeli arms, exchanged staff officers with the IDF and supplied all of Israel's oil until 1967, 50 percent of its needs thereafter.[11] The shah's coziness with Israel and his independent foreign policy, which he dubbed "nonpolarized bilateralism," naturally made him enemies everywhere. With the Soviets broadcasting anti-Pahlavi propaganda from clandestine transmitters in Iran as well as Moscow's National Voice of Iran radio in Soviet Azerbaijan, Muhammed Reza cracked down hard on dissidents.[12]

The shah's notorious, American-designed internal intelligence agency, SAVAK, rooted out communists, as well as rebels among Iran's principal tribes: the Kurds, Qashgais and Bakhtiari.[13] Gamal Nasser's rise in Egypt and the Baath coup in Iraq in 1958 spurred the shah to launch a domestic reform program that would steal some of that Arab nationalist thunder. Nasser and the Baathists impertinently referred to Khuzistan, Iran's principal oil patch, as "Arabistan," and the shah, who ruled a large Arab minority there, felt the heat. In the 1950s and early 1960s, he sought security guarantees from Washington.[14] The Americans gave it; Eisenhower and John Foster Dulles, who had advocated an American-backed "northern tier" from Turkey to Pakistan, viewed Iran as a key piece of the tier. And once Britain officially withdrew from the Gulf in 1971, Iran essentially became the "northern tier."[15] The Turks were wrangling with the Greeks and the Soviets, and the Pakistanis were embroiled with the Indians and Afghans. The region needed a stabilizing force, one that would, as Churchill put it, anchor the emerging pro-Western "Tito-Greco-Turko front," reach through Iraq and Iran and "carry NATO's fingertips to Pakistan."[16]

By the mid-1970s, Iran had become that Western anchor. The Americans took over the old British naval base in Bahrain in 1971 and began basing ships and planes at Diego Garcia, but they relied heavily on the shah's big battalions. Once Nasser passed from the scene in 1970, the shah used his oil wealth to increase Tehran's influence in the region and to separate himself from American tutelage. He spent millions in 1971 on his notorious "Persepolis party." Thrown to celebrate twenty-five hundred years of Persian monarchy, the party—catered by Maxim's, which closed its restaurant in Paris for two weeks so that 180 chefs and staff could be flown to Iran to cook and serve for the shah—underscored Muhammed Reza's determination to promote himself and dominate the region. The Pahlavis, he asserted, were the "Dynasty Blessed by the Gods," the "Great Civilization" with a direct link to Xerxes, Darius and the other Achaemenian emperors. The *shahanshah*, or "king of kings," began the festivities at the Tomb of Cyrus, where he not so subtly suggested—"you are sleeping; we are awake"—that the Pahlavis would revive the hegemony of the Achaemenids and even perhaps reconquer lost Persian provinces in Afghanistan, Pakistan and the Gulf.[17]

The Persepolis party drew a disappointing B-list of dignitaries, men like Spiro Agnew, Josip Broz Tito, Haile Selassie, Jeremy Thorpe and Nicolae Ceausescu. The Queen of England recoiled in horror—her advisers called the party "a creation of royal despotism taking advantage of the bedazzled mass media"—and prevailed upon Prince Charles to go in her place. Evincing his usual diffidence, the Prince of Wales also declined.[18] Few Arabs were comforted by such slights or the shah's clumsy efforts to downplay his rhetoric and militarism: "Countries should believe that we only want their good and nothing else." No matter how hard he tried, the Great Civilizer always came across like a new Xerxes: "In ten years Iran will be a mighty power, for peace, with nothing to gain from war."[19] An American diplomat who toured the United Arab Emirates in 1972 remarked their resentment of "Iran's overbearing and lordly attitude" as well as the shah's "superpower" pretensions and patronizing treatment of the Gulf's "frightened petty princelings."[20] The conservative Arab states also resented Muhammed Reza's pesky subsidies to the Egyptian and Syrian regimes, his provision of cut-price oil to them and his wily encouragement of the Arab-Israeli quarrel to sap the strength of Arab nationalism, increase Israeli dependence on him and give Iran a mediating hand in the region.[21]

THE NIXON DOCTRINE AND THE IRANIAN MILITARY

Threatened by Washington's focus on Vietnam and détente, Nasser's demands for control of the Persian Gulf and the Iraqi drift into the Soviet orbit, the shah went on a military spending spree in the 1960s and 1970s. In a dozen years of wild spending, he made the imperial Iranian military the envy of the Middle East.[22] Seizing the windfall of the 1967 and 1973 oil shocks, the shah increased oil revenues from $1.2 billion in 1970 to $20 billion in 1976 and, prodded by the Nixon Doctrine, which devolved America's global security to "regional power centers" like Iran, plowed the receipts into the fastest, most intensive military buildup ever seen in the Middle East. Weapons imports that averaged $8.5 million annually in the early 1960s increased to $156 million in 1968, $2 billion in 1973 and $4 billion in 1976. A country that had ranked just twenty-ninth in the world in military expenditures in the mid-1960s had climbed to eighth place by the mid-1970s, when Iran was fast closing on Britain, France and West Germany.[23] "In about ten years' time, Iran will be as England and France are today," the shah boasted to the Kuwaiti newspaper *Al-Siyassah* in 1973, and he meant it.[24]

With its 1,620 tanks—most of them late-model American Pattons—and its 640 transport and attack helicopters, the seven-division Iranian army was geared for offensive operations. Shunted around by its choppers and C-130s, it lent a degree of credibility to the Nixon Doctrine. The Imperial Iranian Air Force (IIAF) was as blessed as Israel when it came to top-of-the-line American fighters. With eight squadrons of F-4s and seven squadrons of F-5s—354 aircraft in all—Iran plunked down another $2 billion (more than $9 billion in 2010 dollars) to add 99 F-14 Tomcats in the mid-1970s. By the mid-1980s—had the shah not been swept from power by the Ayatollah Khomeini—Iran would have taken delivery of 250 F/A-18 Hornets and 300 F-16 Vipers. The shah would have refueled and guided that gold-plated escadrille into battle with ten Boeing 707 tankers and ten E-3A AWACs. No wonder key U.S. lawmakers like Scoop Jackson (the "senator from Boeing") and Stuart Symington (whose constituency included the McDonnell Douglas plant in St. Louis) loved the Iranians as much as the Israelis, and turned a blind eye to the shah's increasingly dire missteps.

If delivered, those U.S. combat and surveillance aircraft would have given Iran an air force five times larger than Saudi Arabia's, twice as big as Iraq's, qualitatively better than either India's or Israel's, and one in need of continuous after-sales service for its aircraft and missiles, which included the latest Phoenix, Maverick, Condor and Shrike models.[25] By 1976, the Iranian navy counted eight guided-missile destroyers and frigates. With an oil tanker transiting the Strait of Hormuz every twelve minutes, the navy had a special importance for Tehran; when the shah fell, he was awaiting delivery of four Kidd-class destroyers armed with McDonnell Douglas Harpoon missiles, as well as three diesel-electric submarines. That single purchase would have quintupled the size of the Iranian navy, and, as usual, cost was no object. When the unit cost of the American destroyers jumped from $125 million to $325 million in just three years, owing to runaway U.S. inflation, the shah hardly flinched; he cut his order from six ships to four, but refused even to consider frigates. Iran, he insisted, needed a big ship for deepwater missions at *any* cost.[26] The Iranians routinely patrolled to the Seychelles, the shah grandiosely vowing to control the Indian Ocean to stitch together a "common market from Australia to the Gulf" under *Iranian* military protection.[27]

AN "ISLAND OF STABILITY"?

Incredibly, the high-tech Iranian military cracked by Ayatollah Khomeini's Islamic revolution in 1979 included just one-third of the weapons on order. Still to come were the twenty squadrons of third-generation fighter aircraft (Tomcats, Hornets and Vipers), the Kidd-class destroyers (waggishly renamed the "Ayatollah-class" by the U.S. Navy and resold to the Taiwanese), the submarines, two thousand British main battle tanks, a thousand armored personnel carriers, five hundred self-propelled howitzers and three thousand trucks. Driven by personal ambition and a waning faith in President Jimmy Carter's America, which appeared to be losing the Cold War even more precipitously than Nixon and Kissinger, the shah tried all the harder to make Iran the number three military power in the world. He poured $28 billion into twelve nuclear reactors (two French, two German and eight American), which were widely assumed to be working on uranium enrichment for nuclear weapons. When revolution came, only the Germans had begun building; if all twelve Iranian reactors had entered service, Iran would have generated five times more nuclear power than the Germans and eight times more than the French. This was puzzling—for a poor country with a surplus of oil and gas—and rather alarming.[28] But the shah plowed forward anyway; by the end of his reign, weapons systems were being purchased specifically to surpass the British and West German arsenals. The British in 1973 gasped at the shah's mass purchase of six hundred American helicopters "at a cost and sophistication beyond the British Army's aspirations."[29] Indeed, had Iran taken delivery of the twelve hundred Chieftain tanks on order when the shah fell—to say nothing of the Challengers under consideration—it would have acquired an armored force equal to France's: not bad, considering Iran had just half France's population and one-eighth of its GDP when the order was booked.

This sharp military instrument may have explained President Jimmy Carter's otherwise inexplicable declaration in December 1977 that Pahlavi Iran was "an island of stability in one of the more troubled areas of the world."[30] A year later, U.S. Army colonel Colin Powell toured Iran, inspected the shah's crack troops—the Immortals—and pronounced himself impressed: they filed past "in tailored uniforms, berets, and gleaming ladder-laced boots, men who performed with much shouting and martial flair. The Iranian officer next to me explained: 'Their loyalty is total. The Immortals will fight to the last man to protect the Shah.' "[31] The region quailed, and Nixon and Carter grinned. The shah's determination "to buy early, buy many, and buy the best" fledged a dark little jest in oil-shocked, recessionary America: "What is good enough for Iran is good enough for the United States."[32]

And yet military expenditures on this titanic scale ultimately swamped Muhammed Reza's "island of stability," which, despite the shah's spending and pretensions, remained a Third World country with a Third World GDP. Iran's underdevelopment was such that the shah's military could not even store many of its costly imports, let alone deploy them. Driving north from Shiraz to Isfahan in 1980, a Polish journalist observed hundreds of brand-new American helicopters parked on the shoulder of the highway, half buried in drifted sand.[33] British analysts—who earlier had wondered *how* the shah would integrate and fly those helicopters—deplored the "piecemeal, uncoordinated acquisitions," the inability of "Iranian officers at any level to think for themselves" and the "widening gap between the inflow of highly sophisticated equipment and the necessary training in its use."[34] Impressed as he was by the swank of the shah's Immortals, Colonel Colin Powell was less impressed by the air force; he watched the Iranians train on the F-14 in 1978 and observed that no one bothered to train the backseat weapons systems officer in the use of the plane's attack systems. It was thought sufficient to train the pilot—"from the Iranian upper crust"—to "take off, perform the flashy high speed, low-level passes, and get the plane back on the ground." It was like flying the Tomcat with Maverick but no Goose, or Iceman without Slider. "All you see flying around here is half an airplane," an American trainer scoffed.[35] Still, the shah kept buying with the single-minded mania that would bury his regime. Existing Iranian tanks—to say nothing of the ones on order—were "off the road with the wrong lubricants," and the air force—absorbing hundreds of new planes with inadequately trained pilots and navigators—was "experiencing an increasingly serious accident rate."[36]

Straining to make a virtue of this profligacy, the shah—who handpicked every item in the defense budget—argued that his high-tech military served a critical intellectual and *economic* function. Demanding offsets and technology sharing from foreign suppliers, the imperial military would educate itself in the new technologies, increase its domestic production of advanced technology and help realize the shah's dream of making Iran "the Japan of West Asia."[37] In the 1970s, with the West in recession and heavily dependent on Gulf oil, the shah believed that he could ram Iran into the league of Western great powers in a single generation. In 1975, he vowed to "bring living standards in Iran up to current standards in Europe" within a decade.[38] There was some cause for optimism: Iran's growth in 1966–76 had been stupendous, with GDP increasing from $7 billion to $53 billion over the decade, per capita GDP from $272 to $1,600. The shah's planners calculated that so long as economic growth continued and the population leveled off at 60 million, Iran would leave the Third World and enter the first in the last years of the twentieth century.[39]

On this upward trajectory, the shah's absurdly extravagant military would play a vital role, shielding Iran's oil wealth and driving modernization. The purchase of foreign weapons systems would require local logistics and maintenance facilities that, in time, would burgeon into local assembly and production plants manned and managed by Iranians.[40] This indigenous arms production capability and emphasis on technology would employ an expanding educated workforce, while tens of thousands of previously illiterate, innumerate conscripts wrestled profitably with new concepts and equipment. An expanded military would build modern ports, airfields and garrisons in remote, previously inaccessible provinces.

ROOTS OF THE ISLAMIC REVOLUTION

That was the theory. In practice, the muscle-bound military creamed off most of Iran's 25 percent annual GDP growth in the 1970s, diverted most of the educated elite from more productive civilian occupations and necessitated an influx of foreign technicians, eroding Iran's faith in its own capabilities. Civil-military development projects had to be abandoned for lack of funds. At the same time, masses of landless peasants—bought out by the shah's White Revolution and lured by its third (1962–68) and fourth (1968–73) development plans—migrated to the cities. Tehran swelled from a manageable capital of six million in 1956 to an unmanageable sixteen million by the mid-1970s. In the sprawling slums around the cities, the only social services were increasingly provided by Islamic organizations.[41] Here were roots of the 1979 revolution. Iran's militant clergy, tamed by the shah but never broken, returned to its three favorite themes whenever Iran's misery index worsened: foreign domination, despotism and injustice. The mullahs had successfully campaigned in the past against foreign concessions for railroads, forests, mines, banks, telegraphs, tobacco and oil. Now they began to agitate against the shah's embrace of Western weapons and development plans, which spread wealth to the rich elites, not the masses. One had only to contrast rich northern Tehran with the southern slums to see the impact of Iranian "development."[42] But the shah—lost in his martial reveries—ignored the mullahs and every other critic. "The shah is like a rich man who thumbs through catalogs and orders what takes his fancy without regard to the logistical and technical requirements or the cost," the British military attaché concluded in 1973. "The very catholicity of his tastes and the size of his orders create major problems. There is no coherent objective."[43]

Superficially, the 1970s found the shah at the peak of his powers. He called himself Shahanshah ("king of kings") and Aryamehr ("light of the Aryans"). His armed forces had quadrupled in size since the 1950s and his civilian bureaucracy had more than doubled. In some Iranian towns, more than half the people were employed by the Pahlavi state. The shah ruled as an autocrat, and did not hesitate to use the muscle conferred by his imposing armed forces.[44] He insisted that Bahrain was "the fourteenth province of Iran" until 1971, when he grudgingly recognized the independence of the island state only after the U.S. Navy had crowded in to replace the departing British. To compensate himself for the loss, he seized two disputed islands from the United Arab Emirates.[45] Iraq, which dominated the Shatt al-Arab channel, was forced to accept joint control of the waterway in 1975, or face war with the better-armed Iranians. To fend the shah off, Saddam Hussein permitted the Soviets to build bases in Iraq in exchange for $4 billion in military hardware, a development that raised worried eyebrows in Washington.[46]

Nixon had always viewed the shah as a regional stabilizer. It now appeared that Iran's dizzying military expenditures were producing the opposite effect. They were alarming the neighbors—"it is not only the Baathist dogmatists of Baghdad who see sinister omens in such developments"—and sapping the imperial regime.[47] One British diplomat ventured in 1973 that "if the shah keeps buying, Iraqis and Indians will ask for more from the Soviets, and the shah will have driven his regional rivals into the Soviet pocket by going too far too quickly." Washington wrung its hands over the shah's escalating ambitions. Once content to be a Middle Eastern heavyweight, he now wanted to dominate South and even *East* Asia as well. After India defeated Pakistan in 1971, the shah grandly named himself "the Protector of Pakistan," vowing to "play a much bigger role in a future Indo-Pakistani War than he had in 1971" and to annex Pakistani Baluchistan "if Pakistan ever disintegrated."[48]

Nixon resented the shah's hubris but didn't dare rein him in. Whereas the Israelis bought their American weapons with U.S. foreign aid dollars, the Iranians spent their own dollars, and big sales of advanced weaponry were as good a way as any to quiet Congress and work off America's trade deficit. Thus, the shah got nearly everything he asked for. When Muhammed Reza told an abashed Secretary of Defense James Schlesinger that he needed Harpoon missiles to defend the Indian Ocean and an aerial refueling capability to extend Iranian power as far as Taiwan, Australia and South Africa, Schlesinger swallowed hard and (diplomatically) advised the shah to undertake "a more careful resource analysis," and strive to "integrate what Iran already had and maximize available forces" rather than add costly and possibly unworkable new capabilities. "Superior arms don't always achieve a country's objectives," Schlesinger hinted. And why could the shah not simply relax a bit under the American security umbrella? "We will face the music together," Schlesinger reassured the shah. Unfortunately, the shah wanted the entire orchestra for himself. "I remember the first time I went to the U.S. begging for two battalions of Sherman tanks," he reminisced grandly. "Now we are discussing F-15s! Russia calls Iran the 'self-appointed gendarme of the Persian Gulf.' And why not?"[49] Schlesinger left the question hanging. No one in Washington was ready to prick the shah's bubble, or even press him to reduce oil prices, which were gouging American consumers to fill Iranian arsenals. "The shah is a tough, mean guy. But he is our real friend," Secretary of State and National Security Adviser Henry Kissinger insisted. "We can't tackle him without breaking him."[50]

But someone in Washington *needed* to tackle the shah. Inside Iran, critical development tasks—schools, sanitation, health care and infrastructure—were being starved of funds to pay for the shah's tanks, jets, destroyers and helicopters. Wealth was being spread not to the general population, which was being ravaged by 50 percent annual inflation, but to "privileged elites . . . the royal family and the court, the entrepreneurs (almost all subcontractors for the large Western firms), the powerful merchants, the importers of spare parts and consumer goods, and the speculators fostered by an unbridled capitalism worthy of the nineteenth century."[51] Even a sympathetic American diplomat—"the shah remains our best hope"—wrung his hands at the shah's waste: "The military is a drain of funds and skilled manpower."[52] Worse, the shah's arms mania was accompanied by a creeping strategic paranoia. Armed to the teeth, Muhammed Reza saw enemies everywhere—in the Soviet Union, India, Afghanistan, Iraq and Yemen—but, as the British embassy noted, "this description of devious and linked machinations is about *perceptions* rather than the *actualities* of the perceptions of a lonely and suspicious man." Annual GDP growth of 14 percent in the 1970s was essentially poured down the drain as the shah spent precious billions on "a great deal of sophisticated ironmongery."[53] The CIA, which used Iran as a base to collect Middle Eastern and Soviet intelligence, never ceased worrying; "centuries-old abuses" were not being rectified. "Most reform is more apparent than real." In the early 1960s, the shah had launched his "White Revolution" to improve public health, literacy and development, but the results fell far short of the expectations. By 1970, more than 70 percent of Iranians over the age of ten were still illiterate. Most Iranians eked out a living on just six dollars a month, or less. There was only one doctor per 3,223 people, and just twelve hospital beds for every 10,000 patients. More than 40 percent of Iran's (large) families still lived in a single room.[54]

When Iranians and foreigners complained of the shah's "insolent luxury" and mad military expenditures—33 percent of the Iranian budget in the 1970s—these were the social facts on which they based their complaints. In a typical year, the shah would spend $1 billion or more on defense and just $60 million on health, education and welfare programs.[55] Worse, his weapons buys would—British intelligence concluded—almost certainly be "obsolete by the time Iranians were actually trained to use them."[56] Pledged to an anticorruption campaign, the shah left untouched "the most notorious members of his entourage and family." He apparently left most others untouched too, according to the U.S. embassy's sources in the 1970s: "Corruption permeates the whole of Iranian society from the Royal Family down to the lowest bureaucrat; Iranians are completely cynical about their baksheesh system, and the government's anti-corruption drive has proven futile."[57] Although the shah broke up Iran's feudal estates and redistributed land to smallholders, he never got around to "providing services to the new landholders to supplant those traditionally obtained from feudal landlords." He also didn't resist the temptation to annex some of the lands to his own swollen holdings, or give them to favorite courtiers like SAVAK director General Nematollah Nassiri, who somehow became the biggest landholder around the Caspian Sea on an army salary. This left a new class of peasants stranded in their arid deserts without water, markets, roads, schools, clinics or even enlightened administrators.[58]

An American diplomat who toured the Iranian provinces in 1973 was appalled by the low quality of the shah's bureaucrats. He cited Abdolhassan Jahanandish—governor of Kashmar—as a depressingly typical example.

> Overweight and frustrated, Abdolhassan Jahanandish leads an unhappy life as governor. He speaks a smattering of English and holds degrees from Shiraz in the seemingly unrelated fields of literature and radiology. He was sent to this Class II *farmandarante* [governorship] as purgatory after a scandal with a female *bakhshdar* [district governor]. His wife has contributed to his downfall by having her own affair with another man. He drinks too much and composes obscene parodies of the great Iranian and Arab poets.

Governor Jahanandish bored his American visitor with tearful descriptions of his year in America on a Fulbright scholarship. It was clearly the best thing that had ever happened to him, far better, at any rate, than life as governor of the desert towns of Kashmar, Nain and Yazd, where the White Revolution was not making appreciable inroads. "He has an unending supply of photos from that trip," the American grumbled.[59]

While the imperial administration sputtered, the Shiite clergy emerged as the principal force of opposition in Iran's towns and villages. Whereas Sunni sheikhs are generally state employees, the Shiite mullah lives from contributions of the faithful, "with whom he shares prosperity or poverty, joys and sorrows." Less exposed to SAVAK repression than secular activists, the mullahs enjoyed a small degree of immunity to discuss religion *and* politics with their flock. Prayer leaders inveighed against social injustice, moral rot and corruption, which was widely understood to mean Pahlavi rule and American influence.⁶⁰ That tight political connection between the Shiite clergy and the Iranian people at all levels of society— paid for in blood, several of Iran's ranking ayatollahs were tortured and killed by SAVAK—would explain the speed and ease with which Khomeini's "bare-handed revolutionaries" later swept away the shah and his seemingly invincible imperial army.

"The Shah Is No Longer Willing to Play the Role of American Satellite"

The shah himself was a funny man, afflicted, in the words of the British embassy, with delusions of grandeur—"folie de grandeur"—and strategic paranoia that caused him to "see the Soviet threat everywhere." The CIA also remarked the shah's moodiness—"from deep gloom to firmness"—and his unwillingness to continue "as an American satellite in the Middle East."⁶¹ Flush with oil revenues, the shah suddenly felt richer and tougher than the Western powers, which were energy dependent and suffering stagflation. A journalist noted the parade of Western statesmen to the shah's chalet in St. Moritz, and his condescending treatment of them: "'Now look,' he'd tell the premiers and ministers, 'you don't know how to govern and that's why you don't have any money' . . . The world heard him out meekly and swallowed even the bitterest admonitions because it couldn't take its eyes off the gold pyramid piling up in the Iranian desert."⁶² Washington had tried to trade advanced weaponry for real progress inside Iran—cleaner, more democratic government and improved social services—but had been essentially blackmailed by the shah, who never failed to remind the U.S. embassy that the French, Germans, British and even the Soviets were lining up to sell him all the advanced ships, aircraft and tanks he wanted if the Americans wouldn't.⁶³ "The shah would prefer to make these purchases in the U.S., but has made it clear that he will turn elsewhere if this proves too difficult" was a regular refrain in American diplomatic and intelligence reports. That threat sufficed to free the shah from the strictures of annual State Department reviews of the Iranian economy, which often advised *against* American arms sales. Of course feeding the shah a rich diet of "cake"—the British embassy term for arms sales to Iran—had political consequences, as the American chargé in Tehran warned in 1973: "Our position in Iran is closely associated with the *consequences* of this arms buildup."[64]

"WE DON'T WANT DEMOCRACY AS YOU HAVE IT IN THE WEST"

Political opposition to the shah quickened in the late 1960s, and the "consequences" feared by the U.S. embassy began to emerge. Big-city universities like Tehran, Shiraz and Tabriz were the focal points. There students like future Iranian president Mahmoud Ahmadinejad chafed at the nepotism and corruption of the Pahlavi state. Even the shah's wife did. In a conversation with U.S. ambassador Douglas MacArthur II, Empress Farah deplored the Iranian habits of "flattery and sycophancy." Iran, she scoffed, "is a country where men buy newspaper ads to congratulate their bosses when they get promoted," and "all classes of people had been corrupted."[65] Iranians also bridled at the shah's imperious rejection of democracy as an option for Iran. "We don't want democracy as you have it in the West," Muhammed Reza declared. "Democracy means justice, equality and the right to express yourself." Iranians could not "absorb" such a system; they would never "feel natural in it." They would feel more natural in the Pahlavi system, which became notorious for its tyranny. In 1972, the U.S. embassy protested the typical case of Sadiq Behdad, a successful Tehran lawyer and "pillar of the establishment," who was plucked off the street and thrown in jail for seven years. His crime? To have received a letter of condolence from an exiled Iranian general upon the death of a relative.[66]

Although they shed no tears for connected "pillars of the establishment," Iranian students resented the shah's efforts to control *their* activities and curriculum. In the early seventies, riots and student strikes became regular events on campus. When the shah cracked down on student protests of tuition and bus fare hikes, the protests became overtly political. Tehran University closed its engineering, science and law schools because they had become "hotbeds" of dissent. "The government must reduce the gap between itself and the students," the American ambassador in Tehran wrote home to Washington. Already in 1971, revolution was in the air, and the shah's riot police were making regular forays onto campus armed with tear gas, riot clubs and assault rifles.[67] The shah ordered mass arrests of striking students, jailed student leaders (or packed them off to remote army posts) and planted college-age SAVAK agents on the campus and in the classrooms.

No one was spared. Iran under SAVAK was like East Germany under Stasi. A journalist told the story of an old man at a Tehran bus stop on a hot, humid day. "It's so oppressive," he gasped as he staggered into the shelter. "You can't catch your breath." An alert SAVAK agent posted in the bus shelter hastily followed up: "So it is; it's getting more and more oppressive and people are fighting for air." "Too true," the winded man said, sighing. "Such heavy air, so oppressive." The SAVAK agent stood and marched the graybeard off to jail. "Now you'll have a chance to regain your strength." Younger Iranians understood that words like "oppressive," "dark," "abyss," "burden" or "collapse" were forbidden terms under the shah. The plays of Shakespeare and Molière were banned in Pahlavi Iran because they satirized royal and aristocratic behavior.[68] During Muhammed Reza's thirty-seven-year reign, an estimated five hundred thousand Iranians were arrested, imprisoned or detained in SAVAK's six thousand jails. Thousands were tried in special courts; thousands were tortured and assassinated. The web of vigilance was spun by the agency's sixty thousand agents guided by three million informants.[69] The worst punishment for Iranian students not actually killed, maimed or locked up by riot police or torturers was a peculiarly Iranian form of detention called "living death." Students released into such "lifelong limbo" were promised "no degree, no work, and no travel," which—in status-, travel- and credentials-conscious Iran—was as good as a death sentence. "No wonder," an American diplomat observed, "university students comprise the bulk of terrorists in Iran."[70]

"THE SHAH NOW LISTENS TO SAVAK MORE THAN ANYONE ELSE"

Another American diplomat who traveled with President Nixon during his visit to Iran in 1972 was "struck by the level of internal discontent, even at fairly high levels, and with the degree of disillusionment with corruption in government." Most of all, Iranians resented the "increasing isolation and megalomania of the shah, and his unwillingness to listen to criticism."[71] The shah, an American diplomat observed in 1972, "now listens to SAVAK more than anyone else," but SAVAK was increasingly unreliable; "their corruption has grown with their power." With sixty thousand agents on its payroll by 1972, SAVAK had become an unethical state within a state. It was credibly rumored that SAVAK officers would fling businessmen or public servants into jail as a means of seizing their bank accounts and other assets. "A man needs more than material wealth," an American in Tehran wrote. "He needs spiritual freedom, and *that's* what's missing in Iran today."[72]

Iranian spirits came under attack in the mosque as much as the university. Like his father, Muhammed Reza curbed the powers of the clerics, declaring that "religion has nothing to do with politics and the mullahs should keep away from such matters." Iran, the shah argued, "remained a backward country only because religious priests [had] kept the people ignorant."[73] He feared a scenario sketched by the Americans as early as 1970: Islamic revolution, with left-wing intellectuals allying with the religious right as they had during the Mosaddeq period. The explosiveness of Tehran, Ambassador MacArthur wrote Washington in March 1970, stemmed from its social composition; it contained the most- and the least-educated people in Iran. Seventy-five percent of the nation's college students were there—mainly in northern Tehran—but southern Tehran housed "the bulk of the city's population in slum conditions." That "Persian-style Marxian *lumpenproletariat* was poorly educated and highly ignorant." If "any tendency to activism developed in [southern Tehran], it would be in a reactionary obscurantist direction under the *ulema*." The "left wing intellectuals of the universities"—there were thirty thousand university students enrolled in Iran and thirty-seven thousand abroad when MacArthur wrote—would have to join that essentially right-wing revolution, or be left on the sidelines.[74] MacArthur was predicting with astonishing accuracy the Islamic revolution that would topple the shah eight years later. The mullahs and their masses would seek to end the "great occultation"—and install Khomeini as the long-lost Twelfth Imam—and the student and union radicals would use the Shiite Messiah to sweep away the oppressive monarchy.[75]

"ANTI-AMERICANISM HAS SPREAD AND INTENSIFIED . . ."

The shah's close alliance with the United States and the burgeoning number of U.S. advisers in Iran caused an upsurge of anti-Americanism. That surge set in during the 1960s, when the shah granted "extraterritoriality" to American civilian and military advisers—meaning they could not be tried in Iranian courts for crimes committed in Iran—and when northern Tehran began to take on some of the Americanized qualities of the Baghdad "Green Zone." "One thing that has struck me since coming back to Iran," British diplomat Charles Wiggin wrote the Foreign Office in February 1965, "is the extent to which anti-Americanism has spread and intensified in the last ten years. Our more sophisticated Persian friends are always going on now about the Americans' clumsiness, their way of life, their numbers, their lack of understanding, their fear of Persian food and drink, and so on." The mantle of loathing that had long enveloped the British "seems now to have settled squarely on the Americans' shoulders." Because of their long subjugation to the British and the Russians, the Iranians had a phobia about "foreign domination," which they now attached to the United States.

The Americans had seated the shah in power, propped him up with military, economic and political support, liaised tightly with SAVAK and, as a French critic put it, "pumped the petrodollars out of Iran in exchange for needless armaments, industrial products and consumer goods." To the average Iranian, such "sales" were tantamount to pillage. Khomeini called U.S. exports "looting" in the cassette tapes that he circulated throughout Iran.[76] Wiggin reported that U.S. embassy personnel recognized the problem "but don't know what to do." The "basic problem is the very size of their official and military community" and the dictatorial methods of their ambassador: "The years have not reduced his arrogance, nor granted him tact."[77] In Washington, liberals like Senator J. William Fulbright and Representative Shirley Chisholm launched regular attacks on Nixon's complicity in the shah's despotism, human rights abuses and military spending, which would almost inevitably harm American long-term interests.[78] From his exile in Iraq's holy city of Najaf, Ayatollah Khomeini blasted the Americans and the shah. "You have torn up the very roots of our independence," he wrote Prime Minister Hoveida in 1967. America had replaced Britain as "the head of the imperialist serpent."[79]

CARTER AND KHOMEINI

President Jimmy Carter's administration inherited the bulked-up, increasingly unpopular Pahlavi empire. Its unpopularity was owed in part to the Ford administration, which had tiptoed behind the shah's back in December 1976, persuaded the

Saudis to increase their daily oil production from 8.6 to 11.6 million barrels, driven down oil prices and thus helped wreck the shah's White Revolution.[80] Carter, who emphasized human rights far more than Nixon or Ford, was genuinely alarmed by scandals emanating from Iran, like the Rex Cinema affair in August 1978, when a movie theater in Abadan had been set on fire and its doors chained shut while the wild patrons beat helplessly on the doors until they died. The atrocity was widely blamed on SAVAK, who had chased anti-shah activists into the theater and lost them in the crowd. Although the CIA's National Intelligence Estimate for Iran in 1978—*Iran: Prospect through 1985*—maintained that "Iran is not in a revolutionary or even pre-revolutionary situation," there were powerful dissenters at the State Department, and CIA director Stansfield Turner proved less sanguine than his analysts in his private meetings with Carter's national security adviser, Zbigniew Brzezinski.[81] In October 1978, Stan Turner predicted that the shah would be swept away, not by democracy, but by "undemocratic elements," chief among them the seventy-six-year-old Ayatollah Ruhollah Khomeini, who, having been kicked out of Iraq, was then living in France. Using audiotapes slipped into Iran and played in the mosques, Khomeini—despite his age and fourteen-year exile—had become the most inspiring and generally acceptable voice of the anti-shah resistance. Interestingly, Turner and Brzezinski agreed that even if the liberalizing shah were forced out by religious reactionaries, the U.S. government would be helpless to intervene. "There would be real problems with Congress," Turner wrote. "So many liberal members of Congress believe the Shah is so undemocratic that they would not tolerate a program to keep him in power." The most the Americans would be able to do to arrest the slide toward religious fundamentalism would be *psychological* operations to "inform the world and the Iranians as to the character of the Shah's opposition."[82]

"HE'S A DEFECTIVE PERSONALITY"

The revolution that toppled Shah Muhammed Reza Pahlavi achieved its object surprisingly easily. Having spent three decades arming his military and police to the teeth and staffing SAVAK with agents, vigilantes and informers, the shah was expected to fight to the bitter end. Instead, riddled with cancer, he went out with a whimper. Iran hand Kermit Roosevelt—who had buttressed the shah against

Mosaddeq in 1953 and was consulted again by the State Department in 1978—had always predicted that the shah would fold. "He's a defective personality," Roosevelt told a colleague. He'll be swept away by his own "failure of will."[83] Secretary of State Cyrus Vance had seen this coming. Whereas the CIA—with its heavy reliance on rosy human intelligence from SAVAK—did not "see what was actually happening to the mullahs, merchants and colonels under modernization forced by an auto-cratic, repressive ruler," the State Department—with its big, inquisitive embassy staff in Tehran—did.[84] In the fall of 1978, U.S. ambassador William Sullivan de-scribed the shah as "a man filled with self-doubt, a man who believed nothing could work, who was no longer able to analyze events." For the first time, the shah took no apparent pleasure in the approval of $10 billion in new American military hard-ware. He was alternately lazy and "unhinged," telling Sullivan at one point that he might deliberately install a civilian government so corrupt and incompetent that it would "make the people clamor for an authoritarian military government to pre-vent chaos." When Sullivan suggested that it might be simpler just to go straight for the military crackdown, the shah quailed at the prospect, fearing that mass casualties would make it impossible for his eighteen-year-old son Reza, a cadet at the U.S. Air Force Academy in Colorado Springs, to inherit the throne.[85] Not sur-prisingly, American decision makers were giving up on the shah and looking to the four-hundred-thousand–man Iranian military as the new savior. Even if the shah fell, the generals might be able to negotiate a moderate transition with Khomeini and insist on continuation of a pro-American policy.[86]

The fall and winter of 1978–79 were the critical months. At New Year's Eve celebrations in Tehran, Ardeshir Zahedi threw a party for Western reporters; he raised his champagne glass to the shah's new government, formed by Shahpour Bakhtiar, and announced that it was staffed with Iran's best and brightest and was "ready to roll."[87] The shah continued to waver between halfhearted repression and conciliation. Ambassador Sullivan warned that conciliation—like the mass dis-missal of senior SAVAK officers or amnesty for political prisoners—was just "feeding the crocodiles." The anti-shah coalition of Islamic fundamentalists, students, oil field workers and Tudeh communists alarmed Washington and the Iranian estab-lishment. Americans and Iranians alike began to look past the shah for solutions, like a hard military government, that would clean things up.

General Hossein Rabii visited the U.S. embassy and complained that "His Majesty is simply not being himself. He has got to assert himself, or we'll *make* him assert himself."[88] Khomeini sounded anything but reasonable in his speeches, which dripped venom and foreshadowed a tyranny that might be worse than the shah's: "You intellectuals . . . want all the freedoms . . . freedom that will drag our nation to the bottom . . . Islam says, whatever good there is exists thanks to the sword and in the shadow of the sword! People cannot be made obedient except with the sword! The sword is the key to paradise, which can be opened only for holy warriors!"[89] For now, the imperial army still held the swords, and generals Manuchehr Khosrowdad and Gholam Ali Oveissi talked openly of a coup to keep the shah in power. Younger generals like Rabii—encouraged by the U.S. embassy—were willing to let the shah go, but wanted a purge to wipe out the clerical and communist opposition and seat themselves firmly in power.[90]

RIFTS IN THE CARTER ADMINISTRATION

In Washington, there was a split between Vance's State Department and Brzezinski's NSC. State—guided by Sullivan's cables from Tehran—thought the shah was doomed and that Washington needed to reach some accommodation with the Khomeini camp; Brzezinski, joined by Defense Secretary Harold Brown and Energy Secretary James Schlesinger, thought that the shah might relinquish some domestic authority, but must hold on to military and foreign affairs to maintain Iran as an "island of stability." The fifty-year-old Brzezinski, a Pole whose family had been forced into exile by the Nazis and the Soviets, spoke of an "arc of crisis" in the Middle East—a wave of unrest in Islamic countries, beginning with Iran—that the Soviets were either fomenting or exploiting. "Zbig" persuaded Carter that "secret contacts" with Khomeini could never be kept secret, and would merely demoralize the shah, Bakhtiar and the army.[91] President Carter had grave doubts about the shah, but hesitated to throw him over. "Our friendship and our alliance with Iran is one of our important bases on which our entire foreign policy depends," he said in late October 1978. Graham Allison, the dean of Harvard's Kennedy School of Government, would later cite this wishful "interaction between intelligence analysts and policy-makers" as central to the fiasco of the shah's fall. "Top officials came to regard [the shah's] stability as a premise of American policy." No viable alternatives were worked up; no tough choices made. "So stable was the premise of the shah's survival," the House Intelligence Committee subsequently discovered, "that it limited both the search for an accurate understanding of Iran's internal situation, and the receptiveness of intelligence-users to such analyses."[92]

In Washington to promote such wishful thinking and lobby for even stiffer backing, Iranian ambassador Ardeshir Zahedi worked hard on Brzezinski, Brown and Schlesinger, and also reached out to powerful friends like Henry Kissinger, David and Nelson Rockefeller and eighty-three-year-old John McCloy, who, as chairman of the Chase Manhattan Bank in 1953, had advised Eisenhower and Dulles on Operation Ajax. They all urged the shah to "get tough," to rearrest political prisoners, to shut down the press, to flood the streets with troops and tanks and to secure "hard-line" American aid for a crackdown. Zahedi called Barbara Walters at ABC News, to get her too fretting about "declining U.S. support for the Shah."[93] In Tehran, U.S. ambassador Sullivan resented Zahedi's lobbying, as well as the back-channel efforts of Brzezinski and his staff—David Aaron and Navy captain Gary Sick—to put a gloss on even the worst news out of Iran. "Who is the American ambassador?" Sullivan asked in one of his telegrams. The shah had become a losing proposition, and the more America supported him the more it stood accused of "imperialism." Carter grew frustrated with the infighting and with Sullivan's "smart-ass attitude and smart-ass cables."[94] He sent a harsh note to Stan Turner at the CIA: "I am not satisfied with the quality of political intelligence out of Iran."[95]

"Thinking the Unthinkable"

Violent street battles blazed across Iran on November 5, 1978. The shah complained to Sullivan that he would have no choice but to turn matters over to a military government under General Gholam Reza Azhari and let them "hang ten mullahs or burn ten mosques." The shah and Azhari would try to split the moderate and radical clergy and would try to entice the moderate opposition National Front into a coalition, but the shah held out little hope for either course, telling Sullivan that if his military government failed, "he was finished."[96] Years of SAVAK repression had crushed Iran's secular parties, including Mosaddeq's old National Front; only the Shiite clergy remained intact and powerful as a political force. And Khomeini and the mullahs were attracting broad opportunistic support. In the months before Khomeini's return to Iran in February 1979, all opposition elements—moderate,

Islamic and even communist—marched under the green banner of Islam chanting the name of Allah.[97] To Americans, this was perplexing and unnerving. On November 9, Sullivan sent a despairing telegram to Washington titled "Thinking the Unthinkable." It again recommended making discreet American contacts with Khomeini and the mullahs to assure that they would not push their revolution too far if the shah fell. President Carter exploded when confronted with Sullivan's cable. "No one had warned him that things were *this* serious," with the American ambassador in Tehran actually preparing to dump the shah. Carter summoned Vance, Brzezinski, Stan Turner, Harold Brown and NSA head Admiral Bobby Inman to the White House to explain the lack of early warning. Their explanations were not reassuring: the United States had too long relied on SAVAK for intelligence on the domestic Iranian scene and had focused intelligence assets on the Soviet threat, not the shah's internal opposition. Moreover, Sullivan's embassy had been slow to winkle out the threats posed by the Shiite clergy.[98]

November and December 1978 passed with the diplomats and intelligence operatives alternately sounding gloomy and optimistic. Carter sent Treasury Secretary Michael Blumenthal to Tehran to meet with the shah and report his impressions to the White House. Blumenthal had lunch with Shah Muhammed Reza and was astonished. His State Department briefing packet spoke of a shah "still firmly in power," determined "not to step down." The shah struck Blumenthal as sullen and defeated; the treasury secretary said he had been "shocked by the Shah's demoralized appearance." He appeared not even to hear Blumenthal's repeated assurances that President Carter would stand with the shah in a full-blown crisis. Senate Majority Leader Robert Byrd also posted through Tehran in November and characterized the shah as a beaten man.[99] Carter took Blumenthal's advice to appoint sixty-eight-year-old George Ball as an analyst extraordinaire, to sift through all the conflicting reports from State, the NSC and the CIA to determine just *what* the United States ought to do about Iran. Ball worked hard for two weeks, read classified and unclassified reports from all sources and then met with Carter on December 13, 1978, to render his verdict. The shah was finished, vomited out in "a national regurgitation by the Iranian people." America's wisest course now would be to "work out the transfer of power to responsible hands before Khomeini comes back and messes everything up."

Ball's preferred solution was to turn Iran over to the National Front—a vestige of Mosaddeq—with its broad range of parties from moderates to radical, noncommunist leftists. He specifically recommended forty or fifty "notables" left over from the 1950s, moderates who had worked with Mosaddeq. But the CIA objected that the National Front and its "notables" were "ineffectual," torn by "decades-old ideological and personal feuds that [would] weaken its cohesion." The National Front had no real program other than calling for restoration of the 1906 constitution, which would have made the shah a constitutional monarch. That was not thrilling stuff, and not powerful either. Khomeini, the CIA warned, "can bring out the demonstrators and rioters and plunge Iran into chaos . . . It is the religious leadership that can bring out the mobs, not the National Front." Ball and the CIA agreed that the Iranian military held the wild card: they would "play the pivotal role in future political developments in Iran."[100]

CHAPTER 11

· ⚔ ·

DESERT ONE

PRESIDENT CARTER WAS HEARTENED. The combination of a weak but respectable National Front and a strong army might hold. "I expect the shah to maintain power in Iran and for the present difficulties to be resolved," he told a press conference in mid-December.[1] George Ball urged Carter to tell the shah to leave Iran, turn affairs over to a reliable government and serve as a distant "regent" until things cooled down. "I can't tell another head of state what to do," Carter protested, clearly not relishing such a conversation with the prickly shah. "You can tell a friend what you *think*," Ball persisted. "One of the obligations of friendship is to give advice, particularly to a man who is cut off from the normal sources, who is surrounded by sycophants and out of touch with his people." Carter refused to have that conversation with the shah, and Ball, throwing up his hands in frustration, left for a vacation in Florida.[2]

With Ball in Florida, Zbigniew Brzezinski reopened his attack. Carter must stand by the shah, to reassure allies and deter the Soviets and the Iranian communists. "Geopolitics is not a kindergarten class," Zbig growled to the president.[3] Ball's National Front notables were used-up hacks who wouldn't stand a chance against Khomeini's mobs. No, the United States would have to vest its hopes in the Iranian military, which was still loyal to the shah. Brzezinski drafted a letter for Carter to send to the shah that baldly enjoined him to use force against the demonstrators.

Vance was horrified, and warned Carter that Brzezinski was recommending a course that would end in "a thousand deaths"; others thought tens of thousands. But Carter liked Brzezinski's aggressiveness, and agreed only to let Vance make the recommendation of repression more ambiguous. The letter was never sent, but when Sullivan in Tehran heard of it, he fired off what might have been his last telegram: Carter's policy was "shortsighted and did not understand where U.S. interests lie." Sullivan still wanted American overtures to Khomeini as a hedge against the shah's removal. Carter was furious, barking that he wanted "Sullivan's ass."

"No Coup Would Succeed"

Sullivan's ass was saved by a surge of violence in Tehran, which shifted everyone's attention back to the Iranian streets. Carter sent General Robert Huyser, second-in-command of U.S. forces in Europe, to Tehran on January 3, 1979, to speak with the senior Iranian generals and gauge their attitudes. Huyser discovered that none of them had faith in the new Bakhtiar government—which formed the day Huyser landed in Tehran—and none were prepared to trust the new prime minister. They feared he would sell them out to the opposition. What the generals also feared were corruption investigations; much military spending had stuck to their fingers over the years, and they had gotten rich. Their need to preempt a "clean hands" campaign may have explained their bloodthirstiness. The seven Iranian generals Huyser met with expressed their readiness to kill "a hundred thousand Iranians" if necessary, to restore the shah or an authoritarian regime. What they needed—all seven declared—was unflinching U.S. backing.[4] Huyser would not give it; they must stick with Bakhtiar, he told them. If they freelanced, the United States would dump them.

General Huyser slept at the embassy residence every night, where he argued with Ambassador Sullivan. Huyser was telling Washington that the military command structure was intact and that 80 percent of the troops would follow orders to fire on their fellow citizens. Sullivan heaped scorn on projections like that; the army was near collapse, he said, and would not fire on its countrymen. The Iranian generals felt the air seeping out of the American commitment. Even the influential Brzezinski had failed in his efforts to put the USS *Constellation* with its eighty strike aircraft on station near Iran as an earnest of American support. Carter had deemed the act too provocative and placed the carrier at Singapore instead. U.S. support for the shah and his military was crumbling. On January 13, Ambassador Sullivan sent an aide to meet with Ayatollah Muhammed Behesti, who was Khomeini's man in Tehran. It was the first U.S. contact with the ayatollahs, and Behesti declared himself unimpressed by the Iranian military. "No coup would succeed," he deadpanned.[5]

The shah had been planning to leave Iran for some time, to treat his cancer and permit a "cooling off" of Iran's fraught situation. He flew on January 16, 1979, headed for Walter Annenberg's estate in Palm Springs, California. The moment the shah was in the air, joyous demonstrations broke out in every Iranian city. Vance, Brzezinski and Carter agreed that the shah must not land in the United States when he was so exorbitantly unpopular. They had his flight rerouted to Egypt, where the shah became a guest of Anwar Sadat instead. Sadat, who judged Khomeini "a lunatic madman . . . who has turned Islam into a mockery," welcomed the shah. The Shiite-Sunni divide, which had opened in AD 632 over the question of succession to the Arab caliphate, had since acquired deep political overtones, which Khomeini's rise sharpened.[6] Although Brzezinksi and Brown in Washington and General Alexander Haig at NATO headquarters in Belgium were still for unleashing the Iranian military against the ayatollahs—"Give the officers a go-ahead," Brown urged Brzezinski—Carter refused to roll the dice. Ball and the CIA had always warned against the military crackdown pushed by Brzezinski; if the army mutinied, Iran might dissolve into civil war, and the armed forces would cease to exist as a reliable pillar of order.

When Captain Gary Sick, Brzezinski's Iran specialist, convened an extraordinary meeting of Iran analysts from State and the CIA on January 17, they agreed that a coup had no prospect of success. In Tehran, Huyser had tried to persuade his seven generals to take over the striking oil fields in Khuzistan and use army troops to get them working again, but the generals had balked at even that limited operation. If unwilling to take on the southwestern oil patch, how would they take on the whole country? Sick's working group came to the same conclusion as Huyser: Iran was Khomeini's. America's best course would be to let the ayatollahs take power and exhibit their own incompetence. They were already floundering. "Workers' councils" were taking over the factories and oil fields. Without competent managers, capital or spare parts, Iranian industry was operating at half its prerevolution capacity. Landless peasants were swarming onto the big estates, but without the promised state investments in agriculture. The unemployment rate had shot up to 30 percent. An inflation rate of 50 percent remained a fact of life. Iran's *mostazefin*—

the disinherited poor—suffered cruelly, as did the middle classes.[7] Prime ministers turned over quickly. Bakhtiar, and then his successor, Mehdi Bazargan, and then his successor, Abolhassan Bani-Sadr, all complained of "a dictatorship of the clergy." The already inefficient Iranian administration was clotting up with "ignorant and arrogant mullahs." Instead of fighting a futile rearguard action to save the shah, Washington should cultivate contacts with moderate Islamic clergy, officers and politicians, who would counter Khomeini's radicalism and take over when Khomeini's dream palace crashed back to earth.[8]

On February 1, 1979, Ayatollah Khomeini arrived in Tehran from Paris to a riotous reception. Though Carter, Brown, Brzezinski and even Vance still insisted that the army command held the fate of Iran in its hands, leaks from the State Department told the American press a different story. The shah was finished; Khomeini was ascendant. Leaks threatened to drive policy; if the American people accepted that the shah would fall, Carter would look foolhardy in backing him. Furious, Carter summoned the sixteen most senior State Department officials to the White House and told them that he would fire the head of any department that leaked.

In Tehran, Khomeini moved fast to solidify his "provisional revolutionary government." He fired Prime Minister Bakhtiar—whom Carter press secretary Jody Powell had just told CBS News would not be fired—and appointed Mehdi Bazargan, a moderate from the National Front. Bakhtiar, Khomeini scoffed, was a Western tool: "The superpowers will keep a person for twenty or thirty years in order to use him on a rainy day as their own servant while presenting him in disguise as a national personality, as in the case of Bakhtiar."[9] Even with tepid American backing, the army's hour had seemingly arrived. Khomeini's *komitehs*—Islamic militias and revolutionary courts—were already rounding up Pahlavi courtiers and SAVAK operatives. It would not be long before they moved on to military officers and middle-class businessmen.[10] General Rabii ordered patrols of fighter aircraft and helicopters to orbit Tehran and remind Khomeini where *real* power lay. Rabii and the others made a last appeal to Ambassador Sullivan for support; he relayed the request to Washington, but Vance and Carter offered nothing concrete. Brzezinski knew that Rabii was weighing a coup—despite a pro-Khomeini mutiny in the air force in early February—and called Sullivan to ask whether Rabii's coup would succeed. The Iranian military, after all, was the second most powerful in the Middle East after Israel's. Surely *it* could put a stop to Khomeini's ragtag militants. Sullivan didn't take the call, but later characterized Brzezinski's interest in the coup as "bullshit," and added: "Do you want me to translate that into Polish?"[11]

"ALL OUR INVESTMENT IN AN INDIVIDUAL, RATHER THAN A COUNTRY, CAME TO NAUGHT"

Like the Americans, the Iranian generals threw in the towel. Sullivan cabled Washington on February 27, warning that anti-American sentiment was boiling over in the streets and the press, and that the U.S. embassy could no longer be protected. He and his subordinates recommended that the embassy staff be reduced to "six officers and a vicious dog."[12] (When the embassy was actually seized eight months later, Carter must have wished that he had heeded the warning.) With America in retreat, General Rabii declared his "neutrality," and saw most of his circle arrested or chased into exile before he himself was dragged to a wall and shot by a firing squad.[13] Now the army stood down and let the demonstrations wash over it. The shah's Immortals, reviewed by Colin Powell sixteen months earlier, did not "fight to the last man" after all. They "cracked like a crystal goblet on the first day of fighting," Powell observed from the Pentagon. "In Iran, all our investment in an individual, rather than in a country, came to naught. When the Shah fell, our Iran policy fell with him."[14] In the United States, citizens and lawmakers expressed outrage at the "intelligence failure" over Iran. How could Americans have been caught so unprepared by the shah's sudden and ignominious exit?

As after 9/11, Congress called for a "major program of reconstruction" for America's intelligence services. Human intelligence and "analytic competence" in the Middle East would have to be improved.[15] Eric Rouleau, *Le Monde*'s chief Middle East correspondent, observed that "from the very beginning of the Iranian Revolution, the West—and particularly the United States—seems to have been struck by a peculiar sort of political blindness." The first signs of revolt in the 1970s, the "explosions of rage in the spring of 1978, first in Tabriz and then in Qom," and then the strikes and "immense demonstrations by millions of Iranians" were variously attributed by American analysts to "obscurantist mullahs" or the "'fanaticism' of the Iranian people." Rouleau chided Americans for "labeling an entire people fanatics simply because they were virtually unanimous in expressing their will." Rouleau found that no one in Washington believed that the Iranian masses would choose "a reactionary old cleric in a revolt against a man who had devoted his entire life to modernizing his country." In that respect, Americans failed to grasp that "the concepts of economic development current in the West—where quick material gain is often the only valid criterion—do not necessarily correspond to the true needs and interests of *developing* nations."[16]

The shah spent most of 1979 pleading with the Carter administration for permission to have his cancer treated in New York City. Carter was torn between his desire to succor the shah—an old American ally—and his awareness that to admit the shah into the United States would be a provocative act, in Iran and all across the Middle East. Reckless American policy—aiding the shah politically or militarily—might trigger renewed Arab use of the "oil weapon." Although oil demand was softer in 1979 because of a global recession and the arrival of North Sea and Alaskan supplies, the West was still vulnerable to an oil shock.[17] OPEC raised prices four times in five months in 1979—most sharply in June when war loomed between Iraq and Iran—and no one in Washington wanted to goad the cartel, especially when American inflation was surging past 11 percent and Carter's approval rating was tumbling below 30 percent.[18] In October 1979, Carter finally relented and the shah flew to New York. Viewed in the West as a principled and humanitarian decision, it was seen in Iran as conclusive evidence of American plotting to restore the shah to his throne.[19]

SEIZING THE "DEN OF SPIES"

Two weeks later, on November 4, 1979, sixty Iranian students—"following the Imam's line" to rid Iran of American influence—swarmed over the walls of the U.S. embassy in Tehran, stormed inside and took Americans hostage.[20] It was, as Mark Bowden put it, Iran's "Boston Tea Party," and it briefly united Iranians around the heroic *gerogan-girha*, or hostage-takers, and the gray-haired Imam Khomeini. Hundreds of thousands of Iranians jammed the streets around the embassy to chant hatred of the United States. Many looped laminated images of the Ayatollah Khomeini around their necks to display their allegiance to the Islamic revolution and to Khomeini, whom many believed *was* the long-sought Twelfth Imam—not his deputy—and the heaven-sent Mahdi, or messiah.[21] One of the hostage-takers found an unshredded top secret cable lying on CIA station chief Tom Ahern's desk. It had been written that morning and never sent, presumably because the hostage-takers interrupted Ahern. The telegram had been destined for CIA director Stansfield Turner, and while not exactly a reprise of Operation Ajax, it confirmed the darkest suspicions of the embassy militants:

> You asked me to comment at some point about our prospects for influencing the course of events. Only marginally, I would say, until the military recovers, and that is a process we can do almost nothing to affect. What we can do, and I am now working on, is to identify and prepare to support the potential leaders of a coalition of westernized political liberals, moderate religious figures, and (when they begin to emerge) western-oriented military leaders.[22]

From the American perspective, the most memorable aspect of the Iranian Revolution was the Iranian seizure of the U.S. embassy. That invasion of American territory was justified by the militants on the grounds that it was not an embassy at all, but a "Den of Spies . . . a place of espionage, a center for conspiracy against Iran."[23] The claim was overblown; there were only three CIA officers in Iran in 1979, and none of them spoke Farsi, for CIA collection in Iran had been focused on the Soviets across the northern border. One of the three CIA officers had been in Tehran for less than a week when the embassy was assaulted, and the gloomy warehouse where he and the other hostages were imprisoned was crammed with the data-processing and communications gear used to monitor Soviet broadcasting, communications and missile tests. Another of the three CIA officers, Bill Daugherty, was among the first to assert (in 2005) that Iranian president Mahmoud Ahmadinejad had been among the hostage-takers, and had been one of the most virulent: "I recognized him right off. . . . I remember so much his hatred of Americans. It just emanated from every pore in his body."[24]

The embassy takeover, its purported death blow to "imperialism" and the zeal of true believers like Ahmadinejad was the signal for Khomeini's "second revolution." The sixty most hard-core *gerogan-girha* had planned the embassy seizure to prevent Bazargan from "watering down the revolution" through a normalization of relations with the West, or a repeat of the 1953 coup.[25] Now, with hostages in hand and the Americans inflamed, there appeared to be little hope of normalization. Internally, there were fewer obstacles to what the militants really wanted: *umma*—a tranquil, classless, crime-free Muslim community infused with "the spirit of God."[26] Temporizers like Bazargan were immediately dumped, and the still suspect army was purged by the Islamic *pasdarans*, or revolutionary guards, and *komitehs*. Although Khomeini had not ordered the embassy takeover—indeed had not even known it was in the works—he now recognized its usefulness as a rallying cry. Iran's captains of industry were expropriated and driven into exile; their factories and headquarters nationalized by the Islamic Republic. Iran's prosperous middle class, reviled by Khomeini as "Westernized liberals," were harassed by ardent students. Secret documents procured in the captured U.S. embassy—the notorious "spy den documents," some real, some fabrications, some shredded and laboriously pasted back together—were used by the student leaders to denounce, disgrace and topple uncooperative politicians, tribal leaders and ayatollahs. Foes of the revolution stood accused of "intelligence with the enemy" and "pro-Western counterrevolution," charges that required no elaboration. Their mere mention sufficed to drive moderates into detention or the political wilderness.[27]

KHOMEINI'S ISLAMIC REPUBLIC

The new Khomeini regime made no secret of its totalitarian regional and global ambitions. Khomeini foxily refused to confirm or deny that he was the Twelfth Imam, leaving many Iranians to believe that he was, which made his purges just exactly what he wanted them to be: an assault by absolute good on the darkest evil.[28] A ministry of intelligence and security—answerable only to the supreme leader— took over the functions of SAVAK. The shah's hated Evin prison was emptied of revolutionaries and refilled with "un-Islamic elements." Abolhassan Bani-Sadr, who replaced Bazargan as Iranian president in February 1980, bravely sounded the alarm: "Denunciations, slander, torture, violence, massacres, prisons are nothing more than manifestations of a Stalinist society." Unfortunately, the supreme leader's presidents would be as tame as the shah's prime ministers had been. While Khomeini's handpicked "assembly of experts" drew up a new constitution that would vest near absolute power in the supreme leader (Khomeini, naturally), President Bani-Sadr vainly protested the overinvolvement of the clergy in Iranian politics—"there are too many Richelieus and Mazarins" at work—a remark that merely confirmed the mullahs in their conviction that he was too Westernized in outlook. Although Bani-Sadr was allowed to continue as Iranian president, his protests were gradually silenced by the supreme leader, the legislature (which was packed with Khomeini's creatures) and the supreme court (which was packed with Khomeini's judges). When Khomeini unleashed a "cultural revolution" in April 1980—aimed at the Westernized elites who still held jobs in big business, the universities, the civil service and the armed forces—the last voices of dissent in Iran were strangled. Eventually Bani-Sadr would be disqualified even from choosing his own prime minister; that too would be done by Khomeini and a like-minded "Guardian Council" of twelve intransigents.[29]

Thus empowered, the Iranian ayatollahs vowed to serve "as an example to the rest of the Islamic world." Iran's revolution, Deputy Prime Minister for Revolutionary Affairs Ebrahim Yazdi declared, had triggered "a new era of Islamic struggle." Islam, not liberal capitalism or Soviet-style communism, would "provide the ideological basis for change within Muslim countries." Convinced that Shiite Islam was a modern revolutionary movement as potent as fascism or communism, the Iranian revolutionaries scrapped Iran's hallowed 1906 constitution. The shah had regularly abused it—filling the *majlis* with tractable deputies—but the Iranians had always prided themselves on being a constitutional regime. Mosaddeq had risen to power by asserting his constitutional prerogatives, and the shah had occasionally been curbed by parliamentary foes. Now, as Ayatollah Nuri put it, "dealing with the affairs of the people would be the responsibility of qualified *mujtaheds* [Islamic law specialists], not of any secular representatives." Parliamentary wrangling to "make the law" was "an innovation that is against Islam." Better would be a dictatorial "Council of the Revolution" and "panels of religious scholars" who would interpret God's plan for the Iranian people.[30]

"Economics Is for Donkeys"

The empowerment of Iran's supreme leader, Ayatollah Khomeini, was well under way. Iran had always been a place where "power centers"—the shah's court, the imperial military, the bazaar merchants, National Front moderates, the ayatollahs in Qom—jostled for influence. It now appeared that the clerics had the upper hand, and they had got it, the CIA remarked, with little more than "pious generalities." Khomeini haughtily insisted that "economics is for donkeys" and "we did not make a revolution to cut the price of watermelons," but his selection of Bazargan—a friend of Bakhtiar and a reluctant foe of the shah—suggested that economics and melon prices were as important under the new regime as the old.[31] All of the shah's administration was still intact, as were the army and police. Iran's communist parties—the People's Fedayeen and the People's Mujahidin—were well armed and organized (far better than the *komitehs*), and the bazaar merchants could easily tilt back to the National Front or the army if Khomeini went too far too fast.[32]

Yet, as Bazargan complained to Oriana Fallaci in October 1979, "they've put a knife in my hand, but it's a knife with only a handle; others are holding the blade." The "others" were the mullahs, and the hostage crisis would be the first test of their radicalism.[33] Whereas the men Khomeini scornfully dubbed "the conciliatory officials"—Bazargan, Bani-Sadr and their ilk—saw the advantages of freeing the hostages to salvage American support—or just to temper American anger—the hard-liners around Khomeini and the "embassy militants" wanted to use the hostages as a bargaining chip.[34] They wanted to force Washington to unfreeze Iranian assets and take responsibility for Iran's problems, which would buy the new regime time (and money) to correct them. They also wanted to extort key symbolic concessions like the return of the shah—"our people have been subjected to much torment and suffering at the hands of that very person who is now in the U.S."—to Iran for a show trial.[35]

Although the new Iranian government had no love for Moscow—Khomeini criticized the Soviets for their treatment of Muslims in Soviet Central Asia and their invasion of Afghanistan—he reserved his harshest words for the United States. "We regard the Soviet Union as an expansionist state," he declared, "but the U.S. is a colonialist state." In the Iranian playbook, colonialism and imperialism were the cardinal sins.[36] Indeed despite the "neither East nor West" policy of the Iranian clergy, the Soviets tried to exploit Khomeini's "wrecking of the U.S. position in Iran." A 1980 CIA "straw-man paper" projecting Soviet reaction to the shah's fall had the Kremlin delighting in America's loss of its Iranian base and proxy: "The U.S. has been deprived of its lower-risk intervention option designed to secure the oil fields." Any U.S. incursions into Iran now would involve the certainty of war with the Islamic Republic and a much higher risk of Soviet intervention—to secure "Soviet strategic interests, oil fields and naval bases on the Iranian coast"—which naturally made incursions unlikely for any U.S. government focused on détente and still sweating off the hangover of Vietnam.

Moscow also relished the shah's fall as isolating Pakistan—"the Pak elite will be persuaded that the security of Pakistan depends on coming to terms with the USSR"—and strengthening Russia's hand in Afghanistan.[37] Iran's imprisonment of the U.S. embassy hostages for 444 days drove a wedge into the American-Iranian relationship that was impossible to work around. Iranian loathing of the United States—"Great Satan"—became policy. In addition to the return of the shah and all frozen Iranian cash and assets deposited in American banks, Khomeini demanded a U.S. government apology for America's years of support for the repressive Pahlavis and a guarantee that the United States would never again meddle in Iranian internal affairs. In Washington, Carter felt trapped; to accede to Khomeini's demands would cast the president as a wimpy appeaser. Like his successors, Carter decided to hit back at Iran, freezing their assets in the United States and stopping the import of Iranian oil.[38] Both measures were heavy blows to Iran; the oil boycott cratered Iran's government revenues, and of Iran's total cash reserves of $15 billion, more than half—$8 billion—were on deposit in the United States.[39] (One reason Kissinger, the Rockefellers and John McCloy had been pushing Carter to "get tough" was that the ayatollahs had been threatening to repudiate their debts to the Chase Manhattan Bank and other "imperialist" entities; Carter's asset freeze permitted Chase to declare the Iranian loans in default and seize the shah's cash deposits as compensation.)[40] Any hope the Americans had of empowering moderates in Tehran vanished with the decision to freeze and coerce. In Tehran, Khomeini reacted furiously (and with a sigh of relief); the Americans were beautifully playing the role of "serpent" and "corruption of the earth." Employment or other contact with the shah or Americans was treated as evidence of "espionage" and became grounds for arrest, torture or death. Iranian insiders warned that Khomeini had no incentive to release the hostages; on the contrary, the ayatollah considered that "Iran was less vulnerable to military action, retaliation or other dramatic moves so long as it held the hostages." One exile warned that the hostage crisis would likely become a "semi-permanent situation," with Iran indefinitely hugging the hostages tight to repel American invasion or sanctions.[41]

THE HOSTAGE CRISIS

The fall of the shah and the Iranian "Hostage Crisis," as it became known in the weeks after November 1979, destroyed the Carter presidency. Brzezinski called the hostage crisis "a political calamity for President Carter." America lost face and much else besides: two intelligence stations for monitoring the Soviets and cheap plentiful oil. The higher oil prices caused by the Iranian revolution helped spark the double-digit inflation and the recession that doomed Carter's reelection hopes.[42] Carter unwisely focused all his efforts on freeing the hostages, retreating inside the White House and renouncing travel. The Republicans jeered Carter's "disarray" and "weakness," and the media seized upon the president's "Rose Garden Strategy" and fanned it into a national obsession, network anchors enjoining perseverance and Walter Cronkite signing off nightly thus: "And that's the way it is, Thursday, [whatever date], 1979, the [numbered] day of captivity for the American hostages in Iran."[43] The Iranians relished Carter's predicament, but as one of the hostage-takers reflected in 2004, their cruel treatment of the embassy captives "had caused such tension between Iran and the U.S. that even now, after two decades, no one knows how to resolve it." The hostages were initially tied to chairs and blindfolded. When their captivity lengthened, they were moved to a windowless basement in a warehouse on the embassy grounds, walled off from each other by bookshelves, forbidden to speak and made to sleep on the floor. The CIA officers were regularly interrogated and beaten with rubber hoses. A gambit designed to energize the revolution and isolate reactionary elements had spun out of control: "We lost control of events within twenty-four hours . . . Things got out of hand and took their own course . . . Once the event got out of its student mold and turned into a hostage-taking, it became a long, drawn-out, and corrosive phenomenon."[44]

DESERT ONE

By April 1980, Carter, who had resisted Brzezinski's calls for a military rescue mission and aligned himself with Secretary of State Vance's efforts to find a diplomatic solution, finally relented. Although any U.S. military operation in Iran would be risky—the Soviet news agency TASS warned in December 1979 that any American use of force against Iran "would have the most dangerous consequences," perhaps including even Soviet occupation of northern Iran—the White House was desperate to get Carter out of the Rose Garden—by now ABC was running nightly broadcasts called "America Held Hostage"—and help him fend off increasingly impertinent attacks from Republican challenger Ronald Reagan.[45] Three times in the previous five months, the Iranians had scuttled painstakingly negotiated secret settlements. Khomeini was openly mocking the American president—"Mr. Carter is like a drowning man who would cling to anything coming his way"—and Carter looked weak and despondent.[46] In Paris for the last unsuccessful round of negotiations, the Iranian foreign minister, Sadegh Ghotzbzadeh, confessed to Hamilton Jordan that he simply couldn't take a conciliatory position on the hostages, for that would be "political suicide." Ghotzbzadeh's admission pushed Carter into the Brzezinski camp; he would attempt a rescue mission after all. On April 11, 1980, President Carter met in the White House with General David Jones, the chairman of the Joint Chiefs of Staff, and fifty-one-year-old Colonel Charlie Beckwith, the charismatic, hard-drinking founder of the army's new, elite counterterrorism unit, Delta Force.[47]

The U.S. rescue plan, Operation Eagle Claw, was complex. Eight navy Sea Stallion helicopters painted in Iranian army colors would fly off the USS *Nimitz* in the Arabian Sea with a rescue team to "Desert One," a remote site near Tabas in central Iran that an air force team had already scouted and marked with buried infrared lights. The navy helicopters would be met by a half dozen green-and-black-painted C-130s flying from airfields in Egypt and Oman. Three carried American troops— Delta Force and Rangers—as well as jeeps, dirt bikes, camouflage netting and sheets of aluminum (in case the planes got stuck in the sand); the other three were "bladder planes" carrying fuel for the helicopters in giant rubber balloons. At Desert One, the bladder planes would refuel the choppers, which would then hop over to "Desert Two," a staging area fifty miles southeast of Tehran. There the U.S. rescue team, armed with explosives, grenades and MP-5 submachine guns with silencers, would climb into trucks procured and hidden by CIA operative Dick Meadows and then drive into Tehran to free the hostages. To blend in, Delta Force dyed their hair and beards black and wore black caps and field jackets and blue jeans; to establish their identity as soldiers, not spies, and so conserve their Geneva Convention protection, they sewed American flags—covered by black Velcro patches—onto their sleeves. The patches would be ripped off inside the embassy—to reassure the hostages—or at the moment of capture, to avoid execution as spies.

Vital intelligence on the location of the hostages had been provided by Meadows, posing as an Irish businessman, and an embassy cook, who confirmed that fifty hostages were being held together at the embassy. Three others were being held in the Iranian foreign ministry. Beckwith's plan was to cut power in Tehran, divide the U.S. troops into two assault teams, infiltrate the foreign ministry and the embassy in the darkness, free the hostages—orbiting AC-130 gunships would keep any reacting Iranian forces at bay with their 40 mm chain guns—and rush the hostages to a nearby soccer field, where they would be loaded into the helicopters arriving from Desert Two and flown to Manzariyeh Air Base outside Tehran. That airfield would be seized by an Army Ranger force, which would hold it until the C-130s from Desert One landed to load the hostages and fly them to safety in Saudi Arabia. The air force's six command and communications satellites around the globe provided instant intelligence and communication between the special forces in Iran, the carriers and the Pentagon. U.S. Navy fighter aircraft from the *Nimitz* and *Coral Sea* would be patrolling the Iranian coastline around the clock, ready to jet toward Tehran and shoot down any Iranian fighters bold enough to oppose the rescue. The scheme was almost impossibly convoluted, and made harder by Carter's insistence that no lethal force be used if a crowd formed to stop the extraction of the hostages. The Delta officers were nonplussed. "The only difference between this and the Alamo is that Davy Crockett didn't have to fight his way in," one joked.[48] But seriously, Carter and his secretary of defense, Harold Brown, would later be forced to address and deny rumors that the CIA had projected that 60 percent of the hostages would be killed in the course of the rescue mission. Initial American casualty estimates ran as high as two hundred—rescuers and rescued—and the final ones projected the loss of fifteen to twenty of the fifty-three hostages remaining in Iran.[49] With numbers like that, many wondered why the rescue was even attempted.

Three of the American helicopters broke down because of dust and mechanical problems; one limped back to the *Nimitz*, a second made an emergency landing in the desert with a cracked rotor blade, and a third touched down at Desert One with a broken hydraulic pump. They had flown through haboobs—towering clouds of fine desert sand—that gummed their engines, rotors and navigation devices. Worse, the mission was immediately compromised by the improbable passage of two Iranian pickup trucks and a Mercedes-Benz passenger bus through Desert One at the very moment when the first C-130 touched down. The special forces shot out the tires of the bus and destroyed one of the trucks with an antitank missile, but they lost the other one, which sped away into the salt desert. While Carter—going through the motions of a normal Rose Garden workday back in Washington—debated whether to abort the mission, news arrived that Beckwith's rescue force was down to five choppers, one short of the critical minimum. The mission could not proceed. Standing in a corridor between the Oval Office and his study, Carter absorbed the news and muttered, "Damn. Damn." He scrubbed the mission, certainly giving the lie to Soviet propaganda that "President Carter had prepared death for tens of thousands, perhaps hundreds of thousands of Iranians."[50]

Carter was joined by Brzezinski, Jordan, Walter Mondale, Warren Christopher and Jody Powell. "At least there were no American casualties and no innocent Iranians hurt," the president said with a sigh.[51] Within minutes, even that small consolation would be denied him. After refueling, one of the American choppers lifted off and slammed into one of the bladder planes, igniting the gas tanks on both aircraft and cooking off their ammunition. Desert One shuddered from the explosion, and a fireball rose three hundred feet in the air. Eight U.S. soldiers died, four suffered wounds, and six helicopters and the C-130 were abandoned as flames and explosions crackled across Desert One.[52] In the White House, Hamilton Jordan heard the news, ducked into a restroom and vomited. Secretary of State Cyrus Vance, who had resigned earlier in the day because of his opposition to the rescue mission, approached Carter and said, "Mr. President, I'm very, very sorry."[53] In Tehran, Khomeini used the fiasco to entrench his radical government. The haboobs that felled the Sea Stallions had been stirred up by Allah to thwart the infidels. "Great Satan" had tried to invade and enslave Iran. The burnt aircraft in the desert were all the proof that was needed.

The fiery demise of Operation Eagle Claw triggered a final, thorough purge of the Iranian military. Khomeini accused the Iranian generals of complicity in the American rescue mission. Why were the big, lumbering C-130s and Sea Stallions not picked up on radar and shot down? Although the answer was simple—the American aircraft had flown through predetermined gaps in Iran's air defenses at altitudes of 250 feet or less, well below Iranian radar—the ayatollah had prejudged the issue, and went on a rampage.[54] In the six weeks after Eagle Claw, seven different "plots" were uncovered inside the armed services and used to justify the arrest of several hundred officers. American hopes of a "Pinochet-type regime" seizing power from the ayatollahs in Iran evaporated.[55] Even some hostage-takers were alarmed. "None of us in the revolution believed Iran would ever have an autocratic regime again," Mohsen Miramadi reflected years later. "Yet here we are."[56]

Operation Eagle Claw had big ramifications for the U.S. military as well. Carter was immediately assailed for the lack of military preparedness. Carter lamely explained that "failure to *try*" would have been "a deeper failure than . . . incomplete success."[57] Americans must have wondered just what "incomplete success" he was referring to. The Iranians had captured mission maps and other secret materials at the crash site, and news footage showed jubilant Iranians swarming over the burnt-out wrecks at Desert One. The hostages were more distant than ever, scattered to continually changing prisons and private homes all over Iran—new, secret locations that would be impossible to pinpoint. At an April 30 news conference, Carter insisted that he had "focused the nation's elaborate military capability on this particular equipment used in this operation," but critics wanted to know why only eight helicopters were sent—when a minimum of six were needed—and why none of them had been fitted with sturdier rotors and sandscreens to keep them aloft in the sandstorms and haboobs that regularly swept across the Great Salt Desert south of Tehran. Carter was rumored to have turned down a plan for six hundred troops and thirty helicopters on the grounds that it would be too "provocative" abroad and at home.[58] Reports of poor training, maintenance and missing spare parts led to speculation on the true capabilities of the two million American troops in uniform around the world. If the elite raiding force sent into Iran failed so wretchedly, what could be expected of the regular services?[59]

A "CONFRONTATION STATE" IS BORN

The United States was immediately put on the defensive, but acquired new regional allies. Iran's neighbors—particularly those with large Shiite populations like Iraq, Bahrain and Pakistan—were alarmed. When Ayatollah Khomeini severed diplomatic relations with Cairo after Egypt signed its peace treaty with Israel in March 1979 and then targeted Egypt as the country most vulnerable to Islamist agitation and terminated Iranian subsidies to Egypt, Sadat slid deeper into the American embrace. Sadat's philosophy—"no politics in religion and no religion in politics"—fit nicely with the American preference for secular regimes.[60] The Saudis, with their own unhappy Shiite minority (inconveniently clustered in the kingdom's oil patch), naturally allied themselves even more closely with the United States. The Saudis, Ayatollah Taleghani, a leading Tehran cleric announced, "cannot be considered an Islamic regime."[61] Iran would be the new paradigm; there was not a single truly Muslim government in the world, Khomeini said. Iran would be the first, and its example would promote radical change in every Muslim country.

Radical changes were immediately made to Iranian foreign policy. Whereas the shah had sought stability, the ayatollah pushed revolution. He booted the Israelis out of Tehran and installed Yasser Arafat's PLO in the buildings formerly occupied by the Israeli diplomatic and trade mission. Khomeini summoned Iran's ambassadors home (including Zahedi in Washington), pulled Iran out of its American military agreements, withdrew Iranian blue helmets from Lebanon and the Golan Heights, denounced the Camp David peace treaty between Egypt and Israel as "a crime against Muslims" and extended support and funds to an array of dubious causes: the Polisario Front in the Western Sahara and dissident Muslim groups in Eritrea, Sudan, Pakistan and Malaysia. Iran, armed forces chief of staff General Muhammed Qarani proudly declared, was no longer a Westernized island of stability; it was an Islamic "confrontation state."[62] Writing in December 1979, a senior CIA officer described the new threats posed by Iran: "If Saudi Arabia and the flanking Gulf sheikhdoms contain the ultimate prize of oil, the world of Islam holds the key to the Third World. Already offended by our position in the Arab-Israeli dispute, the Arab world sees in Iran a manifestation of U.S. weakness."[63] The Iranians exerted pressure in three directions: on the Gulf oil supply, on the world's Muslims and on U.S. self-confidence. Carter's fear of appearing "soft on Iran"—and thus encouraging American enemies everywhere—was the same one felt by George W. Bush thirty years later. But Carter went ahead, swallowed his pride and paid up to end the crisis. He restored $8 billion in frozen assets to the Islamic Republic to bring home the hostages, but was unexpectedly subjected to a final humiliation. In a petulant jab at Carter, Khomeini waited till Ronald Reagan had taken the oath of office in January 1981 before releasing the fifty-two hostages still in captivity.[64]

Fortunately for Carter's and then Reagan's America, Iranian jabs and rhetoric were mostly hot air. A glance at the shah's budgets told Khomeini that continued service as regional gendarme was just too expensive. If the Islamic Republic of Iran was going to root itself, it would need to divert funds from defense to basic needs— schools, clinics, roads, and gasoline and food subsidies. Thus, the new Iranian leaders renounced the role of regional policeman. "We'll no longer act as gendarme of the Persian Gulf," defense minister Admiral Ahmad Madani announced. Madani canceled procurement contracts, weeded ships from the fleet and stopped new military construction.[65] Within the Iranian government, leftists and Islamic radicals argued for a complete break with Washington while pragmatists like Bazargan and Foreign Minister Sanjabi recognized that American advisory aid would be essential to operate and maintain the high-tech equipment purchased by the shah in the 1970s.

Internally, as the CIA had predicted in 1978, the clerics—although "popular in the early stages" of their revolution—were "inexperienced and dependent on the same bureaucracy that had failed the Shah, and a constant target for other ambitious elements, including the military."[66] The ayatollahs could not wave a magic wand and get things done. They had to deal with the same obstacles that had slowed the pace of the White Revolution. And moving from the "pious generalities" of the early days to an actual Islamic Republic involved unpopular decisions. First of all, people needed to go back to work. The masses had loved Khomeini in the early days, one of Bakhtiar's ministers recalled, because "there was no Shah. There were no bosses or managers. There was no discipline, and nobody worked or was required to work." That naturally changed. And there was a basic conflict between Iranian nationalism and the Islamic Republic. Bakhtiar had been fired for calling himself "an Iranian first and a Muslim second." An exile noted Khomeini's disdain for the nationalism that had always been a source of pride for Iranians: "Khomeini has no patriotism and no particular interest in Iran as a country. Islam is his only allegiance." He exhibited real concern for the "poor and downtrodden," but that concern coexisted with a desire to "eradicate all modern values in Islamic societies," which was not a widely popular aim. The Iranian exile, who had been Bakhtiar's finance minister, estimated that 95 percent of adult Iranians (secretly) opposed Khomeini and that about 50 percent of students did.[67]

That may have been wishful thinking, for the Islamic militants had momentum on their side. The CIA acknowledged that Khomeini's "prestige is formidable . . . The common man in Iran, religious by nature, is fiercely loyal to him."[68] But Iran was a multinational nation, with big Kurdish, Turkic Baluchi and Arab minorities. All those groups resisted Khomeini's leadership; the Kurds broke into armed revolt. Powerful tribes like the Qashgais quietly extended their power and reach for the anticipated day when Khomeini would fall.[69] In Iran's educated cities, the mullahs could intone all they wanted that "censorship is the prohibition of what is wrong and not of what is right," but that hardly satisfied its many victims. The Iranian media was instructed to publish and broadcast nothing contrary to Islam. Women were put back behind the veil, and education was segregated. The rush to an Islamic Republic was hard to resist. Secular politicians, military officers and moderate ayatollahs all detected Khomeini's strong following and, as American intelligence analysts noted, decided not to "risk getting out of step with him." Even the Tudeh communists made common cause, despite Khomeini's harsh criticism of Moscow. Tudeh—the old bogeyman of 1953—was willing to work within the Islamic Republic "to extirpate the roots of American imperialism." A French analyst noted that it was not a great leap for many Iranian officers, bureaucrats and politicians to rally to the new order and transition from empire to republic; to them, Khomeini's Islamic Republic may have seemed no more radical than had Oliver Cromwell's Puritan Republic or Jean Calvin's Genevan one: "Each had been reviled by its contemporaries as cruel, sectarian, fanatical," but each had developed into a functioning, organized government. Khomeini's "mullahocracy" would find jobs for loyalists—lay and clerical—just as the shah's empire had done.[70]

Strong at home, Iran's Shiites were badly positioned to wreak major changes abroad. As Deputy Director of the CIA Frank Carlucci noted in March 1979, the "paramount leader" concept embodied in Ayatollah Khomeini was a Shiite tendency, not a Sunni one. "The Sunnis are much more inclined to work with a secular government, whereas the Shiites traditionally have been a sect of opposition." One Iranian exile in the United States—a former Iranian bank CEO and finance minister—agreed, writing in November 1979 that "Khomeini is a seventh- to eighth-century man" and an authority "only on the Shiite interpretation of the Koran, and on the history of the Shiite sect itself." The ayatollah "detests everything about the modern world," and he spoke no languages other than "a very layman Farsi."[71] Iran's influence would not "automatically spread to other countries."[72]

Most threatened by Iran was Iraq. Although the Iraqis had provided a safe haven to Khomeini between 1964 and 1978, when he had been hunted by the shah and granted asylum in Najaf, the Baath regime had expelled Khomeini in October 1978. The approach of Islamic revolution in Iran had alarmed the Baathists. Saddam Hussein, who had offered to kill Khomeini for the shah, later reminisced "that the single greatest mistake of his career had been to let the ayatollah leave Iraq alive."[73] The Iraqi leadership worried that Khomeini's Shiite revolution would ignite Iraq's own Shiite majority and tear away Basra and the Iraqi south. They also feared the accent on Islam in Iranian foreign policy, which would militate against Iraq's secular Arab nationalist regime. They also worried about Iraq's Kurds. When the shah collapsed, Iran's Kurds tried to break away, and Iraq's might do the same.[74] In the midst of this regional crisis, Saddam Hussein, who had toiled in the shadow of more senior Baathists, broke through to absolute power in July 1979. Two months later, in September 1979, he invaded Iran, setting off an eight-year war.

Saddam saw opportunity in the Iranian revolution. The vaunted Iranian military had collapsed in the final days of the Bakhtiar government, and the sour relations with Washington implied that whatever Islamic Iranian military replaced the imperial one would have major adaptive problems. The "Iranian military is not worth a damn," an exile told Zbigniew Brzezinski in November 1979. Officers feared for their lives and careers, "stayed out of sight and were reluctant to exercise discipline. Never good even at their peak under the Shah, now they are a group without the ability to organize and operate themselves." CIA analysts concurred: "Iran is unable to present a credible military deterrent to its neighbors."[75] That was an understatement. Of the seventy-six F-14 fighters procured by the shah in the late seventies, only seven were actually operational, and none could fire Iran's Phoenix missiles.[76] Iran was all but helpless, convulsed internally and was effectively disarmed by the purges and defections in the military as well as the U.S. freeze on new parts and platforms. Gauging Khomeini's efforts to rebuild his imploded military, the CIA concluded that Iran would need to jettison its high-tech armaments and hire "Palestinian janissaries" who would help convert the imperial military into PLO-style "combat groups."[77] How the mighty had fallen! The internal convulsions were no less serious than the military ones. Rostam Pirasteh, an exiled former government minister, described the state of Khomeini's Iran: "The Iranian government is operating entirely at random," he told Brzezinski's National Security Council. "There is no underlying program, no plan, and no anticipation of events. Khomeini rules by talking, rambling out loud on whatever topic happens to come up. There is no staff work for his comments, no analysis and no coherent concept or central plan into which his thoughts fit." Pirasteh noted that the Iranian government had no real idea as to the Iranian GDP, unemployment rate or anything else: "They just don't know."[78]

By July 1980, Khomeini was pleading with Iranians to "save the revolution." He and Ayatollah Montazeri called for a "new Islamic revolution" that would "purge satanical elements" from the military and civil service, strengthen the bond between the "masses, the Imam and the genuine clergy" and "impose unity to carry out revolutionary reform." The CIA noted that Bani-Sadr found himself between a rock and a hard place. If he agreed to the "new revolution," his most effective allies would be purged. If he opposed it, he would run up against Khomeini himself, and probably not survive the collision. Looking at the tensions, American analysts felt certain that "effective government is unlikely to exist" in Iran.[79] But there was no U.S. influence either. It had been torn up by the roots, and there was no longer any prospect of a pro-Western coup.

CHAPTER 12

JIHAD

A COUP *HAD* SUCCEEDED just across the Iranian border in Afghanistan. There the Marxist People's Democratic Party of Afghanistan (PDPA) and the Afghan army had seized power in April 1978 and founded a Soviet-style "Democratic Republic of Afghanistan." Four hundred Red Army advisers arrived bearing gifts of the latest Soviet military hardware, and the new Kabul government obediently signed a "treaty of friendship, cooperation and good neighborliness" with Moscow, which authorized Soviet troop deployments into Afghanistan whenever the Afghan government called for them. Problems immediately arose, as swiftly as they did in the wake of the American invasion of 2001. Several months of Russian-style reforms aimed at "uprooting feudalism" and devout Islam soured the conservative Afghan population, and regional revolts flared from Nuristan in eastern Afghanistan across the country. By the spring of 1979, twenty-four of Afghanistan's twenty-eight provinces were up in arms. Already alarmed by the revolutionary situation in Iran—and the possibility of U.S. military intervention there to block the ayatollahs—Moscow pumped in more weapons and advisers.

To Moscow's chagrin, the PDPA never fulfilled its function as a proletarian vanguard; instead, it dissolved into the warring factions that are a fact of Afghan life. On one side stood the Khalq, or Masses, movement of President Nur Muhammad Taraki and Prime Minister Hafizullah Amin, on the other the Parcham, or

Banner, faction, of Babrak Karmal and Muhammad Najibullah.[1] The revolutionary Khalq faction kept the gradualist Parcham faction at bay by various gambits, like the removal of Babrak Karmal to Prague as Afghan ambassador. But the Khalq began to crumble from within. In September 1979, President Taraki was killed in a palace coup—smothered with a pillow by Amin's bodyguards while he slept.

Resistance to the Soviet-backed PDPA was fierce. Well-intentioned PDPA reforms—land redistribution, unveiling women, a mass literacy campaign, broader access to education for boys and girls, limits on dowries and the marriage of minors—ramped up an Islamic backlash against the "Sovietization" of Afghanistan. With the PDPA replacing the Afghan tricolor—striped in Muslim green—with a red communist flag, and trying to expand primary education—which reached only 5 percent of girls and 30 percent of boys before the coup—the rural provinces recoiled in horror. Muslim Brotherhood–inspired parties like Jamaat-e-Islami, or "Muslim Group," vowed to take back Afghanistan and make it a purely Islamic state ruled by sharia law. Teachers presiding over coed classrooms were assassinated, and the mullahs organized the angry peasants against the new regime. Outraged Afghans destroyed the very things that the Soviets were building to improve their lives: schools, hospitals, clinics, telephone lines, trucks and peasant cooperatives. The Afghan army's early successful assaults on growing numbers of Islamist guerrillas—mujahideen—drove the militants into Pakistan, where they found safe haven on the Pakistani side of the fourteen-hundred-mile border, in the seven largely ungoverned tribal areas tucked inside Pakistan's North-West Frontier Province.

Pakistan's leader, General Zia-ul-Haq, was a friend of the mujahideen. The general had seized power from democratically elected prime minister Zulfikar Ali Bhutto in 1977.[2] Fearing Afghan efforts since 1947 to slice the Pashtuns of Pakistan's tribal areas into an independent "Pashtunistan," Bhutto and then Zia succored the mujahideen. Pashtuns were the principal ethnic group in Afghanistan, but there were more of them living in Pakistan—where they were called Pathans—than across the border. If the Afghans fomented secession among the Pathans, Pakistan, already hobbled by its cold war with India, might come apart at the seams. Zia also protected the Islamists because it was a handy way to wring money from the Americans—$3.2 billion after the Soviet invasion—and because he saw the mujahideen as a possible vanguard for a new political movement in Pakistan. He would uproot clubby, connected, secular "Bhuttoism" by emphasizing political Islam—"without Islam, Pakistan will fail"—and jihad. The élan and energy of the mujahideen movement might invigorate his unpopular, repressive dictatorship. In October 1979, as the Soviets prepared to invade Afghanistan and Iranian militants planned to storm the U.S. embassy, General Zia announced that he would create "a genuine Islamic order" in Pakistan; he would empower the violent fundamentalist groups and let them loose. Zia's hypocrisy was breathtaking. "In Islam there is no provision for Western-type elections," he declaimed, which indicated his primary interest in the "genuine Islamic order."[3]

THE SAUDI ANGLE

The Saudis stood ready to play the role of sorcerer's apprentice. Riyadh worried that the Soviet thrust into Afghanistan heralded an attempt by Moscow to attain strategic parity with the United States in the Middle East.[4] With Iran lost to Khomeini and Carter faltering, Pakistan alone anchored Saudi Arabia's eastern flank against the Soviet and Iranian threats. With their own political problems—an obstreperous clergy, a dissatisfied populace and foreign rivals (Iraq, Iran and the Soviets) circling hungrily—the Saudis ramped up their "petrodollar Islam" after 1973, when oil revenues soared, to bankroll fundamentalist movements like Jamaat-e-Islami. The Saudis wanted to spread Wahhabism, push back against secular, pro-Soviet figures like Yasser Arafat—who had praised the Russian invasion of Afghanistan—and beat back Khomeini's Shiite challenge. Khomeini in Tehran was establishing something that looked suspiciously like a Shiite "papacy," which aspired to guide and dominate all Muslims—Shiite and Sunni—by harping on the *secular* themes of Israel, poverty and imperialism. Khomeini's envoys spread alarmingly across the region; Hezbollah, founded in Lebanon with Iranian backing in 1982, would become the most powerful and fearsome party in Lebanon. Superficially, Hezbollah armed itself to prevent southern Lebanon from "sharing the fate of Palestine"—long Israeli occupation— but it was really a new kind of movement: Islamist, revolutionary and wildly popular. Millions of Shiites and Sunnis applauded Hezbollah's embrace of suicide bombings to drive the Israelis, Americans and French out of Lebanon in the 1980s.[5]

As always, the deeply compromised Saudis—Khomeini emphasized their hedonism and corruption at every opportunity—groped for credible ways to undercut Arab nationalist, Shiite, Islamist and communist rivals with a new creed that might appeal to young and disaffected Muslims "from Cairo to Kuala Lumpur." In this rather dastardly way, the Saudis hit upon the "cleansing politics of holy war."⁶ This Saudi strategy—issuing from a notoriously louche kingdom—was dubious at best. King Faisal had been assassinated by a Wahhabi extremist in 1975, and the kingdom had been stunned in 1979, when homegrown jihadis had seized the Grand Mosque in Mecca—reviling the "drunkard, land-grabbing" Saudi princes, who "led dissolute lives" in "luxurious palaces"—and killed or wounded several hundred pilgrims before being slaughtered by French commandos and Saudi national guard troops. Iran had lurked behind that maneuver, Khomeini asserting that the holy places belonged to all Muslims, not the Saudis, and making no secret of his own ambition to manage them. The worried Saudis sought to *export* their problem, close up the Iranian schism and prove their piety by proselytizing abroad. Afghanistan and Pakistan's tribal areas were just the places. There Riyadh could give Islamic fundamentalism "a coat of green paint"—Iran's paint was disturbingly red—and return it to a conservative, traditionalist Sunni track.⁷

Afghans who did not make it to Pakistan to train for jihad were ruthlessly persecuted. Between April 1978 and the Soviet invasion in December 1979, an estimated twenty-seven thousand Afghan political prisoners—the traditional elites, mujahideen and hundreds of mullahs and village headmen—were murdered. The KGB and its Afghan protégés ran amok in this period. Their brief from Moscow was simple: do to Afghanistan what had already been done to Soviet Central Asia— "transform pastoral Islamic societies into insistently godless police states." The transformation had succeeded—more or less—in Uzbekistan, Tajikistan and Kazakhstan. Why not Afghanistan?

The ninety-thousand-man Afghan army began to melt away amid the horrors of the civil war. It lost half its strength in the first year of the conflict. Morale plummeted, desertion spiked and, in March 1979, the Afghan garrison at Herat—just sixty-five miles from the Iranian border and infected by the revolution in Tehran— mutinied and massacred its Soviet advisers, impaling them and their wives and children on pikes. The Red Army replied by forgoing hearts and minds and bombing Herat instead. Twenty-four thousand Afghans died in the attack. Atrocities like that pushed thousands of Afghan army deserters into the ranks of the mujahideen. KGB chairman Yuri Andropov was nonplussed. "Under no circumstances can we *lose* Afghanistan," he told an emergency session of the Politburo in March 1979. Yet how could the Soviets hold it? "The economy is backward, the Islamic religion predominates, and nearly all of the rural population is illiterate. We know Lenin's teaching about a revolutionary situation. Whatever situation we are talking about in Afghanistan, it is not *that* type of situation." Afghanistan was far more influenced by Khomeini's Islamic revolution seeping across the border from Iran. There was no place in such a revolution for Russian atheists.[8]

"DRAW THE SOVIETS INTO THE AFGHAN TRAP"

Casting about for ways to shore up the shaky American position in Iran and stave off the Soviets, President Jimmy Carter and National Security Adviser Zbigniew Brzezinski seized upon the deepening Soviet problem in Afghanistan as an opportunity. Here was a rare chance to beat the Soviets at their own game of Third World subversion and insurgency. "We didn't push the Russians to intervene," Brzezinski reminisced, "but we knowingly increased the probability that they would." Carter signed an executive order in July 1979 authorizing the CIA to conduct covert operations against the Kabul government; Brzezinski judged that "secret operation" an "excellent idea."[9] It "drew the Soviets into the Afghan trap," gave them "their Vietnam War" and distracted them from the deteriorating situation in Iran.[10]

Even at that early date, both Carter and Brzezinski recognized that they were courting "blowback" in Afghanistan by dealing with the reactionary mujahideen. A secret State Department report of August 1979—gleefully published by the Iranians after the embassy takeover—revealed that Washington expected "setbacks . . . for future social and economic reforms in Afghanistan" if the Soviets were rooted out by the Islamist "woman-hating mujahideen." Still, U.S. officials gambled that "the United States' larger interest . . . would be served by the demise of the Taraki-Amin regime," which "would show the rest of the world, particularly the Third World, that the Soviets' view of the socialist course of history being inevitable is not accurate."[11] A vicious jihad in Afghanistan might also prevent World War III. Carter worried that the Soviets might attack Pakistan to destroy the mujahideen camps in the tribal areas. If they did, the United States would have to fight to defend Pakistan. If the Soviets could be mired in an Afghan guerrilla war, they would hesitate to initiate a wider war with Islamabad. Thus, National Security Adviser Brzezinski traveled to Pakistan in February 1980, trekked into the Khyber Pass and was photographed pointing a Chinese-made assault rifle in the direction of the Afghan border.[12]

THE SOVIET INVASION

The Soviets were at least as skeptical of their protégés in Kabul as the Americans had been of theirs in Tehran. Andropov and Defense Minister Dmitri Ustinov set up an emergency commission to study Afghanistan, which concluded that Hafizullah Amin's communist government was probably cultivating secret links to Pakistan, the People's Republic of China and even the United States to survive, yet never ceased calling for greater infusions of Soviet arms and manpower—first helicopter and tank crews in April 1979, then an airborne battalion in July 1979, and then three entire Soviet divisions. By the fall of 1979, there were twelve thousand Soviet troops and advisers in Afghanistan, and Amin's government kept asking for more. Hundreds of Afghan officers trained in the Soviet Union had already become mujahideen. It was clear that Afghan communists would be unable to clean house on their own. Worse, Andropov suspected that Amin was plotting with the Americans to found "a new Ottoman Empire" that would reach from Afghanistan into the Soviet Union's Central Asian republics and one day place Pershing missiles on the USSR's underbelly.[13] The KGB station in Kabul recommended a freewheeling Soviet invasion together with a move against Amin, who would be replaced with more obedient communists less prone to the "harsh repressions" that merely "activated and consolidated the opposition." Yuri Andropov had been Soviet ambassador to Hungary in 1956 and had helped coordinate the Red Army intervention there that removed reformers and crushed a rebellion. He now mistakenly saw parallels in Afghanistan.[14]

On Christmas Day 1979, the Soviet 40th Army threw pontoon bridges across the Amu Darya River and began moving into Afghanistan while Soviet airborne troops landed in Kabul and fanned out across the city. They couched their intervention in the language of the 1978 Treaty of Friendship, Cooperation and Good Neighborliness, but their real motive was to shore up the pro-Soviet PDPA against Amin's intrigues and the swelling Islamist tide. In Pakistan, the notoriously fractious Afghan resistance groups—one-third traditionalist, two-thirds fundamentalist—were meeting and trying to iron out their differences in a *loya jirga*, or grand national assembly, that would exist as an exiled, parallel government in Peshawar. To the Soviet mind, such intrigues were intolerable. The Americans were losing their client in Iran to radical Islam; the Soviets resolved to take better care of theirs.[15] Two days later, seven hundred Soviet Spetsnaz special forces, disguised in Afghan uniforms, seized the presidential palace, shot President Amin and then seized all government and broadcasting facilities. The Soviet army announced that Afghanistan had been "liberated" from Amin's violent rule and turned over to Babrak Karmal, who was brought home from the Afghan embassy in Czechoslovakia and made head of government by a hastily formed Afghan Revolutionary Central Committee. Karmal gratified his new masters by immediately requesting a massive Soviet military intervention, and the Soviets complied. Marshal Sergei Sokolov led a hundred thousand troops and eighteen hundred tanks into Afghanistan in the last days of December 1979. One column advanced down the western end of the country, occupying Herat and Farah; the other pushed through the eastern half to Kabul. Both columns then detached units to Kandahar, where they joined forces. Six million Afghans became refugees, half of them flooding into Pakistan, the other half into Iran.[16]

THE CARTER DOCTRINE

For President Jimmy Carter, who had fumbled away Iran, this Soviet thrust toward the oil-rich Persian Gulf was a disaster of epic proportions. He pronounced the Soviet invasion "the most serious threat to peace since the Second World War" and immediately halted shipments of grain to the Soviet Union and announced a boycott of the 1980 Summer Olympics in Moscow. In his January 1980 State of the Union address, the president announced a "Carter Doctrine" that vowed to treat Soviet adventurism in the Middle East "as an assault on the vital interests of the USA." Although the UN Security Council was stymied by the Soviet veto, the UN General Assembly passed (104 to 18) a resolution that "strongly deplored" the Soviet invasion and demanded a "total withdrawal of foreign troops." India was one of the few countries that actively supported the Soviet thrust; the Indians assumed that the Karmal government would weaken Pakistan and contain the burgeoning jihadist movement that would inevitably flow from Afghanistan and Pakistan into Indian-ruled Kashmir, whose six million Muslims were claimed by Pakistan. Soviet general secretary Leonid Brezhnev simply ignored the UN demand, claiming that the Soviet troops were there "by invitation" of Karmal's Afghan government.

With the Soviets deeply committed and détente in ruins, President Carter authorized Operation Cyclone, which was the CIA program to arm the mujahideen for their guerrilla war against the Karmal regime and the Soviet army. Brzezinski advocated a hard line in Afghanistan. The Soviets would fight harder and more pitilessly than the Americans had in Vietnam, so the Americans would have to ramp up support for the mujahideen, but also for General Zia-ul-Haq. Pakistan, which had been anti-American under Zia's Islamist regime—demonstrators had torched the U.S. embassy in November 1979 while Pakistani police looked on—would be converted into a strategic partner and an essential sanctuary for the mujahideen. Zia would get U.S. cash, weapons, a security guarantee and even license to develop nuclear weapons if he wanted them. (He did.) "Our security policy toward Pakistan cannot be dictated by our nonproliferation policy," Brzezinski incautiously ventured.[17] Carter was impressed by Zia's Anglophile manners and soldierly appearance. Like Musharraf, he trimmed his mustache, slicked his hair with pomade, wore impeccable uniforms and spoke in a smart British accent. Despite his Islamist methods, he kept the clergy out of politics and never authorized Saudi-style religious police or Iranian-style revolutionary guards. He seemed "normal" and Western, a man Washington could do business with.[18]

The incoming administration of Ronald Reagan in 1981 was even more impressed by General Zia. Like the Bush administration partnering with General Pervez Musharraf—sending $10 billion in aid in the years after 9/11—the Reagan administration beefed up support for Zia. Carter had offered Zia $400 million in aid; Reagan increased it to $3.2 billion and even offered advanced platforms like the F-16 that had previously been reserved for NATO allies, Japan, Israel and Pahlavi Iran. Reagan largely ignored the human rights violations that had troubled the Carter administration. His "Reagan Doctrine" sought anticommunist guerrillas wherever they cropped up, whether in Angola, Nicaragua or Afghanistan. Secretary of State George Shultz counseled Reagan to avoid criticism of Zia's martial law regime—or a too close investigation of Pakistan's clandestine nuclear program—and focus on the strategic partnership: "We must remember that without Zia's support, the Afghan resistance, key to making the Soviets pay a heavy price for their Afghan adventure, is effectively dead." President Reagan, British prime minister Margaret Thatcher and the Saudis clapped together a weapons pipeline. Military equipment went by ship to Karachi or by plane to Islamabad, and the cargos were transported to Quetta and Rawalpindi by Pakistan's military intelligence agency—the Inter-Service Intelligence Directorate (ISI)—and there distributed in trucks to the various mujahideen groups. So much ordnance was landed so quickly that much of it had to be stacked up in the ports of entry till there was use for it. One such arms dump detonated on the outskirts of Islamabad in 1988, killing one hundred civilians and injuring one thousand.[19]

PROBLEMS WITH PAKISTAN

The problem—as it would be again under Musharraf—was that Zia's ISI blended its Afghan guerrilla operations with domestic surveillance of enemies and an undeclared war with India. By funding and encouraging the ISI, Washington was underwriting Zia's dictatorship, corroding relations with the Indians and helping establish ISI as a dangerous state within a state—a permanent staff of Pakistani officers seconded to the mujahideen, who would inexorably catch the virus of jihad and spread it to their colleagues. Little attention was paid in Washington to the dysfunctional nature of the relationship between the ISI and Zia, as well as Zia's successors. Whereas the Pakistani army was dominated by generally secular Punjabi officers like Zia and later Musharraf, the ISI included many Pathans—ethnic brothers of the Afghan Pashtuns across the border—who made their Afghan Bureau a stalwart defender of the mujahideen, and a sympathetic coreligionist as well. Under ISI chief General Akhtar Abdul Rahman, the ISI began to embrace jihadist doctrine as a force multiplier in Afghanistan as well as the disputed land of Kashmir.[20]

The CIA went along with these momentous changes, relying heavily on allied assistance from Britain's MI6, the Saudis and China. The Saudi General Intelligence Department (GID), directed by Prince Turki al-Faisal, became ISI's rich uncle, richer even than the Americans. High-priced oil gave the Saudis almost unlimited resources; their five-year government budget ending in 1974 had totaled $9 billion. The next budget, ending in 1979, totaled $142 billion. "We don't do operations," Prince Turki joked to a CIA officer. "We don't know how. All we know how to do is write checks." Saudi operatives carried millions of dollars into Pakistan on Saudi and Pakistani commercial flights, and other funds were distributed from the kingdom's Washington embassy. The total sum injected by the Saudis into Afghanistan is unknown, but could be as high as $20 billion, a sum that was matched dollar for dollar by Washington.[21] There, on the banks of the Potomac, ambassador Prince Bandar bin Sultan would sit on the funds for as long as possible—pocketing interest from "the float"—and then transfer the dollars into Swiss accounts controlled by the CIA.[22] The Saudis—Lawrenceville alumnus and Georgetown dropout Prince

Turki at the forefront—exerted more influence over the mujahideen and the Pakistanis than the Americans did. This was troubling, for, as Steve Coll has brilliantly summarized, Prince Turki was an assiduously corrupt figure who never had Washington's best interests at heart. "A champion of Saudi Arabia's austere Islam, a promoter of women's rights, a multimillionaire, a workaholic, a pious man, a sipper of banana daiquiris, an intriguer, an intellectual, a loyal prince, a sincere friend of the Americans, a generous funder of anti-American causes, Prince Turki embodied Saudi Arabia's cascading contradictions."[23]

OSAMA BIN LADEN APPEARS

Not the least of the Saudi contradictions was the struggle raging for control of the Afghan jihad. Anxious to have direct access to the mujahideen—to "compartment" their network without American or Pakistani supervision—Saudi intelligence competed with the Saudi clergy for control of the guerrillas. That competition—Prince Turki's GID versus Sheikh Abdul bin Baz's Wahhabi ulema—led to a radicalization of the mujahideen. Hungry for Saudi dollars, the mujahideen embraced Wahhabi Islam, founded Wahhabi emirates in remote Afghan valleys, memorized the Koran in Saudi-funded madrassas, and vied for the charitable handouts flown in from Saudi Arabia: "gold jewelry dropped on offering plates by merchants' wives in Jedda mosques; bags of cash delivered by businessmen to Riyadh charities as *zakat*, an annual Islamic tithe; fat checks written from semiofficial government accounts by minor Saudi princes; bountiful proceeds raised in annual telethons led by Prince Salman, the governor of Riyadh; and richest of all were the annual transfers from the Saudi General Intelligence Department to the CIA's Swiss bank accounts."[24]

Those contradictions would fledge Osama bin Laden and the 9/11 plotters, most of whom paid their way into Pakistan and Afghanistan with GID money. The Pakistani ISI put bin Laden in charge of the Makhtab al-Khidamat in 1984, a group organized with Saudi dollars to bring foreign fighters ("Arab Afghans") into the Pakistani tribal areas and eastern Afghanistan to help wage the anti-Soviet jihad. Thirty-five thousand foreign fighters from forty-three countries arrived to fight the Russians; perhaps another fifty thousand came to study in the proliferating religious schools on the Pakistani-Saudi border.[25] Osama bin Laden was typical of the Saudis who went to Afghanistan after the Soviet invasion. The seventeenth of the more than fifty children born to Muhammed bin Laden, Osama had led a typical upper-class Saudi life—with all its weird dichotomies—before he went off to holy war. Not quite motivated enough to make it all the way to university in the United States or Britain, Osama had matriculated at Jedda's King Abdul Aziz University in the 1970s, where he fell under the spell of its Muslim Brotherhood–infused faculty. Devout, rich Saudi Arabia provided jobs aplenty for émigré Palestinian professors like Abdullah Azzam—a spiritual founder of Hamas—and Muhammed Qutb—an Egyptian Islamic radical whose brother had been executed by Nasser—who taught young Saudis the duties of jihad against the West (or its puppets) and the need to live a pure Islamic life.

Qutb's brother, who had studied briefly in Greeley, Colorado, in 1949 and found the experience repugnant—"a reckless deluded herd that knows only lust and money . . . a primitiveness that reminds us of jungles and caves"—had written *Milestones* on his return to Cairo, an Islamist call to arms that advocated an Islamist seizure of power, violence against infidels and a ruthless extirpation of Muslim regimes that dared to govern through Western doctrines, not Islam. Qutb was no different from the 9/11 hijackers, who weirdly mingled lust and chastity, visiting strip clubs the night before they destroyed the World Trade Center and Pentagon. "A girl looks at you, appearing as if she were an enchanting nymph or an escaped mermaid," Qutb had written in 1948, "but as she approaches, you sense only the screaming instinct inside her, and can smell her burning body, not the scent of perfume but flesh, only flesh. Tasty flesh, truly, but flesh nonetheless."[26]

Schooled in Qutb's ignorant teachings—"the soul has no value to Americans"—bin Laden met Afghan mujahideen in Mecca during the hajj, and was spellbound. He had already bewildered his extended Saudi family with his intense religious feeling—so rare for a rich Saudi—and he made his first trip to the theater of war in 1981, when he flew to Lahore with Saudi donations for Jamaat-e-Islami. That first trip established what would become his modus operandi and the seed of al-Qaeda. Bin Laden became a semiofficial liaison between ISI, GID, fundamentalist groups like Jamaat, the Saudi-funded mujahideen commanders and the big Saudi charities like the World Muslim League, the Saudi Red Crescent and the International Islamic Relief Organization. Osama was connected in Riyadh and Islamabad, thanks to his deceased father's construction company. The Saudi Bin Laden Group—which had grown fat from the renovation of the Grand Mosque in Mecca as well as the pharaonic transfer of the Saudi capital from Jedda to Riyadh—had placed the family close to the royal family, especially GID director Prince Turki, and was now building blacktopped roads, caves and bunker complexes in Afghanistan for the mujahideen. The Saudis ran Osama as an agent, courier, fund-raiser and contractor; he coordinated his various functions through the Makhtab al-Khidamat (Services Bureau) in Peshawar. Through this logistical work—which preceded his trips to the fighting front—Osama began to understand how a potent "base"—al-Qaeda—could be formed from stout hearts, superior intelligence, ready cash and shadowy networks.[27]

CHARLIE WILSON'S WAR

Much of the U.S. and Saudi aid was committed to Pakistan, where the ISI—which had been founded in 1948 after Pakistan failed to annex Kashmir in its first war with India—provided safe havens for the mujahideen, and distributed funds, supplies and weapons for the jihad against the Red Army. The Soviets were suffering badly from the jihad: the cost and casualties were mounting, and 35 percent of the Soviet forces in Afghanistan at any given time were pinned down holding villages and outposts that would fall to the guerrillas the instant the Soviets departed.[28] To hasten the fall, the mujahideen received increasingly sophisticated arms, including British Blowpipe and American Stinger shoulder-fired antiaircraft missiles. The portable infrared-homing Stinger had entered service only in 1981 and represented a quantum leap in quality over the Chinese and Egyptian weapons that had initially filled American shipments. The Raytheon-manufactured launcher and missile weighed just thirty-four pounds, and it was deadly accurate.[29] With Stingers alone costing $38,000 each, U.S. expenditures surged, from about $20 million in 1980 to $630 million in 1987. In many ways, it really was "Charlie Wilson's war." "I don't want to know this, Charlie, you just go ahead," Speaker of the House Tip O'Neill used to tell Texas congressman Charlie Wilson when apprised of the congressman's machinations.[30] Wilson and CIA officer Gust Avrakotos negotiated massive increases in aid to Pakistan and the mujahideen. With the Soviets plowing $1 billion a year into their Kabul regime in the early 1980s, the Americans needed to do at least as well. An estimated $20 billion of U.S. aid flowed into Afghanistan through Pakistan. The Gulf states—mainly the Saudis—matched the American contributions dollar for dollar. Those "toxic alliances" with the intelligence services of Saudi Arabia and Pakistan would have awful consequences for the United States.[31]

Having delivered America's purse strings into Pakistani hands, President Reagan was unable to control the final destination (or application) of much funding. Although Zia did not create an Iranian-style "mullahocracy," he did refashion the Pakistani military and intelligence agencies. Before, they had been scrupulously secular and had frowned on religious fervor. Zia had been made general staff chief by Bhutto in large part because peer evaluations praised his lack of religious zeal. Now, striving to refound Pakistan along more militant lines, he encouraged officers to demonstrate their piety and make common cause with the mujahideen. He constructed religious schools—with American aid money—along the frontier with Afghanistan. He instructed his ISI director, Akhtar Abdur Rahman, to keep the Americans out of Afghanistan altogether. Everything would be run by the ISI. Washington would just pay the bills. Zia did not even want his agents or officers socializing with Americans; dollars and strategic backing were enough.[32]

Pakistan poured money into Afghan resistance leader Gulbuddin Hekmatyar, who is currently wanted by the U.S. government for attempts to overthrow Hamid Karzai. As an engineering student at Kabul University in the early 1970s, Hekmatyar had organized rural high school graduates against their more urbane urban peers. Hekmatyar founded a chapter of Muslim Brothers—the Ikhwan—and won control of the university student council in elections. He stood out even among radicals for his Islamic extremism. He condemned every Westernizing tendency and splashed acid in the faces of female students who dared appear unveiled on campus.[33] In 1979, Hekmatyar had fled to Pakistan during a crackdown; there he founded an Islamist party and militia called Hezbi Islami. It operated with ISI approval (and American funding) in the sprawling Afghan refugee camps in Pakistan, established madrassas, clinics and even prisons, and prepared for the day when its earnest *talibs* (pupils) could apply the fundamentalist model to a Soviet-free Afghanistan.

Kept flush by the ISI, Hekmatyar attracted Afghans as well as "transnational Islamists" like Osama bin Laden, who was operating his own outfit in Pakistan—the forerunner of al-Qaeda—that recruited and sustained Afghan Arab volunteers. Radicals like Hekmatyar and bin Laden were linchpins in Pakistani president Zia-ul-Haq's effort to achieve "strategic depth" against India and the Soviets by establishing a reliable, dependent Islamist and Pashtun state in Afghanistan. Zia deliberately diverted money from traditional Afghan royalty and tribal leaders or from non-Pashtun resistance heroes like Ahmed Shah Massoud to more malleable Pashtun protégés like Hekmatyar, whom he expected to coach and dominate during and after the Afghan jihad.[34]

"You Are Creating a Frankenstein"

Zia's nightmare was that Pakistan would be encircled by a Soviet-ruled Afghanistan and a Soviet-allied India. That might be the end of Pakistan. To avert death, he pumped up the rebel (and terrorist) movement. Seven Afghan political parties—four of them Islamist—had their headquarters and bases in Pakistan, but there were also four thousand mujahideen camps in Afghanistan. Commanders led as few as a dozen troops or, in the case of the most successful ones, like Ahmed Shah Massoud (murdered by bin Laden operatives in 2001) as many as ten thousand. Although Pakistani prime minister Benazir Bhutto warned U.S. president George H. W. Bush in 1989 that "you are creating a Frankenstein"—anti-Western Islamists like bin Laden and Hekmatyar—the Americans seemed unconcerned, so long as the mujahideen trained their guns on the Soviets. Key American officials actually *preferred* the Islamists because of their superior zeal, morale and organizational capacity. "Analytically, the best fighters—the best organized fighters—were the fundamentalists," a CIA official confirmed.[35] Still, as one historian's analysis of American support for the West-hating jihadis concludes, Washington, with its "strands" of "clandestine terrorism and clandestine counter-terrorism"—arming the mujahideen with sniper rifle packages, night-vision equipment or Stingers, for example, and then scrambling to buy the weapons back—was "creating the matrix of undeclared war that burst into plain sight in 2001." CIA director Bill Casey assured President Reagan that the mujahideen were playing just "a little part" in his "giant vision" of worldwide struggle against the USSR, but the mujahideen would not content themselves with a bit part forever.[36]

Like the Taliban today, the mujahideen focused on terrorism and sabotage to drive out the Russians and cripple their puppets. They blew up pipelines, cut power lines and placed bombs in government buildings, airports, hotels and cinemas. They scattered land mines all over the country to blow up Soviet tanks, trucks and patrols, and used Stingers to shoot down military and commercial aircraft. They shredded crowds and buildings with car and truck bombs, or left wheelbarrow and bicycle bombs on busy streets. The Russians called the guerrillas *dukhi*—ghosts—for they were nearly impossible to pin down, or even glimpse.[37] When the ghosts materialized, they struck terror into the Russians; Soviet prisoners were skinned alive—slit around the waist, the skin yanked over their heads like a sweater, and left

to die in an agony of heat, pain and flies.[38] The mujahideen regularly blew up innocent civilians, which the CIA lamely defined as "urban sabotage." The CIA boasted
that it had supplied the mujahideen with enough C-4 plastic explosive to "blow up
half of New York." Even the ISI blanched at what they were doing and fomenting.
"We are as good or bad [a] civilized nation as anyone living in the West," General
Muhammed Yousaf confessed, but "when you carry out this sort of operation, it has
a double edge."[39]

Washington's eager sponsorship of Afghan terrorism was all the more remarkable in view of Reagan's simultaneous creation of a "Counterterrorist Center" at the
CIA. Alarmed by Egyptian president Anwar Sadat's assassination by an Islamist
army officer in 1981, Hebzollah's demolition of the U.S. embassy and marine barracks in Beirut in 1983, and the rash of terrorist attacks in 1985 (TWA flight 847, the
Achille Lauro, and the Rome and Vienna airports), Reagan and Casey vowed to scrap
America's hitherto "defensive mentality" and "take the offensive" against terrorism,
which had become "a transnational problem."[40] They now began to put together "hit
teams" to take down terrorists, and sought for ways to burrow into the terrorist
networks. The burrowing was relatively easy in the case of loose-living terrorists like
Abu Nidal, who was as likely to be found in fancy hotel bars as in terrorist camps.
It was far more difficult in the case of pious, abstemious Hezbollah. But even as
Casey labored to defeat terrorism, the ISI was fitting together a terrorist pipeline,
with American dollars. The camps along the Afghan border had become an
American-endowed terrorism university, graduating sixteen to eighteen thousand
guerrillas every year, including thousands of "transnational" Saudis, Algerians,
Egyptians and Palestinians.

One American analyst complained that "terrorism is often confused or equated
with guerrilla warfare." Reagan should have been in no doubt that he was incubating
terrorists, not "freedom fighters." Favorite courses in the Pakistani training camps—
for the best and the brightest—were explosives work, urban sabotage, car bombing
and sniping. The graduates themselves were increasingly interested in bypassing
Afghanistan altogether to take on "corrupt and antireligious governments" across
the Middle East. A small alumni group clustered in the Pakistani city of Peshawar,
which sits at the eastern mouth of the Khyber Pass. It called itself the Islamic Salvation Foundation and submitted to the leadership of Osama bin Laden, who used his
Saudi money to poach the best Arab jihadis from the ISI camps. By 1984, bin Laden
and Abdullah Azzam—who would help found Hamas—were using Saudi and Kuwaiti dollars to cover the expenses ($300 a month) of any Arab from anywhere in

the world who wanted to fight in Afghanistan.⁴¹ Ayman al-Zawahiri returned to Egypt, where he went around the universities dressed like a mujahid—with a turban and a long tunic over baggy pants—and recruited for the jihad in Afghanistan.⁴²

BIN LADEN TAKES AIM AT AMERICA

Meanwhile, bin Laden was tiring of the jihad in Afghanistan, reorienting—by physically separating himself from the mujahideen with Arab-only camps and hospitals—and asking uncomfortable questions: Who was the proper target of jihad? "The communists? The Americans? Israel? The impious government of Egypt? What was the relationship of the Afghan war and the global goals of the Muslim Brotherhood?"⁴³ In Cairo, al-Zawahiri told an American journalist, "Sure, we're taking American help to fight the Russians, but *they're* equally evil." From al-Zawahiri, bin Laden took the notion that Salafist jihad could be twinned with pan-Arab resentment to build a transnational movement that would shake the entire Middle East and create a "global jihad." Al-Zawahiri put Afghanistan in perspective: it was nothing more than "a training course . . . to prepare the Muslim mujahideen to wage their awaited battle against the superpower that now has sole dominance over the globe, namely, the United States." Whereas Washington attributed the Soviet defeat in Afghanistan to imperial overstretch and economic decay (merely aggravated by swarms of holy warriors), the holy warriors saw the Soviet defeat as proof of the invincible power of Islam. Al-Qaeda's game plan emerged: first an Islamic state based on sharia (Afghanistan would serve), and then a steady expansion across the Middle East to smash "the Americans and the Jews," unite the *umma*, grab back Jerusalem and reestablish the caliphate.⁴⁴

Alerted to bin Laden's activities in 1985–86, the Reagan administration downplayed them. The more fighters engaged against the Soviets, the better. Some of Reagan's hard-liners even considered beefing up bin Laden's funding to create a Spanish Civil War–style "International Brigade." CIA deputy director Robert Gates recalled that the Reagan White House actually "examined ways to *increase* their participation . . . coordinate with them . . . not to see them as the enemy." Although evidence of the Soviet Union's decay was accumulating, hard-liners like Reagan, Vice President George Bush, Secretary of Defense Caspar Weinberger and CIA director Bill Casey wanted to "pile on" and deal a death blow to the Soviet empire.⁴⁵

With that larger goal in mind—and much of the CIA "politicized" by the Reagan party line—no one at Langley or the White House took much notice of bin Laden's increasingly sophisticated and menacing methods. Like the CIA itself, which was moving money to the ISI and mujahideen "unilaterals" electronically or by using the ancient and untrackable *hawala* system—delivering cash to a market stall for untraceable delivery to an address thousands of miles away—bin Laden learned to distribute funds and assets invisibly.[46]

REAGAN'S "RABID RIGHT" AND THE JIHAD

In January 1984, CIA director Casey briefed President Reagan on the progress of the Afghan insurgency. The mujahideen had surpassed all expectations. Just four years after the Soviet invasion, they had clawed back 62 percent of Afghanistan, killed or wounded 17,000 Soviet troops, shot down 400 Soviet aircraft, destroyed 2,750 Soviet tanks and armored vehicles, and torched 8,000 Soviet trucks and jeeps. The American-sponsored jihad in Afghanistan went a long way toward erasing Reagan's failures in the Middle East. He had failed to react forcefully when the Israelis had defied American wishes and bombed the Iraqi nuclear reactor at Osirak in 1981 with American F-16s. The strike had brought international condemnation of Israel and the United States, and Secretary of Defense Weinberger had recommended freezing all military and economic aid to Israel, but Reagan had done nothing. In 1982, Reagan and Secretary of State Al Haig had naively blessed an Israeli plan to invade Lebanon, flush out the Syrians and PLO and buttress the Christians. The invasion caused such chaos and suffering that Reagan was forced to dump Haig—exposed as a gullible dupe of Menachem Begin and Ariel Sharon—and deploy marines in 1983 as a peacekeeping force, only to see 241 of them exterminated in their bunks by Hezbollah bombings of the U.S. embassy and marine barracks in Beirut.[47] The issue of Israel had torn the Reagan administration apart—Weinberger, Baker and Bush for bringing the Israelis to heel, Haig and Jeanne Kirkpatrick for giving them free rein. Reagan—who had watched AIPAC shred President Ford's efforts to "reassess" U.S. policy toward Israel in 1975 and nearly defeat Reagan's own efforts to sell AWACS and F-15s to the Saudis—drifted weakly between the two camps.[48] Afghanistan briefly sewed up the rift and gave Reagan his only apparent success in the Middle East; it was a successful campaign that the entire administration could rally behind. The CIA estimated that the war had already cost the Kremlin $12 billion in direct expenses alone—the real number would be much higher—and that its cost would surge if the Kremlin tried to reverse the skid. Casey told Reagan that the Red Army would have to triple or quadruple its troop deployments in Afghanistan to have any hope of beating the mujahideen.[49] On a roll, Casey actually took a page from Hekmatyar's radical playbook and authorized his operatives to cross into Soviet Central Asia and begin inflaming the Muslim Uzbeks, Tajiks, Turkmen and Kazakhs. Casey's agents delivered CIA-printed Korans, perfervid cassette tapes and texts from the Muslim Brotherhood, as well as stirring tales of the jihad in Afghanistan and other anti-Soviet propaganda aimed at "freeing the Muslim lands of Bukhara, Tashkent and Dushabe" from their "infidel regime."[50]

Consensus over Afghanistan was fleeting. As would happen during the neocon-driven George W. Bush administration, there arose in the Reagan administration a basic conflict between what one CIA official called "the sensible bureaucrats . . . and the rabid right." The sensible bureaucrats wanted to keep the mujahideen on a leash and apply moderate pressure to the Soviets. To borrow a phrase from General Zia, they wanted to make Afghanistan "boil at the right temperature," not boil over. The rabid right—Reagan, Casey and Kirkpatrick in the vanguard—threw caution to the wind. They would give the mujahideen *everything* they wanted, and more. Casey took for granted that the Soviets were pursuing a strategy of "creeping imperialism" aimed at two vital crossroads: "the oil fields of the Middle East" and the "isthmus between North and South America."[51] To beat them back in the Middle East, Casey pulled no punches. The CIA would ramp up funding in Afghanistan and even carry the guerrilla war across the Amu Darya River into Soviet Central Asia, hitting Soviet airfields and factories and setting up roadside ambushes to ignite a prairie fire of Islamic revolution.

The Soviet war in Afghanistan was essentially over by 1985. American and Saudi aid to the mujahideen had stymied the Red Army, and a surging heroin trade was filling the coffers of the mujahideen with homegrown revenues as well. Fifty-four-year-old Mikhail Gorbachev came into office, downgraded Afghanistan from a "socialist country" to a "developing" one and vowed to get out. At a Kremlin meeting in November 1986, he voiced his exasperation: "People ask, 'What are we doing there?' Will we be there endlessly? Or should we end this war?" Even with 115,000 troops in country, there was no end in sight.[52] Gorbachev impatiently lowered the bar for success in Afghanistan. Focused on perestroika and glasnost, Moscow would be content with a "neutral country" on its southern border. Gorbachev set a timeline for withdrawal, a year, or two at the most, and then "get out of there." Since the mujahideen refused to negotiate with Babrak Karmal—a discredited, philandering alcoholic—the Soviets brusquely demoted him and installed thirty-eight-year-old Muhammed Najibullah in his place. "Najib the Bull"—nearly twenty years younger than Karmal—was ordered to get the Afghan house in order with an energetic program of "national reconciliation" and prepare for life without Soviet special forces and occupation troops. Gorbachev resented the continuing American aid to the guerrillas. Instead of recognizing that the Soviets—who had rotated a million troops through Afghanistan—had a right to insist on stability in their southern regions, the Reagan administration seemed determined to continue and even intensify the jihad. "The U.S. has set for itself the goal of disrupting a settlement in Afghanistan by any means," Gorbachev protested in December 1986.[53]

Casey, a devout Catholic, was hell-bent on disruption. He welcomed the alliance between fervent Christianity—he covertly funded the Catholic churches in Poland and Nicaragua—and fervent Islam. Reagan too: "I got my ideas of what policy should be from the priests and the Maryknoll nuns," the president liked to say. (Tip O'Neill quipped that he only wished that Reagan had listened more to the nuns and less to cold warriors like Bill Casey.)[54] If the Soviets were trying to secularize the Afghans (or the Yemenis or any of their other clients), the United States would counter by funding religious zealotry. Casey increasingly outsourced the war to ISI director Akhtar: "He is completely involved in this war and certainly knows better than anyone else about his requirements. We simply have to support him."[55] It was an eyes-tight-shut strategy, which the Pakistanis exploited by inserting silver-tongued ISI "barbarian handlers" between the Americans and their mujahideen clients and by choreographing "dog and pony shows" that would appeal to Langley. When Casey insisted in 1984 that he be taken to the Afghan frontier to look at mujahideen camps, the ISI, fearing the impression the real camps would make on Casey, hurriedly built a fake one in the hills behind Islamabad, staffed it with model freedom fighters, then drove Casey around in circles all night—simulating a drive to the tribal areas—before depositing him in the bogus camp before daybreak. Casey was impressed, his belief in the efficacy of jihad confirmed.[56]

Congressman Wilson continued to squeeze extra funding for the mujahideen into federal budgets. Unlike the Nicaraguan contras, the mujahideen were popular everywhere; folklore and romance cloaked their exploits, which explained Charlie Wilson's enthrallment. The hard-drinking politician, who used his government-paid junkets to Pakistan and the Khyber Pass to impress the girlfriends he brought along for the ride, had little sense of the wider dangers posed by the Afghan insurgency, with its anti-Western Saudi and Pakistani minders. Wilson lectured people on the Afghan "cause of freedom," without reflecting on the bigoted ideas being circulated in the Wahhabi madrassas and valley emirates of war-torn Afghanistan.[57] Wilson and Casey secured a stunning expansion of funding for the mujahideen by reaching into the Pentagon budget and diverting unused dollars. When matched by the Saudis, the annual aid surged to $700 million in 1986. Historians looking back for the roots of the Taliban and al-Qaeda can find some in that flood of cash, which armed and empowered the proselytizing ISI generals, but also anti-Western jihadis like Osama bin Laden, Mullah Omar and Gulbuddin Hekmatyar.

With so much American and Saudi money up for grabs, killers like the Egyptian Ayman al-Zawahiri returned to Peshawar. Al-Zawahiri went to work in a Kuwaiti-funded hospital, where the Egyptian terrorist—who had been involved in the plot to assassinate Sadat—came into contact with bin Laden. "I saw this as an opportunity to get to know one of the arenas of jihad that might be a tributary and a base for jihad in Egypt and the Arab region."[58] Hekmatyar, ISI's chief pawn, invested at least as much energy battling rivals like Massoud and propagating radical Islam as he did fighting the Kabul communists. "I would put my arms around Gulbuddin," the CIA station chief in Islamabad recalled, "and we'd hug, you know, like brothers in combat and stuff, and his coal black eyes would look back at you, and you just knew that there was only one thing holding this team together and that was the Soviet Union."[59]

By 1986, the Afghan mujahideen had begun to resent the Arab volunteers who were arriving en masse. The Afghans called them "Wahhabis" because of their hardline Islam—the Arabs regularly desecrated Afghan graves in their campaign against "false idols"—and wished that they would just leave: "They say we are dumb, and we do not know the Koran, and they are more trouble than they are ever going to be worth."[60] For now, Washington turned a blind eye to the growing power of the Saudi-funded Arab Afghans. New money bought new weapons and tactics. Already armed with Stingers and night-vision equipment, the mujahideen now received plastic explosives and sophisticated delay fuses, with which they began launching car bomb attacks. Reagan, who rarely read briefing books, was instead given short videos shot by the CIA or ISI in Afghanistan. He was particularly impressed by the Stinger's debut, mujahideen shrieking "*Allahu Akhbar! Allahu Akhbar!*" as they downed their first Soviet aircraft, Reagan's entourage approvingly noting that "everybody is jumping up and down . . . like some kid at a football game."[61] The more they got, the more fragmented the kids became. "No one should have had any illusions about these people coming together—before or after a Soviet defeat," Robert Gates later wrote. The mujahideen armies were girding for civil war—and the failed state that would fledge the Taliban—even as they administered the death blows to the Soviet army in Afghanistan.

"YOU SEE WHAT OSAMA IS DOING . . ."

Bin Laden moved his family to Peshawar as American and Saudi funding increased. He rented a two-story house and began organizing in a way that alarmed even his Pakistani mentors. He and his Egyptian sidekick, Ayman al-Zawahiri, now denigrated the Afghan war as a mere "incubator" for bigger campaigns to come. Having found no suitable base for jihad in Egypt—"the River Nile runs in its narrow valley between two deserts that have no vegetation or water"—Zawahiri had found one in the wild mountains of Afghanistan. "You see what Osama is doing," one of his aides worriedly noted. "He is collecting and training young people. This is not our policy, our plan. We came to *serve* these people, that's why it's called the Office of Services . . . He is collecting and organizing young people who don't like to participate with the Afghan people."[62] The Arab Afghans had their eyes on a bigger prize, one that soared seventeen hundred feet into the New York sky. Others worriedly noted that al-Zawahiri, bin Laden and their acolytes were committing *takfir*—reversing Islam's core principles (no murder of innocents, for example)—while maintaining a facade of orthodoxy. Islam forbade the terrorism and wanton murder planned by bin Laden, but Osama planned to conceal that fact by creating bogeymen, declaring jihad against them and hammering the fears and resentments of Muslims. A *takfir* apostate himself, with innocent blood on his hands, bin Laden railed against the governments of the Middle East. He called them heretics for their lack of piety and religious zeal.[63]

As a parting gift to Najibullah, the Soviets launched a sequence of attacks in 1987 to rub out as many mujahideen as they could and pinch off the supply lines to Pakistan before they departed. One of their offensives—with two hundred ground troops supported by air strikes and a hailstorm of cluster bomblets—struck at Jaji, Osama bin Laden's Arab-only redoubt near Khost. There, in a week of combat, the legend of Osama was born. Although bin Laden, with his soft hands and weak smile, had been late into combat (visiting the front for the first time in 1984), he and fifty Arab fighters held off four times as many Red Army regulars and Spetsnaz operators for a week before retiring. Fortified with regular insulin injections for his diabetes, bin Laden fought and was wounded in the foot. Though sheltered by a massive CIA-funded tunnel complex fitted with bunkers and hospital beds, he sedulously manufactured the cult of personality that would make him a household name. When the smoke cleared over Jaji, Osama produced a fifty-minute video, showing him leading troops, directing fire, briefing Arab volunteers and scampering along mountain tracks on horseback. Bin Laden distributed the video to sympathetic Arab journalists and posted copies around the Arab world. He twinned this media strategy—to leverage his little Afghan militia into a worldwide movement—with a chilling new goal. He would, as his Egyptian follower al-Zawahiri put it, "hit the snake on the head," which was to say, move past the fading Russians to strike the Americans.[64]

At this critical juncture, Washington lost control of bin Laden forever. With Reagan aging and losing his grip on affairs, Casey dead from brain cancer, Congress and the press asking awkward questions about Iran-Contra and Zia's martial law regime reluctantly liberalizing and shuffling ISI directors, the Afghan portfolio flopped open and scattered its pages. Najibullah had made a good-faith effort to bind up Afghanistan's wounds, erase the Soviet experiment (and presence), bring home the two million refugees in Pakistan and Iran and blend the traditional and fundamentalist strains in Afghan society to restore "normal political life."[65] Washington took no hand in that all-important end game other than to cast a distracted glance—in 1987—at Reagan's radical protégés in Afghanistan. Although the Arab Afghans—the "brigade of strangers" circulating in Peshawar—were still a relatively unknown danger, many analysts and members of Congress were incensed by Gulbuddin Hekmatyar's refusal to travel to Washington to sit down with Reagan and the other American "infidels" who had been bankrolling and arming him for seven years. Milton Bearden, who ran the CIA field office in Afghanistan, defended the tilt toward the Islamists—which was much more pronounced than revealed in congressional audits because of all the secret Saudi funding—in the usual way. The Islamists—Hekmatyar and the Arabs— killed Russians, and the secularists didn't. The CIA, Bearden fumed, was not going to entrust its jihad to "some liberal arts jerkoff." When credible secular mujahideen commanders like Abdul Haq tried to make their voices heard in Washington—and divert funds from the "Wahhabis"—Bearden cut off their access. He would make the strategic decisions, not "Hollywood Haq."[66]

In September 1987, Soviet foreign minister Eduard Shevardnadze had a remarkable meeting with his American counterpart—George Shultz—in Washington. "We will leave Afghanistan," Shevardnadze conceded. The Soviets had poured precious billions into the country; they admitted to twenty thousand dead, but the real number was probably four times that. The timeline to leave was five to twelve months. Gorbachev had authorized Shevardnadze to "associate the United States with the political solution" for Afghanistan, to help build a successor government that would hold back the Pakistani-fostered Islamists. Shultz did nothing with the offer. When Gorbachev invited Vice President Bush to cowrite the last act in Afghanistan—to "avoid a bloody war in the country"—Bush too failed to stir. Both Bush and Shultz were hemmed in by Reagan administration "groupthink" on the Soviets, and did not want to appear "soft." Soviet warnings about the dangers of Islamic radicalism and the *global* threat posed by Afghanistan's mujahideen armies were discounted in the White House and the CIA. Inside Afghanistan, the mujahideen cemented their victory not by joining Najibullah's Commission for National Reconciliation, but by assassinating its leaders and delegates.

Lunching with KGB director Vladimir Kryuchkov in December 1987, acting CIA director Robert Gates heard Kryuchkov's warning that the United States was holding the stirrups in Afghanistan for the rise of a Sunni equivalent of the Shiite regime in Iran. Because two-thirds of the mujahideen were fundamentalists, they had received most of the billions in U.S. and Saudi subsidies delivered over the course of the struggle.[67] Killers and bigots like Hekmatyar and bin Laden had used that money not only to kill Russians, but to build networks for the future. That explained their unwillingness to join Najibullah in reconciling the Afghan factions. They had no interest in Najibullah's moderate vision: a return of King Zahir Shah from exile, a separation of religious and political Islam, private enterprise, women's rights, land reform and a jihad against illiteracy. They wanted a jihad against Westerners, Najibullah's overthrow and an Islamic republic where sharia would be strictly observed.[68] "You seem fully occupied in trying to deal with just one fundamentalist Islamic state," Kryuchkov said. Another one, in Afghanistan, could be just as dangerous, or even more so. Bin Laden and the other Arab jihadis were inculcating a weird cult of death and martyrdom in Afghanistan that frightened even the war-calloused Afghans. With the Soviets beaten, the Arab Afghans were stockpiling unused cash and arms, and—under bin Laden and al-Zawahiri—were creating "the base"—al-Qaeda—for a worldwide assault on the West, "to lift the word of God and to make His religion victorious."

Al-Qaeda, formally created in 1988 as a conglomerate of Islamist terrorist cells in twenty-six countries, planned "to establish the truth, get rid of evil, and establish an Islamic nation." Bin Laden considered the United States a "crocodile"; the Arab world "a helpless child." By the late 1980s, he spoke publicly of killing Americans. Vietnam had killed nearly sixty thousand Americans and provoked antiwar demonstrations. To get the Americans out of Arab affairs—in Lebanon, Palestine and the Persian Gulf—bin Laden proposed more killing: "The Americans won't stop . . . until we give them a lot of blows."[69] But Washington still took little notice of apparent lunatics like bin Laden, and Gates considered Kryuchkov's offer of cooperation in Afghanistan to be a deception and brushed it off. Washington was busy managing the collapse of Soviet power in Europe, owed in no small part to Moscow's investment of $45 billion in the fruitless Afghan War, as well as the end of the Iran-Iraq War in the Persian Gulf. Afghanistan seemed like a sideshow by comparison. Moreover, with its seven warring political parties and innumerable sects and factions, Afghanistan was just too complicated. It was also a mess: 1.3 million Afghans had died in the nine-year war with the Soviets, 1.5 million had become disabled (by land mines and promiscuous Soviet fire), a third of the population had migrated to refugee camps in Pakistan and Iran, and much of the remaining population had flooded into relatively safe cities like Kabul, which filled up with slums and shanties. Nine years of Soviet attacks had smashed roads, schools and houses, and poisoned wells, irrigation systems and farmland. With other matters to deal with and the Soviets gone, Washington defaulted to the strategy that had rooted out the Soviets— Saudi subsidies and "the de facto promotion of Pakistani goals as carried out by Pakistani intelligence." With all their wild talk about the "Islamic tide," wasn't it possible that the Soviets were just manufacturing excuses for their failure, blaming everything on crazy Islamists instead of their own failed system and intervention? Moreover, President George H. W. Bush, who watched the Soviet retreat from Afghanistan, was determined *not* to gloat or make matters worse for the Russians lest they return to imperial policies. Bush would hesitate even to endorse German reunification over Soviet objections; what were the odds that he would dive into Afghanistan to replace Soviet power and influence? No one in Washington gave Afghanistan much thought as the Berlin Wall came tumbling down. Those who did generally reckoned that even if Afghanistan *did* fall apart, it would make sense to let the UN, the Saudis and the Pakistanis—regional experts and U.S. allies—put the country back together.[70]

CHAPTER 13

SADDAM

ONE REASON AMERICANS didn't worry too much about Afghanistan imploding was that the Persian Gulf—a far more important region—was shattering into pieces, and it was unclear who would claim the lion's share, the Iranians or the Iraqis. Neither outcome seemed advantageous to American strategists.

THE IRAN-IRAQ WAR

The Iran-Iraq War had raged for nearly a decade, from 1980 to 1988, when both countries finally collapsed in a welter of casualties and war weariness. Saddam had started the war, knifing into Iran's oil-rich Khuzestan Province in September 1980 to exploit the chaos that attended the fall of the shah and the breakdown of the Iranian military. Saddam had planned to seize Iran's oil fields as well as the Shatt al-Arab waterway. Persia had controlled Iraq until the sixteenth century, when the Ottomans pulled Iraq into their empire; no fewer than eighteen treaties had been concluded between the Turks and the Persians between 1638 and the withering of the Ottoman Empire in 1918, yet somehow the border between Iran and Iraq had never been precisely drawn. That was all the pretext that Saddam—who grouped

Persians with Jews and flies as "three whom God shouldn't have created"—needed to try to push Iraq's border over the Shatt al-Arab and into southwestern Iran. Saddam also wanted to overthrow Ayatollah Khomeini, who was constantly agitating among Iraq's oppressed Shiites.

For his part, Khomeini hated Saddam—"the puppet of Satan." Khomeini wanted to push Iranian control into Iraq to rescue its Shiite majority from their Sunni Baathist masters. He welcomed Saddam's invasion as a useful casus belli. Six months after attacking, the Iraqi invasion stalled—mired in the marshes and barbed wire of Khuzestan—but instead of negotiating an end to the war, Khomeini launched a counterattack on Iraq. In 1982, Iranian forces retook Khorramshahr and drove the Iraqis back across the Shatt al-Arab to Basra. Reproached by a colleague for his indifference to the spiraling casualties on the Iraq front—where Muslims were killing Muslims—Khomeini shrugged: "Do you also criticize God when he sends an earthquake?"[1] Khomeini's coldhearted ferocity and determination to liberate the Shiites not only of Iraq, but of Saudi Arabia and Kuwait as well, persuaded the Gulf Arabs to reach deep into their pockets again. This time they were not supporting Palestinian fedayeen or Afghan mujahideen; this time they offered danegeld to Khomeini to back off. The Saudis and Kuwaitis agreed to supply Saddam with $70 billion, which he would fork over to Khomeini as war reparations. Considerably enriched, it was assumed that Khomeini would lay down his arms and declare the Iran-Iraq War at an end. Saddam even provided a face-saving pretext—if the money wasn't enough. Israel had invaded Lebanon in 1982 to root out the PLO, smash the Syrians and put the Christian Phalange in power. Wasn't it time for Muslim powers to bury the hatchet and make common cause against the Jews and the Crusaders?

Khomeini's reply was not long in coming. In July 1982, he launched the first of a new wave of great offensives into Iraq, declaring that his aim was nothing less than the removal of Saddam Hussein, Saddam's replacement by an Iranian-style Islamic republic and $150 billion in reparations. Iran's human wave attacks were repulsed, and five more Iranian offensives in 1983 were also blocked. In 1984, the Iranians captured a thin band of Iraqi territory, but at the cost of monstrous casualties. Khomeini had converted the war into a struggle for national and revolutionary union, arguing that the survival of Shiite Islam was at stake. Government papers like *Etelaat* wrote paeans to the glory of war and martyrdom: "There is not a single school or town that is excluded from the happiness of waging war, from drinking the exquisite elixir of death or from the sweet death of the martyr, who dies in order to live forever in Paradise."[2] By now, the Iranians were sending attacks with scarcely trained schoolboy militias, or Basiji, in the front as human mine detectors. Those "martyrdom seekers"—seeking paradise—exploded mines (and themselves), inhaled clouds of Iraqi poison gas and cleared assault paths for Pasdaran revolutionary guards and Iranian regular units. Raw Iranian conscripts were visited in their trenches by white-shrouded phantoms on white horses—professional actors hired in Tehran—and given plastic keys. In the event of death—a dead certainty—they were assured that the keys (stamped "Made in Taiwan") would somehow open the doors of paradise. Those senseless "martyrdom operations"—designed to overwhelm Iraqi conventional superiority—were the root of the suicide bombing missions of the 1990s and 2000s.[3]

To discourage the fanatical Iranians, who seemed impervious to rational cost-benefit analysis, Saddam's military hunkered down behind dense field fortifications, smothered and burned the Iranian attackers with gas and high explosives, and began attacking eleven Iranian cities with air strikes and Scud missile attacks. The aerial attacks—answered by the Iranians with air and missile attacks of their own in what became a "war of the cities"—were deliberately indiscriminate, hitting civilian as well as military targets. Saddam had assumed that the Iranians would come to their senses quickly. With most of the fighting confined to the region around Basra—where Khomeini was trying to besiege and annex Iraq's biggest Shiite city—life in Iraq was little affected by the conflict until the third year of the war. By then, under constant Iranian ground and air attack, Saddam's patience (and foreign currency reserves) wore thin. The fact that U.S. arms sales of $200 million to Iraq amounted to less than 1 percent of Iraqi military purchases during the war hinted at the crushing costs of the conflict.[4] The $30 billion in Iraqi reserves in 1980 had been reduced to just $3 billion three years later; Iraq's foreign debt surged that year to $25 billion, in large part because Iraqi oil income—shelled, bombed and blockaded by the Iranians—had plummeted from $26 billion in 1980 to $9 billion in 1982.[5]

REAGAN'S SUPPORT FOR SADDAM HUSSEIN

In view of the outrage expressed by George W. Bush when he made the case for war against Iraq in 2003 and made much of Iraq's air strikes against Kurds and Iranians as evidence of Baathist state terrorism, the actual American hand in those air strikes and the Iran-Iraq War in general was remarkable. In 1984, President Ronald Reagan restored normal diplomatic relations with Iraq—broken during the 1967 Six-Day War—and reinforced a National Security Decision Directive (NSDD) which stated that the United States "would do whatever was necessary and legal to prevent Iraq from losing its war with Iran." The United States, Reagan said, "could not afford to allow Iraq to lose." Saddam Hussein emerged as the indispensable leader—a man who could unite the Baghdad elites under the strain of an unwinnable war and rally Iraq against Iran. Thus, Reagan quietly removed Iraq from Washington's list of state sponsors of terrorism in February 1982 and began channeling export credits, food aid and military support to Saddam. The heavily redacted NSDD tells little about Reagan's "strategic concept for near-term planning"—it's almost entirely blacked out—but it does suggest that Washington's aim was to force acceptance of Israel on Iraq and "strengthen . . . indigenous defense capabilities."[6]

Reagan regretted the Iraqi use of chemical weapons, but he made clear that America's supreme concern was oil: "Because of the real and psychological impact of a curtailment in the flow of oil from the Persian Gulf on the international economic system, we must assure our readiness to deal promptly with actions aimed at disrupting that traffic."[7] This would later become the vision of George W. Bush: compel Iraq to recognize Israel, pump oil and serve as an American base and proxy in the Middle East. To garner those objectives, Reagan sent Donald Rumsfeld to Baghdad as a special envoy in 1983 and again in 1984. In a cordial ninety-minute meeting, Rumsfeld pressed Saddam to build new pipelines across Iraq to Saudi Arabia and Jordan, so that oil exports to the West—cut off by Iranian action in the Gulf and Syria's closure of its pipeline—could be increased.[8] Rumsfeld, who had served as President Gerald Ford's secretary of defense and twenty years later would condemn Saddam's use of chemical weapons, actually appeared in Baghdad and shook hands with Saddam on the very day in 1984 that the UN released a report that sharply criticized the Iraqi president for his *daily* employment of mustard gas and nerve agents like tabun against Iran. It later emerged that Vice President George H. W. Bush coordinated most of the support for Saddam Hussein, which made Bush's war *against* Saddam in 1991 and Bush's son's war against Saddam in 2003 at least as ironic as the fact that Rumsfeld was CEO of the pharmaceutical giant G. D. Searle at the time that he was engaging Saddam and declining to criticize the Iraqi's use of weapons of mass destruction.

Vice President George H. W. Bush became the conduit for satellite-guided battlefield intelligence, cash, agricultural credits, chemicals and weapons to Iraq, as well as dual-use technologies like computers and engines. More controversially, Bush probably provided the dual-use biological agents that would become the germ of Saddam's biological weapons program, a likely ingredient in the mysterious Gulf War Syndrome and a big cause of George W. Bush's invasion of Iraq in 2003: agents like histoplasma, botulin, anthrax, clostridium and West Nile virus, which the Reagan White House surely knew were not being purchased for epidemiological study. In 1988—a year that Washington doubled financial aid to Iraq—Saddam dropped chemical bombs on the Kurdish town of Halabja in northern Iraq, killing as many as seven thousand inhabitants. That atrocity, tolerated by the Americans, was intended to punish Kurdish separatism and contacts with the Iranians, but would later be seized upon by President George W. Bush as an intolerable example of Saddam's record of terrorism and WMD.[9] The Reagan White House coordinated the transfer of weapons—helicopters, tanks, bombs and howitzers—from the armies of Jordan, Egypt, Saudi Arabia and Kuwait to Iraq. Of course America's overriding interest was to maintain a healthy balance of power in the Gulf, so Washington merely "tilted" toward Iraq. Once Iranian might was broken, Washington tilted the other way. Henry Kissinger pithily summarized America's war aim: "It's a pity they both can't lose."[10] Saddam Hussein understood the ambivalent Americans perfectly. In his 1983 meeting with Rumsfeld, he snickered to Reagan's envoy that he fully appreciated the real American position—"to let this group of lunatics bash each other"—but would gladly take American aid anyway.[11]

IRAN-CONTRA

To make Iraq bleed as badly as Iran, Reagan began in 1985 to supply *Iran* with critical spare parts and munitions, as well as complete weapons systems, which were delivered by the Israelis through the intercession of an Iranian arms dealer named Manucher Ghorbanifar. This was the root of the notorious Iran-Contra affair, cooked up by Reagan's national security adviser, Robert McFarlane, when he learned that the Israelis had been blithely selling the Iranians spare (American) parts for years. Although pitched by McFarlane and his deputies—Lieutenant Colonel Oliver North and Vice Admiral John Poindexter as well as future neocons like Elliott Abrams, Otto Reich, John Negroponte and Michael Ledeen—as a way to empower moderates in Khomeini's inner circle, the real reason for American arms sales to Iran was threefold.[12] Cash profits from the sales could be diverted by Israeli or Saudi middlemen to the Nicaraguan contras, for whom U.S. support had been cut off by Congress. Political profits could be used to purchase Iranian pressure on Lebanon's Hezbollah to release American hostages who had been held in Beirut since early 1984. And strengthening Iran would prolong the war, grind down both Gulf powers and magnify U.S. influence.[13] Both Secretary of State George Shultz and Secretary of Defense Caspar Weinberger opposed the sordid scheme, but Reagan, who was aging and briefly hospitalized with colon cancer, plunged ahead, foolishly insisting that he was *not* trading arms for hostages, not negotiating with terrorists and not breaking the law.[14]

In 1987–88, Washington tilted back toward Iraq. The U.S. Navy began flagging Kuwaiti tankers in the Persian Gulf—to shield them from Iranian attacks and protect Iraq's oil revenues—and also began hitting Iranian oil platforms and surface ships.[15] Iran-Contra had kept the Iranian military going until the last year of the war, but at what a price! Oliver North had added a hefty markup to all weapons deliveries to pay for the contras, and Ghorbanifar had added a 41 percent markup of his own to pay himself. Khomeini must have realized that Iran could not go on forever paying premiums like that for its TOWs, Hawks and spare parts. The whole affair had begun to unravel in October 1986 anyway, when a CIA flight of Iranian-funded weapons was shot down in Nicaragua. A Lebanese newspaper reported the covert deal with the Reagan White House, and Ollie North and his secretary, Fawn Hall, were caught shredding NSC documents—including a signed authorization from Reagan himself—relating to the program. Reagan experienced the sharpest drop in approval rating of any president in U.S. history, from 67 percent to 46 percent in November 1986. North and Poindexter were driven into the wilderness, and Iran-Contra folded up amid congressional hearings and indignant press coverage, all of which left the U.S.-built Iranian military vulnerable as never before. International sanctions on Iran—unalleviated by North and Poindexter—cut off vital spare parts, but also weapons. As the war lengthened, the Iraqi advantage in tanks (4 to 1), fighter aircraft (10 to 1), helicopters (3 to 1) and artillery (4 to 1) lengthened too. The crowning blow landed on July 3, 1988, when the Aegis-class guided-missile cruiser USS *Vincennes* shot down an Iranian Airbus with 290 passengers on board. The American skipper claimed that he'd mistaken the Iran Air flight for an Iranian F-14, but Khomeini bought none of that; he assumed that the Americans were actively joining the fight on the side of Iraq, and wearily agreed to end the war.

Saddam emerged from the war with a hatred for the Americans and towering debts. Even as villainous a character as Saddam was struck by the depravity of Iran-Contra, which was publicly pieced together by the 1986 Tower Commission. Not only had Reagan armed the Iranians, he had duped his Iraqi ally, providing the Iraqis with doctored satellite photos that induced them to shift forces *away* from an Iranian offensive that seized the right bank of the Shatt al-Arab as well as Iraq's southernmost city in 1986.[16] Saddam's loss of faith in Washington was compounded by financial worries. The Americans, Japanese and Western Europeans had loaned Saddam about $35 billion, the Saudis $31 billion, Kuwait $14 billion and the UAE $8 billion. Iraq's war costs and economic losses mirrored Iran's—at least half a trillion dollars—and the country emerged from the war with an $80 billion external debt, which it had little hope of repaying, with oil prices sliding down to $13 a barrel as the war petered out and supply picked up.[17] Both sides had lost between five hundred thousand and a million killed and wounded, yet the hotly disputed borderland between the two countries had not shifted an inch. A more wasteful and tragic war could scarcely be imagined.

Bush 41

Surveying the blighted landscape in 1989, the incoming George H. W. Bush administration reiterated that "access to Persian Gulf oil and the security of key friendly states are vital to U.S. national security." Still, Bush 41 evinced far more modesty than his gun-slinging son. The United States would support local Gulf powers "to enable them to play a more active role in their own defense and thereby reduce the necessity for unilateral U.S. military intervention."[18] With huge strategic and financial liabilities—the Reagan administration's "voodoo economics" had burdened the United States with a $2.6 trillion national debt—Washington needed to outsource as much of its national security as possible to "Western allies and Japan" but also to "friendly regional states." Saudi Arabia was the last remaining friend, but Bush yearned for better relations with Iraq, if only Saddam could be persuaded to moderate his anti-Israeli rhetoric and renounce weapons of mass destruction. The Iran-Iraq War had driven Iraq into opposition to Syria—which backed Khomeini—and into a coalition with moderate, pro-American Gulf states like Saudi Arabia.[19] That coalition needed to be strengthened. Iran would also be engaged on the basis of strict "reciprocity": give something to get something. Like the Reagan administration, Bush 41 was still focused on American hostages taken by Shiite militias in Lebanon. If Tehran would arrange their release, relations would be improved.

WOLFOWITZ SOUNDS THE ALARM ON IRAQ

If Bush was moderate on Iraq—hoping for better relations—his undersecretary of defense for policy, Paul Wolfowitz, was not. Wolfowitz had been sounding the alarm on Iraq since 1979, when he, Dennis Ross and Geoffrey Kemp authored a Pentagon study that identified Iraq as *the* chief danger in the Persian Gulf. In what would become a tremendous historical irony, Wolfowitz argued that the collapse of Iran had empowered Iraq, making it a regional heavyweight. Until the fall of the shah, Baghdad had been contained by the offsetting power of Tehran. Suddenly, Wolfowitz argued in 1979, Iraq had no local peers. [Wolfowitz would, of course, engineer the same scenario in reverse in 2003, when he would design a war that would collapse Iraq and leave Iran as the peerless regional heavyweight] Towering over its rivals in 1979, Saddam Hussein's Baath Party made no secret of its resentment of the West, its warm relations with Moscow, its hatred of Israel (and the Arab-Israeli peace process) and its designs on Kuwait. The Iraqis had been claiming Kuwait ever since the British amputated its territory from the Ottoman province of Basra in 1899. Resenting Kuwait's dubious provenance, Iraqis defiantly referred to the sovereign emirate as their "nineteenth province." Kuwait had deep reserves of oil and a long seacoast, which made it far easier for Kuwait to export oil than Iraq. The Iraqis had to rely on the contested Shatt al-Arab waterway, which wended past the guns and airfields of the pugnacious Iranians. Iraq had nearly invaded Kuwait in 1961, backing off only after the British (and then Nasser) sent troops to protect the otherwise impotent al-Sabah dynasty, which coughed up loans to the Iraqis that were never repaid.[20]

The Wolfowitz study of 1979 recommended a more robust American military presence in the Persian Gulf and Southwest Asia "to balance" Iraqi power and influence. "It seems likely that we and Iraq will increasingly be at odds." Not everyone bought into Wolfowitz's fears. Defense Secretary Harold Brown dismissed the study with the observation that revolutionary Iran posed a bigger threat than Baathist Iraq, and certainly the Reagan administration's support of Saddam against Iran over two presidential terms made the same point. Reagan and Weinberger actually *welcomed* Saddam's invasion of Iran in 1980 as a useful check on the ayatollahs. Although Zalmay Khalilzad, a Dick Cheney confidant in the administrations of Bush father and son, attempted to refocus attention on Iraq after George H. W. Bush's inauguration in 1989, he too made little headway against an administration that was distracted by the crumbling Soviet Union and a sense that Iran, not Iraq, was still the principal threat in the Gulf. The Bush 41 administration also took a pragmatic view on Iraq. National Security Adviser Brent Scowcroft had no illusions about Saddam's wickedness, but thought it best to engage him with American wheat sales, investments in Iraq and "nonlethal" training programs in the hope that he could be steered onto a peaceful track. Hardheaded analysis of the Iraqi military also suggested that it was not as mighty as it seemed. Its paper strength was one million, but most of those troops were poorly trained and untested in battle. The guts of the army was the Republican Guard—140,000 strong—and it would be no match for determined, well-equipped Western armies.[21]

In 1989, the Bush administration prepared a top secret National Intelligence Estimate titled "Iraq: Foreign Policy of a Major Regional Power." The NIE concluded that Iraq was a menace, but a weary one incapable of major combat operations. Saddam had acquired long-range strike aircraft and large stocks of chemical and biological weapons, was almost certainly working on nuclear weapons again and had extended the range of his Scud missiles, but would "be reluctant to engage in foreign military adventures" because of the still undigested costs of the Iran-Iraq War.[22] What the Bush administration failed to discern was that it was precisely the high cost of the Iran-Iraq War that would drive Saddam Hussein into military adventures. The Iraqi economy was a shambles, unemployment was high, and the Iraqi military—as employer of last resort—could not be substantially reduced. Saddam was broke, needed money and knew where to get it: Kuwait.

Saddam Takes Aim at Kuwait

Whereas President Bush had assumed that Saddam would demobilize his big army after the war, the Iraqi dictator maintained it intact, with its fifty infantry divisions and six hundred strike aircraft. In 1990, Saddam ordered the U.S. Navy to leave the Gulf, threatened "to burn half of Israel" with his Scuds and began trying to replace the nuclear facilities bombed by the Israelis in 1981. It was now apparent that

Saddam was trying to divert attention from Iraq's foundering economy and recon-struction problems with a bellicose policy toward the West and Israel. He was also seeking pretexts to thrust into Kuwait, the UAE or Saudi Arabia to seize their oil and cash. In July 1990, Saddam's foreign minister, Tariq Aziz, shaped the pretext when he defined Kuwait's refusal to cede territory to Iraq, cut its oil production and forgive its Iraqi war debts as "military aggression." Baghdad also accused Kuwait of "slant drilling" into Iraq's Rumaila field to steal an estimated $2 billion worth of Iraqi oil reserves. The Bush administration suspended grain sales but otherwise accepted the U.S. Central Command's (Centcom) assessment that "Iraq is not ex-pected to use military force to attack Kuwait or Saudi Arabia to seize disputed ter-ritory or resolve a dispute over oil policy."[23]

In Baghdad, U.S. ambassador April Glaspie pressed for a clarification of Iraqi intentions. Iraq had real incentives for annexing Kuwait. The "nineteenth province" would generate $20 million a day in oil revenues and endow Iraq with 20 percent of the world's oil.[24] Glaspie's work became more urgent in the third week of July when Iraqi Republican Guard units began deploying to Basra in preparation for what satellite imagery suggested could only be an invasion of Kuwait. A British of-ficer traveling from Kuwait to Baghdad reported a column of three thousand ve-hicles carrying Iraqi troops and guns to the border. Was this war, or just an elaborate Iraqi bluff—what the Defense Intelligence Agency (DIA) called "intimidation and force posturing"—to drive up oil prices and extort major concessions from Kuwait? Egyptian president Hosni Mubarak and Saudi king Fahd thought Saddam was bluffing; they urged Washington to let the "Arab family" work out its problems and talk the bully down.

Bush's chairman of the Joint Chiefs of Staff, General Colin Powell, also coun-seled patience. His military options to retake Kuwait, Scowcroft grumbled, "had not seemed designed by anyone eager to undertake the task."[25] Powell, whom Reagan had brought in as his last national security adviser to clean up the mess of Iran-Contra, was highly respected in the Bush White House. The general's service in Vietnam had made him wary of "chickenhawk" civilians, who pressed too quickly or eagerly for military solutions. The Weinberger Doctrine—also called the Powell Doctrine—had been conceived by Secretary of Defense Caspar Weinberger and Powell in November 1984 after Reagan's disastrous intervention in Lebanon, and still prevailed in 1990. U.S. forces would only be introduced into conflicts with clear, achievable aims, a visible exit, and strong popular and congressional support.[26] Pow-ell considered that all of those criteria were unfulfilled in the case of Iraq's takeover of Kuwait. He called State Department hawks "the warriors of C Street" and proposed a different strategy: "grind down" Saddam through "a policy of containment or strangulation." Less understandable was Powell's aversion to using U.S. forces—carriers or maritime prepositioning ships—to "signal" American resolve. To Powell, such signaling was a slippery slope that might tip the United States into an unwanted war, like Vietnam. To Saddam, the absence of clear signals suggested that he could probably get away with what he was contemplating.[27]

April Glaspie met with Saddam on July 25, 1990. A regional expert and Arabic speaker, Glaspie believed wholeheartedly in the Bush plan to "moderate" Saddam Hussein. She took as her brief a memo that had arrived from Secretary of State James Baker the previous day. Baker had condemned Iraqi efforts to bully the weaker Gulf states and had noted the peril "of having oil production and pricing policy in the Gulf determined and enforced by Iraqi guns." But Baker also affected "to take no position on the border delineation issue raised by Iraq with respect to Kuwait."[28] Imprecision like that had caused the Korean War forty years earlier, when Secretary of State Dean Acheson neglected to include South Korea in America's East Asian security perimeter. The North Koreans had interpreted that omission as license to invade the south. In 1990, Saddam saw an opening in Baker's apparent indifference on the border issue. What if he left Kuwait largely intact but seized the Rumaila oil field and one or two of Kuwait's islands? Perhaps the Bush administration would permit *that*. The Bush administration itself had no idea what it would do if Saddam invaded Kuwait. Instead of facing the question squarely, President Bush and his key deputies kicked the can down the road and merely hoped that "moderation" would work.

"Do not push us to [invade Kuwait]," Saddam growled to Ambassador Glaspie. "Do not make it the only option left with which we can protect our dignity." After the meeting, Glaspie cabled Baker and urged him to "ease off on public criticism of Iraq" until Saddam had been given the chance to negotiate with the Kuwaitis at a Saudi-arranged conference in Jedda. At the Pentagon, top deputies like Paul Wolfowitz were disturbed by the defeatist tone of Glaspie's cable, but the actual presidential letter to Saddam drafted for Bush's signature by his NSC ran in a Glaspian vein. Saddam's saber-rattling, his accumulation of weapons of mass destruction, his brutal police state and his anti-American and anti-Israeli rhetoric were resolutely downplayed—"certain Iraqi policies and activities"—and Bush pronounced himself "pleased" with Saddam's willingness to attend the Jedda conference that Saddam himself had convened at the point of a gun. Although Bush was about to announce a 25 percent reduction in U.S. armed forces—the post–Cold War "peace dividend"—no cuts had yet been made. Secretary of Defense Dick Cheney's top deputies at the Pentagon recommended a stern rewrite explicitly warning Saddam *not* to attack Kuwait, but the shilly-shallying NSC letter went out over Bush's signature.[29] Nothing was done to reinforce the Kuwaitis, or to open Saudi bases to U.S. forces. A two-thousand-man Marine Expeditionary Unit remained in the Philippines, no B-52s were sent to Diego Garcia, and there was not even a navy carrier in the Gulf or the North Arabian Sea. The nearest U.S. carrier, the *Independence*, was four days away.

SADDAM INVADES KUWAIT

By August 1, it was plain that Saddam intended to invade Kuwait. He had satisfied himself that Washington would not intervene to stop him. Satellite photos depicted corps-strength Iraqi armor and infantry units on the Kuwaiti border, Iraqi marines with bridging equipment opposite Bubiyan Island, dense concentrations of Iraqi strike aircraft and helicopters at air bases in southern Iraq, and all the logistics required for a push down to Kuwait City. The DIA reported that "harsh Iraqi rhetoric" portended "military action" and that troop and aircraft concentrations were sufficient to undertake attacks not only on Kuwait, but "the Eastern Province of Saudi Arabia" as well. Nevertheless, President Bush was preparing to depart for Aspen, Colorado, to announce the "peace dividend," and Centcom commander General Norman Schwarzkopf let his staff go home early on August 2. By seven p.m. Schwarzkopf's staff had all come rushing back from the suburban subdivisions, gyms, Little League diamonds and malls of Tampa; Iraqi mechanized divisions had carved into Kuwait, driven the emir into exile, seized the capital and swiftly defeated weak resistance by the Kuwaiti army. Iraqi troops picked Kuwait clean in a methodical campaign of looting. Containers were loaded with valuables and shipped up to Basra. Iraqi pilots seized Kuwait Airways' jets and flew them up to Baghdad, along with Kuwait airport's runway lights and baggage handling equipment. Cars, trucks, buses, tractors and just about anything with an engine was stolen or stripped for parts. Seats were ripped out of Kuwait's stadiums and movie theaters for use in Iraq. Kuwait's hospitals, universities and libraries were stripped to the bare walls. Beef carcasses were heaved out of Kuwaiti meat freezers and shipped to Iraq. Kuwait's gem market was picked clean, and one million ounces of gold were seized from the Central Bank of Kuwait and deposited in Baghdad. Iraqi emissaries circulated around the Middle East boasting that they had taken $500 billion in cash out of Kuwait; they offered to share the loot with friendly states who would accept the Iraqi invasion and annexation. Iraqi looters, bused in by Saddam to take their places as "Kuwaitis" in case there was a UN referendum on Kuwait's future, swept through Kuwait's shops, houses and apartments stealing everything in sight: televisions, stereos, sinks, toilets, lamps, rugs, curtains, even cutlery and lightbulbs.[30]

No one had predicted that Saddam would actually do something this reckless, but he had always been a reckless operator.[31] Not having made up their minds how to handle an Iraqi invasion, the Bush administration fell to arguing. "Not all wars are avoidable," Scowcroft reflected, "and this was perhaps one of them." Saddam's attack engaged America's superpower interest in oil as well as its determination to shape the new world order that had emerged with the collapse of the USSR. Scowcroft noted a basic divide between those who saw the Iraqi invasion as "the major crisis of our time" (Scowcroft and Cheney) and those who viewed it as a manageable "crisis du jour" (Baker and Powell) that could be handled by sanctions, diplomacy and an embargo on Iraqi oil.[32]

"WE NEED AN OBJECTIVE"

The UN Security Council, the UN General Assembly and the Arab League had all condemned the invasion and there was discussion in the White House of an air and naval blockade of Iraq, but Secretary of Defense Cheney wanted more than just protests, sanctions or a quarantine. Saddam was angling to "dominate OPEC, the Gulf and the Arab world." His tanks were now forty kilometers from Saudi Arabia, and even if he didn't take their oil wells, he would "have an impact . . . The problem would get worse, not better." Saddam's hasty offer in August of a final peace settlement to the Iranians and his evacuation of a thousand square miles of Iranian territory—the only spoils from Iraq's eight-year war with Iran—confirmed that Saddam was clearing the decks and focusing all his energies on a fight with the United States.[33] Cheney enjoined Bush to lay out American aims clearly: "We need an objective." Cheney wanted to fling Saddam out of Kuwait—at a minimum—and perhaps march on to Baghdad to depose him. The United States *had* to maintain a favorable balance in the Gulf. But Cheney also worried that the American people would not support a war to restore the reactionary al-Sabah dynasty, particularly when such a war appeared to benefit Japan—still the export-driven bugbear of Americans in 1990—which imported far more Kuwaiti oil than the United States. Congress also wavered throughout, even a staunch "national security Democrat" like Georgia senator Sam Nunn insisting that only air and naval forces be used against Saddam, no ground troops.

"Kuwait Is an Accident of History"

With Gorbachev's reformers foundering in the face of counterattacks from Soviet hard-liners, could America really afford to embark on war in *Iraq*? The always cautious Powell fed on doubts like that. A war with Iraq would not be easy—"harder than Panama or Libya, this would be the NFL, not a scrimmage"—and such a war as *this* seemed as ill-advised to Powell as Vietnam.[34] He chided Cheney for sounding "Carteresque" in his resolve to defend the Gulf. Carter, of course, had made all the right noises about defending the shah and Iranian moderates, but then collapsed under Khomeini's pressure. Powell reckoned that another defeat like that would destroy American credibility, and he didn't like the sound of a war with Iraq. "The American people," he argued, "don't want their young dying for $1.50 a gallon oil." Defend Saudi Arabia, Powell reasoned, but concede Kuwait to Saddam. "The next few days Iraq will withdraw, but Saddam will put his puppet in. Everyone in the Arab world will be happy." Powell doubted, as New York senator Pat Moynihan witheringly put it, that Americans would agree to put five hundred thousand U.S. troops in harm's way to rescue Kuwaiti princes holed up in Saudi Sheratons, "sitting there in their white robes and drinking coffee and urging *us* to go to war." Moynihan reminded President Bush that Kuwait was an "accident of history," with artificial boundaries drawn by "the bureaucrats of the colonial powers." The implication was clear: Kuwait was not worth the bones of a single American GI.[35]

But General Powell seemed wobbly even on Saudi Arabia, whose sixty-six-thousand-man army would not stand a chance against the Iraqis. "We must communicate to Saddam Hussein that Saudi Arabia is the line," Powell advised Cheney, but then added that even there—the world's biggest oil patch—American intervention would depend on "popular support" from the American people and a "national sense" that the game was worth the candle. President Bush expressed his frustration with the uniformed military to his diary: "We had a long way to go before the military was 'gung ho' . . . Our military is waffling and vacillating in terms of what we can do on the ground."[36] Cheney too bristled at Powell's pessimism. The Iraqis had annexed Kuwait and were within striking distance of Saudi Arabia's Hama oil fields. The Pentagon's job was not to poll public or congressional opinion; it was to advise the president on national security. "I want some options, General," Cheney growled.[37]

On August 2, Bush chaired an NSC meeting that featured sharp exchanges between Powell and the hawks, who now coalesced around Cheney. Thomas Pickering, the U.S. ambassador to the UN, scolded Powell for suggesting that the United States could maintain its policeman's role in the Gulf if it consented to the Iraqi takeover of Kuwait. Bush too worried that Powell was overestimating Iraqi force. "I just didn't see the Iraqis as being so tough," he told Scowcroft.[38] After the meeting, Bush flew to Aspen, where he met with British prime minister Margaret Thatcher; she urged him to take a hard line with Saddam. "If Iraq wins, no small state is safe. They won't stop here. They see a chance to take a major share of oil. It's got to be stopped. We must do everything possible."[39] Thatcher compared the move into Kuwait to Hitler's unopposed moves against Austria and Czechoslovakia in 1938. Hitler had overrun France and Poland with the resources culled from those nations, and Thatcher worried that Saddam would annex the resources of Kuwait and then move on to bigger prey like Saudi Arabia.

Oddly, that bigger prey was reluctant to help the United States roll back Saddam's aggression. Although the Saudis had constructed mammoth ports and air bases to facilitate the arrival of American forces in a crisis, they were slow to define *this* as a crisis. Incredibly, there were not even plans for a U.S. deployment. The Saudis would not permit precrisis planning, nor would they allow the U.S. Marine Corps' maritime prepositioning ships—a brigade's worth of tanks, artillery and fighting vehicles stored in air-conditioned ships at Diego Garcia, seven sailing days from Saudi Arabia—to begin their voyage to the kingdom's ports. Even though Paul Wolfowitz's Carter-era blueprint for defending the Persian Gulf had called for a running start in countering Soviet or rogue-state threats to the kingdom, the Saudis would not even permit a shuffling start. All planning, mobilizing and deploying would have to be carried out in the midst of a crisis, and only when that crisis was defined as such by the cautious Saudi royals.

French president François Mitterrand insisted that the Saudis were the key: "If

Saudi Arabia takes a courageous stand against the annexation of Kuwait, this would bring along all others," but the Saudis were exhibiting no courage, and Bush worried aloud on August 4 that the Saudis "lacked will" and that "they might bug out."[40] By early August, CIA director William Webster was predicting an Iraqi invasion of Saudi Arabia, yet the Saudis still held back from cooperation with the United States. The key player in getting Iraq's invasion of Kuwait defined as a bona fide crisis was Prince Bandar, Saudi Arabia's ambassador in Washington. Bandar, a son of Prince Sultan, had been front and center in the rollback of the Soviets in Afghanistan and had also funneled black money to the Nicaraguan contras on behalf of the Reagan administration. On August 3, Brent Scowcroft asked Bandar if he would accept a major deployment of U.S. troops and air squadrons, and Bandar refused to commit. President Bush made a personal appearance, and expressed his frustration: "It hurts when your friends don't trust you." That afternoon, Bandar was taken to a meeting in Defense Secretary Dick Cheney's office. Powell and Wolfowitz were there. They showed Bandar satellite photos of Iraqi forces in Kuwait and proposed to put a hundred thousand U.S. troops into Saudi Arabia. Bandar still hung back. Like Osama bin Laden, Saddam was accusing the Saudis of being apostates and illegitimate guardians of the holy cities of Mecca and Medina because of their ties to the infidel West. Bandar promised to sound out King Fahd, who, characteristically, consented only to noncommittal meetings in Jedda: "Let the friends come," he said. Secretary of Defense Cheney was named to lead a delegation that would include General Schwarzkopf and Deputy National Security Adviser Robert Gates. Powell remained in Washington in case Saddam detected the friction between Washington and Riyadh and plunged south.[41]

Bush called another NSC meeting on August 3. Baker's principal deputy, Lawrence Eagleburger, pressed for a hard line. If Saddam were given Kuwait, other rogues like Kim Il Sung and Muammar Qaddafi might interpret Western passivity as license to launch their own adventures. Saddam would obtain a choke hold on world oil supplies at no cost. His threats—uttered in March 1990—to rain chemical weapons on Israel would go unanswered. Bush's "new world order" would become a free-for-all, with rogue states helping themselves to territory that had been regarded as untouchable only as long as the Cold War lasted. Turkish prime minister Turgut Ozal reported alarming discussions with Iraqi envoys sent to pry him away from the West. The Iraqis assured the Turks that the West was bluffing, and that Iraq would hold on to Kuwait, "fight to the end" and perhaps advance into the UAE and Saudi Arabia next.[42]

CENTCOM

A hard line, of course, required a war plan. On August 4, Centcom commander General H. Norman Schwarzkopf and his air commander General Chuck Horner flew to Camp David to give President Bush options. Centcom, an outgrowth of the Carter Doctrine and the Rapid Deployment Force created after the Iranian embassy takeover, was a relatively new command. Its insipid name, Central—as opposed to Middle Eastern—Command derived from the hot competition between European Command, which held the Israeli, Lebanese and Syrian "areas of responsibility," and Pacific Command, whose writ ran all the way up to the shores of the Indian Ocean, Arabian Sea and Horn of Africa. Neither command wanted to relinquish responsibility for the Middle East, so a Central Command was slipped in between them as a bureaucratic compromise. When Schwarzkopf got the top job in 1988, it was not as prestigious as the other commands—it had no actual forces, just a headquarters in Tampa—but it earned him a fourth star. No one imagined at the time that Schwarzkopf would actually ever run a war from the "bastard command." Indeed the consensus in the Pentagon was that the fall of the Soviet Union had removed the very threat that had argued for a Central Command: a looming Soviet thrust down to the Persian Gulf and its oil fields.[43] Schwarzkopf, best known for his deputy command of the Grenada invasion in 1983, had done two tours in Vietnam and developed a choleric reputation. At six foot four and 250 pounds, "Stormin' Norman" was a hulking presence with a wild temper. Subordinates spoke of having been "clawed by the bear" or "having their faces ripped off." But Schwarzkopf had been promoted up the ladder because of his distinguished career: service in the army's airborne, mechanized and infantry arms, three Silver Stars in Vietnam, staff jobs in the Pentagon and Pacific Command, study at the Army War College and service as army operations deputy, all of which had given him entrée to the Joint Chiefs of Staff and had earned him promotion to the Centcom job.[44]

"Stormin' Norman" was the son of H. Norman Schwarzkopf, Sr., who had advised Reza Shah and Muhammed Reza during and after World War II. Norman Schwarzkopf, Jr., retained an interest in the Middle East that he had nurtured as a boy. He was fortunate that Cheney was secretary of defense, because Cheney was also focused on the Middle East. Whereas many assumed that the demise of the Soviets had removed threats to the Persian Gulf, Cheney, nudged by Wolfowitz, looked past Moscow in 1989 and identified Iraq ("a robust regional threat") as the next big thing and the reason for a continuing Central Command.[45] Saddam's meetings with Joe Wilson, the American chargé in Baghdad, on August 5 confirmed Cheney's long-held suspicions about the Iraqi leader. Saddam rudely instructed Wilson to tell President Bush that if America wanted to preserve its economic interests in the Persian Gulf, then it would have to bow to Iraqi political supremacy: "You are a superpower and I know you can hurt us, but you will lose the whole area." If America attacked Iraq, Saddam hinted that he would seize Saudi Arabia: "We will not remain idle in the region." When Wilson asked Saddam directly if he planned to invade Saudi Arabia, Saddam replied that so long as the Saudis extended "grants, not loans" to Baghdad, "he would do nothing." In Saddam's Middle East, Saudi Arabia would be reduced to an Iraqi tributary, which was at least as alarming as the annexation of Kuwait.[46]

Cheney, Schwarzkopf and Gates arrived in Jedda on August 6. By now, there were eleven Iraqi army divisions in Kuwait and the Saudis had suddenly become a lot more agreeable. Iraqi patrols were already scouring the border with Saudi Arabia, and two Iraqi divisions were in place to thrust into the kingdom without warning. A six-lane highway ran down the eastern coast of Saudi Arabia to Dhahran—right through the oil patch, just twelve hours' driving time—and the Saudis still had just a single national guard division holding it. Cheney met King Fahd and warned him that without American troops and aircraft, Saudi Arabia would go the way of Kuwait. Saddam's military was the fourth largest in the world. The million-man Iraqi army, with its fifty-seven hundred tanks, was twenty times bigger than Saudi Arabia's. Even as he outlined plans to save King Fahd, Cheney felt compelled to sweet-talk him. He promised to yank American personnel out of Saudi Arabia the moment the Iraqis were defeated, and he pledged to upgrade Saudi Arabia's arsenal as an added incentive. The Saudis argued amongst themselves in Arabic while Cheney looked on. Finally, King Fahd agreed. "Come with all you can bring," he said. Cheney phoned Bush and gave him the green light.[47]

OPERATION DESERT SHIELD

Powell received word so late that he could not begin dispatching forces to the region until August 7. Operation Desert Shield was under way. As the name implied, Pow-

ell initially focused on shielding Saudi Arabia. He had always been opposed to liberating Kuwait, and he had not altered that view, despite President Bush's public
statement that the Iraqi aggression "will not stand." Powell dispatched a brigade of
the 82nd Airborne Division in C-141s to defend the Dhahran airfield, ordered two
carriers—the *Dwight D. Eisenhower* and the *Independence*—toward the Persian Gulf,
belatedly put to sea the prepositioned marine equipment at Diego Garcia and scram-
bled twenty-four F-15s from Langley, Virginia, to Dhahran, where they flew with
Saudi squadrons and American AWACS radar planes to keep watch on the Iraqis.[48]

As American units flowed in, they were undergunned and undersupplied;
Schwarzkopf initially sacrificed logistics and prioritized men over matériel to create
the *impression*—boots on the ground—of American strength. The caches of U.S.
weapons, munitions and fuel that had been prepositioned in Oman, Bahrain and
Diego Garcia since the fall of the shah would fill just a tiny fraction of America's
needs. Even when attention shifted to logistics, the U.S. military was found wanting.
Reagan's massive military buildup had sacrificed unglamorous functions like transport ships ("sealift") and minesweepers to pay for high-tech programs like "Star
Wars," stealth technology, fighter aircraft, attack subs and cruise missiles. The sea-
and airlift problems—even the prepositioning ships in Diego Garcia arrived to
disgorge vehicles with dead batteries, flat tires and no engine oil—would later explain Secretary of Defense Donald Rumsfeld's determination to slim down the
armed services, cut their logistical trains and refocus on "agility" and "mobility"
when he was defense secretary from 2001 to 2006.

President Bush gave a televised address on August 8 explaining the stakes of the
looming conflict to the American people. Iraq already presided over the world's
second largest oil reserves. Annexation of Kuwait would magnify Iraq's influence
over supply and prices at a time when the United States was importing nearly half
the oil it consumed. But, as Powell had earlier warned, Americans would probably
not send their children into harm's way for cheap oil, so Bush tacked on some red,
white and blue bunting. The new post-Soviet era could be "an age of freedom, and
a time of peace," but for that to happen "we must resist aggression or it will destroy
our freedoms."[49]

The marines were the first onto the beach to resist Saddam's aggression, arriving
in al-Jubail from California on August 14. The 7th Marine Expeditionary Brigade
unloaded the prepositioning ships and prepared to test-fire their artillery and M-60
tanks, but were told not to by the Saudis, who considered fire exercises too provocative. The army and air force also had problems with the Saudis, who forbade

low-level training flights and bombing runs and refused to station B-52s at Jedda airport—too close to Mecca—insisting instead that they be based on faraway Diego Garcia, more than twenty-five hundred miles from Kuwait. Schwarzkopf recalled a surreal meeting with the Saudi army commander during which Prince Khalid angrily passed him a bag of U.S. military souvenir T-shirts and demanded that he forbid their sale. The offending shirts depicted palm trees, desert sands and tanks. "What's offensive about this?" Schwarzkopf asked. "We don't like the image of a tank in our desert," Khalid replied. "But there are tanks all over your desert," Schwarzkopf persisted. "Yes, but we don't want this advertised to our people," Khalid concluded. Clearly more diplomacy was needed. "Where's Baker?" Powell grumbled. After his meetings in Russia with Shevernadze, Baker had scheduled a "working vacation" and dropped out of sight at the very moment when he was needed to wrestle King Fahd into line.[50]

The marines' fixed-wing air support—F/A-18s and Harrier jump jets—would not arrive until August 24, another dangerous delay, this one occasioned by interservice friction: the air force would not detach tankers to refuel the marine corps' planes in flight.[51] The first heavy army unit to go was General Barry McCaffrey's 24th Mechanized Division in Fort Stewart, Georgia. It got priority on the navy's eight fast sealift ships, but one of them, the *Antares*, broke down in the middle of the Atlantic with most of the division's helicopters and had to be towed for repairs to Rota, Spain; it would not deliver its choppers to Saudi Arabia until September 23. Meanwhile, most of Schwarzkopf's encoded message traffic continued to pass through the Iraqi-held civilian satellite downlink in Kuwait City. There were no viable alternatives; had Saddam and his Republican Guards only noticed, they could have disabled Desert Shield with one bloodless stroke.[52] All this muddling and improvising gave Schwarzkopf fits; in early August an Iraqi defector had warned him that Saddam was pondering a strike down the coast road to Dhahran or through the western desert to Riyadh, yet Schwarzkopf still had hardly any forces to defend the kingdom, let alone the skeleton force he was assembling at al-Jubail.

The Saudi armed forces—under Auburn University graduate Prince Khalid Bin Sultan al-Saud—had to be treated by the United States not as a subordinate contingent, but as an equal, allied army. Khalid's demands that Schwarzkopf defend the entire northern border of Saudi Arabia, not just the economically vital coast road to Dhahran with its ports, airfields and oil installations, had to be countered with time-consuming diplomacy and endless cups of coffee.[53] The Americans *hoped* the Iraqis would be foolish enough to cross the four-hundred-mile desert to Riyadh and expose themselves to devastating air attack. But Washington had to assume the Iraqis would launch the 150,000 troops and 1,200 tanks they had on the Saudi border toward the closer, more valuable prize: the Gulf oil fields of eastern Saudi Arabia. Meanwhile, Schwarzkopf waited for his troops to arrive; he told a news conference at the Dhahran International Hotel on August 31 that "there is not going to be *any* war unless the Iraqis attack." Powell was trying to limit the U.S. deployment to 150,000 troops, and he still doubted that the American people would back a war for Kuwait.[54]

CONGRESS VOTES FOR WAR

Gradually—using largely foreign-owned transport ships and commandeered civilian airliners—the United States built to a strength of 6 aircraft carrier battle groups, 17 heavy and 6 light army brigades, 9 marine regiments, and 1,376 air force, navy and marine fighter aircraft. In Baghdad, an American air force officer arrived at the airport in August with a briefcase. He drove to the U.S. embassy, opened the briefcase to activate a GPS receiver, took one reading, snapped the case shut and returned to the airport, where he boarded a return flight to Washington. That single, precise reading of the U.S. embassy's GPS coordinates—taken under the noses of the Iraqis—would be used to target all the coalition's Baghdad air strikes five months later. By September 1990, 80 percent of Americans supported Operation Desert Shield, which belied Powell's hand-wringing about scant "popular support." Some yard signs sprouted in American suburbs enjoining "No blood for oil," but a large majority of Americans recognized the need to defend the Western world's energy security. Americans were also moved by a largely spurious $11 million PR campaign paid for by the Kuwaiti government and crafted by Hill & Knowlton. Its most effective piece of propaganda was a lie: that Iraqi soldiers had entered Kuwaiti hospitals, yanked newborn babies out of their incubators and dashed them on the floor before packing up the equipment for shipment to Iraq. That lie was retailed by the daughter of the Kuwaiti ambassador to the United States, pretending to be a Kuwaiti nurse who had witnessed the Iraqi atrocities. In fact, she was not a nurse and had not even been in Kuwait when the Iraqis invaded. Nevertheless, senators and representatives swallowed the story hook, line and sinker.[55] Many of them referenced it when explaining their votes in support of the war, which was narrowly authorized by the Senate 52 to 47 and by the House 250 to 183 on January 12, 1991.

As the numbers suggest, the entire Democratic leadership in both houses voted against the war, and President Bush actually worried about impeachment if the weak congressional support thinned and the war miscarried. That narrow vote to authorize the Gulf War—the narrowest since the War of 1812—was the first congressional approval of military action since the Gulf of Tonkin Resolution of 1964. Iraqi depredations—real and imagined—coupled with the Bush administration's argument that it was also fighting to defend American jobs (that depended on cheap energy) and to punish Saddam's human rights abuses and weapons of mass destruction programs (all of which America had winked at and even supported during the 1980s) awakened American idealism. Here was a war that needed to be fought in defense of American values. Still, the vote was close, and hardly amounted to a national crusade. Massachusetts senator John Kerry blasted Bush for making "a series of unilateral decisions that put us in a box" and "made the war inevitable." His colleague Ted Kennedy beseeched someone, anyone, to "save the President from himself . . . and save thousands of American soldiers in the Persian Gulf from dying in the desert in a war whose cruelty will be exceeded only by the lack of any rational necessity for waging it." Senator Al Gore, weighing his own run for the presidency, agreed to vote for the war only if given the floor for a twenty-minute prime-time television slot (by Republican leader Bob Dole) to advertise his vote. New York senator Pat Moynihan denied that Saddam's invasion of Kuwait amounted to an international crisis that engaged America's values or interests: "Nothing large happened. A nasty little country invaded a littler but just as nasty country."[56]

THE COALITION FORMS

On November 29, 1990, the UN Security Council passed Resolution 678, which gave Saddam till January 15, 1991, to evacuate Kuwait or face eviction by an American-led coalition that had swelled to thirty-four nations. The coalition itself was interesting; it ran the gamut from lightweights like Argentina and Bangladesh to serious combat powers like France and the United Kingdom. Japan and West Germany, big consumers of Gulf oil that were politically reluctant to engage in military operations, chipped in $10 billion and $6.6 billion, respectively, for the costs of the conflict. Egypt joined to get its external debts—$16 billion in 1990—written off. Debt forgiveness on that scale and the peerless opportunity to charge every coalition ship that transited the Suez Canal a $200,000 toll certainly tempered Mubarak's disappointment at having to reject Saddam's bribe of $20 billion, dangled after the seizure of Kuwait.[57] The Saudis deployed their military but, far more important, paid heavily, to the tune of $30 billion for war costs. The Turks deployed a hundred thousand troops along their border with Iraq, which forced Saddam to detach equivalent numbers of his own troops and weaken the force he had available for operations in Kuwait and Saudi Arabia. Saddam's threats to obliterate Israel with his Scud missiles and their payloads of chemical weapons made Israel the coalition's most ardent would-be member, but President Bush kept Tel Aviv at arm's length to ensure the cooperation of Muslim allies like Turkey, Pakistan, Egypt, Syria and Saudi Arabia. Bush extracted a promise from the Israelis not to preempt the Iraqis. In return, Bush tasked U.S. satellites and Aegis air defense cruisers to give Israel early warning of Iraqi missile launches, offered American-crewed batteries of Patriot missiles to shoot down incoming Scuds, dispatched U.S. and British special forces into Iraq's western desert to seek and destroy Scud launchers, and deflected Saddam's insistence that his withdrawal from Kuwait be matched by an Israeli withdrawal from southern Lebanon, the Golan Heights, the West Bank and the Gaza Strip.

To reassure the American Congress and public that he had tried all peaceful means to push Saddam out of Kuwait, Bush sent Secretary of State James Baker to Geneva to meet Tariq Aziz on January 9, 1991. Saddam interpreted the last-minute American parley as evidence of U.S. reluctance to embark on "another Vietnam." Former secretary of defense Robert McNamara, who had run the war in Vietnam, predicted casualties in Iraq of thirty thousand. The Pentagon was predicting as many as thirty thousand deaths in the first twenty days of combat. Former South Dakota senator George McGovern prophesied fifty thousand casualties. The U.S. Air Force predicted the loss of 150 aircraft, with one-quarter of the pilots killed, and another quarter captured "and possibly paraded through the streets of Baghdad." House Majority Leader Dick Gephardt threatened to block all funding for the conflict if Bush proceeded with his essentially Republican authorization to use armed force instead of a formal congressional declaration of war.[58] With terrifying threats, numbers and images like those floating around—and newspaper columnists alternately flaying Bush for his timidity and bellicosity—Saddam assumed that the Americans would shrink from battle, as indeed did nearly every witness called by Georgia senator Sam Nunn's Armed Services Committee to discuss the military option. One after another, the parade of retired flag officers and secretaries— Admiral William Crowe, General David Jones, former secretary of defense James

Schlesinger, former secretary of the navy James Webb and former National Security Agency director William Odom—asserted that a war with Iraq would be wrong-headed and bloody: it would shred the U.S. armed forces and convulse the Middle East. Senator Robert Byrd insisted that even if the United States delivered a "quick knockout," such a blow "would unleash a cascade of outcomes and reactions that would reduce our long-term ability [to] influence events in that region." Let sanctions bite, they all recommended, as did House speaker Tom Foley, who gave Bush a letter signed by eighty-one Democratic members that warned of "catastrophic consequences resulting in the massive loss of lives, including 10,000–50,000 Americans" if America went to war with Saddam.[59]

"WE WILL TURN IRAQ INTO A WEAK AND BACKWARD COUNTRY"

Just in case Bush braved those "catastrophic consequences," Saddam pulled his Republican Guard divisions out of Kuwait so that they would not be chewed up in the first days of a war. He shifted eighty thousand of them to southern Iraq and sixty thousand back to Baghdad to defend the regime. Equivalent numbers of conscripts—largely Kurds and Shiites—were trucked up to the heavily fortified Saddam Line along the Saudi border as cannon fodder. Saddam was disabused of his hopes for American appeasement by Baker's gruff conversation with Aziz. The secretary of state, who had initially aligned himself with Powell against war to avoid antagonizing the Soviets, now threatened a brisk, devastating war that would shatter the Iraqi military and probably unseat Saddam himself. "There will be no UN truce creating a breathing space. It will not be another Vietnam; it will be fought for a quick and decisive end." Baker hinted at the great technological strides that the U.S. military had made since Vietnam: "The strategy used against Iran will [not] succeed here. You will face a completely different force." Unleashed, Baker warned, the U.S. military "will destroy everything you fought to build in Iraq . . . and will turn Iraq into a weak and backward country." The meeting went nowhere; Aziz returned to Baghdad vowing that "it will be a long war," that Iraq—a six-thousand-year-old civilization—would weather it and that America's "friend in the region" would not.[60]

CHAPTER 14

DESERT STORM

HAVING REBUFFED AMERICAN and UN demands that he leave Iraq, Saddam watched the UN deadline—January 15, 1991—come and go. Baker had threatened at Geneva that "midnight of January 15th is a very real date," and indeed it was. The next day, Operation Desert Shield became Operation Desert Storm. Desert Storm began with a massive air campaign—Operation Instant Thunder—whose name was chosen to distinguish it from the pinpricking Lyndon Johnson air campaign in Vietnam—Rolling Thunder—which had gradually increased pressure. Instant Thunder was front-loaded: 100,000 sorties that dropped 88,500 tons of bombs on Iraq immediately. It was the brainchild of Air Force colonel John Warden, who had been on a Caribbean cruise when Saddam invaded Kuwait and did not get back to the Pentagon until August 6.

OPERATION INSTANT THUNDER

Warden was an airpower theorist who in 1988 had tried to bridge the gap between the air force's powerful bomber (SAC) and fighter (TAC) communities with a theory he called "the five rings of airpower." Warden found both the nuclear strike and tactical air superiority notions needlessly polarizing and limiting. His "five rings" theory challenged the air force to use its assets in a new way for a new world: use conventional, precise air raids against enemy "centers of gravity" to collapse resistance. Four rings radiated out from a bull's-eye, like a dartboard. The bull's-eye was the crucial ring—the enemy state's air defenses, and command, control and communications facilities. Without them, the enemy would be unable to thwart air attacks, run its war effort or even police its state internally. The second ring contained the enemy's key military and economic production assets—factories, warehouses, power grids, refineries and, in the case of Iraq, its nuclear, chemical and biological weapons production and storage sites. The third ring represented the enemy's transportation network—roads, bridges, railways, airfields and ports. "Third-ring" attacks would stop enemy mobility cold. The fourth ring was the enemy population itself, as well as its food and water resources. Those had been the principal targets of early airpower advocates like Giulio Douhet and Hugh Trenchard, who, in the 1920s and 1930s, had argued that "morale bombing" would force governments to surrender to protect their terrified, clamoring citizens. But times had changed and no one in Washington had the stomach for air attacks on Iraqi or any other civilians, so Warden pushed that ring well out from the center. The fifth and least important ring, oddly enough, was the enemy's armed forces. If an American air campaign successively hit the bull's-eye, the military-industrial complex, the infrastructure, and the food and water supplies, Warden reasoned that the enemy military would simply wither on the vine—blind, deaf, famished, thirsty and demoralized. The *Washington Post*'s Rick Atkinson wrote that the new American tactics and technology were as revolutionary as "the longbow at Crécy or the machine gun at the Somme." The blending of stealth and smart bombs enabled Americans to "slip unseen into the enemy camp and strike with virtual impunity."[1]

Instant Thunder applied the "five rings" theory. It was war from the inside out, striking the vital centers of gravity first, not last, hurtling over the Iraqi borders and field armies to deal a lethal blow to Saddam in his palaces. Despite the revolutionary nature of the plan, Warden used a historical metaphor to sell it to Schwarzkopf. He called Instant Thunder an aerospace "Schlieffen Plan" that would overwhelm the Iraqi state with crushing blows delivered in just six days of air strikes. Although Warden preferred to ignore Saddam's big army—one million men and five thousand tanks—Powell insisted that he detach some strength to reduce the Iraqi military to less threatening dimensions. Powell envisioned a postwar Iraqi force of just a hundred thousand troops and a thousand tanks. For the rest, he wanted significant attrition and Iraq's ruined "tanks as smoking kilometer fence posts all the way back to Baghdad." Whereas Warden pitched Instant Thunder as a way to win with minimal contact between U.S. and Iraqi forces—a decapitating blow—Powell, Schwarzkopf and Centcom air commander General Chuck Horner chose to implement Instant Thunder—"a Chinese menu" of targets in Schwarzkopf's phrase—as a mere preliminary "to the inevitable air-to-ground attacks on the Iraqi army in Kuwait."[2]

The weeklong "strategic" attacks of Instant Thunder would be followed by pulverizing "tactical" strikes on Iraqi air defenses in Kuwait and the Iraqi forces themselves. Schwarzkopf specifically demanded that the air force create a "kill zone" in Kuwait, where Iraqi units would be "terrorized," "significantly degraded" and made to suffer "maximum casualties." Interestingly, the "five rings" theory was also amended to achieve another Bush administration war aim: "Iraq's ability to export oil *not* significantly degraded."[3] Critical refineries and pipelines were removed from the target list. The navy never liked the plan, which they called "Distant Blunder." They thought it bit off too much too fast. Looking over Iraq's state-of-the-art French-built air defense system—Saddam had upgraded his antiaircraft radars, missiles and artillery after the humiliating Israeli sneak attack on his nuclear reactor at Osirak in 1981—the navy argued for a multiday assault on Iraq's air defenses and ground-based air force command centers, and *then* a transition to bull's-eye and inner-ring targets. The navy had cause for concern. Its A-6 bomber was nonstealthy, slow and on the brink of retirement. It would be a prime target for Iraq's SAMs and antiaircraft guns. A compromise was reached. The navy would keep the A-6s away from Baghdad and rely on Tomahawk cruise missiles fired from its submarines and surface ships in the surrounding seas.

For the air campaign, Baghdad was the hardest target. Iraq's Kari air defense system was centered on the capital, which featured denser, far more lethal air defenses than the USAF had encountered over even thickly defended Hanoi during the Vietnam War. Air planners were projecting the loss of up to 150 American aircraft and 30 to 40 pilots. To cut their way in, the air force studied one of the most stunning air battles of recent memory—the Israeli destruction of Syria's SAM batteries in Lebanon's Bekaa Valley in June 1982. Confronting Syrian pressure on their flank as they invaded Lebanon to flush out the PLO, the Israelis had launched drones into the Bekaa Valley; the Syrian SAMs had fired on the drones, and then Israeli F-16s had swooped down on the empty launchers and cluster-bombed them. In 1991, U.S. air planners devised similar tactics for Baghdad. American drones would trick the Iraqis into switching on their missile radars, and trailing U.S. fighters would lock onto the hot targets and fire high-speed antiradiation missiles (HARMs) that would follow the radar beams down to their station and explode.

The first air corridors into Iraq were opened by air force Apache and Pave Low choppers, which flew over the Saudi-Iraqi border hugging the desert floor, located Iraq's air defense radars using navigational satellites and then peeled off to make way for Army Apache helicopters, which blasted the Iraqi radar sites with Hellfire missiles. By amputating the outlying nodes of the Kari system, the choppers opened corridors for fixed-wing aircraft to fly through. Steered by AWACS battle-management planes, the American fighters jammed the hubs of the Kari system and bombed Iraqi airfields, antiaircraft defenses, telecommunications facilities and fiber-optic arrays. British Tornadoes flew bold, low-level missions over Iraqi runways and churned them up with cluster bombs. F-117 Nighthawk stealth fighters, which were theoretically invisible to surviving radar and SAMs but preceded by EF-111 Raven electronic warfare jamming aircraft just in case, bombed their way into Baghdad, hitting Saddam's palaces, bunkers and security ministries as well as Baath Party headquarters. That second operational test of the black bat-wing F-117—the attack on Noriega in Panama had been the first—was a success, even if the air force was forced by Secretary of State Baker to drop its preferred term for the precision strikes—"decapitation"—and content itself with "incapacitation." Baker considered "decapitation" too brutal, and likely to fray the coalition.[4]

Whether they were decapitating or incapacitating, the precision munitions unveiled in the Gulf War were astonishingly accurate. Whereas the bombs dropped from the F-117s in Panama had gone astray because of the jungle foliage and humidity, the bombs in Iraq fell directly on their targets. Television viewers around the world watched laser and GPS-guided munitions slam home, and the U.S. Air Force divulged some remarkable statistics: F-117s in 1991 were taking out targets with a single "smart bomb" that would have required 9,070 bombs in World War II or 176 in Korea and Vietnam.[5] B-52s flying out of Barksdale Air Force Base in Louisiana—eighteen hours each way—launched AGM-86C cruise missiles, which quietly glided into their targets. The methodical destruction of the strategic targets in Baghdad by the black bat-wing F-117s and the air force and navy cruise missiles, and the whirring of drones, which triggered massive antiaircraft barrages followed by blistering HARM strikes, triggered panic in Baghdad. People who had made their way to the bomb shelters clapping and singing "Palestine belongs to the Arabs, Kuwait belongs to Iraq" now fell dismally silent. Other terrified Iraqis piled into their cars and tried to escape the city. An F-117 pilot looking down at Baghdad at four-thirty a.m. on the first day of the war said the roads out of the city center "looked like the interstate from L.A. to Vegas on a Friday night."[6]

Clouds, fog and smoke from antiaircraft fire made some of the F-117 strikes as chancy as Vegas roulette. Although the air force stressed their stealth and precision, the Nighthawks hit only about half their targets. After much debate about the WMD sites—Schwarzkopf and Horner wanted to bomb them; Powell worried about contaminating the region and infecting American forces—American jets hit Saddam's uranium enrichment sites, as well as his chemical and germ warfare plants and storage bunkers. F-117s, flying from a purpose-built Saudi base, dropped 2,000-pound bombs on the targets, and F-111s then streaked (upwind) of the bunkers strewing cluster bombs to stop the Iraqis from trying to retrieve any toxic material.[7] The number of confirmed WMD sites in 1991 and the ingenuity with which they were hidden and moved around between strikes explained Washington's conviction in 2003 that there *had to be* WMD in Iraq. How could there not be? Saddam in 1991 had the world's biggest chemical weapons program and burgeoning nuclear and biological ones as well.

The entire Iraqi navy was caught fleeing from Basra toward Iranian waters and destroyed from the air. Most of the Iraqi air force was destroyed on the ground or in the air. Once their ground controllers were knocked off-line, the Soviet-trained Iraqi pilots proved helpless against the American fighters. One hundred and fifty Iraqi planes fled into Iranian airspace to escape the American attacks; those aircraft were never returned by the Iranians. The rest of the Iraqi air force pushed their planes into concrete bunkers and refused to fly. The coalition quickly achieved air supremacy; coalition pilots flew 69,000 missions in the war against a mere 910 Iraqi missions. That left the little Scud missiles—with their 300-mile range and light 160-pound warhead—as Saddam's only serviceable air weapon. Though the Scuds, in Schwarzkopf's judgment, were hugely overrated—"the equivalent of a single airplane flying over, haphazardly dropping one small bomb, and flying away"—they were nevertheless a terror weapon that would give the coalition fits for the rest of the war.[8]

Navy Tomahawk cruise missiles—following digitized terrain maps to their targets—slammed into Baghdad, damaging presidential palaces, television stations and government buildings with astonishing accuracy. Because Iraq's terrain was so flat and featureless, the Tomahawks had to be (secretly) launched over western Iran, which had the peaks and valleys the Tomahawk needed to guide itself, before turning left to Baghdad.[9] Air strikes smashed Iraqi power stations and substations, reducing Iraqi electricity production to 4 percent of its prewar levels. Such attacks on the quality of life in Iraq were intended to signal to the Iraqis that they had only to oust their dictator and things would improve: "Hey, your lights will come back on as soon as you get rid of Saddam," one of the American air planners quipped in February 1991. Roads, bridges, ports, oil refineries, pipelines and railroads were also cratered, as were water pumping stations and sewage treatment plants. "I wanted to play with their psyche," General Buster Glosson, who directed Horner's air campaign, explained. He was deliberately returning the Iraqis to a state of nature, where they would "shrivel like a grape when the vine's been cut."[10] Coalition aircraft also attacked Iraq's WMD sites. Stealthy F-117s and nonstealthy F-16s, escorted by F-15s and jamming aircraft, bombed Saddam's nuclear research facility at Tuwaitha. The detonations there and elsewhere scattered poisonous material far and wide, and probably contributed to Gulf War Syndrome. Instant Thunder devastated the Iraqi military's ability to react, or even communicate. It would have been even more devastating had not one-third of coalition airpower been detached for the largely futile "Scud hunt" over Iraq's western desert, where air patrols spun day and night searching for the truck-borne Iraqi Scud launchers. The eight-wheeled mobile launchers hid by day in phosphate mines or under highway culverts and camouflage nets, emerging briefly at night to set up, fire their missiles toward Israel and then race back to their hiding places before allied aircraft could arrive overhead.

Saddam was defiant. He broadcast a rousing reminder that Iraqis were now engaged in "a great duel, the mother of all battles." He promised Iraqis that "the dawn of victory nears as this great showdown begins." Saddam sought an immediate victory in the media war for public opinion. Having lost points by deploying "human shields" before Instant Thunder—Westerners like the little English schoolboy Stuart Lockwood, whom Saddam confined in Baghdad to prevent "the scourge of war"—he now gained points by publicizing the civilian casualties caused by Instant Thunder's "collateral damage." The worst instance was the American strike with two laser-guided bombs on the Amiriyah blockhouse. U.S. targeters identified it as an Iraqi command post; it certainly was, but it also sheltered hundreds of Iraqi civilians: several hundred died and hundreds more were injured when the structure collapsed on them.[11] Saddam reveled in carnage like that. He advertised it, inflated its numbers and then—like Nasser in 1967—invented American air attacks, this time on the Muslim shrines at Karbala and Najaf. Those "big lies" were intended to inflame world opinion against the American-led coalition.

THE GREAT SCUD HUNT

To splinter the coalition, Saddam fired seven Scuds into Israel on January 18, and would continue the missile attacks for six weeks until the end of the war. Striving to expand his derisory coalition beyond its two derisory members—Libya and the PLO—Saddam had defined the conflict as a "holy war against the United States and Israel" and professed a willingness to negotiate on Kuwait if the Israelis would negotiate on Palestine and the occupied territories. The Scud attacks on Israel were Saddam's way of goading the Israelis into counterattacks on Iraq that would drive important Arab states like Egypt and Saudi Arabia out of Bush's coalition. Rejecting all "linkage" between Kuwait and Palestine, Bush put pressure on Cheney, Powell and Schwarzkopf to hit Saddam's Scud launchers and keep the Israelis—who planned massive counterstrikes into western Iraq with two hundred fighter-bombers and airborne commandos—out of the war. Interestingly, Cheney, who may have pressed the Israelis to strike Iran during the Bush 43 administration, did press them to strike Iraq in the Gulf War. Bush 41 was stunned by Cheney's lack of tact— "Cheney's assessment caused dismay . . . he suggested we let them go, go fast, and get it over with"—and the president quickly reeled him in.[12]

But Schwarzkopf's "Great Scud Hunt"—resented by the general and his air commanders as a diversion of precious assets—went badly throughout the war. Saddam had built thirty-six concrete launch pads in western Iraq, which Centcom assumed would be used to attack Israel. In fact, Saddam used the fixed launchers as decoys, and fired his missiles from mobile launchers that were difficult to track and locate. The Iraqis practiced "shoot and scoot," erecting their launchers, firing and racing away before orbiting U.S. strike aircraft could react. When the U.S. warplanes did react, they as often as not fired their expensive missiles into cheap launcher decoys, which the Iraqis scattered around the desert. U.S. intelligence estimated that the Iraqis had as many as seven hundred Scuds. It was imperative that they be destroyed, particularly because Saddam had big stocks of chemical and biological weapons. The coalition had to assume that he would arm his Scuds with weapons of mass destruction and target American troop concentrations in Saudi Arabia as well as Israeli cities. He had fired hundreds of chemical-armed Scuds into Iran during "the war of the cities." Why would he shrink from the same methods in 1991, when the future of his regime was at stake? Schwarzkopf agonized daily over the bulked-up U.S. military presence in Saudi Arabia, which made inviting targets for the Iraqis: "Every dock and airfield in the kingdom was overflowing with American equipment, ammunition and supplies . . . and remote desert roads were experiencing their first traffic jams." Schwarzkopf's agonies would explain Secretary of Defense Donald Rumsfeld's determination to "go light" into Iraq a decade later. The U.S. Air Force had jammed so many aircraft into the Riyadh air base "that it looked like the deck of an aircraft carrier—dozens of jets and a billion dollars' worth of AWACS just lined up on the apron." The army called the eastern Saudi ports, tent camps and dormitory complexes around Ad Dammam and al-Jubail "the Scud bowl," and worried about a "national disaster" if Saddam ever got around to hitting them with his missiles or a stray bomber.[13]

The Israelis chafed at the bit, but President Bush desperately restrained them. The "U.S. would do it all," he assured Prime Minister Yitzhak Shamir, to which Shamir coldly replied: "You treat us like a relative who has a social disease. You want to have nothing to do with us."[14] That much was true, but Bush and National Security Adviser Brent Scowcroft felt confident that the Israelis would not freelance and put their $3 billion American annual aid stipend at risk. Israeli pugnacity was a time-honored ruse to extract gratitude and money from Washington in exchange for Israeli restraint, and this time was no different. In meetings in Tel Aviv with the Israelis in January 1991, Lawrence Eagleburger was startled to receive a bill from the Israeli government for $13 billion—to settle Russian immigrants in the occupied territories and defray Israel's opaque "war costs." Eagleburger peered at the numbers and agreed to take them back to Washington. "But it's kind of expensive, wouldn't you say?"[15]

If the Israelis flew air strikes into Iraq through Syrian, Jordanian or Saudi air space, they might make the war even more expensive, and find themselves at war with one or a combination of those three states. In Washington, Prince Bandar flatly assured the Americans that Saudi Arabia would not tolerate Israeli intervention in the war. Washington also worried that the Saudis might launch their own ballistic missiles on Iraq, which would kill a lot of civilians and cast the coalition in the worst possible light. On January 19, the normally icy Dick Cheney lost his temper and composure for the only time in the war. Looking at the air tasking orders for that day, Cheney told Powell that he wanted more sorties against Iraq's Scud launchers in the western desert. Bush had disabused Cheney of his earlier enthusiasm for Israeli retaliation. Now Cheney too recognized the need to keep Israel out of the war. "Goddamn it, I want some coverage out there. If I have to talk to Schwarzkopf, I'll do it . . . The number one priority is to keep Israel out of the war." In dressing down Powell, Cheney gave a glimpse of the self-confidence that would propel him blindly into Operation Iraqi Freedom in 2003: "As long as I'm Secretary of Defense, the Defense Department will do as I tell them."[16]

The Scud hunt convened a number of Bush 41 players who would reconvene during the administration of Bush 43. Responsibility for keeping Schwarzkopf and Glosson focused on the Scuds was given to Rear Admiral Mike McConnell, whom Cheney would make director of National Intelligence in 2007. Richard Armitage, Powell's deputy at the State Department in 2003, was sent to Amman to gauge the attitude of the Jordanians to Israeli retaliation. Paul Wolfowitz, an architect of the Iraq War in 2003, was sent to Tel Aviv to "hold the Israeli hand."[17] Schwarzkopf loathed the interference from Washington. The politically ordained Scud hunt was absorbing 33 percent of his aircraft and hundreds of daily combat missions to "throw bombs into dunes." Stormin' Norman complained that "Alexander the Great and Napoleon" had never been so constrained in their operations, a Freudian slip relished by his aides. Pressed by Cheney to admit Israeli officers to his Riyadh headquarters, Schwarzkopf exploded: "I couldn't believe I had to explain that the presence of Israelis would wreck Central Command's credibility with the Arabs—assuming the Saudis would even let them into the kingdom."[18] They wouldn't. The British Foreign Office noted the irony; America had been building up Israel since the Truman administration as a military ally, but the "alliance was not particularly useful if it could not be *used* in a crisis like this." Bernard Lewis went further: the Gulf War proved conclusively that "Israel was not an asset, but an irrelevance—some even said a nuisance."[19]

KHAFJI

On January 29, Saddam moved three divisions up to the Kuwait-Saudi border and invaded the kingdom. With most coalition troops still assembling far to the south, Saddam—who traveled from Baghdad to Basra on January 27 to finalize plans for the cross-border attack—hoped to pluck essential ports from the coalition, humiliate the Saudis and inflict enough casualties on the Americans to deflate Congress and U.S. public opinion. Incredibly, he caught the Americans and Saudis off guard, crossed the border and attacked Khafji, where he was eventually fought to a standstill by U.S. Marines, Saudis and Qataris. General Horner received a panicked phone call from Prince Khalid. The Saudi commander had been visiting a unit near Khafji when the Iraqis struck. Pinned down in a bunker near the front, Khalid phoned Horner and demanded B-52 strikes. "Don't tell me how to do the job, tell me what you want done," Horner replied. For three straight days, the Centcom air commander pelted the Iraqis with Navy F/A-18s, Marine Harriers, and Air Force A-10s and B-52s. They plowed up the roads down to Khafji, shattering two Iraqi divisions and blowing up three hundred vehicles. Efforts by the Iraqi commander— Major General Mahmoud—to break off the attack and retreat were vetoed by Saddam, who radioed Mahmoud that Khafji was the first shot in "the mother of all battles." But "the mother is killing her own children," Mahmoud bravely replied. American strike aircraft and attack helicopters were literally stacked above the Khafji battlefield waiting for targets. It was a turkey shoot.[20]

Had he seized Khafji and pressed down the coast road, Saddam could have interrupted the flow of American reinforcements and war material and captured a huge pool of the world's oil. But the Iraqis were stunned by the ferocity of American artillery and air attacks, which, in the worst cases of friendly fire since Vietnam, did not always spare their intended beneficiaries. Eleven marines were killed by their own aircraft and guns at Khafji; the Iraqis fared worse, losing twenty-four hundred killed, wounded and missing in the bloody, blundering action, which turned out to be the biggest battle ever fought on Saudi soil. Saddam had hoped that Khafji would slow the American buildup and inflict punishing casualties on the coalition. In fact, it punished the Iraqis most of all, and revealed them to be all but incapable of sustained, offensive operations. American signals intelligence revealed "virtual command chaos" on the Iraqi side. As the Iraqis retreated into the Saddam Line, it was obvious that they would not be sallying again. Schwarzkopf judged the two-day battle "about as significant as a mosquito on an elephant" but politically important in that it established Saddam again as the aggressor and removed the "colonialist" mantle from U.S. and coalition forces.[21]

The Scud hunt had taken a new turn that radically changed the fortunes and future of American "black world" special operations forces like the Army's Delta Force and the Navy SEALs. Schwarzkopf had cold-shouldered General Carl Stiner's

Special Operations Command (Socom) throughout the war, rebuffing Stiner's offers to rescue the American diplomats being held by the Iraqis in Kuwait City or to kill senior Iraqi leaders in Kuwait and Iraq. The Centcom commander indulged a typical army prejudice against the unbuttoned special operators (long hair, mismatched uniforms, lax discipline) that was compounded by his conviction that U.S. Special Forces had not lived up to expectations in Vietnam and Grenada. Now, prodded by Cheney, IDF chief of staff Ehud Barak and the British military commander Sir Peter de la Billière, who wanted to insert Britain's Special Air Service (SAS), Schwarzkopf ran out of excuses not to use American special forces. He dropped four hundred "snake eaters" into western Iraq to hunt the Scud launchers, which fired ninety missiles into Israel and Saudi Arabia in January and February. The commandos moved in helicopters and dune buggies across a desert the size of Massachusetts, New Hampshire and Vermont, and never actually found a single real Scud. Bedouin rhapsodies about the immensity of the desert were apparently true. Even special operators guided by JSTARS radar planes and Pave Low helicopters couldn't find a missile in the sand sea. American and British commandos blew up about a dozen decoys and unearthed and wrecked a number of Scud hiding places, but couldn't confirm a single kill, even as Iraqi missiles continued to rocket out of the desert toward Tel Aviv, Haifa, Israel's Dimona reactor, Riyadh, Dhahran and King Khalid Military City. The Bush 43 administration's first-term enthusiasm for special operations forces and ballistic missile defense derived in no small part from Bush 41's discovery that there was no effective defense against missiles like the Iraqi Scud, which were easy to buy and launch and would be devastating if loaded with weapons of mass destruction.[22]

By now, Saddam recognized that he was not going to win the "mother of all battles." He grasped desperately at a Soviet-proffered cease-fire proposal on February 22, which would have given him six weeks to pull out of Kuwait without reprisal. The coalition rejected the offer but did agree not to attack Iraqi forces that evacuated Kuwait immediately. By now, the Bush administration was determined to teach Saddam a lesson. Hawks and doves alike agreed that Saddam must not be given an "aperture" to withdraw his troops, reinforce his regime and save face.[23] Still, important coalition elements had begun to waver. The Saudis were refusing to let American officers interrogate Iraqi POWs and deserters—so as not to offend their Muslim sensibilities—and French president François Mitterrand and Egyptian president Hosni Mubarak were urging a suspension of combat operations to arrange a diplomatic settlement.

"Colin, I Can't Let Norm Do This High-Diddle-Diddle Up-the-Middle Plan"

Schwarzkopf had initially planned to bash head-on into the Iraqi defenses on a narrow front. Such a course of action would have sucked the Americans and their coalition allies into the heart of the "Saddam Line"—Iraqi-built minefields, oil-filled ditches, barbed wire, sand berms, bunker complexes and massed artillery batteries on the Kuwait-Saudi border, which Saddam hoped the Americans would attack in the style of the Iranians in the last war. Even if the coalition punched through—alarmists predicted American casualties in the tens of thousands—they would present themselves on the far side of the Saddam Line in such a bedraggled condition that they would be easy prey for Saddam's massed tank divisions and Republican Guard reserves. Even if one assumed that U.S. airpower would significantly weaken Saddam's defenses and mechanized reserves, there would still be hell to pay. Scowcroft and Cheney expressed amazement that Schwarzkopf was even considering such a crude assault. (Schwarzkopf in Riyadh expressed amazement that the White House was asking him to liberate Kuwait with just two hundred thousand troops.) Scowcroft sourly remarked that Centcom's plan resembled the bloody attritional battles of 1864–65 that were being reprised that winter on Ken Burns's hit series *The Civil War* on PBS and eating into American support for the war. A "White House hawk"—reviled but nameless in Schwarzkopf's memoirs, probably Paul Wolfowitz—pompously declared that "Schwarzkopf is just another McClellan," content to pile up armed force, but afraid to attack.[24] Scowcroft and Cheney took a less insulting line; they wisely insisted that coalition forces be extended westward to threaten the Iraqi flank. "Colin, I can't let Norm do this high-diddle-diddle up-the-middle plan," Cheney told Powell.

Powell considered Cheney a serious thinker and a "glutton for information." Never having served in the military, Cheney ordered up fifteen tutorials on topics like "Building an Air Attack Plan" and "Breaching Iraqi Forward Defenses." He peppered Powell and his tutors with questions: "How do tanks work? Patriot missiles? . . . What does armored infantry *do* on a battlefield?" The secretary of defense was determined, as Powell put it, "to know what he was talking about militarily" and to persuade Schwarzkopf to deny Saddam the World War I–style battles that the Iraqi leader was seeking.[25] Cheney favored a "Western excursion" that would threaten Baghdad and maneuver the Iraqi units clustered in Kuwait out of their fortifications, by cutting in behind them. Cheney also wanted to fill Iraq's western desert with coalition troops to make it harder for Saddam to launch Scuds into Israel and Saudi Arabia. Powell protested that an extension of the coalition line to envelop the Iraqis in Kuwait and populate the desert would require at least a second corps from Europe. Cheney promptly set to work delivering one, over Baker's objection that too many U.S. troops might dilute the "international" flavor of the coalition.[26] Few in the Pentagon had any illusions about the coalition's "international" assets. The ones that really mattered in this contingency—the Arab armies—had declared themselves all but useless in advance. Having brought hundreds of thousands of U.S. troops into his kingdom to fight Iraq, Prince Khalid belatedly proposed that the offensive be launched from Turkey, not Saudi Arabia. Having joined the coalition to increase pressure on his rival Saddam Hussein, Syrian president Hafez al-Assad nevertheless severely restricted coalition overflight rights and refused to commit the two divisions he did send to Saudi Arabia to actual combat. The Egyptians also shied away from fighting, which opened up a yawning gap between the marines and the army that would have to be filled by the less than redoubtable Saudis.[27]

Obviously, Schwarzkopf would need a second American corps to stiffen his large but balky coalition. Presented with one by Cheney and Powell, Schwarzkopf began to revise his plan. There was little mystery about Saddam's plan. He took for granted that Americans were soft and casualty-averse and that they relied too much on airpower. Saddam assumed that if he dug in deep enough on his line in Kuwait, he could ride out the air strikes and force the Americans to attack across his minefields—five hundred thousand mines, or one for every member of the coalition, ABC News reported—and into the teeth of his trenches and bunkers.[28] A devious but fundamentally stupid man, Saddam made no allowance for precision munitions—or even dumb ones—and the effect that they might have on his infantry, tanks and gunners, all of which would be visible from the air and easily attacked once Iraq's air cover and SAMs were eliminated. Saddam also had a deluded conception of warfare that held that Westerners were weak and squeamish and would not endure an infantry fight with more virile Arab troops. Reporting on the war from Kuwait, Rick Atkinson marveled at Saddam's strategic folly. The United States had spent $3 trillion upgrading its military in the 1980s, and "Saddam had attacked when world oil supplies were plentiful . . . and when relations between the world powers were better than at any time since the Congress of Vienna in 1815. In confronting the United States, he picked a fight with a nation that had fifteen times the population of Iraq and eighty times its gross national product."[29]

CHENEY'S "WESTERN EXCURSION"

To deny Saddam the battle of attrition he was seeking in Kuwait, Schwarzkopf began shifting his forces away to the west. He rejected as impracticable Cheney's idea of a "Western excursion," which had derived from a Pentagon official's reading of Sir John Bagot Glubb's *A Short History of the Arab Peoples*. Glubb had described the two-pronged British dash from Jordan and Basra to Baghdad in 1941 to suppress the pro-Nazi regime there, and the Pentagon official—Stanford Business School professor Henry Rowen—had recommended a reprise of the maneuver to Paul Wolfowitz, who enthusiastically brought it to Cheney.[30] Schwarzkopf's staff compromised: they left the marines and the French, the British and Prince Khalid's Arab contingents opposite the Iraqi defense lines in Kuwait, and spread their two army corps westward. But not too far west: just far enough to outflank the "Saddam Line," skirt its minefields and then wheel in behind the Iraqi units once they began their inevitable retreat. The process of planning the ground war took a tremendous toll on Schwarzkopf, who felt second-guessed at every turn. Scowcroft and Cheney, on the other hand, entertained serious doubts about Schwarzkopf—too unimaginative—and Powell—too cautious—and leaned hard on the generals to devise a more creative and hard-hitting solution.[31]

Cheney took up Schwarzkopf's revised plan and pushed it even farther west—to As Salman, where the 101st Airborne supported by General Barry McCaffrey's 24th Mechanized Division could stamp out Scud launchers, then pivot east. The 82nd Airborne would cover their desert flank, while the "Screaming Eagles" and the 24th Mech raced to the Euphrates to cut off the Iraqi units in Kuwait and hit any reinforcements coming down from Baghdad in the flank. Major General Rupert Smith's British 1st Armored Division was also pulled west, to join the flanking maneuver, not batter itself uselessly against the Saddam Line. So were the French. Although President Mitterrand had initially refused to put his 6th Light Division under U.S. command, he was so alarmed by the dispositions of the commander he did choose— Saudi Arabia's Prince Khalid—that he secretly applied to Washington for a transfer to American command, which Washington granted, shifting the French from their positions opposite the Saddam Line to the extreme left wing of the left hook, guarding the flank of the 82nd Airborne. As the British took up their new positions, the U.S. Army was struck by their military eccentricity—long hair, officers calling superiors and subordinates alike by their Christian names, tea breaks and casual, improvised uniforms. When General Smith was picked up by an American Humvee, the driver looked at the British tank commander and his staff—a sweater draped raffishly around the general's neck, no signs of rank on display—and asked: "Where you guys from?" "Where do you think we're from?" Smith smiled. "You're sure as hell not in the U.S. Army," the driver replied. "You can't be Mexican. Are you Canadian?"[32]

"POWELL . . . LACKS THE STOMACH FOR WAR"

With prodding from Washington, things were shaping up. Powell assured the Pentagon press corps in late January that the Iraqis were finished: "Our strategy to go after this army is very, very simple. First, we are going to cut it off. And then we are going to kill it." President Bush applauded Powell's "quiet confidence" as "contagious." But Cheney smoldered as Powell kept increasing his demands for troops: another army corps, a doubling of marine forces and air force squadrons, activated reserves and three more carriers.[33] It often appeared that Powell was trying to deter President Bush with the high cost of the deployment as much as he was trying to deter Saddam. Cheney was receiving intelligence that Iraqi army morale was poor—20 to 50 percent of Iraqi troops were already deserting their units—and that Iraqi units in Kuwait had begun stockpiling rags and T-shirts to hold aloft as surrender flags whenever the coalition attacked. Even supposedly elite Republic Guard divisions were losing half their strength to desertions.[34] The impatience with which the neocons would drive to war in 2003 and override Secretary of State Powell's cavils as well as the army's demands for extra troops (for combat and occupation) had its roots in the discovery in 1991 that Powell's army had been too bleak and pessimistic in its estimates.

As G-day approached, the air force reluctantly shifted from strategic targets in Baghdad to tactical targets in Kuwait. The air force had promised to destroy 50 percent of the Iraqi army's tanks, APCs and artillery before the ground war, but its focus on strategic targets in Baghdad, Basra and Mosul had left it well behind on that front. Powell also pulled the air force away from Baghdad after two F-117s hit the Amiriyah bomb shelter on February 13 and killed or wounded six hundred Iraqi civilians. "Powell is a political genius," Schwarzkopf grumbled, "but he lacks the stomach for war." But in the new age of the unblinking twenty-four-hour news cycle, it was hard to stomach errors like Amiriyah. The public relations disaster was sufficient to drag the air force away from Baghdad—Powell and Cheney would henceforth vet all targets there—and down to the Saddam Line.[35]

There too Powell hesitated, pouring bombs on the Iraqis but cautioning Bush to delay the G-day ground attack: "Norm and I would rather see the Iraqis walk out than be driven out. There will be costs. We will lose soldiers in substantial numbers at a time. It will be grisly."[36] For now, all of the grisliness was felt by the Iraqi army. B-52s from Diego Garcia and Missouri pounded the Saddam Line. They dropped explosives as well as "bullshit bombs"—leaflets enjoining the Iraqi troops to save themselves and surrender. ("This is your first and last warning . . . Flee this location now!") F-111s attacked the Kuwait City polo club with laser-guided bombs, killing at least one Iraqi corps commander, who was drinking cocktails in the clubhouse when the bombs struck.[37]

The tactical air attacks were disappointing; to minimize U.S. casualties (as well as the "CNN effect" of downed aircraft and captured pilots) the B-52 raids were carried out in small bombing "cells"—three B-52s instead of six—and at medium and high altitudes that ensured poor accuracy, particularly when the high desert winds were factored in. One officer reflected that it was "like trying to stuff spaghetti up a wildcat's ass."[38] Accuracy became even more problematic when Saddam began lighting Kuwaiti oil wells on fire in February to put his troops and trench lines under a screen of black, oily smoke. (Three billion barrels of Kuwaiti oil—3 percent of the country's total reserves—went up in smoke during the short war.)[39] Marine pilots gave up bombing altogether and dug out Vietnam-era napalm and fuel-air explosives, which they poured over the Saddam Line hoping to burn and smother the Iraqi troops inside. The fuel-air explosives shrouded targets with an aerosol of ethylene oxide, which was then ignited to make an explosion as destructive as a nuclear blast. Men at the aim point were obliterated; men on the fringes suffered burst eardrums, ruptured lungs, crushed internal organs or blindness. It was easy to see why the Iraqi army panicked and ran away. The most successful air-to-ground attacks were carried out by Air Force F-111s and F-15Es and Navy A-6s, which screamed in at eight thousand feet, laser-located the hot, sunbaked Iraqi tanks—even through palls of smoke—and then dropped 500-pound bombs on them. "Tank plinking" worked marvelously; Iraq's ground forces resumed their crumbling at the cost of very few American casualties.

"Cold spots" migrating north on the desert highways began showing up on U.S. airborne sensors; they were recognizable from U.S. analyses of the Iran-Iraq War: twenty-nine-foot refrigerated vans hauling Iraqi corpses to Baghdad for burial. "Bombs R Us," the air force joked. "We live so others may die." That much was true. But the Persian Gulf War was marked by tremendous tension between the air force and the army as well as the marines. The army suspected—and proved—that the air force exaggerated the results of its tactical strikes on Iraqi ground forces. The army, for example, discovered that the air force had destroyed only 26 percent of a Republican Guard division in Kuwait when the air force was claiming to have destroyed 52 percent of it. The CIA and the DIA joined the clamor; both intelligence agencies discovered major discrepancies between the "kills" the air force was reporting and the actual destruction on the ground. The CIA, which relied on satellites, not gun camera footage, would confirm only 358 tank "kills," when Centcom was reporting 1,400. Centcom tried to paper over the interservice and agency wrangling—generally adopting the position of the air force—but never succeeded. Instead of forging a new model of "jointness," the Gulf War merely revealed anew the old tensions between airmen and soldiers.[40]

"THE GOOD LORD HAS A WAY OF TAKING CARE OF DRUNKEN SAILORS AND PISSED-OFF MARINES"

President Bush delivered an ultimatum to Saddam on February 23, ordering the Iraqi leader to begin evacuating Kuwait by noon on February 24. Powell still wanted to bomb the Iraqis into a withdrawal from Kuwait, but Bush now wanted to remove them with ground troops, to drive home the point that aggression would be punished in the "new world order" and to *use* the big coalition army—"we had over 500,000 U.S. troops standing by in the Gulf and our Air Force had flown over 94,000 missions"—before it had to be rotated home. It was a tough call—an example of presidential courage—in a political, media and military environment seething with predictions of slaughter. Even Schwarzkopf, now possessed of a mighty host, still worried that he'd lose five thousand men in the opening assault— "if they choose to dump chemicals on [us], they might even win."[41] On February

24, the marines began their attack, a relatively crude assault into the Saddam Line. Two marine divisions—40 percent of the U.S. Marine Corps—would rake their way through minefields, punch a hole in the Saddam Line and then push straight through in column. The idea was to hit hard on a narrow front, pulling the half million Iraqi troops in Kuwait into battle. Once committed, the Iraqi frontline troops and reserves would be outflanked and destroyed by the army heavy divisions hooking in from the west. Even the limited bite-and-hold operation contemplated by Schwarzkopf and Marine commander General Walt Boomer required a long logistics tail. Planning a "two-division breach" without a running start, the marines were forced to excavate a vast underground supply base right under the guns of the Iraqis: 17,000 tons of ammunition, 4.8 million gallons of fuel, 14 field hospitals, and 1.2 million meals ready-to-eat (MREs). Packed in on a narrow front, the marines were sitting ducks for a chemical weapons attack or even a stray Iraqi shell that might have detonated their fuel and ammunition. "The Good Lord has a way of taking care of drunken sailors and pissed-off Marines," General Boomer reflected. So did the air force, whose plinking and bombing raids over the Saddam Line had culled two tank battalions a day from the Iraqi arsenal and cut the defending force from 362,000 troops down to about 183,000. Many Iraqis had been killed or wounded, but most had just surrendered or run away.[42]

Seventeen thousand marines remained offshore, part of a great feint toward Kuwait's coastline that was never seriously considered because the navy would have needed a month to sweep up Iraqi mines and take out Saddam's Silkworm antiship missiles. Moreover, Schwarzkopf refused marine demands to batter the Kuwaiti coast with air strikes and 16-inch guns and destroy a Kuwaiti liquid natural gas plant that the marines worried might blow up (or be blown up by Saddam) during their landings with the force of a low-yield nuclear weapon. "I intend to destroy every-thing in front of me and on the flanks to try to keep our casualties down," the commander of the marine amphibious force vowed, which worried Schwarzkopf. "I don't want to destroy Kuwait in order to save it," he muttered.[43] Schwarzkopf would later get credit for an amphibious feint that he never seriously considered.

On February 24, the U.S. VII Corps, led by General Frederick Franks, punched into Iraq. A principal American war aim was to smash enough of the Iraqi military to leave Saudi Arabia able to defend itself against "residual Iraqi forces."[44] Now the smashing began in earnest. Although Franks had initially planned to stack his three divisions in a single sixty-mile-long column and bulldoze through the Saddam Line, wiser heads prevailed and he spread his forces wider. Looking at Franks's original plan, one of the general's subordinates mused: "Okay, our first mental task in this war is to change that plan. This is pretty broken." Although Franks had read the German armored warfare theorist Heinz Guderian and taken his emphasis on mass—"fist, not fingers"—to heart, he was ignoring Guderian's insistence on speed, mobility and operational envelopment.[45] Armored forces needed to concentrate and punch hard, but they also needed to seek the enemy's flanks and generate (by their mobility) the element of surprise. "We've got the wrong man commanding [VII] Corps," Cheney grumbled, but it was too late to make a change. Cheney now had to worry about Schwarzkopf too, who hoped that a prolongation of the air campaign would dislodge the Iraqis *without* a ground attack. Schwarzkopf complained that the war had become "political" and that he was being asked to sacrifice U.S. troops for political expediency—so that the president could win a war. "Time is on our side," Stormin' Norman insisted. Schwarzkopf was baffled by Saddam's refusal to extend his lines into the path of the army divisions that were so obviously aimed at his flanks; surely the Iraqi leader had a card up his sleeve—he might be planning "to pop a nuke" in the great empty area that the army would traverse, or make it "a chemical killing sack."[46] Secure in Washington, Wolfowitz joked that Centcom was seeking a "365-day air campaign," and Powell, who had earlier rebuked Schwarzkopf for publicly describing the Iraqis as "on the verge of collapse," now found himself having to buck Schwarzkopf up and prod him into battle. Cheney wanted the ground attack *now*: the logistics were in place, the air commanders were running out of munitions to drop on the Iraqis, and the allied troops had to be thrown into battle before they became stale from inactivity. Cheney also reminded Schwarzkopf that the American objective in the war was not simply to liberate Kuwait, but to destroy Iraq's offensive capability. "Wrap it up," Cheney ordered the Centcom commander.[47]

"LIKE A BEAGLE CHASING A RABBIT"

Schwarzkopf, fond of General William T. Sherman's quotation that "war is the remedy our enemies have chosen, and I say let us give them all they want," now gave the Iraqis all they wanted.[48] Franks's tanks roared forward and Iraqi resistance evaporated. Instead of pulling the Iraqis forward into battle, the marine attacks had driven them backward, in full retreat toward Iraq. Iraqis who didn't retreat were entombed in their trenches by armored marine bulldozers, which roared up to the Saddam

Line, lowered their shovels and pushed the parapets back into the trenches, burying the Iraqi infantry alive. Schwarzkopf had planned to grab the Iraqis by the nose (with the marines) and kick them in the ass (with the army), but the Iraqis had ripped their nose from the marine grasp and begun to run away. The chase was on. Schwarzkopf had joked that the war would be "like a beagle chasing a rabbit," and indeed it was. Could the army "left hook" destroy the bulk of the Iraqi army and annihilate the Republican Guards before they crossed back into Iraq and appealed for a cease-fire? The process was that much harder because the marines and army were slowed by thousands of Iraqi deserters who came across waving white flags and demanding that they be taken prisoner. Driving and fighting with GPS, the Americans knew where they were at all times in the featureless desert, and they knew where the Iraqis were as well. American and British tanks also fought with thermal-imaging equipment, laser range finders and arrow-shaped kinetic energy sabot rounds that zipped downrange a mile a second, permitting the coalition main battle tanks to engage and destroy the obsolete Iraqi tanks from well beyond their effective range. Coalition tanks were effective at *triple* the range of the Iraqi T-55s and T-72s, which dated from the Age of Elvis (Presley and Costello, respectively) and were clad in steel, not ceramic, armor.

The British 1st Armored Division covered Franks's right flank, and the U.S. XVIII Airborne Corps augmented by the French 6th Light Armor Division roared up on Franks's left. The French and the U.S. Airborne Corps were the "left hook" designed to outflank the Iraqi heavy units in VII Corps' path. The coalition units pivoted around to the east and cut into the flank of the Iraqi Republican Guards. Saddam had asked for six weeks to evacuate Kuwait. He now saw that he would not even have that many *days*. Perhaps it was that realization that moved him finally to start targeting the U.S. "Scud bowl" in Saudi Arabia. In a fit of impotent rage, he launched a missile into the American barracks at al-Khobar outside Dhahran. The blast produced more American casualties than any other single action of the war: twenty-eight killed and ninety-eight wounded. The Pentagon and the army were left to ponder how much more slaughter Saddam could have wrought had he sent more Scuds into the American marshaling yards earlier.[49] Under the pressure of coalition attacks, Saddam's troops and tanks began fleeing back across the border on February 26. "It's hard to believe how well we're doing," Cheney exulted to the president. "Thank God," Bush said.[50]

Critics later assailed Schwarzkopf for not immediately implementing the lessons of Khafji, which had exposed the vulnerability of Iraqi forces to air attack as well as their propensity to drop their weapons and run away.[51] Schwarzkopf still proceeded as if he were launching the Schlieffen Plan, "luring" the Iraqis into a fight with the marines that would theoretically pull the Iraqi reserves forward, so that the army could close like a revolving door around the entire Iraqi army (and Republican Guard) in Kuwait. But what if the Iraqis weren't "lured forward" to contest the marine attacks? What if they simply ran up their white flags and surrendered? What if the Republican Guards threw their tanks into reverse and fled back toward Baghdad to yield Kuwait but secure the Saddam Hussein regime? Incredibly, Schwarzkopf made no provision for those *likely* eventualities.

"HIGHWAY OF DEATH"

The most heavily trafficked line of retreat was the principal Iraq-Kuwait highway, which filled with Iraqi infantry columns and vehicles trying to reverse out of Kuwait. Saddam knew that the Arab members of the coalition would *not* join any attacks on Iraqi units once they had left Kuwait, and suspected that other coalition partners like the French would follow suit. Allied forces, racing to hit the Iraqis before they could cross the Euphrates River, pounced on the traffic jams along Highway 8 and slaughtered them. General Barry McCaffrey's 24th Mechanized Division—twenty-six thousand soldiers and eighty-six hundred vehicles—swung up on the left through bogs, wadis and sandstorms with XVIII Corps. McCaffrey's division managed a fast pace of fifteen miles per hour. McCaffrey called the Iraqi units—infantry and armor alike—"tethered goats."[52] Neither the troops nor the officers exhibited any initiative. Alerted by juiced-up pilots who spoke excitedly about their easy kills along the Iraqi lines of retreat, the press began referring to American strikes on Highway 8 as "the turkey shoot," the route itself as the "Highway of Death." "Anything with wings and a bomb rack" was sent aloft to participate in the slaughter.[53] Saddam milked the images of death—burnt-out passenger buses and private cars and even scorched baby carriages—for all they were worth in trying to wring sympathy from the Arab street and world opinion. "The victimizer had become the victim," two historians noted. Coalition forces lurched after the blundering, bleeding Iraqis, Schwarzkopf screaming into the telephone to speed Franks up.[54]

Some of the war's heaviest fighting occurred on the afternoon of February 27, when a Republican Guard armored brigade dug into fighting holes to protect High-way 8 and the approaches to Basra. The M1 tanks of the U.S. 1st Armored Division halted twenty-five hundred yards away—beyond the range of the Iraqi tanks—and methodically blasted them. In just forty-five minutes, Colonel Montgomery Meigs's 2nd Brigade destroyed sixty-nine Iraqi tanks and thirty-eight Iraqi APCs, without the loss of a single American vehicle. American gunners on the flanks worked from the outside in, while gunners in the center fired from the inside out, completing the destruction of the Iraqi armor with remarkable efficiency. "I want you to move gently but deliberately and kill all those people," Meigs ordered.[55] As the marines, VII Corps and the British drove forward—"rather like a grouse shoot," one British commander observed—the air force stopped bombing the coastal high-way running north from Kuwait City through Basra and over the causeway that bridged the Euphrates. That was a grave error exploited by the Iraqis, who poured up the road and out of Kuwait unscathed. It was a signal failure of jointness and "air-land battle," attributable to the growing problem of "friendly fire"—far more dangerous to the coalition than Iraqi fire—and to fears in Washington that a second "highway of death" would be politically calamitous for America's image abroad. There were 1,500 foreign journalists gathered in Riyadh during Desert Storm, 180 of them in pools at the front line, and they were all hungry for a scoop. Bush fretted that he would be accused of "butchering the Iraqis" and "shooting them in the back."[56] President Bush finally conceded a cease-fire after just one hundred hours of combat, on February 27. Schwarzkopf too was in a hurry to end hostilities. If he concluded Desert Storm on February 27, he could call his victory "the Five-Day War," which would best the Israeli victory of 1967 by a day.[57]

The critical meeting in the Bush White House took place at one p.m. on Febru-ary 27. Bush, Scowcroft, Cheney, Powell, Robert Gates and British foreign secretary Douglas Hurd agreed that they needed to force terms on Saddam, not wait for him to request a cease-fire on his own terms. The allies agreed—mistakenly—that they had destroyed Iraq's WMD capabilities, and also that they needed to secure the immediate return of all coalition POWs, including the twenty-five to thirty thou-sand Kuwaitis presumed to be in Iraqi captivity. Although the air force pronounced itself capable of bombing Iraq "until they're down to two stone axes and a pushcart" and coalition ground units were within striking distance of the Iraqi capital—XVIII Corps' 101st Airborne Division sat astride Highway 8 just 150 miles from Baghdad—Hurd was losing the will to go on.[58] Thatcher, who might have argued for a drive on to Baghdad to remove Saddam, had left office in November 1990 and been replaced by John Major, who evinced more caution as well as a desire to end the war. Reflecting the more cautious line, Hurd explained that sanctions—which had not worked before the war—would probably work now because Iraq was weakened and chastened.

Asked about the military situation, Powell explained that the war was won. "We cleaned their clock." Now it was just a matter of chewing up Iraqi equipment: "There are 3,000 destroyed tanks. We are in the home stretch." The war could be wrapped up "today or tomorrow, by close of business . . . a five-day war." Bush listened raptly and called for a "clean end"—or as clean as possible under the circumstances. "This is not going to be like the battleship *Missouri*," he allowed. The main thing, Bush insisted, was to avoid "charges of brutalization," of piling on just to kill Iraqis in the war's last hours. Secretary of State Baker concurred: "We have done the job. We can stop. We have achieved our aims. We have gotten them out of Kuwait." But, like everyone else in the room, Baker worried about "unfinished business." What would become of the Saddam Hussein regime? Would the Americans give it a shove, or let it stand? In Riyadh, Schwarzkopf was declaring victory at the Hyatt Hotel—"the gates are closed . . . we almost completely destroyed the offensive capability of the Iraqi forces"—and assuring the press that going to Baghdad was *not* in the cards. That ingenuous revelation prompted a startled protest from Paul Wolfowitz in the Pentagon, who agreed that the allies probably weren't going to Baghdad, but considered it foolhardy to tell that to the Iraqis. Wolfowitz and the other "Washington hawks"—the neocon architects of the Iraq invasion in 2003—were still hoping for a coup, and wanted to keep pressure on Saddam.[59]

"YOU HAVE GOT TO BE SHITTING ME. WHY A CEASE-FIRE *NOW*?"

In Riyadh, the deputy Centcom commander, General Calvin Waller, also expressed amazement at Washington's hasty, charitable concession of a cease-fire, when only about half of the Republican Guard's equipment had been destroyed and before the last bridges over the Euphrates had been demolished, effectively bottling up the Iraqi army, most of which was still south of Basra, squarely in the sights of the U.S. VII and XVIII corps. American planners had planned to disarm and dismount the

Iraqis and then send them streaming back into Iraq on foot: "Long lines of dispir-
ited Iraqi troops leaving the battlefield like German prisoners marching east after
their defeat at Stalingrad." *That* was the kind of image that would humiliate Saddam
and rock his regime. "You have got to be shitting me. Why a cease-fire *now*?" Waller
expostulated. "One hundred hours has a nice ring," Schwarzkopf chuckled. "That's
bullshit," Waller said. "Then *you* go argue with them," Schwarzkopf said. "Them"
was the Joint Chiefs of Staff, the Pentagon and the Bush White House. Schwarzkopf
had never squared off against Powell and was not about to begin now. He later
explained that lack of starch: "I never knew what was Powell, what was Scowcroft,
what was Cheney, or what was the President." Powell set the tone in the Joint Chiefs
of Staff, and talked the other chiefs into an early end to the war. Desert Storm had
evicted Saddam from Kuwait and erased the stain of Vietnam, so why fight on?

Air Force chief of staff General Merrill McPeak privately protested the "merci-
ful clemency" offered Saddam, but publicly supported Powell. President Bush too
wanted to quit while he was ahead. In Washington, the analogy on everyone's mind
was not Vietnam, but Korea, where a limited American war—to evict the North
Koreans from the south—had slipped (under MacArthur's gung-ho influence) into
an unlimited struggle to destroy the North Korean communists that had dragged
on bloodily and inconclusively for three years and then left American troops as a
permanent fixture in South Korea.[60] Few wanted to risk this easy victory and expand
American liabilities by rolling the dice and pushing north to Baghdad. Powell ridiculed the notion: it was not as if "lots of little Jeffersonian democrats would have
popped up to run for office" in Baghdad on America's coattails. Still, Bush felt tension and incompleteness everywhere. "Why do I not feel elated?" President Bush
asked aloud. He knew why. The instigator of the war had survived to fight another
day, and there was little that Bush could do to change that outcome. In his diary,
Bush wrote of his anger at seeing Baghdad Radio broadcasting *victory* even as U.S.
forces trounced the Iraqis. "It's what concerns me. It hasn't been a clean end—there
is no battleship *Missouri* surrender. This is what's missing to make this akin to
WWII, to separate Kuwait from Korea and Vietnam."[61] But the coalition would not
support continued combat in Iraq or Kuwait merely to "destroy Iraqi forces," nor
would many Americans. The war was not cheap either; 146 Americans had died in
combat, and the bill for the war stood at about $620 billion. "We need to have an
end. People want that. They are going to want to know that we won and that the
kids can come home. We don't want to screw this up with a sloppy, muddled end-

ing." Within a year, two-thirds of Americans would come to believe that President Bush had terminated the war too *soon*, and the unresolved issue would contribute to Bush's defeat in the elections of 1992.[62]

The Hundred Hour War ground to an equivocal close, over Paul Wolfowitz's recondite objection that "hundred-hour war" would be a politically disastrous term since it would evoke memories of the hundred-hour Franco-British-Israeli attack on Egypt in 1956. ("Would 99-hour war work better?" Cheney joked.) Fred Franks's VII Corps had pushed ahead to seize the Safwan road junction between Basra and Kuwait City and McCaffrey had advanced to demolish the Republican Guard when the cease-fire took effect at eight a.m. on February 28. McCaffrey had pushed all the way up to the Rumaila oil field and had subjected the fleeing Iraqis to a vicious artillery barrage. One of his brigade commanders expressed frustration: "I knew that this would be a military decision that would be debated for years to come in terms of where we stopped. The sense was there: 'success, but . . .'"[63] Bush had confidently predicted that the Iraqi "troops will straggle home with no armor, beaten up, 50,000 casualties," but they were more numerous than that, and they had extricated lots of armor.[64] American surveillance photos of southern Iraq revealed the depressing news that Saddam had extricated one-quarter of his tanks and half of his APCs from Kuwait. Worse, the tanks that escaped were largely Republican Guard. Indeed the Republican Guard divisions in Kuwait had escaped largely intact: eighty thousand troops with large numbers of tanks and helicopters. Saddam emerged from the war with three thousand armored vehicles and one thousand heavy guns.

"The end game: it was bad," McCaffrey recalled. "First of all, there was confusion. The objectives were unclear. And the sequence was wrong." McCaffrey's frustration with what appeared to be a desert Dunkirk boiled to the surface on March 2—two days after the war officially ended and while Iraqi officers were en route to Safwan to sign the armistice. McCaffrey ordered his 1st Brigade to demolish Iraqi armored columns—T-72 tanks, APCs, Frog missile launchers and trucks—trying to find a way over the Euphrates. McCaffrey's division destroyed 346 Iraqi vehicles, including 30 T-72s, in the short, sharp exchange. With army loudspeakers blaring, "Get out of your vehicles, leave them behind, and you will not die," the Iraqi crews slithered out the hatches and ran into the marshes, leaving their tanks, trucks and troop carriers to be demolished by McCaffrey's Apaches, artillery and M1 tanks. In Riyadh, Schwarzkopf's headquarters turned a blind eye to the postwar combat: "I don't know, and I don't want to know," a senior army officer commented.[65]

Ordinary Iraqis expressed wonderment at Saddam's continued hold on power. Retreating troops fired their AK-47s into the portraits and murals of Saddam that lined their routes home. An Iraqi cement worker muttered: "Kuwait destroyed by Saddam. Iraq destroyed by combined forces. But Saddam is still in his chair."[66] The Shiites of southern Iraq, who had begun to seethe even before the ground war, exploded into rebellion after the cease-fire. "Saddam is the enemy of God!" Shiite militants chanted as they streamed through the streets of Basra, Karbala, Najaf and Nasiriyah. With phones and power knocked out, factories closed, salaries in arrears and the Baath police in Baghdad unable to jam foreign radio broadcasts, the Shiites listened eagerly to Voice of America, the BBC and the CIA-sponsored, Saudi-operated Voice of Free Iraq.[67] Saddam was weakened and discredited. The moment to rise up had arrived. In northern Iraq, the Kurds made the same calculation. They took President Bush's awkward March 1 declaration as a call to action: "In my own view, I've always said it would be—that the Iraqi people should put him aside and that would facilitate the resolution of all these problems that exist, and certainly would facilitate the acceptance of Iraq back into the family of peace-loving nations."

"And Now We Have Saddam Hussein Still There—the Man That Wreaked This Havoc Upon His Neighbors"

But even as he incited the Iraqis to rebel, Bush forswore any push to Baghdad and conceded Saddam the use of armed helicopters on his side of the border, a concession Saddam requested to enable his officials to get around the war-ravaged country. Saddam promptly exploited the American concession not to vault over shattered roads and bridges but to blast his rebellious subjects from the air. When Scowcroft confronted Powell and Cheney and asked them to revoke the helicopter privilege, Cheney and Powell hesitated to "undercut Schwarzkopf," and added, surely disingenuously, that if deprived of his choppers, Saddam would simply fall back on towed artillery.[68] But how would he have towed heavy guns over blasted roads and bridges? Bush 41 expressed again his mixed feelings about Desert Storm, this time to a (startled) White House press conference: "You know, to be very honest with you, I haven't yet felt this wonderfully euphoric feeling that many of the American people feel." In his hour of triumph, the president sounded anything but triumphant: "I feel much better about it today than I did yesterday. But I think it's that I want to see an end. You mentioned World War II—there was a definitive end to that conflict. And now we have Saddam Hussein still there—the man that wreaked this havoc upon his neighbors." The father's doubts would sow the son's resolve to, as Bush 41 concluded, make sure "the last 't' is crossed, the last 'i' is dotted."[69]

In Iraq, meanwhile, Schwarzkopf traveled to Safwan to accept Saddam's surrender. The whole truce was badly managed. Although President Bush continued to lament the absence of a "battleship *Missouri*" moment, the *Missouri* was actually available, on station in the Persian Gulf, and Schwarzkopf wanted to use it but was deterred by the logistics of transporting herds of coalition representatives and reporters to the battleship on short notice. Safwan—an Iraqi airfield just over the border from Kuwait—would have to do, but Franks did not seize the crossroads, leaving it in the hands of the Iraqis even as the Americans were preparing to accept the Iraqi surrender there. Schwarzkopf, cursing Fred Franks's "slow, ponderous, pachyderm mentality," had to flog Franks forward and *command* him to drive the Iraqis out of Safwan, which Franks grudgingly accomplished.[70] Then the Iraqis tried to send a low-level delegation to the meeting, which Schwarzkopf accepted but Prince Khalid wisely rejected. Still, none of the coalition partners insisted on Saddam's presence at the surrender ceremony, which was a glaring oversight. President Bush *wanted* Saddam there, but recalled that he and his advisers "asked ourselves *what* we would do if he refused." Continue the war? Bad. Retreat from the demand of Saddam's attendance? Worse.[71] Powell and Schwarzkopf thus contented themselves with two four-star Iraqi generals, and Bush did not insist on anything more. The "Washington hawks"—Cheney and Wolfowitz in particular—felt certain that Powell and Schwarzkopf were being played by Saddam, and letting relatively minor military considerations override long-term political ones. Although Westerners treated beaten enemies with respect, Middle Easterners regarded such courtesy as weakness. Was Robert Gates—who would return as secretary of defense for Bush 43—correct or incorrect in urging President Bush on February 28 to stop? "We crushed their forty-three divisions, but we stopped—we didn't want to just kill, and history will look on that kindly."[72] Would it? The U.S. Army, in its haste to get its prisoners released and to get out of the Gulf and back home, was appearing, at best, distracted, at worst, weak. "Norm went in uninstructed," a senior Bush administration official recalled. "He should have had instructions," but he didn't. "The process broke down. The generals made an effort *not* to be guided. It was treated as something that was basically a military decision, not to be micromanaged." Schwarzkopf insisted that he'd been forced to "wing it" precisely because he'd been given no proper instructions. Chas Freeman, the U.S. ambassador to Saudi Arabia, spoke of "a total failure of integration between military and political strategy."[73] The narrow-minded fury with which the neocons would plot and launch the 2003 Iraq War derived in part from their conviction that the cautious army generals had thrown away *real* victory in 1991.

Arriving at Safwan, Schwarzkopf told Tom Brokaw that "this isn't a negotiation. I'm here to tell them exactly what we expect them to do."[74] Schwarzkopf staked out cease-fire lines, ordered a prisoner exchange and demanded details on Iraqi mine-fields, but did not insist that Saddam turn over his WMD or his Scuds. In mid-February, Bush had rather carelessly allowed that "there is another way for the bloodshed to stop, and that is for the Iraqi military and the Iraqi people to take matters into their own hands—to force Saddam Hussein, the dictator, to step aside." The Iraqi military having proven itself weak, tame and coup-proof, the CIA had initiated a plot to raise the Shiites of the south and the Kurds of the north against the Baath regime. As the revolt flared into life—responding to U.S.-funded radio appeals from transmitters in Saudi Arabia—Saddam repressed it viciously. One hundred and seventy thousand Kurds and Shiites fled their towns and villages to escape Saddam's wrath. Having received U.S. permission to fly not only helicopters, but helicopter gunships as well—"So you mean even helicopters that are armed can fly in the Iraqi skies?" General Sultan Hashim Ahmad had asked incredulously; "Yeah," Schwarzkopf had carelessly answered—Saddam turned their rockets and machine guns on the rebellious Kurds and Shiites, none of whom had been given Stingers like the mujahideen.[75] Many hid in the mountains of the north or the marshes of the south or continued into Turkey and Iran as refugees. "When the Iraqi helicopters started coming out, firing on the Iraqis, that's when we knew it was bullshit," a U.S. Army captain bitterly recalled.[76]

Taken off guard amid the hubbub of victory, Bush and his air commanders hastily clapped "no-fly zones" over northern and southern Iraq, expedients that would have been unnecessary had Bush simply demolished the Republican Guards and forbidden the Iraqis to fly. Two historians of the war noted Schwarzkopf's "surprising disinterest in the internal situation in Iraq." To the amazement of the beaten Iraqis, Schwarzkopf "guaranteed" them that the last coalition soldier would leave Iraq the minute the last coalition "ammo and gasoline trucks" were rounded up and put on the road. Bush and Schwarzkopf could have insisted on humane treatment of the Kurds and Shiites, a new constitution or even a new regime. They could have squatted on the Rumaila oil field—seized by McCaffrey in the last hours of the war—until Saddam met their political demands or paid the costs of the war. Instead, in practical military style, they filled their gas and ammo trucks and left. Powell and the Joint Chiefs of Staff vetoed an effort by America's UN ambassador Thomas Pickering to declare Iraq south of Basra a demilitarized zone, a step that would have sheltered the Shiites and held the Rumaila oil field as collateral for Saddam's good behavior. Powell and Schwarzkopf worried that Kurdish and Shiite secessionists might "Lebanonize" Iraq and suck the U.S. military into a civil war, leaving, as Powell put it, Uncle Sam to "sort out 2,000 years of Mesopotamian history."[77] President Bush would not have forgotten just how narrow and precarious support for the war had been in Congress and the press. Virtually everyone had predicted blowback and "mission creep," so the president took pains to avoid both, even at the cost of a partial victory. Limited wars generally end with limited results.[78]

When Army general Steven Arnold prepared a secret Centcom contingency plan that called for a march to Baghdad to remove Saddam and install a friendly regime that would permit a "long-term . . . U.S./Western . . . military presence in the region"—remarkably like the 2003 plan—Schwarzkopf's headquarters recoiled in horror. Arnold's plan implied that Desert Storm had been a partial victory, leaving lots of unfinished business in its wake; Schwarzkopf, Powell and Bush—despite the president's doubts—wanted it recognized as a decisive victory. For its part, the State Department feared that Arnold's suggestion of "attacks . . . across the Euphrates River . . . to provide [political] leverage" against the Saddam regime would tilt America too far toward the Iraqi Shiites.[79] If the Shiite south broke away and rallied to Tehran, America would have fought a war to strengthen the Islamic Republic of Iran. Nobody in Washington wanted that outcome, yet. The debates in 1991 prefigured similar debates in 2003, with the difference that they were more openly contested in 1991, but suppressed by groupthink in 2003.

"MR. PRESIDENT, I KNOW WHAT YOU WANT; I JUST DON'T SEE HOW IT'S GOING TO HAPPEN"

Paul Wolfowitz—eager to loosen Saddam's grip by any means—attempted to reassure the State Department in March 1991 that the Iraqi Shiites were Arabs and would not ally with Iran's Persians. Wolfowitz wanted to incite rebellion in southern Iraq. So did the Saudis, who urged the Americans to equip Iraq's Shiites as they had once equipped the Afghan mujahideen. The Americans demurred, the State Department sensibly pointing out that Lebanon's Hezbollah was also Arab, but a tight, terrorist ally of Iran in spite of that fact. That was also Scowcroft's view in the White House. "Geopolitics," he said, dictated that Washington let Saddam crush the Shiite revolt. It was not in America's interest for Iraq "to fall apart." Iran would be the prime beneficiary of such a development.[80] Scowcroft and his chief Middle East expert, Richard Haass, had reminded Bush throughout the war that regime change in Iraq must *not* be an American aim because a vacuum in Iraq would destroy the regional balance of power as well as Bush's coalition. "Mr. President," Haass told Bush, "I know what you want; I just don't see how it's going to happen."

Scowcroft and Haass had persuaded Bush before the war to stop drawing parallels between Saddam and Hitler—"Saddam is a madman who has shown he will kill"—because statements like that all but committed America to the removal of Saddam Hussein.[81] Powell batted away all talk of intervention to help the Shiites. If the U.S. military intervened to stop the helicopter strikes, would it then have to stop ground attacks as well? Powell warned of mission creep and recommended again that the United States get out quickly and cleanly. "If you want us to go in and stop the killing of the Shiites, that's a mission I understand," the chairman said during a Pentagon strategy session. "But to what *purpose* am I going to stop the killing? If the Shiites continue to rise up, do we then support them for the overthrow of Baghdad and the partition of the country? That's exactly the objective we said we *weren't* interested in."[82] Powell quarreled with Wolfowitz and told him to stop acting as if the question of aiding the Shiites were still open. Wolfowitz grumbled that Powell and Schwarzkopf were seeking "rapid disengagement . . . to preserve the luster of victory."[83]

The ruthless determination with which Cheney, Rumsfeld, Wolfowitz and the rest of the neocons would construct the Iraq War twelve years later derived from their conviction that great opportunities to reinvent Iraq had been squandered at Safwan. "The military's attitude was we have won," Wolfowitz bitterly recalled. "Let's cut this cleanly and not let the civilians load us with a lot of missions. Safwan was too hasty and too dignified."[84] President Bush had commanded the Iraqi skies, had pushed two U.S. Army corps into Iraq, had shattered the Iraqi military and had seized Iraq's richest oil field. Holding all those cards in his hand, Bush had discarded them, asked nothing in return and even, Glosson reflected, "given them a field day against the Shiites." Bush seemed unprepared for a tyrant as ruthless and ungrateful as Saddam. "Tonight in Iraq," President Bush declared on March 6, "Saddam walks amidst ruin. His war machine is crushed. His ability to threaten mass destruction is itself destroyed . . . Now, we can see a new world coming into view. A world in which there is a very real prospect of a new world order . . . a world in which freedom and respect for human rights find a home among all nations."[85]

On March 10, 1991, having upheld Bush's "new world order," the half million U.S. troops in Kuwait and Saudi Arabia began to head home. As they transited Highway 8, they shared the road with panicked streams of refugees fleeing savage Republican Guard attacks in Basra, Karbala and Najaf. The Shiites spoke of atrocities—indiscriminate attacks on women and children, mass executions, the razing of Shiite holy places and threats of chemical weapon attacks. They asked for captured Iraqi weapons caches to defend themselves, but were rebuffed by American engineers, who stolidly withheld the weapons and dynamited them instead. "Bush told us to revolt against Saddam. We revolt against Saddam, but where is Bush? Where is he?" a panicked Shiite fugitive asked U.S. troops on Highway 8.[86] Bush was sticking to the Scowcroft line, to merely "weaken Iraqi popular support for the current government" but not assist in its overthrow. The best outcome for Scowcroft and Bush was an Iraqi coup—"it's the colonel with the brigade patrolling the palace that's going to get [Saddam] if someone gets him."[87] In April 1991, Saddam turned his fire on the restive Kurds, forcing Bush to demarcate a protected enclave in northern Iraq for the Kurds. In late 1992, he formalized a similar "no-fly zone" over the Shiite areas of southern Iraq, too late to save twenty thousand Shiites already butchered, and ineffective anyway against Saddam's ground attacks, which included draining the Euphrates marshes to deprive the Shiites of cover.

"HAD WE TAKEN ALL OF IRAQ, WE WOULD HAVE BEEN LIKE THE DINOSAUR IN THE TAR PIT"

In May 1991, Bush acknowledged that the victory in Kuwait had been anything but decisive when he extended the prewar economic sanctions against Iraq "until Saddam Hussein is out of power." The DIA confirmed that Saddam's nuclear weapons program "had been slowed but not halted" by Desert Storm. After the war, Saddam employed two thousand foreign-trained scientists and eighteen thousand engineers, proof that Saddam was sparing no expense to join the nuclear club. If sanctions and UN inspections ever ceased, Saddam would have a bomb "in two to four years."[88] Bush and Scowcroft later explained their decision not to intervene in Iraq's internal affairs or press on to Baghdad to overthrow Saddam in their joint memoir—*A World Transformed*. Bush noted that the war's object was simple: to eject the Iraqis from Kuwait, restore Kuwait's independence and degrade the Iraqi military. "To occupy Iraq would instantly shatter our coalition, turning the whole Arab world against us, and make a broken tyrant into a latter-day Arab hero." Bush accurately predicted the fate of his less reflective son: "To march into Baghdad . . . would condemn young soldiers to fight in what would be an unwinnable urban guerrilla war. It could only plunge that part of the world into even greater instability and destroy the credibility we were working so hard to establish."[89] Secretary of State Baker concurred, arguing that a drive to Baghdad would have transformed a war to rescue Kuwait into "a U.S. war of conquest" that would have snared the army in "urban warfare and military occupation."[90] Schwarzkopf too was prescient: "I am certain that had we taken all of Iraq, we would have been like the dinosaur in the tar pit—we would still be there." With what sounds like black humor today, Schwarzkopf also noted the prohibitive cost of such a venture, "maintaining or restoring government, education, and other services for the people of Iraq." Surely, Schwarzkopf concluded, "this is a burden the beleaguered American taxpayer would not have been happy to take on."[91] Secretary of Defense Cheney, who would become the sharpest exponent of Operation Iraqi Freedom in 2003, also argued against a push to Baghdad in 1991. "Saddam," Cheney said, "is just one more irritant, but there's a long list of irritants in that part of the world." Cheney argued against an expansion of the war for sensible reasons recounted in a 1992 interview that curiously failed to influence him in 2003:

> I would guess if we had gone in there, we would still have forces in Baghdad today. We'd be running the country. We would not have been able to get everybody out and bring everybody home . . . I don't think you could have done all of that without significant additional U.S. casualties, and while everybody was tremendously impressed with the low cost of the [1991] conflict, for the 146 Americans who were killed in action and for their families, it wasn't a cheap war. And the question in my mind is, how many additional American casualties is Saddam worth? And the answer is, not that damned many. So, I think we got it right, both when we decided to expel him from

Kuwait, but also when the President made the decision that we'd achieved our objectives and we were not going to go get bogged down in the problems of trying to take over and govern Iraq.[92]

Cheney made good points. Even a hard-liner like Margaret Thatcher worried about "getting an arm caught in the mangle," as she put it. Summing up the White House discussions on war termination, Rick Atkinson found that "Bush and his men concluded that the *excessive* price of total victory would be indefinite responsibility for rebuilding a hostile nation with no tradition of democracy but with immensely complex internal politics."[93] Their probity would be confirmed in the years after 2003. Still, the Persian Gulf War left a bad taste in everyone's mouth. Because of his vacillation at Safwan, Bush now found himself precisely where he didn't want to be—"bogged down in a civil war." The suffering of Iraq's Kurds and Shiites was so visible that Bush belatedly rethought his war aims. In April 1991, he abruptly decided that "Saddam is discredited and cannot be redeemed." Having earlier resolved to leave Saddam in place, to ensure a balance of power, Bush now vowed to remove him from office, a task that would have been easier just a month or two earlier, when there were a half million U.S. troops in country. Bush resorted to half-measures: economic sanctions, no-fly zones and a big, apparently permanent U.S. military presence in the region that would embarrass the House of Saud and inflame radicals like Osama bin Laden.

For all his talk of a "new world order" after the Soviets, Bush was an old-world statesman who shrank from the new problems of failed states, civil wars, "loose nukes," drugs, mafias, climate change, immigration and transnational terrorism. Certainly he never saw their seeds in Iraq.[94] A year after the war, Saddam mocked President Bush from Baghdad and claimed victory: "It was George Bush with his own will who decided to stop the fighting. Nobody had asked him to do so."[95] Here were echoes of Churchill's criticism of Eden at Suez thirty-five years earlier: "To go so far and not go on was madness." Seizing on that appearance of presidential weakness, Bill Clinton campaigned that year against President Bush—and beat him—chiding Bush for not putting Saddam and his acolytes on trial for war crimes. Clinton would prove no more effective than Bush in removing Saddam. Neither before nor after the war did anyone seriously seek to *solve* the problem of Iraqi mischief. As Schwarzkopf's chief foreign policy adviser put it in 1991, "We never did have a plan to terminate the war."[96] Instead, they created a situation that endured until 2003 and reminded one U.S. Air Force general of the Cold War over Germany:

air patrols and the occasional incident, "a kind of steady white noise in the background."[97] Perhaps Colin Powell said it best, in his postwar memoirs, when he compared the pressures weighing on Bush's war termination with the pressures weighing on Meade after Gettysburg, or on Eisenhower in 1945 as the Russians raced for Berlin. It was easy to say that the generals should have done more, but at what cost, in lives, treasure and opportunity? That lingering question, which appeared hypothetical when Powell wrote his memoirs, would shortly be answered by President Bush's son.[98]

CHAPTER 15

·✗✗·

9/11

Saddam's defeat rippled across the Middle East as the Soviet Union collapsed. With Moscow as a backstop, inefficient regimes like Nasser's, Assad's and Saddam's had been able to eke out a living and arm themselves. Their anti-Western, anti-Israeli braggadocio had sucked up most of the venom in the Middle East, giving poor, restive, resentful Arabs an outlet for their anger and disappointment.

BIN LADEN'S RESURGENCE

With Saddam humbled and the Soviet Union down the tubes, new personalities and new forces could grasp and direct the fury of the Arab street. Thirty-four-year-old Osama bin Laden, newly returned from the war in Afghanistan, saw the opportunity, and grasped it with both hands. Bin Laden had always detested Saddam Hussein and his secular Baath Party for basing themselves not on Islam and holy war, but on Saddam's dynastic ambition to control the Persian Gulf. In September 1990, as U.S. forces streamed into Saudi Arabia, bin Laden had actually briefed Saudi defense minister Prince Sultan as well as Prince Turki on ways to fight Saddam *without* American backing. Bin Laden took the prophet's injunction—"let there be no two religions in Arabia"—literally. No Christians or Jews should be allowed to cool their heels on the Arabian Peninsula, even if they were there to drive tanks, fly planes and pull triggers to defend the House of Saud. Bin Laden volunteered himself instead. He had set up an Afghan veterans' organization in the kingdom after his return and now proposed to put its members to work for the House of Saud. "I'm ready to prepare a hundred thousand fighters with good combat capability within three months," Osama had assured Prince Sultan. "You don't need Americans. You don't need any other non-Muslim troops. We will be enough." The Saudi Bin Laden Group would excavate trenches and sand traps to stop Saddam's tanks, and Osama's mujahideen would swarm out of the trenches to deal the death blow to Saddam's Republican Guard. "We pushed the Soviets out of Afghanistan," bin Laden boasted. But "there are no caves in Kuwait," Sultan had objected. "We will fight him with *faith*," bin Laden implored.[1]

Ignored in 1990, bin Laden climbed back in 1991. Prince Turki expressed alarm at the "radical changes" in Osama bin Laden. No longer a "calm, peaceful and gentle man," he was now "a person who believed that he would be able to amass and command an army . . . It revealed his arrogance and his haughtiness." Bin Laden now had the confidence to confront the senior Saudi clerics, who had issued a fatwa that had justified U.S. troops in Saudi Arabia on the grounds that they were there to defend Islam. "This is inadmissible," bin Laden had sputtered. It was the first deployment of infidel troops to the Arabian Peninsula "since the inception of Islam." The U.S. military and other Western contingents contained Christians, Jews and even *women*! The presence of female troops in the kingdom had triggered a feminist uprising, with upper-class Saudi women vowing to drive their own cars during Desert Storm, a revolution that drew fatwas and a legal ban on female driving as "a source of depravity." Desert Storm put bin Laden back in the spotlight. He declared that U.S. forces in the kingdom to defend Fahd were analogous to Soviet forces defending Karmal and Najibullah in Afghanistan. Moscow's "fraternal assistance" had attempted to become permanent; bin Laden warned that Washington's would too. He called the Saudi royals "traitors to Islam." Osama was preaching doctrines that most Saudis and many other Arabs applauded. The Saudi clergy was far more sympathetic to bin Laden than the royal house. "My son, Osama, we can't discuss this issue because we're afraid," one of the sheikhs had whispered, merely confirming to bin Laden that he was ranged against infidels, cowards and quislings. The clerics were afraid, but not that afraid. After Saddam's surrender, the Saudi clergy published a "Letter of Demands" that foreshadowed Osama's own

aspirations: strict conformity with sharia, creation of an Islamic army and a "puri-
fied media" with a strict Islamic message.[2]

Part of the religious reaction inside Saudi Arabia was a campaign by the clerics
and more conservative princes to get Osama's passport renewed and restored to
him. It had been seized after his return from Afghanistan. Bin Laden lobbied hard
for its return, got it and returned to Peshawar, Pakistan, in March 1992. Saudi intelligence estimated that between fifteen and twenty-five thousand young Saudi males
had trained to fight in Afghanistan. Tens of thousands of other "Arab Afghans" had
posted through in the course of the jihad against the Soviets. Many of them were
buried there, their dusty graves marked with red and green Arab and Islamic flags
and Koranic verses. The survivors were unwelcome in their home countries, where
they stomped irritably around the mosques in their Afghan battle dress, preaching
revolution. Many of them settled in Pakistan or Sudan; the Pakistani ISI continued
to nurture holy warriors for use in Afghanistan and Kashmir, and Sudan had experienced a successful Islamist military coup in June 1989. Bin Laden traveled to
Pakistan in 1992 to recruit the Arab Afghan diaspora and rebuild al-Qaeda.

SUDAN

Bin Laden had been in contact with Hasan al-Turabi, the ideological brain of the
Sudanese coup, since 1989. By 1992, bin Laden was preparing to move al-Qaeda
lock, stock and barrel into Sudan. "What you are trying to do, it is Sudan!" Osama's
envoys to Khartoum excitedly reported. Osama had worried that Sudan was a "nation of goats," another backwater like Afghanistan. His emissaries—including the
Egyptian Ayman al-Zawahiri—reassured him that al-Turabi's circle were "people
with minds, with professions." Al-Turabi planned nothing less than the founding
of an international Muslim community—the *umma*—in Sudan. All Muslims, regardless of sect, nationality or political coloration, would be welcome there. Al-
Turabi invited in the Palestinian groups Hamas and Abu Nidal, as well as the two
main Egyptian Islamist groups, al-Zawahiri's al-Jihad and Omar Abdul Rahman's
Islamic Group. The Algerian GIA (Groupe Islamique Armé) and Lebanese Hezbollah arrived in the early 1990s, and bin Laden met with Hezbollah's military chief,
Imad Mugniyah—mastermind of the 1983 bombings of the U.S. embassy and
marine corps barracks in Beirut—and worked out a deal by which al-Qaeda mili-

tants would get military training in Lebanon (from Hezbollah's Shiites, a major concession by bin Laden) in return for guns and money. Indeed al-Turabi actively recruited Osama because of his radicalism, and because of his cash and willingness to commit the Saudi Bin Laden Group to Sudanese construction projects. As always in the early days of jihad, Osama mixed business and religion. He committed to build an airport at Port Sudan, established a holding company in Khartoum—Wadi El Aqiq—and officially moved to the Sudanese capital in 1992 (with his four wives and seventeen children) with the promise to establish a construction company—al-Hijira—that would build a three-hundred-kilometer highway through eastern Sudan as a "gift to the nation."[3]

Torn by a civil war between its largely black, animist south and its Arab, Muslim north and bankrupted by capital flight—no foreign investors wanted to be on the hook for al-Turabi's strange *umma*—Khartoum viewed Osama and his gifts as its salvation. The civil war alone was costing $1 million a day, and there was no end in sight. The Saudi expat was rumored to be worth $350 million or more. He generously accepted land in exchange for his construction projects and quickly became the biggest landowner in Sudan. Most of Osama's farms produced tons of fruit and vegetables and herds of livestock; some of them, like Soba Farm ten kilometers south of Khartoum, produced terrorists. Al-Qaeda shipped its entire leftover arsenal from Afghanistan to Sudan, where the weapons were used for training. Bin Laden led a simple life—ambling around Khartoum in a white turban and a simple peasant *gellaba*, fasting, praying, inveighing against music ("the flute of the devil") and tending his burgeoning enterprises—but he felt himself pulled back to jihad. He assembled a *shura* council of advisers, rebuffed early appeals to involve himself against the animist and Christian south, and stewed over the continuing presence of American troops in Saudi Arabia, who remained in the air bases to enforce the "no-fly zones" over Iraq. Bin Laden expressed rage at the introduction of U.S. forces into Yemen and then Somalia during Operation Restore Hope, President George H. W. Bush's last act as president, when he intervened in the Horn of Africa—*after* his 1992 defeat by Bill Clinton—to relieve famine there. (Don't worry, Scowcroft had reassured the incoming Clinton team, combat "could be completed in two weeks"; most of the troops would be out before the inauguration.)[4]

Bin Laden resented the West's purchase of Arab oil; it not only fueled and strengthened the West, its lucrative sale by the Arab states created nothing lasting. In Saudi Arabia, as bin Laden well knew, petrodollar "fortunes melted away like snow in the desert."[5] The West would eventually burn up all the oil in the world and turn to alternate fuels, leaving the Muslim oil states weaker and more marginal than ever. In his theological discussions with al-Turabi, bin Laden's radicalism shined through. He scoffed at al-Turabi's liberal plans for the *umma*, which included knitting up the Sunni-Shiite divide, tolerating the Christians of Sudan, reintroducing music and art to Islam, and empowering women. Such talk was heresy to bin Laden's grim Salafist outlook. It was also a distraction. Although the Americans had bankrolled the jihad in Afghanistan, bin Laden now turned decisively against them. They had been useful idiots; Osama had used them to destroy the Soviets, and that campaign had shifted political momentum in the world from the Christian powers to Islam. Bin Laden slotted the United States and the other Western powers into a broad historical continuum. To Osama, the Crusades had never been resolved, and would never stop until the final victory of Islam. Every Western presence in Muslim territory—whether in Iraq, Saudi Arabia, Yemen, Somalia, Afghanistan or Israel—represented a new Crusade that needed to be rolled back. Islam had been in retreat since the Turkish armies were routed by Christian forces on the outskirts of Vienna on September 11, 1683, but Osama genuinely believed that the mujahideen victory over the Red Army in Afghanistan had turned the tide. The Western powers were weak and faltering; Islam was on the march. "This is a battle of Muslims against global Crusaders," and bin Laden felt certain that the Muslims would win.[6]

"JIHAD AGAINST AMERICA?"

Osama's *shura* council was not so sure. "Jihad against America?" It seemed crazy. "America knows *everything* about us," one al-Qaeda member burst out, "even the labels on our underwear." Incredible as it seemed and still seems, bin Laden, marooned in dirty, backward Sudan, staggering along the muddy banks of the Nile to picnic with his sons, began to plan the great war with the United States that would explode on September 11, 2001, 318 years to the day after the Turkish repulse at Vienna. Osama viewed the post–Cold War American agenda—democracy, human rights, globalization—as little more than a ruse to emasculate and marginalize the Muslim states, which, in his view, needed to seek their renaissance by a strict observance of Islam and its illiberal strictures, and by waging holy war against the still crusading West. Of course nothing would be accomplished so long as America controlled the pace of globalization and patrolled the continents, skies and seas with its invincible military. Thus, even more incredibly, Osama dared to imagine a war with the United States: "a large-scale front, which [America] cannot control."[7]

Bin Laden had learned much from the anti-Soviet jihad, but he also studied Hezbollah. Imad Mugniyah—killed by a car bomb in Damascus in February 2008—had blasted the Americans and French out of Beirut in 1983 with three bloody terrorist attacks. Reagan had sent marines and other Western contingents in to solidify the Christian government of Amine Gemayel, and Mugniyah's Hezbollah suicide bombers—desperate to evict the Westerners before Gemayel's Phalange could root itself—had successively blown up the U.S. embassy, the marine barracks and then the barracks of the French paratroopers, to make the Western powers leave. Leave they did. Two hundred and fifty-eight Americans and fifty-eight French died in the attacks, and the Western powers bolted almost immediately. Two years later, when Hezbollah seized American hostages in Beirut, Reagan secretly negotiated for their release by sending arms and spare parts to Tehran in what became the Iran-Contra scandal. To bin Laden, those events—one tragic, one criminal—were more evidence of Western weakness. Vietnam, Lebanon and Iraq—where the United States had ended the war prematurely to avoid casualties in Baghdad—proved (to al-Qaeda) that Americans were decadent and afraid of death. The United States would quail in the face of terror and casualties; a "large-scale front" of terrorism would demoralize the West and drive it into isolation, leaving the Islamists free to chip away at Israel and rebuild the ancient Muslim caliphate without Western interference.

President Bill Clinton's draggle-tailed retreat from Somalia in 1993—after the loss of just two American helicopters and eighteen troops in Mogadishu—strengthened al-Qaeda's conviction that America lacked guts. "In Somalia . . . our brothers saw the weakness, frailty, and cowardice of U.S. troops . . . they fled in the heart of darkness, frustrated after they had caused great commotion about the New World Order."[8] Osama's contacts with Hezbollah introduced the al-Qaeda chief to "martyrdom operations," which was the terrorist's preferred term for suicide bombing. The Koran expressly forbids suicide—"do not kill yourselves"—but as Hezbollah had demonstrated in Beirut in the 1980s and the Palestinians were showing in the 1990s, suicide bombing was the ultimate stealth weapon. Bin Laden and al-Zawahiri were the first Sunnis to begin justifying and encouraging suicide attacks as a legitimate tactic of jihad. "The way of death and martyrdom is a weapon that tyrants and their helpers, who worship their salaries instead of God, do not have," al-Zawahiri mused. Martyrdom would become al-Qaeda's weapon of choice.[9]

Bin Laden's bloodlust, his willingness to engage in terrorism, propagate suicide and murder innocents, cut against the grain of Islam, which is a kind, gentle faith. Thus, bin Laden and his prayer leader, or imam, Abu Hajer al-Iraqi, rummaged around and rediscovered the thirteenth-century teachings of Ibn Tamiyyah. Tamiyyah had confronted the dilemma of what to do with the Mongols—barbarian brutes who had slaughtered Muslims and then converted to Islam. Did their late conversion to the faith secure them against revenge attacks? No, Tamiyyah had concluded; they were not "true believers," so they could be vengefully slaughtered. Tamiyyah's medieval fatwa had gone further than mere reprisals and was eagerly adopted by al-Qaeda, which was, of course, continuing the process of *takfir*—reversing Islam's core principles—begun in Afghanistan. *Anyone* of *any* faith who aided the Mongols, traded with them or even happened to be standing near them could be killed. If the victims were Muslims, God would sort them out, dispatching the bad ones to hell and the good ones to paradise. As for men, women and children of other faiths, who cared? Bin Laden and Abu Hajer al-Iraqi had discovered a religious rationalization for the mass murder they were planning. It was depraved—"the dead tourist and the hotel worker would find their proper reward"—but it shored up al-Qaeda against guilt feelings and second thoughts, and was a tremendous spur to recruitment.

Anyone who did not embrace al-Qaeda or its allies was an apostate, and was marked for death. Bin Laden approvingly tracked the progress of Algeria's civil war in the 1990s. The old Arab nationalist FLN that had driven out the French had been pronounced corrupt and illegitimate by the Islamist GIA, which received funds and training from bin Laden's offices in Khartoum. The GIA declared that anyone who voted in Algerian elections, attended public schools or had any contact with the secular government was a target, and indeed the Algerian Islamists—"neo-Wahhabis" who had learned to kill in Afghanistan—murdered teachers, administrators, schoolchildren and whole villages. One GIA communiqué declared war on the *entire* population of Algeria, and a hundred thousand Algerians were savagely murdered, the GIA leaders propounding that "there is no neutrality in the war we are waging." Opponents and neutrals alike were slaughtered. Safety could be found only on one's knees, facing Mecca, forehead pressed to the pavement, inside the jihad. In Afghanistan, a new fundamentalist movement nurtured by Pakistan and motivated by the carnage in Algeria was taking hold.[10] Terrorism would be al-Qaeda's weapon against America. Until the 1990s, bin Laden had viewed himself as a mujahid who would conscript Muslim armies to fight godless invaders into Muslim lands, like the

Red Army or Saddam's Republican Guard. He now discarded that model and grasped a new one: terrorism and subversion. America and the West would be subjected to relentless terrorist attacks until they panicked, broke and conceded the world to Muslims.[11]

"Bin Laden Was One of Hundreds of Things to Worry About"

Washington was slow to grasp the new threat of jihad emanating from the Middle East. "What was more important in the world view of history," former national security adviser Zbigniew Brzezinski asked, "the Taliban or the fall of the Soviet Empire? A few stirred-up Muslims or the liberation of Central Europe and the end of the Cold War?"[12] The reasons for American complacency were exposed after 9/11, but had already been the subject of complaints and recriminations before the attack. America's intelligence services were still crammed with Russian-speaking Soviet analysts and operatives, and superior U.S. technology had bred a reliance on electronic—as opposed to human—intelligence that often did not detect off-line al-Qaeda activities. Long before the September 11 attacks, CIA veterans had complained of the unadventurous mentality at Langley, where few operatives sought postings in areas (like Afghanistan) that "included diarrhea as a way of life."[13] Recognizing the threat of transnational terrorism and its Third World sanctuaries in his first term, President Clinton and National Security Adviser Tony Lake had made Richard A. Clarke the "national coordinator for counterterrorism" at the White House.

But Clarke's was just one voice among many. Working closely with John O'Neill, the chief of the FBI's counterterrorism section, Clarke assembled a Counterterrorism Security Group (CSG) that brought together men and women from the CIA, the Pentagon, the NSC, and the Justice and State departments. They met weekly in the White House to examine the threats from al-Qaeda and other groups. Clarke and O'Neill fought bureaucratic inertia to gain new powers—Clinton was persuaded to issue a presidential directive after the Oklahoma City bombing in 1995 that made the FBI the lead agency in counterterrorism in and outside the United States—but their efforts were dissipated by Clinton's preoccupation with other matters. "Bin Laden was one of hundreds of things to worry about," a CIA official observed. One of Clarke's aides compared the practice of sifting all the competing threats to "drink-ing from a fire hose." Iran bulked larger than al-Qaeda as a sponsor of terrorism; the Balkans were in turmoil (requiring U.S. troops) and CIA director John Deutch, who succeeded James Woolsey in 1995, proved disastrously tentative and inept in almost everything he did.[14] Moreover, Washington still suffered from the Cold War–era "lesser included fallacy." It was assumed that arsenals and capabilities designed to contain the Soviets would be potent enough to contain any lesser threat, such as that posed by Arab mujahideen. Bin Laden resolved to target that vulnerability; he would sniff out American weaknesses, and attack them "asymmetrically"—not force against force, but force against unguarded weakness. He also ventured into weapons of mass destruction. With the Sudanese government seeking to purchase chemical weapons for use against the southern insurgents in 1993, bin Laden expressed inter-est in helping, and also began shopping for black-market uranium in the hope that he could build an al-Qaeda bomb.

There was still no constituency for "homeland security" in the United States before 9/11. A maniac like Omar Abdul Rahman, the blind Egyptian sheikh, lived undisturbed in Jersey City, directly across from the World Trade Center. He re-ceived subsidies from bin Laden and wrote fatwas exculpating his followers for robbing banks and killing Jews. He gave sermons in New Jersey mosques that called Americans—who had kindly granted him political asylum from Mubarak's Egypt—"descendants of apes and pigs, who have been feeding from the dining tables of Zionists, Communists and colonialists." For bin Laden, connecting himself to mor-bid killers like Rahman was an extension of the work he had done in Peshawar—linking up the Arab Afghans, straddling the various militias, fund-raising, training and indoctrinating. He now made al-Qaeda a global organization. He aimed to acquire the ability to attack on American soil, or attack American targets overseas, or strike American allies in every hemisphere. He absorbed faltering terrorist groups like al-Zawahiri's al-Jihad—which had been effectively crushed by Egyptian intel-ligence in the early 1990s—and, as one analyst put it, "merged them into one mul-tinational consortium, with common training and economies of scale and departments devoted to everything from personnel to policymaking."[15] Bin Laden slipped agents into the United States and even into the U.S. military. One of his better ones—Ali Abdelsoud Muhammed—had been a major in the Egyptian armed forces. He enlisted in the U.S. Army and, by the 1990s, was teaching al-Qaeda re-cruits American surveillance techniques. Bin Laden sent al-Zawahiri on fund-rais-ing trips to the United States, where he collected the donations that would be used to destroy America. Bin Laden's lieutenants in Khartoum had worried that the all-seeing Americans knew everything about them, down to the "labels on their underwear." The ease with which al-Zawahiri passed in and out of the United States to raise money for al-Qaeda operations in the 1990s proved that the Americans knew next to nothing about the jihadis.

The first attack on American soil came on February 26, 1993, when Ramzi Yousef—the son of a Pakistani father and a Palestinian mother raised in Kuwait and educated in the UK—pulled a rented Ford van loaded with ammonium nitrate and fuel oil into the World Trade Center's underground garage, lit four twenty-foot-long fuses and ran for his life. Yousef had been trained in an al-Qaeda camp in Afghanistan, and was typical of the wandering, hateful misfits enlisted by bin Laden. He boasted that he would kill 250,000 New Yorkers when the World Trade Center fell into the streets of Manhattan. In the event, his massive bomb shattered six floors of steel and cement, killed six and injured 1,042, but failed to collapse the Twin Towers.[16]

Meanwhile, bin Laden's fortune and once unassailable position inside Sudan *were* collapsing. Infuriated by Osama's involvement in terrorism and revolutionary politics, King Fahd revoked bin Laden's Saudi citizenship and cancelled his passport in 1994. Bin Laden's business empire, neglected by his focus on terrorism and eroded by Sudan's triple-digit inflation and sinking currency, fell apart. Bin Laden usually pumped in more Saudi capital when needed, but lost that resource when Fahd confiscated his accounts, whose total sat somewhere between $200 and $300 million. Without that larger sum—Osama retained an estimated $50 million in numbered accounts—bin Laden was less useful to Sudan, and Sudan was becoming less useful to bin Laden.[17] Al-Turabi's complicity in an assassination attempt on Egyptian president Hosni Mubarak in June 1995 as well as his suspected involvement in the World Trade Center bombing drew economic sanctions from the UN. The State Department put Sudan on its list of state sponsors of terrorism, shuttered its Khartoum embassy and moved its operations to Kenya in protest. Counterterrorism units around the world tightened their focus on al-Turabi.

Egypt in particular bore down hard on Sudan. Mubarak's strong presidency became even stronger. The sixty-seven-year-old president made it a crime even to voice sympathy for terrorist movements, constructed five new prisons to house Islamists and then began rounding up thousands of suspects. Brutal methods were used to drag in Islamists: a mother might be stripped naked, paraded in the street and threatened with rape by security forces if her suspected son did not appear. He usually did, only to vanish into an Egyptian jail. Sons of Islamist leaders were kidnapped, drugged, sodomized, photographed and then shown the photographs and ordered to spy on their fathers to keep the rape under wraps. After al-Zawahiri ordered one such boy spy executed—after yanking down his trousers to verify that he had attained puberty—an embarrassed al-Turabi expelled al-Zawahiri from Sudan in 1995. Al-Turabi's *umma* had begun to look sordid, mad and pathetic. Al-Zawahiri drifted around till he found asylum in Yemen. His few remaining followers followed him or returned to Afghanistan. "These are bad times," he grumbled. Bin Laden too was feeling the heat. By expelling al-Zawahiri, al-Turabi had cut out al-Qaeda's Egyptian core. Al-Turabi now pressured bin Laden to leave as well, going so far as to spread the rumor that Osama would be "the next Carlos," a reference to the notorious terrorist "Carlos the Jackal"—Ilich Ramirez Sanchez of the Popular Front for the Liberation of Palestine—who had lived comfortably in Khartoum's Le Méridien hotel until al-Turabi had withdrawn his protection and permitted the French to seize Carlos (from a hospital bed) and fly him to Paris for trial.

BIN LADEN FLEES TO AFGHANISTAN

Cornered, bin Laden dispatched angry letters to Fahd that blasted Saudi Arabia's "oppression of the people, desecration of their sanctuaries, and embezzlement of their wealth and riches." Nasser and Saddam had made similar accusations against the Saudi royal family, but Osama's threats tapped into a deep well of resentment inside the kingdom. Bin Laden escalated his attacks on U.S. forces in the kingdom: "It is unconscionable to let the country become an American colony, with American soldiers—their filthy feet roaming everywhere—for no reason other than protecting your throne and protecting oil sources for their own use. These filthy, infidel Crusaders must not be allowed to remain in the Holy Land."[18] In 1996, CIA operatives met the Sudanese defense minister—General Elfatih Erwa—in a suburban Washington hotel room and urged him to expel bin Laden from his safe haven. "Ask him to leave the country; just don't let him go to Somalia." Erwa replied that if expelled, bin Laden would certainly return to Afghanistan. Osama still had allies there, and a new fundamentalist movement called the Taliban—made up of orphans and other desperadoes from the Soviet-era refugee camps—had been making great strides toward Kabul since 1994, thanks in large part to Saudi and Pakistani support. Afghanistan, an Arab visitor wrote, was the perfect refuge for bin Laden, "a country where jihad seems never-ending."[19] The Taliban had already captured nine of Afghanistan's thirty-two provinces and were arrayed around Kabul bombarding it with artillery. Their fundamentalism would be a natural, dangerous fit with bin Laden's. "Let him," the Americans carelessly replied.[20]

Bin Laden left Sudan on a chartered flight to Afghanistan in May 1996. Having tried and failed to assassinate bin Laden, al-Turabi and the generals confiscated all the investments Osama had made in their blighted country, a loss that totaled somewhere between $20 million (the Sudanese estimate) and $165 million (bin Laden's figure). As he flew away with his sons Saad and Omar to avoid deportation to a Saudi jail, bin Laden groused that al-Turabi's *umma* had been nothing more than "a mixture of religion and organized crime." Sudan had offered to repay Osama not in cash, but in wheat, corn, gum and cattle, which bin Laden, the international fugitive, had no way to possess or market. Poor and alone, bin Laden had little choice but to lay off most of the al-Qaeda members who remained in Sudan. He gave each of them $2,400 and, to those who could actually return to their native countries, a plane ticket home. It seemed like the last gasp of al-Qaeda.[21]

Bin Laden's charter flight—an old Soviet Tupolev on loan from the Sudanese air force—bypassed Kabul, which was still in the hands of two men who most certainly did *not* want Osama bin Laden there—President Burhannudin Rabbani and warlord Ahmed Shah Massoud—and flew on to Jalalabad. The bin Ladens landed, were greeted by Younis Khalis, an old ally of Osama's from the 1980s, and installed at a little farm five miles south of the city. Jalalabad was Taliban country, and Osama's arrival there posed problems. The Saudis—who had just revoked Osama's citizenship and squeezed him out of Khartoum—were pumping money, weapons and vehicles into the Taliban army. How accommodating could the Taliban afford to be to the renegade? Osama shortly found out. He was placed under the personal supervision of the one-eyed Taliban commander Mullah Muhammed Omar.

THE TALIBAN

Omar was a fascinating study. A veteran of the jihad against the Soviets—he had lost the eye battling for Jalalabad in 1989—he was a simple, devout Muslim who had laid down his arms after the Soviet withdrawal and gone to teach at a madrassa near Kandahar. The viciousness of the Afghan civil war—rapes, mass executions, banditry—had pulled Mullah Omar out of retirement and persuaded him to take up arms again. According to Omar, the prophet had appeared to him in a dream and commanded him to restore peace to Afghanistan with a pure, pious regime. "Corruption and moral disintegration had gripped the land," Omar wrote. "Killing, looting and violence had become the norm." He crisscrossed the province of Kandahar on a motorcycle, visiting religious schools to recruit pupils, or *talibs*, for his resurrecting movement. With an army of two hundred believers, many of them recruited from a Saudi-run madrassa, Omar bluffed a local garrison of twenty-five hundred into surrendering and seized their cache of weapons: six MiG-21s, helicopters, armored vehicles, trucks, artillery, rifles and ammunition. The Taliban army was born; within a few months it had grown to twelve thousand troops. A year later, it numbered twenty-four thousand. Casualties were easily replaced by busloads of new *talibs* trucked in from the madrassas in Peshawar and the seven Pakistani tribal areas. Their lives had been contemptible before the Taliban; suddenly they had meaning and a mission. If the Taliban rank and file were young and beardless, the leadership was older, grizzled and, a Pakistani journalist noted, "the most disabled in the world." At war for twenty years—ten against the Soviets and another ten against their fellow Afghans—they hopped around on wooden peg legs, squinted around eye patches and pinned empty sleeves to the sides of their coats.[22]

The battle-hardened Taliban drew heavy support from the Saudis—who praised Mullah Omar's Wahhabi precepts—and the Pakistanis. George Tenet, Clinton's CIA director, believed that the Pakistanis backed the Taliban from "fear of a two-front conflict, with the Indians seeking to reclaim Pakistan and the Taliban mullahs trying to export their radical brand of Islam across the border." Thus, Islamabad weirdly shielded the Taliban and al-Qaeda "to avoid having *their* nation Talibanized." Pakistan also saw the Taliban and al-Qaeda as the lesser of various evils in Afghanistan. Ahmed Shah Massoud's largely Tajik Northern Alliance had been bankrolled for years by the Indians and had achieved fame holding Afghanistan's Panshir Valley against repeated Red Army attacks during the jihad and now against the Taliban government in Kabul. Pakistan could *never* rally to Massoud.[23] The Saudis paid stipends to Omar's *talibs* and their families and also provided arms: the Taliban's emblematic Datsun four-wheel-drive pickup trucks, machine guns, rocket launchers and antiaircraft guns.

More cash was generated by the opium trade. The capture of Kandahar in November 1994 gave the Taliban control of Afghanistan's prime opium-growing region, Helmand Province. Mullah Omar eagerly exploited the crop; in exchange for a 10 percent tax on all shipments, he cleared and policed the roads through the province. The Taliban's war chest grew, as the other warlords saw theirs shrinking with the retreat of their Cold War patrons. The *talibs* themselves were the ultimate holy warriors. Most of them had been raised alone in the madrassas, where they had memorized the Koran and accepted the duty of jihad against evil and unbelievers. None of them had the discernment to question the pseudo-historical explanations that Osama was adducing for jihad. He made much of the Crusades, but also of the Sykes-Picot Agreement of 1916 and the Balfour Declaration of 1917, which he insisted forged the "Christian-Jewish alliance" that had led to the downfall of the Ottoman Empire—no mention was made of Atatürk—and the disappearance of the Islamic caliphate.

The Taliban and Osama bin Laden were not a natural fit. Upon arrival in Jalalabad, Osama had begun to rebuild his life and "brigade of volunteers." He brought in three wives, started a small business in honey and installed the few troops that remained to him in an abandoned Soviet collective farm. The official Taliban line—as propounded by Mullah Omar's information minister—was that "in areas under Taliban control, there are no terrorists," but, like the Sudanese, the Afghans were tempted by Osama's millions. He had been a big spender during the jihad, had run a parallel economy all his own inside Sudan and had never divulged the degree to which he had been cleaned out by al-Turabi, the Sudanese generals, the Saudi king and his own ashamed family. But wealth is a relative thing, and by Afghan standards, bin Laden was still as wealthy as Ali Baba's forty thieves. Even though Mullah Omar was instructed by the Saudis to keep Osama at arm's length, Omar yearned to make use of the rich foreigner. Osama had little trouble connecting with other terrorists in the Taliban zone. Soon after his arrival, he met with World Trade Center bomber Ramzi Yousef's uncle, Khalid Sheikh Muhammed ("KSM"), who had been on the run since nearly being nabbed in the Philippines in 1994 for his part in Operation Bojinka, a failed attempt to blow up eleven American 747s over the Pacific. Bin Laden listened raptly while Khalid Sheikh Muhammed described his bombmaking unit in Manila and its invention of an undetectable nitroglycerin bomb. For the first time, bin Laden started thinking of airplanes as targets, and projectiles.[24]

What virtue the Taliban had was lost when it took Kabul in September 1996. The *talibs* broke into the UN compound where Najibullah had sought asylum, beat and castrated him, dragged his body through the streets behind a jeep, and then shot him in the head. Such *takfiri* mutilation and torture was forbidden by Islam, as was the Taliban's display of Najibullah's corpse on a lamppost, but it would remind any foes of the fate they might expect if they resisted the laws of the new "Islamic Emirate of Afghanistan."

"THROW REASON TO THE DOGS. IT STINKS OF CORRUPTION"

The new Taliban constitution meshed perfectly with bin Laden's worldview. He sought a new caliphate bonded by sharia and a severe observance of Islam that would veer into *takfir* whenever expedient. That was precisely what the Taliban trumped up in Kabul. The narrow-minded *talibs* who had been raised in all-male madrassas displayed a fear of women that struck outsiders as perverse. Women were confined to their homes and permitted outside only in black burkas and veils. They were forbidden to educate themselves, to hold jobs or even to wash clothes in streams and rivers. Men were ordered to grow beards and wear them longer than "the grip of their hand." Men with long "Beatle-y" hair—the Taliban's quaint designation—were seized and shorn on the spot. "Unclean things" were proscribed, which amounted to almost everything: pork, pigs, oil, kites, satellite dishes, movies, music, radios, chess sets, pool tables, computers, VCRs and televisions. The Taliban slaughtered the animals in the Kabul zoo, often in ways that revealed their viciousness; the lion was dispatched with a hand grenade pitched into his cage by a bored *talib*. Afghanistan under the Taliban was a mad world summed up by a sign tacked to the wall of the religious police headquarters: "Throw reason to the dogs. It stinks of corruption."[25]

Al-Qaeda and the Taliban flowed together in their flight from reason. Bin Laden referred to Afghanistan as Khorasan—the ancient Muslim empire that had spanned Central Asia—and viewed himself as a new prophet, and like the old prophet—who had been ridiculed as a fraud and driven out of Mecca in 622—bin Laden chose to regard his flight to Afghanistan as a twentieth-century version of Muhammed's seventh-century hegira. And like the prophet, bin Laden felt certain that he would come back stronger and more popular than before. Symbolism had always been a big part of bin Laden's game, and he now milked his own misery and exile to generate sympathy. He became a symbol for every Muslim who felt cheated and abandoned. He moved his small band of fighters into the caves and tunnels of the Tora Bora Mountains south of Jalalabad, which locals referred to as "bin Laden's emirate."[26] In that remote region, which could be reached only after an arduous journey through Taliban roadblocks and pitted, boulder-strewn mountain roads, he would pose as a pure and noble ascetic—and if things got too hot, he was just miles from the Pakistani border. Like Thoreau taking up residence at Walden Pond, Osama moved into the "Eagle's Nest" cave complex at ten thousand feet and physically separated himself from whatever small evils remained in Taliban Afghanistan. Temperatures plummeted to fifty degrees below zero in winter, and the caves filled with scorpions in summer. "Sheikh bin Laden" seemed to relish the discomfort. A cave near Mecca had been the place where the angel Gabriel had appeared to Muhammed and informed him that he "was the Messenger of God." Even though Osama had scooped out his cave with Bin Laden Group backhoes, tractors and explosives and rigged it with satellite phones, computers and fax machines, he still awaited the apparition of the angel Gabriel.[27]

From his caves and old Soviet barracks around Jalalabad, bin Laden renewed his war on the United States. He seemed even more ludicrous now than he had in Khartoum, which may have accounted for the deeper bite of his rhetoric. "You are not unaware of the injustice, repression and aggression that have befallen Muslims through the alliance of Jews, Christians and their agents." That unholy alliance of infidels was "plundering Muslim blood, money and wealth."[28] Osama became the spokesman of the Arab street. Bin Laden was an early adopter of the Internet, remarking to a visitor in 1996 that "these days the world is becoming like a small village." Every frustrated, paranoid Arab could see a glimmer of truth in Osama's Web-based ravings, which he transmitted from his Afghan caves: the world was skewed against Muslims; the Jews and Americans were responsible for their misery; the UN, the NGOs, the banks, the multinational corporations, and the international media and satellite channels were all tools of the West—all the Arab world's problems stemmed from this external exploitation and an internal neglect of Islam and its pure teachings. Torn asunder by their imperialist past, the Muslim nations ached to be rejoined. "The *umma* is connected like an electric current," Osama insisted. It only needed a spark, and then all Muslims would connect in a new caliphate.[29]

KHOBAR TOWERS

If the Clinton administration thought terrorism was a minor threat, it was disabused of that assumption on June 25, 1996, when bombers struck the barracks of the U.S. 4404th Airlift Wing in the Khobar Towers complex in Dhahran. Nineteen Americans died and nearly four hundred were injured in the blast. The FBI director, Louis Freeh, flew to Dhahran with his counterterrorism chief, John O'Neill, to investigate the attack, but received no help from the Saudis, who, as O'Neill put it, just "shined sunshine up our ass." Instead of sharing suspects with the Americans for interrogation and investigation, the Saudis hastily convicted four men of the Khobar crime and chopped off their heads. Case closed—the Saudis wanted to conceal the fact that Iranian-backed Hezbollah had become active and popular among the Sunni kingdom's persecuted Shiites.[30] Bin Laden conveniently took credit for the blast, stipulated that thirty-three hundred pounds of dynamite had been used and issued his "Declaration of Jihad against the Americans Occupying the Land of the Two Sacred Places," which he faxed to the newspaper *Al-Quds al-Arabi* in London in August 1996.[31] In Washington, a consensus emerged that Khobar had been blasted by the Iranians, perhaps Imad Mugniyah or a Saudi branch of Hezbollah, but President Clinton omitted to name a perpetrator in his comments on the atrocity. "We just learn as we go along," he said wistfully at a news conference. The terror threat was real, and still as fiendishly difficult to grapple with as it would be ten years later. "It's not the Cold War, it's not World War II, but it's an important part of our struggle," Clinton said. "Our generation's time is going to be increasingly preoccupied with terrorists." But how could America *fight* them? Clinton worried that if he hit Iran, Iran would retaliate asymmetrically, with Hezbollah terror attacks on U.S. targets worldwide and possibly even in the United States.[32] "Maybe you have no options," a Saudi agent told O'Neill. "If it's a military response, what are you going to bomb? Are you going to nuke them? Flatten their military facilities? Destroy their oil refineries? And to achieve what? We are next door to them. You are 6,000 miles away."

When CNN's Peter Arnett climbed to bin Laden's hut in the cold mountains above Jalalabad in March 1997, bin Laden, who was still under orders from Mullah Omar to keep out of the spotlight, stepped boldly into it. American support for Israel and American troops in Saudi Arabia as well as the "aggressive policy toward the entire Muslim world" needed to be rolled back. Sitting on blankets in a bare hut, Osama demanded nothing less than an immediate, unilateral U.S. withdrawal from all parts of the world inhabited by Muslims. He had another go at justifying terrorism: "The U.S. today has set a double standard. It wants to occupy our countries, steal our resources, impose on us agents to rule us . . . and wants us to agree to all of these. If we refuse to do so, it will say 'you are terrorists.' " Later, bin Laden told Pakistani reporters that "terrorizing oppressors and criminals and thieves and robbers is necessary for the safety of the people . . . The terrorism we practice is of the commendable kind."[33]

Fearing a backlash, Mullah Omar reeled Osama in, ordering him to relocate from Jalalabad to Kandahar, where the Taliban could track his movements and control his media access. Omar installed bin Laden in Tarnak Farms—a dusty, waterless walled compound without electricity—and parked two T-55 tanks at the gate to discourage forays into the mountains or the airwaves. Al-Zawahiri was in Chechnya during this period, arguing for the creation of a "*mujahid* Islamic belt to the south of Russia that will be connected in the east to Pakistan, which is brimming with mujahideen movements in Kashmir." Afghanistan would be the buckle of that "Islamic belt"—which might serve as the seed of Osama's dreamt-of caliphate—but Osama was not getting any buy-in from the Taliban, which, like the Sudanese, worried about bin Laden's repulsive image abroad. Salvation arrived from Pakistan. The ISI remembered bin Laden's service in the Soviet jihad, and now instructed Mullah Omar to restore Osama's old training camps in Khost so that al-Qaeda could train fighters for combat against the Indians in Kashmir. In a public statement, bin Laden thanked God for the ISI: "As for Pakistan, there are some governmental departments, which, by the Grace of God, respond to the Islamic sentiments of the masses in Pakistan."[34]

Pakistani intervention rescued al-Qaeda from near death. "This place is worse than a tomb," one of Osama's Egyptian militants wrote home from Tarnak Farms. Life was hard. An Arab visitor making his way to bin Laden remarked the lack of food: "an unidentifiable broth with great pools of grease floating on the surface, containing a piece of meat—God only knows where it came from—and half a potato."[35] But things were looking up. With the Pakistanis behind him again, Osama returned to Jalalabad, secured a comfortable compound and began pulling in recruits—new ones as well as old Arab Afghan comrades from the jihad and Sudan. The camps taught the usual weapons training—rifles, machine guns, RPGs, anti-aircraft missiles, Claymore mines—as well as map reading, trenching and celestial navigation.[36] Al-Zawahiri returned from Chechnya in May 1997 and set to work unifying all the mujahideen groups in Afghanistan for a concentrated assault on America: "Our main objective is now limited to one state only, the United States, and involves waging a guerrilla war against all U.S. interests, not only in the Arab region, but also throughout the world."[37] To bin Laden's familiar accusations that America was despoiling the Saudi holy places and propping up Israel, al-Zawahiri added a new accusation: America's punitive strikes and sanctions against Iraq since 1991 had killed one million innocent Arab civilians. That convergence of al-Qaeda interest in Iraq and Iraqi interest in revenge on America explained the only brief contacts between Iraqi and al-Qaeda delegations in Khartoum and Baghdad in the 1990s. The limited contacts went nowhere because Saddam and bin Laden were natural rivals. Bin Laden had funded Kurdish separatists in Iraq, and bin Laden wanted camps in Iraq and a "common strategy," which Saddam would not concede. Perhaps the only tangible result of the al-Qaeda–Iraqi meetings was al-Zawahiri's introduction in Baghdad to a Jordanian killer named Abu Musab al-Zarqawi in 1999. (Al-Zarqawi would lead al-Qaeda in Iraq until his death by an American air strike in 2006.)[38]

"KILL THE AMERICANS AND THEIR ALLIES"

Rebuffed by Saddam, bin Laden turned back to God: the United States, he claimed, was waging "a war on God, his Messenger and the Muslims." To fight back, bin Laden and al-Zawahiri published a bloodcurdling fatwa in February 1998: "The ruling to kill the Americans and their allies—civilian and military—is an individual duty for every Muslim who can do it in any country in which it is possible to do it." That fatwa alone led to an explosion in recruitment. With his usual flair, bin Laden had simplified the struggle and made it real and immediate. Disgruntled Muslims began flooding into Osama's Khaldan training camp from Europe, the Middle East and North America. Among them were Zacarias Moussaoui—a French citizen of Moroccan descent living in London—and Ahmed Ressam, an Algerian living in Montreal, who would be arrested in December 1999 for attempting to cross the Canadian-U.S. border with explosives and timers in the trunk of his car intended to blow up Los Angeles International Airport.[39] (Moussaoui, the "twentieth hijacker," would be arrested in Minneapolis in August 2001 for overstaying his visa and asking suspicious questions at his flight school about the durability of cockpit doors and flight patterns around Manhattan.)

With Pakistani subsidies and an Afghan safe haven, bin Laden could begin paying salaries again, and focus his attack on the United States. The quality of the ten to twenty thousand new recruits who passed through bin Laden's camps was surprisingly good: unlike Mullah Omar's coarse *talibs*, bin Laden's Arab Afghans were university-educated upper- or middle-class Arabs. Many had studied science and engineering in Europe or the United States and spoke several languages, and most came from solid families. If they had one thing in common, it was alienation, either from their own society or from their adopted one. Al-Qaeda lured Algerians from France, Pakistanis from the UK and Egyptians from New York, but also Syrians from Kuwait and Yemenis from Saudi Arabia. They all shared a feeling of drift and impotence.[40] Al-Zawahiri *dared* them to come to the hardscrabble camps, to leave "the life of civilization and luxury" and become "hot-blooded revolutionary strugglers." Muhammed Atta, an Egyptian who arrived in Hamburg in 1992 and studied at the city's Technical University before decamping to bin Laden's Afghan training camp in 1999, was a perfect example of the type: angry, bitter and misogynistic (and perhaps a repressed homosexual). Atta expressed his conflicted nature with hate and fantasies of murder.

It was a testimony to just how far the Arab nations had fallen behind the West in their ability to foster intelligence, careers, ambition and happiness that so many bright young men signed on to al-Qaeda to achieve its three fantastic objectives—the rule of God on earth, martyrdom in the cause of God and purification of the ranks of Islam from the elements of depravity—and to fight its four classes of enemy: Americans, heretics ("the Mubaraks of the world"), Shiites and Israel. Of course the real depravity issued from al-Qaeda itself, as the organization's own manual—*Military Studies in the Jihad Against the Tyrants*—made clear. "The confrontation that we are calling for with the apostate regimes does not know Socratic debates . . . Platonic ideals . . . nor Aristotelian diplomacy. But it does know the dialogue of bullets, the ideals of assassination, bombing and destruction, and the diplomacy of the cannon and the machine gun."[41] There was always a sophomoric quality to al-Qaeda: they wrote like schoolboys trying to impress their teachers with big words that they didn't really understand, and they lashed out at "enemies" (Americans, heretics, Israelis) like cliquish adolescents trying to impress their peers. "Kamikaze camps" were established alongside the more traditional ones at Khost. There suicide bombers trained for their final missions, dressed in special white and gray clothes; they spoke to no one. Al-Zawahiri built labs for chemical and biological weapons research outside Jalalabad and Kandahar. Local Afghans trembled at the fiendish contents of al-Zawahiri's workshops—"hundreds of different kinds of containers, small jars and big jars, sealed with metal lids and containing powders and liquids"—and recalled that stray dogs were regularly trotted out to absorb lethal doses of the mysterious powders and fluids.[42]

Bin Laden's fatwa and the excitement it aroused finally marked him down in Washington for surveillance, arrest or targeted assassination. Distracted by India's test of five nuclear devices and Pakistan's prompt retaliation with five underground tests of its own in May 1998, the CIA nevertheless rehearsed a plan to snatch bin Laden from his compound near Kandahar and fly him out of the country, but concluded that the plan was too risky.[43] CIA director George Tenet decided to enlist the Saudis instead. He flew to Riyadh in May 1998 and asked the Saudis to get bin Laden. Because bin Laden had been urging the overthrow of the Saud dynasty and smuggling weapons into the kingdom, Prince Turki was dispatched to Kandahar in June 1998 to, as Crown Prince Abdullah put it, "finish this." Turki met with Mullah Omar and was astounded by Omar's flat refusal to turn over bin Laden, which Omar claimed would violate the Pashtun tribal code of hospitality. Having tried threats, Turki tried bribes instead; he promised and delivered four hundred four-wheel-drive pickup trucks and other aid—which the Taliban used in August to take Mazar-e-Sharif from its Hazara inhabitants, slaughtering five to six thousand innocents in the process—but *still* the Taliban refused to turn over bin Laden, to the Saudis or anyone else.

With the Saudis offering trucks and bin Laden offering cash—millions each year—it was not hard to see why. Nor did the Saudis try particularly hard to extradite bin Laden; given Osama's intimate links to the more devout members of the Saudi establishment, Prince Turki definitely did *not* want bin Laden interrogated by the Americans. All in all, Turki preferred that Osama rot in Afghanistan.[44] Michael Scheuer, who ran the CIA's anti–bin Laden unit—Alec Station—tried to patch together some old American-backed mujahideen to capture Osama and "rendition" him to a Cairo jail (where he'd be tortured till he gave up names and plots) or kill him. John O'Neill and the FBI objected to that rough treatment and persuaded Attorney General Janet Reno to seek a criminal indictment instead, on the charge, corroborated by a captured laptop computer, that bin Laden had aided the Somalis who killed the American Rangers and special forces in Mogadishu in 1993. The indictment was eventually secured from a federal grand jury in New York in June 1998. Now it only remained to catch bin Laden and bring him to justice.[45]

"THE MOST DANGEROUS NON-STATE TERRORIST ACTOR IN THE WORLD TODAY"

On August 7, 1998, al-Qaeda launched its first confirmed terrorist attacks. Bin Laden–trained operatives exploded truck bombs outside the American embassies in Kenya and Tanzania. In the Nairobi blast, 213 were killed (including 12 Americans), and 4,500 were wounded by the explosion and the rain of concrete chunks, broken glass and splintered office furniture. In Dar es Salaam, the suicide bomber's inability to wrestle his truck past a water tanker truck parked by the wall of the embassy mercifully reduced the blast; only 11 died there and 85 were injured, all of them Africans.[46]

"Now it begins," a Justice Department official said when news of the bombings reached Washington at three thirty a.m. Clinton took to the airwaves and pinned the blame on al-Qaeda: "Behind these attacks were the same hands that killed American and Pakistani peacekeepers in Somalia . . . I'm referring to the bin Laden network of radical groups, probably the most dangerous non-state terrorist actor in the world today."[47] Five hundred FBI agents descended on Africa to work the two cases. In Nairobi, a tipster pointed the FBI to the dingy hotel where a Saudi bomber, Muhammed al-Owhali, had taken refuge. Brought in for questioning, al-Owhali broke down and confessed all: he had been trained at al-Qaeda's Khaldan camp and volunteered for "martyrdom operations." Assigned to the Nairobi crew, he had expressed dismay at not getting an operation inside the United States. Al-Owhali told the FBI that his al-Qaeda handlers had assured him that he was carrying out a critical diversionary attack in East Africa. Al-Owhali then looked at his American interrogators and said: "We have a plan to attack the U.S., but we're not ready yet. We need to hit you outside the country in a couple of places so you won't see what is going on inside. The big attack is coming. There's nothing you can do to stop it."[48]

President Bill Clinton planned a furious response to the embassy bombings: thirteen Tomahawk cruise missiles launched on a suspected al-Qaeda chemical weapons site in Sudan and sixty-six cruise missiles launched on bin Laden's two camps around Khost. But Operation Infinite Reach was an embarrassing bust by any measure. The Khartoum chemical weapons site turned out to be nothing more dangerous than a pharmaceutical factory, and the hits in Afghanistan missed their intended targets, bin Laden and al-Zawahiri. The two senior emirs were in Kabul, not Khost. Even though dozens of the missiles hit their targets, only seven al-Qaeda militants died—three Yemenis, two Egyptians, a Saudi and an Uzbek—but none of them were senior leaders. Half the missiles aimed at Khost fell inside Pakistan, killing two tribesmen as well as twenty Afghans on the other side of the border. With each Tomahawk costing $1 million, that was a poor return on assets. The missiles flew on August 20, 1998, the day that Monica Lewinsky testified to a Washington grand jury that she had performed oral sex on President Clinton during her employment as a White House intern.

Al-Qaeda drolly took the Jewish Lewinsky's affair with the Christian Clinton as physical proof of a Jewish-Christian conspiracy, and they celebrated bin Laden's escape as yet more proof of his exalted role. "Tell the Americans that we aren't afraid of bombardment, threats and acts of aggression," al-Zawahiri exulted. "The war has just begun; the Americans should now await the answer." Bin Laden also went on television. "By the grace of God, I am alive," Osama intoned after the attacks. He implied that God had saved him to fight America, when in fact he had been saved by the cajolery of his bored bodyguards at the Khost-Kabul crossroads. They had successfully persuaded bin Laden to make the turn toward Kabul instead of back to the camps, as the American cruise missiles fluttered off the Arabian Sea and toward Khost. Osama had also been saved by Clinton's libido. Embroiled in the Lewinsky sex scandal, Clinton didn't dare launch an intensive air campaign or insert special forces or CIA operatives into Afghanistan to get bin Laden. Already accused of "wagging the dog" with missile strikes—"I hope and pray," said Republican senator Dan Coats of Indiana, "that the decision wasn't made to save the president's job"—a wider campaign would have convulsed the media and Capitol Hill. Instead, Clinton (and the UN) clamped sanctions on the Taliban regime, freezing its U.S. assets and stopping all commercial and financial transactions. National Security Adviser Sandy Berger's arrest and conviction for stealing classified documents from the National Archives after 9/11 probably stemmed from the damnable hesitation of 1998, when the Clinton team should have hunted and killed bin Laden but decided not to. Richard Clarke drafted "Political-Military Plan *Delenda*"—a reference to the take-no-prisoners battle cry of the Punic Wars, when Romans had said *Carthago delenda*, or "Carthage must be destroyed"—which called for covert action, diplomacy and an air campaign to destroy al-Qaeda and kill bin Laden, but *Delenda* was not implemented.[49]

With American attention focused on Afghanistan (when not focused on Monica), Mullah Omar and the Taliban came under renewed pressure to surrender or expel bin Laden. President Clinton had earlier favored the Taliban as the only force capable of uniting Afghanistan and walling it off from Russian or Iranian influence. The Taliban were Pashtuns, Sunnis, anti-Iranian, anti-Russian, efficient and only too willing to authorize the construction, by the Union Oil Company of California, of a $2.5 billion gas pipeline from Turkmenistan across Afghanistan to Pakistan. Unocal's nine-hundred-mile pipeline would have given U.S. investors access to Turkmenistan's gas (11 percent of world reserves), powered the Indian subcontinent and sneaked the rich prize of what Turkmen were calling "the second Kuwait" onto world markets without a single dollar sticking to Russian or Iranian fingers. But even with rich incentives like that, the pro-Unocal Taliban regime had become too hot to handle by its massacres and ethnic cleansing, its links to transnational terrorists and its repression of women. The last offense was by no means trivial in American eyes; Clinton had appointed Madeleine Albright secretary of state for his second term and pledged that "concerns related to women will be incorporated into the mainstream of U.S. foreign policy."[50] The Taliban, who liked to say that "the only two places for an Afghan woman are in her husband's house and the graveyard," were certainly going to lose Albright's fight, with or without a pipeline. Still safe in his Afghan redoubt, bin Laden mourned the deaths of his seven mujahideen and vowed to "avenge the attack in a spectacular way that would deal a death blow to America that would shake it to its very foundations." Al-Zawahiri encouraged bin Laden to select a high-profile target that would goad the United States into war and overreaction. "This is for the purpose of driving [the Americans] crazy. They are cowboys and they will react without thinking."

Al-Zawahiri and bin Laden wanted to provoke the United States into an armed invasion of the Muslim world, to excite and unify the *umma*. "We must move the battle to the enemy's ground, and burn the hands of those who ignite fire in our countries," al-Zawahiri scribbled. "Small groups could bring frightening horror to the Americans."[51] While al-Zawahiri thought globally and prefigured the 9/11 attacks, Mullah Omar did his bit as well. Exhibiting that weird solipsism peculiar to the Middle East, Omar actually phoned the State Department to urge President Clinton to resign the presidency as a sop to angry Muslim opinion. The State Department official who took the call patiently reminded Omar that Osama was like "a guest who was shooting at the neighbors from the host's windows." Surely even the hospitable Pashtun tribal code—"if even an animal seeks refuge with us, we have no choice but to protect it"—didn't extend protection to guests like *that*.[52]

But Omar had changed; Osama had sworn fealty to the Taliban leader—"we consider you to be our noble emir"—and had begged for his protection. Flattered, Omar gave it, rebuffing first the Americans, and then his principal supports: Saudi intelligence director Prince Turki and ISI director General Naseem Rana, who arrived in Kabul together after the Tomahawk strikes to demand bin Laden. Turki and Rana believed that Omar was a marionette who danced at the end of their purse strings and that he would surrender bin Laden after a token struggle. Instead, Omar dug in his heels and spat defiance at Turki: bin Laden was a "man of honor . . . Instead of seeking to persecute him, you should put your hand in ours and his, and fight against the infidels." By now, Osama—with his big annual subsidies to Mullah Omar—was a key piece of the Taliban economy, and the Taliban's 55th Brigade—manned by al-Qaeda fighters—was one of Omar's best units. It had unflinchingly slaughtered the Shiite Hazaras and won victories against Massoud's Northern Alliance. Bin Laden had also built Omar a nice house. Mullah Omar couldn't *afford* to give bin Laden up. "If you speak to me in the name of America," Omar spat, "do not blame me for speaking in the name of bin Laden."[53]

"What You Are Doing Now Is Going to Bring a Lot of Harm to the Afghan People"

Prince Turki was aroused. His career was at stake; if he couldn't extract bin Laden from an impoverished puppet government recognized by only three nations in the world, what *could* he do? Turki had bankrolled and armed the Taliban, and he must have grasped, as Lawrence Wright put it, that "from now on, Saudi Arabia's place in the world would be held hostage" by Osama bin Laden, the awkward, homicidal hermit living a stone's throw away in Tarnak Farms. As the Saudi and Pakistani spymasters rose to leave, Turki—who would be fired in August 2001 for this failure—growled words that must still echo around the mountain redoubts of Afghanistan: "You must remember, Mullah Omar, what you are doing now is going to bring a lot of harm to the Afghan people." After the meeting, the CIA finally received actionable intelligence that placed bin Laden in their crosshairs; spies in Afghanistan tracked bin Laden's movements and established his daily routine. The intelligence was relayed to Director of Central Intelligence George Tenet, who refused to recommend another cruise missile attack. (Questioned by the 9/11 Commission as to his reasons, Tenet could not recall them.) Without Tenet's recommendation, Clinton also refused to act.[54]

In the spring of 1999, bin Laden met with Khalid Sheikh Muhammed in Kandahar and instructed him to begin planning the attack on the United States with hijacked airplanes that KSM had unsuccessfully pitched to bin Laden three years earlier. Bin Laden believed that America was built on sand—hope and optimism—and that spectacular attacks on "weak spots" would crack the superpower's "unstable foundation" and cause it to "stumble, wither away and relinquish world leadership." The federal union itself might come unglued. Al-Zawahiri egged him on: "The West and the Jews . . . only know the language of interests backed by brute military force." A ruthless attack would defeat the Americans, or bring them to the table. The dullness of al-Zawahiri and bin Laden as historians, strategists or even observant citizens of the world was never more obvious, but their deviousness and ability to exploit the gaps and blind spots in America's security architecture gave the plan some hope of *tactical* success.[55]

Whereas KSM had imagined vengefully crashing airliners into the FBI and CIA headquarters as well as a nuclear power plant, bin Laden preferred targets with vast symbolic importance: he put the White House, the U.S. Capitol and the Pentagon at the top of his list, and threw in New York's World Trade Center at KSM's urging.

Pilots were needed, and although Khaldan had plenty of would-be martyrs, it had few trained pilots. The Saudi jihadis were useful here, because they could painlessly secure visas into the United States and easily enroll in flight schools for training without any questions asked. Before 9/11, Saudis were regarded as thoroughly reliable and solvent visitors. Muhammed Atta arrived in Hamburg at precisely the moment when Khalid Sheikh Muhammed's plan was firming up. Atta's technical education, fluency in English and familiarity with the West made him a natural fit in the plot. Bin Laden set up two teams for the "planes operation": Atta's in Hamburg, which was assigned the task of applying for U.S. visas and flight schools, and a second team in Kuala Lumpur, which had been sent out on a Bojinka-type operation but was now being reassigned to the attack on America.

ATTACK ON THE USS *COLE*

Bin Laden's efforts to coordinate these two teams—the terrorists in Malaysia were mainly Yemenis who had been sent there because they would never qualify for U.S. visas—led to telephone traffic that was picked up by the Saudis and the NSA and passed on to the CIA's Alec Station and the FBI. Although bin Laden had not been using the telephone since 1998, the year the *Washington Times* leaked the news that the NSA was eavesdropping on his satellite phone calls, his underlings were less guarded. "Something nefarious might be afoot," the NSA ventured at the end of 1999, and Prince Turki made the same observation. CIA operatives actually broke into an al-Qaeda terrorist's hotel room, searched it, photographed his passport—including the multientry U.S. visa—and advised that "we need to continue the effort to identify these travelers and their activities, to determine if there is any true threat posed."[56] Had Alec Station taken a deeper interest in them—the CIA neglected, for example, to ask the Malaysians to wiretap the meetings in Kuala Lumpur—they would almost certainly have sniffed out the 9/11 plot, as well as the attack on the USS *Cole* in Aden Harbor on October 12, 2000, when two al-Qaeda operatives steered a little fishing boat packed with C-4 explosive into the port side of the warship, blowing open a gaping hole, killing seventeen sailors and wounding thirty-nine.[57]

John O'Neill and the FBI immediately deployed to Yemen—"a country of 18 million citizens and 50 million machine guns," O'Neill quipped—as they had to East Africa. O'Neill's investigation of the *Cole* attack, which was claimed in the usual bombastic way by bin Laden ("the destroyer represented the capital of the West, and the small boat represented Muhammed"), revealed all the shortcomings of America in the Middle East. Too many agents flew in, and the U.S. embassy protested that their arrival was tantamount to "300 heavily-armed people arriving by plane to take over Des Moines." Only six of the interlopers spoke Arabic. When O'Neill groused at one interrogation that the proceedings were "like pulling teeth," the object of the interrogation—a Yemeni colonel—shot indignantly to his feet. His interpreter had translated O'Neill's phrase as "I'm going to pull out your teeth." Since the worried Yemeni government—pressed on one side by the Americans and on the other by al-Qaeda sympathizers—was still calling the explosion an "accident," pulling out teeth certainly seemed excessive.[58] The *Cole* attack stung the Clinton administration badly. The destroyer had been dispatched to participate in cruise missile attacks on al-Qaeda but had been crippled before it could even arrive on station. Clinton and the *Cole*'s crew were lucky that the ship's ordnance had not cooked off in the blast; the destroyer would have been destroyed and the entire crew would have perished.[59] "We will find out who was responsible and hold them accountable," Clinton said in a hastily convened news conference in the White House Rose Garden. But neither Secretary of Defense William Cohen nor chairman of the Joint Chiefs of Staff General Hugh Shelton showed any interest in inserting U.S. forces into Afghanistan—a country, as Shelton put it, of "extraordinary complexity"—to root out bin Laden and his Taliban sanctuary. Richard Clarke expressed disgust at the play-it-safe culture of Clinton's Pentagon. "Their overwhelming message," he recalled, "was 'we don't *want* to do this.' " So they didn't.[60]

The tension between the FBI and the CIA, lamented after 9/11 and superficially patched by the creation of an intelligence czar, was never more apparent than in the balky efforts to synchronize the handoff of CIA-watched terrorists abroad to the FBI as the terrorists entered the United States. The CIA hated sharing intelligence with the FBI because it would almost certainly end up in an indictment or a public trial and would become useless as intelligence, and it would almost certainly expose and endanger CIA sources and methods as well. For their part, the FBI refused on legal grounds (Rule 6E of the Federal Rules of Criminal Procedure) to share any revelations from grand jury testimony with the CIA, which blocked most intelligence cooperation between the two agencies. Both agencies suffered from the lingering effects of the 1970s, when Nixon had used the FBI, CIA and NSA to spy on political opponents and triggered a congressional crackdown on all infringements of American Fourth Amendment rights.[61] When the FBI searched Zacarias Moussaoui's apartment in Minnesota in mid-August 2001, they seized his laptop computer, but refused to search it without a warrant or probable cause. The laptop would have provided early warning of 9/11 had it been opened and searched. To "throw intelligence over the wall" from the FBI to the CIA or vice versa, information had to be delivered to a secret court in Washington (created by the 1978 Foreign Intelligence Surveillance Act) and arbitrated there. Although the NSA knew that al-Qaeda suspects were living in the United States and knew where they lived, they never shared this information with the FBI because of the FISA "wall" and their own secrecy.

Steve Bongardt, an FBI investigator seeking the identities of two al-Qaeda hijackers known to the CIA but not to the FBI in late August 2001, vented his frustration with a system that had been designed to contain abusive presidents but was now being exploited by al-Qaeda plotters: "If this guy is in the country, it's not because he's going to fucking Disneyland." Bongardt regarded the FISA wall as a "bureaucratic fiction," and wrote his supervisor: "Someday somebody will die—and wall or not—the public will not understand why we were not more effective at throwing every resource we had at certain 'problems.' "[62] Because of their coziness with foreign intelligence agencies (like the Saudis), the CIA was frequently unable to share with the FBI without incriminating *itself.* Unable to spy inside the United States, the CIA might spy through a joint venture with the Saudis or their partner agencies. Thus, the CIA clung tightly to its intelligence, and shared it sparingly, or not at all. Requests from the FBI for elaboration—as, for example, after the *Cole* bombing, when FBI investigators in Aden noticed that al-Qaeda had been wiring money *out* of Yemen on the eve of the *Cole* attack and postulated that another attack might be in the works—were met with silence.[63]

With its paucity of Middle Eastern assets, the CIA also viewed the travel of Arab terrorists into the United States as a way to recruit agents. That might explain one of the great unresolved mysteries of 9/11. Two of the Saudi hijackers landed in Los Angeles twenty-one months before 9/11 and were almost immediately taken under the wing of a suspected Saudi intelligence operative, who moved them to San Diego, introduced them around and eased their way into flight school. In all likelihood, the CIA had handed the al-Qaeda terrorists off to the Saudis in the hope that the Saudis would be able to "turn" them and give the CIA agents inside al-Qaeda.[64] Had the CIA handed them off to the FBI, the most they would have achieved would have been two arrests or deportations. Bureaucratic infighting was another factor. Neither agency wanted to deliver control of an investigation to the other, and the best way to keep control was not to share. In June 2001, FBI and CIA agents met to share notes on al-Qaeda and ended up shouting at each other and *not* sharing: the FBI wanted complete information on the CIA's suspects—to keep them out of the United States, or to locate and arrest them if they were already inside—and the CIA refused to divulge the information so as not to betray sources or sabotage its own counterterrorism operations. (The last of the 9/11 hijackers—known to the CIA but not to the FBI and the immigration agents at U.S. airports—debarked three weeks later at New York's JFK Airport, on the Fourth of July.) Sheer laziness also was a factor. When Doug Miller, the FBI representative in Alec Station, asked for permission to transmit to FBI headquarters the CIA discovery of the meetings in Malaysia and the likely travel of the principals into the United States, his request was initially rebuffed—"this is not a matter for the FBI"—and then ignored. When Kenneth Williams, an FBI agent in Phoenix, warned in August 2001 that Arab students at American flight schools might be al-Qaeda hijackers in training, one of his colleagues (in New York) crumpled the warning and threw it in the trash: "Who's going to conduct the 30,000 interviews? When the fuck do we have time for this?"[65]

Bin Laden had assumed that Clinton would invade Afghanistan after the *Cole* attack and impale himself on the same mountains and caves that had bled the Red Army to death. Osama actually scattered his leadership cadres around the country to avoid death in a cruise missile or special forces attack. But Clinton did not strike. Clinton's director of central intelligence, George Tenet, recalled that Pakistani support was critical for a strike at the roots of al-Qaeda, but Pakistan's ISI and President Pervez Musharraf, who owed his successful coup in 1999 to ISI patronage, would not lift a finger to help, so great were their fears of the Taliban and the Indian-backed Northern Alliance, and so intense was their resentment of Washington for having cut bilateral ties and imposed sanctions on Pakistan after the nuclear tests of 1998.[66] Vice President Al Gore and Governor George W. Bush were vying for the White House, and President Clinton was focused on eleventh-hour negotiations with Yasser Arafat and Ehud Barak for a final settlement of the Palestinian question that never finalized. Clinton also claimed that American intelligence could not verify bin Laden's location, so there seemed little point in missile strikes, a nondecision that his cautious secretary of defense, William Cohen, and his cautious secretary of state, Madeleine Albright, eagerly endorsed. Albright worried that U.S. strikes in Afghanistan would inflame the Arab street at the very moment that Washington was trying to achieve a final settlement, and Cohen, who was trying to revive the dormant U.S.-Pakistani relationship, feared that strikes would embarrass the Pakistani government.[67]

What the Clinton administration *did* do was investigate the possibility of throwing its support behind a more sympathetic "tribal": the so-called Lion of Panshir. Ahmed Shah Massoud had been driven from power in Kabul by the Taliban in 1996, but he remained a potent rival. Like Mullah Omar, Massoud was an Islamist, but he was a Tajik, not a Pashtun, and was more diplomatic and tolerant than the fanatical *talibs*. He built bridges to the Shiite Hazaras, allied with moderate Pashtuns and loathed the Arab Afghans—"bin Laden does more harm than good," he growled. Massoud called for real national reconciliation in Afghanistan and the eviction of Pakistani agents and special forces (who were rumored to be fighting alongside the Taliban), and he criticized the Taliban's destruction in March 2001 of the fifteen-hundred-year-old Buddha statues overlooking the Silk Road at Bamiyan, as well as the accompanying Taliban edict that all Hindus in Afghanistan wear an identifying yellow patch. That last edict, which reeked of Nazi persecution, certainly suggested Pakistani involvement. With a ring of fanatical Pashtuns closing around him—the Taliban and the Pakistanis were murdering the moderate ones, like Hamid Karzai's father, Abdul—Massoud, who still controlled six large territorial pockets in northern, central and western Afghanistan through a United Front of anti-Taliban groups, pumped good intelligence to the Americans. He warned after the *Cole* attack that al-Qaeda was planning an attack inside the United States that would be far bloodier than the East Africa embassy bombings. Richard Clarke wanted to beef up Massoud's United Front armies and unleash them against the Taliban and al-Qaeda, but his planning stalled as Clinton handed over office to Bush, and then went nowhere with the new administration.[68]

"BY FAR YOUR BIGGEST THREAT IS BIN LADEN AND THE AL-QAEDA"

Bill Clinton had been soft on terrorism, but the new administration of George W. Bush was even softer. Bush made ballistic missile defense his top priority and spared little thought for ragamuffins like bin Laden. In a two-hour meeting with Bush after the 2000 election had been decided, Clinton told the incoming president that "by far your biggest threat is bin Laden and the al-Qaeda." Sandy Berger called on Bush's new national security adviser, Condoleezza Rice, and said, "I'm here because I want to underscore how important this issue [of al-Qaeda] is. You're going to spend more time during your four years on terrorism generally and al-Qaeda specifically than on any other issue."[69] Richard Clarke, who shared Berger's view that "terrorism is the most serious threat to American security," briefed Rice on al-Qaeda, but came away with the impression that she had never even heard of the organization. To keep Clarke on the sidelines, Rice downgraded his position—"national coordinator for counterterrorism"—from one with access to principals (the president and his cabinet secretaries) to one that had to wend its way through deputies, like Condi Rice's Stephen Hadley.

Rice was uncomfortable with Clarke's office from the beginning: "It does domestic things and it's not just doing policy, it seems to be worrying about operational issues." Indeed it was; Clarke was obsessed with the operational threat posed by al-Qaeda and the need for an operational response. In January 2001, Clarke greeted the new administration with a memo titled "Strategy for Eliminating the Threat from the Jihadist Networks of al-Qaeda: Status and Prospects." He sent the memo to Condi Rice and asked for an urgent principals meeting on its contents, but never heard back from her. Bush 43's administration was determined to tighten up decision making after the notoriously ragged process of Clinton, whose thirst for information on every subject did not always get molded into coherent strategy. That had certainly been the case in Clinton's on-again, off-again hunt for bin Laden.[70] Director of Central Intelligence George Tenet, like Clarke a Clinton holdover, recalled meeting with Hadley in the same period to push for an immediate offensive against al-Qaeda in its sanctuaries. "You guys need to figure out what your policy is," Tenet chided Hadley. The clock was ticking.[71]

Reports of a looming al-Qaeda attack on America had begun to pour in by early 2001. Bin Laden talked vaguely about the approaching "ignition point," a savage attack on American soil that would shock the *umma* into radical action. "The forces of Islam are coming," he said. Al-Qaeda phone traffic rang with sports metaphors: "The score will be 200 to nothing"; "The Olympics are coming."[72] Most of the nineteen 9/11 hijackers were already installed in the United States awaiting D-day. The NSA reported rising telephone chatter about a coming "spectacular" inside the United States, "another Hiroshima," as one terrorist put it. Massoud issued the same warning, as did Egyptian president Hosni Mubarak, whose jailers had exposed a plot to kill President Bush with "an airplane stuffed with explosives." Even the Taliban foreign minister, Wakil Muttawakil, warned the Americans. He told the American consul general in Peshawar and UN officials in Kabul that al-Qaeda was preparing a "devastating strike on the U.S." With belated foresight, the Taliban official recognized that an al-Qaeda attack on America would lead to an American attack on Afghanistan.

"The Big Wedding"

Bin Laden's terrorist rivals, like the Jordanian Abu Musab al-Zarqawi, who had set up his own jihadi group, al-Tawhid, near Herat (far from al-Qaeda in Jalalabad and Kandahar), expressed alarm at Osama's willingness to strike inside the United States. Such a reckless act would almost certainly result in the loss of the Afghan sanctuary and Taliban support, which, al-Zarqawi believed, were the foundation stones of the globalized jihad. No one knew better than al-Zarqawi that Afghanistan was not only a terrorist base, it was the *only* place in the world where the thousands of outlaws gathered around bin Laden could take up residence. Besides Arabs, there were Chechens, Pakistanis, Bangladeshis, Filipinos, Algerians, Kenyans, Somalis and even Americans, and few of them could leave Afghanistan because they were on wanted lists. Bin Laden knew this, but planned to unleash the desperadoes on a distracted, demoralized world in an escalating jihad. All that was needed was a spark.[73] Jordanian intelligence forwarded the code name of the rumored al-Qaeda attack to Washington: "The Big Wedding." That name alone implied the use of suicide bombers, who would assume that their martyrdom operations would culminate in a "big wedding" to the seventy-two black-eyed virgins of paradise. To spur recruiting, bin Laden shrewdly tapped into the sexual frustration of the young men who came his way. Every *shahid*, or martyr, would maim or kill his victims but blast himself into the better world promised by the Koran: "Therein are rivers unpolluted, and rivers of milk, and rivers of wine, and rivers of clear-run honey." The horny, dead martyrs would lie on the banks of those honeyed rivers with succulent Muslim *houris*—"loving companions of modest gaze with lovely eyes."[74]

In May, Clarke had cautioned Rice: "When these attacks occur, as they likely will, we will wonder what more we could have done to stop them."[75] On July 5, 2001, Clarke convened a meeting of several government agencies—the FBI, the Secret Service, the FAA, the INS and the Coast Guard. "Something really spectacular is going to happen here, and it's going to happen soon," he warned. Five days later, Tenet and Clarke's counterterrorism team met with Rice in the White House and warned her that "attack preparations had been made," that al-Qaeda was about to launch a "spectacular attack" inside America, possibly "multiple and simultaneous attacks with little or no warning." Cofer Black, the CIA's counterterrorist director, warned Rice that "this country needs to go on a war footing now."[76] All over the world, and especially in Afghanistan, al-Qaeda operatives were going to ground; camps were closing, and their recruits were preparing for martyrdom and a constantly referenced "big surprise." Tenet's memoirs give a sense of the tightening circle of al-Qaeda threats—in Europe, America, the Middle East, East Asia and Africa. "The whole world seemed on the edge of eruption."[77] Again, Rice—whose job was to coordinate the views of the cabinet and intelligence agencies on security policy and present them to the president—did nothing. Rice continued to aver that al-Qaeda was a "lesser included" that would be eliminated once her avuncular principals got around to conceiving a broad regional strategy for Pakistan and Afghanistan.

"ALL RIGHT, YOU'VE COVERED YOUR ASS NOW"

"Old-think" like Condi Rice's drove Clarke to distraction. "Al-Qaeda is not some narrow little terrorist issue that needs to be included in a broader regional policy," he reminded her. "Rather, several of our regional policies need to address centrally the transnational challenge to the U.S. and our interests posed by the al-Qaeda network." But Rice and Bush, who evinced a surprising lack of interest in investigating and punishing the *Cole* bombing, turned a deaf ear to Clarke's warnings. On August 6, 2001, Tenet—alarmed at the White House's passivity—ordered a presidential daily brief titled "Bin Laden determined to strike in the U.S." Bush heard it at his ranch in Crawford, Texas, and then jocularly told his briefer: "All right, you've covered your ass now." Rice dismissed the PDB as "historical" and unworthy of the president's urgent attention. Vice President Dick Cheney regarded al-Qaeda as overrated—little more than "noise in the system."

Clarke would not even get to brief President Bush on al-Qaeda until the night of 9/11, when the Pentagon was speared by an airliner and both towers of the World Trade Center lay in smoking ruins. None of the White House speechwriters had even heard the term "al-Qaeda" before 9/11. Rumsfeld's deputy, Paul Wolfowitz, fought a surprisingly obtuse rearguard action against the galloping al-Qaeda threat during this period, protesting that "Iraqi terrorism" would do "at least as much" as bin Laden and that the Iraqi Mukhabarat was more dangerous than al-Qaeda.[78] Stephen Cambone, the undersecretary of defense for intelligence—prodded by Rumsfeld and Wolfowitz—went to see Tenet after the July 2001 meeting and theorized that the "al-Qaeda threats were just a grand deception, a clever ploy to tie up our resources and expend our energies on a phantom enemy that lacked the power and the will to carry the battle to us." The Bush Pentagon had its own priorities— missile defense, China, North Korea, Iraq and Iran—and did not want to get knocked off stride by bin Laden's bloviating. The neocons had made no secret of their contempt for the Oslo Accords and Clinton's interventions in the Israeli-Palestinian peace process. Smash Iraq and Iran, they believed, and the whole "peace process" will fall into place.[79] Bush himself had growled that—unlike Clinton—he would not waste time and energy "swatting flies" like al-Qaeda, Hamas or Arafat. He would focus on *big* issues. His less ideological advisers were alarmed. "No," Tenet replied. "This is real." The intelligence on the al-Qaeda planes operation was convincing, and bin Laden would lose face and funds if he did not carry out his threats. "We are going to get hit."[80]

On September 9, Ahmed Shah Massoud was murdered by two al-Qaeda assassins sent into Afghanistan's Northern Alliance headquarters by al-Zawahiri. The suicide bombers posed as journalists—their preapproved list of questions included several about the future of bin Laden in Afghanistan—and smuggled a bomb into Massoud's office inside their camera battery pack. The blast killed Massoud, his translator and the assassins.[81] Indeed the sole survivor of the blast was Afghanistan's ambassador to India, who described "a dark blue, thick fire rushing towards us," and then death for all but him. The Taliban had been trying to kill Massoud for years. With a twenty-two-thousand-man United Front Army—his Tajik Northern Alliance plus big Uzbek, Hazara and anti-Taliban Pashtun contingents—Massoud was a magnet for every group in Afghanistan that rejected Taliban repression and Pakistani and al-Qaeda meddling.[82] Pakistan's President Musharraf and the ISI feared Massoud, who drew much of his funding from Russia and India. Everyone grasped that Massoud's assassination was a gift to Musharraf and Mullah Omar from bin Laden, and three months later a captured al-Qaeda laptop confirmed that it was.[83] Massoud, who had fought the Russians, Karmal, Najibullah and then Mullah Omar, was a celebrity and the only real rival to the Taliban for control of the country. His murder was baksheesh paid by bin Laden to secure his sanctuary in Afghanistan and the Pakistani tribal areas and to brace the Taliban and Pakistan for the backlash sure to come after al-Qaeda struck inside the United States.

9/11

Bin Laden had sent the signal to launch the Big Wedding—a verse from the Koran: "Wherever you are, death will find you, even in the looming tower." He and the al-Qaeda high command now took to the hills to escape the bombs and cruise missiles that would find them once New York and Washington were hit. The al-Qaeda emirs shipped their wives and children off to safety in Pakistan and returned to the caves around the Lion's Den above Khost, lugging a television set and a satellite dish.[84]

The first plane, an American Airlines Boeing 767 en route from Boston to Los Angeles with ninety-two passengers and nine thousand gallons of jet fuel, slammed into the ninety-fifth floor of the World Trade Center's North Tower at a speed of 429 miles per hour. Fussing with their balky satellite dish, the al-Qaeda leaders in the caves of Tora Bora missed the first reports but finally got a signal from the BBC Arabic service and cheered when they saw images of the burning North Tower. "Wait, wait," bin Laden said. The Big Wedding had been so secret and compartmentalized that most of the senior men in the cave knew nothing about it. When the second plane hit—a sixty-ton United Airlines Boeing 767 slamming at 537 miles per hour into the eightieth floor of the South Tower—Osama wept and prayed, but held up three fingers to his companions. Another attack was coming. When the west face of the Pentagon was smashed by American Flight 77—a Boeing 757 with four tons of fuel traveling at 530 miles per hour—Osama held up four fingers. A fourth attack—United Flight 93, about to crash into a Pennsylvania field—was aimed at the White House or the Capitol.[85]

The looming towers—ten million square feet of crowded office space—fell down into the streets of Manhattan, a shivering mass of concrete, asbestos, lead, fiberglass, paper, cotton, jet fuel and the incinerated corpses of 2,751 people. Their ruins and remains smothered sixteen acres of the world's most precious real estate, and would burn for a hundred days. The smell—like burnt rubber—would drift all the way up Manhattan Island and into every outer borough. Among the dead was John O'Neill, who had left the FBI after the *Cole* attack to become security chief at the World Trade Center. The rest of the victims, Lawrence Wright observed, were "like a universal parliament, representing sixty-two countries and nearly every ethnic group and religion in the world."[86] President Bush, who had been visiting a school in Florida when the terrorists struck, was thunderstruck. "We're going to find out who did this," he told Vice President Cheney, "and we're going to kick their asses."[87]

CHAPTER 16

·✕✕·

ENDURING FREEDOM

BIN LADEN GLOATED in his cave. He had spent $400,000 on the Big Wedding and inflicted $30 billion of damage on New York City and hundreds of billions of dollars in indirect costs to the U.S. economy. The ratio of casualties—19 hijackers killed to 2,973—was just as striking: 1:156. Bin Laden entertained awestruck visitors and walked them through the Twin Towers collapse, boasting that his Saudi Bin Laden Group construction experience had been critical to the planning and execution of the operation: "I was the most optimistic of all because of my expertise in this profession and this business." The Taliban stalled for ten days, and then announced that they would *not* hand bin Laden over to the United States. The Saudi had achieved celebrity status and could not be surrendered. "The Americans are crazy," a Taliban defector remarked. "It's Osama bin Laden who can hand over Mullah Omar, not the other way round."[1] Buoyed, Osama sent a videotape to the studios of Al Jazeera in Qatar that was aired on October 7, in which he taunted the United States, which had just begun bombing the Taliban army. As usual, any scheduled pronouncement by Sheikh bin Laden "emptied the streets in countries like Saudi Arabia, Egypt, Palestine, Syria and Morocco," where people flooded indoors to watch and listen. "There is America, hit by God in one of its softest spots. Its greatest buildings were destroyed, thank God for that. There is America, full of fear from its north to its south, from its west to its east. Thank God for that." He thanked the hijackers—they had "purged the history of the *umma* through their conquests in New York and Washington"—and summoned all believers to come and join the jihad. "These events have divided the whole world into two sides— the side of the believers and the side of the infidels. May God keep you away from them. Every Muslim has to rush to make his religion victorious. The winds of faith have come."[2]

The only winds Osama felt were the whirr of orbiting unmanned aerial vehicles (UAVs) and the rustling of special forces recon teams prowling the darkness. "Go in fast, hard and light," the CIA counseled Bush on September 13, just two days after the attacks on New York and Washington. "Be the insurgents," not the Russians. With bittersweet anticipation, the Russians predicted disaster for the Americans: "Vietnam will be a picnic by comparison; here they will get it in the teeth; they will get it good," a Red Army veteran growled.[3] But CIA teams had been working with Massoud's Northern Alliance since 1999, and they now recommended that Bush take pains not to make this a war of "Americans against Afghans," but an American-bolstered Afghan purge of al-Qaeda and the Taliban. George Tenet, who had underperformed in his duty to fix attention on the terrorist threat, now enjoined the president to turn up the heat on the Taliban by "capitalizing on the Afghan tradition of switching sides." Million-dollar packs of twenty-dollar bills and airdrops— guns, saddles, horse feed and medicine—were aimed at agreeable warlords of the United Front, to build a broad coalition against the Taliban and bin Laden.[4]

The war plan for Afghanistan followed the outlines of U.S. engagement with the now deceased Massoud before 9/11. "Our goal is not to destroy the Taliban," Bush said privately, "but that may be the effect." Pakistan would be bullied into cutting its support for the Taliban. President Musharraf complied, from shame at the barbarity of the al-Qaeda attacks as well as his own fear that his embattled secular government would come under attack from the Taliban, which massed twenty-five thousand troops near the Pakistani border in the days after September 11. Still, even as Musharraf promised to help the United States, ISI agents were in Kandahar tipping the Taliban off about the gathering American storm.[5] With the Pakistanis sidelined, CIA and special forces teams—Army Delta and Navy SEALs—would provide targeting, intelligence and air support for Northern Alliance ground units, which would drive into north-central Afghanistan, seize the crossroads of Mazar-e-Sharif, pull in American supplies from Uzbekistan and then join strengthened assaults on Konduz, Bamiyan and down to Kabul. While two U.S. Navy carrier battle groups pulled into the northern Indian Ocean, air force bombers readied themselves in

Diego Garcia and Missouri, and U.S. troops flew into neighboring Uzbekistan, American planners initially bombed and probed sparingly. The plan, as Tenet put it, was to "create fissures within the Taliban" and get the Pashtuns to switch sides and surrender bin Laden.[6] That would secure victory at a low cost and make a postwar solution easier.

Bush entertained no doubts about the campaign. Cautioned by Senator Tom Daschle and Cofer Black of the CIA to tread softly in Afghanistan, the graveyard of the Red Army, Bush bluffly answered: "That's war. That's what we're here to win."[7] Secretary of Defense Donald Rumsfeld also exuded confidence; his message, according to one of the American planners in Afghanistan, was, "We are not going to repeat the mistakes of the Soviets. We are not going to go in with large conventional forces." The U.S. military would substitute speed and precision for mass and rely on indigenous troops leveraged by American special forces and airpower.

On October 7, Bush launched Operation Infinite Justice, to kill off the Taliban, flush out the Arab Afghans and capture or kill Osama bin Laden. The name struck Muslims as impertinent—only God's justice is infinite—so Bush abashedly renamed it Operation Enduring Freedom. B-52, B-1 and B-2 bombers and strike aircraft from the carriers wiped out Afghanistan's few military aircraft and primitive air defenses, and then moved to hit Taliban military headquarters, bases and terrorist training camps. Navy Tomahawks fired from submarines and surface ships in the Indian Ocean compounded the damage, their only limitation being the lack of suitable targets in primitive Afghanistan, which, Secretary of Defense Rumsfeld smiled, was "not a target-rich environment."[8] Still, twelve thousand bombs and missiles rained down—sixty-seven hundred of them precision-guided—and CIA and special forces A-teams poured in to assist the Northern Alliance. Few of the Americans wore complete uniforms or bothered to cut their hair or beards. They were "black" units—their existence officially denied by the Pentagon—who looked more like Afghans, with their jeans or camouflage pants, dirty T-shirts and fleece jackets. Many of the special operators "cross-functioned" with "white" operators and conventional Rangers to gather intelligence and assist the Northern Alliance in killing off Taliban troops. Although the CIA failed to take an easy opening-day shot at Mullah Omar, who was identified in a convoy fleeing Kabul by a Predator drone with Hellfire missiles, bureaucracy was generally minimized by flattened organizations. U.S. intelligence analysts and communications experts were moved from Bagram Air Base—the principal American headquarters in Afghanistan—into the field to speed the flow of time-sensitive data and "actionable" intelligence like tips and aerial imagery. Using laser target designators, the American ground units located Taliban units, supplies, fortified positions or safe houses, and "painted" them for coalition air strikes.

U.S. Special Forces fought alongside "*shura* troops"—instant militias delivered to the Americans by ingratiating village councils—who wanted a bite of the juicy American apple before it was withdrawn. Task Force 11—twenty-five hundred strong and the biggest group of "black" special operators ever assembled—focused on "high-value targets," which meant "the big three"—Osama bin Laden, Ayman al-Zawahiri and Mullah Omar—and any other senior leadership that cropped up. Seventeen special forces A-teams with overhead support from orbiting fixed-wing aircraft and Hellfire-armed drones pinpointed Taliban ground units and called in air strikes. Whenever American bombers and AC-130 gunships caught Taliban ground units in the open, they pulverized them with 500-pound bombs, 2,000-pound JDAMs (GPS-guided Joint Direct Attack Munitions), cluster bombs, "daisy cutters"—12,600 pounds of explosive designed to clear landing zones in Vietnam without a crater—and volleys of withering fire from the gunships. The Taliban army melted away in mass, terrified desertions. The daisy cutters, with their nine-hundred-foot killing radius and crushing overpressure, were especially demoralizing. The war, which tyros like bin Laden had insisted would become a "quagmire" and a "graveyard," proved astonishingly fast and cheap: just $3.8 billion for the "major combat operations" concluded in December, and another $70 to $100 million in CIA bribes to Taliban commanders and pro-Taliban warlords. For Rumsfeld—who had recently proposed scrapping two of the army's ten divisions to pay for more special forces and precision weapons—it was an exhilarating moment. Operation Enduring Freedom essentially revoked the Powell Doctrine, which had caused so much delay and hesitation in 1990–91—requiring massive deployments of U.S. forces and firepower before combat operations—and was a golden opportunity to showcase "military transformation": lighter, smarter, more agile U.S. forces that could do more with less.[9]

"DEATH TO PAKISTAN"

Unfortunately, more with *more* was needed. As the winter snows approached and bin Laden and Mullah Omar remained at large, Secretary of Defense Rumsfeld leaned hard on Centcom commander Tommy Franks. Army chief of staff General Eric Shinseki and Army secretary Thomas White pushed for a big conventional deployment—perhaps two entire army divisions—to seal pockets like Tora Bora and envelop the al-Qaeda and Taliban leadership still in Afghanistan, but Rumsfeld refused.[10] By November 2001, the administration had already made up its mind to invade Iraq. Rumsfeld had persuaded Bush that the "nexus of terrorism and weapons of mass destruction would not be solved by fighting al-Qaeda inside Afghanistan . . . or focusing narrowly on the perpetrators of 9/11."[11] Iraq needed to be defeated too, and Rumsfeld wanted no unnecessary detachments to Afghanistan, which seemed like a "done deal." But Afghanistan was far from done. The Taliban never splintered, and the Pashtuns, backstopped by their conationals across the border in the Pathan tribal areas of Pakistan's North-West Frontier Province, watched the Tajik, Uzbek and Hazara advance of the United Front—now led by Muhammed Fahim—fearfully. What Pashtuns the United States recruited after pushing into southern and eastern Afghanistan were never enough to overcome the Taliban old guard and their Pakistani patrons. Having promised to cut ties with the Taliban in September, Musharraf was back to supporting them in October. And why not? A *Newsweek* poll revealed that 83 percent of Pakistanis supported the Taliban, not the Americans.[12] Neither the CIA nor the Pentagon could find enough motivated Pashtuns for the American cause. When the Americans tried to bring Pashtun leader Abdul "Hollywood" Haq out of his Dubai exile and back into Afghanistan, the original "Gucci guerrilla"—beloved by Reagan and Casey in the 1980s—was ambushed, lynched and left hanging from a maple tree by Taliban assassins, who were almost certainly tipped off by the ISI about Haq's itinerary.[13] Musharraf's foreign minister warned Washington "not to give support to one side or the other in Afghanistan"—astonishing hypocrisy in view of Pakistan's dogged support for the Taliban—and Secretary of State Colin Powell, on a visit to Islamabad, was induced by his Pakistani hosts to hold out an olive branch to moderate elements in the Taliban, as if there were any.[14] The United Front commanders were shocked by American deference to Pakistan—another symptom of which was Centcom's decision to fight the war from Tampa, not Kabul—and also by the light load of precision bombs dropped on target-poor Afghanistan. "We are all astonished how America and its allies drop three bombs every day on the Taliban, and that's it," one militia commander grumbled.[15] Clearly the Bush administration had Iraq on its mind and was losing interest in Afghanistan. Still, guided by U.S. special operators and air support, the United Front punched the Taliban out of Mazar-e-

Sharif, Herat, a half dozen other cities and then Kabul itself, where crowds cheered the retreat of ten thousand Taliban troops and the arrival of the United Front in November as a liberation, calling out "Death to the Taliban" and, hardly surprisingly, "Death to Pakistan."

While the Kabulis rejoiced in their new freedom to shave, discard burkas and turbans, and watch Bollywood films, the Taliban and the Arab Afghans lived to fight another day. Pounded out of their last footholds in southern and eastern Afghanistan, and in northern pockets like Kunduz, by United Front troops and B-52 strikes, they took to the hills once again. Mullah Omar prudently withdrew $6 million from Afghanistan's national bank before quitting Kabul, and his pious *talibs* looted the capital and its currency shops before leaving the keys of government behind.[16] Those senior leaders who found themselves hopelessly surrounded escaped with Pakistani help. When Kunduz and its several thousand Taliban and al-Qaeda troops were surrounded by United Front forces—Muhammed Daud's Tajiks and Rashid Dostum's Uzbeks, both armies vying for the multimillion-dollar cash rewards offered by Washington for the al-Qaeda leaders inside—Musharraf sheepishly telephoned Washington and requested secret nighttime airlifts out of Kunduz to carry the ISI agents and commandos trapped there to safety. Vice President Cheney, who handled the whole sordid affair, might have been expected to damn Musharraf for his perfidy in running a parallel war against the Americans, but Cheney and Rumsfeld—believing that Musharraf's prestige had to be protected at any price—authorized and cleared the flights, which transported al-Qaeda and Taliban leaders as well as Pakistani agents to safety. Hamid Karzai later confirmed the flights and lamented that "even the Americans didn't know who got away." There were an estimated one thousand Pakistani soldiers and agents inside Kunduz, but Musharraf extracted two or three times that number of fugitives from the city. The ISI jocularly called it "the Great Escape" and was doubtless astonished that Washington never demanded to see who got off the planes in Pakistan. It was an astounding example of strategic and operational incompetence by the George W. Bush administration. U.S. special operators who watched the airlift from the surrounding hills knew exactly who was getting away; they called it "Operation Evil Airlift," but obediently held their fire.[17] Kandahar, the last bastion of the Taliban, fell on December 9, and was pacified by several hundred U.S. Marines who arrived in an operation that was rather too hopefully dubbed Operation Swift Freedom. Mullah Omar, who had determined to make his last stand in Kandahar, wept in frustration at the Taliban's rout, and then vanished into thin air as Hamid Karzai—who had nearly been vaporized by an errant 2,000-pound American bomb four days earlier—led in the liberators. One week later Secretary of State Colin Powell proudly announced, "We've destroyed al-Qaeda in Afghanistan and we've ended the role of Afghanistan as a haven for terrorist activity."[18]

TORA BORA

Not so fast. As Afghan leaders met in Bonn in December 2001 under UN auspices to sew up the nation's wounds and elect Hamid Karzai chairman of an interim authority that would eventually be converted into a post-Taliban government by a *loya jirga*, or national assembly, resistance in Afghanistan still flickered. Hamid Karzai was already backpedaling furiously to dissociate himself from Washington and the eleven-man U.S. Special Forces team (TEXAS 12) that had been protecting him since the start of the campaign. The Pashtun leader, who was uneasily sharing power with at least twenty regional warlords and already opening back-channel contacts to Mullah Omar ("he is a *mujahid* who has worked for the people of Afghanistan"), understood that his long-term future could only be secured in token opposition to the United States, not dutiful obedience. Afghans liked their leaders tough, and Karzai could not afford to look like Bush's poodle.[19] Twelve thousand Taliban had been killed in the short war, twice that number wounded, and another seven thousand were prisoners and likely to perish from the ministrations of United Front warlords like Rashid Dostum, who packed his Taliban captives into shipping containers and left them in the sun to suffocate, and gunned down the rest, flinging them into mass graves in the Afghan desert. "You have to remember that they were terrorists," one of Dostum's Uzbek fighters grinned.[20] About two thousand Taliban, Chechen and al-Qaeda fighters who survived and had nowhere to go withdrew to the old mujahideen tunnel complex high aloft in Tora Bora, the eastern Afghan snow mountains near Jalalabad, which backed onto the Khyber and Kurram tribal areas in Pakistan. Bin Laden had last been sighted in Jalalabad, twenty-five miles northwest of Tora Bora, on November 10, where he had addressed a crowd of a thousand local tribal leaders at the Saudi-funded Institute of Islamic Studies and passed out envelopes stuffed with cash to buy their support or neutrality. He had climbed into a Toyota Corolla after his talk and vanished into the mountains. Light U.S. forces and their Pashtun tribal allies now closed in to pin bin Laden and hundreds of al-Qaeda and Taliban troops in the cave and mountain complex. Delta Force made plans, as one operator put it, "to take the final shot at the trophy buck."[21]

Instead of taking the shot, General Tommy Franks let bin Laden escape into Pakistan. The whole Afghan war was fought against a backdrop of Pentagon theorizing and politics. Rumsfeld had committed the Bush administration to "military transformation," which held that the Cold War army of 1991—"Big Army" with its legions of soldiers, mechanics, technicians, truck drivers, medics and cooks—was too slow, ponderous and logistics-heavy, and the Powell Doctrine too constraining. Rumsfeld saw Operation Enduring Freedom as a golden opportunity to showcase transformation: the ability of stripped-down ground units leveraged with airpower to achieve great results at low cost. If Afghanistan could be done "on the cheap," it would serve as a warning to other terrorist sanctuaries like Yemen or Somalia as well as "rogue states" like Iran and North Korea. Franks, who conducted the war by video link from Florida—nine hours behind and nearly eight thousand miles away—had risen to the Centcom command by dint of his own brave record, but also because of his steady obedience to Rumsfeld. Franks shared Rumsfeld's faith in "transformation" and light fighting—and knew he needed to support the secretary's "force caps"—and thus made no effort to pull in American reinforcements, light or heavy, reassuring Rumsfeld that he would not even ask for them. The war continued to be waged by small parties of enlisted men and junior officers, no U.S. officer above the rank of lieutenant colonel having seen battle in Afghanistan. Franks, still following the war in Florida with AWACS and satellite intelligence and footage from Predator drones, was unperturbed: "There's nothing to be gained from blundering around those mountains and gorges with armor battalions chasing a lightly armed enemy." As Franks undoubtedly knew, no one was asking for armored battalions—just light infantry, field artillery and helicopters. When CIA officer Gary Berntsen pleaded with Franks to send eight hundred Army Rangers into the mountains to block the escape routes into Pakistan, Franks, who was determined to make do with the thirteen hundred American troops that he had scattered around seventeen areas of Afghanistan, stolidly refused to demand the extra troops from Rumsfeld.[22] Franks's refusals gratified Rumsfeld, who wanted all deployments to Afghanistan stopped to facilitate the looming invasion of Iraq, but it meant that there were not nearly enough U.S. boots on the ground. The peaks of Tora Bora soared fourteen thousand feet high and were notched with snow-covered paths and bunkers, and the Afghan boots, trembling with hunger from their

Ramadan fast, failed utterly. So did the Pakistani boots that were supposed to be posted behind Tora Bora. Marine general Mike DeLong, Franks's deputy Centcom commander, recalled a startling conversation with the vice chairman of Pakistan's general staff. When DeLong reminded the Pakistani general to string a cordon of forces along the border, the Pakistani demanded U.S. satellite imagery of Indian forces in Kashmir as a quid pro quo. DeLong naturally replied that he couldn't. The Pakistani then uttered a threat that was apparently enacted: "If you can't tell us, then we may have to pull our forces from the Afghan border."[23]

Like the Pakistani army, Hazrat Ali's Pashtun militia—2,500 strong and hired by the CIA at a cost of $1 million to capture bin Laden—took their American greenbacks and melted away. Some were al-Qaeda spies; others attempted to arbitrage U.S. bounties—one Delta operator noting that a warlord near Tora Bora was offering $1 million for bin Laden's head in the certainty that he could resell the head to the Americans for $25 million.[24] Those allies not in the business of espionage or bounty-hunting "would make an attempt at an attack and then go home and drink tea." The so-called Eastern Alliance Forces had signed on not to hunt bin Laden but simply to drive the Taliban from power and take it themselves. By December, the Taliban—who had lost their base in Kandahar to Hamid Karzai's Popalzai tribe—was finished as a government, and the "*shura* troops" who were supposed to be assaulting Tora Bora and pinching off the "ratlines" to Pakistan drifted away instead, usually enveloped in clouds of soothing hashish. The template that had worked in the north—Afghan Tajiks and Uzbeks bolstered by coalition special forces and airpower—did not fit in the south, where the Afghan Pashtuns had mixed feelings about the vanquished Taliban and fought amongst themselves, even on the slopes of Tora Bora: "This is what Afghanistan is; we kill each other," one of the infighting militia chiefs explained.[25] Some were simply paid off. Arab Afghans trapped in Tora Bora paid an average of $1,200 to be led to safety in Pakistan by their Afghan besiegers, who duly escorted 600 to 800 Arabs out of Tora Bora while Washington (and Tommy Franks) dumbly waited for the news of bin Laden's death or capture. The Afghan warlord who was given $5,000 and a CIA satellite phone to block the eastbound tracks from Tora Bora received a larger bribe from al-Qaeda, and let the Arabs pass through unmolested. One U.S. commando on the ground at Tora Bora recalled studying the faces of every prisoner escorted down the mountain by the Afghans, who were now assumed to be thoroughly crooked allies and jailers. "Hell, it wouldn't have surprised any of us if bin Laden and his cane were strolling along with them."[26] Although Franks knew bin Laden was trapped in Tora Bora—he intercepted Osama's satellite phone and radio calls, a rare breach of communications security by the al-Qaeda chief, who had stayed off the air since 1998—he didn't press the attack hard or fast enough. Hundreds of al-Qaeda leaders and fighters—bin Laden among them—slipped away to Pakistan. Rumsfeld, belatedly understanding that he ought to have sent more troops, seethed in Washington. "Jesus Christ, can't you get them moving any faster?" he scolded Franks. "Hell, I've been up in that altitude skiing before, and I'm sixty-nine years old."

But even if Franks moved faster, he wasn't going to bag the al-Qaeda "squirters," who were getting away. Neither he nor Rumsfeld had summoned sufficient numbers of American ground troops, Centcom foolishly assuming, as Franks's deputy put it, that it would be enough to "force al-Qaeda and the Taliban from the high ground into the caves, and then bomb the hell out of the caves."[27] On the low ground, Mullah Omar climbed back onto the motorcycle from which he had begun his career and vanished into thin air, somehow evading twenty U.S. Special Forces units, a militia of Afghans, and a flight of American gunships and F-16s. On the high ground, bin Laden burrowed into Tora Bora; the bombing went on for four weeks and every day Rumsfeld excitedly called Centcom: "Did we get him? Did we get him?"[28] The 5,000-pound bunker buster bombs—which had been developed to penetrate Saddam's underground command centers in 1991—nearly did. Bin Laden was wounded in the left shoulder and probably subjected to an emergency surgery by al-Zawahiri, who had been to medical school in Egypt before becoming a terrorist.[29] Still, Franks stolidly refused requests for reinforcements—they would take too long to arrive in country—and refused to loosen rules of engagement that were loose over Tora Bora but strict everywhere else. American surveillance planes detected scores of burning heat sources along the ratlines from Tora Bora to Pakistan—obviously al-Qaeda squirters trying to cook and warm up as they fled toward Pakistan—but Franks refused to bomb the campfires. "They might be shepherds," he worried. It was an absurd level of risk aversion: would armies of Afghan shepherds have been tending their flocks in deep snow at ten thousand feet?[30] When the squirters reached Pakistan, most of them dispersed to safety. Bin Laden and a few bodyguards picked their way out of Tora Bora on horseback and rode to safety in the Pakistani tribal area of Kurram. Naturally, no one arrived to arrest Osama. Pakistan's seven "tribal agencies" like Kurram were not called "ungoverned areas" for nothing, and President Bush had merely asked President Musharraf to "do his best to place troops along the Pakistani-Afghan border." Musharraf had done his best, apprehending no more than 150 Tora Bora fugitives while disingenuously asserting that Pakistani regular army units were not permitted in the tribal areas. The best he could do was locally raised "frontier militia," most of which was loyal not to Musharraf, but to the Taliban and al-Qaeda, who paid them.[31]

OPERATION ANACONDA

Tora Bora was a colossal embarrassment for the Bush administration. Of the estimated two thousand fighters in the cave complex, only fifty-four were captured, and none of them were senior leaders. Many were killed in the four-week bombing campaign, but hundreds "squirted" away to safety in Pakistan. A search of the caves and casualties confirmed that twenty-four of the thirty senior al-Qaeda leaders known to be in Afghanistan remained unaccounted for. While twenty al-Qaeda prisoners were flown hooded, drugged and shackled to the U.S. naval base at Guantanamo Bay for detention and interrogation, bin Laden materialized on Al Jazeera to taunt "the shortcomings and ineptitude of the American government and their fragile soldiers." Winter had descended, and Rumsfeld and Franks tardily authorized more U.S. troops to close the yawning gap between mission and assets. Rumsfeld chafed at the manpower demands of the newly inaugurated Hamid Karzai government. Lacking "huge entourages of armed men," the new president relied on a twenty-one-nation International Security Assistance Force (ISAF) to root himself in Afghanistan, which was torn as never before by provincial rivalries and a rising crime wave. Peacekeeping and policing were missions that Bush and Rumsfeld—who had sneered at Clinton's appetite for nation-building—had no intention of fulfilling. "We don't want Afghanistan to become a net importer of security assistance," the Bush administration explained. Even at this early date, all security exports were reserved for Iraq. President Bush gratefully subcontracted ISAF's forty-eight hundred troops to the British and Turks, even as Afghans were tittering over Washington's decision to subcontract the wet work at Tora Bora to Pashtun militias. "The Americans poured money into their pockets," the mayor of Jalalabad chuckled, "but it was not a real war; they were just doing these things for the money."[32] Rumsfeld's "all UW [unconventional warfare], all the time" approach had worked against novices like "American Taliban" John Walker Lindh or fainthearted Taliban peasant levies, who were killed, switched sides or shuffled home to their villages, but it would not work against fervent *talibs* or the al-Qaeda and Chechen diehards who yearned for martyrdom and had no homes to return to anyway. Theirs were in the Arab countries, Chechnya, Uzbekistan, China or Europe. If they went home, they would be turned away, thrown in jail or killed. By January 2002, a month after the Tora Bora fiasco, the wandering militants had begun to dribble back into Afghanistan to collect stragglers and make another stand, this time in the Shahikot, the "Place of Kings," a five-mile ridge of ten-thousand-foot peaks pocked with caves overlooking the Paktia Valley in eastern Afghanistan. Al-Zawahiri had just published *Knights under the Prophet's Banner*, which called for a global "coalition" of holy warriors—"half the road to victory is attained through unity"—to smite the United States.[33] U.S. signals intelligence picked up intensive Arabic telephone and radio communications bouncing around the mountains and valley, which certainly suggested the beginnings of al-Zawahiri's coalition.[34] Afghan locals reported al-Qaeda roadblocks and machine gun nests on all the roads through the Shahikot, as well as speeding al-Qaeda SUVs. Overhead imagery from Predator UAVs and satellites revealed al-Qaeda headquarters buildings. A Taliban defector divulged that there were six or seven hundred al-Qaeda militants entrenched in the Shahikot. They were armed with small arms, machine guns, mortars, sniper rifles and Stingers. Several hundred terrorists were a rich prize, but more "fire and maneuver" conventional forces would be needed to bag them.[35]

Incredibly, Franks and Rumsfeld still hesitated. Rumsfeld considered the Afghan conflict "basically over . . . the enemy was running away."[36] One U.S. officer in Afghanistan recalled continuous pressure from Franks and the Pentagon to prepare for a "general war" in Iraq as early as October 2002, even as thousands of al-Qaeda fighters and their leadership remained at large in Afghanistan. To save troops for Iraq and to reinforce the message of fast and light "transformation," Rumsfeld had imposed a "force cap" on Afghanistan.[37] Even with big al-Qaeda cadres roosting in the Shahikot, Franks would agree to admit no more than a stripped-down combat brigade of the 101st Airborne Division into Afghanistan. To avoid antagonizing Rumsfeld, Franks planned to send the air assault troops without their attack helicopters or artillery and ordered them to rely on air force and navy fixed-wing aircraft flying out of neighboring countries or carriers for their fire support.

Relying on airpower was fine in theory, but troublesome in practice. Whereas field artillery could suppress enemies with nonstop fire, air missions took time to request and approve and relied on fair weather, as well as their parent service's willingness to expend $37,000 GPS-guided smart bombs on close air support missions. "Racking and stacking" orbiting aircraft was no easy task; even harder when the planes failed to show, or simply failed to drop their bombs, as happened when the B-1 and B-52 assigned to hit the Shahikot in March 2002 knocked off instead and returned to their bases with bombs still in their bays. If a plane in the stack had "dumb" bombs on its pylons, not JDAMs, then they might be unusable if the fighting was "danger close." A single B-1 flying in from Saudi Arabia dropped a total of six bombs on the Shahikot massif—less than one bomb per kilometer. Air Force B-52s had pummeled Tora Bora with seven hundred thousand pounds of ordnance three months earlier, and the Americans and their Pashtun allies at Shahikot had expected similar exertions. The air force's AC-130H "Spectre" gunships—whose sensors and 105 mm howitzer could track men and vehicles from fifteen thousand feet in the sky—were never sent aloft in daylight hours or even bright moonlit nights, and when they did deploy over the Shahikot, the AC-130 tragically targeted a column of American Humvees and killed several GIs with "friendly fire."[38] Artillery rounds were cheaper and easier to put on target, and really the only recourse in view of al-Qaeda's choice of positions under overhanging cliffs in the Shahikot that couldn't be hit from the air. Still, Rumsfeld believed—not without reason—that "Big Army was sloppy with manpower" and knew that every U.S. infantryman and gunner needed to be backed by several headquarters and support elements, which invariably ballooned troop numbers alarmingly. Franks didn't dare oppose the secretary of defense in this matter, and indeed tended to anticipate Rumsfeld's objections by slashing troop numbers, lowering the force cap himself and ordering his field officers to fight with "reduced assets," a euphemism for fighting without adequate field artillery and attack helicopters. Indeed Operation Anaconda in March 2002 would be the first American infantry assault since 1942 conducted without artillery support.

General Franks ultimately decided to leave all but three of the 101st Airborne Division's nine battalions "on the shelf" in the United States for Iraq, which, by February 2002, was firmly fixed as Bush's main order of business. The 10th Mountain Division—whose two combat brigades had spent the 1990s shuttling through Somalia, Haiti, Bosnia and Kosovo—was sent instead to serve as the anvil and blocking force in Operation Anaconda. Franks's force cap permitted deployment of only pieces of the division. The Mountain staff joked grimly about the "adhocracy" that had been thrust on them. For the climactic action of the war, Rumsfeld deployed just two thousand troops—less than a brigade strength—scraped together from nine different countries, two army divisions, two special forces groups, a mishmash of aviation units, a handful of CIA operators and six hundred Pashtun militia under a warlord named Zia Lodin.

The Pashtuns displayed their usual avarice and casualty aversion. Many of them were there only because the Americans had offered $4,000 for every Arab prisoner taken. The assault on the al-Qaeda positions in the Shahikot was the highest-altitude battle ever fought by U.S. troops, who were stunned by the ferocity and courage of the defenders, many of whom were local Afghans, inflamed by the impolitic appointment of Zia Lodin to a theater not his own and by President Karzai's dispatch of Tajiks from Kabul to join in the assault. One American soldier, who had assumed that the defenders would fade away under U.S. attack, noted, "We could hear them laughing at us; we weren't used to it; they knew every crevice, every cubbyhole, every cave."[39] It was a desperate muddle on seventy-degree slopes, with friendly fire deaths, helicopter crashes, unnoticed minefields and a miraculous *French* air force rescue of U.S. Army Rangers trapped on a ridge in the Shahikot. Anaconda, like Tora Bora, ultimately failed to kill or capture the enemy. Hundreds of fighters fled down the old mujahideen routes to Pakistan. Franks's appallingly uninformative memoir judged the battle "an unqualified and absolute success," and the Pentagon consoled itself that, as at Tora Bora, it had chased al-Qaeda down another "trail of tears" to Pakistan. But that missed the point.[40] The senior emirs had got away *again*. Even offering a $25 million reward for bin Laden availed nothing here. Many Afghans didn't dare take the blood money, which would have subjected their extended families to vendetta killings for generations to come. Others had no idea how much $25 million would buy. American soldiers would ask Afghan villagers who had seen bin Laden, "Do you have any idea how much money $25 million is?" Typical replies went like this: "$25 million will buy 20 balloons for my children's birthdays, and enough food to feed my family for a year"—a goodly sum, but not enough to turn heads or hearts.[41] The only way to stop al-Qaeda was to *kill* it.

Rested and restored in Pakistan, the hundreds of al-Qaeda fighters who had escaped from the Shahikot—and the senior leaders among them—would live to fight another day. Musharraf's army and ISI slacked off in the tribal areas, and *Wall Street Journal* reporter Daniel Pearl was (conveniently) kidnapped in January and beheaded in February by Pakistani jihadis for his aggressive investigation into the operational links between ISI and the terrorists. A Delta Force officer engaged at the Shahikot ruefully compared Pakistan to Cambodia in the Vietnam War, an inviolable place for Americans, where their enemies could freely move, plan and launch attacks. All of Bush's "with us or against us" rhetoric and Rich Armitage's browbeating of the ISI director after 9/11 had apparently made little real impression on Musharraf and his lieutenants. On March 6, an Australian SAS team covering a streambed that formed a natural escape route off the Shahikot observed a dozen heavily armed bodyguards in black ski masks conducting an "older man with a cane"—probably al-Zawahiri—south toward Pakistan. The Aussies called in an A-10 air strike, but the group split up before the bombs hit and the senior emir escaped.[42] It was a fitting end to an operation that had been mistimed and miscalculated from the beginning.

The U.S. military had decapitated Afghanistan and left it a mess, as receptive to drugs and terrorists after the invasion as before. "Who will run the country?" Bush had asked on the eve of his invasion. No one had even the foggiest idea. Although the Northern Alliance had a clear interest in removing the Taliban, it was a largely Tajik organization pitted against the largely Pashtun Taliban. Even "pro-American" Afghan militias—hopefully labeled AMFs ("Afghan Military Forces")—had proven balky. They often switched sides for a bribe or to "do their Muslim duty." Zia Lodin's militia in Operation Anaconda had simply refused to fight, discouraged by the fury of the al-Qaeda resistance and the absence of American artillery and close air support. U.S. forces fighting in Afghanistan had been convinced of the utter unaccountability and fractiousness of the place. Even had Musharraf and the ISI chiefs cooperated with Washington, it's unlikely that Islamabad would have regained control of events in Afghanistan. Al-Qaeda and the Taliban have found willing hosts among the Kashmiri terrorist groups, which have their own camps and networks in the tribal areas and which the Pakistani government has no interest in eradicating.[43] Then there is the influence of the "Quetta mafia" and other Pakistani organized crime syndicates—all infused with ISI know-how—who reap huge profits from tax-free smuggling through Afghanistan. With the ability to ship everything from flat-panel televisions and laptops to wheat, oil, guns, child prostitutes and heroin across Afghan roads to Russia, Iran, the Gulf emirates and Pakistan, without permits or customs duties, Pakistani mafias increasingly directed not only the Taliban government, but even Taliban offensives, pushing them, in the 1990s, into places like Herat and Kabul to get more roads under their control.[44] Postwar civil war was all but inevitable, particularly since the best U.S. clients were in the north of the country and the vanquished Taliban (and al-Qaeda) were in the south, where they were still discreetly succored by the Pakistanis, all the more so in defeat.

Bush Punts

Hamid Karzai, a Pashtun of a small tribe plucked from Pakistani exile in the fall of 2001, was never a serious player, even with massive American backing and a CIA-supplied satellite phone strapped to his hip. Added to the puzzle were large Chechen and Uzbek pieces—fundamentalist guerrillas who had no interest in a stable Afghanistan. Secretary of Defense Rumsfeld didn't give the matter much thought. "I don't think that leaves us with a responsibility to try to figure out what kind of a government that country ought to have," Rumsfeld ventured. Rice had famously poured scorn on the Clinton-Gore administration during the 2000 campaign for using "the 82nd Airborne to escort kids to kindergarten." She was unlikely to push the "All-Americans" into the breach now. Out of answers, Bush limply fell back on the UN in October 2001: "It would be a useful function for the United Nations to take over the so-called 'nation building'—I would call it the stabilization of a future government—after our military mission is complete." Bush dispatched Zalmay Khalilzad as his special envoy to Afghanistan. Khalilzad was an Afghan-American whose distinguished career had included a stint in the 1990s as liaison between Unocal and the Taliban government. In that capacity, he may have worked with Karzai—rumored to have been a Unocal consultant—and now the two men sat down to lift Clinton-era sanctions, unfreeze Afghan assets in U.S. banks and generally signal that all was well with the new nation, when in fact everything was wrong. The CIA's latest grim estimates warned of "violent chaos" around the corner. Hundreds of thousands of refugees, who had fled into neighboring countries during the war, were now flooding back at a rate of about fifty thousand a week. Airports and other infrastructure were in ruins. Farmers were replanting with poppy to rekindle heroin production. An estimated 175,000 armed men were roaming the country in search of work and plunder; skirmishes were already erupting between rival warlords in important towns like Herat and Mazar; the Russians, Iranians, Indians and Pakistanis were stretching their hands back into Afghanistan to mold the postwar landscape; international donors had pledged (but not actually paid) just $4.5 billion for reconstruction—less than a third of the sum requested by UN secretary general Kofi Annan; and President Karzai's own citizens joked that he was just the mayor of an ISAF-policed Kabul, nothing more.[45]

Before the invasion, George Tenet and Cofer Black had tried to warn Bush and

Cheney that "the war would be driven by intelligence, not the pure projection of power. The challenge wasn't to defeat the enemy militarily. The challenge was to *find* the enemy."[46] As he fled undetected down a ratline into Pakistan in December 2001, Osama bin Laden scribbled his last will and testament: the jihad against America was not going well, but there was hope. "Despite the setbacks that God has inflicted upon us, these painful blows will mark the beginning of the wiping out of America and the infidel West after the passing of tens of years, God willing." Al-Zawahiri returned to Khost in March 2002, to rally the remnants of al-Qaeda. Pinned against the walls of the Shahikot Valley and beaten again, al-Zawahiri escaped again. As he crossed into the Pakistani tribal areas with his masked bodyguards, the unmasked al-Zawahiri called to the Pakistani militia commander, who had a wanted poster with al-Zawahiri's picture on it but no telephone: "May God bless you and keep you from the enemies of Islam. Try not to tell them where we came from, and where we are going."[47]

CHAPTER 17

·⚔·

INTO IRAQ

BIN LADEN'S ESCAPE INTO PAKISTAN with the senior emirs like al-Zawahiri dampened whatever exhilaration President Bush felt after the relatively easy defeat of the Taliban. Although bin Laden had not succeeded in impaling the U.S. military on the jagged peaks of Afghanistan—"we want to bring the Americans to fight us on Muslim land"—that was in part because Bush and Rumsfeld had simply not sent the U.S. military to Afghanistan in significant numbers. They had sent slices of units and reserved the bulk of their forces for Iraq, which had permitted bin Laden, al-Zawahiri, Mullah Omar and hundreds of other terrorist leaders to escape from Kunduz, Kandahar, Jalalabad, Tora Bora and the Shahikot into Pakistan.[1]

America celebrated its nearly bloodless triumph in Afghanistan, and few outside Washington intelligence circles grasped just how incomplete that triumph had been. For Afghans, as one historian put it, the weak Karzai government was not the gallant little democracy flourished by President Bush, but "truly the last stanza in Afghanistan's ballad of despair."[2] Bush had declared a "war on terror," yet Osama bin Laden, his al-Qaeda leadership and their Taliban hosts remained at large, presumably free to prepare new attacks. Al-Qaeda recruitment surged after the 9/11 attack. Mothers pledged children to "Sheikh bin Laden's struggle," and al-Zawahiri—noting the viral spread of al-Qaeda propaganda on the Internet—observed that al-Qaeda no longer needed a territorial base (like Afghanistan) or a cult of personality (like bin Laden).

It was now a global, Web-directed movement that would generate waves of violence with or without Afghan training or Osama's blessing. Eighty percent of al-Qaeda's infrastructure and military organization had been destroyed by Operation Enduring Freedom, and the leadership had been chased into exile, but al-Qaeda survived in fifty to sixty countries and its attacks resumed in 2002, kicked off by the bombing of a synagogue in Djerba, Tunisia, and the demolition of a nightclub packed with Australians in Bali, Indonesia. Even in defeat, al-Qaeda was roaring back.[3] But President Bush was remarkably callow. "This is a big world," he confessed, "and I've got a lot to learn." He had chosen an experienced team of "foreign policy stars"—men like Vice President Dick Cheney, Secretary of State Colin Powell and Secretary of Defense Donald Rumsfeld—precisely because he was so inexperienced, never having been farther from the United States than Canada. "I may not be able to tell you exactly the nuance," he told the *New York Times* before his election, "but I'll ask Condi Rice or I'll ask Paul Wolfowitz or I'll ask Dick Cheney. I'll ask the people who've had experience."[4]

The "people who had experience" also had an agenda that undercut what Bush was now calling the "global war on terrorism." Cheney accepted the vice president's job on the condition that he be given real authority. When former vice president Dan Quayle commiserated with Cheney and warned him that the job was all about "funerals and fund-raising," Cheney tartly replied: "I have a different understanding with the president." Cheney would be given access "to every table and every meeting," as well as all of Bush's memos and e-mails.[5] It was an unprecedented expansion of vice presidential authority. When Cheney visited Bahrain on the eve of the Iraq War, a government spokesman introduced him as America's "deputy president." Cheney built a staff to reflect that power and influence. His chief of staff, I. Lewis "Scooter" Libby, doubled as Cheney's national security adviser and as an assistant to the president as well, which made him National Security Adviser Condoleezza Rice's bureaucratic equal. Cheney and Libby convened a vice presidential national security staff that was four times bigger than Al Gore's had been, and larger even than John F. Kennedy's entire NSC, which had grappled with crises in Berlin, Cuba and Vietnam.[6]

9/11 changed President Bush. His presidency had been fading until the al-Qaeda attack; it revived under the terrible shock. His popularity rating leaped from 55 to 92 percent, which fostered a messianic self-certainty in the president. "I am here for a reason," Bush told his political aide Karl Rove. "I will seize the opportunity to achieve big goals."[7] He was not talking about prescription drug benefits or school lunches; he was talking about a gestating "Bush Doctrine," to abolish terrorism and spread freedom. To mourners at the National Cathedral on September 14, 2001, he said, "Our responsibility to history is clear—to answer these attacks and rid the world of evil."[8]

Even as the U.S. military hunted for bin Laden, it shifted its focus to Iraq. The shift had been under way for several months. Bush's treasury secretary, Paul O'Neill, recalled that at President Bush's first National Security Council meeting in January 2001, finding a reason for a war to remove Saddam Hussein had been the principal order of business.[9] There was some superficial logic in the shift. Having rained chemical weapons on the Iranians as well as the Iraqi Kurds and Shiites during his two wars, Saddam was assumed to have a burgeoning weapons of mass destruction (WMD) program, and, in the panic that followed 9/11, analysts and policy makers, to say nothing of the general public, insisted that al-Qaeda and other terrorist groups must *not* be permitted to get their hands on chemical, biological or nuclear weapons. The Big Wedding attack on New York and Washington had proved that al-Qaeda would stop at nothing. It had to be assumed that bin Laden and al-Zawahiri would try to get WMD from *any* source to annihilate Western targets and transfix the Muslim *umma*. Osama had declared in 1998—just after Pakistan exploded its first nuclear weapon—that "acquiring weapons for the defense of Muslims is a religious duty."

The American capture of al-Qaeda safe houses, laptops and files in Afghanistan in 2001–2 had revealed that Ayman al-Zawahiri was actually running an intensive, structured WMD acquisition program (with separate "CEOs" for chemical, biological and nuclear programs) to inflict mass casualties in the United States.[10] Bin Laden had been trying to establish a working relationship with Pakistani scientist Abdul Qadeer Khan's rogue network of nuclear suppliers for years. For his part, al-Zawahiri was cultivating sympathetic engineers in the Pakistani Institute of Nuclear Science and Technology as well as a former director of Pakistan's Atomic Energy Commission, who had written a profoundly disturbing book titled *Doomsday and Life after Death: The Ultimate Faith of the Universe as Seen by the Holy Koran*. The al-Qaeda number two was cobbling together a bomb, piece by piece, and trying to purchase the fissile material (from the Pakistanis or the Russians) that could be packed into a simple firing system.

While Bush and Cheney embraced Pakistani president Pervez Musharraf and praised him for his (flaccid) efforts in the war on terrorism, a strange dance of death was playing out in Pakistan. There President Musharraf's rivals—like General

Hamid Gul, a former director of the ISI—were entering into alliances with al-Qaeda and the Taliban to undermine Musharraf's relationship with the infidels in Washington. A man like Gul had key contacts and protégés seeded throughout the nuclear development chain and could offer them to bin Laden.[11] Musharraf himself was utterly unreliable in this matter, or any other. To placate Bush, he arrested two thousand Islamist militants in 2002, and then quietly released them. He never moved against the twenty-five thousand Pakistani madrassas that were incubators of terrorism.[12] No wonder Rice told the *New York Times* after 9/11 that the White House had become paranoid. The stream of threat warnings—many issuing from Pakistan—"had a powerful effect on Bush's state of mind and her own. She felt she was constantly on edge, in a state of paranoia, but rational paranoia, as even old threats—and Iraq would soon be one—took on new meaning."[13] It didn't take long for the administration to infer an al-Qaeda–Iraq connection. "Guys in caves can't get WMD" went the mantra, despite the disturbing evidence from Afghanistan and Pakistan. They'd have to get it from Saddam Hussein.

THE BUSH DOCTRINE

The Bush Doctrine was published in September 2002, but its precepts were laid out in Afghanistan. The doctrine held that Washington would use its peerless military power to topple totalitarian regimes that menaced the United States, preempt terrorist attacks and spread democracy. The Bush Doctrine was precisely what neoconservatives like Paul Wolfowitz and Richard Perle had been seeking ever since the Soviet collapse. The neocons had emerged in the wake of Vietnam, détente and Watergate; erstwhile liberals, they embraced conservatism and counterfactual argument to make the case that the Vietnam War should have been intensified (not ended) to uproot communism, that détente was naive self-mutilation that merely strengthened and even legitimized the Soviets, and that Watergate was a hysterical overreaction to routine presidential skullduggery that dangerously limited executive power. In the Bush 43 administration, Rumsfeld and Cheney brought in cadres of neocons like Perle and Wolfowitz, who sprinkled their acolytes around the White House and the Pentagon and pressed the argument that—in a "unipolar" world with no "peer competitors"—the United States alone possessed the raw strength to oust dangerous or merely unappetizing regimes. Whereas Clinton had used economics to expand U.S. power—a "strong dollar," corporate globalization, free markets and the IMF—Bush shifted the focus to the military.[14] America would *use* its raw power—glimpsed in the Persian Gulf War, Serbia and Afghanistan—to redraw the map in the name of Bush's "freedom agenda." Bush's neocons were idealistic and grandiose—they called themselves "hard Wilsonians"—and Saddam Hussein's Iraq bulked large as their first great project.

Afghanistan had proved how *easy* it was to effect regime change. "For a hundred years of war," Bush declared, "military power was used to end a regime by breaking a nation. Today, we have the greater power to free a nation by breaking a dangerous and aggressive regime." That statement encapsulated neocon and Bush Doctrine thought on how the world *ought* to be run. Precise, devastating American weapons could be used either to bluff or bomb hostile regimes out of office. In his regular conversations with Bush, *Washington Post* editor Bob Woodward was struck by the soaring naiveté of the president, who assured Woodward—with a straight face—that "freedom is God's gift to everybody in the world" and that the Bush White House had "a duty to free people."[15] On November 21, 2001—while major combat operations were still going on in Afghanistan—Bush ordered Rumsfeld to make plans to invade and free the *Iraqis*.[16] Whereas Afghanistan was a scrubby country of parched mountains and illiterate peasants, Iraq was the Fertile Crescent, the oil-producing hub of the Middle East where 90 percent of the people could read and there was a large, affluent professional class.

IRAQI OIL

Iraq also had oil, and lots of it. If the president was distracted by his rather credulous "freedom agenda," the rest of his oil-soaked administration had more practical concerns. Bush himself had tried and failed in a career as an oilman before becoming governor of Texas, and Vice President Cheney had been CEO of Halliburton—the world's leading oil services company—in the interregnum between the Bush 41 and Bush 43 administrations. National Security Adviser Condi Rice had served on the board of Chevron; Commerce Secretary Don Evans had chaired a big oil company in Midland, Texas; and one of Bush's biggest backers was Houston-based Enron Corporation, which notoriously gamed and manipulated the California electricity crisis of 2000–2001. Those Enron-induced California blackouts prompted Bush to

appoint Cheney chair of a highly secretive Energy Task Force in 2001, which culmi-
nated in Cheney's National Energy Policy Report.

Dick Cheney's report fleshed out concerns he had aired publicly as CEO of Halliburton, namely that by 2010 the world was going to need "an additional 50 million
barrels [of oil] a day"—six times Saudi Arabia's daily production—yet did not have
six obliging Saudi Arabias standing by to supply it. Instead, the world was stuck
with producers like Iraq, which were government-run businesses that, to put it
mildly, "did not always have America's interests at heart." Iraq had particularly
impressive quantities of oil, which were indicated on the few documents that
Cheney's Task Force and its Big Oil consultants did release to the public. Iraq's
actual production before the U.S. invasion was 3 million barrels a day—a third of
Saudi Arabia's—but with 300 billion barrels of reserves, Iraq had the second largest
reserves in the world after the desert kingdom. And Iraq's oil was cheap to extract,
refine and export. Whereas an Iraqi barrel of oil costs just $1 or $1.50 to produce,
barrels from Malaysia or Oman cost $5, Russian and Mexican barrels cost $6 to
$8, and American and Canadian barrels—pulled from deep wells and shallow
reservoirs—cost $20.[17] Because of price and supply, Iraqi oil had to be at the center
of American energy policy and security for the twenty-first century; one did not
have to adduce a conspiracy of any kind to recognize that fact. Implanting American power and values in Iraq would not only "transform" the Middle East along the
lines of the Bush Doctrine, it would pipe new sources of oil into an energy-hungry
global economy. Cheney's classified report is assumed to have tracked an earlier
one by the James A. Baker Institute at Rice University, which had warned that
Saddam Hussein remained "a destabilizing influence to the flow of oil to international markets from the Middle East." Baker's institute enjoined the Bush 43
administration to lead "in the formation of new rules of the game" in the Middle
East, to "restate goals with respect to Iraq policy" and—a hint of what the new rules
and goals would be—to include "representation from the Department of Defense"
in Cheney's Energy Task Force.[18]

"IRAQ IS NOT AFGHANISTAN"

"Iraq is not Afghanistan," Bush's Future of Iraq Project analysts reminded him
in November 2002. Whereas Afghanistan could be rudely dumped—or so they

thought—once the Taliban and bin Laden were driven from power, the United States needed to "make a commitment to Iraq like Japan and Germany." Just as Tokyo and Bonn had helped prop up the West during the Cold War, a compliant regime in Baghdad would oil the world economy and become a sturdy American sentinel in what policy makers were calling the "long war" against terrorism.[19] Iraq would conclusively and satisfyingly *prove* Bush's arguable contention that there was a hard link between his "universal values"—democracy, freedom, human rights—and global security.

Iraq's importance as a country, an economic asset and an *idea* explained why it came to obsess the Pentagon civilians and the neocons in the White House even as the unfinished war in Afghanistan raged. "Do we wait for Saddam, or do we take preemptive action?" Richard Perle, the neocon maestro on Rumsfeld's Defense Policy Board, asked in November 2001.[20] Secretary of State Colin Powell told a House Committee in February 2002 that Bush was weighing "the most serious set of options one might imagine" to force "regime change" in Baghdad. Powell told the chief UN weapons inspector, Hans Blix, that there were two possible approaches to Iraq: multilateral and bilateral, and that the United States was keeping both options open. Discussing Iraq with Blix in January 2002, Condi Rice told him that the war in Afghanistan had had a useful "demonstrative effect." The same medicine could be administered to Saddam if he didn't fall into line. Vice President Cheney called UN inspections in Iraq a waste of time; they would merely provide "false comfort that Saddam was somehow 'back in his box.'" Neocons like Perle viewed Iraq as just the first shot in an annihilating campaign against anti-Western Islamic obscurantism: next on the list would be Iran, and then (startlingly) Saudi Arabia, which was the paymaster of so much Islamist terrorism.[21]

General Tommy Franks, who had led the underresourced invasion of Afghanistan in 2001, remained Centcom commander in February 2002, when he met with Florida senator Bob Graham, the chairman of the Senate Intelligence Committee. Graham listened as Franks "laid out a very precise strategy for fighting the war on terror. First," Franks said, "we should win the war in Afghanistan. Second, move to Somalia, which [is] anarchy but with a substantial number of al-Qaeda cells; then to Yemen." Franks concluded by urging extreme caution on Iraq. Like his mentor, Marine general Anthony Zinni, who had yielded the Centcom command to Franks in 2000, Franks believed that Iraq had been largely broken by weapons inspections and sanctions and reduced to a "second-rate power." It made no sense to pick a fight with Saddam. "We should be very careful about Iraq because our intelligence

[is] so weak and because we [don't] know what we're getting into."[22] Other officers were less circumspect: "Why Iraq? Why now?" Marine general Gregory Newbold asked. The fight needed to be in Afghanistan. Newbold recalled that the question on most officers' lips was, "What the hell are we doing? Why are we diverting assets and attention?" Newbold retired in frustration, calling himself "a round peg in a square hole."[23] Franks, a square peg in a square hole, never dared express doubts like Newbold's to the White House directly, where all caution had been thrown to the wind anyway. When Powell sent Richard Haass in July 2002 to warn Condi Rice that an Iraq invasion would divert attention from the hunt for bin Laden and the war on terrorism, she replied, "Don't waste your breath; that decision's been made."[24]

PROGRESS IN THE "GLOBAL WAR ON TERRORISM"

The irresponsibility of that decision became clearer with time, but already in 2002 the CIA and other experts were advising Bush to keep his focus on al-Qaeda, not Iraq. Although bin Laden had escaped because of the blundering around Tora Bora, covert, focused American action was beginning to roll up his organization and hit what CIA director George Tenet called "the next tier of leadership, the facilitators, planners, financiers, document forgers, and the like." The CIA was focused on blocking the next attack by taking down the most capable al-Qaeda cadres and "forcing them to move less capable individuals into positions of leadership."[25] Priority one was the planners in charge of operations against the United States. That meant Khalid Sheikh Muhammed (KSM)—coordinator of the 9/11 Big Wedding—who was captured in Rawalpindi, Pakistan, in March 2002; his place was taken by Abu Faraj al-Libi, who would be captured in Pakistan in May 2005. He, in turn, would be replaced by Hamza Rabi'a, who would be killed in Pakistan's North Waziristan Province in November 2005.

Well before the Iraq invasion, American intelligence and its foreign allies were taking the fight to the enemy. Al-Qaeda's number three man, Muhammed Atef, was killed by an American air strike in Afghanistan in November 2001, and the Pakistani police, responding to American tips, captured Abu Zubaydah in Pakistan's third largest city, Faisalabad, in March 2002. KSM and Zubaydah were the first HVDs, or "high-value detainees," taken into American custody. Pakistan's cooperation revealed the complexity of the Washington-Islamabad relationship. Musharraf recognized the need to help Washington—to remain in Bush's pay and good graces—but also continued his unhelpful support for Taliban and al-Qaeda cadres in the tribal areas. He gave with one hand and struck with the other. Still, Tenet was hopeful, observing that "each success cascaded into others." KSM gave up Majid Khan, a senior al-Qaeda financial operator who in turn coughed up the clues that led to the arrest of Hambali and Rusman Gunawan, the leading al-Qaeda figures in Southeast Asia. They disclosed in interrogations that al-Qaeda and its East Asian affiliate, Jemaah Islamiyah, were using bases in the Pacific Rim to expand their reach and sanctuaries and to groom non-Arabs (who would excite less suspicion) for attacks on the United States and other Western targets. Zubaydah divulged the whereabouts of Ramzi bin al-Sibh—the dispatcher who passed messages between al-Qaeda central and the 9/11 hijackers—who was netted in Karachi in September 2002. The HVDs provided what Tenet called "an exhaustive menu and knowledge about how al-Qaeda thinks, operates and trains its members to conduct operations." The CIA foiled at least twenty plots on U.S. infrastructure targets—nuclear power plants, dams, bridges, reservoirs, tunnels and subways—thanks to information gleaned from the first HVDs.

Khalid Sheikh Muhammed not only ratted out minions, he coughed up al-Qaeda's war aims as well. KSM divulged that bin Laden's "highest priority is to spur a revolution in Saudi Arabia and overthrow the government." In May 2003—while U.S. forces were battling in Iraq—al-Qaeda terrorists used the diversion to strike in Saudi Arabia, killing thirty-five (including ten Americans) and wounding two hundred. The CIA briefed the Saudis on the extent of the threat. "Your Royal Highness," Tenet told Crown Prince Abdullah, "your family and the end of its rule is the objective now. Al-Qaeda operatives are prepared to assassinate members of the royal family and to attack key economic targets." Belatedly, the Saudis got serious about al-Qaeda. Al-Zawahiri had been trying to buy stolen Russian nuclear devices in Saudi Arabia, which would either be smuggled to the United States for detonation or exploded in the middle of the kingdom's oil patch, devastating the Saudi and world economies. Al-Qaeda emissaries were trying to persuade Saudi clerics to write fatwas justifying—as one al-Qaeda treatise put it—"the legal use of weapons of mass destruction against infidels." This was *takfir* on a grand scale, and the Saudis struck back furiously; they arrested, imprisoned or killed the senior al-Qaeda plotters in the kingdom. One of their takedowns nabbed Abu Bakr al-Azdi, who confirmed that plots against the United States were being hatched inside the kingdom. Crown Prince Abdullah also intervened with the Wahhabi clergy, pressing them to reject fatwas that condoned terrorism and fund-raising for terrorists. "Patience," Tenet wrote, "had paid off, and we now had the beginnings of a . . . sustained counterterrorism partnership."[26]

PREPARING THE "BAY OF GOATS"

Although ordered in 1991 by the UN Security Council to scrap his ballistic missile and WMD programs, Saddam Hussein had never fully complied. Until 1998, Richard Butler's United Nations Special Commission (UNSCOM) monitored the destruction of Iraqi missiles and WMD and hunted for hidden material and facilities. The inspectors left in December 1998 on the eve of Operation Desert Fox, when President Clinton launched a four-day bombing offensive against illicit Iraqi sites, and then did not return until 2002. Although the American-imposed no-fly zones in northern and southern Iraq remained intact, Saddam's WMD program slipped back into darkness, a situation that struck most Americans as intolerable after the atrocity of 9/11.

Once the inspectors were gone, Saddam tried to trade their right of return for a removal of all sanctions against Iraq, an idea supported by the French and Russians, but not by the Americans.[27] President George W. Bush took a hard line with Saddam from the outset. Not content merely to patrol the no-fly zones, he ordered bombing against Iraqi targets to punish Iraqi antiaircraft fire, to probe Iraqi defenses and to soften up Saddam's military. Operation Southern Focus began in 2002, and the crescendo of bombing was remarkable: no bombs were dropped in March 2002, eight tons were dropped in May, fourteen tons in August and fifty-five tons in September. Southern Focus, pitched to the U.S. public and the international community as a mere *response* to Iraqi pugnacity, was actually an aggressive plan to goad the Iraqis into pugnacious acts—missile shots, antiaircraft fire—that would justify American attacks on the fiber-optic, radar and other infrastructure that needed to be eliminated before a U.S. invasion of Iraq.[28] George Tenet, who straddled the outgoing Clinton and incoming Bush administrations as director of central intelligence, remarked that the new guys "carried a heavy load of aversion to *any* policy the Clinton administration had favored." Brute force and "doing things differently seemed almost an imperative with them."[29] Many of them—including Cheney, Rumsfeld, Wolfowitz and Scooter Libby—had signed on to the Project for the New American

Century in 1998, enjoining then President Clinton to cease his "course of weakness and drift" and get serious about, among other items, "regime change in Iraq." They even had a nickname for themselves—"Vulcans." They were fire-breathing gods of vengeance who would take no prisoners in their struggle against tyranny, terrorism and hand-wringing appeasement. Whereas Clinton had steered clear of what his national security adviser Tony Lake called "wars of murderous naiveté," Bush's Vulcans would steer right into them.[30]

Bush ramped up support for Iraqi dissidents and exile groups. The CIA had been running a covert program since 1991, but first Clinton—with passage of the Iraq Liberation Act in 1998—and then Bush embraced Ahmed Chalabi's Iraqi National Congress (INC) and began to view Chalabi as a successor to Saddam Hussein. Chalabi, who descended from a rich, aristocratic Baghdad family, ought to have filled the Bush administration with alarm, not hope. More appealing than Saddam perhaps, Chalabi had little connection or practical experience with Iraq. His family had fled to Lebanon after the Iraqi military coup in 1958—when the Chalabis were reviled as "plutocrats"—and Ahmed had spent his life in exile, studying at MIT and eventually settling down to a life abroad as a banker (a crooked one) and an exile politician. Chalabi's plan for taking power from Saddam was hopelessly naive. Other exile organizations, like Iyad Allawi's Amman-based (and CIA-funded) Iraq National Accord (INA), aimed to rope in frustrated Baathists and ex-Baathists (like Allawi) and topple Saddam from within by means of a "zipless coup." Chalabi—who had left Iraq when he was a teenager—had different plans. He would raise the Kurds of Iraq (15 percent of the population) against the Baathists, and then march south to Baghdad, whipping up a "popular uprising" as he went, like Napoleon returning from Elba. All he needed, Chalabi assured Pentagon planners at a meeting in Washington on September 19, 2001, was U.S. airpower. He and his "insurgents" would do the rest.[31] Chalabi and his mentors—Cheney, Rumsfeld, Perle, Wolfowitz and the other neocons—were daydreaming. It didn't take hindsight to establish that. When Wolfowitz first proposed the invasion of Iraq by Chalabi's exiles, former Centcom commander Zinni scoffed that it would be a "Bay of Goats," as bad as Kennedy's Bay of Pigs, and maybe worse. "This is going to generate another one of our defeats there, where we get a bunch of people slaughtered."[32]

Iraq's refusal to let UNSCOM back into the country after Clinton's 1998 air strikes gave Bush a useful lever to increase pressure on Saddam and lent credence to American accusations that Saddam was hiding a formidable WMD program. The confluence of Saddam's defiance of UN Security Council resolutions—to disarm in

1991 and to permit the return of UN inspectors in 2002—and bin Laden's rise to infamy led Bush to weigh an invasion of Iraq to discover and destroy the WMD and missile programs and to remove Saddam Hussein, whom Bush linked to bin Laden and placed at the center of his Iran–Iraq–North Korea "axis of evil" in January 2002.

"HITCHE IRAQ TO THE WAGON OF TERROR"

The problem was that powerful, knowledgeable constituencies in Washington detested the power and influence of Saddam and bin Laden, but detected no *connection* between them. CIA analysts did detect occasional contacts between Iraqis and al-Qaeda on matters like chemical and biological weapons as well as training or sanctuary in northeastern Iraq if Afghanistan was lost, but they were always tentative and never pressed home with any conviction. In his meetings with Bush, CIA director George Tenet insisted that there was no linkage between Saddam and 9/11 or Saddam and bin Laden. They represented quite different threats, and indeed were far more likely to be adversaries than allies. The Bush administration's efforts "to hitch Iraq to the wagon of terror" struck advisers like Tenet and Powell as clumsy and unconvincing.[33] Worse, the Bush administration was committing a basic strategic error in its facile overlapping of the al-Qaeda and Iraqi threats. Iraq was a sovereign secular state that was effectively deterred by sanctions, well-armed neighbors and American military overwatch. Al-Qaeda was a shadowy "non-state actor" that was undeterrable because of its vicious, nihilistic philosophy. There was no point in expending precious resources on a deterred and decayed Iraq when the focus so obviously needed to be on al-Qaeda and its various havens, one of which was *not* Iraq.[34]

Not liking the reasonable answers he was getting from Tenet and Powell, Bush turned intelligence on Iraq over to Vice President Cheney and Secretary of Defense Rumsfeld. Cheney, Rumsfeld and Deputy Secretary of Defense Paul Wolfowitz established an Office of Special Plans (OSP) in the Pentagon whose brief was to plan for war with Saddam but also—through OSP's Policy Counterterrorism Evaluation Group—to interpret Iraqi intelligence more "aggressively," to, as Tenet put it, "push the data farther than it deserved" and "make command linkages" where they were murky or nonexistent.[35] If a case for war with Iraq was lacking, President Bush was determined to manufacture one. Vice President Cheney rejected standard CIA analytic tradecraft and operated instead according to a doctrine he dubbed the "1 percent solution"—as in, "if there's a 1 percent chance that Pakistani scientists are helping al-Qaeda build or develop a nuclear weapon, we have to treat it as a *certainty* in our response." That was also Rumsfeld's view; he had chaired a commission on missile defense in the 1990s that concluded that the United States had to reckon "more boldly and imaginatively in projecting missile development in countries like Iran and North Korea."[36] Countermeasures needed to be taken based on what *might* occur, as opposed to what actually *was* occurring.

Condi Rice echoed Cheney, as had become her habit: "Intelligence estimates almost always underestimate capabilities. They rarely overestimate capabilities."[37] What Rice failed to grasp was just how *weird* Cheney's shop had become. Staffed with neocon eccentrics like the Swiss-born David Wurmser—who critics at the time compared with Russell Crowe sketching his mad conspiracy theories across the wall of a shed in *A Beautiful Mind*—the vice president's notorious spider charts wove unrelated threats together to give the appearance of an all-encompassing al-Qaeda–Iraqi plot.[38] Wolfowitz, who had no sense of measure in this matter, had enjoined President Bush in meetings after the 9/11 attacks to include Iraq in any U.S. military response. He had approvingly blurbed a silly book by one of the more venomous neocons in 2000, which had argued that the World Trade Center bombing of 1993 had been instigated by Saddam Hussein as part of his "unfinished war against America."[39] *Washington Post* senior Pentagon correspondent Tom Ricks remarked the oddity of Wolfowitz's prominence in the Iraq War. "It is unusual for so much attention to be focused on a second-level official of subcabinet rank." But Wolfowitz was a workhorse, was devoutly pro-Israel (the *Jerusalem Post* had named Wolfowitz its "Man of the Year" in 2003) and, as Boston University professor Andrew Bacevich noted, "married an extraordinary certainty in the righteousness of American actions to an extraordinary confidence in the efficacy of American arms," which endeared him to Bush, Cheney and Rumsfeld.[40] In 1992, Wolfowitz had drafted a forty-six-page Defense Planning Guidance for Bush 41 that had proven so controversial—it called for unilateral American military dominance in the post–Cold War world—that it had to be rewritten in a more tactful vein by then Secretary of Defense Cheney before its official release.[41]

Bush 43 had none of the qualms of his father. Whereas Bush 41 had been visibly uncomfortable with neocons—formerly left-wing ideologues who viewed crusading, change-the-world *Republican* activism as their best chance to make an impact—Bush

43, encouraged by Cheney and Rumsfeld, embraced them. The new president was impressed by the confident promises of neocons like Perle and Wolfowitz that they could use American military dominance to "drain the swamp" of terrorist groups and states, shatter the amoral "stability" that merely stabilized dictators like Saddam or the Iranian ayatollahs and rebuild the world from democratic materials. Tom Ricks compared the neocons to one of their early influences, sixties radical Jerry Rubin: "They were willing to take a chance and then dance on the rubble," whether in Baghdad, Tehran, Damascus or even Riyadh; the last, oddly, was a particular object of loathing for the neocons because of its medieval government and devious anti-Western initiatives. Wolfowitz—"dangerously idealistic and crack-smoking stupid," in the words of an army officer who met him in Iraq—was let off the leash.[42]

THE OFFICE OF SPECIAL PLANS

Wolfowitz chose Doug Feith—his undersecretary of defense for policy—to head the Office of Special Plans. Feith's judgment was at least as suspect as Wolfowitz's. Many regarded Feith as little more than a pro-Israel hack who had trailed Wolfowitz through various government, academic and think tank positions, cut his teeth with the Jewish Institute for National Security Affairs (JINSA) and the Zionist Organization of America, and then written articles in the 1990s calling for Israel's annexation of the occupied territories and the expansion of settlements there. Feith had worked with Richard Perle on *Clean Break* in 1996, a strategic blueprint for Israel's right-wing Likud Party, which had called for a pitiless military campaign against the Palestinians—instead of negotiations—the ouster of Saddam Hussein and the re-ordering of the entire Middle East.[43] A senior military officer who had flown with Feith on an air force flight from England to the United States on September 12, 2001, recalled that Feith had insisted that the looming campaign against bin Laden's Afghan sanctuaries should make a counterintuitive clean break there as well, and "lead immediately to Baghdad." Back in the Pentagon—which still reeked of fire, smoke and jet fuel—Feith had scolded a (disbelieving) Joint Staff operations officer: "Why are you working on *Afghanistan*? You ought to be working on *Iraq*." This was just a day after 9/11. That same day, Feith's mentor Richard Perle had run into CIA director George Tenet at the White House and said, "Iraq has to pay a price for what happened yesterday. They bear responsibility."[44]

Bush, in short, was bounded by zealots determined to invade Iraq and oust Saddam on any pretext. They alluded often to the high, nagging cost of the no-fly zones—$1 billion a year—and asserted that a short, sharp war to remove Saddam would remove that cost. (By 2005, Bush's war in Iraq would be costing $70 billion a year.)[45] Backed by Bush and Cheney, Feith bypassed the CIA and the State Department—which one neocon snorted was "basically an al-Qaeda cell"—cutting Tenet, Colin Powell and their more prudent analysts out of the loop with the argument that 9/11 necessitated a less cautious approach to intelligence. "The United States can no longer solely rely on a reactive posture as we have in the past . . . We cannot let our enemies strike first."[46] The destruction of the Twin Towers, the 2,751 deaths and the hundreds of billions of dollars of damage to the U.S. economy made it essential not even to run the risk of another attack. "Time is not on our side," Vice President Cheney warned in August 2002. "The risks of inaction are far greater than the risk of action." Oddly but typically, the vice president, not the president, led the charge to war. With Bush relaxing at his ranch in Crawford, Texas, Cheney effectively declared war on Iraq that August in a speech to the VFW National Convention. Working from his doctored intelligence, Cheney stated that there was "no doubt" that Saddam had WMD, and that America must now "take the battle to the enemy."[47] "Nuance" in this or any related matter became a term of derision. Startled by Cheney's saber-rattling, Bush rallied to a vice president that even sympathetic onlookers were referring to as Bush's guiding "regent" and "chancellor." "I don't do nuance," Bush smirked. Nuance was for liberals and apologists like John Kerry and Al Gore. And who could afford to "nuance" intelligence when Saddam might at this very moment be splitting atoms and, as Cheney also asserted in his VFW speech, is "prepared to share [nuclear weapons] with terrorists who intend to inflict catastrophic casualties on the United States." By 2001, the Iraqi dictator had restored Iraqi oil production to pre–Desert Storm levels (2.5 million barrels per day) and was swimming in cash.[48]

THE IRAQI EXILES

Iraqi exiles affiliated with the competing Allawi and Chalabi organizations were only too happy to provide the Bush administration with alarming "facts" of Saddam's weapons programs and links to terrorism. After 9/11, President Bush referred often to the discovery by British intelligence that Saddam could launch weapons of mass destruction in long-range Scuds within forty-five minutes. That assertion was a lie sold to the British by Allawi's INA. Meanwhile, Chalabi's INC supporter Khidhir Hamza published a sensational book in the United States in 2000 titled *Saddam's Bombmaker* (and luridly subtitled *The Terrifying Inside Story of the Iraqi Nuclear and Biological Weapons Agenda*), which put Hamza—subsequently dismissed by insiders as a "documentable fraud" and a "professional liar"—on an author tour and television purveying utterly false "facts" of Saddam's nearly complete nuclear weapons program. Ex-Soviet and East German scientists were in country working around the clock, the exile asserted; the centrifuges were spinning; Iraq was close and needed to be stopped *now*, before it was too late. But Hamza had been knocking around in exile since 1994, living in the Virginia suburbs outside of Washington, D.C. He actually knew very little about the real state of Iraq's WMD programs, which were fading, not rising. Eight years of sanctions had starved them of materials, and Clinton's Operation Desert Fox as well as Bush's 2002 air strikes had wrecked most of their critical infrastructure. General Zinni quipped that Saddam was being contained "day-to-day with fewer troops than go to work every day at the Pentagon."[49] But Wolfowitz welcomed Hamza to the Pentagon as if he were a new defector with fresh, actionable intelligence. Wolfowitz, Feith and the other neocons felt justified in seizing upon fiction like Hamza's and extrapolating the *worst* possible outcomes from it because—in their view—a mistake or underestimation in analysis might lead to nuclear or biological holocaust.

In mid-2002, Tenet recalled that his senior analysts complained that "Scooter Libby and Paul Wolfowitz never seemed satisfied with our answers regarding allegations of Iraqi complicity with al-Qaeda."[50] Libby and Wolfowitz knew the answers they and their bosses wanted, and would get them any way they could. Tenet described how Scooter Libby tried to sell an invasion of Iraq to the CIA. In a "murder board" convened at Langley in November 2002 to weigh the known facts of an al-Qaeda–Iraq connection, Libby skated away from the facts:

Scooter Libby approached it like an artful attorney. An analyst would make a point and Libby would say, okay, this is what you say. But there are other things happening. So, if this were true, would it change your judgment? And the analyst would say, well if that was true, it might. And Libby would say, well, if that's true, what about this? And six "if that were trues" later, I finally had to stop him and say "Yes, there are other bits and pieces out there . . . but the whole does not take us as far as you believe. And everything else is just speculation." That was a push by policy makers to see how far we would go.[51]

THE WILSON AFFAIR

Bush's active "push" for war explained one of the early scandals of the Bush administration. Cheney had been giving speeches in 2002 that warned of an Iraqi nuclear capability "fairly soon." That contradicted CIA analysis, which projected that Iraq would not have nukes "until near the end of the decade," and Tenet recalled being surprised that Cheney never sent his speeches to the CIA for clearance by experts. The vice president and the pet analysts in Feith's shop shot wildly from the hip. Feith's "electrons aren't connected," a retired general complained, "so he arc lights all the time. He can't organize anything."[52] Sadly, President Bush served as a passive, receiving electrode for the disorganized OSP analysis that Cheney forwarded to him. In his State of the Union address in January 2003, Bush claimed as a matter of fact that Saddam had been trying to purchase yellowcake uranium in Niger to build an atom bomb. In July, former ambassador Joe Wilson—who had actually been sent by the CIA to Niger in February 2002 to investigate allegations that Iraq had been shopping there—published an op-ed piece in the *New York Times* which divulged that his mission to Niger had turned up no evidence of Iraqi purchases. Instead of explaining themselves—Iraqis *had* visited Niger to enquire about uranium, they just hadn't bought any—Bush's "White House Iraq Group," an ad hoc committee chaired by Karl Rove and Scooter Libby and tasked with "selling the war in Iraq to the public," sought to discredit Wilson by making him out to be an uxorious fop and dabbler.[53] Richard Armitage, who would later turn on his political masters, leaked the news to journalist Robert Novak that Wilson's wife, Valerie Plame, was a CIA operative and that she had arranged the trip to Niger so that her retired husband would have something to do. Armitage's revelation of Plame's covert employment (a felony) skirted the real issue—that Bush and his White House Iraq Group had grossly exaggerated the Iraq-Niger link to drive the American public toward war—but Wilson's determination not to be maligned or marginalized kept the story in the headlines and drove Cheney (presumably) to instruct Scooter Libby to lie about the origins of the smear campaign, which led to Libby's conviction for perjury, obstruction and lying to the FBI in March 2007.

Anyone who impeded Bush's path to war was smeared by the so-called Mayberry Machiavellis gathered around Rove and Libby. In April 2002, the *Washington Post* reported that Deputy Secretary of Defense Wolfowitz had ordered a CIA investigation of Hans Blix's twenty-five-year career to "provide sufficient ammunition to undermine [Blix] and the UN inspection program." A Pentagon official frankly admitted to the *Post* that "the hawks' nightmare is that inspectors will be admitted, will not be terribly vigorous and will not find anything. Economic sanctions will be eased, and the U.S. would be unable to act."[54]

The administration's harassment of critics like Blix and Joe Wilson baffled the more prudent and methodical CIA. The CIA had already looked into the Niger story and dismissed it. What struck analysts there was not so much the willful distortion practiced by the Bush White House, but the fractured, unintelligent process of distortion. "They were receptive to technical intelligence (the weapons program) where the analysis was wrong, but apparently paid little attention to intelligence on cultural and political issues (post-Saddam Iraq) where the analysis was right," a CIA report released in October 2005 noted. One of the CIA's senior Middle East experts had a run-in with one of Condi Rice's senior NSC officials shortly after 9/11 that summed up the tension. "If you want to go after that son of a bitch to settle old scores, be my guest," the analyst said. "But don't tell us he is connected to 9/11 or terrorism, because there is no evidence to support that. You will have to have a better reason."[55]

As war approached, Saddam's contacts with al-Qaeda picked up, but for reasons that could only be explained by intensifying American pressure. Driven from Afghanistan by American bombs, al-Qaeda fugitives like Abu Musab al-Zarqawi took refuge in the Salafist enclave of Ansar al-Islam—a wedge of ten villages in Iraqi Kurdistan near the border with Iran—that Saddam tolerated because he was kept away by the American-patrolled exclusion zone and because he was preoccupied with the looming American invasion. Bush's pressure on Iraq also achieved something that would previously have been unthinkable. Saddam, a secular strongman who had no time for Islamists, came to regard jihadis like Ansar al-Islam (and al-Qaeda) as potentially useful (as indeed they were) in organizing an insurgency and defeating American troops or their Shiite and Kurdish allies.[56] It would be wrong to assert that Saddam Hussein welcomed or desired the foreign fighters in Iraq. With Saddam distracted and weakened, they were there by dint of their own efforts, not his. But the distinction was not viewed as important in the White House, and Tenet's CIA, one Washington insider noted in 2005, was increasingly reduced to the role of "'facilitator' of policy emanating from President Bush and Vice President Dick Cheney." Policies were concocted in the White House and then confirming intelligence was cherry-picked from CIA files. The Bush White House and the OSP mocked the prudence of analysts in what they dubbed the "reality-based community." Bush and his lieutenants thought it more sensible to create an "alternate reality" that might more accurately reflect Iraqi threats. (Critics called that alternate reality "Feith-based analysis.") George Tenet confided to Bob Woodward that "suddenly there seemed to be no penalty for taking risks and making mistakes." Only analytical caution and due diligence were penalized.[57]

THE PERILS OF "GROUPTHINK"

Groupthink was another problem. No one in Bush's policy circle wanted to get out of step with the president, "hastening the conversion of heavily qualified judgments into accepted fact."[58] That tendency was even more dangerous than usual in the Bush White House because the president was so unreflective. "I'm a gut player," Bush liked to say, "not a textbook player." Bob Woodward had a front-row seat in Bush's war cabinet, and he witnessed the president "scoffing at—even ridiculing—doubt." Advisers would lose their access if they didn't demonstrate "100 percent commitment" to Bush's whims.[59] Bush bullied his subordinates to enforce the groupthink. When told by a senior adviser in 2001 that one of his gut decisions was "bad policy," Bush snapped back: "Bad policy? If I decide to do it, *by definition* it's good policy. I thought you got that."[60] His national security adviser, Condi Rice, certainly "got it." She was supposed to filter and balance the pugnacious recommendations of men like Cheney and Rumsfeld, but she didn't. Rice was overawed by her more senior Vulcans. "I'm by far the baby in this group," she explained. "I don't operate. I don't implement. I coordinate." She saw her role as merely pushing Bush's agenda, not probing it, and, still more dangerously, she sought to "translate Bush's instincts and intuitions into policy." Both of Rice's parents had passed away; she lived alone and had been effectively adopted by George and Laura Bush. She regarded the president with awe. "I've been tremendously influenced by him," she gushed to a friend. "People don't understand, it's not me exercising influence over him. I'm internalizing his world." Instead of asking hard questions and "imposing her own views"—whatever they were—she merely "organized Bush's decision-making," cut her staff by a third and obediently devolved power *back* to Cheney and Rumsfeld and their bulked-up staffs, which left them in charge. One observer called her "an ingénue among wolverines." Rumsfeld was pointedly contemptuous of Rice. During principals meetings, he either refused to attend on grounds that Rice was not a true "principal" (he reduced her to tears at least once) or read memos while she spoke, muttered dismissive comments under his breath and refused to leave her copies of his briefing slides.[61]

The undiminished staffs of Cheney and Rumsfeld enforced the groupthink. Cheney's staff—fearfully called "the Watchers" inside the White House—secretly blind-copied other people's e-mail so that Libby and the vice president could read and manage their thoughts. Whereas Bush resided "high up on the mast"—as one White House counsel put it—Cheney got down "in the wheelhouse below the decks," crushed out mutineers and enforced adherence to his core belief that there was *always* convergence going on between terrorists, rogue states and WMD. Cheney and Libby created an atmosphere of haste and urgency—angrily demanding instant reports from analysts that were half-baked because of the haste—to concoct more raw intelligence that could be plugged into David Wurmser's kooky "spider charts" as yet more evidence of al-Qaeda–Iraqi "connectivity."[62] When an intelligence officer briefed Cheney's staff on why *not* to invade Iraq in September 2002—North Korea was the proliferation threat, not Iraq—Scooter Libby leaned over and stage-whispered to a colleague, "Who *is* this guy?" Others in the room ventured that Iran was a more serious threat than Iraq. Feith scolded them for being "persnickety."[63] The lesson was clear. If you weren't on board with Iraq, then you weren't on board at all. That probably explained Tenet's notorious December 2002 utterance to Bush in the Oval Office that the intelligence on Iraqi WMD was a "slam-dunk case." Even as Bush questioned the sketchy, unconvincing intelligence he was seeing on Iraqi WMD, Tenet, like an obliging puppy, foolishly, tragically hastened to reassure the Boss. Tenet never asserted himself in the bullying atmosphere of the White House. "You paid the biggest price by doubting," he lamented to Bob Woodward. It was easier just to climb on board and nod assent.[64]

Bush's gut-driven groupthink took no prisoners, even among the professional military. Army chief of staff General Eric Shinseki had pronounced Bush's contemplated troop levels for Iraq inadequate. To silence the general, Rumsfeld named Shinseki's successor more than a year before Shinseki's retirement, converting the respected chief of staff into a lame duck. When Shinseki did retire in June 2003, not a single senior civilian official attended his retirement ceremony, a pointed snub.

When Larry Lindsey, President Bush's chief economic adviser, warned in September 2002 that an invasion of Iraq would cost as much as $200 billion—ten times what Bush was projecting at the time and a derisory fraction of the actual cost—Lindsey was fired for spouting "baloney." Treasury Secretary Paul O'Neill characterized Bush-Cheney decision making as "like being in a boat with twenty people, all rowing in the same direction, except you."[65] Secretary of State Colin Powell observed that Bush "is guided more by a powerful inertial navigation system than by intellect. He knows kind of what he wants to do, and what he wants to hear is how to get it done."

Anyone who resisted the pull of Bush's navigation system was cut from the loop. Brent Scowcroft went on CBS's *Face the Nation* in August 2002 and warned that a U.S. invasion of Iraq "could turn the whole region into a cauldron, and thus destroy the war on terrorism." A few days later, Scowcroft published an op-ed in the *Wall Street Journal* titled "Don't Attack Saddam"; it looked skeptically at the Bush administration's weak case for war, warned that the U.S. military would be mired in a long occupation and reiterated that an American war in Iraq would "put at risk our campaign against terrorism as well as stability and security in a vital region of the world." Condi Rice phoned the former national security adviser—who had coordinated the last war against Saddam and launched Condi's own Washington career—to chew him out. "How could you *do* this to us," she growled into the telephone. Scowcroft (who probably wrote with the tacit approval of George W. Bush's own father) was startled. His protégé had become a shill for Cheney's war policy instead of doing her job, which was to examine the proposals of Bush's advisers with a cold, analytical eye. When Secretary of State Colin Powell argued that "Iraq isn't going anywhere. It's in a fairly weakened state . . . we ought to declare our containment policy a success, we have kept [Saddam] in his box," he was shunned. Rice made Powell and his deputies feel "as if they were not on the team"; if Powell attended an important meeting, Rice would end the meeting, and then reconvene it in a new room after Powell (and Tenet) had left.[66]

Vice President Cheney had been gunning for Colin Powell since Powell's appointment as secretary of state, when the general had completely overshadowed the new president at their introductory press conference. Indeed the improbable choice of sixty-eight-year-old Donald Rumsfeld as secretary of defense—he had been a bitter enemy of Bush's father—was pressed by Cheney because Rumsfeld, whom Nixon had called a "ruthless little bastard," would have the moxie not only to stand up to Powell but to defeat him, in alliance with Cheney. In the 1970s, the team of

Cheney-Rumsfeld—Cheney as President Ford's chief of staff, Rumsfeld as Ford's secretary of defense—had crushed the influence of moderate vice president Nelson Rockefeller and orchestrated Rocky's removal and replacement by conservative Bob Dole on the 1976 Republican ticket. Three decades later, abetted by a weak, indulgent Rice, they were an even more potent pair. When Powell sent Richard Haass, his director of policy planning, overseas, Cheney requested secret NSA transcripts of Haass's conversations abroad.[67] Henry Kissinger was only half joking when he quipped on the eve of the Iraq War that Colin Powell's State Department had come to be regarded overseas "as a small country that occasionally does business with the United States."[68]

The vice president's shortcut through the thickets of State Department and CIA intelligence perplexed those who had worked with Cheney in the Bush 41 administration. All had been impressed by the younger Cheney's maturity and judgment, and Bush 41 himself had written a paean to Cheney's Persian Gulf War leadership in his memoirs: "Dick led the way for the military, which I think is the model our Constitution envisioned; armed forces headed by civilians who were leading, not pushing, the military to understanding and fulfilling the missions set for them by the President."[69] Dick Cheney had led brilliantly in 1990–91, but he was *pushing* now. Most of the best intelligence on Iraq recommended caution and denied any al-Qaeda–Iraq connection, but Cheney threw caution to the wind, cozying up to ambitious Iraqi exiles who poured honey in the vice president's ear and told of a future Iraq that would recognize Israel, sell oil concessions to American companies, base U.S. forces, crush terrorists and fundamentalists, and serve as a model, democratic, pro-Western Arab government. The State Department's Future of Iraq Project—a twenty-five-hundred-page dissection of all the potential problems facing a post-Saddam Iraq—was quietly shelved by Cheney, who hoped, as a *Washington Post* reporter put it, "that without a clear blueprint for the political transition," Washington would have no option but to "turn to Chalabi and his band of exiles."[70]

Cheney's shortcut to war was also abetted by ambitious journalists who wrote fearmongering articles in return for privileged access to OSP intelligence. Feith leaked material to his favorite organs—the *National Review* and the *Weekly Standard*—including classified memos (of his own) that purported to show "detailed, conclusive and corroborated" evidence of Iraqi WMD and collaboration with bin Laden. In his speeches, Cheney would reference the Feith-sourced pieces in the conservative magazines "as your best source of information."[71] Some journalists self-censored themselves in deference to the national mood of scared patriotism, which, as a *New York*

Times editor put, fledged a new phenomenon all over the country: the "I-Can't-Believe-I'm-a-Hawk Club." House Majority Leader Dick Armey recalled the same hysteria in Congress, where "everybody was scared to be seen as the guy that didn't want to go cut somebody's throat."[72] Bob Woodward recalled *not* pushing his editors hard to publish a front-page piece for the *Washington Post* that looked at the flimsiness of intelligence on Iraqi WMD.[73] He was deterred in part by Vice President Cheney's constant references to top secret "compartmentalized intelligence" that only Cheney had seen. Journalists had to assume that the vice president of the United States wouldn't lie, or peddle unverified raw intelligence as "fact."

The most reputable and notorious of the journalists beyond Feith's immediate reach was Judith Miller of the *New York Times*. Miller developed a close relationship with Cheney's chief of staff, Scooter Libby, and purveyed scary tales of the Iraqi WMD program in the nation's "paper of record." Miller's front-page pieces—heavily sourced from Ahmed Chalabi as well as Khidhir Hamza's ghoulish account of his career as Saddam's bombmaker—added to the mood of crisis, and were, in turn, milked by Cheney in his appearances on Sunday morning news shows as incontrovertible evidence of Saddam's festering programs and his links to bin Laden. Miller described bubbling Iraqi WMD labs hidden in hospitals and palaces. It was pure science fiction. She also became involved in the Plame affair. Scooter Libby divulged Plame's CIA employment to Miller—and Joe Wilson's "trailing spouse" status—hoping that Miller would leak it into the *New York Times*. Later Miller spent eighty-five days in jail rather than testify against Libby and was fired by the *New York Times* in 2005 for permitting herself (and the *New York Times*) to be misused: first as Cheney's mouthpiece, and then, as *Slate*—which did yeoman's work exposing Miller—put it, as "an eager consumer of defector baloney" from sources like Chalabi and Hamza.[74]

"SHARON'S WAR"

The Israeli government of Ariel Sharon also incited and encouraged Bush's war policy. After the collapse of Bill Clinton's final settlement negotiations at Camp David in 2000—when Arafat had rejected an Israeli offer of Palestinian control of the West Bank and Gaza—the second intifada had broken out. Like the first intifada of the late 1980s and early 1990s, the second featured lots of shouting, fist-shaking and stone-throwing, but, in a new twist, suicide bombers, rocket attacks and targeted assassinations as well. Seventy-three-year-old Ariel Sharon had responded like Bush after 9/11: with the fist. "Sharon is a man who knows only two states of mind," an Israeli pundit commented, "fighting and preparing for fighting."[75] He had fought in every Israeli war since 1948, had been the architect of Menachem Begin's settlements program in the 1970s, and had been the brains behind the disastrous Israeli decision to invade Lebanon in 1982 and push all the way to Beirut. Sharon responded to the second intifada with his trademark aggressiveness. He muscled his way onto Jerusalem's Temple Mount—bruising Muslim sensibilities—and then in 2002 he launched Operation Defensive Shield. The IDF reoccupied the West Bank and Gaza with thousands of troops. Israeli tanks ringed Arafat's *muqata*—PLO party headquarters in Ramallah—knocked holes in the walls and cut off its power and water.

That was the Likud way of doing things. Arafat had spurned Labor prime minister Ehud Barak's pretty fair offer of a Palestinian state at Camp David in 2000, and answered it with intifada. The Likud would not repeat Labor's mistake. Instead, it tried force, implementing a plan that resembled the *Clean Break* strategy that Perle and Feith had helped write in the 1990s for that other Likud paladin, Benjamin Netanyahu. Palestinian leaders were targeted for assassination. Five hundred Palestinians were killed in Defensive Shield; Jewish settlements in the occupied territories were expanded; additional IDF checkpoints were installed; Palestinians were barred from working jobs in Israel; and Sharon began building a "security wall" between Israel and the West Bank that snipped off 12 percent of the Palestinian Authority's land mass without so much as a by-your-leave. When Secretary of State Powell and National Security Adviser Rice threatened to deduct the cost of the controversial security barrier from Washington's annual aid to Israel, a senior Israeli official scoffed: "We are not under any pressure. The United States is a very vibrant democracy and this is a very politically oriented administration. Reality is made sometimes by political constraints." And in the event, Washington bowed to those constraints—New York senator Charles Schumer warning Bush not to "penalize Israel"—and merely slashed Israel's loan guarantees 10 percent, without touching its direct foreign aid.[76]

The Palestinian Authority, established in Oslo in 1994 as the core of a future Palestinian state, seemed as broken and useless as Arafat (who died in November 2004) and his *muqata*, which sat desolate, mute, waterless and powerless under the guns of Israeli tanks and infantry. "We are led by chaos and anarchy alone," a Palestinian official mourned, an impression that was not improved by Sharon's shrewd decision simply to abandon Gaza with its 1.3 million Palestinians and their 70 percent unemployment. Sharon's decision to leave Gaza was a trap designed to snare the Palestinians and Americans. Gaza would almost certainly fail as a political entity because it was so poor, crowded and isolated. Yet the Israelis could sell that loser of a territory for a high price—Bush's credulous endorsement of large, growing Israeli settlements in the West Bank and Bush's agreement that the Palestinian refugees must never return. Bush—hoping that Palestinian elections would prove the wisdom of the Bush Doctrine and return freedom-loving democrats "not compromised by terror"—bought Sharon's pig in a poke and dropped his insistence that Sharon hew to the "road map" toward a negotiated settlement with the Palestinians that Bush had sketched out in 2002. Gaza predictably tumbled into chaos and anarchy, voted for Hamas (instead of the more moderate Fatah) and confirmed Sharon's argument that the PA was just not ready for self-government.[77] Conferring with Bush about Iraq, Sharon's government pressed for a hard line there as well.

For Sharon and the Likud, 9/11 was providential in that it converted the White House to Israeli thinking on terrorism. Clinton had been more like the Europeans, viewing terrorism as the violent expression of political frustration. If "root causes" like borders and refugees could be identified and addressed, then terrorism would stop. Liberal Israelis were sympathetic to that view, but the Likud was not. Sharon believed—not without reason—that even if the Palestinians were given all that they wanted—Jerusalem, the 1967 borders, the "right of return" for all refugees—they *still* would be unable to make a state, put their terrorists in jail and settle down to peace. Arafat had been a weak leader; his successor, Mahmoud Abbas, was even weaker—"He has olives, not balls," an Israeli official sneered—and violent, unappeased, Iranian-backed groups like Hamas and Palestinian Islamic Jihad waited in the wings to inherit power and destroy Israel, with or without a settlement. There was only one way to fight terror and its seductive culture of martyrdom, Sharon said: with haymaker punches and cunning. "In this part of the world," he told a reporter, "declarations, promises, proposals, even signatures are one thing. Only acts are serious." That skepticism and resolve not to "appear weak" fitted with Bush's worldview. "You can't make a peace deal with that guy," Bush said of Arafat. "He screwed President Clinton." Bush vowed that his administration would abandon the pose of evenhandedness and "tilt it back toward Israel."[78]

Bush bought into an Israeli scare campaign that exaggerated the threat of Iraqi WMD. Former Likud prime minister Benjamin Netanyahu traveled to

Washington in April 2002 to meet with senators and journalists and warn them that Saddam was perfecting nuclear "suitcase and satchel bombs" that could be scattered around the United States. A parade of Israeli grandees followed. Shimon Peres told CNN in May 2002 that "Saddam Hussein is as dangerous as bin Laden" and that the United States could not "sit and wait." Ehud Barak placed an op-ed in the *Washington Post* in June that enjoined Bush to "focus on Iraq and the removal of [Saddam Hussein]. Once he is gone, there will be a different Arab world." That "different Arab world" was the ingenuous neocon vision of a democratic Iraq ruled by Shiites, which would undercut the two great Sunni threats: Arab nationalism (not much of a threat since 1991) and Salafist terrorism.[79] That much may have been true, but a democratic Iraq would almost certainly buttress the Shiite threat from Iran or leave an Afghan-style "failed state" that would be exploited by opportunistic terrorists of all stripes. No matter: Sharon, who boasted that "strategic coordination between Israel and the U.S. has reached unprecedented dimensions," confirmed to the Knesset in August 2002 that "Iraq is the greatest danger facing Israel." He sold that threat constellation to Bush, as well as the view that Israel's struggle against Palestinian nationalism was just another fighting front in Bush's "global war against terrorism," not an Israeli problem that needed to be settled by sincere negotiations and concessions.

Bush didn't disappoint. "If people don't fight terrorism, I'm not going to deal with them," the president peevishly told Jordan's King Abdullah. Instead of restarting the peace process after 9/11, Bush transferred it from Powell to Rice and let it wind down. "The Likudniks are really in charge now," a senior U.S. official fumed to the *Washington Post*, a fact proudly trumpeted by Doug Feith's old employer, the Washington-based Jewish Institute for National Security Affairs: "This is the best administration for Israel since Harry Truman." Still, Bush hesitated to state frankly something that his counselors and congressional supporters did: that the war in Iraq derived from the old neocon *Clean Break* strategy and was intended to strengthen Israel by "broadening the conflict to strike fatally the centers of radicalism in the region." Baghdad was just the first of several "centers" that would be fatally struck; next on the list were Damascus, Tehran, Tripoli and Gaza.[80] Washington insider Robert Novak dubbed the looming Iraq conflict "Sharon's War," reporting a closed conversation on the eve of war between the Israeli prime minister and a number of U.S. senators in which Sharon declared, "If they could succeed in getting rid of Saddam Hussein, it would solve Israel's security problems." Joe Klein noted the same collusion in *Time* magazine: "A stronger Israel is very much embedded in the rationale for war with Iraq. It is part of the argument that dare not speak its name, a fantasy quietly cherished by the neoconservative faction in the Bush administration and by many leaders of the American Jewish community." Condi Rice's adviser Philip Zelikow wavered—"this is the threat that dare not speak its name"—but then went ahead and dared. The real Iraqi threat, Zelikow affirmed to an audience at the University of Virginia in September 2002, was "against Israel," not America. "And the American government doesn't want to lean too hard on it rhetorically, because it is not a popular sell."[81]

"MEDIEVAL INQUISITORS CONVINCED OF THE EXISTENCE OF WITCHES"

The British too were wary of what Bush was selling. They watched Bush's embrace of the Likud and his rush to war nervously. On July 23, 2002, Prime Minister Tony Blair convened a meeting of senior political, defense and intelligence officials. Extensively briefed by the Americans, the Labour officials expressed their alarm at Bush's allegations against Iraq in a document that was later leaked to the press and dubbed the "Downing Street memo." Bush and Cheney, the memo noted, "wanted to remove Saddam through military action, justified by the conjunction of terrorism and WMD. But the intelligence and the facts were being fixed around policy." The British, in other words, grasped that Bush and Cheney were fabricating a case for war. Condi Rice said as much to Richard Haass in July 2002. "The decisions were made," she'd said. A war was coming, like it or not. Undersecretary of Defense Doug Feith told a startled conference of U.S., British, French and German officials in Berlin in September 2002 that "war [with Iraq] is not optional." Even more startling was Feith's contention that there was no need "to prove a connection with Iraq and the September 11th attack." Saddam was going to be taken out regardless.[82] This was all the more remarkable in view of the easy, relatively inexpensive containment of Saddam that had been going on since 1991. The no-fly zones were cheap, and not a single U.S. aircraft had been lost to the Iraqis in twelve years of patrolling.[83] No wonder the London-based *Economist,* echoing Blix, called Bush's war cabinet "medieval inquisitors convinced of the existence of witches."[84] Where facts of Iraqi WMD or al-Qaeda connections did not exist, the Bush White House was inventing them.

CIA director Tenet met with Bush in September 2002 and told him that Saddam did *not* have flourishing WMD programs, or even much in the way of WMD at all. The CIA knew this from its agents inside Saddam's inner circle—including the Iraqi foreign minister, who was in French pay—but, characteristically, Bush dismissed the intelligence and certainly did not share it with Congress.[85] Secretary of State Colin Powell, who would brief the UN Security Council on the Iraqi WMD program in February 2003, purveyed inaccurate information, later confessing that he had been working from "deliberately misleading" intelligence, some of it warped by Feith's OSP, the rest mangled by the CIA in a rushed National Intelligence Estimate ordered up by the Senate Intelligence Committee to verify Bush's accusations against Iraq. Tenet excused the CIA failure on the grounds that "we were prisoners of our own history." Since inspectors had been booted out of Iraq in 1998, the CIA had to work from old Clinton-era intelligence, hearsay from defectors and, like Cheney's shop, "extrapolation."[86]

Sometimes the extrapolation verged into lying. The Germans had learned from an Iraqi defector nicknamed "Curve Ball" that Saddam had installed biological weapons labs in trailers that always kept one step ahead of the inspectors. Later, the Germans concluded that Curve Ball was "crazy" and "a fabricator," but his fake allegations remained in Powell's report to the UN. ("Let's keep in mind the fact that this war's going to happen regardless of what Curve Ball said or didn't say," a Pentagon official reminded his colleagues in February 2003.)[87] One of the most outrageous inventions was Bush's assertion—relayed to seventy-five U.S. senators in closed session in October 2002 and repeated by Powell to the UN Security Council—that Saddam had the capability to strike the East Coast of the United States with "lethal microbes" strewn from Iraqi UAVs. Saddam had no such capability—just a duct-taped balsa wood plane and some old South African bomblets—but the House and Senate swallowed the canard and voted on October 10–11, 2002, to authorize President Bush to invade Iraq. With the vote cleverly scheduled for the eve of midterm elections—few members of Congress wanted to risk appearing "soft" on terror or WMD—the House authorized military force against Iraq 296 to 133, the Senate 77 to 23. The votes had been far closer in 1991, 250 to 183 and 52 to 47, respectively. West Virginia senator Robert Byrd noticed the difference: "Why is war now being dealt with not as a last resort, but as a first resort?" There were a few brave echoes— "Why aren't we hearing more about a worst case, and what are we prepared for in that instance?" Rhode Island senator Lincoln Chafee asked at hearings on the pending war—but most members of Congress merely cheered on the Bush administration. When former Centcom commander General Zinni appeared at Senate hearings in February 2003 and mocked Bush's claim that the White House was on the verge of creating a "magnificent democracy" in Iraq, few followed. Really, Zinni concluded, Bush's proposed "transformation" of Iraq came down to this: "Get rid of Saddam Hussein and hope for the best."[88]

Saddam's "Deterrence by Doubt"

As in 1991, Saddam in 2003 was his own worst enemy. Four days after the 9/11 attacks, he had issued an open letter to the American people describing his pleasure that the United States was finally feeling some of the pain that it had routinely inflicted on the Arab world. By the fall of 2002, the Bush Doctrine was complete and summarized for all to see in *The National Security Strategy of the United States of America*, which tumbled out of the Government Printing Office in September. Saddam had only to glance at it to see that the United States would treat any regime that harbored terrorists as a terrorist; that Washington would invade and depose any regime possessed of weapons of mass destruction that *might* threaten attacks on America; that the White House would not tie itself up in endless deliberations at the UN if American national security were at risk; and that the Bush administration would promote democratic change—even at the point of American guns—as the best cure for terrorism and what Bush called "rogue states."[89] A strategy of preemption—discussed and repudiated by Bush 41—had become the organizing concept of Bush 43.

But Saddam wouldn't yield. Sanctions and no-fly zones had conveniently absolved him of responsibility for broad swaths of his own country and society. Iraqi infant mortality had surged under sanctions and handed Saddam a useful new weapon to wield against Washington. "Five hundred thousand Iraqi children are dead as a direct result of UN sanctions," the dictator liked to say, and he was beginning to poke holes in UN sanctions anyway.[90] The corruption he had introduced into the UN Oil-for-Food program convinced him that he could outlast sanctions—even "smart sanctions"—and, once they were removed, rapidly reconstitute his WMD programs. Hans Blix hypothesized that Saddam was like a homeowner who posts a "Beware of Dog" sign, without actually owning a dog, to scare off trespassers. He needed to preserve the illusion of WMD—"deterrence by doubt"—to cow the Saudis, deter the Iranians and Americans, and terrify his own Iraqi citizens, whom he had not hesitated to gas in the past when his regime was threatened. Saddam assumed that Schwarzkopf had not marched on Baghdad in 1991 because of his fear of Iraqi WMD. He took for granted that Tommy Franks would be deterred by the same threat, and he mocked Rumsfeld's military transformation: "No one is as good at absorbing U.S. precision munitions as Iraq. So if that's all the Americans have got, it's not a threat to our national survival." Worst case, Saddam thought that the United States would reprise its forty-three-day Desert Storm bombing campaign, thrust into southern Iraq, annex the eleven hundred wells of the Rumaila oil field, stake out a protected Shiite enclave and then withdraw. Retaining the oil fields of Kirkuk and the rest of Iraq, Saddam felt confident that he would survive this war just as he'd survived the last. "God," Saddam told his officers, would defeat America by "giving his strongest ability to one of his weakest creatures," Iraq.

There was no better statement of Saddam's strategic witlessness, which drove him into a war that he might have avoided had he only cooperated with inspectors.[91] After his capture in December 2003, Saddam told the FBI agent who interviewed him that he had been compelled to bluff on WMD, even at the risk of war with the United States, to keep the Iranians at bay—"you guys just don't understand; this is a rough neighborhood."[92] That "mad dog" posture might have made sense in some contexts, but not in this one, in which Bush's finger was whitening on the trigger. Bush had all but declared war on Saddam in June 2002 at West Point: "We must take the battle to the enemy and . . . confront the worst threats before they emerge." If Saddam was even suspected of concealing threats, then he was a target. "Saddam," Tenet wrote, "gave us little reason to believe that he had changed his stripes or trajectory . . . We knew plenty of countries that were working desperately on WMD programs and trying to conceal that fact. But we had no previous experience with a country that did not possess such weapons but pretended that it did."[93] Blix thought that it didn't matter anyway. The Americans had made it clear that they would be satisfied only with Saddam's removal from power—they had passed an Iraq Liberation Act through Congress and were prepping émigrés like Allawi and Chalabi for power—so why should Saddam bother cooperating with UN weapons inspectors?[94]

Saddam was also an egomaniac, blinded by vanity, paranoia and the cult of personality that he had been constructing for thirty-five years. Despite the sanctions since 1991, he had beefed up his regime, employing seven thousand workers to build a chain of presidential palaces around Iraq that permitted him to sleep in luxury anywhere in the country and change his location daily to thwart assassination attempts, which he took for granted, particularly after 1996, when his son Uday's gold Porsche was riddled with bullets in central Baghdad. He named Baghdad's airport "Saddam International Airport," modeled the city's triumphal arch on his own hands and forearms (clasping crossed swords), and referred to his reign as "the era of Saddam Hussein, protector of Iraq, who rebuilt civilization and rebuilt Babylon." But the braggadocio exposed vulnerabilities as well. So fearful was Saddam of his own safety and U.S. surveillance techniques that he never used the telephone. Insiders swore in 2003 that he had used a phone only twice since 1990. His generals and ministers were taken to meetings with him blindfolded or in cars with blacked-out windows so as not to know his location. There were no intimate meetings with Saddam to talk policy or strategy. Bodyguards were always present.[95]

At one such meeting in 1995, some of Saddam's braver generals had hazarded that if there was a new war with the Americans, Saddam must abandon the concept of 1991—holding the frontiers with the regular army and counterpunching with the Republican Guard—and instead shift to the attritional, defense-in-depth strategy employed by the Russians against Napoleon and Hitler. The Iraqis would trade land for time, falling back, using the Iraqi desert and sandstorms like the Russian steppe and snows, and arming the Sunni tribes to harass American columns. Irregular Fedayeen Saddam units, created in 1994 as proregime vigilantes, would arm and fund themselves from weapons and money caches in Iraqi schools and mosques (or simply buried on Sunni farmland) and launch a guerrilla war against the Americans.[96] The generals counseled against more investment in the tank divisions of the Republican Guard: "So long as the Americans control the air, they will just fly in and destroy the mechanized forces." That conference, two historians noted, "signaled the end of realistic planning" in Baghdad. Saddam pointed to the most outspoken general and said, "If what this officer told you is correct, you'd all be dead, because we'd have lost [in 1991]. You'd have been locked in an American prison or killed on the battlefield. Since we didn't lose, why would we exchange a winning concept for a foreign concept that's not applicable here?" Saddam Hussein genuinely believed that he had *won* in 1991, that his Republican Guard—not George H. W. Bush's scruples—had stopped the U.S. military on the Euphrates and prevented them from advancing to Baghdad. That blindness and ego would explain the rapid collapse of Saddam's military in 2003: generals who expressed pessimism were purged; generals who inflated their capabilities and assured Saddam that they could beat the Americans were funded and promoted. Since Saddam's son Qusay—a military tyro like his father—controlled the Republican Guard Corps, even that potent force stagnated. "Everyone started lying," a captured Republican Guard general confessed to his American interrogators in 2003. "It was like Hitler and his generals after 1944 . . . They watched you go to the bathroom. They listened to everything you said, and bugged everything."[97]

Bush's forward-leaning posture on Iraq—his ambition to change the world in the name of American democracy and national security—made Washington extremely suspect around the world. The Russians and Chinese feared Washington's assumption that it had the right to invade sovereign nations to implant the "universal value" of democracy. The French, who had supported the attack on Afghanistan, resented American arrogance and "hyperpower" in the matter of Iraq, as well as Washington's careless willingness to launch a preemptive "war of choice." There were deep, widening fissures between the United States and the rest of the world. France, Germany, Canada, China and Russia all opposed military action against Iraq—preferring sanctions, inspections and diplomacy. In January 2003, French foreign minister Dominique de Villepin called war with Iraq "the worst solution." Peace demonstrations rippled around the globe. Thirty-six million people took part in more than three thousand protests against the muscular American policy between January and April 2003. Bush merely shrugged. Leadership involves "bucking public opinion," he said.[98]

Saddam continued to buck the Americans, and everyone else. Hans Blix complained in January 2003 that "Iraq appears not to have come to a genuine acceptance—not even today—of the disarmament, which was demanded of it, and which it needs to carry out to win the confidence of the world and to live in peace." Blix noted that Iraq's claim to have destroyed eighty-five hundred liters of anthrax was backed by "no convincing evidence," nor could Saddam account for a thousand tons of missing chemical agents as well as his stocks of VX nerve gas agents. When Colin Powell briefed the UN Security Council on Saddam's WMD capabilities in February 2003, his arguments and evidence were generally accepted, in large part because of Saddam's defiance and secrecy. Still, Blix continued his investigations and reported after Powell's briefing, in March 2003, that "no evidence of proscribed activities has so far been found in Iraq." Blix was making real progress; Bush's first troop deployments to Kuwait seemed to have forced Saddam's hand. The Iraqis destroyed seventy ballistic missiles in March, and Blix pleaded with Powell for more time: "We are not watching the breaking of toothpicks. Lethal weapons are being destroyed."[99]

THE "POTTERY BARN RULE"

Saddam hoped to split the Americans even if he failed to split the coalition. Having learned the lessons of the Persian Gulf War of 1991, he would not fight conventionally this time. He would threaten the use of WMD, unleash the fedayeen irregular bands, fight in the cities where American high-tech was less devastating and confront the Americans with what Thomas Friedman called the "Pottery Barn Rule"; to wit, "You break it, you own it." Powell had explained Friedman's rule to Bush at a dinner meeting in the White House in August 2002. The Iraqi military was not going to resist the United States for long. America would win, and then "you are going to be the proud owner of 25 million people," Powell cautioned the president. "You will own all their hopes, aspirations and problems. You'll own it all." Iraqi nation-building, Powell warned, would pin down 40 percent of the U.S. Army for years to come; it would not be a cakewalk at all.[100] Six months later—after Bush had told a startled Powell that "I really think I have to take this guy out"—Powell's State Department warned the White House and Centcom that they were about to kick over a beehive. Their "focus on primary military objectives and reluctance to take on 'policing roles' " was a recipe for disaster. There were "serious planning gaps for post-conflict public security and humanitarian assistance." A U.S. invasion and removal of Saddam would "suck the oxygen out of everything," leaving a chaotic, dependent Iraq in its wake.[101]

Former secretary of state James Baker later said that Colin Powell was the only man who might have prevented the Iraq War had he only thrown his heart on the table, gone public with his doubts and threatened to resign. But Powell kept in step with the president and, as Bob Woodward observed, "put his war uniform on."[102] The men in real war uniforms nervously monitored the rush to battle. Army chief of staff General Eric Shinseki broke ranks with tamer generals and told the Senate Armed Services Committee in February 2003 that—in pointed contrast to the rosy prognostications of Cheney and Rumsfeld—it would actually take "several hundred thousand troops" to conquer and stabilize Iraq. "We're talking about post-hostilities control over a fairly significant piece of geography, with the kind of ethnic tensions that lead to other problems," Shinseki told Michigan senator Carl Levin. "And so it takes significant ground force presence" to seal Iraq's borders, impose order in the cities (where 75 percent of Iraqis lived), guard the nation's infrastructure against sabotage and looting, and manage the wanderings of a projected one million refugees.[103] Rumsfeld, Wolfowitz, Rice, Hadley and Libby, who were pushing an "Operation Iraqi Freedom" with the argument that it would be fast and cheap, heaped scorn on Shinseki's caution. Big peacekeeping forces were a social-working relic of the Clinton era, they sneered. Real men fought their wars and went home, leaving derisory Afghan-size contingents and UN blue helmets behind.

"HAUL ASS AND BYPASS"

Warned by Powell that he would need more troops to invade and occupy Iraq, Centcom commander Tommy Franks thanked Powell for his advice, but deferred to Rumsfeld. "The military had changed since [Powell] left it," Franks reflected. "Colin was from a generation of generals who believed that overwhelming military force was found in troop strength." That was no longer the case; in the new Pentagon thinking, "effects"—the ability to stun a government, military or population with the "shock and awe" of precision munitions—mattered, not boots on the ground. Even light forces would be able to conquer Iraq, by surprising the defenders, moving fast and annihilating whatever resistance cropped up from the air.[104] With fantasies like that brewing at Centcom—"Haul ass and bypass," as Franks put it—it was no wonder that Bush's team had simply ignored an August 2002 CIA report ("The Perfect Storm: Planning for Negative Consequences of Invading Iraq") that had been included in their Camp David briefing books when they made the first concrete preparations for war in September 2002. The CIA had warned that there would be "anarchy and territorial breakup in Iraq, a surge of global terrorism, deepening Islamic antipathy toward the United States and major oil supply disruptions and severe strains."[105] The Pentagon hawks shrugged off the warning and budgeted for a lightning war: fifty thousand troops would be pulled out within ninety days; the rest would be home within six months.[106] "No one," Richard Perle scoffed on a television talk show, "is talking about occupying Iraq for five to ten years." The war would be "quick." Wolfowitz judged Shinseki's call for more troops "outlandish." Rumsfeld concluded that Shinseki was just another hand-wringing Powell: "the product of old thinking and the embodiment of everything that was wrong with the military."[107] How could it possibly require more troops to secure the peace than win the war? Rumsfeld asked. Wolfowitz piled on: Shinseki is "*way* off the mark."[108]

In fact, Shinseki was on the mark, and it didn't take hindsight to establish that fact. The U.S. military's experience subduing Germany after World War II and Bosnia and Kosovo in the 1990s made plain that a robust ratio of peacekeepers to general population was essential to stability and nation-building. In post–World War II Germany, the U.S. Army had maintained a ratio of 1:10 (or 1.6 million GIs in an American sector that contained 16 million Germans); in Bosnia, a ratio of 1:67; in Kosovo, a ratio of 1:40. In Iraq, where history had carved deep sectarian rifts between the Sunni Arab minority (25 percent of the population) and the more numerous Shiites and Kurds, Rumsfeld and Wolfowitz were arguing for a ratio of just 1:156—or 160,000 coalition troops for a country the size of California, containing 25 million fractious Iraqis. Shinseki was stunned; the army's prevailing Iraq War contingency plan, OPLAN 1003-98, called for 500,000 U.S. troops. In 1999, the U.S. military and Booz Allen had run an Iraq war game called "Desert Crossing," which had concluded that at least 400,000 soldiers would be needed to defeat and stabilize Iraq. Rumsfeld was calling for fewer than half that number for war *and* stabilization.[109]

Marine general Anthony Zinni, who had commanded Centcom during "Desert Crossing," recalled that the preoccupation throughout the game had been postwar "security"—"flooding the towns and villages" with coalition troops to maintain order and critical services like water, sewers, electricity and garbage collection. Zinni recalled that the meltdown projected in 1998 for a postconflict Iraq had "shocked the hell out of me."[110] Bush's own NSC had pondered the question of Iraq troop numbers in February 2003 and concluded that five hundred thousand would be required to establish security along the relatively successful lines of Bosnia and Kosovo. Fewer coalition troops and a smaller ratio, the NSC hypothesized, would deliver failure along the lines of Haiti and Sierra Leone, where the ratios had been 1:350 and 1:400, respectively. The CIA had submitted its own paper titled "The Consequences of Catastrophic Success," which had warned that the Ottomans and the British had "left Iraqis with a deep distrust of occupiers" and predicted that initial euphoria in Iraq would be replaced by "old rivalries and ethnic tensions" as well as fury at the liberator if safety, security, food, shelter, water, electricity and jobs were not forthcoming. The CIA also cautioned that a "U.S.-led defeat of Arab Iraq would probably boost proponents of political Islam and attract many angry young recruits to extremists' ranks."[111]

"The Biggest Risk by Far Is Strategic"

Colonel John Warden, who had shaped the air campaign in 1991, expressed shock at the Bush administration's cavalier approach to the looming war: "The biggest risk by far is strategic." Warden referred Bush's war party to the British experience after World War I, when British troops and officers "found themselves being assassinated from almost the first day." Going light into Iraq and defeating, capturing or disbanding the Iraqi military would also open up the borders to transnational insurgents: "What do we do when small bands of fanatic Muslims start creeping across the border from Iran, Syria or Saudi Arabia?" Warden predicted "years of difficult and very expensive occupation." Retired general H. Norman Schwarzkopf, a Bush family ally and an influential four-star, weighed in in January 2003. Rumsfeld's neocon war party "worried him," as did the insouciant disregard for the anarchy that would be created by a U.S. invasion. "I have picked up vibes that there's going to be this massive strike with massed weaponry, and basically that's going to be it." The Desert Storm commander was dumbfounded: "You're going to walk into chaos . . . What is postwar Iraq going to look like, with the Kurds and the Sunnis and the Shiites? That's a huge question." The U.S. Army, he warned, would have "to become an army of occupation."[112]

But Rumsfeld waved off every counterargument. Deploying small, agile, potent expeditionary forces—as opposed to big, lumbering armies and fleets—was at the heart of the transformation of the U.S. military that Bush had promised in his 2000 run for the presidency and that Rumsfeld had begun to implement in 2001. For Rumsfeld, "transformation" meant creating light units and platforms that could intervene anywhere on the globe on short notice. In his view, Operation Desert Storm in 1991 had been needlessly big, logistics-heavy and time-consuming. It had taken too long to deploy Schwarzkopf's force (Rumsfeld would have preferred a "Storm" without the "Shield"), and once deployed in theater the cumbersome American force had aggravated political relations with Saudi Arabia by its size, enraged Islamists like Osama bin Laden by its proximity to the holy places and become a soft target for Iraqi Scuds. The new U.S. military—which scrapped heavy, fuel-sucking Cold War acquisitions like the forty-three-ton XM2001 Crusader self-propelled howitzer and began shifting to lightweight, transportable fighting vehicles like the Stryker and "future combat systems" that would rely on drones and robots—would move fast and light and deploy anywhere on short notice with adequate combat power.

Under Rumsfeld's direction, the army grudgingly lightened its basic organizing unit, transitioning from ten fifteen-thousand-man Cold War divisions to forty-three four-thousand-man "combat brigades," which could be equipped and moved more swiftly than divisions. Rumsfeld, who had watched Big Army defy or vitiate every effort by Clinton to make changes, viewed the invasion of Iraq as an opportunity to ram changes down the army's throat and showcase the new, evolving capabilities, which Shinseki—a defender of platforms like the Crusader—had expressed skepticism about. The last thing Rumsfeld wanted was to be hemmed in by Shinseki's caution—so reminiscent of Powell's in 1991—and lumbered with hundreds of thousands of reserve and national guard troops who would muddy the impression of speed and ubiquity that he was striving to create. In late 2001, while the war continued in Afghanistan, Rumsfeld ordered his senior military leadership to update its contingency plan for a war with Iraq. The army complied, submitting a plan that called for 500,000 troops; Rumsfeld replied that he wanted the job done with 125,000. The Iraqi army, the defense secretary snorted, was weaker in 2001 than it had been in 1991. Fewer forces would do the job.[113]

"WE WILL, IN FACT, BE GREETED AS LIBERATORS"

There were other factors at work as well. Vice President Cheney sought to showcase the potential of effortless U.S. military superiority. If the Iraqi state and military could be collapsed by a *small* American force, then other rogues like Iran, Syria or even China and Russia would hesitate to make waves. A cheap U.S. victory in Iraq would beg the question: what might a *big* American force accomplish? Army secretary Thomas White—who clashed with Rumsfeld and was forced to resign in 2003—recalled the conviction in Rumsfeld's circle that "liberated people don't misbehave."[114] That explained the public claims by Cheney, Wolfowitz and Ken Adelman that an Iraq invasion would be "a cakewalk" and that the grateful Iraqis would "throw candies" at the invading coalition troops. "The streets of Basra and Baghdad are sure to erupt in joy in the same way the throngs in Kabul greeted the Americans," Vice President Cheney affirmed. On March 16, 2003, three days before the United States attacked Iraq, Cheney told Tim Russert on *Meet the Press* that "things have gotten so bad inside Iraq . . . we will, in fact, be greeted as liberators." Not only did Rumsfeld assume that Iraqis of all sects, tribes and ethnicities would behave, he also took for granted that the United States need no longer pose as the world's fairy godmother, in Afghanistan or Iraq. Tough love was needed to break "the culture of dependency" created by tenderhearted do-gooders like George H. W. Bush and Bill Clinton. At the Pentagon, Doug Feith made a virtue of what he called Rumsfeld's "enabling approach." The absence of U.S. peacekeepers would "enable" the Iraqis to put their own house in order and finance their own reconstruction with oil receipts.[115]

Condi Rice, as usual, went along. "The concept was that we would defeat the army, but the institutions would hold, everything from ministries to police forces. You would be able to bring new leadership, but we were going to keep the body in place." The ruminations of Rumsfeld and Rice exhibited a failure to understand even the most elementary facts about Iraq. It was a police and patronage state built around the core of Saddam Hussein and the Baath Party. "There was no Iraqi who was *not* in the party," an ex-factory manager in Baghdad told an American reporter in April 2003. He meant Iraqis who were "highly educated and technical." Among that cohort, "if you weren't a Baathist, you wouldn't be able to rise in the hierarchy."[116] If Saddam was "taken out" and Iraq "de-Baathified," then Rice and Rumsfeld would find neither body nor leadership to work with, only unquenchable chaos. That was why Middle Eastern leaders had expressed consternation when Clinton had launched Operation Desert Fox against Saddam in December 1998 with 600 bombs and 415 cruise missiles. They didn't like Saddam, but they knew that if he fell, "implosion and chaos" would follow: refugees, economic collapse, civil war and a vastly empowered Iran. "You tip this guy over, you could create a bigger problem for us than we have now" was how Centcom commander Zinni had summarized their fears.[117]

The Rice-Rumsfeld plan, such as it was, was particularly foolhardy because Centcom was planning to "go light" into Iraq on the unexamined assumption that peacekeeping and security would be handled by the Iraqi police and military. But if the indigenous security forces vanished in an ideological campaign of "de-Baathification," who would see to postwar security? So complete was Rice's subjection to Rumsfeld and Cheney by January 2003 that she immediately and unthinkingly agreed to a momentous change, spelled out in National Security Presidential Directive 24 (NSPD 24). Instead of being shared among Defense, State, Treasury and USAID, the postwar stabilization of Iraq would be handled exclusively by Rumsfeld's

Pentagon. Put more bluntly by Tenet: "It gave the Department of Defense"—which had not covered itself in glory in the planning of the Iraq War—"total and complete ownership of postwar Iraq."[118]

Paul Wolfowitz was the most ardent advocate of de-Baathification. He and Feith—who would shortly be given control of post-Saddam Iraq—spread the word that Iraq would be like 1945 Germany or Japan: a supine nation that would permit itself to be molded to American specifications. But first, Wolfowitz averred, the Baath Party needed to be demolished. "Replace 'Baathist' with the word 'Nazi,' " Wolfowitz liked to say, "and you'll know what to do." Wolfowitz and Feith both hailed from families whose ancestors had been killed in Nazi death camps, and they both nursed a Nazi phobia that they unhelpfully applied to Iraq, which never mounted anything like the power, influence or threats wielded by Hitler's Germany. No matter: by comparing Saddam to Hitler, Wolfowitz and Feith put opponents of the war on the defensive and cast all skeptics in the role of appeasers.[119] Wolfowitz— who was horribly gulled by Ahmed Chalabi, who wanted total de-Baathification so that *he* could restaff the Iraqi government, military and statist economy in the same way that Putin had restaffed Russia—ignored the historical fact that U.S. intelligence and occupation forces in defeated Nazi Germany had made liberal use of former Nazis in reconstructing the Allied zones. Feith and Wolfowitz also ignored the wiser counsels of Iraqis and their own State Department and CIA personnel in Baghdad, who argued that what was needed was "more an Iraqi process than a coalition process," something akin to South Africa's Truth and Reconciliation campaign. Powell was for "de-Saddamification": a limited purge of war criminals and senior Baath leadership. The lower cadres without blood on their hands would be left intact to run the country.[120]

While the Pentagon made rushed plans to refashion Iraq—which critics dismissed as "PowerPoint deep," which was to say, not deep at all—Hans Blix itched to resume his weapons inspections.[121] Had he done so, he would have discovered what invading American forces discovered—that there were no weapons of mass destruction in Iraq. But Saddam foolishly kept Blix at arm's length, and Bush, who revealed his thinking in a January 30, 2003, telephone conservation with British prime minister Tony Blair, worried that Blix might report that Saddam was cooperating, thus killing the momentum toward war. Blair's private secretary, who transcribed the call, also noted that Bush's "biggest concern was looking weak."[122] Blix made the same observation. Although "it would prove paradoxical and absurd if 250,000 troops would invade Iraq and find very little . . . can Bush refrain from letting the coiled spring jump without losing face?"[123] Confirming Blix's fears, Bush peremptorily declared that "diplomacy had failed" and that—with or without the UN—the United States would invade Iraq to locate and remove its weapons of mass destruction. "Absence of evidence is not evidence of absence," Rumsfeld ventured as he prepared to unleash the dogs of war. Bush called for a "coalition of the willing," which came together rapidly despite UN secretary general Kofi Annan's protest that an invasion of Iraq would violate the UN charter and the law of nations.[124] Forty countries joined Operation Iraqi Freedom, although the 130,000 U.S. troops and the 30,000 British troops composed the bulk of the coalition.

Bush's haste to override UN inspections stemmed from his determination to fight the war before the summer heat set in. In November 2002, the *New York Times* reported that "many administration officials say they would far prefer a cold rebuff by Mr. Hussein, rather than have him cooperate . . . Speed is important because the cooler winter months, ending in February or March, are the optimal time for an attack against Iraq."[125] An immediate war in the cool season would enable coalition troops to drive to Baghdad and make a purged and renovated Iraq the keystone of the Bush Doctrine. Whereas Bush wanted war for idealistic reasons—to remove a dictator and implant democracy—Vice President Cheney was more realistic. Cheney was focused on threats, not hopes. The vice president recognized that the *greater* threats to America were North Korea, Iran and Pakistan, but he wanted a brusque "takedown" of Iraq for two reasons: it would remove a (lesser) threat, and achieve a powerful "demonstration effect." A crushing victory in Baghdad would demonstrate U.S. resolve and deter the greater threats in Pyongyang, Tehran and Islamabad, to say nothing of Moscow and Beijing. "The ambiguity of purpose at the heart of the war"—Bush calculating like Don Quixote, Cheney like Jack in *Lord of the Flies*— "would do much to explain its undoing," *Washington Post* reporter Barton Gellman surmised.[126]

Cheney never reckoned with his eventual undoing. In 2002, he stepped up what can only be called a misinformation campaign to push the United States into the demonstrative war. He crushed out the resistance of House Majority Leader Dick Armey—a rock-ribbed Texas Republican in armadillo boots who was an embarrassing foe of Operation Iraqi Freedom—by spinning him yarns. Saddam Hussein, Cheney assured Armey, has direct personal ties and "operational links" to al-Qaeda. The Iraqi leader would have nuclear weapons "within a year," as well as "suitcase nuclear weapons" that could be handed off to bin Laden for detonation inside the United States. The only reason those hair-raising "facts" were not common knowledge, Cheney confided, was because the threat from Iraq was "more imminent than we want to portray to the public at large." Armey's intuition rebelled—he felt "bullshitted" by Cheney—but the senior House Republican didn't dare continue his opposition to the White House on the off chance that Cheney just might be telling the truth.[127]

"SCIENTIFIC WILD-ASSED GUESSES"

The army keeled over more easily than Armey. Tommy Franks had been on board since 2001. Although he had quietly expressed skepticism about the Iraq invasion, he publicly fell into line, embraced the chain of command—which ran from the field, through the combatant commanders like Franks at Centcom, to the defense secretary and on to the president—and kowtowed to Rumsfeld. Asked by the president for his opinion, Franks tamely replied: "Sir, I think exactly what my secretary thinks, what he's ever thought, what he will think, or whatever he thought he might think."[128] Franks, who was disliked by many in Centcom headquarters as a bullying yes-man, obligingly cut down the force for Operation Iraqi Freedom, from 500,000 to 385,000, then to 200,000. Each time he submitted his plan to Rumsfeld, the defense secretary shook his head. Through what Franks called their "iterative process," they finally agreed on 145,000 troops. "There was always pressure from OSD [Office of the Secretary of Defense]," one Centcom colonel recalled. "Could we do it smaller?"[129] Removed from Franks's iterative process were the Joint Chiefs, who had figured so prominently in the 1991 war with Iraq. Rumsfeld and Franks agreed that the chiefs were bothersome bureaucrats who could be ignored; Franks called them "Title Ten Motherfuckers"—a reference to their chief responsibilities (under Title 10 of the Goldwater-Nichols Act) of training and procurement, not combat command. Driven by Rumsfeld, whom Franks privately called "his nibs," Franks concocted a "new paradigm" to fit the slight troop numbers. "You know, the doctrines that existed for our armed forces several years ago really don't apply to the first war of the twenty-first century," Franks hazarded.[130] Instead of a broad-front invasion and occupation of Iraq, the army would target key "slices" of Saddam's regime to make it fall: leadership, Republican Guard and internal security targets, suspected WMD sites and infrastructure. Where military science didn't support Franks's optimism, he relied on SWAGS—"scientific wild-assed guesses"—that would later cost many American lives. Groupthink bound Franks's Centcom as tightly as it did the White House and the Pentagon: "Everything has to be good news stuff," one officer groused. Officers and analysts would "pull information out of their hats" to satisfy Franks's desire to satisfy Rumsfeld. "You would find out that you can't tell the truth."[131]

Rumsfeld referred Franks to a recent study by defense thinkers Harlan Ullman and James Wade titled *Shock and Awe*. The book argued that volleys of air-, ship- and submarine-launched precision weapons could "paralyze" an adversary and achieve the "rapid dominance" that used to require sustained ground and air attacks. In 2002–3, Rumsfeld pored over every request for troops for Iraq with a red pen. He was constantly slashing to keep the force small and ordered the generals to be ready to "off-ramp" all reinforcements destined for Iraq if the regime fell quickly. Cheney, Rumsfeld and Wolfowitz were obsessed with keeping the force small and beating Saddam on the cheap. Still, when senators Joe Biden and Chuck Hagel visited Qatar in December 2002 to observe a classified war game that sketched the pending invasion of Iraq, Biden told General Franks that it was the postcombat phase that most "worried America." What was being done to create security and stability in the wake of war?[132]

CHAPTER 18

·✗✗·

IRAQI FREEDOM

As IN 1991, the defeat of Iraqi conventional forces proved easy. An effort to "decapitate" Saddam on the first night of the war with Tomahawks and two F-117s missed the mark, requiring a ground invasion and a drive to Baghdad. The nonchalance with which Americans talked about killing Saddam in 2003 made a sharp contrast with 1991, when then secretary of defense Cheney had fired the air force chief of staff for declaring in public that Saddam was "the focus of our efforts."[1] Indeed American methods in 2003 were altogether different from the last time around. "We are at a crease in history," General Tommy Franks told his officers. Outnumbered six to one, the Americans would nevertheless prevail because of "precision, experience, flexibility and adaptability." The war would be "fast and final."

Centcom had counted on the use of Turkey to open a second front in Iraq's north and secure Kirkuk and its oil fields before the Kurds and Arabs fell to fighting over them, but, fearing Iraqi Scuds, Muslim backlash and military cooperation between Turkish and Iraqi Kurds if things went badly in Iraq, the Turkish parliament refused permission, leaving Franks in a much less advantageous position. "Fuck Turkey. Fuck their families. Fuck their dogs," Franks cursed. Later, he calmed down. "With the Turks we win. Without the Turks we win," the Centcom commander assured Washington, and then Franks drove at the Iraqis on March 21, 2003, from what he called "a cold start" in Kuwait: three U.S. Army divisions, one marine division, a British division, and 247 tanks. That small number of troops—145,000 in all—supported by air cover, drove fast toward Baghdad.[2] "I go where they send me, but I win where I go," Franks had boasted to Bahrain's defense minister. And win he did.

Expecting a long Desert Storm–type air campaign, the Iraqi army was stunned by the simultaneous delivery of air and ground attacks. Rumsfeld had waved off the air force's request for a sixteen-day air campaign and had insisted instead on precise air attacks timed to coincide with the advance of coalition ground units. Saddam and his son Qusay—who commanded the Republican Guard units in the war—refused to believe that the relatively light force barreling up from Kuwait was the main thrust. Saddam kept his eyes peeled to the west, expecting another 1991-style "left hook." When U.S. forces stormed through Baghdad on April 3 to seize the international airport, the Iraqis were taken completely off guard. They had only antiaircraft batteries there, with Republican Guard troops and tanks entrenched in the runways, expecting an airborne assault—not one from the ground, least of all from the south.[3] In this case, the "shock and awe" Franks had read about before the war worked. The Iraqis went limp under the American jabs, losing untold thousands of dead—estimates ranged from 13,000 to 45,000—to the onrushing allies against just 139 U.S. and 33 British deaths; about 7,000 Iraqi civilians died in the initial air and ground attacks, and the rest of the population appeared stunned by the speed of the coalition advance. The Iraqis called it the "Disney War"—flashes of light and noise but little perceptible damage. In contrast to the air campaign in the 1991 Gulf War, this one spared infrastructure targets that would be essential to postwar reconstruction. Bridges, dams, power plants, electrical grids and oil refineries were left unscathed, adding to the impression of a Disney War.[4]

"TELL ME HOW THIS ENDS"

Franks had predicted that he'd be in Baghdad within eleven days of crossing the "line of departure" in Kuwait. German intelligence warned Washington that Saddam had drawn a "Red Line" south of Baghdad along the roads from Karbala and Hillah to Kut that would be defended with every weapon in the Iraqi arsenal, including WMD.[5] In the event, there was no stoutly defended "Red Line," and Baghdad fell on April 9; Saddam's hometown of Tikrit fell six days later.[6] The British took Basra—a city of 1.25 million people—on April 6 with the loss of just three men. The advance struck stiff resistance in only a few places. The marines had to wrest Nasiriyah from Uday's Fedayeen Saddam units, which held the city for several days, inflicted heavy casualties, coaxed the marines into friendly fire incidents and then melted into surrounding villages, where they began to churn up what would shortly be called the insurgency. Advance units of the U.S. Army V Corps encountered the same opposition at Najaf: Fedayeen and Republican Guards with mortars, RPGs and machine guns who shuttled along Highway 8, struck and then sped away in pickup trucks. The commander of the 101st Airborne Division, General David Petraeus, watched the fight for Najaf beside embedded journalist Rick Atkinson. It was a meeting of two historians: Atkinson had written one of the better books on the Persian Gulf War and was taking time off from his bestselling World War II trilogy; Petraeus had earned a Ph.D. from Princeton with a dissertation on the impact of Vietnam on America's military. They now wondered—in March 2003—how *this* sputtering little war would affect America's reach and power. "Tell me how this *ends*," Petraeus said to Atkinson. "Eight years and eight divisions?" Petraeus was mischievously quoting General Matthew Ridgway, who had given that dispiriting estimate to President Eisenhower after the French collapse at Dien Bien Phu, when Ike had asked Ridgway what it would take to pacify Vietnam and secure a friendly government.[7]

Fifty years later, American main battle tanks were jouncing through an eerie sandstorm, or *shamal*, their crews regarding the unexpected outbreak of guerrilla war through what Petraeus called "a tornado of mud." U.S. forces took the capital, seized Saddam's palaces and the key Baath ministries, and pulled down the iron statue of Saddam. "Speed kills," Tommy Franks smiled. He had busted into the "decision cycle" of Saddam and his armed forces and "exploited operational advantage" to neutralize them. Gushing Pentagon buzzwords, Franks paused to congratulate himself and Rumsfeld for having ignored "strategic kibbitzers" like Shinseki and Powell, who had recommended more troops. Still, on a visit with Petraeus's 101st Airborne Division, Franks was shown Iraqi arms caches that the Americans were unearthing and expressed shock: "*The whole country is one big weapons dump*, I thought. *There must be thousands of ammo storage sites. It will take years to clear them all*."[8]

General Franks assumed that the retreating Baaathists would arm themselves from the caches and make a last stand in Tikrit, but that city too fell surprisingly easily. The resources that Saddam had set aside for guerrilla warfare in the Sunni Triangle around Tikrit were immense. A single cache of $9.5 million, 1.5 billion Iraqi dinars and 1,071 gold bars was unearthed, as well as heaps of rifles, machine guns, RPGs, ammunition and even thirty-one Iraqi army helicopters, which were found parked in a grove of palm trees.[9] Tikritis were immediately shown the difference between the marines and the army. Marines had always emphasized counterinsurgency; the army hadn't really practiced it since Vietnam. When General Ray Odierno's 4th Infantry Division relieved the marines in Tikrit, they substituted force and intimidation—"the 4th Infantry guys looked mean and ugly, they stood on top of their trucks, their weapons pointed directly at the civilians"—for the "velvet gloves" and "budding cooperative relationship" of the Marine Corps. The 4th Infantry "acted like a colonial power, trying to hold on to a restive province." They took a misplaced pride in their hard tactics, described by one of Odierno's colonels thus: we were "there to kill the enemy, not win their hearts or minds."[10]

In the north—which was supposed to have been the province of Odierno's 4th Infantry, who had been marooned off the coast of Turkey before being shipped through the Suez Canal to Kuwait—Franks initially ran an "economy of force" operation. Small parties of U.S. Special Forces guided Kurdish Peshmerga guerrillas into the rear and flanks of the twelve Iraqi divisions deployed on the Green Line separating Saddam's Iraq from the American-protected exclusion zone. The Iraqi units—all regular army—dissolved under the Kurdish attacks and air strikes from B-52s, F/A-18s and F-14s. In the north, American worries swerved from Iraqi resistance to Kurdish looting and marauding, which threatened to pull in the Turks—not to bash Saddam, but to crush the Peshmerga. "Fuck the Turks," Franks grumbled again to an aide. With the Kurds and Arabs trying to drive each other out of Kirkuk and Mosul, marine and army units hastened to divide the combatants. The Iraqi V Corps surrendered without firing a shot: "It looked like Woodstock with guns," an American officer laughed. But the bigger problem was the ethnic cleansing being waged by Arabs and Kurds in the northern cities, and the slack American response. "They were all about fighting Iraqis and force ratios and how they were going to handle the threat," an American colonel judged his colleagues. "They just couldn't come around to the realization that *that* wasn't their problem."[11] Saddam's 150,000 troops in the north had shrugged off their uniforms and gone home. They had "self-demobilized."

Fears that Baghdad would hold out like Stalingrad, Hue, Mogadishu, Grozny or Jenin—all cases of urban warfare studied by army and marine planners—never materialized. The Saddam regime collapsed like a house of cards. General Scott Wallace's V Corps ringed the city with two cordons—to keep senior Baathists from escaping and to contain the flow of WMD—and then ran raids into the city center to disrupt and weaken the defense and "take down" the government. The "thunder runs" into the heart of Baghdad were so unexpected that army vehicles had to share the road on April 5 with Iraqi commuters driving to work. The Iraqi information minister, Muhammed Saeed Sahhaf (better known as "Baghdad Bob"), gave surreal press conferences in which he insisted that U.S. forces were being cut to pieces in the desert even as they were cutting into the heart of Baghdad. Too late, Saddam ordered his Republican Guard units to disband and fight house to house. The urban warfare would have to be waged mostly by Fedayeen Saddam and hundreds of Arab volunteers, many of whom had fought and trained with Hezbollah, Hamas and al-Qaeda.[12]

DE-BAATHIFICATION

The White House had confidently predicted an "early regime collapse" detonated by the arrival of America forces. But there were few mass surrenders like the ones of 1991, and most of the Iraqi army seemed to be melting away to fight another day. Far from being greeted as "liberators," U.S. forces were met with fusillades and roadside bombs, many of them issuing from embittered servants of the old regime who were laid off in a May 2003 Rumsfeld-ordained program of "de-Baathification" that had the predictable effect of sending the Iraqis best trained in explosives, firearms and military tactics—three hundred thousand ex-officers, security forces and servicemen—into the welling insurgency. Iraq, with a population of twenty-five million and thousands of miles of unguarded borders as well as terrain that offered mountains, urbanized spaces, and natural and artificial waterways cloaked in vegetation, would become a hell for the occupier if a serious insurgency broke out. Insurgents would have no trouble finding places to hide, and foreign fighters, money and weapons could be brought in over the open borders with impunity.[13] "Vacuums are going to be filled with stuff you and I aren't going to like, and it's going to take a long time to get rid of that," Jay Garner, who had run the Kurdish safe haven in 1991, warned General Franks. "It's almost as if, unintentionally, we were working with [al-Qaeda in Iraq] to create the maximum amount of chaos possible," a senior army officer observed.[14] An Iraqi expressed his hurt at American conduct and attitudes: "The sense that our people, our leaders, our country, our culture and our history were being spat on by U.S. soldiers, themselves pitifully lacking in history, education, culture and respect, was too much to bear."[15]

No one in the Pentagon was listening to those early warnings and complaints. Indeed Rumsfeld and Franks considered firing the V Corps commander, General Scott Wallace, for giving an interview to the *New York Times* in which he allowed that "the enemy we're fighting is a bit different than the one we war-gamed against."[16] The mood of glowing optimism had to be upheld, at least for now. Rumsfeld and Cheney plunged ahead with the reconstruction of Iraq. Secure in NSPD 24, the Pentagon hawks simply stopped telling the CIA and the State Department what they were doing. When American officials in Baghdad asked for retired general Anthony Zinni to help run the country, Rumsfeld—who feared the former Centcom commander's swagger and independence—curtly replied, "Anybody but Zinni."[17] Powell's deputy Rich Armitage offered eighty Arabic-speaking Iraq experts from the State Department to set up an American embassy-in-waiting in Baghdad, but Undersecretary of Defense Doug Feith—who had been entrusted with the postwar reconstruction of Iraq—rebuffed him. Powell and Armitage, the *Washington Post*'s Baghdad bureau chief observed, "regarded the presence of seasoned diplomats and Arabic-speaking Middle East specialists within [U.S.-occupied Baghdad] as a bulwark against attempts to hand power over to Chalabi and other exiled politicians." Feith, of course, intended to knock down that bulwark, or preempt its construction. Instead of using the regional experts, Feith placed a partner from his old law firm in charge of Iraqi civil administration. The lawyer, Michael Mobbs—who had no Middle Eastern experience—convened meetings and then vanished. "He was not a leader," an ex-ambassador on his team recalled. "He didn't know what to do; he just cowered in his room most of the time."[18] Sidelined by the Pentagon, CIA director Tenet recalled having to ask the British for news "because we were getting no political reporting" from Rumsfeld. Powell's deputies asked State Department personnel in Baghdad to send back-channel memos on their personal Yahoo and Hotmail accounts, to skirt the surveillance of Cheney's "Watchers" and the veil of silence lowered by Rumsfeld.[19]

The CIA pointed out that de-Baathification affected not only good and bad servants of the old regime, but "brothers and sisters and aunts, uncles and cousins." The negative impact would be enormous, affecting far more than the 1 percent of Iraqis carelessly cited by Feith in Washington. Forty thousand Iraqi schoolteachers were fired on Feith's orders for having been party members. The Iraqi university system—375,000 students on twenty-two campuses—fell apart. Professors were fired and unguarded university buildings were looted. Idle students drifted into the streets; many became insurgents—along with their bitter, unemployed teachers.[20] The Iraqi military and police forces that Condi Rice's "enabling approach" had assumed would assure order, were instead dissolved by the enablers themselves. "The only thing left for me is to blow myself up in the face of the tyrants," a disappointed Iraqi officer told Al Jazeera. General David Petraeus looked anxiously around his area of responsibility and warned that the de-Baathified Iraqi security forces were "really tinder out there just waiting for a spark."[21]

General Tommy Franks, who was as subservient to Rumsfeld in Iraq as he had been in Afghanistan, made no preparations of the sort recommended by Shinseki. Asked by President Bush three months before the invasion how he would maintain law and order *after* an invasion, Franks had replied: "It's all taken care of, sir. I have an American officer who will be lord mayor of every city, town and hamlet."[22] Baghdad and the other cities, towns and hamlets of Iraq now cascaded into a frenzy of looting and vandalism. "Democracy is wonderful. Now we can do whatever we want," an English-speaking Iraqi yelled to an American reporter as the Iraqi drove down the wrong side of the street into oncoming traffic. The lord mayors and even Bush were surprised at the lawlessness. General Petraeus, who took Najaf in March 2003 with his 101st Airborne Division, recalled scouring the city in search of the mayor, or *any* mayoral figure. "I mean *everything* just disappeared. You could just feel that this was going to be really hard." Petraeus instantly grasped the problem—Rumsfeld and Franks had "taken the top off with a pretty thin density of troops." That "leadership structure" and the fear it inspired were all that had ever held Iraq together. Petraeus recalled his bemusement: "And so it's, like, okay—what's next?"[23]

"FREEDOM'S UNTIDY"

Rumsfeld, pushed by Cheney, had disbanded the Iraqi military and intelligence agencies without even consulting the president, his national security adviser or the secretary of state. Franks, who had off-ramped a hundred thousand Iraq-bound U.S. reinforcements in April to placate Rumsfeld, now found himself with no troops on hand to defend vital facilities or even escort occupation personnel, who ended up huddling fearfully in the American-protected "Green Zone" of Baghdad. "Well, the policy was to keep the [Iraqi] army intact," Bush mused. "Didn't happen."[24] "Freedom's untidy" was Rumsfeld's unhelpful comment. "Stuff happens. That's what free people do." (No, one of Rumsfeld's friends reminded him, "that's what *barbarians* do.")[25] Instead of buttressing the prestige and strength of the United States as an occupying power, Rumsfeld's overriding concern remained—as he put it—"to avoid being stampeded into just sending units over." He personally plucked the 1st Cavalry Division from Franks's outstretched hands (America's First Team—"yeah, first to go home," the Cav grumbled) and insisted that Franks mop up and stabilize the country with the small numbers he had on hand. Rumsfeld wanted the whole U.S. invasion force home within six months. "The nature of Rumsfeld," Army secretary Tom White confided, "is that you just get tired of arguing with him."[26]

Jay Garner, whom Rumsfeld and Feith had selected to run the occupation through an Office of Reconstruction and Humanitarian Assistance (ORHA), was also tired. Rumsfeld aide Lawrence Di Rita came to Baghdad and deprecated Garner's fears about the spreading chaos: "We don't *owe* these people a thing. We gave them their *freedom.*" Di Rita was in Iraq to ensure that the United States did not do another open-ended Bosnia or Kosovo; the war needed to end, and end now.[27] Garner was staggered at the disconnect between Rumsfeld's ends and means. Each day of anarchy eroded big chunks of goodwill between the Americans and the Iraqis. There wasn't much left. Garner called the wholesale de-Baathification of Iraq "madness." Yet doubts like that were intolerable in Rumsfeld's Pentagon. Abruptly and unceremoniously replaced by Lewis Paul "Jerry" Bremer's Coalition Provisional Authority (CPA), Garner marched to Bremer's office to demand that Bremer draw the line with Rumsfeld and put de-Baathification on hold: "Don't do this. You're going to drive 50,000 Baathists underground before nightfall," and effectively undo what little rebuilding work had been accomplished by ORHA. Baathists were "the brains of the government." But Bremer, who took his orders from Rumsfeld, ignored Garner. "We are determined to eradicate Saddamism," he said. Not only did Rumsfeld and Bremer fail to anticipate the looting, the collapse of ministries and public works, and the expanded insurgency, they refused to detach troops to guard any "static sites" other than two—the Republican Palace and the Ministry of Oil.[28] The entire Iraqi power grid was disassembled as if by an army of termites. "They just started at one end of the transmission line and worked their way up, taking down the towers, taking away the valuable metals, smelting it down, and selling it into Iran and Kuwait." Looters stripped the computerized control centers bare. Raw sewage gushed untreated into the Tigris. Trash piled up in the streets. Perhaps ORHA needed the name change to CPA, because just one month into the war, Americans and Iraqis alike were calling it the "Organization of Really Hapless Americans."[29]

Doug Feith's muddling alienated most of the Iraqi population—the Sunnis in particular—and "gave oxygen to the rejectionists." When Garner appealed directly to the Pentagon, demanding that Rumsfeld stop de-Baathification, Feith replied for his boss: reversing de-Baathification was out of the question, for such a step "would undermine the entire moral justification of the war." Bremer too told Garner not to waste his breath—the decision to disband had come from "above Rumsfeld's pay grade," which could only mean Vice President Cheney. When the CIA arranged a meeting between General Rick Sanchez, who commanded all U.S. Army troops in Iraq, and fifty-seven former Iraqi generals—a meeting that was intended to find ways to tamp down the insurgency—Bremer ordered Sanchez to skip the meeting. "We will not engage with the enemy," he said. Bremer's smug view was that "we dominate the scene and we'll continue to impose our will on this country." General Petraeus recalled the army's "astonishment" that Bremer never consulted with American officers on the changes he was decreeing; planning was isolated in the Green Zone.[30] Meanwhile, looters ransacked homes, shops, businesses, government buildings and museums, and they tore apart power generation and telecommunications installations for their copper wire and other valuable scrap. The impact on an infrastructure that was already decrepit after ten years of sanctions and neglect was catastrophic. Trash rotted and stank in the streets, lights and air-conditioning died, and potable water stopped flowing. Gangs and demobilized troops snatched up the huge weapons and explosives caches that Saddam had distributed around the country for his Fedayeen units. Those weapons and explosives—an estimated one million tons of explosives, guns and ammo—would shortly arm the insurgency. From his hideout on the Afghan-Pakistan border, Osama bin Laden angrily offered "10,000 grams of gold to whoever kills the Occupier Bremer."[31]

The Pentagon estimated that looters made off with 250,000 tons of explosives in the days after the fall of Baghdad. With more troops, coalition forces could have secured those caches, which instead would be turned into the improvised explosive devices (IEDs) and car bombs that would kill, concuss and maim tens of thousands of American and British troops. Regarding de-Baathification, a disbanded Iraqi colonel growled to the *New York Times* on May 25, "We have guns at home. If they don't pay us, if they make our children suffer, they'll hear from us."[32] National

Security Adviser Condi Rice's assurance that Bush would merely cut off Iraq's diseased head and leave the healthy body intact now looked more whimsical than ever. The CIA lamented that the Pentagon's mismanagement "had taken large numbers of common Iraqis and given them few prospects beyond being paupers, criminals or insurgents." Worse, de-Baathification, which struck a broad blow against the Sunnis, got Iraqis thinking of themselves in sectarian, not national terms, the exact opposite of what had been intended.[33] Rice wearily referred critics to the "Pentagon chain," which proved as addled as she was. Criticized by the CIA station in Baghdad, Paul Wolfowitz haughtily brushed them off: "You don't understand the policy of the U.S. government, and if you don't understand the policy, you are hardly in a position to collect the intelligence to help that policy succeed."[34]

To help his stumbling policy succeed, Bush first dispatched Jay Garner and then Jerry Bremer to manage the transition from Saddam's shattered rule to a new representative government in the mold of the Bush Doctrine. With his troops in possession of Baghdad, Tommy Franks was negotiating a multimillion-dollar book deal. Recognizing that his triumph was about to be erased by the spreading stain of the insurgency—"the enemy's tactics were becoming more unorthodox and brutal"—Franks abruptly retired, pausing only to proclaim Doug Feith—the author of so much misery in Iraq—"the dumbest fucking guy on the planet."[35] It wasn't all Feith's fault; Franks had never expressed much interest in the post-Saddam phase of the war—"You take care of the day after and I'll take care of the day of" had been his message to Rumsfeld—but Franks had been distracted by the war in Afghanistan and his exhausting eighteen-month "iterative process" with OSD over Iraq invasion plans and force size.[36] Tommy Franks was also a typical product of an army that had focused on operations, not strategy, ever since Vietnam, when despair at the length of that war and exhilaration at the speed and decisiveness of the technology-boosted Arab-Israeli wars had persuaded the army brass to focus *everything* on, as their field manual put it, "winning the first battle in the next war." But operations and tactics, as T. E. Lawrence famously put it, were just "the steps in the staircase" to strategy, and, with its focus on technology and speed in *all* environments, the army seemed to have lost sight of strategy. Desert Storm had been an example of that tendency; the U.S. military had collapsed Iraqi power and then zipped away, leaving behind an unrepentant Saddam and a scourged population that had no sense of the extent or meaning of its defeat, or even if it had been defeated at all. With army hopes and doctrine focused on a quick victory and an even quicker exit—a preference that had explained Powell's caution in 1991 and again in 2003—there had never been much interest inside "Big Army" in counterinsurgency.[37]

"THE ISRAELIS WON IN SIX DAYS—BUT HAVE BEEN FIGHTING EVER SINCE—FOR THIRTY YEARS"

Franks was replaced by the Arabic-speaking General John Abizaid, who would have to learn quickly about counterinsurgency and "stability and support operations." Franks had "put his pack down" in May and June 2003, trying to arrange a restorative weekend in the Bahamas with his wife while Iraq spun into chaos, and the situation on the ground reflected that lack of attention.[38] Abizaid, a Lebanese-American described in his West Point yearbook as "an Arabian Vince Lombardi," was discouraged by the military intelligence he was hearing. One analyst wisely observed, "It's premature to be doing victory laps. The hard part is going to be the occupation. The Israelis won in six days—but have been fighting ever since—for thirty years." Abizaid had predicted before the invasion that American troops would not be welcomed by Iraqis as "liberators," but would instead be regarded as "an antibody in their society."[39] Indeed they were. Coordinated bombings of the Jordanian embassy and the UN and Red Cross headquarters in Baghdad inaugurated the insurgency in August 2003. As terrorist attacks rippled across Iraq, increasingly aggressive American patrols—"large and in charge"—enraged the Iraqis, as did the contrast between the proliferating American bases—with showers, mess halls, coffee bars, air conditioners, satellite dishes—and the hot, decaying Iraqi cities around them. "Millions of dollars were being spent, and not a goddamn thing being done for the people downtown," an air force colonel recalled. "We looked like an occupation power, and we were; we behaved like one." Desperate to strangle the insurgency at birth, the Americans experimented with Israeli tactics—collective reprisals—which only made things worse. U.S. troops chopped down date and citrus trees, bulldozed homes and farms, and subjected the inevitably hostile villagers to deafening rock music at maximum volume.[40] The results were depressing. Traveling with a U.S. convoy, a reporter watched the troops scatter candies to Iraqi kids by the side of the road. "Don't touch it, don't touch it!" the Iraqi children squealed. "It's poison from the Americans; it will kill you!"[41]

AMERICAN VICEROY

Jerry Bremer was unlikely to calm things down. The sixty-one-year-old Bremer had been selected for his reliable political credentials (Republican, conservative) from a short list that had included Rudy Giuliani, James Baker III, Bob Dole, Bill Cohen and William Weld. Garner's brusque, unexpected replacement with Bremer reflected spreading panic in the White House, where Bush and Rice—who had relied on the optimism of Wolfowitz and Feith—finally recognized that they were going backward in Iraq. They had torpedoed Garner's smartest recommendation—to stand up a broad government of Iraqi exiles and "internals" that would include secular and religious Shiites, Sunnis and Kurds—only to discover that in so doing they had fatally undermined Garner. Jerry Bremer, bulging with ego and work ethic and nicknamed for his patron saint, Jerome, was dispatched as a take-charge strongman who might just work a saintly miracle.[42] Bremer, who had converted to Roman Catholicism (and embraced Saint Jerome) at the age of fifty-three, would wrestle the unraveling Iraqi scene back into some semblance of manageability, so that a Pentagon-approved government could be elected and installed. The stakes were high; rumor had it that Bremer might replace Powell as secretary of state if he succeeded.

Bremer, who had grown up in Hartford, Connecticut, before attending Andover, Yale and Harvard, moved into a villa by the Republican Palace. Visitors to his office noted its simplicity—a Dell desktop computer, a copy of Rudy Giuliani's *Leadership* and a box of raisin bran. Bremer's new CPA, headquartered in Saddam's Republican Palace in what was now called the "Green Zone," was accompanied by the Iraq Survey Group (ISG), which was a fourteen-hundred-member international inspection team organized by the Pentagon and the CIA to replace Hans Blix's UNMOVIC (United Nations Monitoring, Verification and Inspection Commission) and hunt more aggressively for Saddam's weapons of mass destruction. Bush and Cheney had promised that the invasion of Iraq would create a "moment of truth," when Iraq's hidden WMD arsenals would be yanked from "totalitarian darkness" for the world to see. They found nothing, in the dark or the light. It embarrassingly appeared that Saddam's nuclear weapons program had indeed withered on the vine and that the dictator *had* destroyed most of his chemical and biological weapons in 1991, and the rest in the ensuing years under the pressure of UN inspections.[43]

Bush—who improbably asserted that Saddam must have moved his WMD to

Syria or buried them in the desert—was still optimistic that he could bring Iraq under control. Perhaps he was taken in by Bremer's imperious confidence. Bremer had demanded near absolute powers in Baghdad. He scoffed at the "squirrel cage" of the interagency process, where State, CIA, the NSC and the Pentagon would all reserve the right to review and "chop on" his arrangements. Refusing to be twisted and turned by "an 8,000-mile-long screwdriver," Bremer agreed only to report occasionally to Rice and her deputy, Steve Hadley, and to his masters in the Pentagon, who, startlingly, had forgotten that he worked for *them*. "He works for you, Don," Condi Rice reminded Rumsfeld in 2003, but Rumsfeld wanted nothing more to do with Bremer or Iraq. "No, he doesn't," Rumsfeld (wrongly) protested. "He's been talking to the NSC; he works for the NSC." The master bureaucrat was trying to pass the buck; he even told a startled Bremer that he was "bowing out of the political process" after having expended so much effort monopolizing it, and cutting out the State Department, the CIA, Treasury, Justice and everyone else before the war.[44] Left to his own devices in Baghdad, Bremer sidelined veteran diplomats seconded to him as advisers and relied instead on what Rajiv Chandrasekaran, the *Washington Post*'s Baghdad bureau chief, called "a coterie of sycophantic young aides, most of whom had never worked in government before and were too junior to be beholden to anyone back home. Their only loyalty was to the viceroy."[45]

When the CIA reestablished a presence in the Green Zone—the four-square-mile U.S. enclave in central Baghdad—it was appalled by the incompetence of Bremer's fifteen-hundred-member viceroyalty. "Boss," one officer reported to Tenet, "that place runs like a graduate school seminar, none of them speaks Arabic, almost nobody's ever been to an Arab country, and no one makes a decision but Bremer." Zinni called Bremer's administration "a pickup team," and people joked in Baghdad and Washington that CPA stood for "Can't Produce Anything," a worthy successor to Garner's "Organization of Really Hapless Americans." Green Zone culture erected a wall between America and Iraq. Everything was contracted out. Food was flown in from the United States; laundry was bagged up and driven to Kuwait for washing. Security was provided by Gurkhas or American contractors. Sex was confined to coalition couples, usually in portable toilets or against the wall in a dark quarter of the Green Zone, because no one below the senior executive cadres had any privacy. "Are we in teething problems or fatally flawed in concept?" a senior Pentagon administrator wrote as his team settled into the Republican Palace. "Military and OSD cannot make the transition from military to political-military mission." Out of ideas, Bush asked Congress for $87 billion to begin rebuilding Iraq, an admission of defeat by a president who had promised that Iraqi reconstruction would be "self-financing."[46]

"PASTING TOGETHER FEATHERS, HOPING FOR A DUCK"

Money was being spent promiscuously, but little effort was spent reconciling Shiites and Sunnis or figuring out how to break the insurgency, whose "precision was astounding," a reporter observed. Every well-meaning Iraqi who had stepped forward in the months after April 2003 to help build a better country was being systematically exterminated: "They went to the slaughter. Thousands and thousands of them: editors, pamphleteers, judges and police officers."[47] Instead of shielding and promoting those indispensable Iraqi faces of the new Iraq, Bremer's CPA veered off in weird directions. "What CPA seemed to be getting were people anxious to set up a Baghdad stock exchange or try out a flat-tax system." They were trying to convert one of the most centralized states in the world into a privatized free market that would light a path for George W. Bush's America, but they were trying out their schemes before even basic security had been established.[48] A *Washington Post* reporter confirmed the CIA's impression in 2004: "Most people in the palace had simply given up, they repaired to the bar in the al-Rasheed Hotel, where they drank Turkish beer, Lebanese wine, and third-rate blended Scotch . . . but a few bureaucrats remained cloistered in their air-conditioned offices, toiling for 18 hours a day to check off one more item on the grand to-do list before they flew home." They were, as one participant put it, "pasting together feathers, hoping for a duck," and the duck was not materializing. The only universally safe topic of conversation in the Green Zone was "praise of 'the mission'—the Bush administration's campaign to transform Iraq into a peaceful, modern, secular democracy where everyone, regardless of sect or ethnicity, would get along."[49]

For a while, Bremer and his aides seemed to be everywhere in their convoys of armored GMC Suburbans, bristling with heavily armed security provided by Blackwater USA and other private security firms. Bremer dropped in on schools, hospitals, factories and soccer fields. He and his team were active participants in what Bob Woodward called the "Kabuki" of generals and administrators knowing they were losing in Iraq but telling the White House what it wanted to hear.[50] Bremer—

who would have seen disturbing graffiti smeared on walls, such as, "Anyone who helps the Americans is a dirty traitor worth killing"—had expectantly forwarded Rumsfeld a copy of a May 2003 Rand Corporation report that called for five hundred thousand coalition troops to stabilize Iraq.[51] That report had reaffirmed many of the points made by General Shinseki before the war; namely, that there is "an inverse ratio between force levels and the level of risk," for the simple reason that fewer peacekeepers on the ground encourages insurgents to shoot at them. Fewer peacekeepers also compels the peacekeepers to rely on excessive force, to cow potential insurgents and protect themselves. As the U.S. Army learned in Iraq, that reliance on force begets more, not fewer, insurgents.[52] But Rumsfeld, who was yearning to draw down the 145,000 troops actually in Iraq, never replied. So Bremer fell back on symbolism and photo ops. "Bremer," one reporter observed, "was keen to demonstrate that he was no Jay Garner. The way to do that was to be out and about, in front of the cameras, with the air of a head of state."[53]

"MISSION ACCOMPLISHED"

Bush too put on airs, which explained his theatrical flight on May 1, 2003, to the USS *Abraham Lincoln*, where the president landed on the carrier in a flight suit, mugged for the cameras and later, as the sun set on San Diego, gave his "Mission Accomplished" speech. "In the battle of Iraq, the United States and our allies have prevailed," he intoned. In fairness, Bush was responding to a request from Tommy Franks to acknowledge the valiant exertions of his troops, as well as the legal need to proclaim "major combat operations" over so that less valiant nations would join the coalition for peacekeeping duties; however, as one historian wrote, proclaiming the mission accomplished in May 2003 was like "tearing down the goalposts at halftime." Meanwhile, the May issue of *Vanity Fair* hit the streets with Deputy Secretary of Defense Paul Wolfowitz's surprising admission that the war in Iraq had not really been about WMD after all. The Bush war cabinet had merely "settled on" WMD "because it was the one issue that everyone could agree on," and the one most likely to engage all strands of the federal bureaucracy and grab the attention of "Joe Public."[54]

Meanwhile, the insurgency flamed across Iraq. Although Rumsfeld, Garner and then Bremer—"the proconsul in desert boots and rep tie"—called the insurgents "FREs" (former regime elements) or "Anti-Iraqi Forces," they were in fact largely

Iraqis fighting for various, entirely predictable Iraqi agendas. Bremer articulated a three-step plan to pacify Iraq—restore electricity, water and other basic services; reopen banks and resume paying salaries; and wean Iraqis from the Baath's socialist precepts—but the insurgency raged on regardless, and made services, security and job creation difficult.[55] Bush, Cheney and Rumsfeld tried for a time to forbid the use of the word "insurgency." *State of Denial*, the third volume of Bob Woodward's quartet on Bush's war, made the point that everyone who mattered in the Bush administration "remained inured to harsh truths." But the media had no aversion to harsh truths, and they kept using the word "insurgency," and, by and by, Bush, Cheney and the army did too.[56] There were lots of violent criminals mixed in with the insurgents. They had been released by Saddam in a prewar general amnesty that filled Iraq's towns and villages with sociopathic killers who were only too happy to take up arms against Americans and Iraqis alike.

In the "Sunni Triangle"—which extended from Saddam's hometown of Tikrit southwest to Ramadi and southeast to Baghdad—the insurgents were Baathists and Sunni tribesmen battling for power and survival against what they took to be a swelling tide of American-backed Kurds and Shiites. "The old Baathists are everywhere in Iraq," a forty-four-year-old Sunni engineer told the *Los Angeles Times* in July 2004. Saddam had provided jobs and status; now both were in short supply. Towns and villages sloughed off irregular mujahideen, who would gang up to attack American troops and then blend back in with the general population.[57] "De-Baathification" had left old Sunni elites and just plain old Sunni cops and soldiers with nothing to do or earn. The insurgency beckoned as an alternate career. The Sunnis embarked on a campaign of ethnic cleansing, using death squads and terrorism to force Shiites and Kurds out of contested areas. Wherever U.S. forces interfered, they too were targeted. Until 2007, 70 to 80 percent of U.S. casualties were generated by IEDs, car bombs, suicide bombers, snipers, mortars and rocket-propelled grenade attacks in the Sunni areas: Baghdad, Anbar and Salah ad Din provinces. Why Feith's OSP never reckoned with the wrath of the Sunni Arabs—20 percent of the population and Iraq's privileged caste—was a question on everyone's mind as the insurgency accelerated. "Blood draws more blood," a leading Iraqi politician fretted.[58] Only occupation troops and patient, peaceful methods could have stanched the bleeding. "Plans are nothing," the great Prussian general Helmuth von Moltke had famously observed. "But planning is everything."

Plans or no plans, Bush still felt that he had matters in hand. Not having made any arrangements for a long-term stay in Iraq—Shinseki had called Bush's approach "a twelve-division strategy for a ten-division army"—Bush turned to private contractors to fill the gaps in housing, food, fuel, telephones, Internet and other logistics services. The demands on Houston-based Halliburton were so intense and unexpected—by the Pentagon civilians, not the dissenting brass—that the army was forced to revise its contract with Halliburton every other day in 2003 and 2004. Corruption flourished in a poorly audited atmosphere of hasty no-bid contracts that totaled over $100 billion. Halliburton alone took $18 billion of Iraq work in 2004; it was accused by Pentagon auditors of billing the government for $200 million of meals that were never served. Titan Corporation of San Diego was accused of overbilling the government to the tune of $4.9 million.[59] Senator Ted Stevens of Alaska, driven from office by felony charges in 2008, earmarked billions of dollars in no-bid Iraq work for "Alaska Native corporations," most of which was subcontracted to non-Alaskan contractors like Lockheed Martin and Bechtel.[60] Some U.S. Army personnel and civilian officials in Iraq and Kuwait lined their pockets too: a U.S. Army major in Kuwait took $9 million in no-bid kickbacks; his successors more than $1 million. Iraqi government ministers expected 5 percent kickbacks for every development project in their portfolios; with billions of dollars of American direct aid flowing in, the Iraqi bureaucracy got at least as rich—on U.S. taxpayer money—as their crooked American mentors. An Australian journalist revealed how a contract was bid by Iraq's ministry of electricity: "The work was worth $15 million, but the minister's staff wanted a rake-off of about $40 million. They advised the bidder to inflate the price to $70 million so that they could have their cut and the bidder could make a good profit too."[61] Eventually, the Iraqi government wearied of the revelations of its corruption and simply dismissed the anticorruption auditors who had been attached to every ministry in the early days of the new Iraq.[62] President Bush remained sanguine despite the paucity of troops, the mediocre performance of the contractors and the stench of corruption emanating from his Iraqi leaders. "Bring 'em on," Bush taunted the insurgents on July 2, 2003, with the trademark swagger that would be decreasingly on display as the war ground on.[63]

"BRING 'EM ON"

Bush's fighting words were spectacularly ill chosen, since insurgent attacks—like the "Ramadan Offensive"—were drawing a widening torrent of American blood. There were successes in the summer of 2003. Troops from the 101st Airborne Division and Task Force 20 cornered and killed Saddam's sons—Uday and Qusay—in Mosul in July 2003, and by summer's end more than three hundred senior Baath officers and bureaucrats had been killed or arrested. But Wolfowitz's postwar solution for Iraq—a pro-American satrapy run by the malleable Ahmed Chalabi—had come spectacularly, humiliatingly unglued. Inside Iraq, General Rick Sanchez had been given field command of all 180,000 coalition troops, an abrupt promotion from a division command of 20,000 that may have surprised Sanchez as much as those around him. Sanchez's peers thought him the embodiment of the Peter Principle—he had been promoted up to his level of incompetence. A State Department colleague was withering in his assessment of Sanchez: "All trees, no forest, not a strategic or political thought." Like Bremer, with whom he had frosty relations, Sanchez was remote, aloof and dictatorial, which would explain how the grotesque scandals of Abu Ghraib were not detected and corrected early. The three-star general concerned himself chiefly with logistics and "metrics": trying to measure and assert "progress," like Westmoreland in Vietnam.[64]

Six thousand miles away in Washington, Bush finally recognized that Rumsfeld and Wolfowitz had made a hash of the war. In October 2003, he transferred some of Rumsfeld's powers to Condi Rice, who belatedly created an Iraq Stabilization Group in the White House. Rumsfeld resented the interference, which he compared to "Iran-Contra," but this time he was ignored.[65] By December 2003, the Americans had still not found any WMD in Iraq, nor had they established a connection between Saddam and al-Qaeda. It doesn't matter, President Bush assured the nation. If Saddam didn't have WMD, he would have *tried* to get them. As for the al-Qaeda–Iraq connection, which the president and Cheney had made much of before the war, a document revealing contacts between the leader of the 9/11 hijackers and Saddam materialized in Baghdad in December 2003. On closer examination, it proved to be a forgery.[66]

AHMED CHALABI AND THE EXILES

The world and Iraq would be a better place with Ahmed Chalabi in charge, President Bush asserted. Seated behind the First Lady at Bush's State of the Union address in January 2004, Chalabi had swum smilingly into focus each time the cameras glanced at Laura Bush. He was George W. Bush's great white hope—and the darling of Cheney and Wolfowitz—but he was about to fall.[67] Chalabi had promised to raise a fifteen-thousand-man "Iraqi Freedom Force" (IFF) among Iraqi exiles in Europe, America and the Middle East, but only ninety-five volunteered. Although Powell's State Department and Tenet's CIA warned that Chalabi had no popular base or legitimacy—and Franks had sputtered, "I don't have time for this fucking bullshit"— Cheney insisted that the "control" offered by Chalabi's IFF trumped considerations of popular legitimacy, and Feith insisted that "*we* can legitimize them." It was the exact opposite of the healthier policy pursued in Afghanistan, where Hamid Karzai had been deployed on the battlefield and then certified by an Afghan *loya jirga* before being hoisted into power. The CIA's mission manager for Iraq grumbled that, in this case, the neocons were pursuing a different Afghan solution: "It was as though Defense and the vice president's staff wanted to invite comparison with the Soviet invasion of Afghanistan," when Soviet troops toppled the government and flew Babrak Karmal in from Moscow.[68]

Inserted into Iraq behind American troops, Chalabi and his ninety-five merry men—who had been sensibly downgraded from troops to translators—were instantly reviled by Iraqis as American stooges. Despite massive U.S. backing, Chalabi's party got few votes and no seats in Iraqi parliamentary elections.[69] With no electoral prospects, Chalabi played the Iranian ace that he had always kept up his sleeve. The Iranian ayatollahs liked Chalabi for the same reasons that the Americans did. Chalabi was a Shiite and anti-Saddam, and, for Tehran, he was cheap, because the Americans were paying his bills—an estimated $30 million in bills since the early 1990s. With American support faltering—he was despised by virtually everyone, including UN special representative for Iraq Lakhdar Brahimi—Chalabi converted overnight into a sectarian Shiite politician. Ironically, the conversion was facilitated by Paul Wolfowitz, who had the bright idea of augmenting Chalabi's derisory corps of translators with several hundred members of the Iraqi Badr Brigades, fundamentalist Shiite militiamen who had been armed and protected by the Islamic Republic of Iran since 1979.[70]

No longer the lapdog of the Americans, Chalabi—with the Pentagon's witless help—would become the lapdog of the Iranians. He would ally with Iraq's leading Shiite cleric, Grand Ayatollah Ali al-Sistani, as well as its most violent one, Moqtada al-Sadr, to hunt down Sunni Baathists and facilitate Shiite majority rule in Iraq. Brahimi, who had knit Afghanistan back together after the U.S. departure in 2002 by inviting some of the most disreputable warlords back into government, had never seen anyone quite so disreputable as Chalabi. To appease his mentors in

Tehran, Chalabi was now angling for an Iraqi Islamic Republic, which was not the sort of "representative government" that the Bush Doctrine had been seeking. Just four months after Chalabi had attended Bush's State of the Union address, a Navy SEAL team and Iraqi police drove up to the exile's Baghdad headquarters, surrounded it, arrested two of his aides, put a gun to Chalabi's head and carted off most of his files and computer drives. Chalabi was accused of developing an operational relationship with the Iranian government and bad-mouthing the U.S. occupation. "The electricity still doesn't work, thousands are dead and the U.S. has lost the moral high ground in the Middle East," Chalabi snarled. Bush was stunned. "What the hell is going on with Chalabi?" he fumed at a White House meeting. "Is he working for you?" he asked Tenet. No, Tenet replied; Langley assumed that Chalabi was working for the Pentagon. All eyes swiveled to Rumsfeld, who promised to "check his status." In fact, Chalabi's status was well known in the executive ring of the Pentagon—a $350,000 per month American subsidy and support from all the heavy hitters. Not getting anything out of Rumsfeld, Bush weakly trailed off: "I don't think he ought to be working for us."[71]

With Chalabi discredited—Garner called him "a thug, very sleazy"—Jerry Bremer cast about for someone more acceptable and hit upon Chalabi's chief rival: fifty-nine-year-old Iyad Allawi. Bremer made Allawi "interim prime minister of Iraq," with the brief to oversee elections and a constitutional convention. Like Chalabi, Allawi was a Shiite who had been living in exile for thirty years, which commended him to Bremer. Iraqis predictably viewed him as a "Western puppet" borne to Baghdad on American bayonets, a reputation that was not improved by credible rumors that Allawi—a former Baathist—had tortured communists in the 1960s, befriended Saddam Hussein and shot several terrorism suspects in cold blood in a Baghdad police station a week before he took office. His American handlers called him "Saddam Lite." President Bush showed no interest in Allawi's murky past. When apprised of the transfer of power from Bremer's CPA to Allawi's interim government, Bush jotted—without irony—"Let freedom reign!"[72]

"LET FREEDOM REIGN!"

Let terror reign was more like it. Whereas President Bush still viewed Iraq as a place where free men were being liberated from Baathist oppressors, many Iraqis took a different view. By promoting the Shiites, Bush was declassing Iraq's traditional Sunni elite, and—some Iraqis said—wrecking Islam by snatching Iraq from its "true" Sunni guardians and handing it over to "heretical Shiites."[73] Bremer grasped the dangers and actually handed the reins of government over to Allawi two days *early*, to foil the inevitable terrorist attacks. That's how insecure even the Green Zone had become. But Allawi's image and Baathist "dead-enders" proved to be the least of America's problems. Iraqi attitudes toward the U.S. occupation, Ambassador John Negroponte observed, were "the black, the gray, and the white," with black predominating in 2004.[74] Other groups joined the guerrilla war after Saddam's capture just before the New Year. Now it was obviously a fight for Iraq's future, and as Viceroy Bremer passed the baton to Ambassador Negroponte, he left more U.S. troops behind in Iraq than had been there when he arrived.

The lingering U.S. troops were sensibly transferred from the disastrous leadership of Rick Sanchez—"the William Westmoreland of the Iraq War," in Andy Bacevich's judgment—to that of a more effective general, George Casey. Abizaid proved little help to either Sanchez or Casey because he regarded Iraq as a bottomless pit of distractions from his strategic responsibilities in the wider Centcom theater, which included Pakistan, Iran, Saudi Arabia and the grinding war in Afghanistan.[75] While Casey wrote a twenty-five-page campaign plan—oddly, neither Franks nor Sanchez had ever drafted one, preferring uncoordinated "kill and capture" missions—foreign fighters streamed across Iraq's open borders to join Abu Musab al-Zarqawi's al-Qaeda in Iraq, and Iraq's Shiites began to form militias like Moqtada al-Sadr's Mahdi Army to defend their enclaves and drive out coalition-backed Iraqi security forces. The Syrians funneled $1.2 million a month into Ramadi to fuel the Sunni insurgency and lock America into an unwinnable war. American troops (and journalists) were struck by the local pride that sustained the insurgency, which was really a collection of insurgencies. "You want to overthrow Saddam Hussein's regime?" an insurgent in Nasiriyah had barked to an American reporter. "Go to Baghdad. What are you doing *here*?" No one in the Sunni areas seemed to mind Saddam's record of brutality. They reeled at the naiveté of the Bush Doctrine, which, they felt, *had* to cloak some darker motive and conspiracy: "In Iraq, if there is a leader who is fair, he will be killed. He must be tough, or he will be killed the next day."[76]

"IT IS . . . BETTER TO BE DEALING WITH TERRORISTS IN IRAQ THAN IN THE UNITED STATES"

Insurgents seized control of Fallujah in the Sunni Triangle and drew the United States into its heaviest combat of the war—a forty-seven-day battle that killed 95 Americans and 1,350 insurgents whose ranks included large numbers of foreign fighters from Yemen, Kuwait, Saudi Arabia, Jordan, Palestine, Syria, Algeria, Pakistan, China and the Philippines. "If you kill my brother, then I will kill yours," said one Fallujan. That would be a lot of brothers: in their battle to retake Fallujah in November 2004, the marines flattened the city under four thousand artillery rounds, ten thousand mortar shells and ten tons of aerial bombs. "We cannot afford many more victories like Fallujah," a former marine officer concluded. The marines had fought heroically—house to house and room to room. They gave the lie to bin Laden's prediction in his 1996 "Declaration of Jihad against America" that "your problem will be how to persuade your troops to fight, while our problem will be how to restrain our youths."[77] The marines needed no persuading, but, as another marine reflected, "what's the impact on a ten-year-old kid when he goes back in and sees his neighborhood destroyed? And what's he going to do when he's eighteen years old?" Still, the U.S. military had little option but to eliminate insurgent bases like Fallujah, which fed the violence in Baghdad, or Tal Afar in the north, which fed Mosul with a steady stream of suicide bombers. The apparition of foreign fighters in places like Fallujah and Tal Afar—fewer than 2 percent of total insurgents—was nevertheless seized upon by President Bush as evidence that the Iraq invasion had been essential. "We have to deal with threats *before* they come on our shore," he now asserted.[78]

In July 2004, Bush dismissed Senate criticism of his flawed rationale for the war—Saddam's weapons of mass destruction—by recasting the war altogether. David Kay had stepped down from leadership of the Iraq Survey Group in January 2004 and made a startling declaration. Saddam had *not* possessed WMD after all. "Everyone was wrong," Kay concluded. Saddam had destroyed everything in the early 1990s and merely bluffed to maintain an image of power. But Bush had already moved on, ignoring Kay's revelations as well as those of the 9/11 Commission in June 2004, which conclusively demonstrated that there had been no evidence of a "collaborative, operational relationship" between Iraq and al-Qaeda.[79] Bush ignored those emerging truths. America, Bush now asserted, had *really* invaded Iraq as a means of "taking the fight to the enemy . . . defending the peace, protecting the peace and extending the peace."[80] Rumsfeld hazarded the same argument: "It is, in my view, better to be dealing with terrorists in Iraq than in the United States."

Both men skipped over the inconvenient fact that, by their invasion of Iraq, they had essentially taken a Russian problem—Chechnya—and made it into an American one. In 2004–5, the "underground railroad" that had fed the long jihad in Chechnya diverted to Iraq; the hundreds of foreign fighters who had made the trip through Azerbaijan and Dagestan to Grozny now made their way through Syria to the Iraqi border city of Qaim, where they made arrangements to kill Americans. Worse, an Arab analyst noted that al-Qaeda seemed impervious to the costly "war on terror" in Iraq. On the contrary, Iraq became al-Qaeda's "training ground" and "recruitment officer," and killing al-Qaeda fighters in Iraq did nothing to constrain continuing al-Qaeda attacks in Jordan, Egypt and Morocco. If Iraq, as Bush stated, was the "central front" in the war with al-Qaeda, small victories there had little or no effect on the peripheral fronts, and indeed *strengthened* the revived jihad in Afghanistan, where foreign fighters fled whenever the military pressure intensified in Iraq.

Saudi and Israeli studies made during the Iraq War arrived at the same disturbing conclusion: most of the foreign fighters in Iraq had not been jihadis *before* the U.S. invasion; they had "been radicalized by the war itself."[81] Polling in late 2003 revealed that more than half of Saudis approved of bin Laden's message and that more Egyptians approved of bin Laden than of George W. Bush, whose annual subsidies kept Egypt afloat.[82] While Russian president Vladimir Putin's approval ratings soared because of his entirely accidental reprieve by Operation Iraqi Freedom, Bush's sank.[83] For the first time, a majority of Americans polled—51 percent— said that the Iraq War was going badly. A *Washington Post*/ABC poll revealed that 53 percent of Americans now considered that the war was not worth fighting. Pundits who had supported the invasion—Thomas Friedman, David Brooks, Fouad Ajami, Fareed Zakaria and others—joined a stampede in the opposite direction. It became as fashionable to hate this war as it once had been to support it. "A year or so ago, it was our war, and we claimed it proudly," Ajami wrote. "But gone is the hubris. Let's face it, Iraq is not going to be America's showcase in the Arab-Muslim world."[84]

New and old critics of the Bush administration goggled at the president's effrontery in redefining the war after his original arguments had proven false. Even casual observers knew that peace had reigned in Iraq until the U.S. invasion—"Iraq was not a failed state in 2002," as one analyst put it—and that al-Qaeda, loathed and feared by Saddam Hussein, had only entered Iraq in strength because of the vacuum created by the exclusion zones, the U.S. invasion and the dictator's fall. Operation Iraqi Freedom, not Saddam's plotting, had made Iraq "a magnet for international terrorist activity," the CIA concluded in January 2005.[85] Common sense suggested that the average Iraqi insurgent—paid $200 to "pray and spray" with an assault rifle—was not the sort of terrorist who was ever going to obtain a passport and visa and make it to the United States. He was a purely Iraqi phenomenon *created* by Franks's invasion. Indeed an internal Pentagon report confessed that "the disaster that is the reconstruction of Iraq has been the *key* cause of the insurgency." A CIA briefing for Rice and Hadley in November 2003—it was repeated for Cheney and Libby—lamented that the United States had offered "Iraqi factional leaders . . . the greatest jihad yet, against Americans in the Arab heartland." On the ropes in 2003, al-Qaeda would use Bush's war "to keep itself alive and make a comeback." At a briefing for Bush in November, another CIA analyst let the president in on the bad news: "Iraq came along at exactly the right time for al-Qaeda." It "inspired a permanent jihadist movement and pulled Iraqis—hitherto isolated by Saddam's police state—into the fight," waged in now chaotic Iraq by the same "experienced facilitators" the CIA had encountered in Afghanistan, Chechnya and Bosnia, as well as some new ones.[86]

ABU GHRAIB

With old and new insurgents swarming around them—there were 26,496 insurgent attacks on coalition and Iraqi security forces in 2004—the Americans desperately sought "human intelligence," or HUMINT, to unravel the guerrilla networks. Nothing was working. "Everything we do helps us lose," an army officer observed. "More patrols—bad. Less patrols—bad. How do we get out of it? I don't know."[87] The CPA had been folded up in June 2004 and converted into a U.S. embassy, but the transition had not been attended by any reduction in violence. For the history books—where the Bush administration had hoped to inscribe a quick, bloodless victory—the Iraq War in mid-2004 surpassed the War of 1812, the Mexican War and the Spanish-American War in numbers of U.S. casualties. Who was killing and maiming all those Americans? General John Abizaid referred in briefings to a total of five thousand insurgents in Iraq at a time when he had five thousand suspected insurgents in his prisons. Sunni FREs who had worked in the military, police and intelligence services directed loose networks of "angry young men"—unemployed and criminal Sunnis—to attack American and Iraqi government targets.[88] General Casey finally called the war what it was—an insurgency—and roughed up a strategy to defeat it: contain the guerrillas, expand the Iraqi security forces, rebuild the Iraqi economy and use carrots and sticks to bring the Sunnis back on board. In the prison of Abu Ghraib, twenty miles west of Baghdad, American guards and interrogators preferred sticks to carrots. They subjected Iraqi prisoners to harsh abuse to extract information, abuse that was exposed in April 2004 by *60 Minutes II* and by a piece in the *New Yorker* by Seymour Hersh, who had exposed the My Lai massacre and cover-up in 1969 (and won a Pulitzer Prize).

The misconduct at Abu Ghraib—one of the vilest prisons in Iraq during the Saddam era—reflected Rumsfeld's frustration with the impenetrability of the Iraqi insurgency, but also with Washington's legal constraints on rapid action in the war on terrorism. One officer described Rumsfeld in the fall of 2001 as "kicking a lot of glass and breaking doors." He wanted to remove the legal barriers to renditions, targeted assassinations of al-Qaeda and Taliban leaders, and rough interrogations.[89] Instead of embarking on a time-consuming counterinsurgency strategy, Cheney, Rumsfeld and Undersecretary of Defense for Intelligence Stephen Cambone authorized the U.S. military's Iraq interrogators to use the tough methods on Iraqi prisoners that had previously been reserved for al-Qaeda suspects. Code-named "Copper Green," the secret Pentagon program subjected Iraqi prisoners to extreme physical and mental abuse and sexual humiliation. Even with harsh interrogation techniques that amounted to torture, it was hard to unravel the insurgent network precisely because the insurgents were not networked. As one analyst wrote in the summer of 2004, the Iraqi insurgency was a "netwar" against a flat, segmented adversary, not a pyramidal, unified one. With its multitude of Sunni, Islamist, Shiite and criminal factions—most Iraqi, some foreign—the insurgency had no clear leader, no reigning ideology, no fixed organization and no concerted plan to seize and hold power in Iraq. Where the insurgents did take cities—most notably Fallujah in 2004—they cooperated loosely and retreated under heavy attack, never to return. Loosely affiliated cells swam into one another, traded weapons and intelligence (often gleaned from turncoat Iraqi police or Iraqi employees of the CPA), launched opportunistic attacks and then drifted apart.

That lack of structure and intelligence combined with America's paucity of troops—not enough to guard the borders and manage growing numbers of detainees—drove Rumsfeld, Cambone and General Geoffrey Miller, who had traveled from Guantanamo to Baghdad in August 2003, to insist that "detention operations be used as an enabler for interrogation."[90] Since the army had no real counterinsurgency doctrine, officers did what they had been trained to do. They ran raids into sullen neighborhoods, grabbed suspects and detained them—an estimated forty thousand detainees in the months after the U.S. invasion. The population of Abu Ghraib had swelled to seven thousand inmates by October 2003. That restive horde was guarded by just 360 demoralized military police officers. With a 1:20 ratio of guards to prisoners, General Miller decided to "Gitmoize" Abu Ghraib in the hope that harsh measures would restore discipline and yield intelligence. Everything was allowed—prisoners were stripped naked, beaten with chairs, placed in stress positions, exposed to extremes of heat and cold, threatened with snarling guard dogs, denied sleep, sodomized with broom handles and fluorescent lightbulbs, dressed in women's underwear and made to masturbate in front of chortling female guards.[91]

The foul methods—stop "running a country club," Miller growled—yielded more and sometimes better intelligence, but at a high cost to America's global standing and to army morale. Reserve Brigadier General Janis Karpinski, who ran Abu Ghraib as well as the other military prisons in Iraq, was expected to wink at the harsher prison conditions and all the secret interrogators in civilian clothes—some military, some CIA, some private security contractors—going in and out of Abu Ghraib on Cambone's orders. Yet Karpinski was later blamed for "leadership failures." Seven enlisted members of the 372nd Military Police Company were scapegoated for their sadistic part in the "Gitmoization" ordered by their superiors. And many innocent Iraqis—"cabdrivers, brothers-in-law and people pulled off the streets"—were raked over the coals for nothing. The foul play at Abu Ghraib was an extension of the foul play in the streets of Iraq, where abuse of detainees by U.S. troops—"PUC [person under control] fucking," in army parlance—became commonplace. One journalist ascribed this in part to "strategic confusion." Told by their commander in chief that they were in Iraq to fight al-Qaeda and retaliate for 9/11, many unreflecting troops came to regard *all* Iraqis as terrorists.[92] After gunning down an Iraqi woman who stood between him and an insurgent, an army sergeant told a (shocked) reporter: "I'm sorry, but the chick was in the way."[93] The army's most culturally sensitive troops—the special forces—resigned in droves to join private security firms like Blackwater USA in part because of their frustration with the regular army's sledgehammer approach. One such early retiree called Sanchez's Coalition Joint Task Force "a mammoth elephant trying to squish a mouse." Another, Dave Scholl—who had taken the trouble to learn Arabic—lamented, "We are a hated occupier. How many Iraqis have seen an American who wasn't pointing a gun at them?"[94]

"I'M A NEOCONSERVATIVE WHO'S BEEN MUGGED BY REALITY"

Returning to Baghdad in February 2004 for the first time since May 2003, George Tenet wrote that he'd "never seen so many stressed-out young people in one place in my life." Even CIA analysts showed up for meetings in body armor.[95] A U.S. official charged with rebuilding Iraq's universities threw up his hands in despair. "I'm a neoconservative who's been mugged by reality," he told the *Washington Post*.[96] The impact of the insurgency on U.S. combat troops was dreadful. Already in 2004, 20 percent of U.S. soldiers returning from Iraq suffered serious mental health problems because of the randomness of death and maiming in Iraq from suicide bombers, IEDs, RPG attacks, snipers, ambushes, mortars and mines. "Iraqis look at you like they don't want you here," an eighteen-year-old private in the 1st Armored Division told *USA Today* in June 2004. "And it's just scary that your life might just end right there. That scares me a lot."[97] IEDs were the emblem of the Iraq War; they evolved quickly from primitive booby traps—hardwired artillery shells and mortar rounds—to remote-controlled roadside bombs made from C-4 plastic explosive or TNT and detonated with cell phones or garage door openers. Hidden amid rubble, beneath piles of trash or inside the carcasses of dead dogs, IEDs were difficult to detect, especially as the temperatures soared to 120 degrees and tempers, stamina and patience frayed.

The rate of posttraumatic stress disorder in Iraq was far higher than had been the case in the Persian Gulf War (10 percent or less) or even the Vietnam War (15 percent). Serious brain injuries spiked, as the blasts from IEDs stuffed into tree branches or hung from light poles concussed soldiers who survived the flying fragments. The percussion heaved brains around inside the skull in a way that nature had never intended.[98] The insurgency was also stretching the U.S. military to the breaking point because of its demand for boots on the ground. "The war in Iraq is wrecking the Army and the Marine Corps," retired navy captain John Byron wrote in July 2004. "Troop rotations are in shambles, and the all-volunteer force is starting to crumble as we extend combat tours." Pentagon investments in hardware and readiness were being cut to pay for the nonstop operational tempo in Iraq.[99] Bush, who had vowed to defeat Iraq on the cheap without dipping into reserves and national guards, now found himself scraping the bottom of the barrel everywhere. The U.S. Army of 2004 was one-third smaller than the U.S. Army of 1991, and it was stretched thin. "The math was the math," JCS chairman General Peter Pace lamented. He worried that President Bush, in his panic to win a war that had gone horribly wrong, was "using the reserve assets of the United States inappropriately."[100]

Bush was. The army reserves (205,000 troops) and national guards (350,000) were called up—"thrown into missions for which they hadn't been designed"—and the active-duty army (499,000 troops) shifted soldiers from service to combat jobs, lowered recruiting standards, redeployed forces from South Korea and even sent elite training units to Iraq.[101] Those measures too proved inadequate, which explained the Bush administration's deepening, problematic reliance on private security firms, which provided more troops to Bush than all of his "coalition of the willing" allies put together—about sixty thousand contractors in all, of which fifteen to twenty thousand were "shooters." But those armed contractors, employed by firms like Dyn-Corp, Halliburton and Blackwater, had an entirely different mission than the army and marines. The firms had to protect their "principals"—officers, officials, dignitaries and businessmen—and had no qualms about shooting into crowds or barreling onto crowded sidewalks in armored SUVs to accomplish that, practices that undermined all efforts to win over the Iraqi people.[102] Rumsfeld had vowed after 9/11 that he would not repeat the mistake of the Soviets in Afghanistan—going in heavy to become bogged down in a quagmire. Curiously, he was now doing just that in Iraq.

"This Is a War against Terrorism and Iraq Is Just *One* Campaign"

For all the unease that attended Bush's escalation of the war and its impact on Americans—the recall of inactive veterans, his extension of combat tours from twelve to fifteen months, his "stop-loss" orders, which forced thousands of troops to remain in Iraq after their contracts had expired, as well as the revelations of prisoner abuse at Abu Ghraib—Bush won reelection in November 2004 to a second term. Unlike Barack Obama in 2008, John Kerry in 2004 sketched no credible alternative to the Bush war policy. His was, as a sympathetic critic put it, a "me too, only better" approach that inspired few swing voters to switch horses in midstream.[103] Bush, Cheney and the neocons regarded Bush's reelection as a validation not only of their decision to invade Iraq, but of the Bush Doctrine and its call for "transformation" in the Middle East. Wolfowitz and Feith were rehabilitated; Rumsfeld recovered his bounce. Porter Goss replaced George Tenet at the CIA and oversaw a purge of dissidents in the Directorate of Intelligence. Analysts who continued to criticize the Bush-Cheney approach to the Middle East were let go or reassigned. "Apostates" were replaced with "true believers."

Lebanon's "Cedar Revolution" in early 2005 suggested that Bush finally had the wind at his back. After Rafik Hariri, a popular Lebanese politician, was assassinated for demanding a withdrawal of all Syrian forces in Lebanon—who had been there for thirty years—Lebanese crowds demanded their sovereignty back and shamed the Syrians into withdrawing their fourteen-thousand-man garrison. Even though the Israelis warned that the Cedar Revolution was more hype than substance—the "Syrian intelligence services and their claque of Lebanese collaborators" as well as Hezbollah remained in charge—the Bush administration eagerly advertised Lebanon as the first great success of the Bush Doctrine. (The name, "Cedar Revolution," was coined in Washington, not Beirut, where it was simply called an independence intifada.)[104] With the Cedar Revolution coming hot on the heels of Bush's second inaugural, Rumsfeld reportedly met with the Joint Chiefs and told them that the American people had voted for Bush, again, and that there must be no more second-guessing. The gist of Rumsfeld's message—according to an insider—was this: "This is a war against terrorism and Iraq is just *one* campaign. The Bush administration is looking at this as a huge war zone. Next we're going to have the Iranian campaign . . . This is the last hurrah—we've got four years, and want to come out of this saying we won the war on terrorism."[105]

Even as it stumbled in Iraq, the Bush administration weighed military operations against Iran. Indeed they were already under way. American special forces were clashing with Iranians along the border, the Americans trying to stem the flow of Iranian cash, weapons and operatives into Iraq. But the Bush administration wanted to knock over the mullahs, open the gates to secular reformers in Iran and strike a deadly blow against the Iranian nuclear program, which, most Western intelligence agencies (including the United States) believed in 2005 was three to five years away from a nuclear warhead. The Islamic Revolution of 1979 and the expropriation of private savings and assets—banks, hotels, businesses and industries—had given the mullahs deep pools of unaccounted money, much of which was siphoned off to secret accounts in Switzerland and Luxembourg or buried in the *bonyads* (religious foundations) that later became a useful place to hide funds that could be spent on the nuclear program, terrorism and the war in Iraq. Possessing 10 percent of the world's oil and 15 percent of its natural gas gave Iran even more leverage as oil and gas prices began to climb with world demand.[106] Iran had been a good customer of Pakistan's black-market nuclear weapons program since the mid-1980s; just how good a customer the Bush administration discovered in 2004, when Pakistani engineer A. Q. Khan was placed under house arrest for having covertly sold the Iranians gas centrifuges for uranium enrichment. To Pakistan's other crimes in the war on terrorism—sheltering bin Laden, not policing its border regions, succoring the Taliban—was added this one, as Khan made it clear that General Musharraf, Bush's key ally in the war on terrorism, had been a silent partner to the "tens of millions of dollars" of technology sales to Iran and Libya.

Tensions with Iran and Pakistan simmered throughout the Iraq War, as the Bush administration seriously contemplated attacks on Iran's nuclear sites despite the fact that they were hardened, dispersed and, in the view of the International Atomic Energy Agency (IAEA) in 2008, dormant. Although Bush minimized that revelation—correctly noting that the Iranians could restart enrichment at any time—he was reluctant to launch another attack on Iranian or *any* WMD if they were not verifiably there. "There is," a U.S. intelligence official chuckled, "no education in the second kick of a mule." Having eyed the cocked Iranian hoof for several years, President Bush finally retreated in July 2008, grasping that any "hits" in Iran—to nuclear, chemical and missile sites—would be partial (even with A. Q. Khan's cooperation on targeting) and open to retaliation by Iran's long-range ballistic missiles, SAMs, antiship missiles, drones and Hezbollah clients in Lebanon and Iraq. Even if the Iranians didn't immediately retaliate—"We'll come down on the Israelis like a hammer and crush their bones," Iranian general Rahim Safavi warned in August 2004—they would certainly renounce the Nuclear Non-Proliferation Treaty after a U.S. or Israeli strike, and, as one analyst put it, "it's better to have them cheating *within* the system." Bush also grasped that the old neocon theory that a successful attack on Iran's WMD sites would trigger an uprising against the ayatollahs was fatuous. Iranians were nationalists first, partisans second, and would almost certainly rally behind the mullahs if the Americans (or Israelis) struck their military infrastructure.[107]

"YOU HAVE ALLOWED THE PERSIANS TO TAKE OVER IRAQ"

Even though prospects for an American invasion of Iran were better than they'd ever be—U.S. forces could invade Iran from Iraq *and* Afghanistan—Bush had no stomach for augmenting his already massive liabilities. Every move Bush made seemed to strengthen, not weaken, Iran. The Saudi foreign minister disgustedly noted this fact on his visit to Washington in September 2005. The United States and Saudi Arabia, Prince Saud al-Faisal reminded his hosts, had propped up Baghdad in the Iran-Iraq War and limited its violence against Iraq during the 1991 war "to keep Iran out of Iraq . . . Now we are handing the whole country over to Iran without reason."[108] Eighty-two-year-old King Abdullah made the same point to President Bush in April 2007: "You have allowed the Persians to take over Iraq."[109] Bush's invasion of Iraq had converted a weak, internally riven Sunni state into "the first modern Arab Shiite-dominated state." His support for the Israeli invasion of Lebanon in 2006 had made it possible that the Iranian-backed Shiites—just one-third of the Lebanese population—would take power there as well, by vaunting their anti-American and anti-Israeli credentials.[110] The Iraq insurgency was fueled by the conservative Sunni states around Iraq—Saudi Arabia, Kuwait and Jordan—which were willing to try *anything*, even Sunni terrorism that killed U.S. troops, to stop the spread of militant Shiism under the banner of Iran and reestablish their own waning credibility. That was the dirty little secret of the insurgency that no one dared utter in Washington: "War on America is now war on Shiism, and war on Shiism is now war on America." Of the twelve hundred foreign fighters detained in Syria between 2003 and 2005, 85 percent were Saudis, young men driven to Iraq by their *Saudi* prayer leaders. Their exodus addressed two problems for Riyadh: removing extremists from the kingdom and enlisting them against the Iraqi Shiites.[111]

Bush's horribly conceived wars had run the U.S. national debt to $7 trillion and converted Clinton's surplus into a $413 billion deficit, the biggest in American history, at a time when Iraq—its security, administration and infrastructure underwritten by U.S. taxpayers—was running a budget *surplus*. Bush's approval rating continued to plummet, and other threats crowded in. Henry Kissinger observed that even as Bush flailed in Iraq and Afghanistan—burning up $10 billion a month—"China's emergence as a great power and a potential superpower is already a principal element in shifting the international center of gravity to Asia."[112] Bush had wrong-footed America in the great game of geopolitics. He had promised that "when the Iraqis stand up, we will stand down"—in order to rebalance America's strained military—but there was no cohesive Iraqi nation to stand up and facilitate an American withdrawal. Instead, Iraq was fracturing into ethnic enclaves and terrorist havens. Kurds and Shiites voted in the elections of January 2005 for an "Iraqi Transitional Government," but most Sunnis boycotted the vote. Poland's president, who had committed a contingent to Bush's "coalition of the willing," lamented after the elections that "we've failed totally at nation-building in postwar Iraq." While 81 percent of Iraqis viewed the Americans as "occupiers," not "liberators," only 13 percent of Iraqis judged the U.S. invasion "morally justified." Pro-insurgent music cassettes and CDs sold well on Iraqi streets, with lyrics like this:

America has come and occupied Baghdad
The army and the people have weapons and ammunition
Let's join the fight and call out the name of Allah.[113]

The White House had hoped to turn Iraq over to the new government and begin withdrawing—two years after the "Mission Accomplished" speech—but May 2005 proved to be the bloodiest month since the invasion. Sunni suicide bombers—Iraqis, Saudis and Syrians—struck Shiite gatherings and holy places to discourage the Shiites from settling in Sunni areas or using their raw numbers to take control of an Iraqi democracy. The murder of Shiite political leader Ayatollah Muhammed Bakir Hakim in August 2003 had lit the fuse of sectarian struggle and deprived the United States of one of its most credible allies. Now the country descended into civil war, with 34,131 insurgent attacks in 2005, up from 24,496 the previous year. The Jordanian terrorist Abu Musab al-Zarqawi—who had stepped into bin Laden's empty shoes and opportunistically renamed his al-Tawhid organization "al-Qaeda in Iraq"—threw his weight behind the Sunni whirlwind, and made plans to reap it once the Americans cut and ran. Al-Zarqawi defined the Shiites as "the lurking serpent; they can inflict more damage on the *umma* than the Americans." They were "a sect of treachery and betrayal," heretics and atheists whom al-Zarqawi and many Iraqi Sunnis assumed were secretly conspiring with the Americans to take control of Iraq through Shiite stooges like Chalabi, Allawi or al-Maliki.[114]

In July 2005, al-Zawahiri wrote al-Zarqawi a letter in which he reminded the Jordanian terrorist that "the aftermath of the collapse of American power in Vietnam—and how they ran and left their agents—is noteworthy. We must be ready, starting now."[115] To help things along, al-Zarqawi's terrorists bombed the al-Askari Mosque in Samarra—one of the Shiite holy places—in February 2006. That atrocity set off the wave of killings that al-Zarqawi had been hoping for—the murder rate in Baghdad tripled after the bombing—as Shiites and Sunnis savagely settled scores. A 2006 study by the Johns Hopkins University Bloomberg School of Public Health estimated that more than six hundred thousand Iraqis had died since the war began, and two-thirds of them had died at the hands of their fellow Iraqis.[116] Refugees—terrified by the sectarian killings—flooded out of the country. By 2006 there were 1.6 million Iraqis living abroad—a tremendous brain drain, since the ones who left were usually the best educated.[117] Decent Sunnis wrung their hands at the carnage their coreligionists were inflicting—and Sunni Arab governments were abetting—in the name of Islam. "No Arab government raises its voice in condemnation," Abdul Rahman al-Rashed wrote in the Saudi daily *Asharq al Awsat*, "although most of them shrilly objected when the new Iraqi Constitution failed to mention that the country was part of the Arab Nation."[118]

What Arab governments did raise their voice to condemn was Operation Iraqi Freedom. In September 2005, the Saudi foreign minister called the chaos in Iraq "very threatening. It will draw the countries of the region into conflict."[119] Launched by Bush to create stability, OIF was creating the opposite. President Bush meanwhile hustled the Iraqis toward elections in December 2005, which would usher out Interim Prime Minister Allawi and produce a new parliament and prime minister and perhaps tranquilize the Iraqi political scene. To keep Americans focused on the war, Bush warned of "Islamofascists" marching to take over the world. In an October 6, 2005, speech, Bush warned that the Iraqi insurgents were seeking nothing less than "a totalitarian empire that denies all political and religious freedom." Although the neocons had faded away, they were still apparently writing the president's speeches, taking al-Zawahiri's July 2005 letter to al-Zarqawi as their text: "The militants believe that controlling one country will rally the Muslim masses, enabling them to overthrow all moderate governments in the region and establish a radical Islamic empire that spans from Spain to Indonesia."[120] Saddam Hussein at his worst had been unable to dent Iran or even conquer Kuwait, but the beleaguered terrorists were considered capable of taking over the world.

IRAQ 2.0

Prime Minister Nouri al-Maliki took office on May 20, 2006, to embark upon what the *Washington Post* called "Iraq 2.0," a beta version led by Iraqi, not American, officials.[121] The new government, which needed months to pull itself together, had even less success than the transitional government in stemming the sectarian violence. "Maliki was nobody's pick," the Baghdad CIA station chief lamented. "His name came up late. He has no real power base in the country or in parliament." Iraq's relations with its neighbors were strained; it was obvious, as former president Bill Clinton put it, that the war would not be won or settled "within the four corners of Iraq" alone.[122] Foreign fighters poured unchecked over the Syrian border. Iran erected a fifth column inside al-Maliki's Iraq by subsidizing and arming the Shiite parties and militias. Al-Maliki, who leaned heavily on the Shiite fundamentalist parties for support, did little to arrest the slide. When the Saudis protested Iran's growing military and political influence in Iraq, Bayan Jabr, the Iraqi finance minister (who hailed from the Iranian-backed Supreme Council for the Islamic Revolution in Iraq party) told the Saudis to shut up. "The Saudis have one god, he is the king . . . A whole country is named after a family." In contrast, Jabr boasted, "Iraq is the cradle of civilization that taught humanity reading and writing, and now some Bedouin riding a camel [Saudi foreign minister Prince Saud al-Faisal] wants to teach *us*." Anbar Province—populated in parts by Sunni Bedouins on camels—flared into indignant revolt, with insurgents taking control of Ramadi, the provincial capital. Baghdad continued to burn as Shiite and Sunni militias battled for neighborhoods. The bloodiest day of the war to that point was November 23, 2006, when Sunni militants exploded car bombs and fired mortar rounds into Sadr City—Baghdad's chief Shiite enclave, a slum the size of the Bronx—killing 215 and wounding 257. That atrocity led to matching atrocities by the Shiite militias and death squads, which attacked the Sunni neighborhoods.

In testimony before the Senate Armed Services Committee, Centcom commander Abizaid glumly agreed that Shinseki had been correct three years earlier: "General Shinseki was right that a greater international force contribution, U.S. force contribution, and Iraqi force contribution should have been available immediately after major combat operations."[123] The reference to "Iraqi force contribution" was odd, since no one had expected Iraqis to join the battle against Saddam in 2003, but it did reflect the obsession in 2005: to arm and train Iraqis to take over their own security. Virtually every Centcom and Pentagon briefing alluded to the improvement in Iraqi security forces, but somehow they were never ready, never able to conduct fully independent operations, and their minimum required numbers were always rising. In September 2005, the Pentagon said that 270,000 Iraqi police and soldiers would suffice to break the insurgency. In October, they revised the estimate upward to 325,000.[124] The new Iraq, an American official concluded, "was like a gardener without a trowel. We're still building the factory to make the trowel," which was a dismal and fitting epitaph for Operation Iraqi Freedom.[125]

Dismal 2006 was the backdrop for the dismal Iraq Study Group Report, which was supervised by former secretary of state James Baker (a Republican) and former congressman Lee Hamilton (a Democrat) and released to the public in December 2006. The bipartisan study group concluded that "the situation in Iraq is grave and deteriorating." They worried that Bush had blundered into a quagmire: "U.S. forces seem to be caught in a mission that has no foreseeable end." Thomas Friedman averred in the *New York Times* that "we must not throw more good American lives after good American lives for people who hate others more than they love their own children."[126] As if on cue, the weekly rate of insurgent attacks on civilians, coalition and Iraqi forces hit a new high in December 2006—1,057 attacks per week.[127] Pentagon plans to reduce the number of U.S. combat brigades in Iraq from fifteen to twelve by year-end 2006 were quietly shelved. President Bush, who had pinned his hopes on the Iraqi elections—"political progress will drive security gains"— finally admitted, within the walls of Camp David and the White House in late 2006, that the war was unwinnable unless the rampaging violence could *somehow* be reduced. That was the cue for General David Petraeus's counterinsurgency strategy to replace the failed Bush-Rumsfeld approach, which had been essentially: kick ass, take names, install the exiles and leave.

GENERAL DAVID PETRAEUS

Saddam Hussein was hanged for crimes against humanity on December 30, 2006, after a yearlong trial. For 2007, Bush replaced General George Casey—commander of Multinational Force Iraq—with General Petraeus. In the November 2006 mid-term elections, antiwar Democrats had won control of both houses of Congress, compelling Bush finally to dump Rumsfeld and to persuade Petraeus to fashion a strategy that would satisfy "both ends of Pennsylvania Avenue": the White House *and* Congress. Petraeus, who had gloomily projected an eight-year struggle in March 2003, was halfway there when he assumed Casey's command. With Princeton doctoral work on Vietnam under his belt and a keen interest in counterinsurgency, Petraeus advocated a twenty-thousand-troop "surge" to defeat the spreading insurgent attacks and establish security in key Iraqi towns and neighborhoods. "Surge" was a euphemism for "escalation" or "increase" at a time when Americans were yearning for a troop *withdrawal*, and when the British—recoiling at London's $16 billion in war costs—were pulling their entire contingent out of Iraq. One thing the British withdrawal did surge was the U.S. share of the "U.S.-led coalition," which remained a "coalition" in name only, with U.S. forces composing 92 percent of coalition troops and coalition force levels down 75 percent from 2003. The only big contingents left were the (departing) British, two thousand troops from Georgia and twelve hundred South Koreans. The Spanish, Japanese and Italians had already left; the Poles and Australians were leaving; and so were the British, Georgians and South Koreans. When asked why a surge of five U.S. combat brigades would work—doubly difficult now that the British were leaving Basra to its Iranian-backed Shiite militias, death squads and self-appointed "morals police"—President Bush lamely replied "because it has to."[128]

David Petraeus and the new U.S. ambassador to Iraq, Ryan Crocker, set to work drafting a Joint Campaign Plan for Iraq, which President Bush, guided by National Security Adviser Stephen Hadley, wearily signed in November 2007. The Petraeus plan envisioned stability only after a vigorous campaign along four "lines of operation—security, politics, diplomacy and economics." It was accompanied by the usual cheerleading from the White House intended to buck up sagging public opinion and interest. "Advance America's Interests, Preserve Iraqi Independence," Condi Rice's State Department ventured. "Accelerate the Transition to Self-Reliance," the Defense Department admonished. "Surge and Fight, Create Breathing Space," Steve Hadley's NSC suggested. If the daily violence could be snuffed out, U.S. forces would shift from an active role to "overwatch," and the three hundred U.S. military bases and outposts in Iraq could be sharply reduced. Bush procured an additional twenty thousand troops for Petraeus by a variety of dodges. Tours were extended for U.S. troops already in Iraq—which wore on already strained marriages, families and mental health, to say nothing of morale—and entry standards were sharply reduced for new recruits. Aptitude minimums were lowered, and far more convicted felons than usual were given "conduct waivers" and admitted into the army and marines.[129] Rumsfeld, who opposed the surge—"we need to be pushing responsibility onto the Iraqis"—was let go and replaced with Texas A&M president Robert Gates, whom Vice President Cheney hoped would be a "more troops man."[130]

Petraeus had won praise in the early stages of the war for his successful pacification of northern Iraq and the ethnic tinderbox of Mosul with his 101st Airborne Division. Whereas neighboring generals had fought an anti-insurgency campaign, Petraeus had waged a true counterinsurgency by securing his zone, then getting Iraqis inside it back to work. Petraeus bent over backward to restore confidence; when Iraqis in his area accused U.S. troops of using their night-vision equipment to look through women's clothing, he invited the tribal leaders to try the goggles on and see for themselves. "Hostile contacts" fell sharply.[131] U.S. soldiers were converted from "trigger pullers" to "warrior-builder-diplomats," or, as wags put it, from "carnivores" to "herbivores." That was a complete reversal of everything President Bush—with his disdain for nation-building—had advocated after his election in 2000. Under Petraeus's influence, the army changed its doctrine, from the heavy combat of the Rumsfeld era to "stability operations" and the resuscitation of "fragile states" like Iraq and Afghanistan. An administration that had mocked Clinton's use of U.S. troops to "walk kids to kindergarten"—Condi Rice's infelicitous phrase—now unashamedly measured progress in Iraq by the number of kids in kindergarten, development projects completed, kilowatt hours of electricity generated, barrels of oil exported, palm trees sprayed against pests and chickens imported.[132]

The surge, which increased U.S. forces in Baghdad from seventeen to forty thousand, generally succeeded. Its emphasis on "population security"—already begun by Casey—drove down violence in the hotly contested capital, but at the cost of higher U.S. combat deaths. Republican senator Chuck Hagel, one of the more redoubtable critics of the war, blasted the very idea of the surge. "What is the *point* of bringing the violence down?" he asked. Was it to create "the peace and security" that would permit Iraq's Kurds, Sunnis and Shiites to reconcile? But those groups were making no serious effort to reconcile—witness their complete failure to agree on how to divide Iraq's oil production and reserves. So why was Washington continuing to pour in American blood and hundreds of billions of dollars in war costs? The effort was merely "undermining our interests around the world" while providing no assurance that there wouldn't be a civil war in Iraq the moment Petraeus relaxed the surge, or even if he didn't.[133]

In March 2008, U.S. combat deaths in Iraq reached four thousand. That sad milestone reminded Americans of Bush's old pledge that "Americans would stand down when the Iraqis stood up." When would the Iraqis stand up? It was a question that infused the 2008 presidential campaign, with Republican John McCain arguing that U.S. forces were critical to consolidate Iraq and Democrat Barack Obama arguing, like Senator Hagel, that Iraq was a strategic drain and distraction, and that Iraqis would have no incentive to "stand up" until the Americans "stood down." Bush and McCain were expecting the Iraqis to stand up while the United States was still standing up. "How long will this take? And at what point do we say, 'Enough'? " Obama asked Petraeus at a Senate hearing on the Iraq War in September 2007. "If we're there—the same place—a year from now," do we withdraw troops, or continue to hang around? Senator McCain had none of Obama's impatience. He would make his approach to the war "conditions based." Only when conditions improved would troops be withdrawn. Although the Republicans labored to paint Obama as a weakling, the senator evinced more strategic acuity than McCain. In his conversations with Petraeus, Obama made clear that he worried that Iraq was a quagmire that was degrading and exhausting U.S. military and financial resources for no appreciable return, as Washington's poor working relationship with the al-Maliki government in Baghdad (and the Karzai government in Kabul) made obvious. Most important for Obama was preserving America's strategic flexibility and resources and nailing down a minimum achievement in Iraq against rising Iraqi nationalism—"to make sure that we reach a tipping point where [al-Qaeda in Iraq and some of the Shiite militias] can't reconstitute themselves." Beyond that, he wanted the Iraqis to fend for themselves, and create their own future.[134]

Petraeus was not the commander in chief of this administration or the next, so he could only mutter, "We are where we are," and get on with what he had been ordered to do.[135] He authored a counterinsurgency strategy for Iraq that sought to win hearts and minds, provide neighborhood security and win back urban and desert areas from the insurgents. It was a serious, creative plan, and it bore fruit.

U.S. combat deaths fell from 126 in May 2007 to a wartime low of five in July 2008. The army and marines reoccupied neighborhoods and villages that had been written off. They tightened their rules of engagement to spare Iraqi civilians, and they patrolled with interpreters, which gave the occupation a more human and comprehensible face. "We will not commute to fight" was Petraeus's mantra, and it motivated U.S. troops to face danger, endure pain and excel, no small feat in view of the fact that many U.S. troops were on their second or third rotation and thoroughly exhausted by the interminable war.[136]

Petraeus helped bring about the "Anbar Awakening," which was the conversion of the formerly anti-American Sunni tribes of Anbar Province to the American cause. By arming, bribing and flattering the Anbar sheikhs—he hired a hundred thousand "Sons of Iraq" at a monthly rate of $300 per son—Petraeus turned the tribes against al-Qaeda in Iraq. Abu Musab al-Zarqawi dismayed even the most aggrieved sheikhs with his savagery—mortaring playgrounds and beheading enemies in mosques—and his nihilistic worldview: "If the enemy wins, we'll burn everything." None of the sheikhs mourned the al-Qaeda emir's death when U.S. F-16s bombed al-Zarqawi's safe house in June 2006 and killed him, triggering a covert and apparently unsuccessful scramble for the $25 million bounty on al-Zarqawi's head.[137] Pacifying Anbar vastly simplified the American war effort—indeed was arguably more important than the U.S. troop surge in turning Iraq around. Anbar sprawled west from Baghdad, contained the insurgent hotbeds of Ramadi and Fallujah, and had long, leaky borders with Saudi Arabia, Jordan and Syria. Paid "Sons of Iraq" were also instrumental in pacifying Baghdad's violent neighborhoods.

"WE HAVEN'T TURNED ANY CORNERS"

Petraeus flew to Washington to testify to Congress on April 8, 2008. He discouraged troop withdrawals, and remarked, "We haven't turned any corners; we haven't seen any lights at the end of the tunnel." Indeed the army hadn't. A long-awaited Iraqis-only security operation in Basra in March had been brutally and humiliatingly routed by Moqtada al-Sadr's Mahdi Army. Heartened, the Shiite militias rose in Sadr City and drove out their security forces, compelling the Iraqi government to ask its own citizens to flee the neighborhood. If that was the Iraqi army "standing up," then there certainly was no "light at the end of the tunnel." Dual loyalty and timidity remained the chief characteristics of the American-trained Iraqi forces.[138] Although President Bush and Senator McCain insisted that the colossal expenditures in Iraq were making the United States safer and that Iraq remained a "central front in the war on terrorism," Petraeus was not so sure. History, he told Virginia senator John Warner, would decide whether the war had strengthened or weakened America. When Delaware senator Joe Biden asked Petraeus which was the more important front against al-Qaeda—Iraq or Afghanistan—Petraeus indicated Afghanistan. Bush and McCain had long been fudging the issue; Petraeus made it plain, and implied what Bush's Democratic critics had been saying all along: that the excursion into Iraq had sucked life and focus from the more important front in Afghanistan, where al-Qaeda and the Taliban were regrouping, reclaiming power and finding a ready source of funds in the heroin trade. Several lawmakers lamented the cost of the Iraq War and reconstruction and wondered how much longer American taxpayers would have to bear it while the Iraqi government banked its rising oil revenues. "By the end of 2008," West Virginia senator Robert Byrd told his Senate Appropriations Committee, "the war in Iraq will have cost over $600 *billion*. That is $600 for every minute since Jesus Christ was born. *You got that?*"[139] By late 2008, with American banks failing, credit drying up, the Big Three automakers teetering toward bankruptcy and the U.S. economy plunging into a deep, long recession, everyone got it.

In September 2008, Petraeus was promoted to the Centcom command, which put him in charge of all U.S. forces from Egypt east to Pakistan. He replaced Admiral William Fallon, who had been nudged into an abrupt retirement after criticizing the administration's confrontational approach to Iran in a March 2008 interview published in *Esquire*.[140] General Ray Odierno—on his third Iraq tour—replaced Petraeus in Iraq, which showed just how deeply counterinsurgency had penetrated the army. In 2003, Odierno's 4th Infantry Division had been criticized for its brutal methods in the Sunni Triangle: kicking down doors, bulldozing homes and arresting and killing indiscriminately in their hunt for Saddam Hussein, who was captured by Odierno's troops. That was the occasion—in December 2003—for Odierno's memorable boast that "the insurgency is over." In the intervening years, Odierno came to understand the damage that his hard methods caused, and he embraced the counterinsurgency doctrine drafted and implemented by Petraeus and Lieutenant Colonel John Nagl.[141]

The rise of Petraeus was remarkable. Beginning in 2007, President Bush all but gave up on the Iraq War, and subcontracted every question on it to Petraeus. "I trust David Petraeus" became the president's signature answer to most queries. Onlookers were struck by the unprecedented power shift from Washington to Baghdad, from the commander in chief to the regional field commander.[142] Petraeus became a weird totem on the 2008 presidential campaign trail as well, with candidates John McCain and Sarah Palin vying to outdo each other in total obeisance to the boyish general. McCain and Palin sprinkled every debate and talking point with earnest adherence to the general's wishes. Whereas Obama and Biden insisted on civilian leadership of the war and a hard-nosed articulation of ends and means, McCain and Palin (like Bush) devolved everything to Petraeus—"our great general," as Palin put it, "one of the great military leaders in American history," said McCain—implying that independent thought on the matter was treasonous. Meanwhile, Petraeus was turning the war crafted by Bush, Cheney and Rumsfeld inside out. Whereas Bush's war cabinet had disdained stabilization operations and peacekeeping à la Bosnia, Petraeus and Secretary of Defense Robert Gates made them the first order of business. A new National Defense Strategy paper issued by Gates in the summer of 2008 and heavily influenced by Petraeus noted that the army would become as good at righting failed states as it was at high-intensity combat.[143]

Iraq, of course, was far more than just an electoral football for the 2008 campaign. Bush's war there raised the larger question of the viability and desirability of such operations. "If we convince ourselves that it was the surge that was the primary cause for the lowering of violence, that may convince us that we can tackle another problem like Iraq in the future and have the same results," West Point historian and Iraq veteran Colonel Gian Gentile warily observed in 2008. Violence in Iraq was arguably reduced more by the "Anbar Awakening"—the decision by the Sunni sheikhs to switch sides—and by Moqtada al-Sadr's unexpected decision to stand down his Shiite Mahdi Army and work with the government than by the surge in U.S. troops. Moreover, Petraeus's "bottom-up" approach—appeasing the Shiite militias, empowering the Sunni sheikhs and embracing the Kurds—suggested an eventual partition of the country more than a union. Bush and Petraeus premised the surge on a dogged effort by the Iraqi government to mend its sectarian divisions and share out oil revenues, but that progress remained illusory a year after the surge. "We're midwifing the dissolution of the country," a former Clinton official observed. David Kilcullen, an Australian counterinsurgency expert, observed that the surge had failed in its principal aim: to buy time for a "grand bargain" at the national level between Iraq's contending groups. It had achieved the opposite effect, splintering Iraq into ethnic ghettos—Sunnis, Shiites and Kurds—that achieved security on their own terms but made no concessions to one another in Baghdad. The United States, in other words, was sitting on a powder keg.[144]

Instead of pulling itself together behind the shield of the surge, Iraq seemed to be going the way of Yemen, lapsing into "warlordism" and "tribalism." It was hard to imagine that the empowered Sunnis, Kurds and Shiites would convene peacefully after American troops and minders left, not least because Petraeus—pressured by queasy Republicans, antiwar Democrats, manpower-strained Joint Chiefs and a demoralized president—didn't dare ask for the one thing that might stabilize Iraq: more troops and more time. Iraq's "three strategic nodes"—Mosul, Baghdad and Basra—were put back under government control, but that left vital cities like Kirkuk, "the land the surge forgot," effectively uncontrolled.[145] Bush signed a status of forces agreement in December 2008 that guaranteed the departure of all U.S. forces from Iraq's cities by 2009 and from the rest of the country by 2011. "We're creating dependencies in a decentralized state that will be at risk when we leave," the Clinton official concluded. Senator Joe Biden shared those doubts; the hundred thousand "Sons of Iraq" recruited for the "Anbar Awakening" were armed and dangerous. Unless al-Maliki or his successors brought them into the government fold, they would restart the civil war the minute the surge wound down. "Guess what," Biden observed "They're awakened . . . They want a piece of the action, and they're not getting any"—owing to al-Maliki's preference for Shiites and Iran's support of radical Shiite parties. Petraeus may not have saved Iraq; he may just have prolonged its post-Saddam agony. Or, as Steve Coll wrote after an extended visit to Iraq, Petraeus's "constructive opportunism"—his collaboration with any tribe or warlord that would help stem the violence—may not have stopped Iraq's civil war; it may just have paused it, and left Washington stranded in a "strategic cul-de-sac." *Best* case, Coll concluded, Iraq might settle down to become an "Algeria or a Colombia—unstable and troubled by internal violence, but secure within its borders."[146] Such an inglorious and unhelpful future was certainly not the one breezily projected by George W. Bush and his Vulcans in 2003.

CONCLUSION

QUICKSAND BEGAN WITH BURKE'S ENJOINDER never to suffer the "unpitied calamity" of forgetfulness of the past. Burke also scolded those—like the neocons—who would restlessly "consult invention and reject experience." *Clean Break* and the Iraq War flowed from those mothers of invention, and just plain idiocy. Even as Iraq spun into insurgency and mayhem in 2005, Bush's occupation planner, Doug Feith, told a reporter—with a straight face—that the war was defensible and even desirable because "George W. Bush has more insight, because of his knowledge of human beings and his sense of history, about the motive force, the craving for freedom and participation in self-rule, than do many of the language experts and history experts and culture experts."[1] Although Feith's predecessors in the Eisenhower administration had weighed their own Operation Iraqi Freedom—to oust General Kasim and put in their own exiles—and then rejected such an operation as certain to fail in the face of Iraqi pride and sectarian divisions, Bush 43 and his Vulcans pushed ahead without even a nod to those important debates that had flared through the White House forty-five years earlier. President Obama, thankfully, seems more of a history and experience man. He has heeded Eisenhower's warning that to strike out alone in the Middle East makes Washington "just another adventurer, like Genghis Khan." Obama has deepened our coalition, refocused attention on al-Qaeda and dialed back expectations for Iraq and Afghanistan, even as the United States works through a painful recession exacerbated by the colossal expenditures and distractions of the Iraq War.

Obama inherits Iraq, which is not the hoped-for neocon bastion of American power, but a crumbling, infighting place that may even become a "failed state." American prestige is at stake there—so much having been invested and lost—so continued engagement, even beyond the 2011 deadline, is anticipated. The U.S. Army has preemptively draped a "Vietnam narrative" over Iraq, saying, in effect, that the shipwreck there was the fault of politicians—a neocon "war of murderous naiveté"—not the military. That said, it was as noteworthy in Iraq as in Vietnam that no senior flag officer resigned his commission to protest the folly of the politicians. So it is their war too. With attention shifting to Afghanistan, there is a "phony war" quality to Iraq, a calm before the storm punctuated by increasing numbers of car bombs. Can anyone credibly argue that the enormous U.S. investment in Iraq has been worth it? The Iraqi state teeters on the edge of civil war; al-Qaeda has been pushed away, but only as far as Yemen, where it skulks and awaits new opportunities. The WMD threat merely suspected in Iraq has become all too real in Iran, where the ayatollahs have glimpsed the *limits* of American power advertised in Iraq and Afghanistan and redoubled their efforts to build nuclear weapons and mount them on ballistic missiles.

Washington has historically looked to Iran as a potential makeweight in the region. Persian, not Arab, Shiite, not Sunni, the Iranians have been a natural wedge against menacing movements like Arab nationalism or Sunni fundamentalism. The Iranian revolution of 1979 eradicated our influence and deepened our problems because the Iran of Khomeini sought to broaden its footprint by extending a creed of "Islamic revolution" to Sunnis and Shiites alike, underwriting terrorist groups all over the world and plowing Tehran's oil receipts into a major nuclear weapons program. Today's nuclear standoff with Iran strikes Washington as a necessary effort to stop proliferation; it strikes the Iranians as an infringement on their sovereignty, for nuclear weapons have become as much a political status symbol as a military weapon. Meanwhile, our intelligence on Iran is fogged by the same bewildering kaleidoscope of political actors—mullahs, moderates and militants—that made predictions about Operation Ajax and the shah's fall so uncertain. The Iranian regime is clearly in trouble because of its own political and economic ineptitude. Even if the ayatollahs survive the 2009 demonstrations, they will have their work cut out for them hiring and inspiring a youthful population of seventy-four million that is tired of unemployment, isolation and humorless piety. Ironically, the Iranian security forces today are taking their cues from the shah and SAVAK; because the shah was so gentle, he fell. The revolutionary guards and their vicious boy militias on dirt bikes will not make the same mistake, or so they say. Meanwhile, the Guardian Council—which polices the otherwise supreme leader—is undoubtedly thinking about throwing the reigning president and supreme leader overboard to save the increasingly shopworn and unpopular Islamic revolution. Whatever regime emerges to placate and employ Iran's frustrated population, security problems will remain. With daily oil receipts of $100 million—sustained by inflation, not production, which has declined more than a third since the more businesslike shah ruled—Iran in 2010 possesses a serious ballistic missile and nuclear weapons program built around the reactor breeding of plutonium and the enrichment of uranium by five thousand centrifuges. The involvement of the Chinese and Russians—the Chinese to work off their swelling imports of Iranian oil and liquefied natural gas, the Russians to sell something usable and poke the American eagle—makes the billion-dollar-a-year Iranian nuclear program even harder to extirpate. Iran's curious animosity toward Israel—historically they were allies—makes the situation especially fraught, for it makes Israeli preemption or massive retaliation all but inevitable. Can Israel be expected to sit passively while the peevish "confrontation state" born in 1979 successfully tests missiles capable of striking Israel, a former Iranian president (Rafsanjani) ventures that "one nuclear bomb inside Israel" will kill the Israelis but merely wound the Islamic world, and a sitting president (Ahmadinejad) declares that "Israel should be wiped off the face of the map"? The sitting president may go, and the Islamic Republic may wilt, but the Iranians will probably retain their nuclear ambitions. As two analysts direly concluded in 2009, nuclear weapons have only intensified America's problems in the Middle East: "The cradles of civilization once swung on the Carthage-Tehran axis, but three millennia later, those cities, and many in between, now host different embryos: the dragon's egg of nuclear disaster."[2]

The Russians always predicted disaster for America in Afghanistan, and Moscow may still have its bittersweet moment. Obama has sensibly repackaged the grinding war in Afghanistan into something he calls "AfPak," shorthand that captures the interdependence of the Taliban war and its Pakistani logisticians. And Obama seems to have made more progress in Pakistan in a year than Bush did in eight. That has much to do with Pakistan's belated recognition of its own vulnerability to the Taliban and al-Qaeda. Pakistani polls reveal (at last!) that al-Qaeda and the Taliban are unpopular. Three years ago more than 70 percent of Pakistanis admired the terrorist groups; nowadays the ratio is reversed, a loathing shared by the government in Islamabad, which has finally decided that the al-Qaeda and Taliban threats to Pakistan's secular regime outweigh their usefulness against India. Still, Pakistani sympathy—as far as it goes—will not guide us out of Afghanistan. Obama more than doubled U.S. force levels in 2009—from thirty-two thousand to sixty-eight thousand—and vowed to secure the Afghan population, break the Taliban and restore the country to a semblance of civilized normalcy. The results have been mixed, occasional successes offset by rising coalition casualties—twenty times higher in late-2009 than in the period from 2001 to 2004—as well as surging Taliban affiliation, tribalism, corruption and heroin production. President Karzai's August 2009 reelection was achieved under such a cloud of fraud—hundreds of dummy polling sites stuffed with hundreds of thousands of Karzai ballots—that the UN and international observers indignantly demanded a recount and audit. Some worried—not without reason—that the vanquished Abdullah Abdullah, a former aide to Ahmed Shah Massoud and a born Afghan vote-getter (Pashtun father, Tajik mother), would tip Afghanistan into civil war in retaliation for Karzai's rigged election. In Afghanistan, even more than Iraq, one grasps the meaning of General Douglas MacArthur's judgment that "all military occupations are failures." They hand you problems that you are culturally, financially, politically and militarily unequipped to solve.

From the Balfour Declaration to the Bush Doctrine, the United States has struggled to find its stride in the Middle East, as our latest stumbles in Iraq and Afghanistan merely confirm. During World War I, there was little urgency to get into stride. President Woodrow Wilson interested himself in the region only to the extent that it fitted with his ideas about postwar national self-determination and, belatedly, because the "Jewish national home" promised by British foreign secretary Arthur Balfour all but forced the U.S. government to take a position, for or against. Wilson's first inclination was against. His Fourteen Points could not be squared with plans by European Zionists to take over Arab land in Palestine, and "assimilationist" Jews in America—as in Britain and Europe—feared and resented the idea of a Jewish state anyway, for it reinforced the cliché of the "wandering Jew" by implying that Jews were stateless. But Wilson was lobbied hard on the matter by Supreme Court justice Louis Brandeis and other Zionists who talked the president around using an old variant of a now familiar Israeli talking point: namely, that the Jewish state would be a vital U.S. ally. During World War I, Justice Brandeis and Jewish Agency chief Chaim Weizmann argued that Balfour's Jewish national home would "form a powerful barrier against waves of German-Turkish ambitions, a wall to prevent the spread of German might over the world." Hence, Weizmann hopefully concluded, "Jewish Palestine must become a war aim for America." Too preoccupied with German ambitions to worry about German-Turkish ones, Wilson did not give the Jewish state much thought, but he did give it a skeptical thumbs-up. More than a million European Jews had settled in key electoral pockets like New York between 1890 and 1914, and—for all his internationalism—Wilson knew that all politics are ultimately local. With the Americans on board, Balfour and the Zionists got Israel up and running.[3]

The birth of Israel and the discovery of vast pools of oil in Saudi Arabia in the 1930s focused American attention on the Middle East as never before, and wove the Middle East into U.S. domestic politics. American strategy in the Middle East has been muddled and confused over the years because it has been addressed politically, not strategically. The nature of Israel's creation—from a legally cloudy "national home" to a militarily dominant and religiously exclusive state—appears to have engendered eternal bitterness in the Arab world. Initially the bitterness was at the mere fact of the expulsion of the Palestinians by the Jews. By and by, it became a political reflex, with Arab regimes voicing lamentations on behalf of the Palestinians that they would never dream of voicing on behalf of their own oppressed or merely neglected citizens. Meeting with Saudi king Ibn Saud in 1945, President Roosevelt expressed surprise at the Saudi's strong feelings on the subject of Palestine, which—to FDR—hardly seemed warranted by the "barren and rocky land" he had flown over on his way to Yalta.[4] If FDR evinced ambivalence on the Middle East—his early support for the Zionists evaporating the more he listened to *enragés* like Ibn Saud—his successor, Harry Truman, did not. Truman had cut his teeth as a Missouri county commissioner and a cold warrior; he took his political and military allies where he found them, and Israel seemed remarkably convenient.

The Truman instinct on Israel became the abiding American instinct. Every U.S. president after Truman tailored his electoral campaigns—as well as midterm congressional ones—to the exigencies of what gradually came to be known as the "Israel lobby." Truman admitted as much to his Middle Eastern ambassadors in 1945: "I am sorry, gentlemen, but I have to answer to hundreds of thousands who are anxious for the success of Zionism; I do not have hundreds of thousands of Arabs among my constituents."[5] The Israel lobby developed a bullying reputation—

pointing out that American Jews were concentrated in critical states with vital blocs of electoral votes and that they gave generously to friendly political campaigns and not at all to unfriendly ones. It became difficult for American presidents to "reassess" Middle Eastern policy or to "downgrade Israel" in U.S. assessments for the simple reason that there was a potentially lethal political price to pay. Although Eisenhower boasted that he would "handle our affairs exactly as though we don't have a Jew in America," he didn't, fearing—as he put it in 1956—the loss of "New York, New Jersey, Pennsylvania and Connecticut, at least." Kennedy too treaded warily—quailing before what John Foster Dulles had called "the terrific control the Jews have over the news media and the barrage the Jews have built up on Congressmen"—and so did not punish Israel's clandestine nuclear program in the early 1960s despite his passion for nonproliferation. JFK had narrowly beaten Nixon in 1960 and knew that he would need Jewish votes in 1964.[6] Nixon didn't lean on the Israelis because of the narrowness of *his* victory over Humphrey, and Ford, pushing in 1975 for an Arab-Israeli "reassessment," was slammed down by the "Letter of 76," not a bicentennial fillip, but a letter commanding undiminished support for Israel signed by seventy-six of one hundred U.S. senators. Presidents and members of Congress got the message, summarized in 2002 by New York's Jewish daily *Forward*: "You don't cross these people, or they take you down."[7]

Domestically produced U.S. support for Israel created a strategic problem, which reinforced the no-nonsense Truman instinct. As long as the Cold War smoldered, Moscow incited the Arab regimes against the West using Israel as "exhibit A" of American malevolence. Israel was alleged to be an "American pawn," a conspiracy "minted on Wall Street," and so on. The fact that none of this was true—America seemed as much a pawn to Israeli intrigues as the other way around—did not diminish the canard's effectiveness in pulling important countries like Iraq, Syria and Egypt into opposition to the West. The proximity of those opportunistic Soviet allies to the Suez Canal and the oil fields and pipelines of the Persian Gulf alarmed Washington and empowered Tel Aviv. Israel could now pose as the indispensable ally, committed to uphold not only the West's influence, but its energy security as well. Long before the neocons, there was a parade through many administrations of White House advisers arguing the folly of any policy other than a pro-Israel one for the simple reason that the Israelis were pro-American and the Arabs were not.

Until the fall of the Soviet Union, there was little incentive in Washington to ask *why* the Israelis were so pro-American—because they usually got what they wanted—or to revisit the security relationship with Israel. American complacency was reinforced by a concerted Israeli campaign—in the United States and the Middle East—to isolate Washington. During the Cold War, Israeli policy and lobbying involved driving a wedge between Washington and the Arabs. In a 1970 memo titled "Washington and Tel Aviv—Clashing Interests amidst Interdependence," the State Department noted the tremendous "paradox" that "Israeli military initiatives" like the Six-Day War had begun to "function as the catalyst and arbiter of *American* actions in the region": a case of the tail wagging the dog. The Israelis nurtured a red scare in the 1970s and insisted that brute force against Moscow's "Arab proxies" was the solution. The State Department discerned Israel's larger agenda: "Tel Aviv needs 100 percent American backing in all fields, and such backing can best be assured if Washington is bereft of options, if the Middle East is effectively polarized between the Arabs/Soviet Union and the Israelis/U.S." Nowadays, the threat is Arabs/al-Qaeda or Arabs/Hezbollah, and the Israelis labor to create the same polarization that worked until the fall of the Soviets, this time pitting Washington and Tel Aviv against transnational terrorism and its state sponsors.[8] Israeli and neocon connivance in Operation Iraqi Freedom has opened eyes in Washington to the perils of this isolating dynamic, but the "interdependence" of Israel and America, forged in Congress and on the campaign trail, remains. *Quicksand* is filled with anecdotes from successive administrations in which presidents and their foreign policy advisers were coldly told—by the Israel lobby, its members of Congress or the Israelis themselves—to "think again" and not rock the boat. But that political refusal to "think again" on questions like borders, occupied territories, settlements and refugees merely sharpened the strategic problem—how to penetrate and harness the Arab world?

Making the Arab world *like* the United States became a strategic priority because of the Cold War, the "global war on terrorism" and Saudi oil. *Quicksand* has spanned a period in which the United States went from being a net exporter of oil—powering the great coalition against Germany and Japan in World War II—to an energy-dependent importer of foreign oil. In the early days of the U.S.-Saudi relationship, when American "Great White Fathers" gave Saudi princes the proverbial jeweled Cadillacs in exchange for access to their oil, no one in Washington worried too much about Middle Eastern politics. Indeed after World War II, Harold Ickes, oil czar to FDR and Truman, thought the best place to leave America's billion-barrel strategic petroleum reserve—"for war, if needs must, and for peace, in any event"—was in the ground in Saudi Arabia. The kingdom appeared *that* reliable.

But times changed, politics evolved and the angry Wahhabi clerics inside Saudi Arabia never resigned themselves to an American presence in the kingdom. Even the sybaritic royal family found it increasingly difficult to advertise its American alliance at a time when the Palestinian nationalist movement—rebranded as an international cause célèbre by the PLO in the 1970s—had scarified the Arab street in Saudi Arabia and everywhere else. Thus, in 1973, the Saudis did the unthinkable: they bit the hand that fed them, clamping an oil embargo on the superpower that protected them against Soviet attack because of Washington's support for Israel in the Yom Kippur War. Since then, the Saudis have tried to square the circle—privately befriending Washington while publicly giving every international crisis "a coat of green paint." That militant Muslim green—mixed with guns and terrorism—was acceptable only so long as it was daubed on the Soviet bear. Since 1990, it has been quite unacceptable—in Western eyes—leading to continuous tension with the United States that has yet to be resolved.

Every modern president has had to walk the tightrope negotiated by Nixon and Kissinger in 1973, and it remains our principal, unsteady avenue into the Middle East. Some administrations have inched cautiously along the tightrope; others have stomped irritably along it, hardly seeming to care if they fell into the nets below. Temperament and provenance seem to be the critical variables. Steeped in oil, the George H. W. Bush administration had far less patience with Israeli bluster and cajolery and far more patience with Saudi complaints. Secretary of State James Baker could be withering in his treatment of Israeli diplomats and lobbyists. Baker nearly expelled Israel's ambassador during Desert Storm for pressuring the administration, and the secretary of state rarely bothered to conceal his contempt for the Likud's zeal on settlements and inaction on occupied territories and refugees. "When you're serious about peace, call us," Baker challenged Prime Minister Yitzhak Shamir (and Housing Minister Ariel Sharon) in hearings on Capitol Hill. To underscore the insult, Baker then read aloud the White House phone number.[9] The contrast between Bush father and son on Israel was one of the many curiosities of the George W. Bush administration. Bush 43 was also steeped in oil and derived in no small part from the men of Bush 41, but his had none of the earlier administration's skepticism about Israeli motives and methods. Perhaps the key difference was Bush 43's affiliation with Christian conservatives, who had allied themselves with the neocons as an odd but powerful couple—the "New Right"—since the 1970s and who, like the neocons, looked expectantly to the day when the Jews would complete their settlement of Greater Israel. It hardly mattered that the neocons were seeking "strategic depth" while the Christian fundamentalists sought rapture and last judgment in a Holy Land emptied of Muslims. So long as the aim was Greater Israel, the New Right facilitated Israeli expansion and obduracy.[10]

Every administration has engaged in the Arab-Israeli "peace process," but some more than others. Carter brokered the historic peace between Israel and Egypt in 1979. Clinton nearly founded the Palestinian state in 2000. "You are a great man," Arafat told Clinton after the Camp David talks. "I am not a great man," Clinton replied. "I am a failure, and you made me one."[11] The near miss in 2000 has been blamed on both sides as well as Clinton's eagerness to secure a legacy, but Camp David missed chiefly because neither Arafat nor Barak could agree on how to divide Jerusalem and what to do with the Palestinian refugees, whose number had grown from about 750,000 in 1948 to nearly 4 million in 2000. Most fundamentally—and this remains the crucial problem—Clinton's two-week Camp David summit failed because of a divergence in narratives. The Israelis saw themselves as generously giving Palestinians over 90 percent of the West Bank and all of Gaza; the Palestinians grumbled that they were being pressed to accept just 22 percent of the Palestine that had been wrested from them in 1948. Israel and the Palestinian Authority are like an eternally divorcing couple, the husband feeling he is giving too much, the wife complaining she is being assigned the crumbs from the table. Some resolution of the refugee, territory and settlement problems has always been central to the peace process—and any practicable resolution will have to be forced on the Israelis by Washington. But Colin Powell recalled being shocked by George W. Bush's outline of the matter in 1998: "We flew over the Palestinian camps; looked real bad down there. I don't see much we can do over there at this point."[12]

Modern European history and the Cold War explain many of America's problems in the Middle East. Germany, more than any other state, is responsible for the entrenchment of Israel in Palestine and the ensuing rancor. *Quicksand* suggests that the Jewish state might not have flourished had the Germans not hounded the Jews out of Germany and Austria, sparked a wave of anti-Semitic regimes across East Central Europe and then embarked on the genocidal Holocaust. Until the 1930s, Arabs and Jews struggled inconclusively for control of the Holy Land. The Zionists spoke disarmingly about a Jewish-Arab "commonwealth," not a Jewish state. But the flood of Jews driven from Europe by Hitler had to go somewhere and—in a resolutely Christian West that pinched off Jewish immigration even after the Nazi seizure of power—Palestine became the catch basin, even more so after 1945, when Western presidents and prime ministers, looking for a place to send Europe's

500,000 Jewish "displaced persons," settled upon Palestine at a time when there were 600,000 Jews and 1.2 million Arabs there. Everyone could do the math on that one. Jews, who had been a minority in Palestine—surging from 17 to 30 percent of the population thanks to the European pogroms of the 1930s—suddenly glimpsed the opportunity to become a majority in one fell swoop after 1945. Because of the Holocaust, Jews had also lost any guilt feelings they may have had about displacing the Arabs. Because of Axis atrocities and genocide, the new Jewish immigrants felt capable of *anything*, even hunting the Palestinians into ghettos, exile or the grave.

Soviet mischief in the Cold War also wrong-footed America in the Middle East. By turning the Arab nationalist regimes in Egypt, Syria and Iraq against the United States, Moscow left backward Saudi Arabia—as Ike put it—"the only stone on which to build." Riyadh was and remains a loose and slippery stone to build on— "the losing horse, a certain loser," as the British disgustedly put it more than fifty years ago. Soviet pressure also cornered the United States in Iran. Historians may argue that the United States tragically erred in ousting Mosaddeq in 1953 and backing the shah until 1979, but what were Washington's options? For all his brilliance, Mosaddeq was old and whimsical and, to cold warriors in Washington, an intolerable liability. His duel with the Anglo-Iranian Oil Company had opened the doors to the Soviet-backed Iranian communists, who may have planned to use Mosaddeq as a useful idiot before toppling him in a Bolshevik coup. Iran's proximity to Russia and Moscow's interest in Persian Gulf bases and oil made the Pahlavi empire a vital front in the Cold War. American support for the shah and SAVAK must always be weighed—in fairness—against Soviet intrigues with Tudeh and later the ayatollahs. That same logic applied everywhere else. The more the USSR supported the Iraqis or the Syrians, the more the United States was forced back on Israel, the Wahhabis of Saudi Arabia or the Maronite Phalange in Lebanon. Still, even amid the Cold War—and certainly before and after it—there was room for American maneuver. Under pressure to accept the Israeli seizure of Gaza and the Sinai in 1956, the Eisenhower administration instead ordered the Israelis out, calculating that Israeli-occupied territories would make American leadership and defense of the Middle East impossible. Briefly installed in Lebanon in 1958, Ike spurned the hawks who wanted him to press the attack against the pro-Moscow regimes in Damascus and Baghdad: "A big operation that could run all the way through Syria and Iraq [would be] far beyond anything I have the power to do constitutionally"—or even practically.[13]

The Arab "oil weapon" brandished in 1973 increased the tendency to fit U.S.

Middle Eastern policy and strategy to domestic political constituencies (Big Oil and its gas-guzzling customers) that were rarely in the best interest of Washington's foreign policy. By the 1970s, everyone knew that the Saudis were a terrific liability—archaic, hypocritical, involved in terrorism, anti-Israeli and un-American—but no presidential administration dared move against them, lest they cut off oil, stop buying U.S. treasuries or collapse and make way for a Soviet-backed Arab nationalist or Islamist regime. Thus, one administration after another winked at Saudi wiliness. Just as the British had opposed the extension of secular Young Turk reforms to the kingdom during World War I—as a means of keeping Mecca and Medina under Britain's imperial thumb—so the United States encouraged Wahhabism as a check on communism and Arab nationalism in the decades after World War II. President Eisenhower proposed making King Saud "the great gookety gook of the Muslim world" to steal Nasser's thunder. Every Cold War president viewed Saudi religion (and petrodollars) as the best insurance against the spread of communism. Only 9/11—where fifteen of nineteen hijackers and two-thirds of the first "Arab Afghans" captured in Enduring Freedom and flown to Guantanamo were Saudis—gave the White House pause. Rumsfeld's Office of Special Plans belatedly began pondering regime change for the Saudis as well, but the timing and the agenda (another neocon "clean break," not a flowering of freedom on Saudi terms) were not propitious.

A new president and a new administration inaugurated in 2009 can look back on a century of American engagement in the Middle East and seek answers of their own. But this administration, like every one since Woodrow Wilson's, is also a prisoner of that past. Obama will have to negotiate that thorny "Carthage-Tehran axis" in the company of Israeli prime minister Benjamin "Bibi" Netanyahu, an old Likudnik, who last crossed swords in Washington with President Bill Clinton and Secretary of State Madeleine Albright. Dealing with Bibi, Albright once said, is "like negotiating in hell."[14] While Obama and Secretary of State Hillary Clinton argue for a Palestinian state, Bibi argues, as he has always done, for a mere entity with continuing Israeli settlements as well as Israeli control of borders, airspace, military affairs and—a nod to the twenty-first century—electronic communications. While Obama speaks—like every president since FDR—of yet another "historic opportunity" to make peace in Palestine, Netanyahu, practiced at running out the clock on "historic opportunities," answers, "Yes, but . . ." Leaving Obama at one end of Pennsylvania Avenue in May 2009, Bibi traveled to the other end and told congressional lawmakers that peace would come only if the Palestinians dismantled "militant groups," the Iranians renounced nuclear weapons, the "Arab countries [took] concrete steps to improve relations with Israel" and so on. By the fall of 2009, Obama—like his predecessors—seemed to have surrendered lock, stock and barrel to the Israelis. Against Netanyahu's decision to flout Obama's requested settlement freeze and plow ahead with three thousand new housing units in the occupied territories, Obama mustered nothing more punitive than a "philosophy of persistence," which he *hoped* would temper the Israelis, mollify the Palestinians and bring peace to the Holy Land. In that fond hope, history is not on the president's side.

The history related in *Quicksand* suggests some policy guidance for Washington. Every president since Wilson has wrestled with the quandaries of Saudi Arabia and Israel. Many have begun their administrations with a determination to do things differently, to reinvent the relationships on a cleaner, more sustainable footing. Each has been deterred by distractions, lobbying and just plain old attrition. Will Saudi Arabia run out of oil, or will the world shift to alternative fuels and renewable energy? Either way, our Saudi problem will eventually dissipate like a cloud of smoke. Still, we will be shrouded in that oily smoke for some years to come. So much that passes between Riyadh and Washington is classified that it is hard to know the level of real cooperation and amity between the two governments. It is extraordinary—even maddening—to research today in Western diplomatic and intelligence archives and witness the special treatment that is still accorded the Saudi royal family. Every other country sees its diplomatic and intelligence reports declassified after thirty years, with rare exceptions. Saudi files that describe the behavior of the royals remain classified for half a century, or longer. Those that are released are often all but illegible because of all the material that is blacked out. Clearly we—and the British—are abashed by our own connivance and hypocrisy in the affairs of the Saudis, but it is clear that so long as we wink at the obscurantism of Saudi Arabia—the bankrolling of terrorists, the denigration of women, the shunning of Shiites, the rejection of democracy, the squandering of public funds—our campaigns against those things in other parts of the region (Afghanistan, Pakistan, Iran or Iraq) will lack punch or even believability. The Iraq War was so foolish in part because it played out against the backdrop of a Saudi Arabia that, in most respects, was even more obnoxious than Baathist Iraq. If, as Ibn Saud chortled back in the 1930s, the United States is concerned only to "get the oil out" without "getting into politics," then we need to extend that pragmatism to every regime. Operation Iraqi Freedom was a strategic absurdity because Saddam's Iraq was probably less dangerous to American security than Saudi Arabia, whose charitable pet-rodollars and zealous youth fueled the Taliban and al-Qaeda as well as numerous other Islamist groups.

The United States can either accept Saudi Arabia's cultural and political differ-ences, or work to reform them. The latter is a slippery slope. What the Middle East has taught us more than anything is the folly of idealistic conceptions about democ-racy, fair play, freedom, nationalism or even independence. "We must push the Arabs in a liberal direction," a British diplomat wrote after the Six-Day War, "but this does *not* mean advocating the adoption of Western democratic forms where they have no relevance, or dismantling the internal security systems without which no Middle Eastern regime can survive." The problems of the brittle region can only be managed, not solved—much less magically "transformed" by a presidential doc-trine. Still, there has been a fractured quality to U.S. policy over the past decades. We rail against Taliban misogyny while tolerating Saudi misogyny; we denounce Saddam's links to terrorists while overlooking Riyadh's; we protest the spread of Wahhabi madrassas without tackling the Wahhabis. Such equivocation undercuts our every effort to make our public diplomacy heard. Are we going to defend the Saudis with American blood for no specified price, or are we going to urge them to earn that protection with a modern state, a modern culture and a reasonably trans-parent policy? Simply put, we must make up our minds how we are going to deal with the Saudis, or confess (privately) that we are just making use of them and let-ting them make use of us until their oil runs out. Until we speak with a coherent voice on Saudi Arabia—and why shouldn't we, now that the Cold War is over and jihadi terrorism has been exposed as the new great danger?—we will not have a credible policy for Iran, Afghanistan, Pakistan, Iraq, Syria, Lebanon or the Palestin-ian Authority.

We must have our reckoning with Israel too. No U.S. policy maker wishes to place the Jewish state in jeopardy, but the quicksand that sucks at our boots in the Middle East is especially sticky because the states of the region are so furious at our two-faced policy on Israel. FDR, it was said, tried hard "to be King of the Jews and King of the Arabs." He died before the futility of that position became fully appar-ent. No matter what we do, we are going to make ourselves unpopular in some quarter, but we do need to act. Every president since Wilson has succumbed to the bluster of the Israel lobby. Most have consoled themselves that they are merely succoring a reliable ally and a functioning democracy. That much is true; helped by astonishing sums of U.S. foreign aid and intimate cooperation with Washington, the Israelis have built a prosperous economy, a potent military and a vibrant democracy. Those building blocks permit them to deride their more stagnant and backward neighbors, and hazard poor odds for the success of a peaceful Palestinian state. Scorn for the neighbors and the Palestinians is infectious, especially when it is conflated with the inhuman violence and persecution in places like Iraq and Afghanistan and the repression in Iran. Why *should* the Israelis return land or even sovereignty to the Palestinians when they might just use those gifts for crime, repression and terrorism—or merely spurn them, as Arafat did in 2000? That's the Israeli narrative, which Bush 43 swallowed without chewing.

But what emerges from *Quicksand* is the craven neglect of *our* policy on Israel and Palestine. Already in 1948, the Truman administration regretted the arrogance and brutality of Jewish ethnic cleansing in the Arab parts of Palestine but did nothing about it because of Cold War rivalry and fear of what Truman called the "pressure boys" of the Israel lobby. Each subsequent administration cried foul— "Henry, they can't do this to us *again*," Nixon wailed to Kissinger in 1973—but failed to crack down on Israeli foul play because of the same worries that creased Truman's brow. Today, the Cold War threat has been replaced by the terrorism threat, all the more reason to exert massive pressure on the Israelis to concede a real Palestinian state that will gather in lots of foreign aid and interest, and either sink or swim by its own efforts. To security hawks, who would say that conditions do not permit such an experiment, the answer is simple enough. The Israelis had decades to compensate or resettle the refugees and restore the occupied territories; they never did. They have always harped on the dangers of the Palestinians and presumably always will, and have always counted on collusion in Washington, as Golda Meir put it, "because of the Jewish vote." As in the case of Saudi Arabia, the United States cannot exert real influence for positive change in the Middle East until it first breaks a lance for the people who were run out of their homes in 1948. Kissinger reminded the Israelis in the 1970s that they are "*not* the Prussians," free to annex territories and expel or intimidate the inhabitants. The world of the UN, the NGO, the Internet and the sleepless news cycle is not so permissive, and the Palestinian question lights fires everywhere—even in faraway Malaysia, where Malays who have no idea what Palestine is nowadays chant electoral slogans (for their Muslim candidates) that vaunt the rights and power of Palestine. As Ike and John Foster Dulles agreed in an earlier chapter, U.S. policy will never work to the advantage of "the total situation, from Dakar to the Philippine Islands" until America's Israel policy is straightened out.

Between those poles—in the heart of the "total situation"—resides Iran, and this administration must make up its mind how it is going to engage the regional heavyweight. The continuing cold war between Tehran and Washington serves no one's interests, and is driven by the bitter resentments of 1979 as well as Tehran's blatant support for terrorist groups like Hamas and Hezbollah and its determined pursuit of nuclear weapons. Does continued confrontation with the "confrontation state" suit the American book, or would we be wiser to seek common ground and slot Iran into a Middle Eastern security architecture that would help pacify Iraq and Afghanistan, lower our security costs in the region and even dissuade Tehran from funding terrorism and pursuing the nukes that the Iranians began pursuing under the shah? We can offer foreign aid, investment, the hand of friendship, a face-saving deal on Palestine and a greater international legitimacy. They can offer a more stable and prosperous region, and become part of the solution, not the problem, in Iraq and Afghanistan. The joker in the deck, as always, is Tehran's Revolutionary Guard. How fiercely will they cling to power? Will they shoot demonstrators in the street, torture political prisoners, bait Great Satan, and transform the Islamic Republic into a military dictatorship? That outcome—and all the challenges *it* will pose—is at least as likely as reform and rapprochement.

General Petraeus famously asked how long the war in Iraq would take, and hazarded an answer—"eight years and eight divisions." Eight years have passed and at least eight divisions have been exhausted in the process. Afghanistan looks likely to be as exhausting; the name *Enduring* Freedom was aptly chosen, but suggests the freedom to kill and maim more than anything else. The war begun after 9/11 was costing $4 billion/month eight years later, and killing U.S. soldiers at ten times the rate of 2002. Today's Taliban—centered on Aghanistan's Pashtuns, who constitute 45 percent of the population—has morphed into a layered movement that is far harder to eradicate than the old Mullah Omar government ever was. To the traditional fundamentalists must be added new talibs: drug-runners, wily tribal chiefs, Pakistani volunteers and revenge killers activated by every clash with NATO or the Afghan security forces. But the bulk of Taliban support will come from ordinary Afghans, who, if present trends continue (rising Afghan combat and flagging Western interest), will calculate that the wind is going out of the sails of Karzai and Obama, and that the time is ripe to drop the pilot and switch sides, before it is too late.

Long ago, during the Suez Crisis, military thinker Basil Liddell Hart was already warning against "the Napoleonic fallacy" that one or a handful of "decisive battles" could win wars in the developing world. Looking around at his democratic, materialistic, media-dizzied age, Liddell Hart predicted the emergence of a *new* Western way of war that would be impatient with long, costly, attritional struggles in faraway places and would content itself—for want of anything better—with basic security and containment, not new dawns of hope and change. He also discouraged the sort of technological triumphalism that infused the "Project for a New American Century" crowd that jeered at Clinton and drove Bush 43 into military adventures: "The object in war is to attain a better peace . . . If you concentrate exclusively on victory, with no thought for the after-effect, you may be too exhausted to profit by the peace, while it is almost certain that the peace will be a bad one."[15]

The Bush Doctrine, juiced up on the technological capabilities of a "revolution in military affairs," dared to believe that a return to Napoleon—crushing victory and a dictated peace—was possible. It wasn't. Critics had warned Eden that even if he tipped over Nasser in 1956, he would have years of thankless work ahead of him. Critics warned Bush 43 of the same thing, but he plunged ahead, confident that a "decapitated" Iraq would somehow get all its limbs and organs back to functioning, cheaply and quickly. For Afghanistan, Bush made no such predictions—limply asking, "Who's gonna run the country?"—and accepting Rumsfeld's reply that such questions could be left to "the Afghans." Unfortunately, Afghans appear to be as thin on the ground as Iraqis. More obvious are the well-armed, boisterous subgroups: Hazaras, Pashtuns, Tajiks, Uzbeks, Kurds, Arabs, Shiites and Sunnis. Without responsible "Afghans" or "Iraqis" to make a new state, the job becomes ours, in accordance with Thomas Friedman's "Pottery Barn Rule": we broke it, so we own it. To paraphrase Liddell Hart, the "after-effect" of the most recent U.S. forays into the Middle East has been bad, and the "peace"—such as it is—even worse.

Military force is good at precision strikes against sites, leaders or select units, but not much good at wars in the developing world, as Liddell Hart foretold. Saddam's last boast, that "Iraq is better than any country at absorbing U.S. precision munitions," was arguably true. The tendency, revealed in Iraq and Afghanistan for precision munitions to go astray and kill innocent civilians in large numbers adds a new level of complexity. It strengthens the (intended) targets of those munitions, weakens the targeters, and has exposed coalition forces to greater risk; they must now patrol and strike without the heavy fire support they used to enjoy. Fears of collateral damage, host government outcries and media scrutiny have eviscerated the American way of war. Obama and Petraeus know all of this. Their war in Afghanistan will be a template, one suspects, for all future battles in the "long war." They are dialing back artillery and air strikes, creating security through continuous NATO force presence in contested areas (not "commuting to fight"), crushing out the sanctuaries on either side of the AfPak border and hoping for the best. They are also aware of something that right-thinking people like Tenet, Powell, Shinseki and even Tommy Franks recognized before the Iraq invasion: that the war with the jihadis would not be won on a "central front" like Iraq. It will flicker and smolder as long as there are sanctuaries like Afghanistan, Yemen, Somalia, Iraq and Pakistan. Energy, resources, troops and morale must always be conserved for the *next* battle in the *next* place, which is why it's called a long war. In his decolonizing post-1945 world— torn by struggles of national liberation—Liddell Hart saw this coming: beware of "self-exhaustion," he wrote; fight in "the most strength-conserving way." Needless to say, building elaborate new nations in places like Iraq and Afghanistan is not "strength-conserving." It is strength-exhausting, and the strength needs to be conserved for the fight with the terrorists, who can be engaged from friendly enclaves within the stumbling new countries.

A Western diplomat in Baghdad observed in May 1967 that "there is no rational political discourse in the Middle East. Our policy must be that of Abbé Sieyès"— that great survivor of several French revolutionary regime changes—"'to survive and wait for better days.'" "Better days," of course, always seem over the horizon in the Middle East. There, realism—a pragmatic embrace of half-measures and expedients—may be the best possible course because there is no other that will satisfy the clashing constituencies. "Change is something the Arabs must do for themselves," a British official in Baghdad concluded in 1966. "We have no alternative but to sit this one out . . . until the ranting and shadow-boxing about 'imperialism' is treated as dépassé," until "another general elbows in insisting on a more balanced, pragmatic outlook on the world." A new sequence will emerge: liberation, leadership by a popular hero, tyranny, and then eventually "re-liberation."[16] Because of the general prickliness about imperialism—al-Qaeda in July 2009 weirdly accused Pakistan of becoming an American pawn and "Crusader state"—Washington and the West cannot speed or steer this sequence. They can only wait for it, taking care to assure their own safety through shrewd diplomacy and public relations, deftly targeted foreign aid, improved intelligence and, where absolutely required, armed force. There are tough calls Washington must make, about the nature of its relationships with Riyadh, Tehran and Tel Aviv, as well as its tolerance for nuclear proliferation, but beyond that, America can only discreetly steer the more worrisome nations of the Middle East, confident that they themselves are becoming exhausted with the nihilism of the jihadis and the excuse-mongering of their governments.

Quicksand in a state of nature is surprisingly viscous and buoyant; the weight of beasts and humans causes it to liquefy and sink a trapped body, whose panicked exertions cause the awful stuff to become viscous again, and inescapable. Let us move deliberately and powerfully to the edge of the morass, and climb out.

ACKNOWLEDGMENTS

Quicksand is dedicated to my sons Matias and Winslow, who earned the dedication of my last book, and have repeated the feat here. They are the light of my life. Whether we are traveling, hanging around the house, or lining up at the ballpark for a game, we have so much fun together that the days pass like hours and the hours like minutes. Mati and Win give me all the joy of a father's love for two growing, jostling boys, who are always ready to throw and catch whatever ball is in season, go skiing, play nine holes of golf, or sit down with their dad to watch the Patriots, Red Sox or Tour de France. They are great kids, and they make my life happier and fuller. With or without them, I invariably think of Douglas MacArthur's *Father's Prayer*, and how my boys fulfill it: they are "proud and unbending," yet "humble and honest," serious, but never too serious, full of strength *and* compassion. Marianne Cook was also a source of love and companionship throughout the writing of this book. Whether in Dallas or abroad—Marianne joined me on a two-week trek through Lebanon and Syria in the midsummer heat—she invigorated my work and made it far easier, as T. E. Lawrence once said, "to heave at that beastly book of mine."

My mother, Judith Stoughton Wawro, has been a tremendous support and role model, helping me raise the boys and providing me with a cool New England haven from the hot Dallas summers. Her kindness, energy, curiosity, independence and selflessness at the age of eighty-six are awe-inspiring. My brother David has been a shrewd reader of this book through many drafts, and my brother Mark has arranged periodic escapes to Park City, Utah, which have been good for morale. As always, my sister Jill has been a great friend and confidante, as have brothers George and Peter, and my nephew Marc Bataillon. Speaking of friends, Chuck LeSauvage has been a great one.

I wish I could thank everyone in the Middle East who assisted me in my research and travels, but most asked not to be named. My driver and guide in Iran, Bagher Vali, was as good a best friend as one could make in just two or three weeks of traveling. Our picaresque road trip from Tehran to Qom, Isfahan, Kerman, Mashad, Shiraz and Bandar Abbas will always be one of my most agreeable memories. In the presidential libraries and the archives in Washington and London, the level of indexing, computerization and digitization is so advanced that there is no one to thank in this instance, except the taxpayers and public servants who have made those archive collections so accessible. Where I did meet obstacles—in my search for high-resolution photos—the ever-helpful Tim Nenninger of the National Archives put me on the right track to secure the images for this book.

I wrote this book at two institutions—the Naval War College in Newport, Rhode Island, and the University of North Texas. I have debts at both places. In Newport, I wish to thank all of my colleagues in the Center for Naval Warfare Studies—and indeed all around the college—for educating me on the intricacies of the global military balance. In particular, I must thank Alberto Coll, who brought me back to Newport after a visiting appointment and gave me a number of superb opportunities to travel in the Middle East and elsewhere, and to research, write and teach. At UNT, I must thank my excellent colleagues in the Department of History and in the Military History Center. Mike Leggiere and Rob Citino have helped me keep the center growing and on track, and have been good friends as well. Guy Chet, Todd Smith and Aaron Navarro have kept my tennis game sharp. Harold Tanner, Richard Lowe and Mike Campbell have been wise and helpful colleagues. Thanks also to Bob and Bette Sherman, Warren Burggren, Stan Walker, Al Hurley and Jerry Farrington, for helping us build a superb military history program.

At the Penguin Press, I want to thank editor in chief Eamon Dolan, who has been a generous and painstaking reader, and has provided critical feedback at every turn. Scott Moyers, Eamon's predecessor, signed the book and kept me going in the early days, when I felt hopelessly stuck in archival quicksand. My agent, Tina Bennett at Janklow & Nesbit, has also kept me moving along, reading carefully and seeing to it that the manuscript was read by specialists. They have all improved my work, and any errors of fact or judgment that remain are mine alone.

Dallas, Texas

2011

NOTES

INTRODUCTION

1. Elie Kedourie, *In the Anglo-Arab Labyrinth: The McMahon-Husayn Correspondence and Its Interpretations 1914–39*, Cambridge: Cambridge University Press, 1976, p. xiii.
2. British National Archives, London (BNA), War Office (WO) 106/189, Cairo, Feb. 28, 1919, General Clayton to War Office.
3. Kermit Roosevelt, *Arabs, Oil and History: The Story of the Middle East*, New York: Harper, 1949, p. 162.
4. Martin Amis, *Koba the Dread: Laughter and the Twenty Million*, London: Vintage, 2002, p. 93.
5. George Kirk, *Survey of International Affairs: The Middle East in the War*, London: Oxford University Press, 1952, p. 407.
6. Anwar el-Sadat, *In Search of Identity: An Autobiography*, New York: Harper & Row, 1977, p. 137.
7. Cited in Geoffrey Wheatcroft, "Tony's Tories," *Wall Street Journal*, May 4, 2005.
8. Sadat, p. 126.
9. BNA, Foreign Office (FO) 371/40285, London, Aug. 23, 1944, Eastern Department, "Personalities in Saudi Arabia."
10. BNA, FO 371/3061, London, Dec. 1917, Balfour to Sykes.
11. Malcolm Brown, ed., *T. E. Lawrence in War and Peace: An Anthology of the Military Writings of Lawrence of Arabia*, London: Greenhill, 2005, p. 9.
12. National Archives and Records Administration, Washington (NARA), M 1642, 46, Colonel Bonner Fellers, GSC, Sep. 30, 1942, "Memorandum for Gen. Strong." Also Nov. 2, 1942, "Memorandum for Col. Donovan."
13. Roosevelt, *Arabs, Oil and History*, p. 9.
14. Arnold Toynbee, "Introduction," in Kirk, *Middle East in the War*, pp. 1–2.
15. Kermit Roosevelt, *Countercoup: The Struggle for Control of Iran*, New York: McGraw Hill, 1979, p. 40.
16. NARA, M 1642, 122, Washington, Feb. 22, 1942, Colonel Donovan to BG Raymond E. Lee, "Report of a Meeting of Prominent Germans in Buenos Aires on January 24."
17. Ian Frazier, "Invaders: Destroying Baghdad," *New Yorker*, Apr. 25, 2005, pp. 50–52.
18. Roosevelt, *Arabs, Oil and History*, pp. 200–201.
19. From Eothen, cited in Harry St. John Philby, *Sa'udi Arabia*, New York: Arno Press, 1972 [orig. 1955], pp. 298–99.
20. BNA, FO 371/3061, Calcutta, Aug. 1917, Chief Political Officer IEF, "A Sketch of the Political History of Persia, Iraq and Arabia."
21. Chantal Metzger, *L'Empire colonial français dans la stratégie du Troisième Reich, 1936–1945*, 2 vols., Brussels: Peter Lang, 2002, vol. 1, p. 176.
22. Cited in Senator Elbert Thomas, "We demand . . . ," *The New Palestine*, Nov. 20, 1942.
23. Mark Wischnitzer, *To Dwell in Safety: The Story of Jewish Migration since 1800*, Philadelphia: Jewish Publication Society of America, 1948, pp. 282–85.
24. Michael J. Cohen, *Truman and Israel*, Berkeley: University of California Press, 1990, pp. 87–8.
25. NARA, M 1642, 83, Washington, Aug. 25, 1942, William J. Donovan, "Memorandum for Operations Division, War Department."
26. Herbert Feis, *The Birth of Israel: The Tousled Diplomatic Bed*, New York: Norton, 1969, pp. 16–17.
27. BNA, FO 371/90236, Tunis, Dec. 19, 1950, Calvert to R. Allen.

28. NARA, LM 163/2, Washington, Jan. 30, 1945, "Memo of Conversation between Acting Secretary Grew and Egyptian Minister Maymoud Hassan."

29. Herbert Feis, *Seen from E.A.: Three International Episodes,* New York: Knopf, 1947, p. 94.

CHAPTER 1: ZION

1. Andrew Roberts, *A History of the English Speaking Peoples since 1900,* New York: HarperCollins, 2007, p. 182.

2. Cited in John Laughland, "Georgia on Their Mind," *Guardian,* Apr. 1, 2004.

3. Margaret MacMillan, *Paris 1919: Six Months That Changed the World,* New York: Random House, 2001, pp. 413–15.

4. BNA, FO 78/5479, Cairo, Nov. 29, 1902, Lord Cromer to Marquess of Lansdowne. London, Jun. 19, 1903, Marquess of Lansdowne to Theodor Herzl.

5. MacMillan, p. 416.

6. Edward Atiyah, *An Arab Tells His Story: A Study in Loyalties,* London: John Murray, 1946, p. 205.

7. Gordon Wright, *France in Modern Times,* 5th ed., New York: Norton, 1995, pp. 242–45.

8. Howard M. Sachar, *A History of Israel: From the Rise of Zionism to Our Time,* 2nd ed., New York: Knopf, 1998, p. 21. Michael Burns, *France and the Dreyfus Affair,* Boston: Bedford, 1999, pp. 53–7.

9. Wischnitzer, p. 55.

10. David Fromkin, *A Peace to End All Peace: The Fall of the Ottoman Empire and the Creation of the Modern Middle East,* New York: Henry Holt, 1989, pp. 271–73.

11. Carl E. Schorske, *Fin-de-Siècle Vienna: Politics and Culture,* New York: Vintage, 1981, pp. 162–68. Niall Ferguson, *The House of Rothschild: The World's Banker, 1849–1999,* New York: Viking, 1999, p. 257.

12. Benny Morris, *Righteous Victims: A History of the Zionist-Arab Conflict, 1881–2001,* New York: Vintage, 2001, p. 7. Sachar, p. 36.

13. Ferguson, *The House of Rothschild: The World's Banker,* pp. 279–80, 282. Sachar, pp. 40–2.

14. Morris, *Righteous Victims,* p. 5.

15. Sachar, pp. 163–64.

16. Benny Morris, *The Birth of the Palestinian Refugee Problem Revisited,* Cambridge: Cambridge University Press, 2004, p. 41.

17. Wischnitzer, pp. 133, 154.

18. Sachar, p. 43.

19. Ahron Bregman, *Israel's Wars: A History since 1947.* 2nd ed. London, Routledge, 2002, p. 3.

20. Fromkin, p. 42.

21. BNA, FO 78/5479, Jerusalem, Jan. 4 and Feb. 9, 1899, N. R. O'Connor, "Immigration of Jews into Palestine." Haifa, Oct. 25, 1901, J. H. Monahan.

22. Morris, *Birth,* p. 42.

23. Sachar, pp. 30–34, 87–8, 165. Morris, *Righteous Victims,* pp. 106–7.

24. BNA, FO 371/61931, London, Apr. 24, 1947, Mr. H. Beeley, "The Political History of Palestine under British Administration."

25. Sachar, pp. 89–90.

26. John Keay, *Sowing the Wind: The Seeds of Conflict in the Middle East,* New York: Norton, 2003, p. 136.

27. NARA, M 1037/2, Washington, Feb. 1, 1937, Reverend Benjamin Haffiz to Cordell Hull.

28. Tom Segev, *One Palestine Complete: Jews and Arabs under the British Mandate,* New York: Henry Holt, 1999, pp. 120–21.

29. Ferguson, *The House of Rothschild: The World's Banker,* p. 450. Sachar, pp. 98–9. Fromkin, pp. 276–79, 290.

30. Ferguson, *The House of Rothschild: The World's Banker,* p. 281.

31. Khalidi, *Resurrecting Empire: Western Footprints and America's Perilous Path in the Middle East,* Boston: Beacon Press, 2004, p. 1.

32. Jill, Duchess of Hamilton, *First to Damascus: The Story of the Australian Light Horse and Lawrence of Arabia,* Sydney: Kangaroo Press, 2002, p. 97.

33. MacMillan, p. 416.

34. BNA, FO 608/107, London, Military Section, Jun. 14, 1919, Lt. Colonel Gribbon, "Defense of Suez Canal and Egypt."

35. Royal Institute of International Affairs, *Great Britain and Palestine, 1915–36*, London: Chatham House, 1936.
36. BNA, FO 608/107, London, Military Section, Jun. 14, 1919, Lt. Colonel Gribbon, "Defense of Suez Canal and Egypt." Sachar, pp. 100, 119.
37. BNA, FO 371/3052, London, , Apr. 28, 1917, Balfour to General Wingate.
38. Royal Institute of International Affairs, *Great Britain and Palestine*. BNA, FO 371/3053, Bern, Oct. 2, 1917, Heron-Goodhart to Balfour.
39. Brown, *T. E. Lawrence*, p. 105. Roosevelt, *Arabs, Oil and History*, p. 176. Donald Macintyre, "The Birth of Modern Israel: A Scrap of Paper That Changed History," *Independent*, May 26, 2005.
40. BNA, FO 371/3053, Bern, Oct. 2, 1917, Heron-Goodhart to Balfour. Ferguson, *The House of Rothschild: The World's Banker*, p. 451. Fromkin, pp. 295–96.
41. BNA, FO 371/3054, London, Oct. 24, 1917, Weizmann to Balfour.
42. BNA, FO 371/3054, Petrograd, Nov. 26, 1917, General Barter to CIGS.
43. BNA, Foreign and Colonial Office (FCO) 371/3054, Geneva, Dec. 5, 1917, American Vice Consul Edelmann, "The Zionist Movement." Naomi W. Cohen, *Jacob H. Schiff: A Study in American Jewish Leadership*, Hanover, NH: Brandeis University Press, 1999, pp. 47, 106. Laurel Leff, *Buried by the Times: The Holocaust and America's Most Important Newspaper*, Cambridge: Cambridge University Press, 2005, pp. 24–5.
44. Wischnitzer, pp. 120 and 125.
45. BNA, WO 106/189, London, Feb. 6, 1919, General Staff, "Notes on Zionism," secret. FCO 371/3054, Washington, Dec. 28, 1917, Spring-Rice to Foreign Office.
46. BNA, FO 371/3054, Odessa, Nov. 30, 1917, British Consul to Foreign Office.
47. Sachar, p. 109.
48. Robert Graves and Alan Hodge, *The Reader over Your Shoulder: A Handbook for Writers of English Prose*, New York: Macmillan, 1944, p. 21.
49. BNA, FO 608/107, London, Military Section, Jun. 12, 1919, Lt. Colonel Gribbon. Hashim Behbehani, *The Soviet Union and Arab Nationalism, 1917–1966*, London: KPI, 1986, pp. 73–4.
50. BNA, WO 106/189, London, Feb. 6, 1919, General Staff, "Notes on Zionism," secret. Henry Moskowitz, "Zionism No Remedy: A Voice from America," *New York Times*, Jun. 10, 1917. NARA, M 1037/2, Leonard Stein, "Zionism."
51. Segev, *One Palestine*, pp. 100–1, 119. Ferguson, *The House of Rothschild*, p. 452. Bernard Lewis, "The Palestinians and the PLO," *Commentary*, Jan. 1975.
52. BNA, FO 371/3054, Cairo, Dec. 20 and 31, 1917, General Wingate to Balfour. WO 106/189, London, Feb. 6, 1919, General Staff, "Notes on Zionism," secret. MacMillan, pp. 420–21.
53. Segev, *One Palestine*, p. 9.
54. Ritchie Ovendale, *The Origins of the Arab-Israeli Wars*, 2nd ed., London: Longman, 1992, p. 60.
55. BNA, FO 371/61931, London, Apr. 24, 1947, Mr. H. Beeley, "The Political History of Palestine under British Administration."
56. Roosevelt, *Arabs, Oil and History*, p. 189.
57. Joseph B. Schechtman, *The Mufti and the Fuehrer*, New York: Yoseloff, 1965, pp. 24–5.
58. "Britain in the Middle East: Tremendous and Indefinite Liabilities in Mesopotamia and Palestine," *Evening Standard*, Jun. 1, 1920.
59. Nigel John Ashton, *Eisenhower, Macmillan and the Problem of Nasser: Anglo-American Relations and Arab Nationalism 1955–59*, London: Macmillan, 1996, p. 30.
60. Sachar, p. 126–27.
61. BNA, FO 371/3061, London, Dec. 27, 1917, Balfour to Spring-Rice. FO 371/61931, London, Apr. 24, 1947, Mr. H. Beeley, "The Political History of Palestine under British Administration." BNA, WO 106/189, Vatican, Mar. 17, 1919, Count de Salis to Foreign Office. London, Mar. 5, 1919, Balfour to Count de Salis.
62. "Britain in the Middle East," *Evening Standard*, Jun. 1, 1920.
63. BNA, FO 371/61931, London, Apr. 24, 1947, Mr. H. Beeley, "The Political History of Palestine under British Administration."
64. Sachar, p. 130.
65. BNA, FO 371/61931, London, Apr. 24, 1947, Mr. H. Beeley, "The Political History of Palestine under British Administration."
66. BNA, WO 106/189, London, Feb. 6, 1919, General Staff, "Notes on Zionism," secret. Sachar, pp. 131, 134.

67. BNA, FO 371/61931, London, Apr. 24, 1947, Mr. H. Beeley, "The Political History of Palestine under British Administration."
68. BNA, WO 106/189, London, Feb. 6, 1919, General Staff, "Notes on Zionism," secret.
69. Bregman, p. 3.
70. Roosevelt, *Arabs, Oil and History*, p. 124.
71. Kirk, *Middle East in the War*, pp. 228–29. BNA, FO 371/61931, London, Apr. 24, 1947, Mr. H. Beeley, "The Political History of Palestine under British Administration."
72. Sachar, pp. 148, 154–55, 160. Kirk, *Middle East in the War*, p. 236.
73. Roosevelt, *Arabs, Oil and History*, pp. 23–4.
74. Bregman, p. 4.
75. NARA, M 1037/1, Washington, Jan. 18, 1930, Wallace Murray, "Memorandum of Conversation." Margin comments by P. Knabenshue, Jerusalem, Apr. 13, 1930.
76. BNA, FO 371/104735, Tel Aviv, Dec. 22, 1953, Anthony Moore to Eden. Kirk, *Middle East in the War*, pp. 232–33.
77. Bregman, p. 6. Raymond Aron, *De Gaulle, Israel and the Jews*, New York: Transaction, 2004 [orig. 1969], p. xvii. BNA, FO 371/61931, London, Apr. 24, 1947, Mr. H. Beeley, "The Political History of Palestine under British Administration." Sachar, pp. 135–39.
78. BNA, WO 106/189, London, Feb. 6, 1919, General Staff, "Notes on Zionism," secret.
79. Rabbi Stephen Wise, "In Reply to King Ibn Saud," *Life*, Jun. 21, 1943.
80. BNA, FO 371.35035, Washington, May 25, 1943, Halifax to Eden.
81. NARA, M 1037/2, New York, Sep. 1, 1936, Zionist Organization of America to Cordell Hull.
82. Richard Slotkin, *Lost Battalions: The Great War and the Crisis of American Nationality*, New York: Henry Holt, 2006, pp. 416–21.
83. Shlomo Aronson, *Hitler, the Allies, and the Jews*, Cambridge: Cambridge University Press, 2004, p. 10.
84. Wischnitzer, p. 154.
85. NARA, M 1037/2, Kew Gardens, UK, Sep. 8, 1936, G. D. Kheirallah to President Roosevelt.
86. Macintyre, "The Birth of Modern Israel." Segev, *One Palestine*, p. 36.
87. Kirk, *Middle East in the War*, pp. 249–50. Wischnitzer, p. 173.
88. Wischnitzer, p. 172.
89. Philip Mattar, *The Mufti of Jerusalem: Al-Hajj Amin al-Husayni and the Palestinian National Movement*, New York: Columbia University Press, 1988, p. 102. Zvi Elpeleg, *The Grand Mufti: Haj Amin al-Hussaini*, London: Frank Cass, 1993, p. 65.
90. NARA, M 1037/1, Washington, Jan. 18, 1930, Wallace Murray, "Memorandum of Conversation."
91. NARA, M 1037/2, "Senators' Statement on Holy Land Crisis," *New York American*, Sep. 18, 1936.
92. NARA, M 1037/2, Washington, Sep. 13, 1936, Wallace Murray to Hull.
93. BNA, FO 371/61931, London, Apr. 24, 1947, Mr. H. Beeley, "The Political History of Palestine under British Administration."
94. Mark Sykes, margin comment on BNA, FO 371/3054, Bern, Dec. 10, 1917, Horace Rumbold to Balfour.
95. Atiyah, p. 201. NARA, M 1037/1, Jerusalem, Jan. 11, 1930, P. Knabenshue, "Political Situation in Palestine—Conclusions."
96. Cited in Kirk, *Middle East in the War*, p. 325. Arthur Koestler, *Promise and Fulfillment*, New York: Random House, 1976, p. ix.
97. BNA, FO 371/61931, London, Apr. 24, 1947, Mr. H. Beeley, "The Political History of Palestine under British Administration."
98. Wischnitzer, pp. 193, 217, 242.
99. Ibid., p. 202.
100. Kirk, *Middle East in the War*, p. 234.
101. BNA, FO 371/61931, London, Apr. 24, 1947, Mr. H. Beeley, "The Political History of Palestine under British Administration."
102. Harry St. John Philby, *Arabian Jubilee*, New York: John Day, 1953, pp. 210–11.
103. Kirk, *Middle East in the War*, pp. 319–20.
104. David Remnick, "Blood and Sand," *New Yorker*, May 5, 2008.
105. David Tal, "Between Intuition and Professionalism: Israeli Military Leadership during the 1948 Palestine War," *Journal of Military History* 68 (Jul. 2004), p. 887.

106. Mattar, p. 31.
107. Morris, *Righteous Victims*, pp. 111–12. Kirk, *Middle East in the War*, p. 332. Segev, *One Palestine*, pp. 303, 438–39.
108. BNA, FO 371/61931, London, Apr. 24, 1947, Mr. H. Beeley, "The Political History of Palestine under British Administration."
109. Ibid.
110. Bregman, p. 7.
111. Wischnitzer, p. 216.
112. Bregman, p. 6. Kirk, *Middle East in the War*, pp. 23, 241.
113. Atiyah, p. 204.
114. Metzger, *L'Empire colonial français*, vol. 1, pp. 328–31. Kirk, *Middle East in the War*, p. 229.
115. Metzger, *L'Empire colonial français*, vol. 1, pp. 551–52.
116. Mattar, p. 104.
117. Metzger, *L'Empire colonial français*, vol. 1, p. 553.
118. Kirk, *Middle East in the War*, p. 239.
119. Ibid., p. 249.
120. Aron, p. 14.
121. Morris, *Birth*, pp. 45–8.
122. The phrase was coined not by Herzl but by Lord Shaftesbury in his 1854 memoirs. Morris, *Righteous Victims*, p. 42.
123. BNA, FO 371/45406, May 2, 1945, J. A. de C. Hamilton, "Possibility of Arab Disturbances in Palestine." Segev, *One Palestine*, p. 456. Sachar, p. 247.
124. Kirk, *Middle East in the War*, p. 308.
125. Ibid., p. 324.
126. BNA, WO 208/1705, Jerusalem, Oct. 2, 1944, "Terrorist Activities—From Palestine," top secret.
127. Kirk, *Middle East in the War*, p. 322.
128. Segev, *One Palestine*, p. 475.
129. BNA, FO 371/61931, London, Apr. 24, 1947, Mr. H. Beeley, "The Political History of Palestine under British Administration." Kirk, *Middle East in the War*, pp. 331–32.
130. Kirk, *Middle East in the War*, pp. 14, 325. Harry Levin, *Jerusalem Embattled,* London: Gollancz, 1950, p. 25.
131. Mattar, pp. 104–7.
132. American Christian Palestine Committee, *The Arab War Effort: A Documented Account,* New York: ACPC, 1947, pp. 21–2.
133. Segev, *One Palestine*, pp. 375–76.

CHAPTER 2: OIL

1. Roosevelt, *Arabs, Oil and History*, pp. 22–3.
2. Wilfred Thesiger, *Arabian Sands,* New York: Dutton, 1959, pp. xvii, 75.
3. Roosevelt, *Arabs, Oil and History*, p. 18.
4. NARA, LM 168/3, Beirut, Jan. 15, 1947, Kuniholm, "Jedda Clinic."
5. NARA, LM 168/3, Headquarters, USAFIME, Dec. 16, 1944.
6. BNA, FO 371/3061, Calcutta, Aug. 1917, IEF, "A Sketch of the Political History of Persia, Iraq and Arabia."
7. Lawrence Wright, *The Looming Tower: Al Qaeda and the Road to 9/11,* New York: Knopf, 2006, p. 63.
8. Frederick F. Anscombe, *The Ottoman Gulf: The Creation of Kuwait, Saudi Arabia and Qatar,* New York: Columbia University Press, 1997, pp. 16–18, 42.
9. BNA, FO 608/107, London, Military Section, Jun. 12, 1919, Lt. Colonel Gribbon.
10. BNA, FO 371/40285, London, Aug. 23, 1944, Eastern Department, "Personalities in Saudi Arabia."
11. Fromkin, pp. 424–25. Anscombe, p. 154.
12. Madawi Al-Rasheed, *A History of Saudi Arabia,* Cambridge: Cambridge University Press, 2002, p. 61.
13. Ibid., p. 40.
14. Harry St. John Philby, *Sa'udi Arabia,* New York, Arno Press, 1972 [orig. 1955], pp. 268–69. Anscombe, pp. 164–66.
15. Philby, *Sa'udi Arabia*, p. 259.

16. BNA, FO 371/3052, Berlin, Feb. 22, 1917, "Korrespondenzblatt Nr. 10," Dr. Martin Hartmann.
17. Anscombe, p. 6.
18. BNA, FO 371/3054, Cairo, Nov. 28, 1917, General Wingate to Balfour.
19. BNA, FO 371/3054, Cairo, Jul. 10, 1917, Commander D. G. Hogarth, "Note on the Anglo-French-Russian Agreement about the Near East."
20. Anthony Cave Brown, *Oil, God and Gold: The Story of Aramco and the Saudi Kings*, Boston: Houghton Mifflin, 1999, p. 6.
21. BNA, FO 371/3053, Berne, Oct. 2, 1917, Heron Goodhart to Balfour.
22. Philby, *Sa'udi Arabia*, pp. 271–72.
23. Brown, *Oil, God and Gold*, p. 7.
24. BNA, FO 371/3054, Jeddah, Jul. 29, 1917, Lawrence to Wingate.
25. Ibid.
26. Al-Rasheed, pp. 49–51.
27. BNA, FO 371/3046, Basra, Dec. 3, 1916, Percy Cox to India Office.
28. BNA, FO 371/3054, Jeddah, Jul. 29, 1917, Lawrence to Wingate.
29. BNA, FO 371/3054, Jan. 20, 1917, Arthur Hirtzel, "British Interests in Arabia."
30. Al-Rasheed, pp. 45–6.
31. BNA, FO 371/3054, Jeddah, Jul. 29, 1917, Lawrence to Wingate.
32. Wright, *Looming Tower*, p. 61.
33. Philby, *Sa'udi Arabia*, p. 290.
34. Roosevelt, *Arabs, Oil and History*, p. 157.
35. Ibid., p. 47.
36. BNA, FO 371/40285, London, Aug. 23, 1944, Eastern Department, "Personalities in Saudi Arabia." Michael Sheldon Cheney, *Big Oil Man from Arabia*, New York: Ballantine, 1958, p. 215.
37. Tore T. Petersen, *The Middle East between the Great Powers*, London: Macmillan, 2000, p. 54.
38. NARA, LM 169/2, Washington, Feb. 12, 1952, Charles Bohlen to Fred Awalt, "Col. Eddy's Manuscript Regarding the Meeting of President Roosevelt with Ibn Saud."
39. BNA, FCO 17/9, London, Aug. 11, 1967, Willie Morris, "Revolutionary and Non-Revolutionary Regimes in the Middle East."
40. Roosevelt, *Arabs, Oil and History*, p. 159.
41. Philby, *Sa'udi Arabia*, pp. 326–27.
42. Ibid., pp. 304–5.
43. Ibid., p. 319.
44. BNA, FO 141/665, Jedda, Jul. 8, 1926, S. R. Jordan, "Report on the Activities of the Soviet Delegations to the Moslem Conference at Mecca, Jun. 1926." Behbehani, p. 7.
45. BNA, CO 732/33-8, London, Mar. 1928, Sir Samuel Hoare, "Instructions to Sir Gilbert Clayton." BNA, FO 371/45543, London, Nov. 30, 1945, "Anglo-American Relations in Saudi Arabia."
46. NARA, LM 168/1, Jedda, Jan. 13, 1945, William Eddy, "Saudi Arabia." Matthew R. Simmons, *Twilight in the Desert: The Coming Saudi Oil Shock and the World Economy*, Hoboken, Wiley, 2005, p. 10. Kirk, *Middle East 1945–50*, p. 368.
47. NARA, M 1642, 33, Washington, Jul. 3, 1942, "Memo on Saudi Arabia."
48. Kirk, *Middle East 1945–1950*, pp. 354–56, 357. NARA, LM 168/1, Jedda, Jan. 13, 1945, William Eddy, "Saudi Arabia."
49. Roosevelt, *Arabs, Oil and History*, p. 27.
50. Daniel Yergin, *The Prize: The Epic Quest for Oil, Money and Power*, New York: Simon & Schuster, 1991, pp. 288–89. Cheney, pp. 140, 151.
51. Roosevelt, *Arabs, Oil and History*, pp. 159–61. Cheney, pp. 146–47.
52. Philby, *Sa'udi Arabia*, pp. 331–32.
53. Kirk, *Middle East 1945–1950*, pp. 346–47, 354–55, 358.
54. Feis, *Seen from E.A.*, pp. 102–3, 156.
55. Roosevelt, *Arabs, Oil and History*, p. 27.
56. BNA, FO 141/1047, "Cairo Conversations Feb. 1945: Record of Conversations with King Abdul Aziz Ibn Saud in the Fayoum, 12:30–3:30 p.m., 17 February 1945."
57. NARA, M 1642, 33, Washington, Jul. 3, 1942, "Memo on Saudi Arabia." NARA, CIA-RDP78-01617A0004002100001-0, Apr. 5, 1949, Intelligence Memorandum no. 156, confidential.
58. Kirk, *Middle East 1945–1950*, p. 3.

59. Philby, *Sa'udi Arabia*, p. 351. Kirk, *Middle East 1945–1950*, p. 26.

60. NARA, LM 169/2, Washington, Feb. 24, 1951, Colonel Eddy to Charles Bohlen.

61. Roosevelt, *Arabs, Oil and History*, p. 8.

62. NARA, LM 169/4, Jedda, Jan. 31, 1945, Eddy to Stettinius.

63. BNA, FO 371/45542, Jedda, Feb. 21, 1945, Jordan to Eden, top secret.

64. BNA, FO 371/45543, Jedda, Apr. 7, 1945, R. E. Ellison to Eden.

65. Roosevelt, *Arabs, Oil and History*, p. 28.

66. NARA, LM 163/3, Washington, Jun. 28, 1945, Stanley Woodward to Holmes. BNA, FO 371/40285, London, Aug. 23, 1944, Eastern Department, "Personalities in Saudi Arabia."

67. NARA, LM 163/3, Washington, Riyadh, Apr. 21, 1948, Childs to Marshall.

68. Ashton, p. 17.

69. BNA, FO 371/45543, London, Apr. 4, 1945, Foreign Office Minute.

70. NARA, CIA-RDP78-01617A0004002100001-0, Apr. 5, 1949, Intelligence Memorandum no. 156, confidential.

71. Ibid.

72. BNA, FO 371/45543, London, Nov. 30, 1945, "Anglo-American Relations in Saudi Arabia."

73. BNA, FO 371/45543, Jedda, Mar. 17, 1945, Grafftey-Smith to Campbell, "Anglo-American Relations in Saudi Arabia." FO 371/45543, London, Apr. 4, 1945, Foreign Office Minute.

74. Feis, *Seen from E.A.*, pp. 117–18.

75. NARA, LM 163/3, Riyadh, Apr. 22, 1948, Childs to Marshall, top secret.

76. Kirk, *Middle East 1945–1950*, pp. 356, 363.

77. Ibid., pp. 356–57.

78. Al-Rasheed, p. 47.

79. NARA, LM 168/1, Jedda, Feb. 21, 1945, Eddy to Stettinius, "Visit of His Majesty Abdul Aziz al Saud to the President of the United States."

80. Feis, *Seen from E.A.*, p. 156.

81. NARA, LM 168/1, Washington, Dec. 11, 1944, Forrestal to Acheson.

82. Feis, *Seen from E.A.*, p. 93.

83. Kirk, *Middle East 1945–1950*, p. 474. Feis, *Seen from E.A.*, p. 176.

84. Roosevelt, *Arabs, Oil and History*, p. 31.

85. Bruce R. Kuniholm, *The Origins of the Cold War in the Near East: Great Power Conflict and Diplomacy in Iran*, Princeton: Princeton University Press, 1980, p. 183. NARA, LM 168/1, Washington, Jan. 27, 1945, Murray to Acheson, top secret. Roosevelt, *Arabs, Oil and History*, p. 31.

86. Kirk, *Middle East 1945–1950*, p. 360.

87. Feis, *Seen from E.A.*, pp. 95–6.

88. Cordell Hull, *The Memoirs of Cordell Hull*, 2 vols., New York: Macmillan, 1948, vol. 2, p. 1517.

89. Kirk, *Middle East 1945–1950*, p. 367. *New York Herald Tribune*, Sep. 30, 1943. *New York Times*, Oct. 6, 1943. Feis, *Seen from E.A.*, pp. 96, 99–100.

90. Feis, *Seen from E.A.*, p. 99.

91. James A. Bill and William Roger Louis, *Musaddiq, Iranian Nationalism and Oil*, Austin: University of Texas Press, 1988, pp. 151–53.

92. Roosevelt, *Arabs, Oil and History*, p. 18.

93. Cohen, *Truman and Israel*, p. 93. Kirk, *Middle East 1945–1950*, pp. 345–47. Feis, *Seen from E.A.*, pp. 103–6.

94. Cheney, pp. 105–6.

95. Kirk, *Middle East 1945–1950*, pp. 353–54.

96. Philby, *Sa'udi Arabia*, p. 335.

97. BNA, FO 371/3054, Jan. 20, 1917, Arthur Hirtzel, "British Interests in Arabia."

98. Fritz Grobba, *Männer und Mächte im Orient*, Göttingen: Musterschmidt, 1967, pp. 110–13.

99. Metzger, *L'Empire colonial français*, vol. 1, p. 344–45.

100. BNA, FO 371/31450, Riyadh, Feb. 26, 1942, Stonehewer to Bird.

101. Kirk, *Middle East 1945–1950*, p. 352. Philby, *Sa'udi Arabia*, pp. 338–39.

102. NARA, LM 163/3, Jedda, Jul. 8, 1945, William Eddy, "Visit to Riyadh to Receive King's Reply to Proposals for U.S. Military Mission."

103. NARA, LM 168/3, Jedda, Dec. 27, 1948, J. Rives Childs, "Some Observations on the Strategic Importance of Saudi Arabia."

104. BNA, FO 371/127201, Feb. 26, 1957, "Mankind's Stake in Middle Eastern Oil," an address by B. Brewster Jennings, Chairman of the Board of Socony Mobil Oil Co. to the American Institute of Mining, Metallurgy and Petroleum Engineers Annual Meeting in New Orleans.

105. Roosevelt, *Arabs, Oil and History*, p. 154.

106. Cheney, pp. 111–16.

107. Roosevelt, *Arabs, Oil and History*, pp. 25, 31.

108. Kirk, *Middle East 1945–1950*, pp. 363–67. Feis, *Seen from E.A.*, pp. 142, 147, 154, 168. Herbert Feis, *Petroleum and American Foreign Policy*, Palo Alto: Food Research Institute, Stanford University, 1944, p. 1.

109. Kuniholm, pp. 181–84. Feis, *Seen from E.A.*, pp. 171–72.

110. NARA, LM 163/3, Riyadh, Apr. 21, 1948, Childs to Marshall.

111. NARA, LM 168/1, Washington, Jan. 27, 1945, Murray to Acheson, top secret.

112. Ashton, p. 13.

113. NARA, LM 168/1, Cairo, Apr. 26, 1948, S. Pinkney Tuck to Marshall.

114. Kirk, *Middle East 1945–1950*, pp. 24–5. Cheney, pp. 140–41.

115. Cheney, pp. 111–16, 142–43.

116. David Holden and Richard Johns, *The House of Saud*, London: Sidgwick & Jackson, 1981, p. 151.

117. George McGhee, *Envoy to the Middle World: Adventures in Diplomacy*, New York: Harper & Row, 1983, p. 192.

118. Bill and Louis, p. 149. Holden and Johns, p. 154.

119. Kirk, *Middle East 1945–1950*, p. 3.

120. Bill and Louis, p. 149.

121. Roosevelt, *Arabs, Oil and History*, p. 26.

122. Philby, *Sa'udi Arabia*, p. 344.

123. Cheney, pp. 215–16.

124. Philby, *Sa'udi Arabia*, p. 351.

125. Thesiger, *Arabian Sands*, pp. xiii–xiv.

126. Ashton, p. 34.

127. Douglas Little, *American Orientalism: The United States and the Middle East since 1945*, Chapel Hill: University of North Carolina Press, 2002, p. 138.

128. Philby, *Sa'udi Arabia*, pp. 342–43.

129. Cheney, p. 2.

130. NARA, LM 168/1, Jedda, Jan. 13, 1945, William Eddy, "Saudi Arabia."

131. Roosevelt, *Arabs, Oil and History*, p. 32.

132. NARA, LM 168/1, Jedda, Jan. 6, 1948, J. Rives Childs to Marshall.

133. NARA, LM 168/1, Jedda, Jan. 13, 1945, William Eddy, "Saudi Arabia."

134. Cheney, p. 219.

135. Roosevelt, *Arabs, Oil and History*, pp. 35–8.

136. NARA, LM 163/3, Riyadh, Apr. 21, 1948, Childs to Marshall.

137. NARA, LM 168/3, Jedda, Sep. 5, 1946, Childs to Byrnes.

138. NARA, LM 168/1, Jedda, Jan. 13, 1945, William Eddy, "Saudi Arabia." Petersen, p. 72.

139. Cheney, pp. 146–47.

140. Petersen, p. 58.

141. Salim Yaqub, *Containing Arab Nationalism: The Eisenhower Doctrine and the Middle East*, Chapel Hill: University of North Carolina Press, 2004, pp. 102–3.

142. BNA, FCO 8/1505, Jedda, Mar. 9, 1970, Craig to Arthur. Al-Rasheed, p. 41.

143. Dore Gold, *Hatred's Kingdom: How Saudi Arabia Supports the New Global Terrorism*, Washington, D.C.: Regnery, 2003, p. 8.

144. Petersen, pp. 36–7, 48.

145. Ibid., pp. 26–8.

146. BNA, FO 371/127201, Feb. 26, 1957, "Mankind's Stake in Middle Eastern Oil," an address by B. Brewster Jennings, Chairman of the Board of Socony Mobil Oil Co. to the American Institute of Mining, Metallurgy and Petroleum Engineers Annual Meeting in New Orleans.

147. Khalidi, p. 109.

148. Petersen, p. 28. Cheney, pp. 148–49.

149. NARA, LM 168/1, Jedda, Dec. 4, 1947.

150. Ray Takeyh, *The Origins of the Eisenhower Doctrine: The US, Britain and Nasser's Egypt, 1953–57*, New York: Macmillan, 2000, p. 116. Petersen, p. 58. Ashton, p. 17.

151. Yaqub, pp. 162–63.

152. BNA, FCO 8/812, Jedda, Sep. 18, 1968, Morris to Stirling.

153. Little, *American Orientalism*, p. 138.

154. Ashton, pp. 16–17. Petersen, pp. 52, 56.

155. BNA, FO 141/866, Jedda, Mar. 13, 1943.

156. BNA, FO 141/866, London, Jun. 29, 1943, "Copies of Letters Exchanged between Ibn Saud and President Roosevelt."

157. NARA, LM 168/3, Jedda, Dec. 27, 1948, J. Rives Childs, "Some Observations on the Strategic Importance of Saudi Arabia."

158. NARA, LM 168/1, Jedda, Feb. 4, 1945, Eddy to Stettinius.

159. Elliott Roosevelt, *As He Saw It*, New York: Duell, Sloan and Pearce, 1946, pp. 243–44.

160. NARA, LM 168/1, Jedda, Feb. 21, 1945, Eddy to Stettinius, "Visit of His Majesty Abdul Aziz al Saud to the President of the United States."

161. The friend was Bernard Baruch. Roosevelt, *As He Saw It*, p. 244. NARA, LM 168/1, Jedda, Feb. 21, 1945, Eddy to Stettinius, "Visit of His Majesty Abdul Aziz al Saud to the President of the United States."

162. NARA, LM 168/1, Washington, Oct. 3, 1948, J.S.M., "Memorandum for the President—King Ibn Saud."

163. BNA, FO 141/1047, "Memo of Conversation between HM Abdul Aziz Al Saud, King of Saudi Arabia, and President Roosevelt, 14 Feb. 1945, aboard the USS *Quincy*."

164. NARA, LM 168/1, Jedda, Feb. 21, 1945, Eddy to Stettinius.

165. NARA, LM 168/1, Washington, Oct. 3, 1948, J.S.M., "Memorandum for the President—King Ibn Saud."

CHAPTER 3: EXODUS

1. Kirk, *Middle East in the War*, p. 307.

2. Segev, *One Palestine*, pp. 406–7.

3. BNA, FO 371/61931, London, Apr. 24, 1947, Mr. H. Beeley, "The Political History of Palestine under British Administration."

4. Kirk, *Middle East in the War*, pp. 312–13.

5. Roosevelt, *Arabs, Oil and History*, p. 185. Jews from 65,000 to 600,000, Arab Muslims from 515,000 to 1.1 million.

6. NARA, LM 168/1, Jedda, Feb. 4, 1945, Eddy to Stettinius, top secret.

7. Wilson D. Miscamble, *From Roosevelt to Truman: Potsdam, Hiroshima and the Cold War*, Cambridge: Cambridge University Press, 2007, p. 82.

8. Hull, vol. 2, pp. 1528–31.

9. Kirk, *Middle East in the War*, pp. 314–15.

10. *New York Times*, Apr. 13, 1943.

11. NARA, LM 163/2, Washington, Jan. 23, 1945, "Memo of Telephone Conversation."

12. Wright, p. 11.

13. Hull, vol. 2, p. 1531.

14. Philby, *Arabian Jubilee*, pp. 211–18. Kirk, *Middle East in the War*, p. 317.

15. Feis, *Birth of Israel*, pp. 23, 43–4.

16. BNA, FO 371/35035, Washington, Jun. 12, 1943, Halifax to Eden, "Report by Dr. Weizmann of an Interview with President Roosevelt."

17. NARA, LM 163/23, Prague, Jun. 3, 1948, Steinhardt to Marshall.

18. BNA, WO 208/1705, London, Jan. 20, 1944, Major Claud Dewhurst, M.I. 2. Also London, Mar. 9, 1944, Lt. Colonel G.S., M.I. 2.

19. Hull, vol. 2, p. 1534.

20. Kirk, *Middle East in the War*, pp. 316–19.

21. Donald Neff, *Fallen Pillars: US Policy towards Palestine and Israel since 1945*, Washington, D.C.: Institute for Palestine Studies, 1995, p. 43. Feis, *Birth of Israel*, p. 19.

22. BNA, FO 371/35035, Jedda, May 10, 1943, Wikeley to Eden.

23. NARA, LM 168/1, Jedda, Feb. 4, 1945, Eddy to Stettinius, top secret.

24. Kirk, *Middle East in the War*, p. 327.

25. Aronson, p. 233. Leff, pp. 135–37, 271–77. Wischnitzer, pp. 252–59.

26. BNA, FO 371/35035, Washington, May 25, 1943, Halifax to Eden.

27. Isaac Alteras, *Eisenhower and Israel: US-Israeli Relations 1953–1960*, Gainesville: University Press of Florida, 1993, p. 29.
28. Atiyah, p. 204.
29. Wischnitzer, pp. 260, 265.
30. Arthur Max, "Holocaust Files Finally Opening to the Public," Associated Press, Nov. 19, 2006.
31. Wischnitzer, p. 261.
32. Ibid., p. 262.
33. Feis, *Birth of Israel*, pp. 27–8.
34. Kirk, *Middle East in the War*, p. 311.
35. Ovendale, *Origins*, p. 48.
36. Kirk, *Middle East in the War*, p. 250.
37. Segev, *One Palestine*, p. 9.
38. BNA, FO 371/61931, London, Apr. 24, 1947, Mr. H. Beeley, "The Political History of Palestine under British Administration."
39. Kirk, *Middle East in the War*, pp. 233, 235.
40. NARA, LM 187, "Palestine: UN activities 1945–49."
41. BNA, FO 371/68402, Washington, Jan. 5, 1948, Lord Inverchapel to Bevin.
42. Cohen, *Truman and Israel*, p. 90.
43. Wischnitzer, p. 271.
44. Ibid., p. 269.
45. Kirk, *Middle East in the War*, p. 247.
46. Alteras, p. 2.
47. Ovendale, *Origins*, p. 130.
48. Cohen, *Truman and Israel*, pp. 88–91, 279.
49. Neff, p. 29.
50. Ovendale, *Origins*, p. 126.
51. Kirk, *Middle East in the War*, p. 25.
52. BNA, FO 371/68402, London, Jan. 1, 1948, Foreign Office to Lord Inverchapel.
53. NARA, LM 187/4, New York, Apr. 12, 1948, Senator Warren Austin to George C. Marshall.
54. David McCullough, *Truman*, New York: Simon & Schuster, 1992, pp. 615–16. NARA, LM 187/4, New York, Apr. 9, 1948, Senator Warren Austin to George C. Marshall.
55. Wischnitzer, p. 284.
56. NARA, LM 187/4, New York, Apr. 7, 1948, Senator Warren Austin to George C. Marshall.
57. T. G. Fraser, *The USA and the Middle East since World War II*, New York: St. Martin's Press, 1989, p. 27.
58. NARA, LM 169/2, Washington, Feb. 24, 1951, Colonel Eddy to Charles Bohlen.
59. McCullough, pp. 615–16.
60. NARA, LM 187/4, Apr. 2, 1948, League of Women Voters, "Brief for Action."
61. George F. Hofmann, *Through Mobility We Conquer*, Lexington, KY: 2006, pp. 461–62.
62. Miscamble, p. 284.
63. Ibid., pp. 323–24.
64. Ibid., pp. 39–40.
65. Feis, *Birth of Israel*, p. 46.
66. Behbehani, pp. 58–9, 65.
67. Bregman, p. 9.
68. Aron, p. xxiii.
69. Fraser, *USA*, pp. 33–5.
70. Ibid., p. 28.
71. Bregman, p. 9.
72. Kirk, *The Middle East 1945–1950*, p. 270.
73. Benny Morris, *1948: A History of the First Arab-Israeli War*, New Haven: Yale University Press, 2008, pp. 125–28.
74. BNA, FO 371/75268, Haifa, Oct. 18, 1949, C. N. Ezard, "Grievances Entertained by the Arabs of Northern Palestine against the Israeli Authorities."
75. Morris, *1948*, pp. 149–50.
76. Morris, *Birth*, p. 185. Bregman, p. 12.
77. Roosevelt, *Arabs, Oil and History*, p. 21.

78. BNA, WO 208/1705, Jan. 16, 1944, C-in-C Middle East to War Office, most secret.
79. Kirk, *Middle East 1945–1950*, p. 272. Roosevelt, *Arabs, Oil and History*, pp. 117, 123.
80. Morris, *1948*, p. 170.
81. Morris, *Birth*, pp. 432–35. Bregman, p. 12. Morris, *1948*, p. 99.
82. NARA, M 1642/2, May 18, 1946, Joint Intelligence Committee, "Intelligence Estimate on Palestine," top secret. Kirk, *Middle East 1945–1950*, pp. 308, 339.
83. BNA, WO 208/1705, Jan. 16, 1944, C-in-C Middle East to War Office, most secret.
84. BNA, FO 371/45406, May 2, 1945, J. A. de C. Hamilton, "Possibility of Arab Disturbances in Palestine." Bregman, pp. 10–11.
85. NARA, M 1642/2, May 18, 1946, Joint Intelligence Committee, "Intelligence Estimate on Palestine," top secret.
86. BNA, WO 208/1705, Jan. 16, 1944, C-in-C Middle East to War Office, most secret.
87. BNA, FO 371/45406, May 2, 1945, J. A. de C. Hamilton, "Possibility of Arab Disturbances in Palestine."
88. Morris, *Birth*, pp. 30–1.
89. Ibid., p. 34.
90. Bregman, pp. 11, 13.
91. Morris, *Birth*, pp. 67–9, 72–4, 137–38.
92. Feis, *Birth of Israel*, pp. 48–9.
93. Anthony Nutting, *Nasser*, New York: Dutton, 1972, pp. 25–7.
94. Alteras, p. 9. Feis, *Birth of Israel*, pp. 60–2.
95. Morris, *1948*, p. 59. Neff, pp. 62–3. Bregman, p. 14.
96. Nutting, pp. 25–8.
97. Morris, *1948*, p. 114.
98. NARA, LM 187/4, New York, May 4, 1948, Rusk to Marshall and Lovett.
99. Wright, *Looming Tower*, p. 14.
100. Cohen, *Truman and Israel*, p. 98.
101. Cheney, pp. 64–6.
102. Neff, pp. 60–1. Cohen, *Truman and Israel*, p. 100.
103. Kirk, *Middle East 1945–1950*, p. 273.
104. Morris, *Righteous Victims*, pp. 216–18. Tal, "Between Intuition and Professionalism."
105. Bregman, pp. 15–16.
106. Kirk, *Middle East 1945–1950*, p. 277.
107. Bregman, p. 18.
108. Morris, *Birth*, p. 69.
109. Ibid., p. 35. Bregman, p. 13.
110. Alteras, p. 4.
111. BNA, FO 371/75268, Haifa, Oct. 18, 1949, C. N. Ezard, "Grievances Entertained by the Arabs of Northern Palestine against the Israeli Authorities." Edwin M. Yoder, Jr., *Joe Alsop's Cold War*, Chapel Hill: University of North Carolina Press, 1995, p. 148.
112. Alteras, p. 8.
113. Ashton, p. 18.
114. Feis, *Birth of Israel*, p. 66.
115. Morris, *1948*, pp. 201–2. Bregman, p. 16.
116. McGhee, p. 27. Behbehani, p. 65.
117. Morris, *1948*, p. 310. Cohen, *Truman and Israel*, pp. 262–63.
118. Cohen, *Truman and Israel*, pp. 264–65.
119. Kirk, *Middle East 1945–1950*, p. 287.
120. Cohen, *Truman and Israel*, p. 268.
121. Ibid., p. 270.
122. Bregman, p. 21. Morris, *Birth*, pp. 317–18.
123. Morris, *Birth*, p. 40.
124. Roosevelt, *Arabs, Oil and History*, p. 117.
125. Neff, pp. 76–8.
126. McGhee, pp. 36–7.
127. Cohen, *Truman and Israel*, p. 271.
128. Alteras, p. 20.

129. Feis, *Birth of Israel*, p. 36.
130. Cohen, *Truman and Israel*, p. 271.
131. Feis, *Birth of Israel*, p. 65.
132. Ibid., p. 21.
133. Alteras, p. 20.
134. Roosevelt, *Arabs, Oil and History*, pp. 44–5.
135. Behbehani, pp. 65–6.
136. Morris, *Birth*, p. 361.
137. NARA, LM 163/2, Tel Aviv, Jan. 3, 1949, "Ben-Gurion Speech on 'Ingathering of Exiles Day.'"
138. Morris, *Birth*, p. 361.
139. Ibid., pp. 319–20, 356–58.
140. McGhee, p. 34.
141. Ibid., pp. 27–8.
142. Aron, pp. 97, 99.
143. Neff, pp. 77–8.
144. Alteras, pp. 4–5. Kirk, *Middle East 1945–1950*, pp. 278, 283.
145. Kirk, *Middle East 1945–1950*, p. 284.
146. Alteras, p. 6.
147. McGhee, pp. 30–31.
148. Alteras, p. 7.
149. Keay, pp. 386–87.
150. BNA, FO 371/75268, Tel Aviv, Oct. 31, 1949, Sir Knox Helm to Bevin.
151. BNA, FO 371/104735, Tel Aviv, Jun. 5, 1953, Francis Evans to Foreign Office, "John Wilson's Impressions of Israel."
152. Morris, *Birth*, p. 467. Kirk, *Middle East 1945–1950*, p. 295.
153. Yoder, p. 148.
154. Wischnitzer, p. 66.
155. BNA, FO 371/45406, May 2, 1945, J. A. de C. Hamilton, "Possibility of Arab Disturbances in Palestine."
156. McGhee, p. 38.
157. Said K. Aburish, *Nasser: The Last Arab*, New York: St. Martin's Press, 2004, pp. 24–5. Philby, *Sa'udi Arabia*, p. 28.
158. Kirk, *Middle East 1945–1950*, p. 292.
159. Ibid. p. 271.
160. NARA, LM 187/5, Damascus, May 14, 1948, Memminger to Marshall.
161. BNA, FO 371/68402, London, Jan. 1, 1948, Bevin to Inverchapel.
162. Cohen, *Truman and Israel*, p. 273.
163. BNA, FO 371/98245, Mar. 19, 1952, "Record of a Conversation between the Jordan Minister and Mr. Ross." Alteras, pp. 18, 38.
164. Alteras, p. 13. Wright, *Looming Tower*, p. 9.

CHAPTER 4: AJAX
1. Kuniholm, pp. 192, 204–6.
2. McGhee, p. 19.
3. Miscamble, pp. 294–95, 322, 326.
4. Kuniholm, pp. 195–200.
5. Roosevelt, *Arabs, Oil and History*, p. 196.
6. P. Avery, G. R. G. Hambly and C. Melville, eds., *The Cambridge History of Iran*, vol. 7, Cambridge: Cambridge University Press, 1991, p. 437.
7. Mark J. Gasiorowski and Malcolm Byrne, *Mohammad Mosaddeq and the 1953 Coup in Iran*, Syracuse: Syracuse University Press, 2004, pp. 103–4. Stephen Dorril, *MI6: Inside the Covert World of Her Majesty's Secret Intelligence Service*, New York: Free Press, 2000, p. 572. Roosevelt, *Countercoup*, pp. 53–6, 59.
8. William Engdahl, *A Century of War: Anglo-American Oil Politics and the New World Order*, 2nd ed., Ann Arbor: Pluto Press, 2004, p. 93. James Bamberg, *British Petroleum and Global Oil, 1950–75*, Cambridge: Cambridge University Press, 2000, p. 102.

9. John Prados, *Safe for Democracy: The Secret Wars of the CIA*, Chicago: Ivan R. Dee, 2006, p. 99. Jonathan Bloch and Patrick Fitzgerald, *British Intelligence and Covert Action*, Kerry, Ireland: Brandon, 1983, p. 109.

10. Roosevelt, *Arabs, Oil and History*, p. 26.

11. Bill and Louis, p. 28. Avery et al, vol. 7, p. 431.

12. Roosevelt, *Countercoup*, p. 59.

13. Avery et al, vol. 7, pp. 433–35.

14. Bill and Louis, pp. 48–51.

15. Kinzer, *Overthrow*, p. 118.

16. Yergin, p. 460.

17. Roosevelt, *Countercoup*, p, 85.

18. Prados, p. 99. Bloch and Fitzgerald, p. 109.

19. Stephen Kinzer, *All the Shah's Men: An American Coup and the Roots of Middle East Terror*, Hoboken: Wiley, 2003, pp. 123–24.

20. Roosevelt, *Countercoup*, pp. 104–5.

21. Bill and Louis, pp. 148, 154–55, 273.

22. Petersen, pp. 19–20.

23. Bill and Louis, pp. 228–29.

24. Gasiorowski and Byrne, p. 9. Kinzer, *Overthrow*, p. 118.

25. Ashton, pp. 10–11.

26. Petersen, p. 55.

27. Roosevelt, *Arabs, Oil and History*, p. 117.

28. Bill and Louis, pp. 228–29.

29. Yergin, pp. 484–85. Ashton, pp. 11–12, 81.

30. Engdahl, p. 89.

31. Evelyn Shuckburgh, *Descent to Suez: Diaries 1951–56*, New York: Norton, p. 71. Petersen, p. 73. Bill and Louis, p. 244.

32. Roosevelt, *Arabs, Oil and History*, p. 7.

33. Dorril, pp. 566, 572.

34. Bamberg, pp. 16–17.

35. Kinzer, *Overthrow*, p. 120.

36. Bill and Louis, pp. 230, 244–45.

37. Dorril, p. 567.

38. NARA, CIA-RDP79S01011A000800020002-8, Oct. 14, 1952, "Special Estimate: Prospects for Survival of Mosaddeq Regime in Iran." Avery et al, vol. 7, p. 441.

39. Gasiorowski and Byrne, pp. 179–81.

40. Roosevelt, *Arabs, Oil and History*, p. 203.

41. Roosevelt, *Countercoup*, p. 86. Eric Rouleau, "Khomeini's Iran," *Foreign Affairs*, Fall 1980, p. 3. Roosevelt, *Countercoup*, p. 71. Bill and Louis, p. 32.

42. NARA, CIA-RDP79T01146A00300440001-1, Washington, Aug. 21, 1951, "Eastern Section 2," top secret. Roosevelt, *Arabs, Oil and History*, p. 236.

43. NARA, LM 73/44, Tehran, Aug. 20, 1952, Henderson to Acheson, Apr. 24, 1953, Henderson to Acheson.

44. NARA, CIA-RDP79S01011A001100020001-5, Aug. 26, 1953, "Special Estimate: The Current Outlook in Iran," secret.

45. Roosevelt, *Countercoup*, p. 99.

46. Yergin, p. 466. Roosevelt, *Countercoup*, p. 77.

47. NARA, LM 73/44, Tabriz, Nov. 10, 1952, Iams to Acheson.

48. Petersen, p. 26.

49. Yergin, p. 467.

50. Petersen, pp. 21–2.

51. NARA, CIA-RDP80R01443R000100070006-9, n.d., "The Iranian Situation."

52. Kinzer, *Overthrow*, p. 120. Dorril, p. 566.

53. Roosevelt, *Arabs, Oil and History*, p. 239.

54. Miles Copeland, *The Game of Nations: The Amorality of Power Politics*, London: Weidenfeld & Nicolson, 1969, p. 13.

55. Dorril, p. 568.

56. NARA, CIA-RDP70-00058R000200120139-3, Prague, *Mladá Fronta*, Sep. 17, 1961, "The Master of Futility." Gasiorowski and Byrne, p. 231. Kinzer, *Overthrow*, pp. 111–16.

57. Roosevelt, *Countercoup*, pp. 10–11.

58. NARA, CIA-RDP79S01011A000800020002-8, Oct. 14, 1952, "Special Estimate: Prospects for Survival of Mosaddeq Regime in Iran." NARA, CIA-RDP80R01731R000300090046-4, Cambridge, Apr. 29, 1959, Max Thornburg to Allen Dulles, "Notes on Iraq." NARA, CIA-RDP78-00915R00915R000400030005-9, Jan. 1955, "Communist Techniques of Infiltrating Armed Forces: The Officers' Organization of the Tudeh Party." Gasiorowski and Byrne, pp. 103–4. Dorril, p. 573.

59. NARA, CIA-RDP79S01011A000800020002-8, Oct. 14, 1952, "Special Estimate: Prospects for Survival of Mosaddeq Regime in Iran." NARA, CIA-RDP79T00975A000900240001-5, Nov. 7, 1952, "Current Intelligence Bulletin," top secret. Dorril, p. 567.

60. NARA, CIA-RDP78-00915R00915R000400030005-9, Jan. 1955, "Communist Techniques of Infiltrating Armed Forces: The Officers' Organization of the Tudeh Party." Dorril, p. 574.

61. Yergin, p. 468.

62. NARA, CIA-RDP80T00942A000600070002-0, Jan. 1979, "The Iranian Constitution: A Reference Aid," confidential.

63. Yergin, p. 467.

64. NARA, CIA-RDP80T00942A000600070002-0, Jan. 1979, "The Iranian Constitution: A Reference Aid," confidential. NARA, CIA-RDP79S01011A000800020002-8, Oct. 14, 1952, "Special Estimate: Prospects for Survival of Mosaddeq Regime in Iran." NARA, CIA-RDP80R01443R000100070006-9, n.d., "The Iranian Situation."

65. Roosevelt, *Arabs, Oil and History*, pp. 198–99, 209.

66. Bill and Louis, pp. 24–5, 91–3. Gasiorowski and Byrne, pp. 13–14, 29–31.

67. Engdahl, pp. 95–6.

68. Bill and Louis, p. 275.

69. Dorril, pp. 568, 580–83.

70. Yergin, pp. 470–78. Gasiorowski and Byrne, p. 184.

71. Yergin, p. 464.

72. Kinzer, *Overthrow*, pp. 122–24. Yergin, p. 468.

73. Kuniholm, p. 174. BNA, FO 371/98245, Ankara, Apr. 5, 1952, Helm to Bowker.

74. NARA, CIA-RDP80R01443R000100070002-3, Mar. 4, 1953, "DCI Briefing: Iranian Situation," top secret.

75. Kinzer, *Overthrow*, p. 122.

76. NARA, CIA-RDP80R01443R000100070002-3, Mar. 4, 1953, "DCI Briefing: Iranian Situation," top secret.

77. NARA, CIA-RDP80-00809A000700210036-4, Feb. 27, 1953, "Indications of Pro-USSR Policy by Mosaddeq."

78. NARA, CIA-RDP80R01443R000100070002-3, Mar. 4, 1953, "DCI Briefing: Iranian Situation," top secret.

79. Gasiorowski and Byrne, p. 72. Bill and Louis, p. 287.

80. Kinzer, *Overthrow*, pp. 122–23. Dorril, p. 579.

81. NARA, CIA-RDP80R01443R000100070002-3, Mar. 4, 1953, "DCI Briefing: Iranian Situation," top secret.

82. Dorril, p. 580.

83. NARA, CIA-RDP80R01443R000100070002-3, Mar. 4, 1953, "DCI Briefing: Iranian Situation," top secret.

84. Dorril, p. 574.

85. Ibid., p. 580.

86. Bill and Louis, p. 275. Gosiorowski and Byrne, p. 274.

87. Dorril, p. 575.

88. Bill and Louis, p. 113.

89. Kinzer, *Overthrow*, pp. 123–24.

90. Petersen, p. 23. Dorril, pp. 584–87.

91. Roosevelt, *Countercoup*, pp. 3, 5–10, 14, 18.

92. NARA, CIA-RDP80R01443R000100290001-0, Aug. 5, 1953, "Briefing Notes for the NSC—The Situation in Iran," top secret.

93. Ibid.

94. Yergin, p. 462.

95. Roosevelt, *Countercoup*, pp. 147–49.

96. NARA, CIA-RDP91T01172R000200330011-3, Aug. 17, 1953, CIA, Office of Current Intelligence, "Assessment of the Iranian Situation," top secret.

97. NARA, CIA-RDP80R01443R000100290001-0, Aug. 5, 1953, "Briefing Notes for the NSC—The Situation in Iran," top secret.

98. Roosevelt, *Countercoup*, p. 85.

99. Dorril, pp. 592–93.

100. Bill and Louis, p. 112.

101. Gosiorowski and Byrne, pp. 13–14, 79, 254. Bill and Louis, p. 113–15.

102. Roosevelt, *Countercoup*, p. 151.

103. Gosiorowski and Byrne, pp. 254–55.

104. Roosevelt, *Countercoup*, p. 171.

105. Dorril, pp. 576, 584.

106. Gasiorowski and Byrne, p. 256. Roosevelt, *Countercoup*, p. 187.

107. Kinzer, *Overthrow*, pp. 127–28. Dorril, p. 594.

108. Roosevelt, *Countercoup*, p. 199. Dorril, p. 594.

109. Dorril, p. 597.

110. Gasiorowski and Byrne, pp. 188–89.

111. Ibid., p. 25.

112. Bill and Louis, p. 65.

113. Ibid., pp. 17–18.

114. Roosevelt, *Arabs, Oil and History*, pp. 208–9.

115. Dorril, p. 583.

116. NARA, CIA-RDP79S01011A000800020002-8, Oct. 14, 1952, "Special Estimate: Prospects for Survival of Mosaddeq Regime in Iran."

117. NARA, CIA-RDP79T01146A001200310002-4, Sep. 22, 1952, "Top Secret Supplement to the Current Intelligence Digest."

118. Gasiorowski and Byrne, pp. 184–87, 257.

119. NARA, CIA-RDP79S01011A001100020001-5, Aug. 26, 1953, "Special Estimate: The Current Outlook in Iran," secret. Chalmers Roberts, "Helms, the Shah and the CIA," *Washington Post*, Dec. 29, 1972.

120. Richard Helms, *A Look Over My Shoulder: A Life in the Central Intelligence Agency*, New York: Random House, 2003, p. 117.

121. Gasiorowski and Byrne, pp. 183, 257.

122. NARA, CIA-RDP79S01011A001100020001-5, Aug. 26, 1953, "Special Estimate: The Current Outlook in Iran," secret. Dorril, p. 595.

123. Khalidi, pp. 90–2.

124. NARA, CIA-RDP78-01617A000400210001-0, Apr. 5, 1949, "Intelligence Memo: Will and Ability of Certain Countries to Support and Develop Their Armed Forces," top secret.

125. BNA, FO 371/115511, London, May 10, 1955, Evelyn Shuckburgh, Foreign Office Minute.

126. Avery et al, vol. 7, pp. 444–45.

127. Ryszard Kapuscinski, *Shah of Shahs*, New York: Vintage, 1982, pp. 39–40.

128. Gasiorowski and Byrne, p. 257.

129. Dorril, p. 596.

130. NARA, CIA-RDP78-00915R00915R000400030005-9, Jan. 1955, "Communist Techniques of Infiltrating Armed Forces: The Officers' Organization of the Tudeh Party."

131. Seymour M. Hersh, "Preparing the Battlefield: The Bush Administration Steps Up Its Secret Moves Against Iran," *New Yorker*, Jul. 7 and 14, 2008.

132. NARA, CIA-RDP79S01011A001100020001-5, Aug. 26, 1953, "Special Estimate: The Current Outlook in Iran," secret.

133. Avery et al, vol. 7, pp. 441–42.

CHAPTER 5: NASSER

1. Prados, p. 98. Nutting, p. 30.
2. Roosevelt, *Arabs, Oil and History*, pp, 92–3, 151–53.
3. "Arabs v. Communists: Thanks But No Thanks," *Time*, Aug. 9, 1971.
4. Wright, p. 24.
5. McGhee, p. 376.
6. Roosevelt, *Arabs, Oil and History*, pp. 89–95, 151–52.
7. Ibid., p. 97.
8. Nutting, p. 6.
9. Roosevelt, *Arabs, Oil and History*, pp. 88–9.
10. Israel Gershoni and James Jankowski, *Redefining the Egyptian Nation 1930–45*, Cambridge: Cambridge University Press, 2002, pp. 99–100.
11. Nutting, pp. 19–20.
12. Behbehani, p. 105. Prados, p. 98.
13. Ashton, p. 27.
14. NARA, CIA-RDP78-02771R000500030002-9, 1956, "Egypt's Role in the Muslim World." Roosevelt, *Arabs, Oil and History*, pp. 87, 255.
15. NARA, LM 163/3 Cairo, Jun. 23, 1949, Patterson to Marshall.
16. NARA, CIA-RDP78-02771R000500030002-9, 1956, "Egypt's Role in the Muslim World." David W. Lesch, "Abd-al Nasser and the United States: Enemy or Friend?" in Elie Podeh and Onn Winckler, *Rethinking Nasserism: Revolution and Historical Memory in Modern Egypt*, Gainesville: University Press of Florida, 2004, pp. 206–7.
17. Guy Wint and Peter Calvocoressi, *Middle East Crisis*, London: Penguin, 1957, pp. 40–1. Sadat, p. 13. Nutting, p. 13.
18. Takeyh, p. 51. Wint and Calvocoressi, pp. 39–40. Sadat, p. 16.
19. Nutting, pp. 9–10.
20. Aburish, pp. 28, 33.
21. Petersen, p. 4.
22. Ashton, pp. 19–20.
23. Aburish, p. 43. Roosevelt, *Arabs, Oil and History*, p. 94.
24. "Arabs v. Communists" *Time*.
25. Keith Kyle, *Suez*, New York: St. Martin's, 1991, p. 55. Jean Lacouture, *Nasser*, London: Secker & Warburg, 1973.
26. Nutting, p. 7. Sadat, p. 20.
27. Sadat, pp. 99–100.
28. Nutting, pp. 27–8.
29. BNA, FO 371/96986, Cairo, Sep. 18, 1952, Creswell to Reilly. Cairo, Sep. 20, 1952, Duke to Allen.
30. Sadat, p. 103.
31. Kyle, pp. 40–1. Nutting, p. 31.
32. Kyle, p. 52. Prados, p. 98.
33. Sadat, pp. 106–7.
34. Nutting, p. 37.
35. Sadat, p. 107.
36. Grobba, p. 103.
37. NARA, CIA-RDP75-00001R000400380006-7, Washington, May 1966, "The Ba'th: Ideology and Practice."
38. "Nasser: Defeat, Hyperbole, Survival," *Wall Street Journal*, Jan. 8, 1968.
39. Aron, pp. 67, 76. Israeli per capita GDP was ten times higher than Egypt's.
40. Petersen, p. 6.
41. Kyle, p. 49.
42. Sadat, p. 108. Petersen, p. 10.
43. Miscamble, pp. 318–21.
44. Alteras, pp. 30–31.
45. Petersen, p. 17.
46. Ibid., pp. 49–50.
47. Nutting, p. 41.

48. Sadat, p. 119.
49. Nutting, pp. 30, 44.
50. Takeyh, p. 52. Kyle, p. 60.
51. BNA, FO 371/96986, Cairo, Sep. 18, 1952, Creswell to Reilly.
52. Behbehani, pp. 109–10. Kyle, pp. 49, 55.
53. Kyle, p. 48. Nutting, p. 40. Sadat, pp. 121–24.
54. Kyle, p. 54.
55. BNA, FCO 39/242, Panama, Jun. 11, 1968, Henkey to Spears, "From UAR Ambassador to Panama."
56. Behbehani, pp. 113–16. Nutting, p. 46.
57. BNA, FO 371/96986, Cairo, Sep. 20, 1952, Duke to Allen. Behbehani, p. 106. Sadat, pp. 124–25, 133.
58. Gershoni and Jankowski, pp. 82, 94–5.
59. Nutting, p. 11.
60. NARA, CIA-RDP79R00890A000200030001-1, Washington, Jan. 21, 1954, NSC Briefing, "Moslem Brotherhood Threat in Egypt."
61. Atiyah, p. 192.
62. Petersen, p. 7.
63. Prados, p. 98.
64. Nutting, p. 46.
65. Sadat, p. 141.
66. Henry J. Taylor, "Egypt Is Caught in a Red Trap," *Baltimore News American,* Dec. 10, 1972.
67. Lesch, "Nasser," in Podeh and Winckler, p. 207.
68. Sadat, p. 129.
69. Ashton, p. 28.
70. Chalmers Roberts, "A Breathtaking Biography of Gamal Abdel Nasser," *Washington Post,* Nov. 1, 1971.
71. Aburish, p. 90. BNA, FCO 39/242, Panama, Jun. 11, 1968, Henkey to Spears, "From UAR Ambassador to Panama."
72. Sadat, pp. 130–31.
73. Copeland, pp. 216, 221.
74. BNA, FO 371/108315, Cairo, Mar. 11, 1954, Stevenson to Foreign Office. Sadat, pp. 122, 137.
75. Copeland, p. 215.
76. Ashton, p. 21.
77. BNA, FO 371/119133, Brussels, Aug. 29, 1956, E. B. Boothby to Adam Watson.
78. Petersen, p. 44.
79. BNA, FO 371/108315, Cairo, Sep. 27, 1954, Stevenson to Foreign Office. Roosevelt, *Arabs, Oil and History,* p. 100.
80. Copeland, p. 215.
81. Petersen, p. 8. Sadat, p. 127.
82. Alteras, p. 47.
83. Ibid., pp. 43, 90.
84. Takeyh, p. 21.
85. BNA, FO 371/104735, Tel Aviv, Dec. 22, 1953, Anthony Moore to Eden.
86. Alteras, pp. 102, 133.
87. Kyle, p. 67.
88. BNA, FO 371/128225, Tel Aviv, Aug. 28, 1957, R. M. Tesh, "Israel-Syria."
89. BNA, FO 371/104735, Tel Aviv, May 5, 1953, F. Evans to Winston Churchill. Alteras, pp. 45–6, 80, 83, 89. Kyle, p. 66.
90. Ovendale, *Origins,* p. 192.
91. Kyle, pp. 70–1.
92. Zeev Maoz, *Defending the Holy Land,* Ann Arbor: University of Michigan Press, 2006.
93. Takeyh, p. 81. Alteras, p.137.
94. http://weekly.ahram.org.eg, Sep. 15–21, 2005, "Popular hero or homme d'état?" Kyle, pp. 73–6.
95. Behbehani, p. 70.
96. Ibid., pp. 113, 122.
97. William I. Hitchcock, *The Struggle for Europe: The Turbulent History of a Divided Continent 1945–2002,* New York: Doubleday, 2002, pp. 123–24. Aron, p. 133.
98. Aburish, p. 84. Behbehani, pp. 89–90, 106, 113.

99. Bregman, p. 33.
100. NARA, CIA-RDP78-02771R000500030002-9, 1956, "Egypt's Role in the Muslim World."
101. Kyle, pp. 62–4. Takeyh, p. 74.
102. Bregman, p. 32. Kyle, p. 107.
103. Kyle, pp. 63, 65. Alteras, pp. 86–7, 92–7.
104. BNA, FO 371/104735, Tel Aviv, Jun. 5, 1953, Francis Evans to Foreign Office, "John Wilson's Impressions of Israel." Fraser, *USA*, pp. 88–9.
105. BNA, FO 371/115867, Cairo, Apr. 27, 1955, Ralph Stevenson, "Notes for Discussion with Mr. Attlee."
106. BNA, FO 371/104735, Tel Aviv, May 5, 1953, F. Evans to Winston Churchill. Alteras, pp. 98–9, 102.
107. NARA, CIA-RDP75-00001R000400380006-7, Washington, May 1966, "The Ba'th: Ideology and Practice."
108. Sadat, p. 135.
109. Lesch, "Nasser," in Podeh and Winckler, p. 208. Ashton, pp. 51–2.
110. Maoz, p. 88.
111. Ashton, p. 35.
112. Bregman, p. 26.
113. Ian Black and Benny Morris, *Israel's Secret Wars: A History of Israel's Intelligence Services*, New York: Grove Weidenfeld, 1991, pp. 110–14. Sadat, p. 147.
114. BNA, FO 371/108349, Cairo, Jan. 12, 1954, Stevenson to Eden.
115. Alteras, p. 30.
116. Ashton, pp. 18–19. Alteras, pp. 21–2, 26, 32.
117. Lesch, "Nasser," in Podeh and Winckler, p. 209. Takeyh, p. 50.
118. NARA, CIA-RDP79S00427A000427A000400060002-8, Washington, Dec. 6, 1961, "The Arab-Israeli Situation," secret. Takeyh, p. 95.
119. Alteras, pp. 58, 71–3.
120. Ibid., pp. 50, 63, 67.
121. Ashton, p. 40.
122. Petersen, pp. 10–11.
123. Alteras, p. 68.
124. Ibid., pp. 55–6.
125. Ibid., pp. 33–7, 41–2, 76.
126. Kyle, p. 98.
127. Takeyh, p. 24.
128. Ashton, p. 40. Lesch, "Nasser," in Podeh and Winckler, p. 209.
129. Kyle, p. 57. Ashton, pp. 28–9, 41.
130. Petersen, p. 60. Ashton, pp. 46–51, 61. Kyle, p. 59.
131. Miscamble, p. 329.
132. BNA, FO 371/115511, London, May 13, 1955, Evelyn Shuckburgh to Ralph Stevenson.
133. Petersen, pp. 62, 71.
134. NARA, CIA-RDP79T00975A002600380001-1, Jul. 13, 1956, Current Intelligence Bulletin, "Iraqi Chief of Staff Makes Last-Hour Appeal for More U.S. Arms," top secret.
135. Alteras, p. 109. Ashton, p. 55.
136. Ashton, p. 78.
137. Kyle, pp. 146, 228, 258.
138. Sadat, pp. 133–34.
139. Kyle, pp. 56–7.
140. Ibid., pp. 82–3.
141. Ibid., p. 96.
142. Alteras, pp. 165–66. Kyle, pp. 96–7.
143. Alteras, pp. 171–72.
144. Takeyh, pp. 70–71.
145. Peter G. Boyle, *The Eden-Eisenhower Correspondence 1955-57*, Chapel Hill, University of North Carolina Press, 2005, p. 104. Kyle, pp. 99–101. Petersen, pp. 62–3.
146. Aburish, p. 84. Takeyh, p. 121.
147. Herman Finer, *Dulles over Suez: The Theory and Practice of His Diplomacy*, Chicago: Quadrangle, 1964, pp. 51, 54.

148. Kyle, p. 130.
149. Sadat, p. 142. Alteras, p. 189. Kyle, pp. 132–33.
150. Petersen, p. 76.
151. Hugh Thomas, *Suez,* New York: Harper & Row, 1966, p. 64.
152. Behbehani, pp. 140–41.
153. Roberts, *History,* p. 432.
154. Boyle, p. 165.
155. Thomas, p. 94.
156. Kyle, pp. 159–61. Finer, pp. 95–7.
157. Kyle, pp. 68–9, 532.
158. Boyle, pp. 14–15, 19. Roberts, "A Breathtaking Biography."
159. Kyle, pp. 62, 68–9, 190, 206, 257.
160. Thomas, p. 90.
161. BNA, FO 371/119078, London, "PM's Answer in the House This Morning."
162. Thomas, pp. 75, 81.
163. Boyle, p. 15.
164. André Beaufre, *The Suez Expedition 1956,* New York: Praeger, 1969, p. 28. Petersen, p. 82.
165. Kyle, pp. 111–12, 276. Takeyh, pp. 127–28.
166. BNA, FO 371/119078, London, Jul. 30, 1956, "Record of Secretary of State's Conversation with the French Ambassador." Petersen, p. 82.
167. Beaufre, p. 31.
168. Thomas, p. 83.
169. BNA, FCO 17/28, London, Jun. 28, 1967, Foreign and Colonial Office Research Section, "French Policy in the Middle East 1957–67."
170. BNA, FO 371/121345, London, Jun. 30, 1956, Morris to Hadow. Aron, p. 14. Kyle, pp. 218, 291, 344. Bass, p. 150. Stephanie Cooke, *In Mortal Hands,* New York: Bloomsbury, 2009, p. 235.
171. BNA, FO 371/115868, Cairo, Aug. 31, 1955, H. Trevelyan to Foreign Office. Alteras, pp. 144–45, 172, 186–87.
172. Petersen, p. 82.
173. Bregman, p. 22.
174. Ibid., pp. 28–31.
175. BNA, FO 371/104735, Tel Aviv, May 5, 1953, F. Evans to Winston Churchill. FO 371/110814, Paris, Sep. 1, 1954, G. Jebb to French Minister of Foreign Affairs, "Aide Mémoire." FO 371/115868, London, Sep. 8, 1955, "Arms in Egypt and Israel." Bregman, pp. 24, 38.
176. Thomas, p. 88. Beaufre, pp. 66–8. Kyle, pp. 318–19.
177. Bregman, p. 37. Kyle, pp. 297–98.
178. Kyle, pp. 118, 298.
179. Alteras, pp. 142–44, 155–56, 160, 180, 184–85.
180. BNA, FO 371/104735, Tel Aviv, Dec. 22, 1953, Anthony Moore to Eden.
181. Thomas, pp. 112, 115.
182. Kyle, pp. 206, 264, 266–71, 315–17. Alteras, pp. 197–99, 203–4.
183. Thomas, p. 86.
184. Kyle, pp. 318–19.
185. Thomas, p. 81. Finer, p. 379.
186. BNA, FO 371/121792, Amman, Nov. 5, 1956, C. Duke to Foreign Office. Alteras, pp. 192–93, 203. BNA, FO 371/121792, AFHQ, Nov. 7, 1956, Ralph Murray to Foreign Office.
187. Sadat, p. 143.

CHAPTER 6: SUEZ

1. Petersen, p. 17.
2. Kyle, pp. 154–55.
3. Ibid., p. 181.
4. Ibid., pp. 293–94, 300.
5. Ibid., pp. 344–45.
6. Alteras, pp. 218–19. Thomas, pp. 103–5. Kyle, pp. 293–94.
7. Kinzer, *Overthrow,* p. 166.

8. Kyle, p. 309.
9. Thomas, p. 87. Kyle, p. 317.
10. Kyle, pp. 298–99, 320–21, 370, 375. Petersen, p. 90. Alteras, pp. 199, 202.
11. Beaufre, p. 96. Kenneth M. Pollack, *Arabs at War: Military Effectiveness 1948–1991*, Lincoln: University of Nebraska Press, 2002, pp. 39–40.
12. Thomas, p. 108.
13. Kyle, pp. 347–50.
14. Thomas, p. 123.
15. Ibid., p. 111.
16. Pollack, pp. 39–40. Kyle, pp. 368–70.
17. Sadat, pp. 144–45. Pollack, p. 46.
18. Kyle, pp. 380–81, 385. Thomas, p. 130.
19. Behbehani, p. 147. Thomas, p. 125.
20. Petersen, p. 92. Alteras, p. 229.
21. Thomas, pp. 117, 127.
22. Finer, pp. 1–5, 370–71. Kinzer, *Overthrow*, p. 159.
23. James Srodes, *Allen Dulles: Master of Spies*, Washington, D.C.: Regnery, 2000, p. 474. Thomas, pp. 129–32.
24. Diane B. Kunz, *The Economic Diplomacy of the Suez Crisis*, Chapel Hill: University of North Carolina Press, 1991, p. 121. Kyle, p. 354.
25. Alteras, p. 226.
26. Petersen, p. 93. Kyle, p. 409.
27. Sadat, p. 145.
28. Finer, p. 440. Kyle, p. 357.
29. Kyle, pp. 469–70.
30. Ibid., p. 515.
31. Ibid., pp. 425–27.
32. Alteras, p. 293.
33. Petersen, pp. 88–9.
34. Finer, pp. 375–76. Kyle, pp. 47, 220.
35. Kyle, p. 253.
36. Ibid., pp. 207–9, 386. Finer, p. 381.
37. Alteras, p. 244.
38. Kyle, pp. 477–78. Alteras, p. 246.
39. Finer, pp. 412–13. Thomas, p. 114. Kyle, p. 399.
40. Kyle, p. 332.
41. Pollack, pp. 37–8. Kyle, pp. 172–74.
42. Kyle, p. 176.
43. Ibid., p. 375.
44. Beaufre, pp. 29, 38, 49, 54, 66. Thomas, pp. 66–7. Kyle, p. 177.
45. Thomas, p. 136. Kyle, pp. 236–40, 382–83.
46. Beaufre, pp. 56, 63.
47. Kyle, pp. 169, 382–83, 456. Beaufre, p. 97.
48. Beaufre, pp. 50, 54–5, 80.
49. Thomas, p. 131. Kyle, pp. 416–17.
50. BNA, FO 371/119133, Moscow, Sep. 12, 1956, Parrott to Foreign Office.
51. Finer, p. 372.
52. Kunz, p. 125. *Washington Post*, Nov. 8, 1956. Finer, p. 418. Thomas, pp. 142–44. Kyle, pp. 426, 456–58.
53. Sadat, p. 146. Alteras, p. 247.
54. Boyle, p. 45.
55. Kyle, p. 412.
56. Ibid., p. 262.
57. Yergin, p. 492.
58. Kunz, pp. 131–33. Kyle, p. 257. Thomas, p. 145. Finer, pp. 428, 454.
59. Thomas, p. 146. Kyle, pp. 500–502, 510.
60. Douglas Little, "From Even-Handed to Empty-Handed: Seeking Order in the Middle East," in

Thomas G. Paterson, ed., *Kennedy's Quest for Victory: American Foreign Policy 1961–63*, Oxford: Oxford University Press, 1989, p. 156.

61. Kunz, p. 124. Kyle, p. 386. Beaufre, p. 63.
62. Bamberg, pp. 94–99. Yergin, pp. 491–95. Kyle, pp. 522–25. Kunz, p. 131.
63. Petersen, pp. 94, 103.
64. Ibid., pp. 94–5.
65. Kyle, p. 174. Thomas, p. 146.
66. Thomas, pp. 69–70, 132–33, 147.
67. Ibid., pp. 93, 98–9.
68. Beaufre, p. 63.
69. Thomas, p. 139. Kyle, pp. 377–79.
70. Kyle, pp. 188–89.
71. Ibid., p. 190.
72. Ibid., p. 404.
73. Ibid., p. 405.
74. Ibid., p. 441.
75. Finer, p. 426. Thomas, p. 151. Kyle, pp. 404–5, 467–68.
76. Roberts, "A Breathtaking Biography."
77. Kyle, pp. 489, 504.
78. Roberts, *History*, p. 430.
79. Kyle, pp. 390–96, 401–4, 451.
80. Petersen, p. 95, Alteras, pp. 240–41.
81. Kyle, pp. 505, 513. Petersen, p. 98.
82. BNA, FO 371/121792, London, Nov. 5, 1956, Eden to Eisenhower. Petersen, p. 83. Kyle, pp. 179, 386–87.
83. Kyle, pp. 365–66, 376.
84. Thomas, p. 148.
85. Kyle, p. 400.
86. Patrick Tyler, *A World of Trouble: The White House and the Middle East from the Cold War to the War on Terror*, New York: Farrar, Straus and Giroux, 2009, p. 61.
87. Tyler, p. 56. Finer, p. 473. Sadat, p. 146. Kyle, pp. 364–67.
88. Boyle, p. 37.
89. Takeyh, p. 137. Kyle, p. 507. Finer, p. 456.
90. Petersen, pp. 99–101.
91. NARA, CIA-RDP80B01676R004200140014-8, Apr. 5, 1957, "Report to the President on the Vice President's Visit to Africa, February 28–Mar. 21, 1957," secret.
92. Petersen, p. 122.
93. Finer, p. 2.
94. Kyle, p. 527.
95. NARA, CIA-RDP85S00362R000200080018-2, Jan. 29, 1957, Intelligence Advisory Committee, "The Algerian Situation," secret. Kyle, p. 542.
96. Yaqub, p. 53. Finer, pp. 379, 434.
97. NARA, CIA-RDP80B01676R004200140014-8, Apr. 5, 1957, "Report to the President on the Vice President's Visit to Africa, February 28–Mar. 21, 1957," secret. Ashton, p. 156. Kyle, p. 530.
98. NARA, RG 59, 1613, Box 2381, Baghdad, Nov. 29, 1972, Lowrie to Rogers. Kyle, pp. 274–75, 466. Roberts, *History*, pp. 433–34.
99. BNA, FO 371/91715, Tel Aviv, May 19, 1951, A. K. Helm to Herbert Morrison.
100. Alteras, pp. 223–24.
101. Kyle, pp. 477–79.
102. BNA, FO 371/115867, Cairo, Apr. 1 and 6, 1955, Ralph Stevenson to Evelyn Shuckburgh, top secret.
103. BNA, FO 371/115867, Washington, Apr. 27, 1955, Harold Caccia to Foreign Office.
104. BNA, FO 371/115883, Tel Aviv, Nov. 21, 1955, Jack Nicholls to Foreign Office.
105. BNA, FO 371/121792, Tel Aviv, Nov. 7, 1956, Jack Nicholls to Foreign Office.
106. BNA, FO 371/115883, Washington, Nov. 21, 1955, R. Makins to Foreign Office.
107. Kyle, p. 473. Finer, pp. 448, 470, 476–77.
108. BNA, FO 371/115867, Washington, Apr. 27, 1955, Harold Caccia to Foreign Office.
109. Yaqub, p. 74.

110. Ibid., p. 116. Kyle, p. 538.
111. BNA, FO 371/104735, Tel Aviv, Jun. 5, 1953, Francis Evans to Foreign Office, "John Wilson's Impressions of Israel."
112. BNA, FO 371/121792, Tel Aviv, Nov. 7, 1956, Jack Nicholls to Foreign Office.
113. Yaqub, p. 151.
114. Kyle, p. 539. Alteras, pp. 249, 256.
115. Alteras, p. 257.
116. Ibid., pp. 260, 270, 299–300.
117. Yaqub, pp. 106–8. Alteras, pp. 265–66, 270–71, 294.
118. Sadat, p. 148. Kyle, p. 549.
119. NARA, C 0028/1, Cairo, Dec. 17, 1956, Hare to Dulles. CIA-RDP78-02771R000500030002-9, 1956, "Egypt's Role in the Muslim World." Behbehani, pp. 115–16. Alteras, p. 166. Kyle, pp. 54–6.
120. NARA, C 0028/1, Alexandria, Jul. 27, 1957, Cross to Secretary of State. Beirut, Jul. 29, 1957, Heath to Secretary of State.
121. Kyle, pp. 519–20.
122. BNA, FO 371/128224, Washington, Aug. 22, 1957, Dulles to Macmillan. David W. Lesch, *Syria and the United States: Eisenhower's Cold War in the Middle East.* Boulder: Westview, 1992, pp. 106–7. Finer, pp. 468, 478.
123. Yaqub, p. 108.
124. Lesch, *Syria*, pp. 106–7. Yaqub, pp. 104, 121.
125. Takeyh, pp. xviii, 113.
126. Ashton, p. 111.
127. Yaqub, p. 102.
128. Ibid., p. 103.
129. Ashton, p. 76. CIA-RDP80B01676R003800170048-3, Washington, Dec. 1957, anonymous to anonymous.
130. NARA, CIA-RDP80-01065A000200080053-0, Apr. 18, 1952, "Ideological Warfare," secret.
131. BNA, FCO 39/242, Aden, May 23, 1967, E. F. Penrose to Humphrey Trevelyan.
132. Ashton, pp. 34–5, 78.
133. NARA, CIA-RDP78-02771R000500030002-9, 1956, "Egypt's Role in the Muslim World."
134. Aburish, pp. 146–47. Petersen, p. 59.
135. Kyle, pp. 518, 563. Petersen, p. 125.
136. Roberts, *History*, p. 434. Kyle, pp. 508, 542.
137. Little, *American Orientalism*, p. 133. Yaqub, pp. 113–14.
138. Finer, pp. 500–501.
139. Little, *American Orientalism*, p. 131.

CHAPTER 7: THE EISENHOWER DOCTRINE

1. Kyle, pp. 546–49. Yaqub, pp. 76–7, 112. Little, *American Orientalism*, pp. 132–33.
2. Tyler, p. 59. Ashton, p. 109. Petersen, pp. 110–11.
3. BNA, FO 370/2875, London, "Syria and Communism 1954–66," secret. NARA, C 0028/1, Washington, Jan. 1958, Hugh Cumming, Jr., to Secretary of State, "Intelligence Note: The Prospects for Syro-Egyptian Federation," secret. Ashton, pp. 32–3.
4. Aburish, p. 182. Thomas Thompson, "U.S. Humiliation—A Diary from Cairo," *Life*, Jun. 30, 1967.
5. BNA, FO 371/133799, Washington, Jul. 19, 1958, "The Middle East—American Press and Radio Comment." Matthew Elliot, *'Independent Iraq': The Monarchy and British Influence 1941–1958*, London: I. B. Tauris, 1996, pp. 139, 158–59. Khalidi, pp. 96–101.
6. NARA, CIA-RDP78-00915R000900090011-1, Jul. 15, 1959, "Assessment of the Threat of Communist Subversion in the Baghdad Pact Area," secret. NARA, CIA-RDP80R01731R000300090046-4, Cambridge, Apr. 29, 1959, Max Weston Thornburg, "Notes on Iraq."
7. Yaqub, p. 222.
8. Ibid., pp. 175, 178–80.
9. Thomas, p. 86. Yaqub, p. 148. Kyle, p. 58. Copeland, p. 209.
10. NARA, RG 59, 1970–73, Box 2452, Washington, Jun. 25, 1973, "Memo of Conversation: Franco-U.S. Middle Eastern Consultations—Syria and Lebanon." Nicholas Watt, "No Regrets over Trip to Syria,"

Guardian, Nov. 3, 2001. NARA, RG 59, 1970–73, Box 2614, Beirut, Jan. 25, 1971, Houghton to State Department. Roosevelt, *Arabs, Oil and History,* pp. 130, 136.

11. NARA, C 0051/6, Beirut, Oct. 14, 1958, Higgs to Dulles, "The Roots of the Lebanese Revolution."

12. BNA, FO 371/134117, Beirut, May 16, 1958, Middleton to Foreign Office. Ashton, pp. 33–4. Roosevelt, *Arabs, Oil and History,* p. 131. NARA, C 0028/1, Beirut, Jan. 28, 1958, McClintock to Secretary of State.

13. Yaqub, p. 209. Roosevelt, *Arabs, Oil and History,* p. 130.

14. Yaqub, p. 189.

15. Copeland, pp. 196–99, 211.

16. Ibid., p. 200. Yaqub, pp. 100, 142. Roosevelt, *Arabs, Oil and History,* p. 130.

17. Roosevelt, *Arabs, Oil and History,* pp. 133–34.

18. Ibid., p. 136.

19. NARA, C 0028/1, Washington, Jan. 25, 1958, Lampton Berry to Secretary of State.

20. Ashton, p. 110.

21. NARA, C 0051/2, New York, May 21, 1958, Lodge to Dulles, "Lebanese Situation."

22. NARA, C 0051/2, Washington, May 19, 1958, Dulles to American embassies Beirut, Paris, London.

23. Copeland, pp. 201–2.

24. NARA, C 0051/2, Cairo, May 21, 1958, Hare to Dulles.

25. NARA, C 0051/2, Beirut, May 19, 1958, McClintock to Dulles.

26. Yaqub, p. 143.

27. Copeland, p. 220.

28. Yaqub, pp. 189–92, 200.

29. Michael B. Oren, *Power, Faith and Fantasy: America in the Middle East, 1776 to the Present,* New York: Norton, 2007, p. 517. Petersen, p. 118. Ashton, p. 168. Little, *American Orientalism,* p. 135.

30. Yaqub, pp. 223, 225, 242.

31. NARA, CIA-RDP79S00427A000500070002-6, Mar. 30, 1961, "Lebanon," secret. BNA, FO 371/134117, Baghdad, May 14, 1958, Wright to Foreign Office.

32. NARA, C 0051/6, Beirut, Oct. 24, 1958, McClintock to Dulles. Copeland, p. 203. Yaqub, p. 228.

33. NARA, C 0051/2, Washington, May 23, 1958, Dulles to McClintock.

34. NARA, C 0051/6, Beirut, Nov. 3, 1958, McClintock to Dulles, "Memorandum of Conversation on Current Situation in Lebanon."

35. Ibid.

36. Ibid.

37. Ibid.

38. Little, *American Orientalism,* p. 135.

39. Yaqub, p. 214.

40. Ibid., p. 228.

41. Finer, p. 501. Petersen, p. 118. Yaqub, pp. 143, 214.

42. Ashton, p. 170.

43. NARA, C 0051/2, Beirut, May 19, 1958, McClintock to Dulles.

44. NARA, C 0028/1, Washington, Jan. 1958, Hugh Cumming, Jr., to Secretary of State, "Intelligence Note: The Prospects for Syro-Egyptian Federation," secret. Ashton, p. 31. Yaqub, p. 189.

45. Yaqub, p. 219.

46. BNA, FO 371/128225, Beirut, Aug. 29, 1957, Ian Scott to Michael Rose. FO 370/2875, London, P. D. Wheeler, "Syria and Communism, 1954–66," secret. FO 371/128225, Tel Aviv, Aug. 28, 1957, R. M. Tesh, "Israel-Syria." Ashton, p. 162. Yaqub, pp. 124, 149–50.

47. BNA, FO 371/128225, Beirut, Sep. 2, 1957, Ian Scott to Michael Rose. Washington, Sep. 6, 1957, Caccia to Foreign Office.

48. Little, *American Orientalism,* p. 136. BNA, FO 371/128225, Beirut, Aug. 29, 1957, Ian Scott to Michael Rose.

49. Little, *American Orientalism,* p. 135.

50. NARA, C 0051/6, Beirut, Oct. 29, 1958, McClintock to Dulles. Oren, *Power, Faith, and Fantasy,* pp. 517–18.

51. Yaqub, p. 240.

52. Copeland, p. 204.

53. Little, "From Even-Handed to Empty-Handed," in Paterson, pp. 158–59.

54. Copeland, p. 215.
55. NARA, C 0051/6, Beirut, Oct. 18 and Dec. 10, 17, 21, 1958, McClintock to Dulles. NARA, C 0051/6, Beirut, Oct. 28, 1958, McClintock to Dulles.
56. NARA, C 0051/6, Beirut, Oct. 11, 1958, McClintock to Dulles.
57. Ibid.
58. Yaqub, pp. 130, 142, 239–40, 247. NARA, C 0051/6, Beirut, Oct. 28, 1958, McClintock to Dulles. BNA, FO 371/134117, Beirut, May 16, 1958, Middleton to Foreign Office.
59. Yaqub, pp. 134–35, 140.
60. Ibid., pp. 217, 243.
61. BNA, FO 371/133799, Washington, Jul. 19, 1958, "The Middle East—American Press and Radio Comment."
62. Lesch, "Nasser," in Podeh and Winckler, p. 214.
63. Little, "From Even-Handed to Empty-Handed," in Paterson, p. 156.
64. Little, *American Orientalism*, p. 183. Copeland, p. 221.
65. Copeland, pp. 225–26, 236.
66. Burton I. Kaufman, *The Arab Middle East and the United States: Inter-Arab Rivalry and Superpower Diplomacy,* New York: Twayne, 1996, pp. 34–6. Kyle, p. 55.
67. NARA, RG 59, 1970–73, Box 2587, Aug. 3, 1973, Department of State Research Study, "A USSR-Saudi Arabian Relationship? Never Say Die."
68. Little, "From Even-Handed to Empty-Handed," in Paterson, p. 167.
69. Bass, p. 137.
70. Little, "From Even-Handed to Empty-Handed," in Paterson, p. 157. Ovendale, *Origins*, pp. 191–92. Kaufman, p. 39.
71. Copeland, pp. 225–26.
72. BNA, FO 371/180655, Washington, Mar. 23, 1965, Stewart to Foreign Office. Oren, *Power, Faith, and Fantasy,* p. 520. Kaufman, p. 37. Douglas Little, "From Even-Handed to Empty-Handed," in Paterson, pp. 167–69, 183–84. Bass, pp. 140–43. Copeland, p. 230.
73. NARA, CIA-RDP86B00269R000400060002-9, Apr. 12, 1960, "UAR Developments."
74. Bass, p. 143.
75. NARA, CIA-RDP75-00149R000200280007-6, Washington, Jan. 17, 1967, "The Egyptian Intelligence Service."
76. Eric Pace, "After Ten Months, Southern Yemen Has Made Little Progress," *New York Times,* Sep. 22, 1969.
77. "Israel: The Free-Booters," *New Republic,* Apr. 1963. Black and Morris, pp. 196–99.
78. NARA, CIA-RDP78-02771R000500030002-9, 1956, "Egypt's Role in the Muslim World."
79. NARA, CIA-RDP80T01002A000200040028, May 30, 1974, "Syria's Rulers and Their Political Environment," secret.
80. NARA, CIA-RDP75-00001R000400380006-7, Washington, May 1966, "The Ba'th: Ideology and Practice."
81. NARA, CIA-RDP79S00427A000427A000400060002-8, Washington, Dec. 6, 1961, "The Arab-Israeli Situation," secret.
82. NARA, CIA-RDP79T00975A007000210001-0, Washington, May 18, 1963, Central Intelligence Bulletin, "UAR-Syria," top secret.
83. NARA, CIA-RDP71T00730R000200020004-5, Dec. 30, 1963, "Briefing Notes for DCI," secret.
84. BNA, FCO 17/9, London, Aug. 11, 1967, Willie Morris, "Revolutionary and Non-Revolutionary Regimes in the Middle East."
85. Yaqub, p. 202.
86. Copeland, pp. 222–23.
87. NARA, CIA-RDP79S00427A000427A000400060002-8, Washington, Dec. 6, 1961, "The Arab-Israeli Situation," secret. Little, "From Even-Handed to Empty-Handed," in Paterson, pp. 163–65. BNA, FO 371/91715, New York, May 11, 1951, UK Delegation to UN, Gladwyn Jebb to Herbert Morrison.
88. Little, "From Even-Handed to Empty-Handed," in Paterson, p. 166.
89. Ibid., p. 157.
90. Bass, pp. 144–45.
91. Little, "From Even-Handed to Empty-Handed," in Paterson, p. 171. Bass, p. 151.

92. Oren, *Power, Faith, and Fantasy*, p. 524. Ovendale, pp. 192–93. BNA, FO 371/180658, Amman, Oct. 23, 1965, Parkes to Morris. Kyle, p. 55.

93. BNA, FO 371/180658, Amman, Oct. 23, 1965, Parkes to Morris.

94. BNA, FCO 371/180647, London, Mar. 25, 1965, Ramsbotham to Brown.

95. NARA, C 0028/1, Cairo, Aug. 14, 1957, Hare to Secretary of State.

96. Bass, p. 146.

97. Little, "From Even-Handed to Empty-Handed," in Paterson, pp. 159, 171–72.

98. Fraser, *USA*, pp. 84–6.

99. Oren, *Power, Faith, and Fantasy*, p. 521.

100. Bass, pp. 149–50, 164–65.

101. Yaqub, p. 266.

102. Mordechai Gazit, *President Kennedy's Policy Toward the Arab States*, Tel Aviv: Shiloah Center, 1983, p. 46. Little, "From Even-Handed to Empty-Handed," in Paterson, pp. 159–60.

103. BNA, FO 371/180655, Feb. 1965, Foreign Office Minute, "Points from Mr. Thomson's Discussions in Washington, Jan. 15–16, 1965," secret.

104. BNA, FO 371/180655, Washington, Mar. 23, 1965, Stewart to Foreign Office.

105. Tyler, p. 68. Oren, *Power, Faith, and Fantasy*, p. 523.

106. Bass, p. 250. Copeland, pp. 226–27.

107. Oren, *Power, Faith, and Fantasy*, p. 521. Kaufman, p. 45. "The New LBJ: A Tougher Line," *U.S. News and World Report*, May 3, 1965. BNA, FO 371/180655, Amman, Apr. 9, 1965, Phillips to Crawford. BNA, FO 371/180655, Feb. 1965, Foreign Office Minute, "Points from Mr. Thomson's Discussions in Washington, Jan. 15–16, 1965," secret. Little, "From Even-Handed to Empty-Handed," in Paterson, pp. 185–86.

108. Copeland, p. 228.

109. Yaqub, p. 9.

110. Little, "From Even-Handed to Empty-Handed," in Paterson, p. 185.

111. BNA, FO 371/180655, Amman, Apr. 9, 1965, Phillips to Crawford. Michael B. Oren, *Six Days of War: June 1967 and the Making of the Modern Middle East*, Oxford: Oxford University Press, 2002, p. 39.

112. NARA, CIA-RDP78-03061A000300060001-3, Apr. 1971, "Aswan on the Nile." BNA, FO 371/180655, Amman, Apr. 9, 1965, Phillips to Crawford.

113. BNA, FCO 17/11, Washington, Jan. 6, 1967, Everett to Morris.

114. Ibid.

115. BNA, FCO 17/9, Washington, Mar. 30, 1967, Stewart.

116. BNA, FO 371/180655, Washington, Jun. 8, 1965, Everett to Crawford, confidential.

117. BNA, FO 371/180655, London, Mar. 12, 1965, Hope to Crawford.

118. BNA, FCO 17/11, Washington, Jan. 6, 1967, Everett to Morris.

119. Eric Downton, "Change in the Air in Cairo," *Daily Telegraph*, Oct. 17, 1968.

120. NARA, CIA-RDP79T00975A004900030002-3, Jan. 6, 1960, Central Intelligence Bulletin, "Nasir Still Faces Difficulties in Syria."

121. "How Do Arabs Grow?" *Economist*, Apr. 1, 1967.

122. BNA, FCO 17/9, London, Aug. 11, 1967, Willie Morris, "Revolutionary and Non-Revolutionary Regimes in the Middle East." Yaqub, pp. 138–40.

CHAPTER 8: A SIX-DAY WAR

1. Avner Cohen, *Israel and the Bomb*, New York: Columbia University Press, 1998, p. 117. Behbehani, pp. 127, 149.

2. Kaufman, pp. 48–9. Robert M. Citino, *Blitzkrieg to Desert Storm: The Evolution of Operational Warfare*, Lawrence, KS: University Press of Kansas, 2004, pp. 158–68.

3. Yaqub, p. 265.

4. Copeland, p. 238.

5. NARA, RG 59, 1970–73, Box 2642, Moscow, Jan. 21, 1970.

6. Tom Segev, *1967: Israel, the War, and the Year That Transformed the Middle East*, New York: Metropolitan, 2005, pp. 202–17. Kaufman, p. 53. Oren, *Six Days*, pp. 46–7. Bregman, p. 43. Copeland, p. 237.

7. NARA, CIA-RDP79S00427A000427A000400060002-8, Washington, Dec. 6, 1961, "The Arab-Israeli Situation," secret.

8. BNA, FO 371/180654, Jerusalem, Apr. 13, 1965, Saunders to Goodson.

9. NARA, RG 59, NND939522, 1963, Box 3733, Washington, Apr. 3, 1963, President's Press Conference. Apr. 4, 1963, Memorandum of Conversation, "German Scientists in the UAR."

10. Warren Bass, *Support Any Friend: Kennedy's Middle East and the Making of the U.S.-Israel Alliance,* Oxford: Oxford University Press, 2003, pp. 208–16, 223, 239. Black and Morris, p. 199.

11. Bregman, p. 43. Bass, pp. 208–11.

12. Bregman, p. 65.

13. Oren, *Six Days,* p. 163.

14. Citino, p. 166.

15. NARA, CIA-RDP78-03061A000400060002-1, Jun. 1967, "Preliminary Assessment of the Military Equipment and Training Provided to the Arabs by the USSR."

16. BNA, FO 371/180856, Tel Aviv, Mar. 31, 1965, Beith to Crawford.

17. BNA, FCO 17/11, Washington, Jan. 17, 1967, Everett to Goodison.

18. Clayton Fritchey, "What Next from the Staff on Mideast Policy?" *Washington Star,* Jul. 17, 1967.

19. BNA, FCO 17/9, Tel Aviv, May 5, 1967, Hadow to Weir.

20. Little, *American Orientalism,* p. 142.

21. Ibid., pp. 139–41.

22. BNA, FCO 17/11, Washington, Feb. 23, 1967, Everett to Moberly.

23. BNA, FCO 17/11, Washington, Apr. 11, 1967, Owen to Foreign Office, "Julius Holmes Report Has Been Leaked." "U.S. Looks at Tomorrow's Crisis: Alarms Ring from Mideast to Atlantic," *Washington Post,* Apr. 9, 1967.

24. BNA, FCO 17/11, Washington, Apr. 11, 1967, Owen to Foreign Office, "Julius Holmes Report Has Been Leaked." "U.S. Looks at Tomorrow's Crisis," *Washington Post.*

25. BNA, FCO 17/11, Washington, Apr. 11, 1967, Owen to Foreign Office, "Julius Holmes Report Has Been Leaked." "U.S. Looks at Tomorrow's Crisis," *Washington Post.*

26. Fritchey, "What Next?"

27. Little, *American Orientalism,* pp. 141–42.

28. BNA, FCO 17/11, Washington, Mar. 8, 1967, Everett to Morris. Little, *American Orientalism,* pp. 140–43.

29. Yaqub, p. 75.

30. Adeed Dawisha, *Arab Nationalism in the Twentieth Century: From Triumph to Despair,* Princeton: Princeton University Press, 2003, 234–35. NARA, RG 59, 1970–73, Box 2470, Jedda, Feb. 14, 1968, Eilts, "Saudi Arabia Takes Another Look at the Arabian Peninsula."

31. Little, *American Orientalism,* pp. 186–87. Bregman, pp. 42–3.

32. BNA, FCO 17/11, Tel Aviv, Jul. 11, 1968, George Chalmers, "American View of the Problem of Peace in the Middle East." Oren, *Six Days,* p. 45.

33. Little, *American Orientalism,* pp. 186–87.

34. BNA, FCO 17/11, Tel Aviv, Jul. 11, 1968, George Chalmers, "American View of the Problem of Peace in the Middle East."

35. "Soviet Blunder That Led to Mideast War," *U.S. News and World Report,* Jul. 17, 1967.

36. BNA, FCO 17/11, Tel Aviv, Jul. 11, 1968, George Chalmers, "American View of the Problem of Peace in the Middle East." Bregman, pp. 45–7.

37. Copeland, pp. 235–36.

38. NARA, CIA-RDP70S00385R000100310008-9, May 24, 1967, Memorandum for the Record, "Intelligence Support Required of ORR."

39. BNA, FCO 17/11, Washington, Dec. 15, 1967, Urwick to Moore, "Eugene Rostow's Speech to the University of Mississippi Law School on 'The Middle Eastern Crisis and Beyond.'"

40. Bregman, p. 46.

41. Little, *American Orientalism,* p. 187.

42. Fritchey, "What Next?" Oren, *Six Days,* pp. 94–5.

43. David G. Nes, "Washington's Policy in the Middle East Held to Forestall the Peace It Professes," *Baltimore Sun,* Aug. 11, 1968.

44. Kaufman, p. 55.

45. Oren, *Six Days,* pp. 142–43, 164.

46. John J. Mearsheimer and Stephen M. Walt, *The Israel Lobby and U.S. Foreign Policy,* New York: Farrar, Straus and Giroux, 2007, p. 85. Copeland, p. 237.

47. Citino, pp. 165–67. Oren, *Six Days,* pp. 149, 151.

48. Sadat, p. 173. Kaufman, p. 56.
49. Oren, *Six Days*, p. 42.
50. Ibid. p. 159.
51. Bregman, p. 51.
52. "The Periscope: Why the Soviets Blundered in the Middle East," *Newsweek*, Jul. 17, 1967.
53. Tyler, p. 72. Bregman, pp. 54–5. Oren, *Six Days*, pp. 146–47.
54. Kaufman, p. 55. Oren, *Six Days*, p. 165.
55. Little, *American Orientalism*, p. 187.
56. James Reston, "Washington: A Steadier Administration," *New York Times*, Jun. 28, 1967.
57. Ray Vicker, "Israel's Spies Play for Keeps," *Wall Street Journal*, Feb. 12, 1970. Oren, *Six Days*, pp. 170–71.
58. NARA, CIA-RDP78-03061A000400060002-1, Jun. 1967, "Preliminary Assessment of the Military Equipment and Training Provided to the Arabs by the USSR."
59. Pollack, pp. 84–6, 88. Bregman, pp. 55–7. Oren, *Six Days*, p. 163.
60. Oren, *Six Days*, p. 188.
61. Thompson, "U.S. Humiliation."
62. NARA, CIA-RDP70S00385R000100310008-9, May 24, 1967, Memorandum for the Record, "Intelligence Support Required of ORR."
63. Oren, *Six Days*, p. 226.
64. Ibid., p. 209. Kaufman, p. 58.
65. Thompson, "U.S. Humiliation." Roberts, "A Breathtaking Biography." Oren, *Six Days*, p. 217.
66. Lyndon Baines Johnson, *The Vantage Point: Perspectives of the Presidency, 1963–1969*, New York: Holt, Rinehart & Winston, 1971, p. 299. Segev, *1967*, pp. 364–65.
67. Oren, *Six Days*, p. 45.
68. Ibid. p. 192.
69. Segev, *1967*, pp. 482–85. Oren, *Six Days*, p. 208.
70. Bregman, p. 57.
71. Ibid., p. 50.
72. Segev, *1967*, p. 369. Bregman, p. 53.
73. Oren, *Six Days*, p. 202.
74. Taylor, "Egypt Is Caught in a Red Trap."
75. Copeland, p. 234.
76. Lester Velie, "The Week the Hot Line Burned," *Reader's Digest*, Aug. 1968. Oren, *Six Days*, pp. 196–97.
77. Oren, *Six Days*, p. 197.
78. Kaufman, p. 60.
79. Thompson, "U.S. Humiliation."
80. NARA, CIA-RDP78-03061A000400060002-1, Jun. 1967, "Preliminary Assessment of the Military Equipment and Training Provided to the Arabs by the USSR."
81. Bass, p. 149.
82. Segev, *1967*, pp. 352, 372. Pollack, pp. 76–9. Oren, *Six Days*, p. 201. Tyler, p. 99.
83. NARA, CIA-RDP78-03061A000400060002-1, Jun. 1967, "Preliminary Assessment of the Military Equipment and Training Provided to the Arabs by the USSR."
84. Bregman, p. 56.
85. James Scott, *Attack on the Liberty*, New York: Simon & Schuster, 2009, pp. 325–31. Segev, *1967*, pp. 386, 568–70. Oren, *Six Days*, pp. 266–71. Tyler, pp. 99–101.
86. Joseph Alsop, "Extent of Mideast Arms Aid Shows Aims of Soviet Union," *Washington Post*, Jun. 5, 1970.
87. Segev, *1967*, pp. 386–88.
88. Oren, *Six Days*, pp. 148, 154, 317.
89. Pollack, pp. 460–62. Oren, *Six Days*, p. 154.
90. Bregman, p. 58.
91. Ibid., pp. 58, 61.
92. BNA, FCO 8/812, Rabat, Jan. 23, 1968, Holliday to Spears.
93. Bregman, p. 59.
94. Kaufman, p. 60.
95. BNA, FCO 17/9, London, Jun. 16, 1967, Foreign and Colonial Office to Certain Missions.
96. Roberts, "A Breathtaking Biography."
97. Tyler, p. 84. BNA, FCO 17/11, Washington, Jun. 15, 1967, Dean to Foreign Office.

98. Bregman, p. 65.

99. Mearsheimer and Walt, p. 99. Segev, *1967*, pp. 369, 403–7.

100. Ovendale, pp. 209–10. Segev, *1967*, p. 404.

101. BNA, FCO 17/11, Washington, Jul. 7, 1967, Urwick to Morris.

102. Nes, "Washington's Policy."

103. BNA, FCO 17/9, London, Jun. 16, 1967, Foreign and Colonial Office to Certain Missions.

104. "Prisoners of Self-Deception," *Pravda*, Feb. 2, 1968.

105. *Congressional Record*, Oct. 17, 1967.

106. Tyler, p. 101. Dawisha, pp. 254–56. Copeland, p. 239.

107. Aburish, p. 277. "Nasser: Defeat, Hyperbole, Survival," *Wall Street Journal*, Jan. 8, 1968.

108. Thompson, "U.S. Humiliation." Tyler, pp. 101–2.

109. BNA, FCO 39/242, London, Jun. 22, 1968, Speares to Adams.

110. BNA, FCO 39/242, Beirut, Jun. 15, 1968, Sanders to Walker.

111. BNA, FCO 39/242, London, Jun. 22, 1968, Speares to Adams.

112. Ibid.

113. BNA, FCO 17/11, Washington, Jul. 7, 1967, Urwick to Morris.

114. Oren, *Six Days*, p. 155.

115. Washington, NARA, RG 59, 1970–73, Box 2384, Tel Aviv, W. B. Zurhellen, "Political Commentary for January 1970," secret.

116. *Congressional Record*, Dec. 2, 1967.

117. Tyler, p. 102. BNA, FCO 17/17, Moscow, Feb. 13, 1968, Symons to Cliff.

118. Gershom Gorenberg, "Israel's Tragedy Foretold," *New York Times*, Mar. 10, 2006.

119. BNA, FCO 17/11, Washington, Jul. 11, 1967, Dean to Foreign Office. Oren, *Six Days*, p. 100.

120. BNA, FCO 17/11, Washington, Dec. 15, 1967, Urwick to Moore, "Eugene Rostow's Speech to the University of Mississippi Law School on 'The Middle Eastern Crisis and Beyond.'"

121. BNA, FCO 17/11, London, Jul. 12, 1967, Willie Morris, "The State Department and the Middle East."

122. Scott, p. 141.

123. Oren, *Six Days*, pp. 234–35, 253–55.

124. I. F. Stone, "The Future of Israel," *Ramparts*, Jul. 1967.

125. Fraser, *USA*, pp. 84–5.

126. BNA, FCO 8/812, Rabaat, Jan. 23, 1968, Holliday to Spears.

127. BNA, FCO 17/11, London, Jul. 12, 1967, Willie Morris, "The State Department and the Middle East."

128. Copeland, p. 127.

129. Fraser, *USA*, pp. 82–3.

130. Segev, *1967*, pp. 572–73.

131. Maoz, passim.

132. Robert Allen and John Goldsmith, "Johnson Still Bars Jets for Israelis," *Northern Virginia Sun*, Sep. 17, 1968.

133. BNA, FCO 17/11, Washington, Apr. 22 and May 7, 1968, Alan Urwick to Foreign Office.

134. Tyler, p. 131. Fraser, *USA*, p. 85. Mitchell G. Bard, "The 1968 Sale of Phantom Jets to Israel," Jewish Virtual Library (www.jewishvirtuallibrary.org).

135. Tyler, p. 104.

136. Nes, "Washington's Policy."

137. Scott, p. 222.

138. Kaufman, pp. 61–2. NARA, RG 59, 1970–73, Box 2389, Department of State Research Study, May 7, 1970, David Mark, "Washington and Tel Aviv: Clashing Interests amidst Interdependence," secret.

139. Fraser, *USA*, pp. 83–4.

140. Little, *American Orientalism*, p. 188.

141. Fritchey, "What Next?" Nes, "Washington's Policy."

CHAPTER 9: THE NIXON DOCTRINE

1. Kaufman, p. 70.

2. Fraser, *USA*, pp. 89–91.

3. BNA, FCO 8/2102, Baghdad, Dec. 18, 1973, Meluney to Burton, "Iraq's Oil Policy Explained."

4. BNA, FCO 8/2051, V. Semenov, "The Oil Crisis and Iran," Jul. 10, 1973. A. Vasilev, "Persian Gulf: Oil and Politics," *Pravda*, Jun. 11, 1973.

5. Alsop, "Extent of Mideast Arms Aid."

6. NARA, RG 59, 1970–73, Box 2614, Apr. 7, 1971, Talcott Seelye and Ghaleb Kayali, Memorandum of Conversation, "Syrian-U.S. Relations: Current Situation." BNA, FCO 17/17, Washington, Jan. 16, 1968, Bendall to Smith.

7. Rachel Bronson, *Thicker Than Oil: America's Uneasy Partnership with Saudi Arabia*, New York: Oxford University Press, 2006, pp. 110–11. Little, *American Orientalism*, pp. 136–37, 188.

8. BNA, FCO 8/2053, Jedda, Nov. 20, 1973, J. S. Laing to Foreign Office. "Why the Shah Was Gentle to Israel," *Financial Times*, Nov. 1, 1973.

9. BNA, FCO 8/1737, Jedda, Nov. 3, 1971, Ian Winchester to Robert McGregor.

10. BNA, FCO 17/11, Washington, May 7, 1968, Urwick to Foreign Office. Little, *American Orientalism*, pp. 143–44. Kaufman, p. 77.

11. NARA, RG 59, 1613, Box 2587, Jedda, Mar. 16, 1970, Rogers to American Embassy.

12. NARA, CIA-RDP79-00891A001300080001-1, Dec. 1972, "Saudi Arabia Handbook," secret.

13. Ibid.

14. Ibid.

15. Wright, p. 155.

16. NARA, RG 59, 1970–73, Box 2587, Jedda, Apr. 1, 1971, Thacher to Rogers, secret.

17. Ibid.

18. BNA, FCO 8/1505, Jedda, Feb. 1, 1970, Morris to Acland. NARA, CIA-RDP79-00891A001300080001-1, Dec. 1972, "Saudi Arabia Handbook," secret. NARA, RG 59, 1970–73, Box 2472, Jedda, Mar. 15, 1967, Eilts, "Modernization Coming to Buraida." NARA, RG 59, 1613, Box 2567, May 29, 1971, "Memo of President's Conversations with King Faisal." BNA, FCO 8/1737, Jedda, Nov. 3, 1971, Ian Winchester to Robert McGregor.

19. BNA, FCO 8/1734, Jedda, Dec. 31, 1970, Morris to Sir Alec Douglas-Home.

20. BNA, FCO 8/812, Jedda, Sep. 18, 1968, Morris to Stirling.

21. NARA, LM 169/2, Mar. 7, 1954, "Address of HM the King at Inaugural Ceremony of the Council of Ministers."

22. BNA, FCO 8/812, Jedda, Jan. 30, 1967, Long to Eyers.

23. NARA, RG 59, 1970–73, Box 2470, Jedda, Jan. 2, 1969, Eilts, "Monthly Commentary."

24. NARA, RG 59, 1970–73, Box 2587, Dhahran, Dinsmore.

25. BNA, FCO 8/812, Jedda, Sep. 18, 1968, Morris to Stirling.

26. Steve Coll, *Ghost Wars: The Secret History of the CIA, Afghanistan, and Bin Laden, from the Soviet Invasion to September 10, 2001*, New York: Penguin Press, 2004, p. 35. NARA, RG 59, NND 959000, Box 1675, Jedda, Nov. 27, 1965, Richard Murphy, "The Saudi Army Officer's Role in National Affairs."

27. NARA, CIA-RDP79-00891A001300080001-1, Dec. 1972, "Saudi Arabia Handbook," secret.

28. NARA, RG 59, 1970–73, Box 2587, Jedda, Apr. 1, 1971, Thacher to Rogers, secret.

29. Ibid.

30. NARA, RG 59, 1970–73, Box 2587, Dec. 15, 1973, "Memo of Conversation with Hisham Nazir, Prince Saud, Prince Turki, Henry Kissinger, James Akins, Joseph Sisco, and Alfred Atherton."

31. NARA, RG 59, 1970–73, Box 2585, Dhahran, May 5, 1971, Countryman to Rogers.

32. NARA, RG 59, 1970–73, Box 2585, Jedda, [1970], American Embassy to Rogers.

33. NARA, RG 59, 1970–73, Box 2585, Dhahran, Aug. 26, 1971, Dinsmore, "Saudi Official Comments on his Government." Dhahran, May 5, 1971, Countryman to Rogers.

34. NARA, RG 59, NND 959000, Box 1745, Jedda, Nov. 3, 1966, C. J. Quinn.

35. NARA, CIA-RDP79-00891A001300080001-1, Dec. 1972, "Saudi Arabia Handbook," secret.

36. NARA, RG 59, NND 959000, Box 1675, Jedda, Nov. 27, 1965, Richard Murphy, "The Saudi Army Officer's Role in National Affairs."

37. Ibid.

38. NARA, RG 59, 1970–73, Box 2587, Jedda, Apr. 1, 1971, Thacher to Rogers, secret.

39. Ibid.

40. NARA, RG 59, NND 959000, Box 1675, Jedda, Nov. 27, 1965, Richard Murphy, "The Saudi Army Officer's Role in National Affairs."

41. BNA, FCO 8/812, Jedda, Mar. 23, 1968, Brig. H. E. R. Watson, "General Notes on the Present State of the National Guard," secret.

42. NARA, RG 59, 1970–73, Box 2378, Tehran, Jan. 9, 1973, Farland, "Political Assessment Report from Iran." Little, *American Orientalism*, p. 145.

43. NARA, RG 59, 1970–73, Box 2384, Tel Aviv, Feb. 10, 1973, Zurheller, "Decision Making in an Election Year."

44. NARA, RG 59, 1970–73, Box 2641, Tel Aviv, Mar. 23, 1972, Ambassador Barbour, "An Estimate of Israel's Territorial Expectations."

45. NARA, RG 59, 1970–73, Box 2388, Aug. 7, 1973, Sisco to Rogers, "Israel: New Departures in Occupation Policies."

46. BNA, FCO 17/896, London, Feb. 27, 1969, Appleyard to Tripp, "Israel after Mr. Eshkol."

47. Ovendale, p. 210. NARA, RG 59, 1970–73, Box 2385, Dec. 10, 1970, Sisco to Rogers, "Briefing Memo." Box 2641, Tel Aviv, Mar. 23, 1972, Ambassador Barbour, "An Estimate of Israel's Territorial Expectations."

48. Idith Zertal and Akiva Eldar, *Lords of the Land: The War over Israel's Settlements in the Occupied Territories, 1967–2007*, New York: Nation, 2007, p. 46. NARA, RG 59, 1970–73, Box 2388, Aug. 7, 1973, Sisco to Rogers, "Israel: New Departures in Occupation Policies."

49. NARA, RG 59, 1970–73, Box 2614, Feb. 21, 1973, "Internal Developments in Israel."

50. Tyler, p. 134. NARA, CIA-RDP79T00975A018400040002-2, Mar. 2, 1971, "Central Intelligence Bulletin: Egypt," top secret.

51. Wright, p. 39.

52. Kaufman, p. 78. NARA, CIA-RDP79T00975A020100100001-6, Oct. 2, 1971, Central Intelligence Bulletin, "Egypt," secret. NARA, RG 59, 1970–73, Box 2641, Feb. 26, 1971, Ray Cline to Rogers, "UAR-Sadat on a Tight Rope," secret.

53. NARA, RG 59, 1970–73, Box 2613, Beirut, Sep. 13, 1972, "Syrian Policy Gets Tougher."

54. NARA, RG 59, 1970–73, Box 2614, Apr. 7, 1971, Talcott Seelye and Ghaleb Kayali, Memorandum of Conversation, "Syrian-U.S. Relations: Current Situation." Fraser, *USA*, pp. 93–4.

55. NARA, RG 59, 1970–73, Box 2641, Tel Aviv, Mar. 23, 1972, Ambassador Barbour, "An Estimate of Israel's Territorial Expectations." Box 2386, American Embassy Paris, Jan. 27, 1970.

56. NARA, RG 59, 1613, 1860, Tel Aviv, Oct. 14, 1971, Zurheller to Atherton, secret.

57. NARA, RG 59, Box 2387, Jerusalem, Mar. 24, 1971, Campbell to State.

58. NARA, RG 59, 1970–73, Box 2641, Tel Aviv, Mar. 23, 1972, Ambassador Barbour, "An Estimate of Israel's Territorial Expectations."

59. Washington, NARA, RG 59, 1970–73, Box 2384, Tel Aviv, Feb. 4, 1970, W. B. Zurheller, "Political Commentary for January 1970," secret.

60. NARA, RG 59, 1970–73, Box 2386, Office of the Secretary of Defense, Feb. 28, 1973, "MemCon—Visit of Mrs. Meir," secret. NARA, RG, 1613, NND 969027, 1860, Secretary of Defense, Feb. 27, 1973, "Memo for the President—Israel's Requests for Aircraft and Aircraft Production Assistance," secret.

61. BNA, FCO 17/1007, Washington, Feb. 13, 1970, Stewart, "Arms Supply to Middle East."

62. NARA, RG 59, 1970–73, 1613, 1860, Tel Aviv, Mar. 14, 1973, American Embassy to Rogers. Tel Aviv, Dec. 8, 1972, "Memo of Conversation: U.S.-Israeli Relationship."

63. NARA, RG, 1613, NND 969027, 1860, Washington, Feb. 21, 1973, Sisco to Rogers, "Memo for the President—Aircraft Supply and Production Assistance for Israel."

64. NARA, RG 59, 1970–73, Box 2389, Department of State Research Study, May 7, 1970, David Mark, "Washington and Tel Aviv: Clashing Interests Amidst Interdependence," secret.

65. Mearsheimer and Walt, pp. 37–8. Kaufman, p. 72.

66. NARA, RG 59, 1970–73, Box 2386, Tel Aviv, Apr. 7, 1972, Zurheller and Barbour, "Israel: The Trend to the Right." RG 59, 1970–73, 1613, Washington, Dec. 16, 1972, Rogers to American Embassy Tel Aviv.

67. Tyler, p. 124. Mearsheimer and Walt, pp. 42–3. NARA, RG 59, 1970–73, Box 2385, Oval Office, Dec. 11, 1970, "Memorandum of Conversation," top secret.

68. Ovendale, *Origins*, p. 210.

69. BNA, FCO 17/1022, Feb. 25, 1970, "The Middle East: The Arab-Israeli Dispute, Brief by the FCO."

70. Kaufman, p. 51. Fraser, *USA*, pp. 94–5.

71. NARA, RG 59, 1970–73, Box 2452, Department of State, Jun. 25, 1973, Memorandum of Conversation, Joseph Sisco and Guy de Commines de Marsilly, "Franco-U.S. Middle East Consultations, Jun. 25—Syria and Lebanon."

72. NARA, RG 59, 1970–73, Box 2385, Oval Office, Dec. 11, 1970, "Memorandum of Conversation," top secret.

73. Kaufman, p. 75.

74. Ibid.

75. NARA, RG 59, 1970-73, Box 2613, Washington, Nov. 19, 1970, William P. Rogers, "Memo for the President: An Analysis of the Latest Events in Syria." Beirut, Nov. 3, 1970, "Situation in Syria." Box 2614, Nov. 25, 1970, Department of State, "Intelligence Note: Syria—Latest Chapter in Continuing Power Struggle Guarantees Neither Moderation nor Stability."

76. Fraser, *USA*, pp. 96–7.

77. NARA, RG 59, 1613, 1860, Jan. 31, 1972, "Intelligence Note—Egypt/USSR: Sadat's Moscow Visit."

78. Kaufman, pp. 73, 80. Taylor, "Egypt Is Caught in a Red Trap."

79. NARA, RG 59, 1970–73, Box 2386, Tel Aviv, Apr. 7, 1972, Zurheller and Barbour, "Israel: The Trend to the Right."

80. Kaufman, p. 76.

81. Khalidi, p. 130.

82. NARA, RG 59, 1970–73, 264, Feb. 18, 1970, Department of State Research Study, "UAR: Reading between the Lines."

83. Pollack, pp. 103–4.

84. NARA, CIA-RDP83M00171R001800070002-0, Washington, Mar. 21, 1975, "Crisis Management Relationships between the NMCC and Other Key Washington Centers." NARA, CIA-RD-P79B01737A002100130001-4, "Correction of Deficiencies Shown by Analytic Shortcomings in the Period before Outbreak of Hostilities in the Middle East—Oct. 1973."

85. NARA, CIA-RDP83M00171R001800070002-0, Washington, Mar. 21, 1975, "Crisis Management Relationships between the NMCC and Other Key Washington Centers."

86. Fraser, *USA*, pp. 101–2.

87. Henry Kissinger, *Crisis: The Anatomy of Two Major Foreign Policy Crises*, New York: Simon & Schuster, 2003, pp. 122–23. Pollack, pp. 111–12.

88. Pollack, p. 112.

89. Ibid., p. 125.

90. NARA, CIA-RDP80T00942A001000030001-0, May 1979, "Politics in Syria: An Intelligence Assessment," confidential.

91. NARA, CIA-RDP79B01737A002100160001-1, Dec. 3, 1974, "Syria's Negotiating Tactics."

92. Fraser, *USA*, pp. 102–3.

93. Pollack, pp. 104–5.

94. Ibid., p. 112.

95. Kaufman, p. 81. Kissinger, *Crisis*, p. 109. Pollack, p. 490.

96. Kissinger, *Crisis*, p. 111.

97. Fraser, *USA*, pp. 103–4.

98. Marilyn Berger, "Oil, Foreign Policy and the Energy Crisis," *Washington Post*, Apr. 16, 1972. Bronson, pp. 111–12.

99. Bamberg, p. 476.

100. "The Oil War," *New York*, Oct. 14, 1974.

101. Roberts, *History*, p. 431.

102. BNA, FCO 8/2102, Baghdad, Dec. 18, 1973, Meluney to Burton, "Iraq's Oil Policy Explained."

103. Bronson, pp. 113–14.

104. "The Oil War," *New York*. Tyler, pp. 146–47.

105. Bamberg, pp. 474–76.

106. Berger, "Oil, Foreign Policy and the Energy Crisis."

107. Andrew Tobias, "War—The Ultimate Antitrust Action," *New York*, Oct. 14, 1974.

108. Bamberg, p. 484.

109. BNA, FCO 8/2102, Baghdad, Dec. 18, 1973, Meluney to Burton, "Iraq's Oil Policy Explained."

110. "The Oil War," *New York*.

111. BNA, FCO 8/2053, Tehran, Nov. 1, 1973, Arbuthnott to Hunt.

112. Kissinger, *Crisis*, pp. 56–7, 64.

113. NARA, RG 59, 1970–73, Box 2389, Washington, Nov. 2, 1973, Memorandum of Conversation, Kissinger, Sisco, Rodman, Meir, Sinitiz, top secret.

114. Kissinger, *Crisis*, p. 146.

115. Mearsheimer and Walt, p. 43. Kissinger, pp. 63, 85–9, 96–7, 109, 111, 116.

116. Kissinger, *Crisis*, p. 122.

117. Ibid., p. 198.

118. Ibid., p. 181.
119. Ibid., p. 228.
120. Ibid., pp. 125, 151, 207.
121. Fraser, *USA*, pp. 104–5. Kissinger, *Crisis*, pp. 123, 151, 200–201.
122. Kissinger, *Crisis*, pp. 86–7, 94, 254–56.
123. Tyler, pp. 142–45.
124. Kissinger, *Crisis*, p. 112.
125. Citino, pp. 181–84. Kissinger, *Crisis*, p. 141.
126. Kissinger, *Crisis*, p. 123.
127. Ibid., pp. 122–23, 190. Pollack, pp. 345–48.
128. Tyler, p. 141. Pollack, p. 497.
129. Kaufman, p. 81. NARA, RG 59, 1970–73, Box 2614, Dec. 1, 1973, "Background Paper: Syria."
130. Kissinger, *Crisis*, pp. 122–23, 139–41. Tyler, pp. 140–41.
131. Lyle J. Goldstein and Yuri M. Zhukov, "A Tale of Two Fleets: A Russian Perspective on the 1973 Naval Standoff in the Mediterranean," *Naval War College Review* 57/2 (Spring 2004), pp. 42, 54. NARA, RG 59, 1970–73, Box 2452, Department of State, Memorandum of Conversation, Jun. 25, 1973, Joseph Sisco and Guy de Commines de Marsilly, "Franco-U.S. Middle East Consultations, Jun. 25 —Syria and Lebanon."
132. Tyler, pp. 125, 147–48. Kissinger, *Crisis*, pp. 169, 208.
133. Oren, *Power, Faith and Fantasy*, p. 534. Kissinger, *Crisis*, pp. 212, 217. Tyler, pp. 152–53.
134. Bamberg, p. 478. Kissinger, *Crisis*, p. 253.
135. Bamberg, p. 478.
136. "The Oil War," *New York*. Bamberg, p. 480.
137. Pollack, pp. 116–24.
138. Ibid., p. 128.
139. Goldstein and Zhukov, p. 51.
140. Alsop, "Extent of Mideast Arms Aid."
141. Kissinger, *Crisis*, pp. 173, 262.
142. Ibid., pp. 299, 314.
143. Fraser, *USA*, pp. 106–7.
144. Kissinger, *Crisis*, p. 307.
145. David Binder, "An Implied Threat Spurred U.S. Forces' Alert," *New York Times*, Nov. 21, 1973.
146. BNA, FCO 93/254, Moscow, Oct. 9, 1973, Killick to Foreign Office.
147. Kissinger, *Crisis*, pp. 198, 253, 340, 343.
148. Ibid., pp. 229, 331.
149. NARA, RG 59, 1970–73, Box 2389, Washington, Nov. 2, 1973, Memorandum of Conversation, Kissinger, Sisco, Rodman, Meir, Sinitiz, top secret.
150. Ibid. Fraser, *USA*, pp. 108–10.
151. Tyler, p. 169. Kissinger, *Crisis*, p. 369.
152. Fraser, *USA*, p. 112.
153. NARA, RG 59, 1970–73, Box 2389, Washington, Nov. 2, 1973, Memorandum of Conversation, Kissinger, Sisco, Rodman, Meir, Sinitiz, top secret.
154. NARA, CIA-RDP85T00875R000600050069-2, Nov. 1973, secret. BNA, FCO 93/254, Amman, Paul Balfour to Foreign Office.
155. Wright, pp. 40–1.
156. Kaufman, p. 83. Bamberg, p. 479.
157. Tyler, p. 174.
158. Bronson, pp. 119–20. Tobias, "War—The Ultimate Antitrust Action."
159. Kissinger, *Crisis*, pp. 285, 325.
160. NARA, RG 59, 1970–73, 1613, Washington, Nov. 28, 1973, Marshall Wright to Kissinger.
161. NARA, RG 59, 1613, Box 2587, Riyadh, Dec. 15, 1973, Memorandum of Conversation, Kissinger, Sisco, Akins, Nazir, Princes Saud, Faisal and Turki.
162. NARA, RG 59, 1970–73, Box 2390, Washington, Dec. 6, 1973, Sisco to Kissinger, "Your Meeting with Moshe Dayan."
163. NARA, RG 59, 1613, Box 2587, Riyadh, Dec. 15, 1973, Memorandum of Conversation, Kissinger, Sisco, Akins, Nazir, Princes Saud, Faisal and Turki.

164. NARA, CIA-RDP79B01737A002100160001-1, Dec. 3, 1974, "Syria's Negotiating Tactics."

165. NARA, CIA-RDP79-01194A000300110001-1, Apr. 1971, "Aswan on the Nile."

166. Tyler, p. 131. NARA, RG 59, 1970–73, Box 2641, Washington, Sep. 28, 1970, R. P. Davies to Rogers and Kissinger aboard the USS *Saratoga*.

167. NARA, RG 59, 1970–73, Box 2641, Jul. 26, 1971, Ted Eliot, "Memo for Mr. H. A. Kissinger: Sadat's Jul. 23 Speech."

168. NARA, RG 59, 1970–73, Box 2641, May 16, 1971, Rogers, "Memo for the President: Sadat Consolidates His Position."

169. Avraham Rabinovich, *The Yom Kippur War: The Epic Encounter that Transformed the Middle East,* New York: Kindle, 2005, pp. 507–8.

170. Anthony McDermott, "A Rough Ride on Sadat's Hunt for Alternatives," *Guardian,* Aug. 12, 1971.

CHAPTER 10: GREAT CIVILIZATION

1. NARA, RG 59, 1970–73, Box 2472, Dhahran, Jun. 9, 1969, L. Dinsmore, "The Shia Community."

2. Roosevelt, *Arabs, Oil and History,* pp. 77–8.

3. Kirk, *Middle East in the War,* p. 131.

4. Avery et al, vol. 7, pp. 220–26.

5. Petersen, p. 78.

6. Vali Nasr, *The Shia Revival: How Conflicts within Islam Will Shape the Future,* New York: Norton, 2006, pp. 123–24. Rouleau, p. 2.

7. Avery et al, pp. 225–39.

8. Barry Rubin, "Iran Seeks Supremacy in the Gulf, *National Guardian,* Feb. 16, 1972.

9. Kirk, *Middle East in the War,* pp. 28–9.

10. Avery et al, pp. 245–50.

11. NARA, CIA-RDP79T00865A002600100001-3, May 29, 1975, CIA Memorandum, "Iran's Mediatory Role in the Middle East," secret. CIA-RDP80T00942A000800100001-5, Mar. 1979, "New Directions in Iranian Foreign Policy: An Intelligence Assessment," secret.

12. NARA, CIA-RDP81B00401R0005001600, "Intelligence Memorandum: National Voice of Iran Broadcasts, Jan.–Mar. 1980," secret. NARA, CIA-RDP78-00915R000900090011-1, Jul. 15, 1959, "Assessment of the Threat of Communist Subversion in the Baghdad Pact Area," secret. BNA FO 371/126842, Tehran, Apr. 13, 1957, Stevens to Foreign Office.

13. NARA, CIA-RDO79S00427A000500070002-6, Mar. 30, 1961, "Iran," secret.

14. NARA, CIA-RDP86B00269R000400060002-9, Tehran, Apr. 15, 1960, "Eighth CENTO Ministerial Council Session: Politico-Economic Situation of Iran, Background Paper," secret. NARA, CIA-RDP80B01676R000400190058-7, Washington, May 7, 1966, George Carroll to R. J. Smith.

15. Petersen, pp. 11, 120.

16. Ibid., p. 17.

17. Geoffrey Wawro, "Letter from Iran," *Naval War College Review,* Winter 2002.

18. Ibid.

19. BNA, FCO 8/2053, Kuwait, Nov. 29, 1973, J. R. Young, "Ahmed Jarallah's Interview."

20. NARA, RF 59, 1970–73, Box 2381, Tehran, J. L. Washburn.

21. NARA, CIA-RDP79T00865A002600100001-3, May 29, 1975, CIA Memorandum, "Iran's Mediatory Role in the Middle East," secret. BNA, FCO 8/2051, Tehran, May 29, 1973, Ramsbotham to Carrington, "The View from Niavaran."

22. NARA, CIA-RDP86B00269R000400060002-9, Tehran, Apr. 15, 1960, "Eighth CENTO Ministerial Council Session: Politico-Economic Situation of Iran, Background Paper," secret.

23. George Lenczowski, ed., *Iran under the Pahlavis,* Stanford: Hoover Institute Press, 1978, p. 425. Robert E. Looney, "The Role of Military Expenditures in Pre-Revolutionary Iran's Economic Decline," *Iranian Studies* 21 (1988), p. 54.

24. BNA, FCO 8/2053, Kuwait, Nov. 29, 1973, J. R. Young, "Ahmed Jarallah's Interview."

25. Alvin J. Cottrell and James E. Dougherty, *Iran's Quest for Security: US Arms Transfers and the Nuclear Option,* Cambridge, MA: Institute for Foreign Policy Analysis, 1977, pp. 16–17. Shahram Chubin, "Iran's Security in the 1980s," *International Studies* 2 (Winter 1978), p. 60. Tom Baranauskas, "Air Power in the Iran-Iraq War," *Asian Defence Journal,* Mar. 1987, p. 52. R. D. M. Furlong, "Iran: A Power to Be Reckoned With," *International Defense Review,* Jun. 1973, p. 727.

26. John T. Hayward, "The Shah's Navy," *Government Executive,* Oct. 1976, p. 38. Chubin, pp. 58–9. Cottrell and Dougherty, pp. 18–19.
27. NARA, RG 59, 1613, NND 969027, Box 1859, American Embassy Tehran, Jun. 22, 1971. Avery et al, p. 455.
28. Cottrell and Dougherty, pp. 21–2. Ahmed S. Hashim, "Civil-Military Relations in Iran: A Case Study," unpublished MS, 1999, p. 137.
29. Kapuscinski, p. 62. BNA, FCO 8/2051, Tehran, May 22, 1973, Ramsbotham to Douglas-Home, "The Iranian Armed Forces: A Contrast of Strength and Weakness."
30. James T. Patterson, *Restless Giant: The United States from Watergate to Bush v. Gore,* New York: Oxford University Press, 2005, p. 124.
31. Colin L. Powell with Joseph E. Persico, *My American Journey,* New York: Random House, 1995, p. 240.
32. Chubin, p. 61. Furlong, p. 727.
33. Kapuscinski, p. 62.
34. BNA, FCO 8/2051, London, May 31, 1973, B. Smith, "The Iranian Armed Forces: Three Dispatches from Tehran."
35. Powell, pp. 240–41.
36. BNA, FCO 8/2051, Tehran, May 22, 1973, Ramsbotham to Douglas-Home, "The Iranian Armed Forces: A Contrast of Strength and Weakness."
37. Furlong, p. 721.
38. Cottrell and Dougherty, p. 23.
39. Chubin, pp. 77–8.
40. Ibid. pp. 67–8.
41. Vanessa Martin, *Creating an Islamic State,* London: I. B. Taurus, 2000, pp. 21–3, 73. Chubin, pp. 64–5.
42. Rouleau, p. 3.
43. BNA, FCO 8/2051, Tehran, May 22, 1973, Ramsbotham to Douglas-Home, "The Iranian Armed Forces: A Contrast of Strength and Weakness."
44. Hashim, "Civil-Military Relations in Iran," p. 141.
45. Maqsud Ul Hasan Nuri, "Regional Military Involvement: A Case Study of Iran under the Shah," *Pakistan Horizon* 37/4 (1984), pp. 33–4.
46. Marion Farouk-Sluglett and Peter Sluglett, *Iraq since 1958: From Revolution to Dictatorship,* London: KPI, 1987, pp. 171–72. Alvin J. Cottrell, "Iran's Armed Forces," in Lenczowski, *Iran under the Pahlavis,* p. 402. Manucher and Roxane Farmanfarmaian, *Blood and Oil: A Prince's Memoir of Iran, from the Shah to the Ayatollah,* New York: Random House, 1997, pp. 448–49.
47. BNA, FCO 8/2051, Tehran, May 29, 1973, Ramsbotham to Carrington, "The View from Niavaran."
48. NARA, RG 59, 1970–73, Box 2378, Tehran, Jan. 9, 1973, Farland, "Political Assessment Report from Iran." NARA, RG 59, 1970–73, Box 2378, Jun. 4, 1973, Intelligence Note, "Iran and Pakistan: Bhutto Visit Reveals Emerging Alliance."
49. NARA, RG 59, 1970–73, Box 2378, Jul. 26, 1973, Secretary of Defense Schlesinger, Memorandum of Conversation, "Meeting with the Shah of Iran."
50. Borzou Daragahi, "U.S. Policies May Have Contributed to Iran Revolution, Study Says," *Los Angeles Times,* Oct. 17, 2008.
51. Rouleau, p. 4.
52. NARA, RG 59, 1970–73, Box 2378, Tehran, Jan. 9, 1973, Farland, "Political Assessment Report from Iran." "CIA Deputy Director Offers Insight on U.S. Prestige," *Harrisburg Evening News,* Mar. 12, 1979.
53. BNA, FCO 8/2051, Tehran, May 29, 1973, Ramsbotham to Carrington, "The View from Niavaran." NARA, RG 59, 1970–73, Box 2378, Jul. 26, 1973, Secretary of Defense Schlesinger, Memorandum of Conversation, "Meeting with the Shah of Iran."
54. Rouleau, p. 4.
55. NARA, CIA-RDP80-01601R0000600030001-5, Aug. 9, 1972, Fred Lowe, "Iran's Burden of Reaction."
56. BNA, FCO 8/2051, London, May 31, 1973, B. Smith, "The Iranian Armed Forces: Three Dispatches from Tehran."
57. NARA, RG 59, 1970–73, Box 2378, Tehran, Jan. 9, 1973, Farland, "Political Assessment Report from Iran."
58. NARA, CIA-RDP86B00269R000400060002-9, Tehran, Apr. 15, 1960, "Eighth CENTO Ministerial Council Session: Politico-Economic Situation of Iran, Background Paper," secret. NARA, RG 59, 1970–

73, Box 2378, Tehran, Sep. 9, 1972, Farland, "Unchecked SAVAK Power Constitutes Long-Term Danger to Iranian Regime."

59. NARA, RG 59, 1970–73, Box 2378, Tehran, Jun. 14, 1973, S. T. Escudero, "Trip to Nain, Yazd, and the Towns and Villages of the Central and Northeastern Iranian Desert."

60. Rouleau, p. 5.

61. BNA, FCO 8/1884, Tehran, Ramsbotham to Foreign Office, "President Nixon's Visit to Iran, 30–31 May 1972." BNA, FCO 8/2051, Tehran, May 29, 1973, Ramsbotham to Carrington, "The View from Niavaran." BNA, FCO 8/2051, London, May 31, 1973, B. Smith, "The Iranian Armed Forces: Three Dispatches from Tehran." NARA, CIA-RDP86B00269R000400060002-9, Tehran, Apr. 15, 1960, "Eighth CENTO Ministerial Council Session: Politico-Economic Situation of Iran, Background Paper," secret.

62. Kapuscinski, pp. 54–5.

63. BNA, FO 371/180794, Tehran, Nov. 23, 1965, Dean to Morris.

64. NARA, CIA-RDP79T00826A000600010057-7, CIA Intelligence Memorandum, "U.S.-Iranian Relations," May 6, 1966, secret. NARA, RG 59, 1970–73, Box 2378, Tehran, Jan. 9, 1973, Farland, "Political Assessment Report from Iran."

65. NARA, RG 59, 1970–73, Box 2379, Tehran, Jan. 20, 1971, MacArthur, "Portrait of an Empress."

66. NARA, RG 59, 1970–73, Box 2378, Tehran, Sep. 9, 1972, Farland, "Unchecked SAVAK Power Constitutes Long-Term Danger to Iranian Regime."

67. NARA, RG 59, 1970–73, Box 2378, Tehran, May 10, 1971, MacArthur, "Student Disturbances at the Universities in Tehran." Washington, Jun. 12, 1973, Department of State Intelligence Note, "Iran: Internal Dissidence—A Note of Warning."

68. Kapuscinski, pp. 44–6.

69. Rouleau, p. 4.

70. NARA, RG 59, 1970–73, Box 2378, Tehran, Sep. 9, 1972, Farland, "Unchecked SAVAK Power Constitutes Long-Term Danger to Iranian Regime."

71. BNA, FCO 8/1884, London, Jun. 14, 1972, Wright to Mellunish.

72. NARA, RG 59, 1970–73, Box 2378, Tehran, Sep. 9, 1972, Farland, "Unchecked SAVAK Power Constitutes Long-Term Danger to Iranian Regime."

73. BNA, FCO 8/2053, Kuwait, Nov. 29, 1973, J. R. Young, "Ahmed Jarallah's Interview."

74. NARA, RG 59, 1970–73, Box 2378, Tehran, Mar. 23, 1970, MacArthur, "South Tehran: The Urban Mass."

75. NARA, CIA-RDP76M00527R000700200001-1, 1968, "Iran," secret.

76. Rouleau, p. 4.

77. BNA, FO 371/180786, Tehran, Feb. 19, 1965, Wiggin to Morris.

78. NARA, RG 59, 1970–73, Box 2378, Tehran, Mar. 23, 1970, MacArthur, "South Tehran: The Urban Mass."

79. Rouleau, p. 5.

80. Daragahi, "U.S. Policies."

81. Scott Armstrong, "The Fall of the Shah: U.S. Urged 'Crackdown' on Opposition," *Washington Post*, Oct. 27, 1980.

82. NARA, CIA-RDP81B00401R002000120002-9, Oct. 30, 1978, Stansfield Turner, "Meeting with Dr. Brzezinski, 27 Oct. 1978."

83. Armstrong, "U.S. Urged 'Crackdown' on Opposition."

84. Graham Allison, "An Intelligence Agenda," *New York Times*, Dec. 21, 1980.

85. Armstrong, "U.S. Urged 'Crackdown' on Opposition."

86. Scott Armstrong, "The Fall of the Shah: U.S. Rejects Coup Options," *Washington Post*, Oct. 30, 1980.

87. Ibid.

88. Armstrong, "U.S. Urged 'Crackdown' on Opposition."

89. Wright, p. 47.

90. Armstrong, "U.S. Rejects Coup Options."

91. Ibid.

92. Allison, "An Intelligence Agenda."

93. Armstrong, "U.S. Urged 'Crackdown' on Opposition."

94. Scott Armstrong, "The Fall of the Shah: Vance Deflects a Call for Toughness," *Washington Post*, Oct. 28, 1980.

95. Allison, "An Intelligence Agenda."

96. Armstrong, "U.S. Urged 'Crackdown' on Opposition."

97. Rouleau, pp. 5–6.
98. Armstrong, "Vance Deflects a Call for Toughness."
99. Ibid.
100. Ibid.

CHAPTER 11: DESERT ONE

1. Armstrong, "Vance Deflects a Call for Toughness."
2. Ibid.
3. Tyler, p. 230.
4. Armstrong, "U.S. Rejects Coup Options."
5. Ibid.
6. Wright, p. 47.
7. Rouleau, pp. 15–16.
8. Armstrong, "U.S. Rejects Coup Options." Rouleau, p. 8.
9. NARA, CIA-RDP81B00401R000500060014-9, American Embassy Ankara, Nov. 1979, "Khomeini Reply to Message from Pope."
10. Rouleau, pp. 7–8.
11. Tyler, p. 232. Armstrong, "U.S. Rejects Coup Options."
12. Armstrong, "U.S. Rejects Coup Options."
13. General Robert E. Huyser, *Mission to Tehran,* New York: Harper & Row, 1987.
14. Powell, pp. 242–43.
15. Allison, "An Intelligence Agenda."
16. Rouleau, p. 1.
17. NARA, CIA-RDP83B00100R000100090001-6, NFAC Contribution to DCI Annual Report, "1978 in Intelligence," secret.
18. Patterson, p. 127.
19. Tyler, pp. 240–42. Rouleau, p. 10.
20. Rouleau, p. 8. Patterson, p. 125.
21. Mark Bowden, "Among the Hostage-Takers," *Atlantic Monthly,* Dec. 2004. Nasr, p. 131.
22. Ibid.
23. NARA, CIA-RDP81B00401R000500060014-9, American Embassy Ankara, Nov. 1979, "Khomeini Reply to Message from Pope."
24. Daniel Pipes, "Iranian President Mahmoud Ahmadinejad and the 1979–81 U.S. Embassy Takeover," Nov. 20, 2006, Capitalism Magazine (www.capmag.com).
25. Bowden, "Among the Hostage-Takers."
26. Ibid.
27. Rouleau, pp. 11–13.
28. Nasr, p. 132.
29. Rouleau, pp. 14–15.
30. NARA, CIA-RDP80T00942A000600070002-0, Jan. 1979, "The Iranian Constitution: A Reference Aid," confidential. Rouleau, p. 8.
31. NARA, CIA-RDP81B00401R002000120002-8, Nov. 3, 1978, "The Opposition to the Shah." Nasr, p. 134.
32. Rouleau, p. 9.
33. Ibid.
34. NARA, CIA-RDP81B00401R000500130009-7, Mar. 27, 1980, "Moscow's View of the US-Iranian Hostage Crisis Since Afghanistan," secret.
35. NARA, CIA-RDP81B00401R000500060014-9, American Embassy Ankara, Nov. 1979, "Khomeini Reply to Message from Pope."
36. NARA, CIA-RDP80T00942A000800100001-5, Mar. 1979, "New Directions in Iranian Foreign Policy: An Intelligence Assessment," secret.
37. NARA, CIA-RDP81B00401R000500160019-3, Dec. 6, 1979, John H. Waller to Deputy Director of Central Intelligence, "Soviet Attitude toward Iran." NARA, CIA-RDP81B00401R000500130018-7, Washington, Feb. 19, 1980, "A Soviet 'Best Case' for Military Intervention in Iran," secret.
38. Patterson, p. 125.
39. Rouleau, p. 16.
40. Tyler, pp. 241–42.

41. NARA, CIA-RDP81B00401R000500100028-9, The White House, Nov. 30, 1979, Al McDonald to Zbigniew Brzezinski, "Impressions on Iran."

42. Ivo Daalder and I. M. Destler, *In the Shadow of the Oval Office: The Presidents and Their National Security Advisers from JFK to George W. Bush,* New York: Simon & Schuster, 2009, pp. 147–48.

43. Patterson, p. 125.

44. Bowden, "Among the Hostage-Takers."

45. NARA, CIA-RDP81B000401R000500160019-3, Dec. 6, 1979, John H. Waller to Deputy Director of Central Intelligence, "Soviet Attitude toward Iran."

46. NARA, CIA-RDP81B00401R000500060014-9, American Embassy Ankara, Nov. 1979, "Khomeini Reply to Message from Pope."

47. Mark Bowden, "The Desert One Debacle," *Atlantic Monthly,* May 2006.

48. Ibid.

49. John K. Cooley, "Iran Fiasco Rekindles Debate on U.S. Military Readiness," *Christian Science Monitor,* May 1, 1980.

50. NARA, CIA-RDP81B00401R000500140045-6, Apr. 30, 1980, FBIS Trends, "USSR Caustic on Rescue Mission."

51. Bowden, "Desert One Debacle."

52. "Raging Debate over the Desert Raid," *Time,* May 12, 1980.

53. Bowden, "Desert One Debacle."

54. Ibid.

55. Rouleau, pp. 15, 20.

56. Bowden, "Among the Hostage-Takers."

57. "Raging Debate over the Desert Raid," *Time.*

58. Ibid.

59. Cooley, "Iran Fiasco." "Raging Debate over the Desert Raid," *Time.*

60. Wright, p. 49.

61. NARA, CIA-RDP80T00942A000800100001-5, Mar. 1979, "New Directions in Iranian Foreign Policy: An Intelligence Assessment," secret.

62. Ibid.

63. NARA, CIA-RDP81B000401R000500160019-3, Dec. 6, 1979, John H. Waller to Deputy Director of Central Intelligence, "Soviet Attitude toward Iran."

64. Patterson, p. 126.

65. NARA, CIA-RDP80T00942A000800100001-5, Mar. 1979, "New Directions in Iranian Foreign Policy: An Intelligence Assessment," secret.

66. NARA, CIA-RDP81B00401R002000120002-8, Nov. 3, 1978, "The Opposition to the Shah."

67. NARA, CIA-RDP81B00401R000500100028-9, The White House, Nov. 30, 1979, Al McDonald to Zbigniew Brzezinski, "Impressions on Iran."

68. NARA, CIA-RDP81B000401R000500160019-3, Dec. 6, 1979, John H. Waller to Deputy Director of Central Intelligence, "Soviet Attitude toward Iran."

69. NARA, CIA-RDP81B000401R000500160019-3, Dec. 6, 1979, John H. Waller to Deputy Director of Central Intelligence, "Soviet Attitude toward Iran."

70. Rouleau, pp. 1–2, 18.

71. NARA, CIA-RDP81B00401R000500100028-9, The White House, Nov. 30, 1979, Al McDonald to Zbigniew Brzezinski, "Impressions on Iran."

72. "CIA Deputy Director Offers Insight on U.S. Prestige," *Harrisburg Evening News,* Mar. 12, 1979. NARA, CIA-RDP79T00912A002200010020-3, "East Asia Review," Mar. 13, 1979, secret. Nasr, p. 121.

73. Nasr, p. 140.

74. NARA, CIA-RDP80T00942A000800100001-5, Mar. 1979, "New Directions in Iranian Foreign Policy: An Intelligence Assessment," secret.

75. Ibid.

76. "Raging Debate over the Desert Raid," *Time.*

77. NARA, CIA-RDP81B000401R000500160019-3, Dec. 6, 1979, John H. Waller to Deputy Director of Central Intelligence, "Soviet Attitude toward Iran."

78. NARA, CIA-RDP81B00401R000500100028-9, The White House, Nov. 30, 1979, Al McDonald to Zbigniew Brzezinski, "Impressions on Iran."

79. NARA, CIA-RDP81B004001R000500110030-5, Bureau of Intelligence and Research, Jul. 6, 1980, "Iran: Khomeini's 'Revolution within the Revolution.'"

CHAPTER 12: JIHAD

1. William Maley, *The Afghanistan Wars*, New York: Palgrave, 2002, pp. 28–30.
2. Peter Marsden, *The Taliban: War, Religion and the New Order in Afghanistan*, New York: Zed Books, 1998, pp. 22–4. Dilip Hiro, *Holy Wars: The Rise of Islamic Fundamentalism*, New York: Routledge, 1989, pp. 245–46, 250–51.
3. Maley, pp. 69–71.
4. Coll, *Ghost Wars*, p. 81.
5. Nasr, pp. 136–37, 141–42.
6. Coll, *Ghost Wars*, pp. 25–7, 61, 73.
7. Nasr, pp. 147–49. Coll, *Ghost Wars*, pp. 27–9.
8. Gregory Feifer, *The Great Gamble: The Soviet War in Afghanistan*, New York, HarperCollins, 2009, pp. 28–33. Hiro, *Holy Wars*, pp. 254–55. Coll, *Ghost Wars*, pp. 39–41.
9. George Crile, *Charlie Wilson's War: The Extraordinary Story of the Largest Covert Operation in History*, New York: Atlantic, 2003, p. 354.
10. Wright, p. 99. "How Jimmy Carter and I Started the Mujahideen," Interview with Zbigniew Brzezinski, *Le Nouvel Observateur*, Jan. 21, 1998.
11. William Blum, *Killing Hope*, New York: Common Courage, 1995, p. 347.
12. Daalder and Destler, p. 156. Coll, *Ghost Wars*, p. 43.
13. Coll, *Ghost Wars*, p. 49.
14. Ibid., p. 38.
15. Marsden, p. 26. Hiro, *Holy Wars*, p. 257.
16. Marsden, p. 28.
17. Coll, *Ghost Wars*, pp. 51, 58.
18. Ibid., p. 61.
19. Feifer, pp. 130–31. Maley, pp. 79–81, 147. Coll, *Ghost Wars*, p. 62.
20. Michael Griffin, *Reaping the Whirlwind: Afghanistan, Al-Qa'ida, and the Holy War*, revised ed., London: Pluto Press, 2003. Griffin, p. 204. Maley, pp. 72–4. Coll, *Ghost Wars*, p. 65.
21. Abdel Bari Atwan, *The Secret History of al Qaeda*, Berkeley: University of California Press, 2006, p. 44.
22. Wright, pp. 147–48. Coll, *Ghost Wars*, pp. 72, 79, 82.
23. Coll, *Ghost Wars*, p. 73.
24. Atwan, pp. 44–5. Coll, *Ghost Wars*, pp. 83–4.
25. Ahmed Rashid, *Taliban: Militant Islam, Oil and Fundamentalism in Central Asia*, New Haven: Yale University Press, 2000, p. 130.
26. Atwan, pp. 42–3, 73–4. Wright, pp. 7–12.
27. Rashid, *Taliban*, p. 131. Maley, pp. 253–54. Coll, *Ghost Wars*, pp. 84–7, 112. Wright, pp. 66–8, 100–103.
28. Maley, p. 47.
29. Coll, *Ghost Wars*, p. 11. Maley, p. 80.
30. Crile, p. 166. Hiro, *Holy Wars*, p. 266.
31. Coll, *Ghost Wars*, p. 16.
32. Ibid., p. 63.
33. Hiro, *Holy Wars*, p. 245. Coll, *Ghost Wars*, p. 113.
34. Marsden, p. 29. Coll, *Ghost Wars*, pp. 67–8.
35. Marsden, p. 34. Coll, p. 120.
36. Coll, *Ghost Wars*, pp. 15–16, 147.
37. Ibid., p. 17.
38. Feifer, p. 109.
39. Coll, *Ghost Wars*, p. 133.
40. Ibid., p. 139.
41. Ibid., p. 155.
42. Wright, p. 43.
43. Coll, *Ghost Wars*, pp. 156–58.
44. Atwan, pp. 50, 83. Wright, p. 46.

45. Rashid, *Taliban*, p. 131. Coll, *Ghost Wars*, pp. 144–46.
46. Coll, *Ghost Wars*, pp. 151–52, 159–60.
47. Tyler, pp. 252–58, 273–81.
48. Mearsheimer and Walt, pp. 144, 158.
49. Coll, *Ghost Wars*, p. 89.
50. Hiro, *Holy Wars*, p. 259. Coll, *Ghost Wars*, pp. 103–4.
51. Coll, *Ghost Wars*, p. 97.
52. Feifer, pp. 4, 146, 185–86.
53. Maley, pp. 92, 99, 105–6, 130–31. Hiro, *Holy Wars*, p. 265. Coll, *Ghost Wars*, pp. 158–60, 167.
54. Crile, p. 266.
55. Coll, *Ghost Wars*, p. 99.
56. Ibid., pp. 100, 132.
57. Ibid., pp. 90–2.
58. Ibid., pp. 154–55.
59. Ibid., p. 120.
60. Ibid., pp. 152–53.
61. Ibid., pp. 129, 150.
62. Wright, p. 44. Coll, *Ghost Wars*, p. 164.
63. Atwan, p. 78. Wright, pp. 124–26.
64. Rashid, *Taliban*, p. 132. Hiro, *Holy Wars*, p. 265. Coll, *Ghost Wars*, pp. 162–63.
65. Hiro, *Holy Wars*, pp. 266–68.
66. Wright, p. 105. Coll, *Ghost Wars*, pp. 165–67.
67. Rashid, *Taliban*, p. 18.
68. Maley, pp. 120–25.
69. Wright, pp. 106–7, 133, 142, 151.
70. Feifer, pp. 255–56. Rashid, *Taliban*, p. 13. Maley, pp. 154–59, 226–28. Coll, *Ghost Wars*, pp. 167–69. Wright, p. 137.

CHAPTER 13: SADDAM
1. Nasr, p. 120.
2. *Etelaat*, Apr. 4, 1983.
3. Nasr, p. 132.
4. Stockholm International Peace Research Institute, *Arms Transfers to Iraq, 1970–2004*.
5. Charles Tripp, *A History of Iraq*, 2nd ed., Cambridge: Cambridge University Press, 2002, p. 235.
6. George Washington University National Security Archive (GWU NSA, www.gwu.edu/~nsarchiv), National Security Decision Directive 99, Washington, Jul. 12, 1983, "United States Security Strategy for the Near East and South Asia," top secret.
7. GWU NSA, National Security Decision Directive 114, Washington, Nov. 26, 1983, "U.S. Policy toward the Iran-Iraq War," top secret.
8. GWU NSA, London, Dec. 21, 1983, American Embassy to Secretary of State, "Rumsfeld Mission: December 20 Meeting with Iraqi President Saddam Hussein," secret.
9. Bob Woodward, "CIA Aiding Iraq in Gulf War; Target Data From U.S. Satellites Supplied for Nearly Two Years," *Washington Post*, Dec. 15, 1986.
10. William Shawcross, *Allies: The U.S., Britain, Europe, and the War in Iraq*, New York: Public Affairs, 2004, pp. 168–69.
11. GWU NSA, London, Dec. 21, 1983, American Embassy to Secretary of State, "Rumsfeld Mission: December 20 Meeting with Iraqi President Saddam Hussein," secret.
12. "The Return of the Iran-Contra Brigade," *Observer*, Dec. 8, 2002.
13. Tyler, pp. 310–13. Timothy Naftali, *Blind Spot: The Secret History of American Counterterrorism*, New York: Basic Books, 2005, pp. 160–62.
14. Magnus Ranstorp, *Hizb'allah in Lebanon: The Politics of the Western Hostage Crisis*, New York: St. Martin's Press, 1997.
15. "What's the Chinese Word for Chutzpah?" *Newsweek*, Nov. 9, 1987. "Bull Market in Silkworms," *New York Times*, Nov. 9, 1987. Michael R. Gordon and Bernard E. Trainor, *The Generals' War*, Boston: Little, Brown, 1995, p. 39.

16. Stephen Pelletière, *America's Oil Wars*, Westport, CT: Praeger, 2004, pp. 92–4.
17. Rick Atkinson, *Crusade: The Untold Story of the Persian Gulf War*, Boston: Houghton Mifflin, 1993, p. 28.
18. Federation of American Scientists archive (www.fas.org), The White House, Oct. 2, 1989, National Security Decision Directive 26, secret.
19. GWU NSA, Defense Estimative Brief, Prospects for Iraq, Sep. 25, 1984.
20. Gordon and Trainor, *Generals' War*, p. 7.
21. Jack Anderson and Dale Van Atta, "Saddam Pulls Back Elite Forces," *Washington Post*, Nov. 5, 1990. Gordon and Trainor, *Generals' War*, pp. 9–12.
22. Gordon and Trainor, *Generals' War*, p. 10.
23. Atkinson, p. 28. Gordon and Trainor, *Generals' War*, p. 14.
24. Atkinson, pp. 28, 52–3.
25. George Bush and Brent Scowcroft, *A World Transformed*, New York: Knopf, 1998, p. 431.
26. Caspar W. Weinberger, *In the Arena: A Memoir of the 20th Century*, Washington, D.C.: Regnery, 2001, pp. 308–13.
27. Atkinson, pp. 121–22. Gordon and Trainor, *Generals' War*, pp. 19–20, 29–30.
28. Gordon and Trainor, *Generals' War*, p. 20.
29. Ibid. pp. 23–4.
30. Atkinson, p. 460. Gordon and Trainor, *Generals' War*, p. 27. Bush and Scowcroft, pp. 339, 374.
31. Michael R. Gordon and Bernard E. Trainor, *Cobra II: The Inside Story of the Invasion and Occupation of Iraq*, New York: Pantheon, 2006, p. 59.
32. Bush and Scowcroft, pp. 313, 317.
33. Ibid., pp. 323, 336, 347.
34. Ibid., pp. 324, 358–59, 372.
35. Tyler, p. 380. Atkinson, p. 193. Gordon and Trainor, *Generals' War*, p. 33. Bush and Scowcroft, p. 396.
36. H. Norman Schwarzkopf, *It Doesn't Take a Hero: The Autobiography*, New York: Bantam, 1992, p. 340. Bush and Scowcroft, pp. 381–83.
37. Gordon and Trainor, *Generals' War*, p. 34.
38. Daalder and Destler, p. 255.
39. Bush and Scowcroft, p. 319.
40. Ibid., pp. 326–28.
41. Gordon and Trainor, *Generals' War*, pp. 39, 47–50. Bush and Scowcroft, pp. 325–26.
42. Bush and Scowcroft, pp. 331–33.
43. Atkinson, pp. 72–3. Gordon and Trainor, *Generals' War*, p. 43.
44. Atkinson, pp. 68–9. Gordon and Trainor, *Generals' War*, pp. 41–2.
45. Gordon and Trainor, *Generals' War*, p. 46.
46. Tyler, pp. 376–77. Bush and Scowcroft, p. 337.
47. Wright, pp. 156–57.
48. Daalder and Destler, p. 254. Gordon and Trainor, *Generals' War*, pp. 54–5.
49. Bush and Scowcroft, pp. 340–41.
50. Schwarzkopf, p. 334. Gordon and Trainor, *Generals' War*, p. 65.
51. Gordon and Trainor, *Generals' War*, p. 61.
52. Schwarzkopf, p. 348. Gordon and Trainor, *Generals' War*, p. 64.
53. Atkinson, p. 72.
54. Schwarzkopf, pp. 332–33. Gordon and Trainor, *Generals' War*, p. 65.
55. John R. MacArthur, *Second Front: Censorship and Propaganda in the Gulf War*, Berkeley: University of California Press, 1992, pp. 63–77.
56. Tyler, pp. 380–81. Alan Simpson, "Gore Traded Vote on the Gulf for Prime-Time TV," Bnet.com, Nov. 6, 2000. Bush and Scowcroft, pp. 445–46.
57. Bush and Scowcroft, p. 339.
58. Anderson and Van Atta, "Saddam Pulls Back Elite Forces." Bush and Scowcroft, pp. 425, 432, 436.
59. Bush and Scowcroft, pp. 389, 417–18, 428.
60. James A. Baker III with Thomas M. DeFrank, *The Politics of Diplomacy: Revolution, War and Peace, 1989–92*, New York: G. P. Putnam's Sons, 1995, pp. 359–61. Daalder and Destler, p. 252. Gordon and Trainor, *Generals' War*, pp. 197–98. Atkinson, p. 56. Bush and Scowcroft, pp. 441–42.

CHAPTER 14: DESERT STORM

1. Atkinson, pp. 34, 56–62. Gordon and Trainor, *Generals' War*, pp. 78–9.
2. Gordon and Trainor, *Generals' War*, pp. 84, 90.
3. Ibid., pp. 188, 190.
4. Atkinson, pp. 44–5. Gordon and Trainor, *Generals' War*, pp. 136, 188.
5. Gordon and Trainor, *Generals' War*, p. 189.
6. Atkinson, p. 49. Gordon and Trainor, *Generals' War*, p. 219.
7. Gordon and Trainor, *Generals' War*, pp. 191–93.
8. Schwarzkopf, p. 417. Gordon and Trainor, *Generals' War*, p. 224.
9. Gordon and Trainor, *Generals' War*, p. 116.
10. Atkinson, pp. 64–5, 217. Gordon and Trainor, *Generals' War*, pp. 314–15.
11. Atkinson, pp. 285–86.
12. Tyler, pp. 386–87. Bush and Scowcroft, pp. 346, 452. Schwarzkopf, pp. 417–19.
13. Schwarzkopf, pp. 350–51, 391. Gordon and Trainor, *Generals' War*, p. 240.
14. Atkinson, pp. 90–2.
15. Tyler, pp. 387–88. Atkinson, p. 131.
16. Atkinson, p. 97. Gordon and Trainor, *Generals' War*, pp. 231–34.
17. Bush and Scowcroft, p. 456.
18. Powell, p. 512. Gordon and Trainor, *Generals' War*, pp. 237–39. Schwarzkopf, pp. 416–21.
19. Mearsheimer and Walt, p. 58.
20. Atkinson, pp. 208–10. Gordon and Trainor, *Generals' War*, pp. 283–84.
21. Schwarzkopf, p. 355. Gordon and Trainor, *Generals' War*, p. 287. Atkinson, p. 212.
22. Atkinson, pp. 144–48. Gordon and Trainor, *Generals' War*, pp. 244, 247.
23. Gordon and Trainor, *Generals' War*, p. 334.
24. Schwarzkopf, pp. 356–67.
25. Powell, p. 503.
26. Atkinson, pp. 94–5. Gordon and Trainor, *Generals' War*, pp. 138–41. Schwarzkopf, pp. 368–70.
27. Schwarzkopf, pp. 401–3. Gordon and Trainor, *Generals' War*, p. 252.
28. Bush and Scowcroft, p. 467.
29. Atkinson, pp. 55, 316.
30. Gordon and Trainor, *Generals' War*, pp. 143–44.
31. Atkinson, pp. 108–15.
32. Schwarzkopf, p. 390. Atkinson, pp. 382, 400–401.
33. Powell, pp. 509–10. Bush and Scowcroft, p. 469. Atkinson, p. 162. Gordon and Trainor, *Generals' War*, p. 266.
34. Gordon and Trainor, *Generals' War*, pp. 153–55, 164, 172, 185–86, 352–54.
35. Atkinson, p. 73. Gordon and Trainor, *Generals' War*, pp. 324–27.
36. Bush and Scowcroft, p. 477.
37. Atkinson, pp. 335–37. Gordon and Trainor, *Generals' War*, pp. 314–15.
38. Atkinson, pp. 99–100, 220.
39. Ibid., p. 493.
40. Schwarzkopf, pp. 431–32, 438–39. Atkinson, pp. 263–66, 366–67. Gordon and Trainor, *Generals' War*, pp. 322–24, 329, 334–35.
41. Bush and Scowcroft, pp. 477–79. Schwarzkopf, pp. 439–42.
42. Atkinson, p. 342.
43. Ibid., p. 170. Gordon and Trainor, *Generals' War*, pp. 293–98.
44. Gordon and Trainor, *Generals' War*, p. 188.
45. Ibid., pp. 302–4.
46. Schwarzkopf, p. 439.
47. Atkinson, pp. 270, 344. Gordon and Trainor, *Generals' War*, pp. 307–8.
48. Schwarzkopf, p. 430.
49. Bush and Scowcroft, p. 484. Atkinson, pp. 345, 420. Gordon and Trainor, *Generals' War*, p. 239.
50. Atkinson, p. 399.
51. Gordon and Trainor, *Generals' War*, p. 289.
52. Ibid., pp. 400–401.

53. Atkinson, p. 450.
54. Powell, p. 518.
55. Atkinson, pp. 465–67.
56. Gordon and Trainor, *Generals' War*, pp. 407–8, 412, 414.
57. Schwarzkopf, p. 439. Powell, p. 520. Atkinson, p. 446. Gordon and Trainor, *Generals' War*, pp. 405.
58. Atkinson, p. 448.
59. Powell, p. 523. Bush and Scowcroft, pp. 485–86.
60. Atkinson, pp. 297, 471, 475–76.
61. Bush and Scowcroft, pp. 486–87.
62. Gordon and Trainor, *Generals' War*, pp. 415–24. Atkinson, pp. 452, 475–76.
63. Gordon and Trainor, *Generals' War*, p. 425.
64. Bush and Scowcroft, p. 487.
65. Thomas E. Ricks, *Fiasco: The American Military Adventure in Iraq*, New York: Penguin Press, 2006, p. 6. Gordon and Trainor, *Generals' War*, p. 432–38. Schwarzkopf, p. 466.
66. Gordon and Trainor, *Generals' War*, pp. 432–33.
67. Ibid., pp. 434–35.
68. Bush and Scowcroft, p. 490.
69. Ibid., p. 472. Gordon and Trainor, *Generals' War*, pp. 443, 446.
70. Schwarzkopf, pp. 473–78. Atkinson, p. 268.
71. Bush and Scowcroft, pp. 489–90.
72. Ibid., pp. 487.
73. Schwarzkopf, p. 480. Daalder and Destler, p. 259.
74. Schwarzkopf, p. 483.
75. Gordon and Trainor, *Generals' War*, p. 446.
76. Ricks, *Fiasco*, p. 5.
77. Atkinson, pp. 299, 490.
78. Bush and Scowcroft, p. 489.
79. Gordon and Trainor, *Generals' War*, p. 452.
80. Gordon and Trainor, *Cobra II*, pp. 11–12.
81. Daalder and Destler, p. 256.
82. Atkinson, p. 490.
83. Ricks, *Fiasco*, p. 7. Gordon and Trainor, *Generals' War*, pp. 447–48, 455–56.
84. Gordon and Trainor, *Generals' War*, p. 448.
85. Wright, p. 160.
86. Robert Fisk, *The Great War for Civilization: The Conquest of the Middle East*, New York: Knopf, 2005, pp. 646–48. Gordon and Trainor, *Generals' War*, pp. 448–51.
87. Jeffrey Record, *Dark Victory: America's Second War Against Iraq*, Annapolis: Naval Institute Press, 2004, p. 3. Daalder and Destler, p. 258.
88. Gordon and Trainor, *Generals' War*, p. 457.
89. Bush and Scowcroft, p. 464.
90. Record, p. 4.
91. Schwarzkopf, p. 498.
92. Ricks, *Fiasco*, pp. 6–7. Charles Pope, "Cheney Changed His View on Iraq," *Seattle Post-Intelligencer*, Sep. 29, 2004.
93. Atkinson, pp. 300–301.
94. Daalder and Destler, pp. 260–63.
95. Record, p. 7.
96. Gordon and Trainor, *Generals' War*, p. 461.
97. Ricks, *Fiasco*, p. 14.
98. Powell, p. 524.

CHAPTER 15: 9/11
1. Rashid, *Taliban*, p. 133. Wright, pp. 156–57.
2. Atwan, pp. 45–6. Wright, pp. 158–60. Rashid, *Taliban*, p. 133.
3. Naftali, pp. 254–55. Atwan, pp. 47–8. Wright, pp. 164–65.
4. Daalder and Destler, p. 282.

5. Wright, p. 172.

6. Ibid., p. 209.

7. Coll, *Ghost Wars*, pp. 268–70. Wright, pp. 170–72.

8. Wright, pp. 188–89.

9. Atwan, pp. 94–8. Wright, p. 219.

10. Rashid, *Taliban*, p. 135–36. Wright, pp. 189–90.

11. Wright, pp. 174–75.

12. Rashid, *Taliban*, p. 130.

13. Griffin, p. 278.

14. Naftali, pp. 252–53, 274.

15. Wright, pp. 183–84.

16. Ibid., p. 178.

17. Atwan, p. 52.

18. Wright, pp. 209–15, 219.

19. Atwan, p. 20.

20. Wright, p. 221.

21. Atwan, pp. 31, 49–52. Wright, pp. 222–23.

22. Coll, *Ghost Wars*, pp. 287–88. Rashid, *Taliban*, p. 17. Wright, pp. 224–29.

23. Maley, pp. 89–90. George Tenet with Bill Harlow, *At the Center of the Storm: My Years at the CIA*, New York: HarperCollins, 2007, pp. 139–41.

24. Naftali, p. 270. Atwan, p. 54. Wright, pp. 235–36.

25. Coll, *Ghost Wars*, pp. 333–35. Wright, pp. 230–31.

26. Atwan, p. 25.

27. Wright, p. 233.

28. Ibid., p. 234.

29. Atwan, pp. 30, 34.

30. Richard A. Clarke, *Against All Enemies: Inside America's War on Terror*, New York: Free Press, 2004, pp. 112–15. Wright, p. 238–39.

31. Atwan, pp. 36, 53.

32. Naftali, pp. 248–50.

33. Wright, pp. 247, 263.

34. Rashid, *Taliban*, p. 138. Naftali, pp. 261–62. Wright, pp. 249–51.

35. Atwan, p. 22.

36. Wright, p. 302.

37. Ibid., pp. 259–61.

38. Ibid., p. 295.

39. Naftali, p. 275.

40. Atwan, pp. 104–5.

41. Tenet, pp. 159, 200–205. Wright, pp. 302–5, 336.

42. Griffin, p. 335. Wright, pp. 303–4.

43. Clarke, pp. 148–49. Naftali, pp. 261–62.

44. Rashid, *Taliban*, p. 138. Naftali, p. 263.

45. Atwan, p. 36. Wright, pp. 264–68.

46. Coll, *Ghost Wars*, pp. 403–5.

47. Naftali, pp. 266–67.

48. Griffin, pp. 227–29. Wright, p. 279.

49. Clarke, pp. 184–90, 204. Rashid, *Taliban*, p. 134. Maley, pp. 248–50. Naftali, pp. 267–69. Atwan, pp. 55–6. Daalder and Destler, pp. 318–19. Wright, pp. 284–86.

50. Griffin, pp. 98–104, 148, 154. Maley, pp. 227–28. Coll, *Ghost Wars*, pp. 311–13.

51. Atwan, pp. 79, 83.

52. Rashid, *Taliban*, p. 140. Atwan, p. 55. Wright, p. 287.

53. Atwan, p. 56.

54. Rashid, *Taliban*, p. 139–40. Naftali, p. 271. Wright, p. 289.

55. Atwan, p. 84. Wright, *Looming Tower*, p. 308.

56. Naftali, pp. 270–71. Wright, pp. 310–11.

57. Wright, pp. 319–20.

58. Ibid., pp. 323–25.
59. Naftali, pp. 278–79.
60. Coll, *Ghost Wars*, pp. 532–34.
61. Barton Gellman, *Angler: The Cheney Vice Presidency*, New York: Penguin Press, 2008, p. 141.
62. Wright, pp. 353–54.
63. Ibid., pp. 329–30.
64. Ibid., pp. 314–15, 342–44.
65. Ibid., pp. 269, 310–11, 340–41.
66. Tenet, p. 142. Naftali, pp. 262–63.
67. Naftali, pp. 280–81.
68. Rashid, *Taliban*, p. 133. Maley, pp. 256–57. Naftali, pp. 280, 287. Wright, pp. 331, 337.
69. Daalder and Destler, p. 320.
70. Clarke, pp. 229–30. Naftali, p. 289.
71. Tenet, pp. 142–44. Daalder and Destler, pp. 336–37. Naftali, pp. 263, 288–89.
72. Coll, *Ghost Wars*, p. 560. Atwan, pp. 36–7.
73. Rashid, *Taliban*, p. 136. Atwan, pp. 196–97.
74. Atwan, pp. 102–3. Wright, pp. 337–38.
75. Naftali, p. 284.
76. Tenet, pp. 150–55. Wright, p. 344.
77. Tenet, pp. 155–56.
78. Clarke, pp. 230–32. Naftali, pp. 292–93. Daalder and Destler, pp. 337–41.
79. Olivier Roy, *The Politics of Chaos in the Middle East*, New York: Columbia University Press, 2008, p. 14.
80. Gordon and Trainor, *Cobra II*, pp. 5–6. Tenet, p. 154. Naftali, pp. 289–90, 299–302.
81. Maley, p. 251.
82. Anthony Davis, "Ahmadshah Massoud: Commander of Afghanistan's United Front," *Jane's Defence Weekly*, Jun. 27, 2001.
83. Paul Haven, "Spanish Report: Document Says Pakistan Spy Agency Helped Taliban," Associated Press, Oct. 2, 2008.
84. Wright, pp. 350, 356.
85. Griffin, pp. 259–62. Maley, pp. 251–52. Wright, pp. 358–60.
86. Wright, pp. 361, 368.
87. Bob Woodward, *Bush at War*, New York: Simon & Schuster, 2002, p. 39.

CHAPTER 16: ENDURING FREEDOM
1. Griffin, pp. 280, 327.
2. Atwan, pp. 39, 99, 110. Wright, pp. 369–70.
3. Griffin, pp. 273–74.
4. Tenet, pp. 207–8.
5. Griffin, pp. 270–72. Maley, pp. 259–60.
6. Tenet, pp. 214–15.
7. Woodward, *Bush at War*, p. 52.
8. Maley, p. 263.
9. Ahmed Rashid, *Descent into Chaos: The United States and the Failure of Nation Building in Pakistan, Afghanistan and Central Asia*, New York: Viking, 2008, pp. 96–7.
10. Sean Naylor, *Not a Good Day to Die: The Untold Story of Operation Anaconda*, New York: Berkley, 2005, p. 18. Griffin, p. 285.
11. Gordon and Trainor, *Cobra II*, p. 10.
12. Griffin, p. 290.
13. Ibid., pp. 297–98. Tenet, p. 218. Maley, p. 264.
14. Maley, pp. 264–65.
15. Griffin, p. 301.
16. Ibid., p. 306.
17. Rashid, *Descent*, pp. 90–94. Griffin, pp. 312–15.
18. Maley, pp. 266–68. Griffin, p. 320.
19. Griffin, pp. 311, 317–18, 322–23.

20. Tom Lasseter, "Afghanistan: Mass Grave Site Still Unprotected," *Miami Herald,* Dec. 19, 2008. Griffin, pp. 316, 361–62. Rashid, *Descent,* pp. 93–94.

21. Dalton Fury, *Kill Bin Laden: A Delta Force Commander's Account of the Hunt for the World's Most Wanted Man,* New York: St. Martin's, 2008, p. xxii. Griffin, p. 320.

22. Griffin, pp. 273, 338. Tommy Franks, *American Soldier,* New York: Regan Books, 2004, p. 324. Rashid, *Descent,* p. 99.

23. Michael DeLong with Noah Lukeman, *Inside CENTCOM: The Unvarnished Truth about the Wars in Afghanistan and Iraq,* Washington, D.C.: Regnery, 2004, p. 50.

24. Fury, p. 244. Griffin, pp. 321–22.

25. Griffin, p. 324.

26. Fury, p. 269. Griffin, pp. 321, 325.

27. DeLong, p. 55.

28. Ibid., p. 56.

29. Atwan, p. 62.

30. Naylor, pp. 20–21.

31. Rashid, *Descent,* pp. 98–99. Tenet, pp. 226–27. DeLong, p. 57. Griffin, p. 331.

32. Griffin, pp. 325, 330–32, 356–57.

33. Atwan, pp. 82–3.

34. Ibid., p. 122.

35. Franks, p. 379.

36. Naylor, pp. 55–6.

37. Ibid., p. 86.

38. Ibid., p. 131.

39. Griffin, pp. 345–49.

40. Franks, p. 381.

41. DeLong, p. 76. Griffin, p. 321.

42. Naylor, pp. 376–77. Griffin, p. 350.

43. Gary C. Schroen, *First In: An Insider's Account of How the CIA Spearheaded the War on Terror in Afghanistan,* New York: Ballantine, 2005, p. 361.

44. Griffin, pp. 118–21. Rashid, *Taliban,* pp. 189–90.

45. Gordon and Trainor, *Cobra II,* pp. 5–6. Daalder and Destler, pp. 346–47. Griffin, pp. 356–59.

46. Tenet, p. 176.

47. Wright, pp. 372–73.

CHAPTER 17: INTO IRAQ

1. Atwan, p. 179.

2. Griffin, p. 368.

3. Atwan, pp. 87–8, 180–81.

4. Daalder and Destler, pp. 321–22.

5. Gellman, pp. 57–60.

6. Gordon and Trainor, *Cobra II,* pp. 38–41. Daalder and Destler, pp. 324–25.

7. Ricks, *Fiasco,* p. 134. Daalder and Destler, p. 344.

8. Daalder and Destler, p. 344.

9. Ron Suskind, "What Bush Meant," *Esquire,* Oct. 2008.

10. Tenet, pp. 259–60.

11. Ibid., pp. 261–62.

12. Dexter Filkins, "The Long Road to Chaos in Pakistan," *New York Times,* Sep. 28, 2008. Steve Coll, "The Back Channel: India and Pakistan's Secret Kashmir Talks," *New Yorker,* Mar. 2, 2009.

13. Daalder and Destler, p. 345.

14. Engdahl, pp. 246–47.

15. Bob Woodward, *Plan of Attack,* New York: Simon & Schuster, 2004, p. 187. Record, pp. 18–19.

16. Daalder and Destler, pp. 347–48.

17. Atwan, p. 184.

18. Engdahl, pp. 246–50.

19. Future of Iraq Project, U.S. Department of State, Nov. 1, 2002.

20. Hans Blix, *Disarming Iraq,* New York: Pantheon, 2004, p. 230.

21. Roy, *Chaos*, p. 17. Record, p. 24.
22. Gordon and Trainor, *Cobra II*, p. 27. "U.S. Prepared for Iraq Long Before Attack, Book Says," *Baltimore Sun*, Sep. 6, 2004. Blix, pp. 58, 70.
23. Ricks, *Fiasco*, pp. 40, 67.
24. Daalder and Destler, p. 358.
25. Tenet, pp. 239–42.
26. Ibid., pp. 242–43, 248–49, 254, 272–75.
27. Blix, pp. 58–9.
28. Gordon and Trainor, *Cobra II*, p. 69.
29. Tenet, p. 139.
30. Ricks, *Fiasco*, p. 17. Daalder and Destler, p. 281.
31. Gordon and Trainor, *Cobra II*, p. 18.
32. Ricks, *Fiasco*, pp. 22–3.
33. Gordon and Trainor, *Cobra II*, p. 127. Tenet, pp. 341, 350–55.
34. Record, p. 89. Ricks, *Fiasco*, pp. 308–9.
35. Jeffrey Goldberg, "A Little Learning—What Douglas Feith Knew and When He Knew It," *New Yorker*, May 9, 2005. Tenet, p. 354.
36. Tenet, p. 332.
37. Daalder and Destler, pp. 345, 361.
38. Gellman, pp. 222–25.
39. Tenet, p. 342.
40. Mearsheimer and Walt, p. 239. Ricks, *Fiasco*, p. 7.
41. Gellman, p. 88.
42. Record, pp. 20–24. Ricks, *Fiasco*, p. 17.
43. Mearsheimer, and Walt, p. 239.
44. Gordon and Trainor, *Cobra II*, p. 15. Tenet, pp. xix, 306. Ricks, *Fiasco*, pp. 47–8.
45. Ricks, *Fiasco*, p. 15.
46. Gellman, p. 112. Blix, p. 70.
47. Blix, p. 71.
48. Thomas C. Reed and Danny B. Stillman, *The Nuclear Express: A Political History of the Bomb and Its Proliferation*. Minneapolis: Zenith, 2009, pp. 282–85. Ricks, *Fiasco*, pp. 49–51.
49. Reed and Stillman, p. 20.
50. Tenet, p. 302.
51. Ibid., pp. 343–44.
52. Ricks, *Fiasco*, p. 78. Tenet, p. 315.
53. Gellman, pp. 240–43. "Leak Probe Focus Seems to Widen," *Wall Street Journal*, Oct. 12, 2005.
54. Blix, p. 61.
55. Tenet, pp. 307, 373.
56. Atwan, pp. 190–91.
57. Suskind, "What Bush Meant." Seymour M. Hersh, "The Coming Wars: What the Pentagon Can Now Do in Secret," *New Yorker*, Jan. 24 and 31, 2005.
58. John Diamond, "Review Faults Prewar Plans," *USA Today*, Oct. 12, 2005.
59. Bob Woodward, *Bush at War*, p. 113.
60. Suskind, "What Bush Meant."
61. Griffin, p. 233. Daalder and Destler, pp. 329–31, 356–57. Gordon and Trainor, *Cobra II*, pp. 147–48. Gellman, pp. 240–42.
62. Gellman, pp. 51–3, 225.
63. Tenet, p. 319.
64. Woodward, *Plan of Attack*, pp. 247–50.
65. Ron Suskind, *The Price of Loyalty: George W. Bush, the White House, and the Education of Paul O'Neill*, New York: Simon & Schuster, 2004, p. 327. Joseph E. Stiglitz and Linda J. Bilmes, *The Three Trillion Dollar War: The True Cost of the Iraq Conflict*, New York: Norton, 2008, pp. 7–9.
66. Blix, p. 259. Daalder and Destler, pp. 348–56, 359–60. Ricks, *Fiasco*, pp. 13, 47.
67. Gellman, p. 105.
68. Daalder and Destler, p. 327–29, 354.
69. Bush and Scowcroft, p. 354.

70. Rajiv Chandrasekaran, *Imperial Life in the Emerald City: Inside Iraq's Green Zone,* New York: Knopf, 2006, pp. 29–31. Gordon and Trainor, *Cobra II,* p. 159.

71. Tenet, pp. 356–58.

72. Gellman, p. 216.

73. Bob Woodward, *The War Within: A Secret White House History 2006–2008,* New York: Simon & Schuster, 2008, p. 117. Ricks, *Fiasco,* p. 93.

74. Michael Isikoff and David Corn, *Hubris: The Inside Story of Spin, Scandal and the Selling of the Iraq War,* New York: Crown, 2006, pp. 56–61, 207, 215–21. Ricks, *Fiasco,* pp. 35, 381–84.

75. David Remnick, "Checkpoint," *New Yorker,* Feb. 7, 2005.

76. Mearsheimer and Walt, p. 216.

77. Suskind, *Price of Loyalty,* pp. 288–90. Roger Cohen, "Ariel Sharon Deploys a Paradoxical Strategy," *International Herald Tribune,* Jul. 21, 2004. Daalder and Destler, pp. 370–71.

78. James Bamford, *A Pretext for War: 9/11, Iraq and the Abuse of America's Intelligence Agencies,* New York: Doubleday, 2004, p. 265. Daalder and Destler, p. 369.

79. Roy, *Chaos,* pp. 23–4.

80. Bamford, pp. 266–69.

81. Mearsheimer and Walt, pp. 231–35. Remnick, "Checkpoint."

82. Tenet, pp. 309–10.

83. Ricks, *Fiasco,* p. 15.

84. Blix, p. 263.

85. Walter Pincus, "Ex-Iraqi Official Unveiled as Spy," *Washington Post,* Mar. 23, 2006. Sidney Blumenthal, "Bush Knew Saddam Had No Weapons of Mass Destruction," Salon.com, Sep. 6, 2007.

86. Tenet, pp. 321–33, 375–83.

87. Gordon and Trainor, *Cobra II,* pp. 133–34.

88. Colum Lynch, "UN: Iraqi Drones Were No Threat," *Washington Post,* Sep. 5, 2004. Blix, pp. 221–28. Gordon and Trainor, *Cobra II,* pp. 128–29. Ricks, *Fiasco,* pp. 62, 86.

89. Blix, p. 70.

90. Record, pp. 9–10.

91. Gordon and Trainor, *Cobra II,* pp. 66, 121.

92. Ibid., p. 65. Tenet, p. 332.

93. Ricks, *Fiasco,* p. 38. Tenet, pp. 331–32.

94. Blix, p. 265.

95. Gordon and Trainor, *Cobra II,* p. 57.

96. Atwan, p. 186.

97. Gordon and Trainor, *Cobra II,* pp. 58–9.

98. Blix, p. 185.

99. Ibid., p. 190.

100. Gordon and Trainor, *Cobra II,* p. 71. Daalder and Destler, pp. 349–50.

101. GWU NSA, Feb. 7, 2003, "State Department Experts Warned CENTCOM before Iraq War about Lack of Plans for Postwar Iraq Security." Daalder and Destler, pp. 357–58.

102. Jill Abramson, "The Final Days," *New York Times Book Review,* Sep. 28, 2008.

103. "Army Chief: Force to Occupy Iraq Massive," Associated Press, Feb. 25, 2003.

104. Franks, pp. 394–97. Gordon and Trainor, *Cobra II,* pp. 103–5.

105. Tenet, pp. 317–18.

106. Richard Whittle, "General: Iraq 'Stretching the Army,'" *Dallas Morning News,* Jul. 13, 2004.

107. Isikoff and Corn, p. 207. Ricks, *Fiasco,* pp. 96–100.

108. "Administration Fends Off Demands for War Estimates," Mar. 3, 2003, CNN.com. Gordon and Trainor, *Cobra II,* p. 102.

109. Tenet, p. 420.

110. Ricks, *Fiasco,* p. 20.

111. Barbara Slavin and Dave Moniz, "How Peace in Iraq Became So Elusive," *USA Today,* Jul. 22, 2003. Tenet, pp. 424–25.

112. Ricks, *Fiasco,* pp. 82–3, 103.

113. Gordon and Trainor, *Cobra II,* pp. 3–5, 95–7. Ricks, *Fiasco,* pp. 68–9.

114. Slavin and Moniz, "How Peace in Iraq Became So Elusive."

115. Woodward, *War Within,* pp. 147–51. Gordon and Trainor, *Cobra II,* p. 142.

116. Chandrasekaran, p. 48.
117. Ricks, *Fiasco*, p. 20.
118. Gordon and Trainor, *Cobra II*, pp. 72–4. Blix, p. 71. Daalder and Destler, pp. 363–65. Tenet, pp. 420–21. Slavin and Moniz, "How Peace in Iraq Became So Elusive."
119. Ricks, *Fiasco*, p. 77.
120. Ibid. pp. 16, 163–64. Chandrasekaran, pp. 49, 69. Gordon and Trainor, *Cobra II*, pp. 160–63.
121. Gordon and Trainor, *Cobra II*, p. 145.
122. Douglas Jehl, "Bush Cited Two Allies over Arms, Book Says," *New York Times*, Oct. 14, 2005.
123. Blix, pp. 110, 112, 194.
124. "Iraq War Illegal, Says Annan," BBC News, Sep. 16, 2004.
125. Blix, p. 91.
126. Gellman, pp. 229–33.
127. Ibid., pp. 215–22. "Armey Says Cheney Misled Him about Iraq," *Dallas Morning News*, Sep. 16, 2008.
128. Daalder and Destler, pp. 350–51.
129. Ricks, *Fiasco*, p. 42.
130. Gordon and Trainor, *Cobra II*, p. 93. Ricks, *Fiasco*, p. 33.
131. Ricks, *Fiasco*, p. 33.
132. Gordon and Trainor, *Cobra II*, pp. 25–9, 35, 47, 92, 97–8.

CHAPTER 18: IRAQI FREEDOM

1. Atkinson, p. 273.
2. Gordon and Trainor, *Cobra II*, pp. 35, 112–14.
3. Ibid., pp. 346–47, 357–58.
4. Atwan, p. 198. Tenet, pp. 396–97. Gordon and Trainor, *Cobra II*, pp. 89, 209.
5. Gordon and Trainor, *Cobra II*, p. 124.
6. Dexter Filkins, *The Forever War*, New York: Knopf, 2008, p. 105.
7. Steve Coll, "The General's Dilemma," *New Yorker*, Sep. 8, 2008. Gordon and Trainor, *Cobra II*, pp. 257–59.
8. Franks, pp. 466, 477, 522.
9. DeLong, p. 118.
10. Ricks, *Fiasco*, pp. 125, 141, 232–35. Gordon and Trainor, *Cobra II*, p. 446.
11. Roy, *Chaos*, pp. 110–11. Gordon and Trainor, *Cobra II*, pp. 448–53.
12. Gordon and Trainor, *Cobra II*, pp. 342, 408–9.
13. Martin Van Creveld, *The Changing Face of War: Lessons of Combat from the Marne to Iraq*, New York: Ballantine, 2006, pp. 248–49.
14. Chandrasekaran, p. 42. Ricks, *Fiasco*, p. 99.
15. Ahmed Hashim, *Insurgency and Counter-Insurgency in Iraq*, Ithaca: Cornell University Press, 2006, pp. 99–124. Atwan, pp. 200–201.
16. Franks, p. 508. Gordon and Trainor, *Cobra II*, pp. 311–12. Ricks, *Fiasco*, pp. 124–25.
17. Ricks, *Fiasco*, p. 80.
18. Chandrasekaran, pp. 32–5.
19. Ibid., p. 64.
20. Ibid., pp. 4–5. Tenet, pp. 426–27.
21. Ricks, *Fiasco*, p. 164.
22. Tenet, p. 420.
23. Coll, "The General's Dilemma."
24. Daalder and Destler, p. 367. Ricks, *Fiasco*, pp. 83–4.
25. Woodward, *War Within*, pp. 147–51.
26. Ricks, *Fiasco*, pp. 84, 120–23, 136. Gordon and Trainor, *Cobra II*, pp. 460–61.
27. Gordon and Trainor, *Cobra II*, p. 464.
28. Ibid., p. 476. Chandrasekaran, pp. 40–42, 70–71.
29. Gordon and Trainor, *Cobra II*, pp. 467–68. Chandrasekaran, p. 30.
30. Ricks, *Fiasco*, p. 180. Tenet, pp. 428–30, 441–42.
31. Atwan, p. 199. Ricks, *Fiasco*, p. 145.
32. Tenet, p. 429.
33. Ibid., p. 430.

34. Ibid., p. 430.
35. Franks, pp. 489, 530–31. Ricks, *Fiasco*, p. 78.
36. Ricks, *Fiasco*, p. 79.
37. Peter R. Mansoor, *Baghdad at Sunrise: A Brigade Commander's War in Iraq*, New Haven: Yale University Press, 2008, pp. 344–46. Record, p. 11. Ricks, *Fiasco*, pp. 130–33.
38. Ricks, *Fiasco*, pp. 155–56.
39. Gordon and Trainor, *Cobra II*, pp. 163, 486. Ricks, *Fiasco*, pp. 135, 183.
40. Atwan, p. 201. Ricks, *Fiasco*, p. 200.
41. Filkins, *Forever War*, p. 82.
42. Chandrasekaran, pp. 54–5.
43. Blix, pp. 256–57.
44. Ricks, *Fiasco*, pp. 181–82.
45. Gordon and Trainor, *Cobra II*, pp. 475–76. Chandrasekaran, pp. 63–4.
46. Chandrasekaran, pp. 50, 56–7. Ricks, *Fiasco*, p. 213.
47. Filkins, *Forever War*, p. 82.
48. Tenet, pp. 422–23. Chandrasekaran, pp. 28–9.
49. Ricks, *Fiasco*, pp. 203–4. Chandrasekaran, pp. 4, 11.
50. Woodward, *War Within*, p. 110.
51. Filkins, *Forever War*, p. 83.
52. Gordon and Trainor, *Cobra II*, pp. 477–78.
53. Chandrasekaran, pp. 58–64.
54. Ricks, *Fiasco*, p. 145. Tenet, pp. 321, 361.
55. Chandrasekaran, p. 61.
56. Tenet, pp. 437–38.
57. Patrick J. McDonnell and Suhail Ahmed, "Resentment Is Festering in 'Little Falloujas,'" *Los Angeles Times*, Jul. 13, 2004. Seymour Hersh, "The Gray Zone," *New Yorker*, May 24, 2004.
58. David Ignatius, "A Report from Iraq 2.0," *Washington Post*, Jul. 13, 2004.
59. T. Christian Miller, "Pentagon Waste in Iraq May Total Billions, Investigators Say," *Los Angeles Times*, Jun. 16, 2004. Chandrasekaran, pp. 13–15.
60. T. Christian Miller, *Blood Money: Wasted Billions, Lost Lives, and Corporate Greed in Iraq*, New York: Little Brown, 2006, pp. 57–61.
61. "Government Watch: U.S. Bribery in Iraq," *Parade*, Oct. 26, 2008. Atwan, pp. 211–12.
62. "Iraq: Fraud Fighters Quietly Fired," *Dallas Morning News*, Nov. 18, 2008.
63. Ricks, *Fiasco*, p. 172.
64. Ibid., pp. 175–76.
65. Ibid., p. 157. Daalder and Destler, pp. 367–68.
66. Suskind, "What Bush Meant." Blix, p. 269.
67. DeLong, pp. 77–8.
68. Gordon and Trainor, *Cobra II*, pp. 106–7. Tenet, pp. 418–20.
69. Tenet, pp. 397–99, 440.
70. Ibid., pp. 398–99.
71. Ricks, *Fiasco*, pp. 123, 388–89. Tenet, pp. 445–46.
72. Jon Lee Anderson, "A Man of the Shadows," *New Yorker*, Jan. 24 and 31, 2005. Ricks, *Fiasco*, pp. 154, 390.
73. Nasr, pp. 244–45.
74. Ignatius, "A Report from Iraq 2.0."
75. Ricks, *Fiasco*, pp. 391–92.
76. Filkins, *Forever War*, pp. 89–90.
77. Atwan, p. 64.
78. Ricks, *Fiasco*, pp. 330–37, 344–46, 401–5, 409. Gordon and Trainor, *Cobra II*, p. 462. "Iraq by the Numbers," *Atlantic Monthly*, Jul.–Aug. 2004. Blix, p. 230.
79. Ricks, *Fiasco*, pp. 375–78.
80. Amy Goldstein, "'We Were Right to Go into Iraq,' Bush Says," *Washington Post*, Jul. 13, 2004.
81. Atwan, pp. 10, 63, 206.
82. Ibid., p. 39.
83. C. J. Chivers, "Power: The Vladimir Putin Story," *Esquire*, Oct. 2008.
84. Ricks, *Fiasco*, pp. 380–81.

85. Ibid., pp. 430–31.

86. Tenet, pp. 434–36. Ricks, *Fiasco*, p. 350. Hersh, "The Gray Zone."

87. Ricks, *Fiasco*, p. 362.

88. Bruce Hoffman, "Plan of Attack," *Atlantic Monthly*, Jul.–Aug. 2004. Ricks, *Fiasco*, pp. 392–98.

89. Hersh, "The Gray Zone."

90. Ricks, *Fiasco*, pp. 197–200. Hersh, "The Gray Zone."

91. Kevin Lamarque, "U.S. Major General Geoffrey Miller Testifies before the Senate Armed Services Committee on Capitol Hill about Iraqi Prisoner Abuse on May 19, 2004," Reuters, May 15, 2009. Seymour Hersh, "Torture at Abu Ghraib," *New Yorker*, May 10, 2004. Ricks, *Fiasco*, pp. 292–93.

92. Ricks, *Fiasco*, pp. 270–74. Hoffman, "Plan of Attack."

93. Filkins, *Forever War*, p. 91.

94. Ricks, *Fiasco*, p. 369.

95. Tenet, pp. 417–18.

96. Chandrasekaran, p. 5.

97. Steven Komarow, "Army Division Sees Its Iraq Tour Extended and Its Casualties Rise," Associated Press, Jun. 16, 2004.

98. Ricks, *Fiasco*, pp. 217–21.

99. Georgie Anne Geyer, "Troubling Army Omens," *Washington Times*, Jul. 13, 2004.

100. Coll, "The General's Dilemma."

101. Ricks, *Fiasco*, p. 363.

102. Ibid., pp. 372–73.

103. William M. Arkin, "Kerry: A Lighter Shade of Bush," *Los Angeles Times*, Jun. 20, 2004.

104. Eyal Zisser, "The Withdrawal of Syrian Forces from Lebanon," *Tel Aviv Notes*, Sep. 27, 2004.

105. Hersh, "The Coming Wars."

106. Paul Klebnikov, "Millionaire Mullahs: Who Controls Today's Iran?" *Forbes*, Jul. 7, 2003. Seymour M. Hersh, "Shifting Targets: The Administration's Plan for Iran," *New Yorker*, Oct. 8, 2007.

107. "Iran Reports Successful Test of New Ballistic Missile," *International Herald Tribune*, Aug. 12, 2004. Hersh, "The Coming Wars."

108. Nasr, pp. 241–42.

109. Woodward, *War Within*, pp. 346–47.

110. Thomas P. M. Barnett, "Hassan Nasrallah," *Esquire*, Oct. 2008.

111. Nasr, pp. 242–46.

112. Henry A. Kissinger, "Center of Gravity Shifts in International Affairs," *San Diego Union-Tribune*, Jul. 4, 2004.

113. Atwan, pp. 210, 213.

114. Ibid., pp. 198, 204.

115. "Al-Qaeda Seeks Plan if U.S. Deserts Iraq," *Dallas Morning News*, Oct. 12, 2005.

116. "Updated Iraq Survey Affirms Earlier Mortality Estimates," Johns Hopkins Bloomberg School of Public Health, Oct. 11, 2006.

117. "UNHCR Worried about Effect of Dire Security Situation on Iraq's Displaced," Office of the United Nations High Commissioner for Refugees, Oct. 13, 2006.

118. Thomas Friedman, "This War Is Over if the Sunnis Don't Get on Board," *New York Times*, Sep. 29, 2005.

119. "Iraq Tensions Seething, U.S. Told," *Dallas Morning News*, Sep. 23, 2005.

120. "Bush Warns Militants May Take Over Iraq if U.S. leaves," *Dallas Morning News*, Oct. 7, 2005.

121. Ignatius, "A Report from Iraq 2.0."

122. Woodward, *War Within*, pp. 115, 226.

123. "Senate Armed Services Committee Holds Hearing on Current Situation in Iraq and Afghanistan," Congressional Transcripts, *Congressional Quarterly*, Nov. 15, 2006.

124. David Cloud and Eric Schmitt, "Pentagon Says Iraqi Forces Are Improving, But Still Can't Fight Alone," *New York Times*, Oct. 14, 2005.

125. Jon Lee Anderson, "A Man of the Shadows," *New Yorker*, Jan. 24 and 31, 2005.

126. Thomas Friedman, "This War Is Over if the Sunnis Don't Get on Board."

127. "Attacks in Iraq at All-Time High, Pentagon Report Says," Online NewsHour, PBS, Dec. 19, 2006.

128. "Government Watch: Who's Left in the Coalition?" *Parade*, Jan. 13, 2008. David E. Sanger, "The Struggle for Iraq: Bush Adding 20,000 U.S. Troops; Sets Goal of Securing Baghdad," *New York Times*, Jan. 11, 2007.

129. Thomas E. Ricks, *The Gamble: General David Petraeus and the American Military Adventure in Iraq, 2006–2008*, New York: Penguin Press, 2009, pp. 244–54. Lolita Baldor, "More Convicted Felons Allowed to Enlist in Army, Marines," Associated Press, Apr. 21, 2008.
130. Woodward, *War Within*, p. 223. Daalder and Destler, pp. 379–80. Coll, "The General's Dilemma."
131. Ricks, *Gamble*, pp. 228–32.
132. Mansoor, pp. 342–48. "U.S. Army: Doctrine Stresses Nation-Building," *Dallas Morning News*, Oct. 5, 2008. Coll, "The General's Dilemma."
133. Woodward, *War Within*, pp. 379–81. Connie Bruck, "Odd Man Out: Chuck Hagel's Republican Exile," *New Yorker*, Nov. 3, 2008.
134. Coll, "The General's Dilemma."
135. Ibid.
136. Mansoor, pp. 234–35.
137. Woodward, *War Within*, p. 381. Filkins, *Forever War*, p. 175. Coll, "The General's Dilemma."
138. Ricks, *Gamble*, pp. 278–83.
139. Robert Draper, "Old as the Hill," *GQ*, Sep. 2008.
140. Ricks, *Gamble*, pp. 274–75. Woodward, *War Within*, pp. 408–9.
141. "Changed General Takes Over," *Dallas Morning News*, Sep. 17, 2008. Gordon and Trainor, *Cobra II*, p. 447.
142. Andrew J. Bacevich, "Sycophant Savior: General Petraeus Wins a Battle in Washington—If Not in Baghdad," *American Conservative*, Oct. 8, 2007.
143. Coll, "The General's Dilemma."
144. Ricks, *Gamble*, pp. 260–72, 196. Woodward, *War Within*, pp. 383–84.
145. Ricks, *Gamble*, pp. 286, 296–97.
146. Coll, "The General's Dilemma."

CONCLUSION

1. Goldberg, "A Little Learning."
2. Reed and Stillman, pp. 291–301.
3. BNA, WO 106/189, London, Feb. 6, 1919, General Staff, "Notes on Zionism," secret.
4. Fraser, *USA*, p. xi.
5. Kirk, *The Middle East 1945–1950*, p. 247.
6. Yaqub, p. 116. Kyle, p. 538.
7. Mearsheimer and Walt, pp. 38, 158–59. Alteras, p. 226.
8. NARA, RG 59, 1970–73, Box 2389, Department of State Research Study, May 7, 1970, David Mark, "Washington and Tel Aviv: Clashing Interests Amidst Interdependence," secret.
9. Tyler, pp. 387–88.
10. Kevin Phillips, *American Theocracy: The Peril and Politics of Radical Religion, Oil and Borrowed Money in the 21st Century*, New York: Viking, 2006, pp. 250–55.
11. Bill Clinton, *My Life*, New York: Knopf, 2004, p. 944.
12. Bamford, pp. 265–66.
13. Yaqub, pp. 217, 243.
14. Tyler, p. 490.
15. Liddell Hart, *Strategy*, p. 353.
16. BNA, FCO 17/9, London, Aug. 11, 1967, Willie Morris, "Revolutionary and Non-Revolutionary Regimes in the Middle East."

BIBLIOGRAPHY

ABRAHAMIAN, ERVAND. *Khomeinism: Essays on the Islamic Republic.* Berkeley: University of California Press, 1993.

ABURISH, SAID K. *Nasser: The Last Arab.* New York: St. Martin's, 2004.

ACHARYA, AMITAV. *U.S. Military Strategy in the Gulf.* London: Routledge, 1989.

ADELSON, ROGER. *London and the Invention of the Middle East: Money, Power and War.* New Haven: Yale University Press, 1995.

ALAM, ASADOLLAH. *The Shah and I: The Confidential Diary of Iran's Royal Court.* New York: St. Martin's, 1991.

ALI, SHEIKH R. *Oil and Power: Political Dynamics in the Middle East.* New York: St. Martin's, 1987.

AL-RASHEED, MADAWI. *A History of Saudi Arabia.* Cambridge: Cambridge University Press, 2002.

ALTERAS, ISAAC. *Eisenhower and Israel: US-Israeli Relations 1953–1960.* Gainesville: University Press of Florida, 1993.

AMERICAN CHRISTIAN PALESTINE COMMITTEE. *The Arab War Effort: A Documented Account.* New York: ACPC, 1947.

AMIRAHMADI, HOOSHANG and NADER ENTESSAR. *Reconstruction and Regional Diplomacy in the Persian Gulf.* London: Routledge, 1992.

AMUZEGAR, JAHANGIR. *The Dynamics of the Iranian Revolution.* Albany: State University of New York Press, 1991.

ANDERSON, IRVINE H. *Aramco, the United States and Saudi Arabia: A Study of the Dynamics of Foreign Oil Policy, 1933–50.* Princeton: Princeton University Press, 1981.

ANSCOMBE, FREDERICK F. *The Ottoman Gulf: The Creation of Kuwait, Saudi Arabia and Qatar.* New York: Columbia University Press, 1997.

ARON, RAYMOND. *De Gaulle, Israel and the Jews.* New York: Transaction, 2004. Originally published 1969.

ARONSON, SHLOMO. *Hitler, the Allies, and the Jews.* Cambridge: Cambridge University Press, 2004.

ASHTON, NIGEL JOHN. *Eisenhower, Macmillan and the Problem of Nasser: Anglo-American Relations and Arab Nationalism 1955–59.* London: Macmillan, 1996.

ASLAN, REZA. *No god but God: The Origins, Evolution, and Future of Islam.* New York: Random House, 2005.

ATIYAH, EDWARD. *An Arab Tells His Story: A Study in Loyalties.* London: John Murray, 1946.

ATKINSON, RICK. *Crusade: The Untold Story of the Persian Gulf War.* Boston: Houghton Mifflin, 1993.

ATWAN, ABDEL BARI. *The Secret History of al Qaeda.* Berkeley: University of California Press, 2006.

AVERY, P., G. R. G. HAMBLY and C. MELVILLE. *The Cambridge History of Iran,* vol. 7. Cambridge: Cambridge University Press, 1991.

BAKER, JAMES A. III with THOMAS M. DEFRANK. *The Politics of Diplomacy: Revolution, War and Peace, 1989–92.* New York: G. P. Putnam's Sons, 1995.

BALFOUR-PAUL, GLEN. *The End of Empire in the Middle East.* Cambridge: Cambridge University Press, 1994.

BAMBERG, JAMES. *British Petroleum and Global Oil 1950–1975: The Challenge of Nationalism.* Cambridge: Cambridge University Press, 2000.

BAMFORD, JAMES. *A Pretext for War: 9/11, Iraq and the Abuse of America's Intelligence Agencies.* New York: Doubleday, 2004.

BARAHENI, REZA. *The Crowned Cannibals: Writings on Repression in Iran.* New York: Vintage, 1977.

BARGHOUTI, MOURID. *I Saw Ramallah.* New York: Anchor, 2003.

BARRACLOUGH, GEOFFREY. *Survey of International Affairs: 1956–1958.* London: Oxford University Press, 1962.

BARRACLOUGH, GEOFFREY and RACHEL F. WALL. *Survey of International Affairs: 1955–1956.* London: Oxford University Press, 1960.

BASS, WARREN. *Support Any Friend: Kennedy's Middle East and the Making of the U.S.-Israel Alliance.* Oxford: Oxford University Press, 2003.

BAYOUMI, MOUSTAFA and ANDREW RUBIN, eds. *The Edward Said Reader.* New York: Vintage, 2000.

BEAUFRE, ANDRÉ. *The Suez Expedition 1956.* New York: Praeger, 1969.

BEGIN, MENACHEM. *The Revolt: Story of the Irgun.* New York: Schuman, 1951.

BEHBEHANI, HASHIM A. *The Soviet Union and Arab Nationalism 1917–1966.* London: KPI, 1986.

BELL, CORAL. *Survey of International Affairs: 1954.* London: Oxford University Press, 1957.

BENAZET, HENRY. *L'Afrique française en danger.* Paris: Fayard, 1947.

BERKOWITZ, MICHAEL. *Western Jewry and the Zionist Project 1914–33.* Cambridge: Cambridge University Press, 2003.

BILL, JAMES A. and WILLIAM ROGER LOUIS. *Musaddiq, Iranian Nationalism and Oil.* Austin: University of Texas Press, 1988.

BLACK, IAN and BENNY MORRIS. *Israel's Secret Wars: A History of Israel's Intelligence Services.* New York: Grove Weidenfeld, 1991.

BLIX, HANS. *Disarming Iraq.* New York: Pantheon, 2004.

BLOCH, JONATHAN and PATRICK FITZGERALD. *British Intelligence and Covert Action: Africa, Middle East and Europe since 1945.* Kerry, Ireland: Brandon, 1983.

BORDEN, MARY. *Journey down a Blind Alley.* New York: Harper, 1946.

BOYLE, PETER G. *The Eden-Eisenhower Correspondence 1955–57.* Chapel Hill: University of North Carolina Press, 2005.

BREGMAN, AHRON. *Israel's Wars: A History since 1947,* 2nd ed. London: Routledge, 2002.

BRONSON, RACHEL. *Thicker Than Oil: America's Uneasy Partnership with Saudi Arabia.* New York: Oxford University Press, 2006.

BROWN, ANTHONY CAVE. *Oil, God and Gold: The Story of Aramco and the Saudi Kings.* Boston: Houghton Mifflin, 1999.

BROWN, MALCOLM, ed. *T. E. Lawrence in War and Peace: An Anthology of the Military Writings of Lawrence of Arabia.* London: Greenhill, 2005.

BRYSON, THOMAS A. *American Diplomatic Relations with the Middle East 1784–1975: A Survey.* Metuchen, NJ: Scarecrow, 1977.

BULLARD, SIR READER. *Britain and the Middle East: From the Earliest Times to 1950.* New York: Hutchinson's, 1951.

BURNS, MICHAEL. *France and the Dreyfus Affair.* Boston: Bedford, 1999.

BUSH, GEORGE and BRENT SCOWCROFT. *A World Transformed.* New York: Knopf, 1998.

CALVOCORESSI, PETER. *Survey of International Affairs: 1951.* London: Oxford University Press, 1954.

———. *Survey of International Affairs: 1952.* London: Oxford University Press, 1955.

———. *Survey of International Affairs: 1953.* London: Oxford University Press, 1956.

CAROE, OLAF. *Wells of Power: The Oil Fields of Southwestern Asia.* London: Macmillan, 1951.

CHANDRASEKARAN, RAJIV. *Imperial Life in the Emerald City: Inside Iraq's Green Zone.* New York: Knopf, 2006.

CHENEY, MICHAEL SHELDON. *Big Oil Man from Arabia.* New York: Ballantine, 1958.

CHUBIN, SHAHRAM and CHARLES TRIPP. *Iran and Iraq at War.* Boulder: Westview, 1988.

CITINO, ROBERT M. *Blitzkrieg to Desert Storm: The Evolution of Operational Warfare.* Lawrence, KS: University Press of Kansas, 2004.

CLARK, MARK W. *Calculated Risk.* New York: Harper, 1950.

CLARKE, RICHARD A. *Against All Enemies: Inside America's War on Terror.* New York: Free Press, 2004.

CLINTON, BILL. *My Life.* New York: Knopf, 2004.

COHEN, AVNER. *Israel and the Bomb.* New York: Columbia University Press, 1998.

COHEN, MICHAEL J. *Palestine to Israel: From Mandate to Independence.* London: Frank Cass, 1988.

———. *Truman and Israel.* Berkeley: University of California Press, 1990.

COHEN, MICHAEL J. and MARTIN KOLINKSY, eds. *Britain and the Middle East in the 1930s: Security Problems 1935–39.* New York: St. Martin's, 1992.

———. *Demise of the British Empire in the Middle East: Britain's Responses to Nationalist Movements 1943–55.* London: Frank Cass, 1998.

COHEN, NAOMI W. *Jacob H. Schiff: A Study in American Jewish Leadership.* Hanover, NH: Brandeis University Press, 1999.

COLL, STEVE. *Ghost Wars: The Secret History of the CIA, Afghanistan, and Bin Laden, from the Soviet Invasion to September 10, 2001.* New York: Penguin Press, 2004.

COPELAND, MILES. *The Game of Nations: The Amorality of Power Politics.* London: Weidenfeld & Nicolson, 1969.

CORDESMAN, ANTHONY H. *The Gulf and the Search for Strategic Stability.* Boulder: Westview, 1984.

———. *Iran's Military Forces in Transition: Conventional Threats and WMD.* Westport, CT: Praeger, 1999.

———. *The Iraq War: Strategy, Tactics and Military Lessons.* Westport, CT: Praeger, 2003.

———. *Saudi Arabia: Guarding the Desert Kingdom.* Boulder: Westview, 1997.

CORDESMAN, ANTHONY H. and AHMED S. HASHIM. *Iran: Dilemmas of Dual Containment.* Boulder: Westview, 1997.

COTTRELL, ALVIN J. and JAMES DOUGHERTY. *Iran's Quest for Security: US Arms Transfers and the Nuclear Option.* Cambridge, MA: Institute for Foreign Policy Analysis, 1977.

CRILE, GEORGE. *Charlie Wilson's War: The Extraordinary Story of the Largest Covert Operation in History.* New York: Atlantic, 2003.

CURTISS, RICHARD H. *Stealth PACs: Lobbying Congress for Control of U.S. Middle East Policy.* Washington, D.C.: American Educational Trust, 1991.

DAALDER, IVO and I. M. DESTLER. *In the Shadow of the Oval Office: The Presidents and Their National Security Advisers from JFK to George W. Bush.* New York: Simon & Schuster, 2009.

DANIEL, NORMAN. *Islam, Europe and Empire.* Edinburgh: Edinburgh University Press, 1966.

DANN, URIEL. *The Great Powers in the Middle East 1919–39.* New York: Holmes & Meier, 1988.

DAWISHA, ADEED. *Arab Nationalism in the Twentieth Century: From Triumph to Despair.* Princeton: Princeton University Press, 2003.

DE FELICE, RENZO. *Fascismo e l'Oriente: arabi, ebrei e indiani nella politica di Mussolini.* Bologna, 1988.

DELONG, MICHAEL with NOAH LUKEMAN. *Inside CENTCOM: The Unvarnished Truth about the Wars in Afghanistan and Iraq.* Washington, D.C.: Regnery, 2004.

DORRIL, STEPHEN. *MI6: Inside the Covert World of Her Majesty's Secret Intelligence Service.* New York: Free Press, 2000.

DUCHESS OF HAMILTON, JILL. *First to Damascus: The Story of the Australian Light Horse and Lawrence of Arabia.* Sydney: Kangaroo Press, 2002.

DUGDALE, BLANCHE E. C. *Arthur James Balfour*, 2 vols. New York: Putnam's, 1937.

EHTESHAMI, ANOUSHIRAVAN. *After Khomeini: The Iranian Second Republic.* London: Routledge, 1995.

EHTESHAMI, ANOUSHIRAVAN and RAYMOND HINNEBUSCH. *Syria and Iran: Middle Powers in a Penetrated Regional System.* London: Routledge, 1997.

ELLIOT, MATTHEW. *"Independent Iraq": The Monarchy and British Influence 1941–1958.* London: I. B. Tauris, 1996.

ELPELEG, ZVI. *The Grand Mufti: Haj Amin al-Hussaini.* London: Frank Cass, 1993.

ENGDAHL, WILLIAM. *A Century of War: Anglo-American Oil Politics and the New World Order*, 2nd ed. Ann Arbor: Pluto Press, 2004.

FAOUR, MUHAMMAD. *The Arab World after Desert Storm.* Washington, D.C.: USIP Press, 1993.

FEIFER, GREGORY. *The Great Gamble: The Soviet War in Afghanistan.* New York: HarperCollins, 2009.

FEIS, HERBERT. *The Birth of Israel: The Tousled Diplomatic Bed.* New York: Norton, 1969.

———. *Petroleum and American Foreign Policy.* Palo Alto: Food Research Institute, Stanford University, 1944.

———. *Seen from E.A.: Three International Episodes.* New York: Knopf, 1947.

FERGUSON, NIALL. *The House of Rothschild: Money's Prophets, 1789–1848.* New York: Viking, 1998.

———. *The House of Rothschild: The World's Banker, 1849–1999.* New York: Viking, 1999.

FIELD, MICHAEL. *Inside the Arab World.* Cambridge, MA: Harvard University Press, 1995.

FILKINS, DEXTER. *The Forever War.* New York: Knopf, 2008.

FINER, HERMAN. *Dulles over Suez: The Theory and Practice of His Diplomacy.* Chicago: Quadrangle, 1964.

FISHER, JOHN. *Curzon and British Imperialism in the Middle East 1916–19.* London: Frank Cass, 1999.

FISK, ROBERT. *The Great War for Civilization: The Conquest of the Middle East.* New York: Knopf, 2005.

FRANKS, TOMMY. *American Soldier.* New York: Regan Books, 2004.

FRASER, T. G. *The Middle East, 1914–79.* New York: St. Martin's, 1980.

———. *The USA and the Middle East since World War II.* New York: St. Martin's, 1989.

FREIBERGER, STEVEN. *Dawn over Suez: The Rise of American Power in the Middle East.* New York: Ivan Dee, 2007.

FROMKIN, DAVID. *A Peace to End All Peace: The Fall of the Ottoman Empire and the Creation of the Modern Middle East.* New York: Henry Holt, 1989.

FULLICK, ROY and GEOFFREY POWELL. *Suez: The Double War.* London: Pen & Sword, 2006.

FURY, DALTON. *Kill Bin Laden: A Delta Force Commander's Account of the Hunt for the World's Most Wanted Man.* New York: St. Martin's, 2008.

GASIOROWSKI, MARK J. and MALCOLM BYRNE. *Mohammad Mosaddeq and the 1953 Coup in Iran.* Syracuse: Syracuse University Press, 2004.

GAZIT, MORDECHAI. *President Kennedy's Policy toward the Arab States.* Tel Aviv: Shiloah Center, 1983.

GELLMAN, BARTON. *Angler: The Cheney Vice Presidency.* New York: Penguin Press, 2008.

GERGES, FAWAZ. *America and Political Islam: Clash of Cultures or Clash of Interests.* Cambridge: Cambridge University Press, 1999.

———. *The Far Enemy: Why Jihad Went Global.* Cambridge: Cambridge University Press, 2005.

———. *The Superpowers and the Middle East: Regional and International Politics 1955–1967.* Boulder: Westview, 1994.

GERSHONI, ISRAEL and JAMES JANKOWSKI. *Redefining the Egyptian Nation 1930–45.* Cambridge: Cambridge University Press, 2002.

GOLD, DORE. *Hatred's Kingdom: How Saudi Arabia Supports the New Global Terrorism.* Washington, D.C.: Regnery, 2003.

GOLDSTEIN, LYLE. J. and YURI M. ZHUKOV. "A Tale of Two Fleets: A Russian Perspective on the 1973 Naval Standoff in the Mediterranean." *Naval War College Review* 57/2, Spring 2004.

GOODE, JAMES F. *The United States and Iran: In the Shadow of Musaddiq.* New York: St. Martin's, 1997.

GORDON, MICHAEL R. and BERNARD E. TRAINOR. *Cobra II: The Inside Story of the Invasion and Occupation of Iraq.* New York: Pantheon, 2006.

———. *The Generals' War.* Boston: Little, Brown, 1995.

GRIFFIN, MICHAEL. *Reaping the Whirlwind: Afghanistan, Al-Qa'ida, and the Holy War,* revised ed. London: Pluto Press, 2003.

GROBBA, FRITZ. *Männer und Mächte im Orient.* Göttingen: Musterschmidt Verlag, 1967.

GUNTHER, JOHN. *Roosevelt in Retrospect.* London: Hamish Hamilton, 1950.

HAHN, PETER. *Caught in the Middle East: U.S. Policy Toward the Arab-Israeli Conflict, 1945-61.* Chapel Hill: University of North Carolina Press, 2004.

HART, LIDDELL. *Strategy,* second edition. London: Plume, 353

HASHIM, AHMED. *Insurgency and Counter-insurgency in Iraq.* Ithaca: Cornell University Press, 2006.

HEIKAL, MUHAMMED HASSANEIN. *Autumn of Fur: The Assassination of Sadat.* London: Corgi, 1984.

———. *Cutting the Lion's Tai: Suez through Egyptian Eyes.* Westminster, MD: Arbor House, 1987.

HELMS, RICHARD. *A Look over My Shoulder: A Life in the Central Intelligence Agency.* New York: Random House, 2003.

HERSH, SEYMOUR M. *Chain of Command: The Road from 9/11 to Abu Ghraib.* New York: HarperCollins, 2004.

HIRO, DILIP. *Holy Wars: The Rise of Islamic Fundamentalism.* New York: Routledge, 1989.

———. *Iran under the Ayatollahs.* London: Routledge, 1987.

———. *The Longest War: The Iran-Iraq Military Conflict.* New York: Routledge, 1991.

HIRST, DAVID. *The Gun and the Olive Branch: The Roots of Violence in the Middle East.* New York: Nation, 2003.

HIRSZOWICZ, LUKASZ. *The Third Reich and the Arab East.* London: Routledge, 1966.

HITCHCOCK, WILLIAM I. *The Struggle for Europe: The Turbulent History of a Divided Continent 1945–2002.* New York: Doubleday, 2002.

HOFMANN, GEORGE F. *Through Mobility We Conquer: The Mechanization of U.S. Cavalry.* Lexington, KY: University Press of Kentucky, 2006.

HOLDEN, DAVID and RICHARD JOHNS. *The House of Saud.* London: Sidgwick & Jackson, 1981.

HOSKINS, HALFORD L. *The Middle East: Problem Area in World Politics.* New York: Macmillan, 1956.

HULL, CORDELL. *The Memoirs of Cordell Hull,* 2 vols. New York: Macmillan, 1948.

HUYSER, ROBERT E. *Mission to Tehran.* New York: Harper & Row, 1987.

ISIKOFF, MICHAEL and DAVID CORN. *Hubris: The Inside Story of Spin, Scandal and the Selling of the Iraq War.* New York: Crown, 2006.

JOHNSON, LYNDON BAINES. *The Vantage Point: Perspectives of the Presidency, 1963–1969.* New York: Holt, Rinehart & Winston, 1971.

JUDD, DENIS. *Balfour and the British Empire: A Study in Imperial Evolution 1874–1932.* London: Macmillan, 1968.

KAPUSCINSKI, RYSZARD. *Shah of Shahs.* New York: Vintage, 1982.

KATZMAN, KENNETH. *Warriors of Islam: Iran's Revolutionary Guard.* Boulder: Westview, 1993.

KAUFMAN, BURTON I. *The Arab Middle East and the United States: Inter-Arab Rivalry and Superpower Diplomacy.* New York: Twayne, 1996.

KEAY, JOHN. *Sowing the Wind: The Seeds of Conflict in the Middle East.* New York: Norton, 2003.

KEDDIE, NIKKI R. *Iran and the Muslim World: Resistance and Revolution.* New York: NYU Press, 1995.

KEDOURIE, ELIE. *In the Anglo-Arab Labyrinth: The McMahon-Husayn Correspondence and Its Interpretations 1914–39.* Cambridge: Cambridge University Press, 1976.

KEEGAN, JOHN. *The Iraq War.* New York: Knopf, 2004.

KERR, MALCOLM H. *The Arab Cold War: Gamal Abd Al-Nasir and His Rivals 1958–1970.* London: Oxford University Press, 1971.

KHADDURI, MAJID. *The Gulf War: The Origins and Implications of the Iraq-Iran Conflict.* Boulder: Westview, 1988.

KHALIDI, RASHID. *Resurrecting Empire: Western Footprints and America's Perilous Path in the Middle East.* Boston: Beacon Press, 2004.

KINZER, STEPHEN. *All the Shah's Men: An American Coup and the Roots of Middle East Terror.* New York: Wiley, 2003.

———. *Overthrow: America's Century of Regime Change from Hawaii to Iraq.* New York: Henry Holt, 2006.

KIRK, GEORGE, ed. *Survey of International Affairs: The Middle East 1945–1950.* London: Oxford University Press, 1954.

———. *Survey of International Affairs: The Middle East in the War.* London: Oxford University Press, 1952.

KISSINGER, HENRY. *Crisis: The Anatomy of Two Major Foreign Policy Crises.* New York: Simon & Schuster, 2003.

KLIBANSKY, RAYMOND, ed. *The Mussolini Memoirs 1942–1943.* London: Phoenix Press, 2000. Originally published 1949.

KOLINSKY, MARTIN. *Britain's War in the Middle East: Strategy and Diplomacy 1936–42.* London: Macmillan, 1999.

———. *Law, Order and Riots in Mandatory Palestine, 1928–35.* London: St. Martin's, 1993.

KROSNEY, HERBERT. *Deadly Business: Legal Deals and Outlaw Weapons: The Arming of Iran and Iraq 1975 to the Present.* New York: Four Walls Eight Windows, 1993.

KUNIHOLM, BRUCE ROBERT. *The Origins of the Cold War in the Near East: Great Power Conflict and Diplomacy in Iran, Turkey, and Greece.* Princeton: Princeton University Press, 1980.

KUNZ, DIANE B. *The Economic Diplomacy of the Suez Crisis.* Chapel Hill: University of North Carolina Press, 1991.

KYLE, KEITH. *Suez.* New York: St. Martin's, 1991.

LACOUTURE, JEAN. *Gamal Abdel Nasser.* Paris: Bayard, 1973.

LA GUARDIA, ANTON. *War Without End: Israelis, Palestinians and the Struggle for a Promised Land.* New York: Thomas Dunne, 2001.

LANGER, WILLIAM L. *Our Vichy Gamble.* Hamden, CT: Archon, 1965.

LAQUEUR, WALTER. *The Struggle for the Middle East: The Soviet Union in the Mediterranean 1958–1968.* New York: Macmillan, 1969.

LAVERGNE, BERNARD. *Une Révolution dans la politique coloniale de la France: le problème de l'Afrique du nord.* Paris: Mercure, 1948.

LEFF, LAUREL. *Buried by the Times: The Holocaust and America's Most Important Newspaper.* Cambridge: Cambridge University Press, 2005.

LENCZOWSKI, GEORGE, ed. *Iran under the Pahlavis.* Stanford: Hoover Institute Press, 1978.

————. *Russia and the West in Iran, 1918–1948: A Study in Big-Power Rivalry.* Ithaca: Cornell University Press, 1949.

LESCH, DAVID W. *Syria and the United States: Eisenhower's Cold War in the Middle East.* Boulder: Westview, 1992.

LEVIN, HARRY. *Jerusalem Embattled.* London: Gollancz, 1950.

LEVRAN, AHARON. *Israeli Strategy after Desert Storm: Lessons of the Second Gulf War.* London: Frank Cass, 1997.

LILIENTHAL, ALFRED M. *The Zionist Connection: What Price Peace.* New York: Dodd Mead, 1978.

LITTLE, DOUGLAS. *American Orientalism: The United States and the Middle East since 1945.* Chapel Hill: University of North Carolina Press, 2002.

LOCKMAN, ZACHARY. *Contending Visions of the Middle East: The History and Politics of Orientalism.* Cambridge: Cambridge University Press, 2004.

LONDON, LOUISE. *Whitehall and the Jews 1933–48.* Cambridge: Cambridge University Press, 2003.

LOUIS, WILLIAM ROGER. *The British Empire in the Middle East 1945–1951.* Oxford: Clarendon, 1984.

LUCAS, W. SCOTT. *Divided We Stand: Britain, the U.S. and the Suez Crisis.* London: Hodder & Stoughton, 1991.

LYTLE, MARK HAMILTON. *The Origins of the Iranian-American Alliance 1941–53.* London: Holmes & Meier, 1987.

MacARTHUR, JOHN R. *Second Front: Censorship and Propaganda in the Gulf War.* Berkeley: University of California Press, 1992.

MACKEY, SANDRA. *Passion and Politics: The Turbulent World of the Arabs.* New York: Dutton, 1992.

MacMILLAN, MARGARET. *Paris 1919: Six Months That Changed the World.* New York: Random House, 2001.

MAKIYA, KANAN. *Cruelty and Silence: War, Tyranny, Uprising, and the Arab World.* New York: Norton, 1993.

————. *The Monument: Art, Vulgarity and Responsibility in Iraq.* London: I.B. Tauris, 2004.

————. *Republic of Fear: The Politics of Modern Iraq.* Berkeley: University of California Press, 1989.

MALEY, WILLIAM. *The Afghanistan Wars.* New York: Palgrave, 2002.

MAMDANI, MAHMOOD. *Good Muslim, Bad Muslim: America, the Cold War, and the Roots of Terror.* New York: Pantheon, 2004.

MANN, JAMES. *The Rise of the Vulcans: The History of Bush's War Cabinet.* New York: Viking, 2004.

MANSOOR, PETER R. *Baghdad at Sunrise: A Brigade Commander's War in Iraq.* New Haven: Yale University Press, 2008.

MAOZ, ZEEV. *Defending the Holy Land.* Ann Arbor: University of Michigan Press, 2006.

MARLOWE, JOHN. *The Persian Gulf in the Twentieth Century.* London: Cresset, 1962.

MARSDEN, PETER. *The Taliban: War, Religion and the New Order in Afghanistan.* New York: Zed Books, 1998.

MATTAR, PHILIP. *The Mufti of Jerusalem: Al-Hajj Amin al-Husayni and the Palestinian National Movement.* New York: Columbia University Press, 1988.

McCULLOUGH, DAVID. *Truman.* New York: Simon & Schuster, 1992.

McGHEE, GEORGE. *Envoy to the Middle World: Adventures in Diplomacy.* New York: Harper & Row, 1983.

McLOUGHLIN, LESLIE. *Ibn Saud: Founder of a Kingdom.* New York: St. Martin's, 1993.

MEARSHEIMER, JOHN J. and STEPHEN M. WALT. *The Israel Lobby and U.S. Foreign Policy.* New York: Farrar, Straus and Giroux, 2007.

METZER, JACOB. *The Divided Economy of Mandatory Palestine.* Cambridge: Cambridge University Press, 2002.

METZGER, CHANTAL. *L'Empire colonial français dans la stratégie du Troisième Reich, 1936–1945,* 2 vols. Brussels: Peter Lang, 2002.

MIKESELL, RAYMOND F. and HOLLIS CHENERY. *Arabian Oil: America's Stake in the Middle East.* Chapel Hill: University of North Carolina Press, 1949.

MILLER, T. CHRISTIAN. *Blood Money: Wasted Billions, Lost Lives, and Corporate Greed in Iraq.* New York: Little, Brown, 2006.

MILLSPAUGH, ARTHUR C. *Americans in Persia.* Washington, D.C.: Brookings, 1946.

MISCAMBLE, WILSON D. *From Roosevelt to Truman: Potsdam, Hiroshima and the Cold War.* Cambridge: Cambridge University Press, 2007.

MONROE, ELIZABETH. *Britain's Moment in the Middle East 1914–56.* Baltimore, Johns Hopkins, 1963.

MORRIS, BENNY. *1948: A History of the First Arab-Israeli War*. New Haven: Yale University Press, 2008.

———. *The Birth of the Palestinian Refugee Problem Revisited*. Cambridge: Cambridge University Press, 2004.

———. *Righteous Victims: A History of the Zionist-Arab Conflict, 1881–2001*. New York: Vintage, 2001.

MORTON, H. V. *Through the Lands of the Bible*. New York: Dodd Mead, 1938.

MURRAY, WILLIAMSON and ROBERT H. SCALES, JR. *The Iraq War*. Cambridge, MA: Belknap, 2003.

NAFTALI, TIMOTHY. *Blind Spot: The Secret History of American Counterterrorism*. New York: Basic Books, 2005.

NASR, VALI. *The Shia Revival: How Conflicts within Islam Will Shape the Future*. New York: Norton, 2006.

NAYLOR, SEAN. *Not a Good Day to Die: The Untold Story of Operation Anaconda*. New York: Berkley, 2005.

NEFF, DONALD. *Fallen Pillars: US Policy towards Palestine and Israel since 1945*. Washington, D.C.: Institute for Palestine Studies, 1995.

NICOLSON, HAROLD. *Peacemaking 1919*. New York: Universal Library, 1965.

NUTTING, ANTHONY. *Nasser*. New York: Dutton, 1972.

OREN, MICHAEL B. *Power, Faith and Fantasy: America in the Middle East, 1776 to the Present*. New York: Norton, 2007.

———. *Six Days of War: June 1967 and the Making of the Modern Middle East*. Oxford: Oxford University Press, 2002.

OVENDALE, RITCHIE. *Britain, the United States and the Transfer of Power in the Middle East 1945–1962*. London: Leicester University Press, 1996.

———. *The Origins of the Arab-Israeli Wars*, 3rd ed. London: Longman, 1999.

PALMER, MICHAEL A. *Guardians of the Gulf: A History of America's Expanding Role in the Persian Gulf 1833–1992*. New York: Free Press, 1992.

PATERSON, THOMAS G., ed. *Kennedy's Quest for Victory: American Foreign Policy 1961–63*. Oxford: Oxford University Press, 1989.

PATTERSON, JAMES T. *Restless Giant: The United States from Watergate to Bush v. Gore*. New York: Oxford University Press, 2005.

PELLETIÈRE, STEPHEN. *America's Oil Wars*. Westport, CT: Praeger, 2004.

PETERSEN, TORE T. *The Middle East between the Great Powers: Anglo-American Conflict and Cooperation 1952–57*. London: Macmillan, 2000.

PHILBY, HARRY ST. JOHN. *Arabian Jubilee*. New York: John Day, 1953.

———. *Sa'udi Arabia*. New York: Arno Press, 1972. Originally published 1955.

PHILLIPS, KEVIN. *American Theocracy: The Peril and Politics of Radical Religion, Oil and Borrowed Money in the 21st Century*. New York: Viking, 2006.

PODEH, ELIE and ONN WINCKLER. *Rethinking Nasserism: Revolution and Historical Memory in Modern Egypt*. Gainesville: University Press of Florida, 2004.

POLK, WILLIAM R. *Understanding Iraq: The Whole Sweep of Iraqi History from Genghis Khan's Mongols to the Ottoman Turks to the British Mandate to the American Occupation*. New York: HarperCollins, 2005.

POLLACK, KENNETH M. *Arabs at War: Military Effectiveness 1948–1991*. Lincoln: University of Nebraska Press, 2002.

POSNER, GERALD. *Secrets of the Kingdom: The Inside Story of the Secret Saudi-U.S. Connection*. New York: Random House, 2005.

POWELL, COLIN L. with JOSEPH E. PERSICO. *My American Journey*. New York: Random House, 1995.

PRADOS, JOHN. *Safe for Democracy: The Secret Wars of the CIA*. Chicago: Ivan Dee, 2006.

RABINOVICH, AVRAHAM. *The Yom Kippur War: The Epic Encounter That Transformed the Middle East*. New York: Kindle, 2005.

RASHID, AHMED. *Descent into Chaos: The United States and the Failure of Nation Building in Pakistan, Afghanistan and Central Asia*. New York: Viking, 2008.

———. *Taliban: Militant Islam, Oil and Fundamentalism in Central Asia*. New Haven: Yale University Press, 2000.

RECORD, JEFFREY. *Dark Victory: America's Second War Against Iraq*. Annapolis: Naval Institute Press, 2004.

REED, THOMAS C. and DANNY B. STILLMAN. *The Nuclear Express: A Political History of the Bomb and Its Proliferation*. Minneapolis: Zenith, 2009.

RICKS, THOMAS E. *Fiasco: The American Military Adventure in Iraq*. New York: Penguin Press, 2006.

————. *The Gamble: General David Petraeus and the American Military Adventure in Iraq, 2006–2008.* New York: Penguin Press, 2009.

ROBERTS, ANDREW. *A History of the English Speaking Peoples since 1900.* New York: HarperCollins, 2007.

ROBERTS, MARK J. *Khomeini's Incorporation of the Iranian Military.* Washington, D.C.: NDU Press, 1996.

ROOSEVELT, ELLIOTT. *As He Saw It.* New York: Duell, Sloan and Pearce, 1946.

ROOSEVELT, KERMIT. *Arabs, Oil and History: The Story of the Middle East.* New York: Harper, 1949.

————. *Countercoup: The Struggle for Control of Iran.* New York: McGraw Hill, 1979.

ROSTOW, EUGENE V., ed. *The Middle East: Critical Choices for the United States.* Boulder: Westview, 1976.

ROULEAU, ERIC. "Khomeini's Iran." *Foreign Affairs,* Fall 1980.

ROY, OLIVIER. *Globalized Islam: The Search for a New Ummah.* New York: Columbia University Press, 2004.

————. *The Politics of Chaos in the Middle East.* New York: Columbia University Press, 2008.

RUBIN, BARRY. *Cauldron of Turmoil: America in the Middle East.* New York: Harcourt Brace Jovanovich, 1992.

————. *The Great Powers in the Middle East 1941–1947: The Road to the Cold War.* London: Frank Cass, 1980.

SACHAR, HOWARD M. *A History of Israel: From the Rise of Zionism to Our Time,* second edition. New York: Knopf, 1998.

SADAT, ANWAR EL. *In Search of Identity: An Autobiography.* New York: Harper & Row, 1977.

SAFRAN, NADAV. *Saudi Arabia: The Ceaseless Quest for Security.* Cambridge, MA: Belknap, 1985.

SALEM, PAUL. *Bitter Legacy: Ideology and Politics in the Arab World.* Syracuse: Syracuse University Press, 1994.

SARRASIN, PAUL-EMILE. *La Crise algérienne.* Paris: Cerf, 1949.

SCHECHTMAN, JOSEPH B. *The Mufti and the Fuehrer.* New York: Yoseloff, 1965.

SCHORSKE, CARL E. *Fin-de-Siècle Vienna: Politics and Culture.* New York: Vintage, 1981.

SCHROEN, GARY C. *First In: An Insider's Account of How the CIA Spearheaded the War on Terror in Afghanistan.* New York: Ballantine, 2005.

SCHULZ, ANN TIBBITS. *Buying Security: Iran under the Monarchy.* Boulder: Westview, 1989.

SCHWARZKOPF, H. NORMAN. *It Doesn't Take a Hero: The Autobiography.* New York: Bantam, 1992.

SCOTT, JAMES. *Attack on the Liberty.* New York: Simon & Schuster, 2009.

SEGEV, TOM. *1967: Israel, the War, and the Year that Transformed the Middle East.* New York: Metropolitan, 2005.

————. *One Palestine Complete: Jews and Arabs under the British Mandate.* New York: Henry Holt, 1999.

SHAWCROSS, WILLIAM. *Allies: The U.S., Britain, Europe, and the War in Iraq.* New York: Public Affairs, 2004.

————. *The Shah's Last Ride: The Fate of an Ally.* New York: Simon & Schuster, 1988.

SHLAIM, AVI. *The Iron Wall: Israel and the Arab World.* New York: Norton, 2001.

SHUCKBURGH, EVELYN. *Descent to Suez: Diaries 1951–56.* New York: Norton, 1986.

SHWADRAN, BENJAMIN. *The Middle East, Oil and the Great Powers.* New York: Wiley, 1973.

SICK, GARY. *All Fall Down: America's Tragic Encounter with Iran.* New York: Random House, 1985.

SICKER, MARTIN. *The Bear and the Lion: Soviet Imperialism and Iran.* Westport, CT: Praeger, 1988.

SIMMONS, MATTHEW R. *Twilight in the Desert: The Coming Saudi Oil Shock and the World Economy.* Hoboken: John Wiley, 2005.

SIMPSON, JOHN. *Inside Iran: Life under Khomeini's Regime.* New York: St. Martin's, 1988.

SLOTKIN, RICHARD. *Lost Battalions: The Great War and the Crisis of American Nationality.* New York: Henry Holt, 2006.

SOROS, GEORGE. *The Bubble of American Supremacy: Correcting the Misuse of American Power.* New York: Public Affairs, 2004.

SRODES, JAMES. *Allen Dulles: Master of Spies.* Washington, D.C.: Regnery, 2000.

STIGLITZ, JOSEPH E. and LINDA J. BILMES. *The Three Trillion Dollar War: The True Cost of the Iraq Conflict.* New York: Norton, 2008.

STIVERS, WILLIAM. *America's Confrontation with Revolutionary Change in the Middle East 1948–83.* New York: St. Martin's, 1986.

————. *Supremacy and Oil: Iraq, Turkey and the Anglo-American World Order 1918–1930.* Ithaca, NY: Cornell University Press, 1982.

SUSKIND, RON. *The Price of Loyalty: George W. Bush, the White House, and the Education of Paul O'Neill*. New York: Simon & Schuster, 2004.

TAKEYH, RAY. *The Origins of the Eisenhower Doctrine: The US, Britain and Nasser's Egypt, 1953–57*. New York: Macmillan, 2000.

TEICHER, HOWARD and GAYLE RADLEY TEICHER. *Twin Pillars to Desert Storm: America's Flawed Vision in the Middle East from Nixon to Bush*. New York: William Morrow, 1993.

TENET, GEORGE with BILL HARLOW. *At the Center of the Storm: My Years at the CIA*. New York: HarperCollins, 2007.

THESIGER, WILFRED. *Arabian Sands*. New York: Dutton, 1959.

————. *The Marsh Arabs*. New York: Dutton, 1964.

THOMAS, HUGH. *Suez*. New York: Harper & Row, 1966.

TRIPP, CHARLES. *A History of Iraq*, second edition. Cambridge: Cambridge University Press, 2002.

TYLER, PATRICK. *A World of Trouble: The White House and the Middle East from the Cold War to the War on Terror*. New York: Farrar, Straus and Giroux, 2009.

VAN CREVELD, MARTIN. *The Changing Face of War: Lessons of Combat from the Marne to Iraq*. New York: Ballantine, 2006.

VAUCHON, GEORGES. *Gamal Abdel-Nasser et son équipe*, 2 vols. Paris: Juillard 1959–60.

WAWRO, GEOFFREY. "Letter from Iran." *Naval War College Review*, Winter 2002.

WEINBERGER, CASPAR W. *In the Arena: A Memoir of the 20th Century*. Washington, D.C.: Regnery, 2001.

WEST, BING and RAY L. SMITH. *The March Up: Taking Baghdad with the 1st Marine Division*. New York: Bantam, 2003.

WILSON, MARY CHRISTINA. *King Abdullah, Britain and the Making of Jordan*. Cambridge: Cambridge University Press, 1990.

WILSON, PETER W. and DOUGLAS F. GRAHAM. *Saudi Arabia: The Coming Storm*. Armonk, NY: M. E. Sharpe, 1994.

WINT, GUY and PETER CALVOCORESSI. *Middle East Crisis*. London: Penguin, 1957.

WISCHNITZER, MARK. *To Dwell in Safety: The Story of Jewish Migration since 1800*. Philadelphia: Jewish Publication Society of America, 1948.

WOODWARD, BOB. *Bush at War*. New York: Simon & Schuster, 2002.

————. *Plan of Attack*. New York: Simon & Schuster, 2004.

————. *State of Denial*. New York: Simon & Schuster, 2006.

————. *The War Within: A Secret White House History 2006–2008*. New York: Simon & Schuster, 2008.

WRIGHT, LAWRENCE. *The Looming Tower: Al Qaeda and the Road to 9/11*. New York: Knopf, 2006.

YAPP, M. E. *The Near East since the First World War*. London: Longman, 1991.

YAQUB, SALIM. *Containing Arab Nationalism: The Eisenhower Doctrine and the Middle East*. Chapel Hill: University of North Carolina Press, 2004.

YERGIN, DANIEL. *The Prize: The Epic Quest for Oil, Money and Power*. New York: Simon & Schuster, 1991.

YODER, EDWIN M., Jr. *Joe Alsop's Cold War*. Chapel Hill: University of North Carolina Press, 1995.

ZABIH, SEPEHR. *The Iranian Military in Revolution and War*. London: Routledge, 1988.

ZEBEL, SYDNEY. *Balfour: A Political Biography*. Cambridge: Cambridge University Press, 1973.

ZERTAL, IDITH. *Israel's Holocaust and the Politics of Nationhood*. Cambridge: Cambridge University Press, 2005.

ZERTAL IDITH and AKIVA ELDAR. *Lords of the Land: The War over Israel's Settlements in the Occupied Territories, 1967–2007*. New York: Nation, 2007.

INDEX

leaves Iran in January 1979, 356
military buildup of 1960s and 1970s, 335–41, 343–44
Nixon asks for protection from, 297, 332
overthrow, 348–59
after overthrow of Mosaddeq, 150–52
in overthrow of Mosaddeq, 142, 143, 144–45, 147, 149, 332
political opposition of 1960s and 1970s, 344–45
relations with Mosaddeq, 127, 128–29, 134, 135, 138, 144
SAVAK, 151, 333, 342, 343, 345–48, 351, 352, 357
Shiite clergy curbed, 346
Soviet encroachment opposed, 126, 332–33
Soviet vilification, 141
strategic paranoia, 341, 343
superpower pretensions, 334, 339–40
as U.S. client, 148, 150, 151, 332
U.S. gives up on, 355–57
U.S. weapons wanted, 297
Western aid sought, 135
White Revolution, 127, 291, 339, 341, 342, 348
mujahideen:
Afghan army deserters join, 377, 379
Benazir Bhutto's warning about, 387
bin Laden meets, 384
"blowback" for U.S. support, 378
camps in Afghanistan, 387
fundamentalism, 379, 396
girding for civil war, 394
Pakistan as sanctuary, 375, 381, 385
radicalization, 383
Saudi influence, 383
Soviet attacks of 1987, 394–95
successes, 390, 391
terrorism, 387–88
U.S. arms, 381–82, 385, 387–88, 391, 392, 393–94
al-Zawahiri unifies, 474
Zia's support, 386
Musharraf, Pervez:
in airlift of Pakistani agents from Afghanistan, 497
fails to prevent Taliban escape, 501–2
and Massoud assassination, 490
military rivals undermine relationship with U.S., 511–12
and Pakistani support for Taliban, 493, 496, 505–6
refuses to aid U.S. after *Cole* attack, 485
in technology sales to Iran, 580
in war against al-Qaeda, 516–17
Muslim Brotherhood, 168–69
bin Laden influenced by, 384, 389
Egyptian defeat in 1948 and, 122
in Egyptian radicalism after Yom Kippur War, 324

Israeli intransigence and, 283
membership in 1950s, 154, 168
Nasser has members arrested, 167
in overthrow of Farouk, 160, 161
as pro-Nazi, 155
Sadat criticized, 299
Soviets on Jewish state and, 102
Muslims, *see* Islam

Naguib, Muhammed, 155–56, 167, 169, 171, 172, 182
Nairobi embassy bombing, 477
Najibullah, Muhammed, 375, 392, 394–96, 469–70
Nasser, Gamal Abdel, 159–60
agrarian reform, 166, 170
anti-Americanism, 224–25
in Arab-Israeli war of 1948, 160
Arab nationalism, 11, 12, 159, 163, 166, 169, 171, 192, 242, 244, 284
attempts to revive UAR, 245, 246
on British withdrawal from Egypt, 186
bureaucracy created, 168, 171
Byroade as ambassador to, 175
Chinese advice to, 276
comes to power, 122, 161–62
dictatorial powers assumed, 167–68
Dulles and, 182, 242
economic difficulties, 246
Eden on, 169, 171, 217, 235
Eisenhower and, 80, 163–64, 169, 187, 242, 289
first phase of revolution of, 165–66
in free officers' movement, 157, 159–60
gallant pose struck, 244–45
Holmes Report of 1967 on, 258–59
in Iraqi coup of 1958, 231
and Israeli Gaza Strip action of 1955, 176–77
Israel opposed, 163, 187
Johnson and, 250–51
Kennedy and, 240, 242, 243, 249, 250
Kuwait defended against Iraq, 246
in Lebanon crisis of 1958, 231, 232–35, 237, 238
Muslim Brotherhood opposes, 168–69
Nasserism, 162–66, 235, 252
on Negev Desert, 174
negotiates with Britain over Suez Canal, 171
neutralism, 184, 262
on Palestinian question, 122
and PLO, 247
rubber stamp party of, 252
seen as martyr after Six-Day War, 278–79
in Six-Day War, 262–63, 265, 266, 267–69, 270, 272, 274
socialism, 162, 168, 170–71, 252
as Soviet client, 168, 175, 176, 179, 185, 187–89, 237, 247, 262–63
in Suez Crisis, 188–92, 196, 197, 199–202, 204, 206–10, 218, 224

To Chris —
all the best!

Aneck Reuers

CNN
1981-2010